W9-CAM-380

the Unofficial Guide® to

Washington D.C.

7th Edition

Also available from Wiley Publishing:

Beyond Disney: The Unofficial Guide to Universal, SeaWorld, and the Best of Central Florida

Inside Disney: The Incredible Story of Walt Disney World and the Man Behind the Mouse

Mini Las Vegas: The Pocket-Sized Unofficial Guide to Las Vegas

Mini-Mickey: The Pocket-Sized Unofficial Guide to Walt Disney World

The Unofficial Guides to Bed & Breakfasts and Country Inns:
California   Great Lakes States   Mid-Atlantic
New England   Northwest   Rockies   Southeast   Southwest

The Unofficial Guides to the Best RV and Tent Campgrounds:
California and the West   Florida and the Southeast
Great Lakes   Mid-Atlantic States   Northeast   Northwest
Southwest   U.S.A.

The Unofficial Guide to Branson, Missouri

The Unofficial Guide to Central Italy: Florence, Rome, Tuscany, and Umbria

The Unofficial Guide to Chicago

The Unofficial Guide to Cruises

The Unofficial Guide to Disneyland

The Unofficial Guide to Disneyland Paris

The Unofficial Guide to Florida and the Keys

The Unofficial Guide to the Great Smoky and Blue Ridge Region

The Unofficial Guide to Golf Vacations in the Eastern U.S.

The Unofficial Guide to Hawaii

The Unofficial Guide to Las Vegas

The Unofficial Guide to London

The Unofficial Guide to New Orleans

The Unofficial Guide to New York City

The Unofficial Guide to Paris

The Unofficial Guide to San Francisco

The Unofficial Guide to Skiing in the West

The Unofficial Guide to South Florida, including Miami and the Keys

The Unofficial Guides to Traveling with Kids:
California   Florida   Mid-Atlantic   New England and New York
Southeast   Walt Disney World

The Unofficial Guide to Walt Disney World

The Unofficial Guide to Walt Disney World for Grown-Ups

The Unofficial Guide to Washington, D.C.

The Unofficial Guide to the World's Best Diving Vacations

the Unofficial Guide® to Washington, D.C.

7th Edition

Joe Surkiewicz
and
Bob Sehlinger
with
Eve Zibart

WILEY
Wiley Publishing, Inc.

For Tom Nugent, aka the Enemy of Comfort—J. S.
To Dick Wood, who infected me with this strange contagion we call book publishing.—B. S.
To D.—E. Z.

Please note that prices fluctuate in the course of time, and travel information changes under the impact of many factors that influence the travel industry. We therefore suggest that you write or call ahead for confirmation when making your travel plans. Every effort has been made to ensure the accuracy of information throughout this book, and the contents of this publication are believed correct at the time of printing. Nevertheless, the publishers cannot accept responsibility for errors or omissions or for changes in details given in this guide or for the consequences of any reliance on the information provided by the same. Assessments of attractions and so forth are based upon the authors' own experience, and therefore, descriptions given in this guide necessarily contain an element of subjective opinion, which may not reflect the publisher's opinion or dictate a reader's own experience on another occasion. Readers are invited to write the publisher with ideas, comments, and suggestions for future editions.

Published by:
Wiley Publishing, Inc.
909 Third Ave.
New York, NY 10022

Produced by Menasha Ridge Press
Cover design by Michael J. Freeland
Interior design by Michele Laseau

For information on our other products and services or to obtain technical support please contact our Customer Care Department within the U.S. at (800) 762-2974, outside the U.S. at (317) 572-3993, or fax (317) 572-4002.

Wiley also publishes its books in a variety of electronic formats. Some content that appears in print may not be available in electronic formats.

ISBN 0-7645-6740-3

ISSN 1071-6440

Manufactured in the United States of America

5 4 3 2 1

Contents

Part Ten Entertainment and Nightlife 355

Part Twelve Exercise and Recreation 386

Index 403

List of Maps and Illustrations

Acknowledgments

Eve Zibart, author of several books including *The Eclectic Gourmet Guide to Washington, D.C., The Unofficial Guide to New Orleans, The Unofficial Guide to Walt Disney World for Grown-Ups,* and *The Ethnic Food Lover's Companion,* is a feature writer and dining columnist for the *Washington Post;* she drew on her intimate knowledge of D.C.'s diverse after-hours scene and the area's vast array of dining spots when writing our entertainment and restaurant sections. Eve also scoped out where to find the best deals for our chapter on shopping.

Officer Rod Ryan of the Washington Metropolitan Police gave us the straight skinny on how to avoid street crime in Washington.

Metro's Phil Portlock provided photos of the subway system and, among other things, the correct spelling of the U Street–Cardozo station; Gary Barton supplied his detailed knowledge of Washington's streets and spent a Saturday chauffeuring us to suburban Metro stations; renowned bicycling writer (and former D.C. resident) Arlene Plevin shared suggestions on cycling around town; mega-boater Steve Garrison blessed our section on whitewater canoeing; and Ann Lembo pitched in with some last-minute editorial assistance.

To fulfill their tasks, hotel inspectiors, Alisa Bralove, Grace Walton, and Diane Kuhr, endured sore feet, crowds, and notoriously bad D.C. traffic.

Finally, many thanks to Molly Merkle, Nathan Lott, Carolyn Hassett, Frances Moore, Annie Long, Steve Jones, and Michelle Sanders, the pros who managed to transform all this effort into a book.

Introduction

Washington without the Hassle

Before we begin rhapsodizing about the joys of visiting Washington, D.C., we have a small confession to make: Sometimes we hate being visitors in D.C.

It's not that we are immune to the spell of this beautiful city on the Potomac. We've done our share of gaping in patriotic awe from the top of the Washington Monument and have witnessed in utter fascination the histrionics of long-winded U.S. senators ramrodding a pork barrel project through Congress. For us, as for others, the locus of government is intoxicating. We thrive on the constant tension arising from the polarity of powerful people and ideas. Washington, unquestionably, is one of the most exciting cities on the planet.

Where else but in Washington can you watch fire-and-brimstone politicians debate the rights of men and women on the floor of the U.S. Senate or marvel at the eloquence of barristers arguing a case before the Supreme Court—or discover, perhaps, how politics really works by eavesdropping on a couple of veteran lobbyists as they plot strategy over dry martinis in a hip Georgetown pub?

Then, of course, there is the beauty, the magnificence, the majesty of the city. America's capital city boasts some of the most stunning monuments ever created, as well as world-class museums and lush, verdant parks. Broad, shaded boulevards, meticulously laid out by Pierre-Charles L'Enfant, radiate like spokes from the heart of the city, punctuated by stately plazas, ornate bridges, and breathtaking sculpture.

Our problem with D.C. is very simple: We cannot stand the peculiarly Washingtonian hassles that routinely get in the way of enjoying this extraordinary city—the sweltering summer heat and humidity, the Rube Goldberg street plan, the agonizing lack of legal parking, the elbow-to-elbow crowds that can wipe out your high spirits before lunch.

In response, we've become absolute fanatics when it comes to warning Washington visitors away from Washington's worst torments. Here's the short list: long lines that never seem to move, lousy food (when D.C. boasts some of the finest restaurants on earth!), industrial-strength traffic jams, outrageous prices for mediocre hotel rooms, bored tour guides that herd tourists like sheep . . .

We do get quite grumpy when things go amiss on a Washington visit.

It doesn't have to be this way for you.

This book is the reason why. Its primary purpose can be expressed in exactly ten words: We're going to take the misery out of touring Washington!

While we can't guarantee great weather and small crowds, we'll tell you when you've got the best chances of encountering both, and we'll give you tons of information that will save your feet and your wallet, not to mention your temper.

You'll also find suggestions for things to do and see off the beaten track on hot August afternoons when a stroll on the Mall invites heat stroke and when crowds flock to the best-known attractions. At the same time, we'll introduce the best of what D.C. has to offer after the museums close, places where the people who live and work in Washington like to go after hours: the great ethnic restaurants, theaters, and nightspots. We'll also tell you about the best places around to shop, walk, take a hike, get a workout, or ride a bike.

This guide is designed both for folks planning a family trip to Washington to see its famous monuments, halls of government, historic places, and museums, and for business travelers who want to avoid the city's worst hassles. The *Unofficial Guide* also shows how you can see a side of Washington that most visitors miss: a re-creation of a Roman catacomb, $90 million worth of antiques in one place, and the mansion and gardens of a fabulously rich heiress, among other things.

The bottom line: We'll help you see Washington like a native. Of course, we can't promise that your D.C. visit will be perfect. But this guidebook can help you eliminate most of the needless irritations that so frequently spoil the fun for Washington tourists.

And who knows? Maybe you'll discover, as we did while researching this book, that there's nothing left to "hate" about being a Washington visitor!

About This Guide

How Come "Unofficial"?

Most "official" guides to Washington, D.C., tout the well-known sights, promote the local restaurants and hotels indiscriminately, and leave out a lot of good stuff. This one is different.

Instead of pandering to the tourist industry, we'll tell you if the food is bad at a well-known restaurant, we'll complain loudly about D.C.'s notorious high prices, and we'll guide you away from the crowds and lines for a break now and then.

Visiting Washington requires wily strategies not unlike those used in the sacking of Troy. We sent in a team of evaluators who toured each site, ate in the city's best restaurants, performed critical evaluations of its hotels, and visited Washington's wide variety of nightclubs. If a museum is boring, or standing in line for two hours to view a famous attraction is a waste of time, we say so—and, in the process, hopefully make your visit more fun, efficient, and economical.

Creating a Guidebook

We got into the guidebook business because we were unhappy with the way travel guides force the reader to work to get any usable information. Wouldn't it be nice, we thought, if we were to make guides that are easy to use?

Most guidebooks are compilations of lists. This is true regardless of whether the information is presented in list form or artfully distributed through pages of prose. There is insufficient detail in a list, and prose can present tedious helpings of nonessential or marginally useful information. Not enough wheat, so to speak, for nourishment in one instance, and too much chaff in the other. Either way, these types of guides provide little more than departure points from which readers initiate their own quests.

Many guides are readable and well researched, but they tend to be difficult to use. To select a hotel, for example, a reader must study several pages of descriptions with only the boldface hotel names breaking up large blocks of text. Because each description essentially deals with the same variables, it is difficult to recall what was said concerning a particular hotel. Readers generally must work through all the write-ups before beginning to narrow their choices. The presentation of restaurants, nightclubs, and attractions is similar except that even more reading is usually required. To use such a guide is to undertake an exhaustive research process that requires examining nearly as many options and possibilities as starting from scratch. Recommendations, if any, lack depth and conviction. These guides compound rather than solve problems by failing to narrow travelers' choices down to a thoughtfully considered, well-distilled, and manageable few.

How *Unofficial Guides* Are Different

Readers care about the authors' opinions. The authors, after all, are supposed to know what they are talking about. This, coupled with the fact that the traveler wants quick answers (as opposed to endless alternatives), dictates that authors should be explicit, prescriptive, and above all, direct. The authors of the *Unofficial Guide* try to do just that. They spell out alternatives and recommend specific courses of action. They simplify complicated destinations and attractions and allow the traveler to feel in control in the most unfamiliar environments. The objective of the *Unofficial Guide* authors is not to give the most information or all of the information, but to offer the most accessible, useful information.

An *Unofficial Guide* is a critical reference work; it focuses on a travel destination that appears to be especially complex. Our experienced authors and research team are completely independent from the attractions, restaurants, and hotels we describe. *The Unofficial Guide to Washington, D.C.,* is designed for individuals and families traveling for the fun of it, as well as for business travelers and conventioneers, especially those visiting D.C. for the first time. The guide is directed at value-conscious, consumer-oriented adults who seek a cost-effective, though not spartan, travel style.

Special Features

The *Unofficial Guide* offers the following special features:

- Friendly introductions to Washington's most fascinating neighborhoods.
- "Best of" listings, giving our well-qualified opinions on things ranging from bagels to baguettes, 4-star hotels to 12-story views.
- Listings that are keyed to your interests, so you can pick and choose.
- Advice to sight-seers on how to avoid the worst of the crowds; advice to business travelers on how to avoid traffic and excessive costs.
- Recommendations for lesser known sights that are away from the huge monuments of the Mall but are no less spectacular.
- A zone system and maps to make it easy to find places you want to go to and avoid places you don't.
- Expert advice on avoiding Washington's notorious street crime.
- A Hotel Information Chart that helps you narrow down your choices fast, according to your needs.
- Shorter listings that include only those restaurants, clubs, and hotels we think are worth considering.
- Detailed index to help you find things fast.
- Insider advice on crowds, lines, best times of day (or night) to go places, and, our secret weapon, Washington's stellar subway system.

What you *won't* get:

- Long, useless lists where everything looks the same.
- Information that gets you somewhere you want to go at the worst possible time.
- Information without advice on how to use it.

How This Guide Was Researched and Written

While a lot of guidebooks have been written about Washington, D.C., very few have been evaluative. Some guides come close to regurgitating the hotels' and tourist offices' own promotional material. In preparing this work, nothing was taken for granted. Each museum, monument, federal building, hotel, restaurant, shop, and attraction was visited by a team of trained observers who conducted detailed evaluations and rated each according to formal criteria. Team members conducted interviews with tourists of all ages to determine what they enjoyed most and least during their Washington visit.

While our observers are independent and impartial, they did not claim to have special expertise. Like you, they visited Washington as tourists or business travelers, noting their satisfaction or dissatisfaction.

The primary difference between the average tourist and the trained evaluator is the evaluator's skills in organization, preparation, and observation. The trained evaluator is responsible for much more than simply observing and cataloging. While the average tourist is gazing in awe at stacks of $20 bills at the Bureau of Engraving and Printing, for instance, the professional is rating the tour in terms of the information provided, how quickly the line moves, the location of rest rooms, and how well children can see the exhibits. He or she also checks out things like other attractions close by, alternate places to go if the line at a main attraction is too long, and the best local lunch options. Observer teams use detailed checklists to analyze hotel rooms, restaurants, nightclubs, and attractions. Finally, evaluator ratings and observations are integrated with tourist reactions and the opinions of patrons for a comprehensive quality profile of each feature and service.

In compiling this guide, we recognize that a tourist's age, background, and interests will strongly influence his or her taste in Washington's wide array of attractions and will account for a preference for one sight or museum over another. Our sole objective is to provide the reader with sufficient description, critical evaluation, and pertinent data to make knowledgeable decisions according to individual tastes.

Letters, Comments, and Questions from Readers

We expect to learn from our mistakes, as well as from the input of our readers, and to improve with each new book and edition. Many of those who use the *Unofficial Guides* write to us asking questions, making comments, or sharing their own discoveries and lessons learned in Washington. We appreciate all such input, both positive and critical, and encourage our readers to continue writing. Readers' comments and observations will frequently be incorporated into revised editions of the *Unofficial Guide,* and will contribute immeasurably to its improvement.

How to Write the Authors:

Bob, Joe, Eve
The Unofficial Guide to Washington, D.C.
P.O. Box 43673
Birmingham, AL 35243

When you write, be sure to put your return address on your letter as well as on the envelope—sometimes envelopes and letters get separated. And remember, our work takes us out of the office for long periods of time, so forgive us if our response is delayed.

Reader Survey

At the back of the guide you will find a short questionnaire that you can use to express opinions about your Washington visit. Clip the questionnaire out along the dotted line and mail it to the above address.

How Information Is Organized: By Subject and by Geographic Zones

In order to give you fast access to information about the *best* of Washington, we've organized material in several formats.

Hotels Since most people visiting Washington stay in one hotel for the duration of their trip, we have summarized our coverage of hotels in charts, maps, ratings, and rankings that allow you to quickly focus your decision-making process. We do not go on, page after page, describing lobbies and rooms which, in the final analysis, sound much the same. Instead, we concentrate on the specific variables that differentiate one hotel from another: location, size, room quality, services, amenities, and cost. The hotels are compared by rankings in a concise chart (pages 62–69) and all the vital information for all hotels is provided in a second chart (pages 72–85).

Attractions Attractions—historic buildings, museums, art galleries—draw visitors to Washington, but it's practically impossible to see them all in a single trip. We list them by type as well as location (see pages 179–186) and then evaluate each one, including its appeal to various age groups. These descriptions are the heart of this guidebook and help you to determine what to see and when.

Restaurants We provide a lot of detail when it comes to restaurants. Since you will probably eat a dozen or more restaurant meals during your stay, and since not even you can predict what you might be in the mood for on Saturday night, we provide detailed profiles of the best restaurants in and around Washington. They are also listed by cuisine and location (pages 264–270).

Entertainment and Nightlife Visitors frequently try several different clubs or nightspots during their stay. Since clubs and nightspots, like restaurants, are usually selected spontaneously after arriving in Washington, we believe detailed descriptions are warranted. The best nightspots and lounges in Washington are profiled as well (see pages 372–385).

Geographic Zones Once you've decided where you're going, getting there becomes the issue. To help you do that, we have divided the city into geographic zones and the suburbs into sub-zones:

- Zone 1 The Mall
- Zone 2 Capitol Hill
- Zone 3 Downtown
- Zone 4 Foggy Bottom
- Zone 5 Georgetown
- Zone 6 Dupont Circle/Adams-Morgan
- Zone 7 Upper Northwest Washington
- Zone 8 Northeast Washington
- Zone 9 Southeast Washington
- Zones 10 A–D Maryland Suburbs
- Zones 11 A–C Virginia Suburbs

All profiles of hotels, restaurants, and nightspots include zone numbers. If you are staying at the Carlyle Suites, for example, and are interested in Japanese restaurants within walking distance, scanning the restaurant profiles for restaurants in Zone 6 (Dupont Circle/Adams-Morgan) will provide you with the best choices.

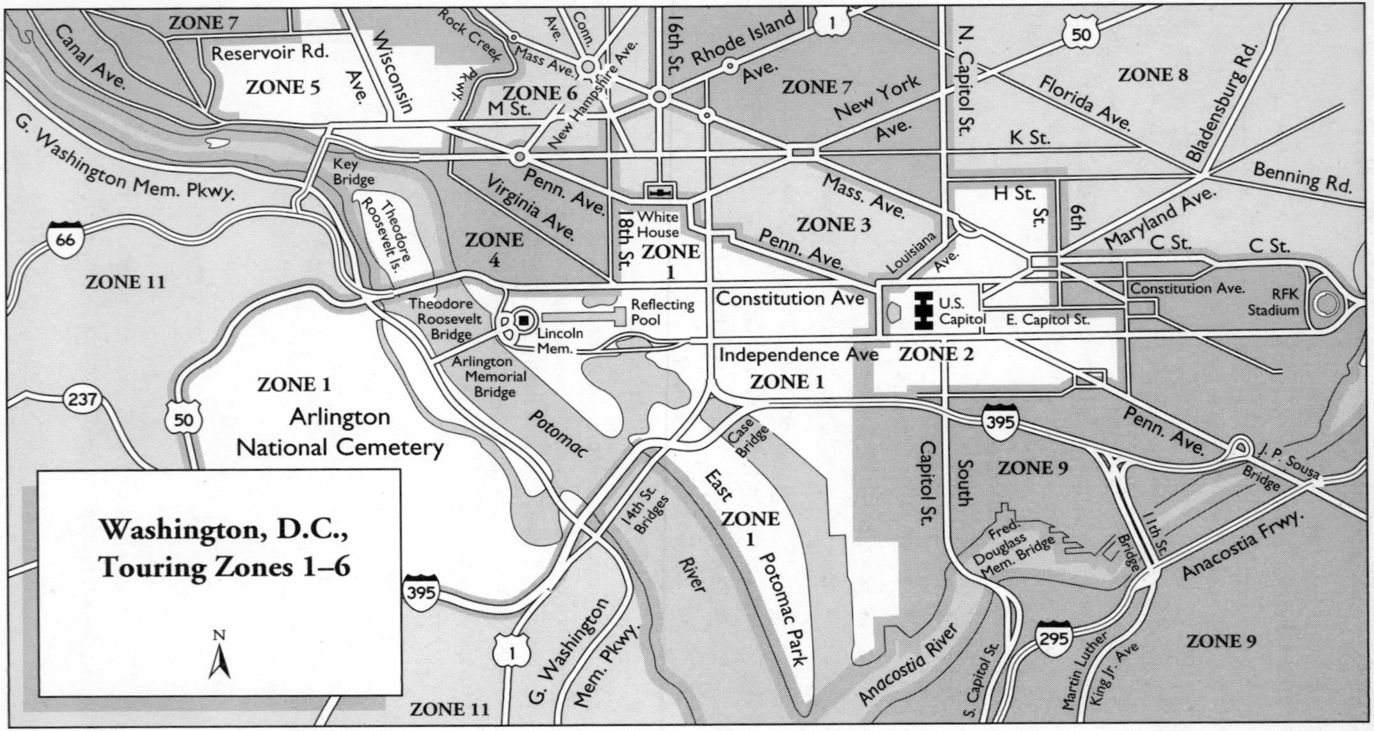
Washington, D.C., Touring Zones 1–6
N
ZONE 7
Reservoir Rd.
ZONE 5
Canal Ave.
Wisconsin Ave.
Rock Creek Pkwy.
Mass Ave.
Conn. Ave.
ZONE 6
M St.
New Hampshire Ave.
16th St.
Rhode Island Ave.
1
ZONE 7
New York Ave.
N. Capitol St.
50
ZONE 8
Florida Ave.
Bladensburg Rd.
K St.
Benning Rd.
G. Washington Mem. Pkwy.
Key Bridge
Theodore Roosevelt Is.
Penn. Ave.
Virginia Ave.
ZONE 4
18th St.
White House
ZONE 1
Mass. Ave.
ZONE 3
Penn. Ave.
Louisiana Ave.
H St.
St.
6th
Maryland Ave.
C St.
C St.
66
ZONE 11
Theodore Roosevelt Bridge
Reflecting Pool
Lincoln Mem.
Constitution Ave
U.S. Capitol
E. Capitol St.
Constitution Ave.
RFK Stadium
Independence Ave
ZONE 2
ZONE 1
Arlington Memorial Bridge
ZONE 1
Arlington National Cemetery
237
50
Potomac
Case Bridge
395
Penn. Ave.
J. P. Sousa Bridge
Capitol St.
South
ZONE 9
East
ZONE 1
Potomac Park
14th St. Bridges
River
Fred. Douglass Mem. Bridge
Bridge
11th St.
Anacostia Frwy.
395
1
G. Washington Mem. Pkwy.
Anacostia River
S. Capitol St.
295
Martin Luther King Jr. Ave
ZONE 9
ZONE 11

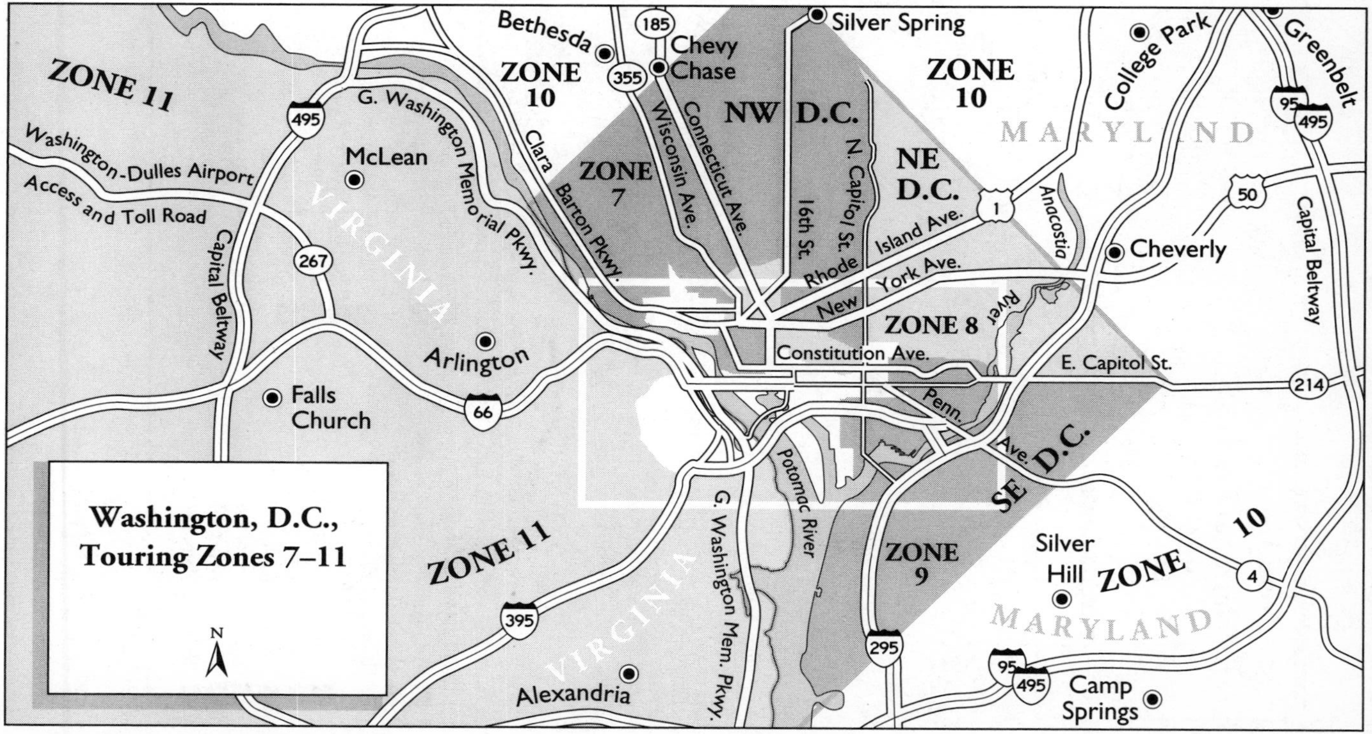

Washington, D.C., Touring Zones 7–11

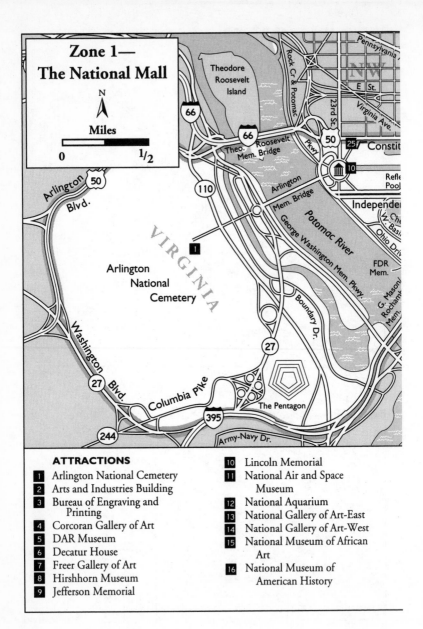

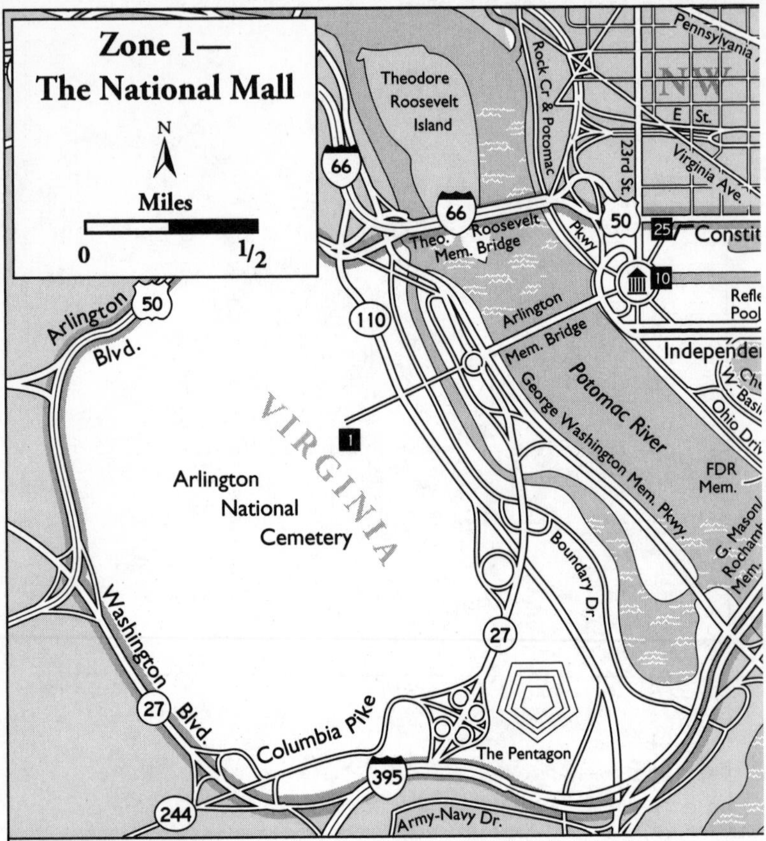

ATTRACTIONS

1 Arlington National Cemetery
2 Arts and Industries Building
3 Bureau of Engraving and Printing
4 Corcoran Gallery of Art
5 DAR Museum
6 Decatur House
7 Freer Gallery of Art
8 Hirshhorn Museum
9 Jefferson Memorial
10 Lincoln Memorial
11 National Air and Space Museum
12 National Aquarium
13 National Gallery of Art-East
14 National Gallery of Art-West
15 National Museum of African Art
16 National Museum of American History

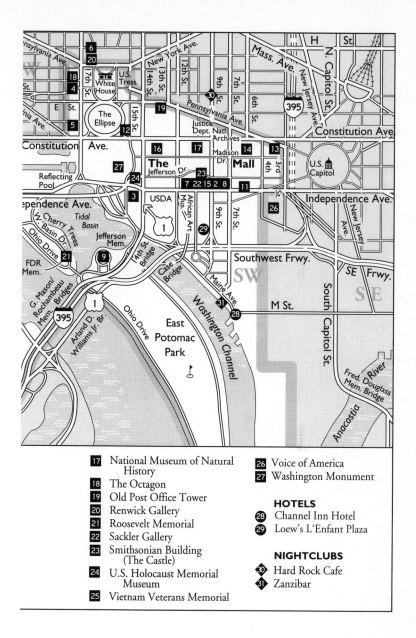

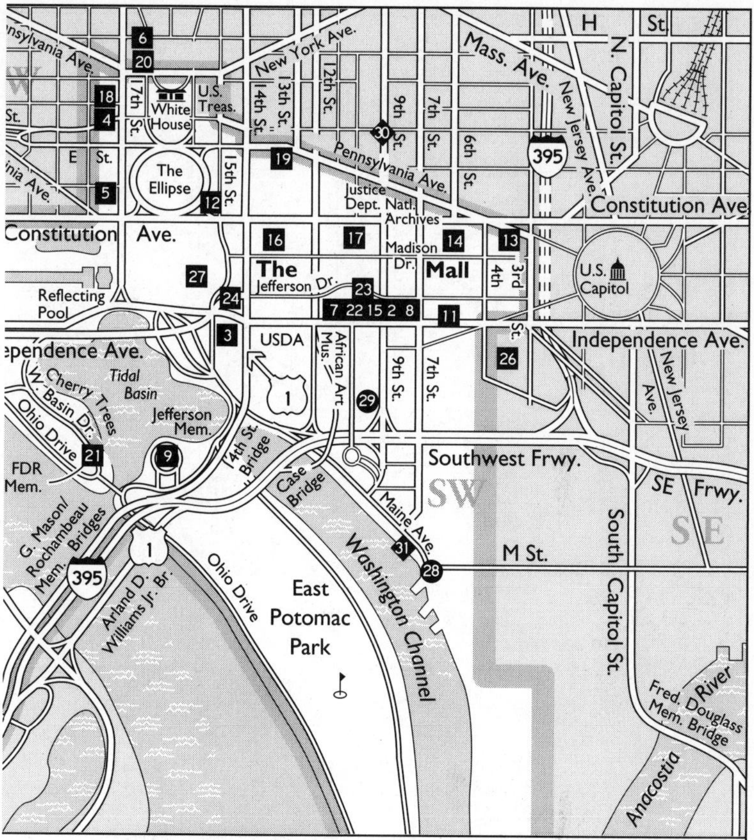

- 17 National Museum of Natural History
- 18 The Octagon
- 19 Old Post Office Tower
- 20 Renwick Gallery
- 21 Roosevelt Memorial
- 22 Sackler Gallery
- 23 Smithsonian Building (The Castle)
- 24 U.S. Holocaust Memorial Museum
- 25 Vietnam Veterans Memorial
- 26 Voice of America
- 27 Washington Monument

HOTELS

- 28 Channel Inn Hotel
- 29 Loew's L'Enfant Plaza

NIGHTCLUBS

- 30 Hard Rock Cafe
- 31 Zanzibar

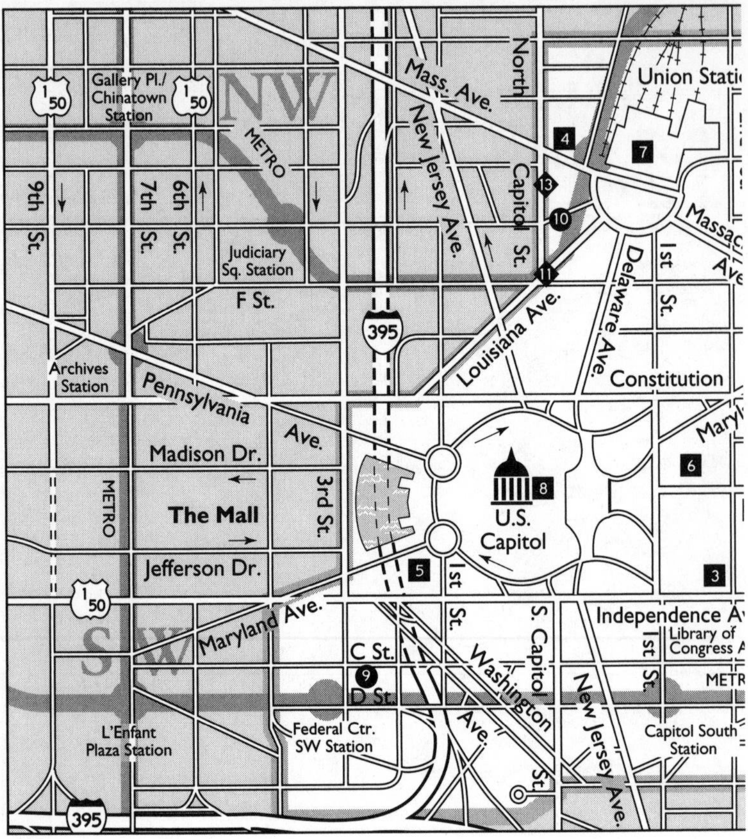
Gallery Pl./
Chinatown
Station
NW
METRO
Mass. Ave.
North
Union Station
New Jersey Ave.
Capitol St.
9th St.
7th St.
6th St.
Judiciary
Sq. Station
F St.
395
Louisiana Ave.
Delaware Ave.
1st St.
Massachusetts Ave.
Constitution
Archives
Station
Pennsylvania Ave.
Madison Dr.
The Mall
METRO
3rd St.
U.S.
Capitol
Jefferson Dr.
1st St.
50
Maryland Ave.
C St.
D St.
S. Capitol St.
Washington Ave.
New Jersey Ave.
Independence Av
Library of
Congress
1st St.
METR
SW
L'Enfant
Plaza Station
Federal Ctr.
SW Station
Capitol South
Station
395

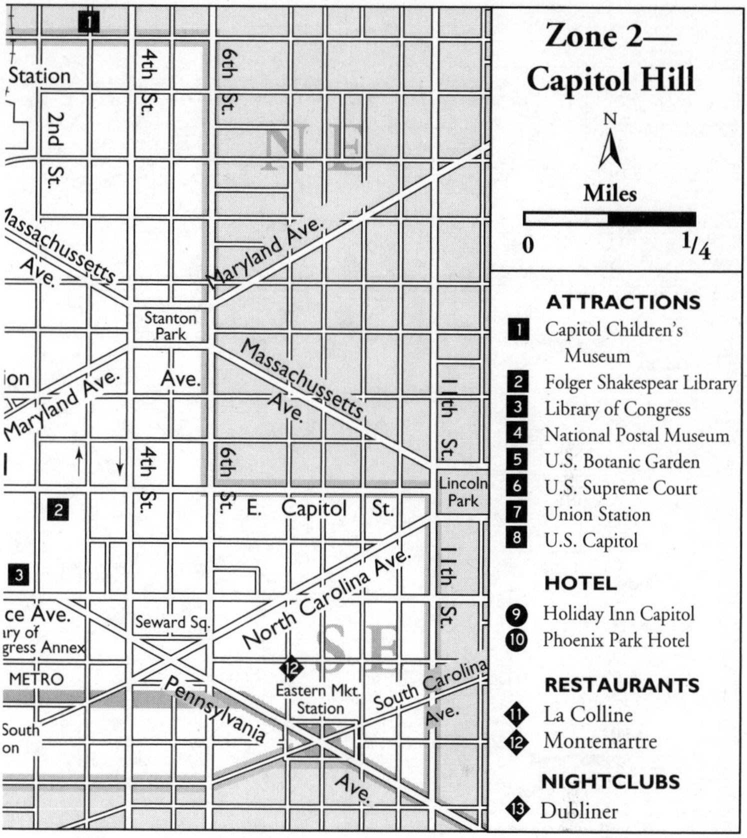
Zone 2—
Capitol Hill
N
Miles
0
1/4
ATTRACTIONS
1 Capitol Children's Museum
2 Folger Shakespear Library
3 Library of Congress
4 National Postal Museum
5 U.S. Botanic Garden
6 U.S. Supreme Court
7 Union Station
8 U.S. Capitol
HOTEL
9 Holiday Inn Capitol
10 Phoenix Park Hotel
RESTAURANTS
11 La Colline
12 Montemartre
NIGHTCLUBS
13 Dubliner
Station
2nd St.
4th St.
6th St.
NE
Massachussetts Ave.
Maryland Ave.
Stanton Park
Ave.
11th St.
Lincoln Park
E. Capitol St.
North Carolina Ave.
ce Ave.
ary of
gress Annex
Seward Sq.
METRO
Pennsylvania Ave.
Eastern Mkt. Station
South Carolina Ave.
SE
South

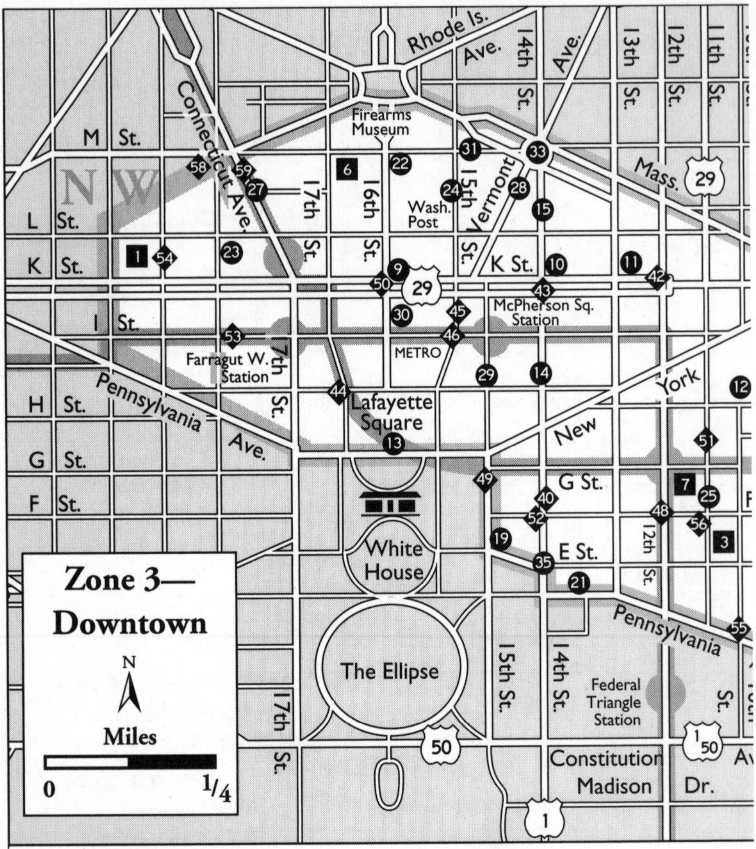

ATTRACTIONS

1 B'Nai B'rith Klutznick Museum
2 FBI
3 Ford's Theatre/Petersen House
4 International Spy Museum
5 National Building Museum
6 National Geographic Society
7 National Museum of Women in the Arts

HOTELS

8 Best Western Capitol Hill
9 Capitol Hilton
10 Crowne Plaza
11 Four Points Sheration Downtown
12 Grand Hyatt Washington
13 Hay-Adams Hotel
14 Hilton Garden Inn
15 Holiday Inn Downtown
16 Holiday Inn on the Hill
17 Hotel George
18 Hotel Monaco
19 Hotel Washington
20 Hyatt Regency Capitol Hill
21 J.W.Marriott Hotel
22 Jefferson Hotel
23 Lincoln Suites
24 Madison Hotel
25 Marriott Metro Center
26 Red Roof Inn Downtown
27 Renaissance Mayflower Hotel
28 Residence Inn Thomas Circle
29 Sofitel Lafayette
30 St. Regis
31 The Wyndham Washington

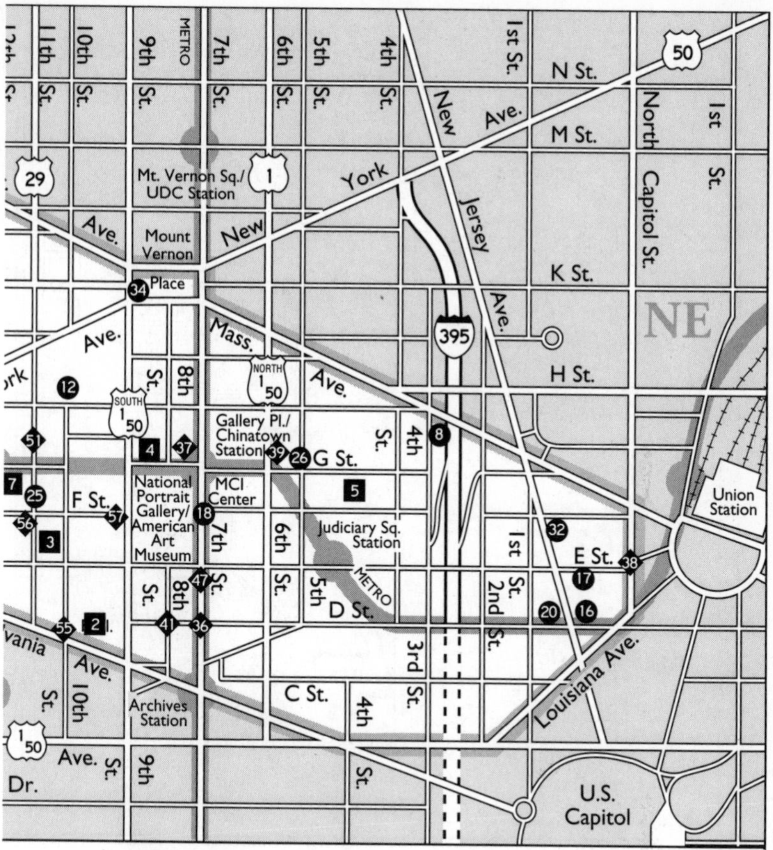

32 Washington Court Hotel
33 Washington Plaza Hotel
34 Washington Renaissance Hotel
35 Willard Inter-Continental

RESTAURANTS

36 Andale
37 Austin Grill
38 Bistro Bis
39 Burma
40 Butterfield 9
41 Cafe Atlantico
42 Courduroy
43 D.C. Coast
44 Equinox
45 Georgia Brown's
46 Gerard's Place
47 Jaleo
48 Oceanaire
49 Old Ebbitt Grill
50 Olives
51 Ortanique
52 Red Sage
53 Taberna del Alabardero
54 Teatro Goldini
55 TenPenh
56 Tosca

NIGHTCLUBS

57 The Improv
58 Ozio
59 Platinum

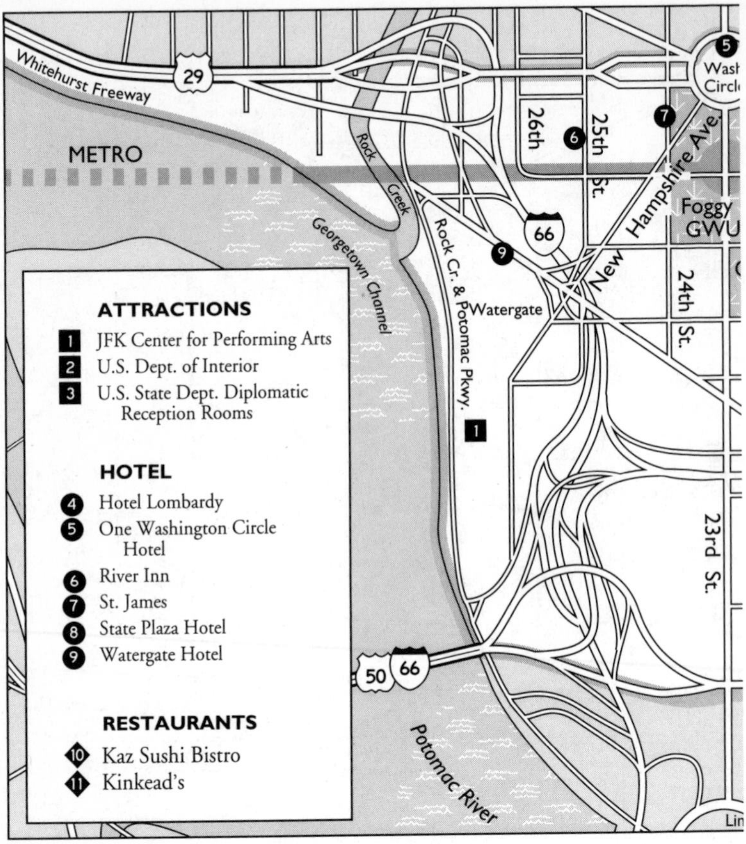
Whitehurst Freeway
29
METRO
Rock Creek
Georgetown Channel
Rock Cr. & Potomac Pkwy.
Watergate
26th
25th St.
New Hampshire Ave.
66
24th St.
23rd St.
Foggy
GWU
Wash
Circl
50
66
Potomac River
Lin
ATTRACTIONS
1 JFK Center for Performing Arts
2 U.S. Dept. of Interior
3 U.S. State Dept. Diplomatic Reception Rooms
HOTEL
4 Hotel Lombardy
5 One Washington Circle Hotel
6 River Inn
7 St. James
8 State Plaza Hotel
9 Watergate Hotel
RESTAURANTS
10 Kaz Sushi Bistro
11 Kinkead's

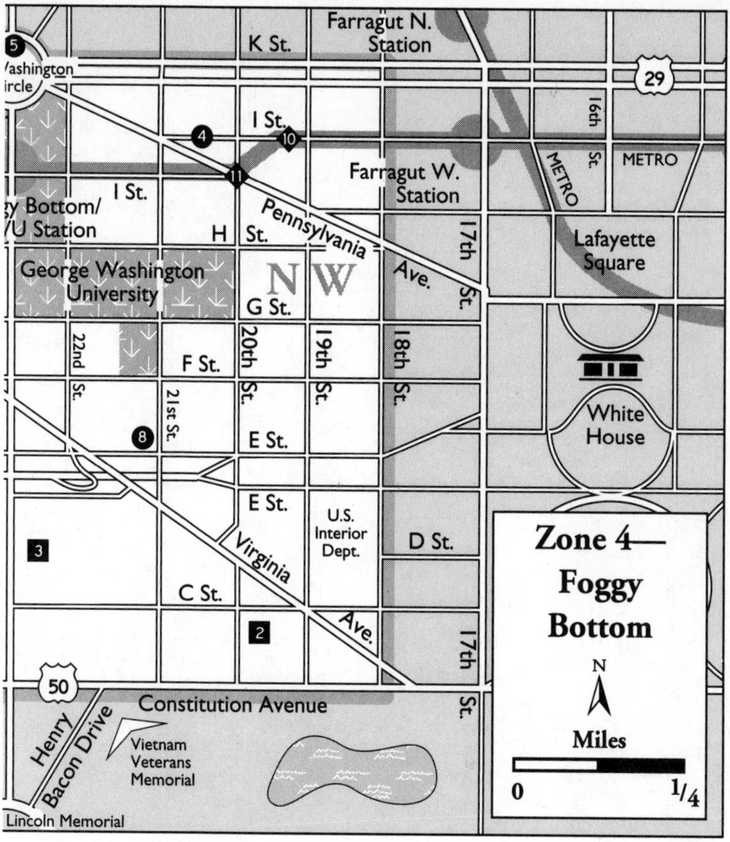
Farragut N. Station
K St.
Washington Circle
29
16th St.
I St.
Farragut W. Station
METRO
METRO
I St.
Bottom/
U Station
H St.
Pennsylvania Ave.
17th St.
Lafayette Square
George Washington University
NW
G St.
22nd St.
F St.
20th St.
19th St.
18th St.
21st St.
White House
E St.
E St.
U.S. Interior Dept.
D St.
Zone 4—Foggy Bottom
Virginia Ave.
C St.
17th St.
50
Constitution Avenue
N
Miles
Henry Bacon Drive
Vietnam Veterans Memorial
0
1/4
Lincoln Memorial

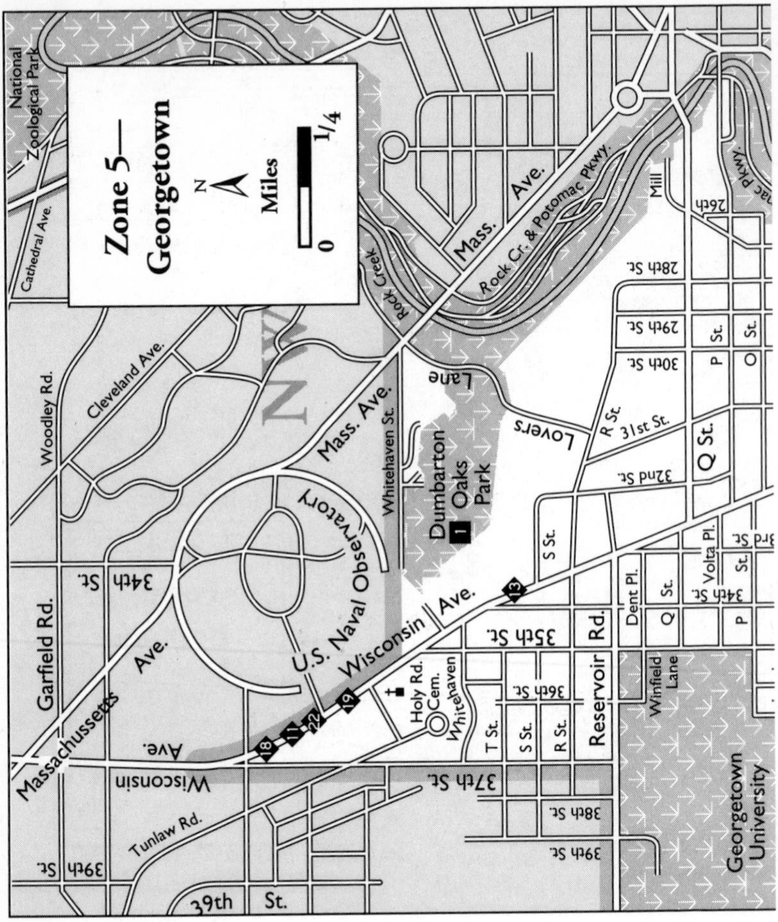

Zone 5—
Georgetown
N
Miles
0
1/4
National Zoological Park
Cathedral Ave.
Woodley Rd.
Cleveland Ave.
Garfield Rd.
34th St.
Massachussetts Ave.
Wisconsin Ave.
Tunlaw Rd.
39th St.
U.S. Naval Observatory
Mass. Ave.
Whitehaven St.
Dumbarton Oaks Park
Lovers Lane
Rock Creek
Rock Cr. & Potomac Pkwy.
Mill
26th
28th St.
29th St.
30th St.
R St.
31st St.
32nd St.
Q St.
P St.
O St.
S St.
Dent Pl.
Volta Pl.
35th St.
Reservoir Rd.
36th St.
T St.
Holy Rd. Cem.
Whitehaven
Winfield Lane
37th St.
38th St.
Georgetown University
1
11
13
18
19
22

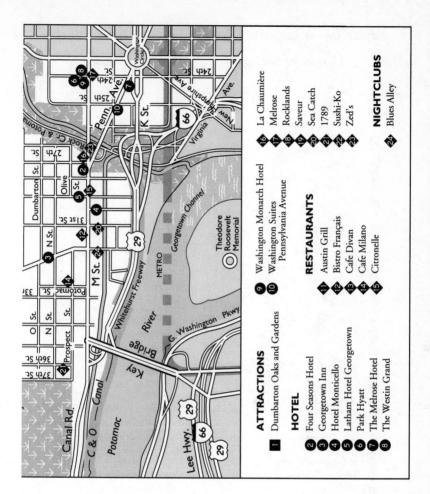

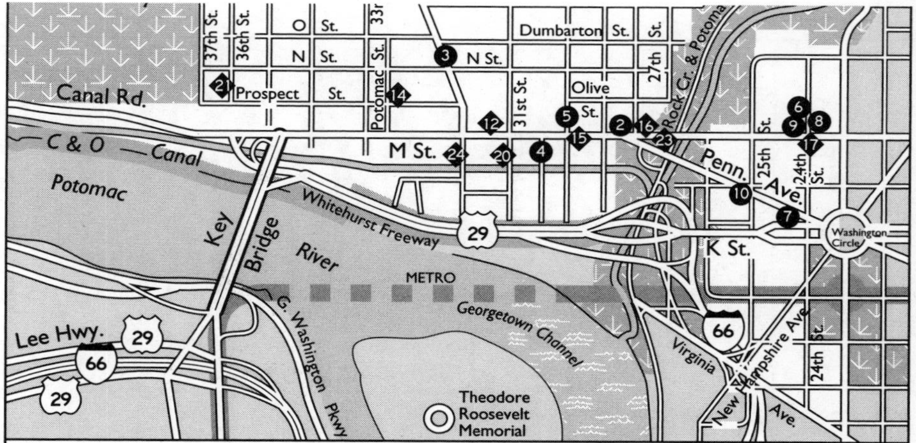

ATTRACTIONS

1 Dumbarton Oaks and Gardens

HOTEL

2 Four Seasons Hotel
3 Georgetown Inn
4 Hotel Monticello
5 Latham Hotel Georgetown
6 Park Hyatt
7 The Melrose Hotel
8 The Westin Grand
9 Washington Monarch Hotel
10 Washington Suites Pennsylvania Avenue

RESTAURANTS

11 Austin Grill
12 Bistro Français
13 Cafe Divan
14 Cafe Milano
15 Citronelle
16 La Chaumière
17 Melrose
18 Rocklands
19 Saveur
20 Sea Catch
21 1789
22 Sushi-Ko
23 Zed's

NIGHTCLUBS

24 Blues Alley

Zone 6—Dupont Circle/ Adams-Morgan

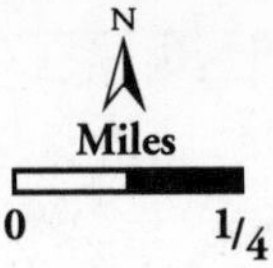

ATTRACTIONS

1 Christian Heurick House Mansion
2 House of the Temple
3 Islamic Center
4 Meridian International Center
5 Phillips Collection
6 Society of the Cincinnati
7 Textile Museum
8 Woodrow Wilson House

HOTEL

9 Best Western New Hampshire Suites
10 Carlyle Suites Hotel
11 Churchhill Hotel
12 Courtyard Embassy Row
13 Courtyard Washington
14 Embassy Inn
15 Embassy Row Hilton
16 Embassy Square Summerfield Suites
17 Embassy Suites Downtown
18 The Governor's House
19 Hotel Madera
20 Hotel Rouge
21 Hotel Topaz
22 Jurys Normandy
23 Kalorama Guest House
24 Radisson Barceló Hotel
25 Residence Inn Dupont Circle
26 The Ritz-Carlton
27 St. Gregory Luxury Hotel & Suites
28 Tabard Inn
29 Washington Hilton & Towers
30 Washington Marriott Hotel
31 Westin Fairfax
32 Windsor Park Hotel
33 Wyndham City Center

RESTAURANTS

34 Asia Nora
35 Bacchus
36 Etrusco
37 Gabriel
38 Galileo
39 i Ricchi
40 Johnny's Half Shell
41 Marcel's
42 Meskerem
43 Nora
44 Obelisk
45 Pizzeria Paradio
46 Tabard Inn
47 Vidalia

NIGHTCLUBS

48 Black Cat
49 Brickskeller
50 Buffalo Billiards
51 Chi-Cha Lounge
52 Lulu's Night Club
53 MCCXXIII

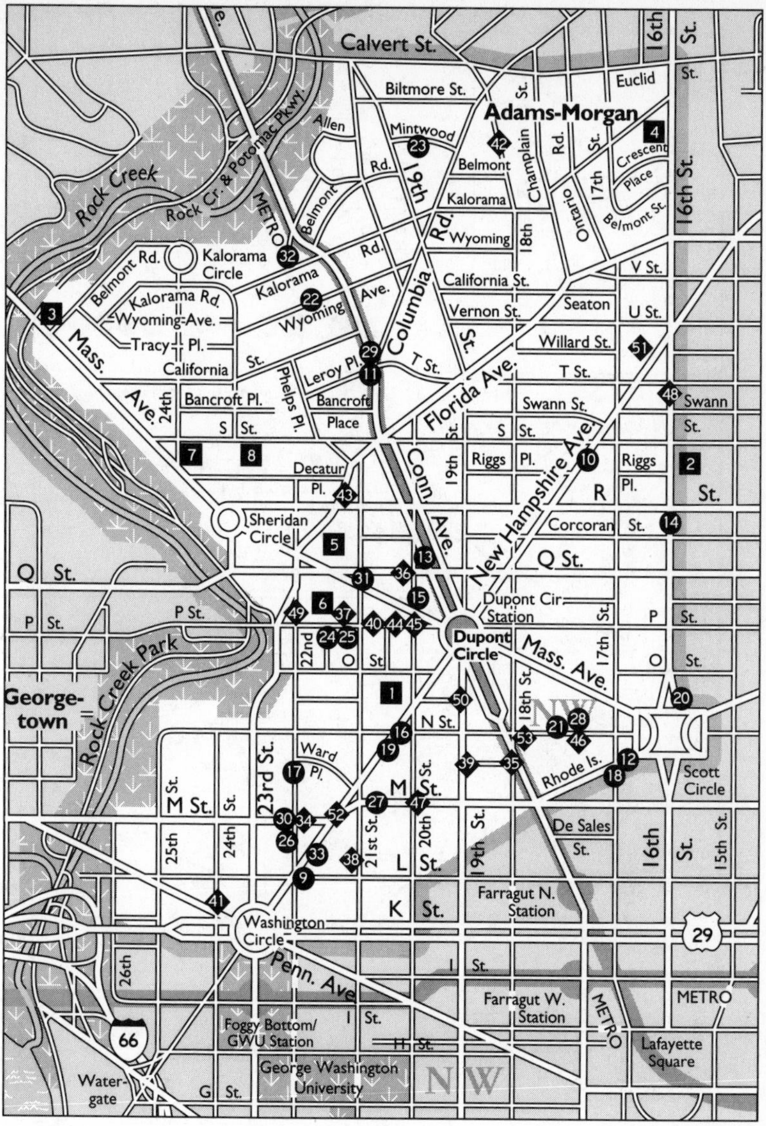
Calvert St.
Biltmore St.
Euclid
Adams-Morgan
Allen
Mintwood
Belmont
Champlain
Rd.
St.
Crescent
Place
Belmont St.
16th St.
Rock Creek
Rock Cr. & Potomac Pkwy.
METRO
19th
Kalorama
Ontario
17th
Columbia Rd.
Wyoming
18th
Kalorama Circle
Belmont Rd.
Kalorama Rd.
Wyoming Ave.
Tracy Pl.
California St.
Vernon St.
Seaton
V St.
U St.
Willard St.
Mass. Ave.
Leroy Pl.
T St.
Florida Ave.
Phelps Pl.
Bancroft Pl.
Bancroft Place
24th
S St.
Swann St.
Swann
Riggs Pl.
New Hampshire Ave.
Riggs
Decatur Pl.
R St.
Conn. Ave.
Sheridan Circle
Corcoran St.
Q St.
P St.
Dupont Cir. Station
Dupont Circle
22nd
O St.
Mass. Ave.
Rock Creek Park
Georgetown
N St.
18th St.
NW
Ward Pl.
23rd St.
M St.
Rhode Is.
Scott Circle
25th
21st St.
20th St.
L St.
19th St.
De Sales St.
16th St.
15th St.
K St.
Farragut N. Station
Washington Circle
29
I St.
Penn. Ave.
26th
Farragut W. Station
METRO
66
Foggy Bottom/ GWU Station
H St.
Lafayette Square
Watergate
G St.
George Washington University
NW

Zone 7—Upper NW

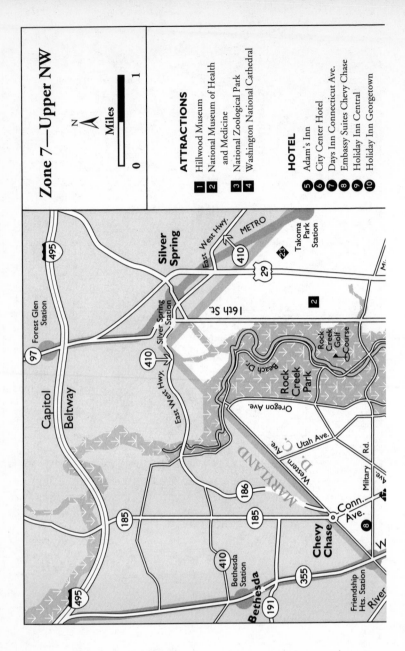

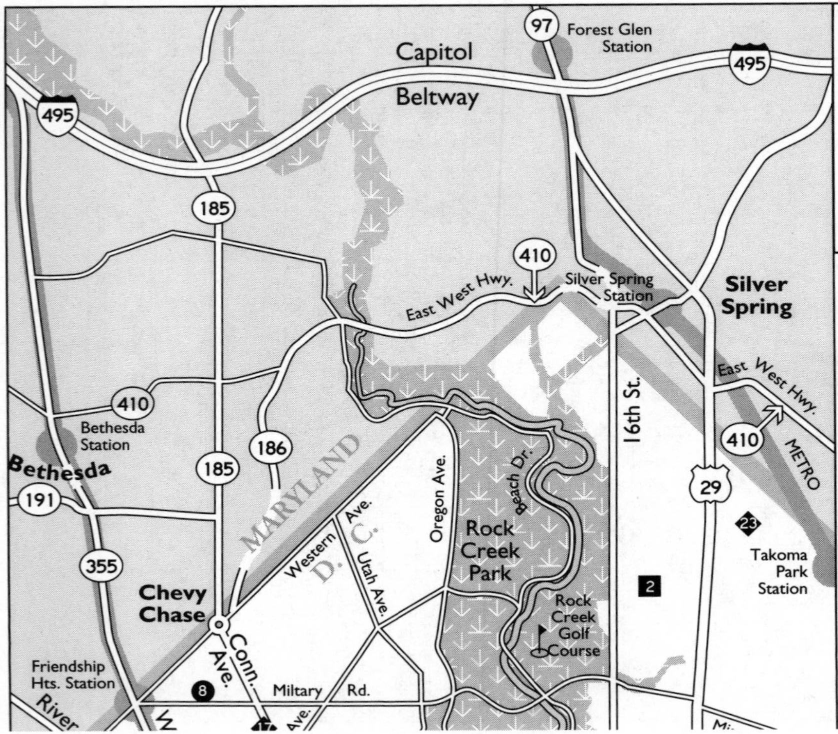

ATTRACTIONS

1. Hillwood Museum
2. National Museum of Health and Medicine
3. National Zoological Park
4. Washington National Cathedral

HOTEL

5. Adam's Inn
6. City Center Hotel
7. Days Inn Connecticut Ave.
8. Embassy Suites Chevy Chase
9. Holiday Inn Central
10. Holiday Inn Georgetown

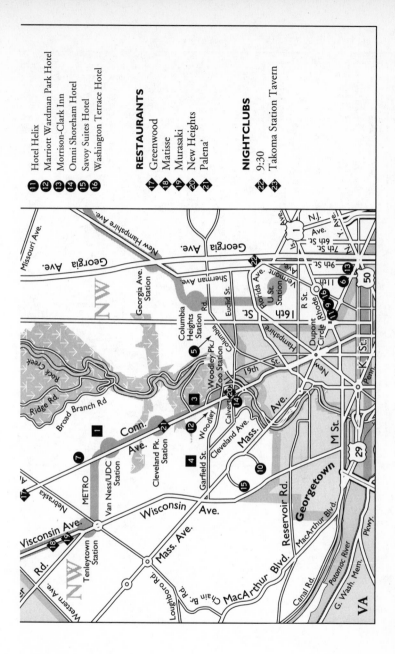

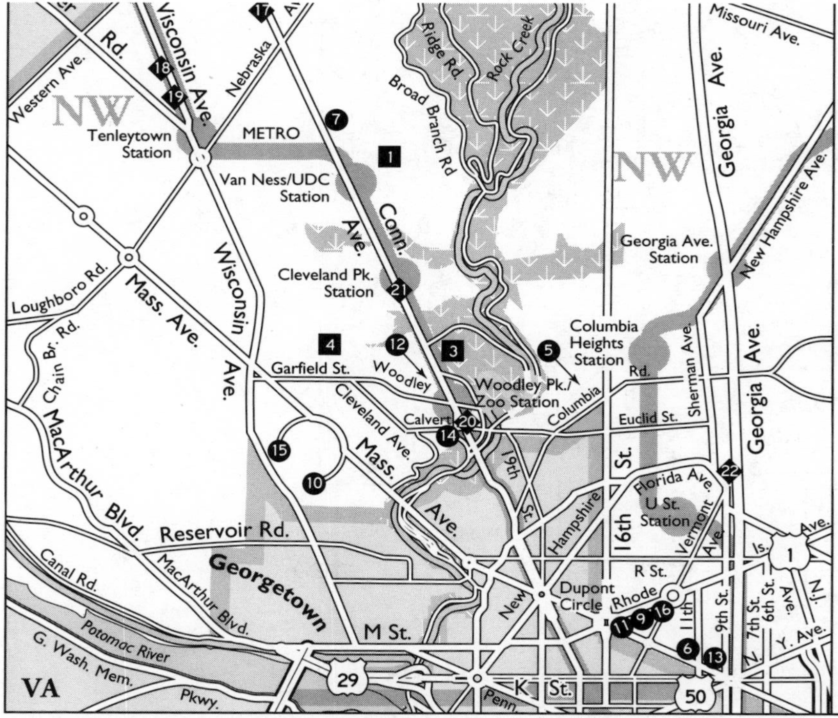

- 11 Hotel Helix
- 12 Marriott Wardman Park Hotel
- 13 Morrison-Clark Inn
- 14 Omni Shoreham Hotel
- 15 Savoy Suites Hotel
- 16 Washington Terrace Hotel

RESTAURANTS

- 17 Greenwood
- 18 Matisse
- 19 Murasaki
- 20 New Heights
- 21 Palena'

NIGHTCLUBS

- 22 9:30
- 23 Takoma Station Tavern

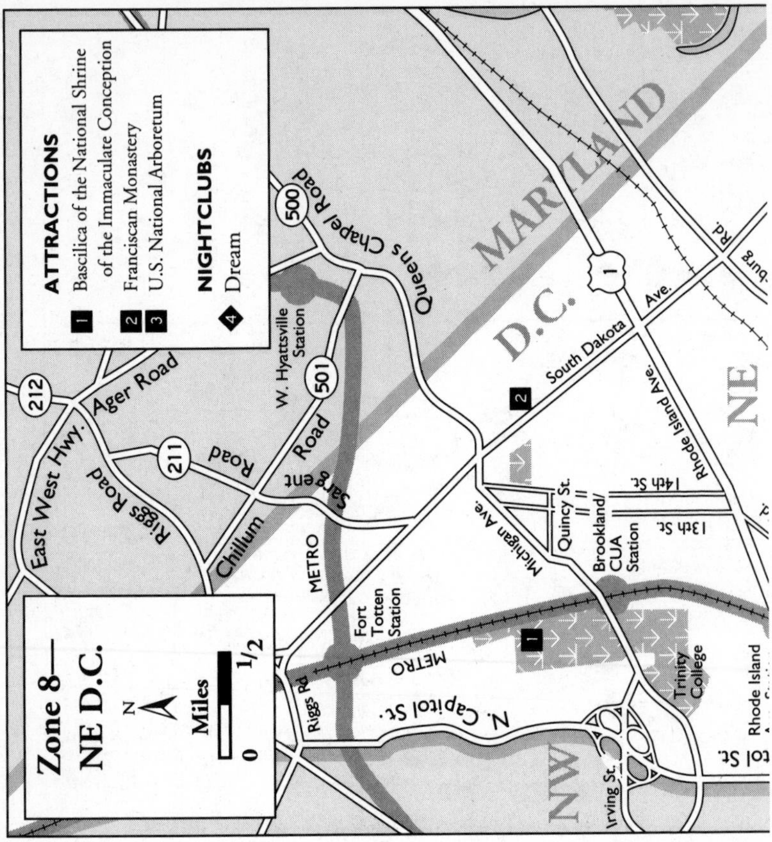

Zone 8—
NE D.C.
N
Miles
0
1/2
ATTRACTIONS
1 Basilica of the National Shrine of the Immaculate Conception
2 Franciscan Monastery
3 U.S. National Arboretum
NIGHTCLUBS
4 Dream
MARYLAND
D.C.
NE
NW
East West Hwy.
Ager Road
Riggs Road
Chillum Road
Sargent Road
Queens Chapel Road
W. Hyattsville Station
Fort Totten Station
METRO
Riggs Rd
N. Capitol St.
Michigan Ave.
South Dakota Ave.
Rhode Island Ave.
Quincy St.
14th St.
13th St.
Brookland/ CUA Station
Trinity College
Irving St.
212
211
501
500
1

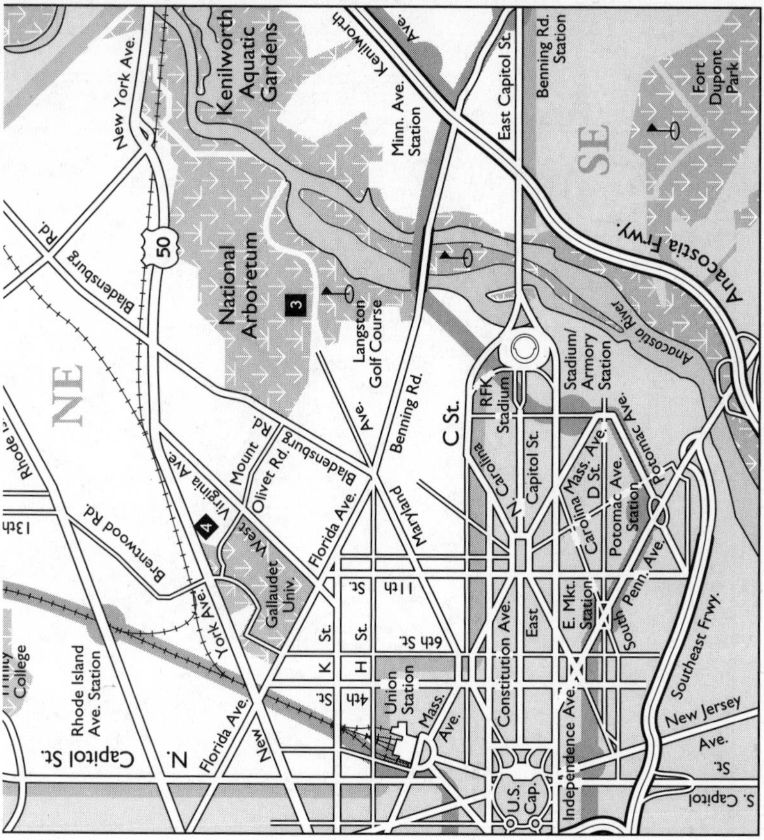

NE
SE
National Arboretum
Kenilworth Aquatic Gardens
Langston Golf Course
Gallaudet Univ.
Trinity College
Rhode Island Ave. Station
Union Station
U.S. Cap.
RFK Stadium
Stadium/ Armory Station
Minn. Ave. Station
Benning Rd. Station
Potomac Ave. Station
E. Mkt. Station
Fort Dupont Park
New York Ave.
Bladensburg Rd.
Brentwood Rd.
West Virginia Ave.
Mount Olivet Rd.
Florida Ave.
Benning Rd.
Maryland Ave.
C St.
N. Carolina
East Capitol St.
Constitution Ave.
Independence Ave.
Mass. Ave.
D St.
Potomac Ave.
South Penn. Ave.
Southeast Frwy.
New Jersey Ave.
S. Capitol St.
N. Capitol St.
Anacostia Frwy.
Anacostia River
Kenilworth Ave.
13th
11th St.
6th St.
4th St.
K St.
H St.
50
3
4

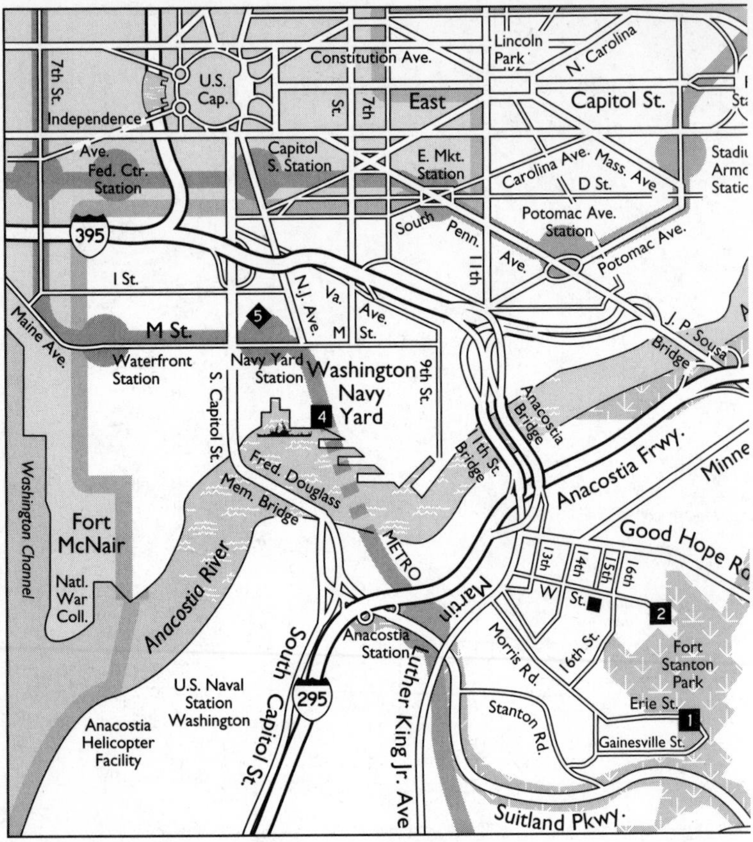

Lincoln Park
N. Carolina
Constitution Ave.
U.S. Cap.
7th St.
Independence Ave.
St.
7th
East Capitol St.
Capitol S. Station
E. Mkt. Station
Carolina Ave.
Mass. Ave.
D St.
Stadium Armory Station
Fed. Ctr. Station
395
Potomac Ave. Station
South Penn. Ave.
11th
Potomac Ave.
I St.
N.J. Ave.
Va. Ave.
M St.
Maine Ave.
5
M St.
J. P. Sousa Bridge
Waterfront Station
Navy Yard Station
Washington Navy Yard
9th St.
4
S. Capitol St.
Anacostia Bridge
11th St. Bridge
Anacostia Frwy.
Fred. Douglass Mem. Bridge
Washington Channel
Fort McNair
Natl. War Coll.
Anacostia River
METRO
Good Hope Rd.
13th
14th
15th
16th
W St.
2
Martin Luther King Jr. Ave
Anacostia Station
Morris Rd.
16th St.
Fort Stanton Park
South Capitol St.
295
U.S. Naval Station Washington
Anacostia Helicopter Facility
Stanton Rd.
Erie St.
1
Gainesville St.
Suitland Pkwy.

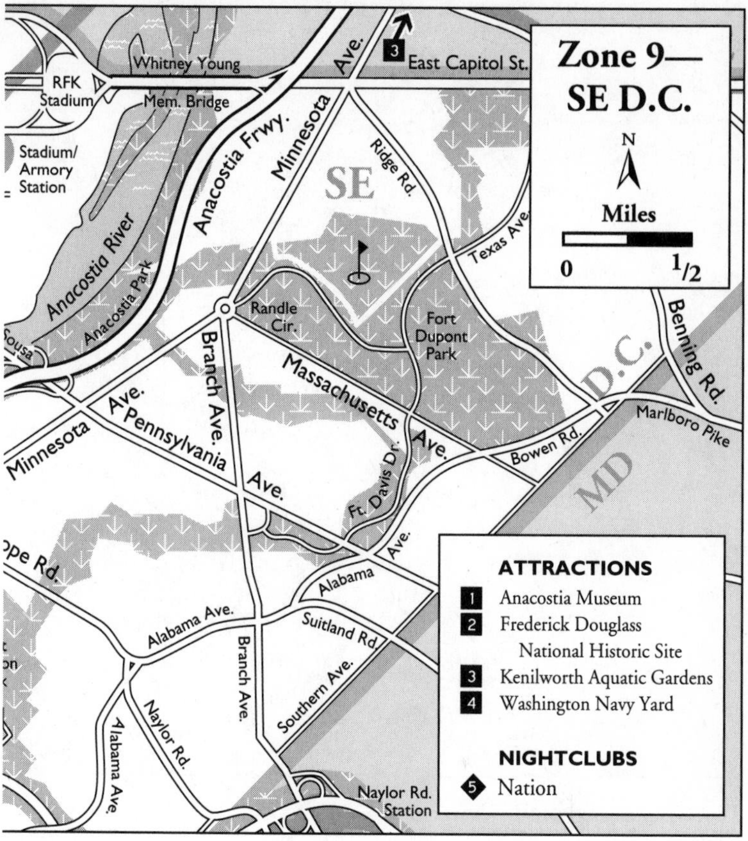
Zone 9—
SE D.C.
N
Miles
0
1/2
Whitney Young
Mem. Bridge
RFK
Stadium
Stadium/
Armory
Station
East Capitol St.
Anacostia River
Anacostia Frwy.
Anacostia Park
Minnesota Ave.
Ridge Rd.
SE
Texas Ave.
Benning Rd.
Randle
Cir.
Fort
Dupont
Park
Branch Ave.
Massachusetts Ave.
D.C.
Marlboro Pike
Bowen Rd.
MD
Minnesota Ave.
Pennsylvania Ave.
Ft. Davis Dr.
Alabama Ave.
Suitland Rd.
Southern Ave.
Naylor Rd.
Naylor Rd.
Station
ATTRACTIONS
1 Anacostia Museum
2 Frederick Douglass
National Historic Site
3 Kenilworth Aquatic Gardens
4 Washington Navy Yard
NIGHTCLUBS
5 Nation

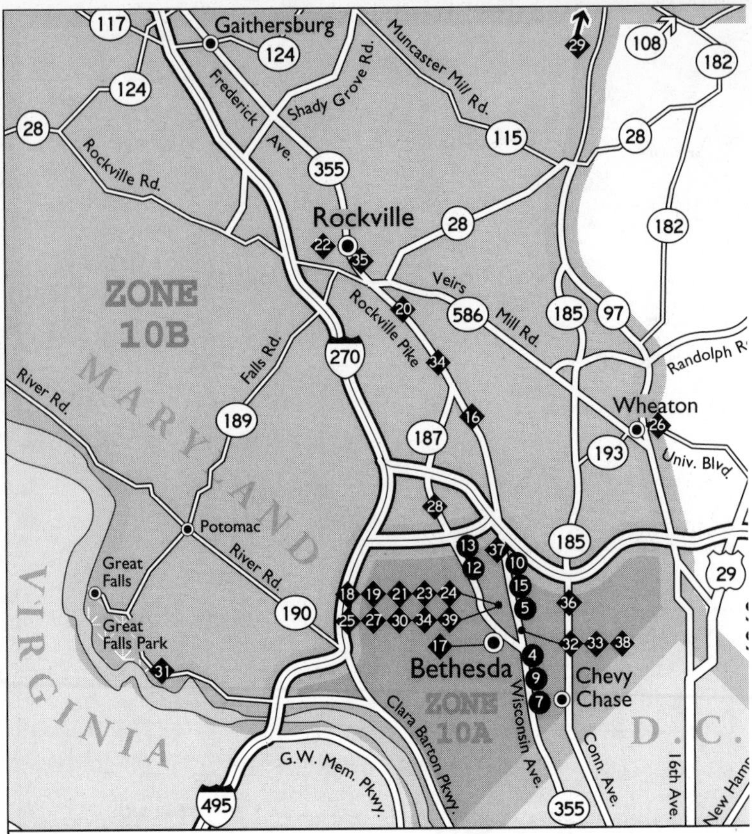

ATTRACTIONS

1 NASA/Godard Space Flight Center
2 National Cryptologic Museum
3 National Wildlife Visitor Center

HOTEL

4 American Inn of Bethesda
5 Bethesda Court Hotel
6 Courtyard New Carrollton
7 Four Points Sheraton Bethesda
8 Hilton of Silver Spring
9 Holiday Inn Bethesda
10 Holiday Inn Chevy Chase
11 Holiday Inn Silver Spring
12 Hyatt Regency Bethesda
13 Marriott Hotel Bethesda
14 Quality Inn College Park
15 Residence Inn Bethesda

RESTAURANTS

16 Addie's
17 Austin Grill

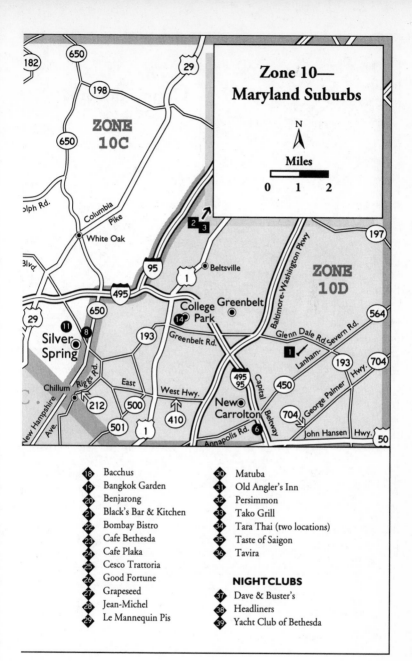

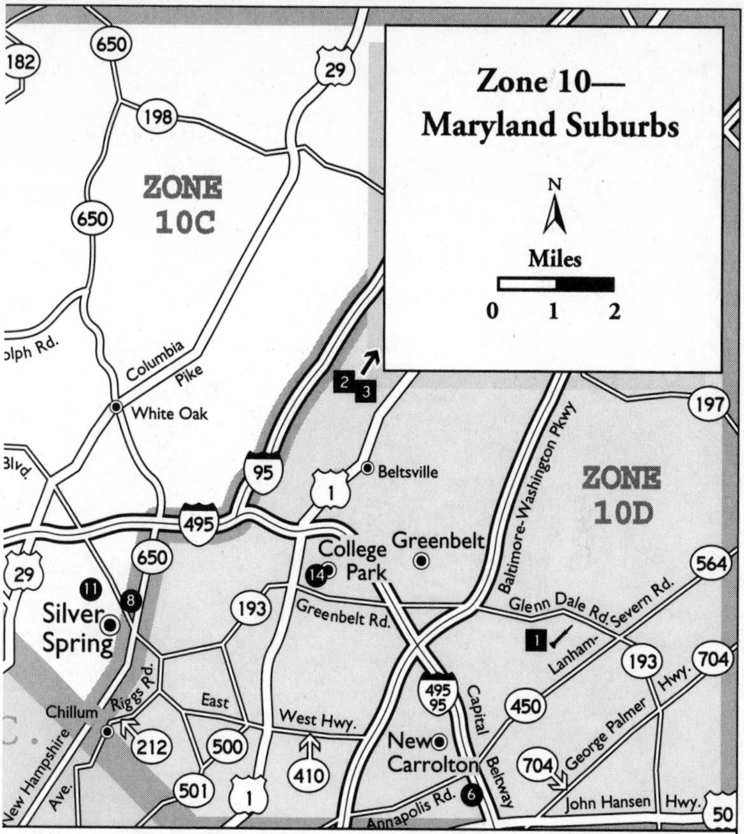

18 Bacchus
19 Bangkok Garden
20 Benjarong
21 Black's Bar & Kitchen
22 Bombay Bistro
23 Cafe Bethesda
24 Cafe Plaka
25 Cesco Trattoria
26 Good Fortune
27 Grapeseed
28 Jean-Michel
29 Le Mannequin Pis
30 Matuba
31 Old Angler's Inn
32 Persimmon
33 Tako Grill
34 Tara Thai (two locations)
35 Taste of Saigon
36 Tavira

NIGHTCLUBS

37 Dave & Buster's
38 Headliners
39 Yacht Club of Bethesda

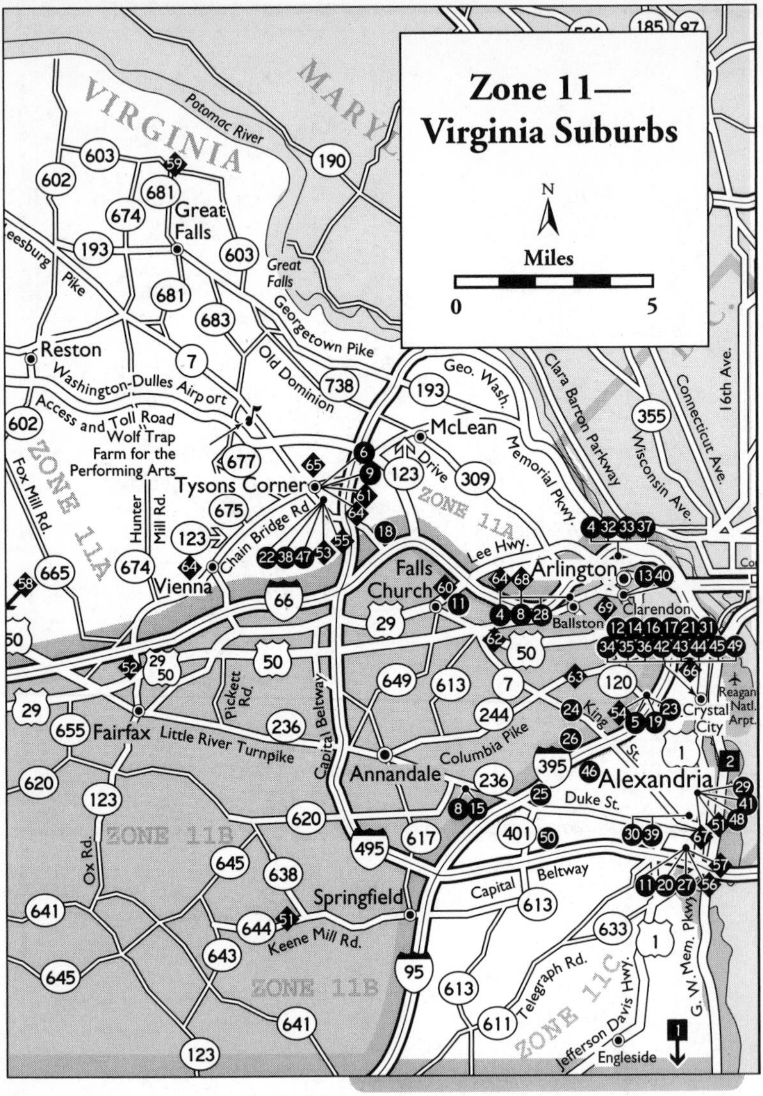
Zone 11—
Virginia Suburbs
N
Miles
0
5
VIRGINIA
MARYLAND
Potomac River
Great Falls
Reston
McLean
Tysons Corner
Vienna
Falls Church
Arlington
Clarendon
Ballston
Fairfax
Annandale
Springfield
Alexandria
Crystal City
Reagan Natl. Arpt.
Engleside
Leesburg Pike
Georgetown Pike
Old Dominion
Washington-Dulles Airport Access and Toll Road
Wolf Trap Farm for the Performing Arts
Chain Bridge Rd.
Geo. Wash. Memorial Pkwy.
Clara Barton Parkway
Wisconsin Ave.
Connecticut Ave.
16th Ave.
Lee Hwy.
Fox Mill Rd.
Hunter Mill Rd.
Pickett Rd.
Capital Beltway
Little River Turnpike
Columbia Pike
King St.
Duke St.
Ox Rd.
Keene Mill Rd.
Telegraph Rd.
Jefferson Davis Hwy.
G. W. Mem. Pkwy.
ZONE 11A
ZONE 11B
ZONE 11C

ATTRACTIONS

1 Mount Vernon
2 Old Town Alexandria

HOTEL

3 Arlington Virginia Hilton
4 Best Western Key Bridge
5 Best Western Pentagon
6 Best Western Tyson's Westpark
7 Comfort Inn Arlington
8 Comfort Inn Landmark
9 Comfort Inn Vienna
10 Comfort Inn Washington Gateway
11 Courtyard Alexandria
12 Courtyard Crystal City
13 Courtyard Rosslyn
14 Crowne Plaza National Airport
15 Days Inn Alexandria
16 Days Inn Crystal City
17 Doubletree Hotel Crystal City
18 Doubletree Hotel Tysons Corner
19 Econo Lodge National Airport
20 Embassy Suites Alexandria
21 Embassy Suites Crystal City
22 Embassy Suites Tysons Corner
23 Four Points Sheration Pentagon
24 Hampton Inn Alexandria
25 Hampton Suites
26 Hilton Alexandria at Mark Center
27 Holiday Inn and Suites
28 Holiday Inn Arlington
29 Holiday Inn Hotel and Suites
30 Holiday Inn National Airport
31 Holiday Inn Rosslyn at Key Bridge
32 Holiday Inn Select Old Town
33 Hyatt Arlington
34 Hyatt Regenceny Crystal City
35 Marriott Crystal City
36 Marriott Crystal Gateway
37 Marriott Hotel Key Bridge
38 Marriott Tysons Corner
39 Morrison House
40 Quality Inn Iwo Jima
41 Radisson Plaza Hotel Old Town
42 Residence Inn Pentagon City
43 Ritz-Carlton Pentagon City
44 Shearaton Crystal City
45 Sheraton National Hotel
46 Sheraton Pentagon South
47 Sheraton Premiere Tysons Corner
48 Sheration Suites Alexandria
49 Washington National Airport Hilton
50 Washington Suites Alexandria

RESTAURANTS

51 Austin Grill (two locations)
52 Bombay Bistro
53 Busara
54 Carlyle Grand Cafe
55 Colvin Run Tavern
56 Elysium
57 Geranio
58 The Inn at Little
59 L'Auberge Chez Francois
60 La Côte D'Or Cafe
61 Maestro
62 Mark's Duck House
63 Matuba
64 Tara Thai
65 Taste of Saigon
66 Woo Lae Oak

NIGHTCLUBS

67 Birchmere
68 Iota
69 Whitey's

Part One

Planning Your Visit to Washington

When to Go

Going When the Weather Is Good

The best times to visit Washington are in the spring and fall, when the weather is most pleasant and nature puts on a show. The city's fabled cherry blossoms bloom in late March or early April, while fall brings crisp, cool weather and, by mid-October, a spectacular display of gold, orange, and red leaves.

The summers—mid-June through September—can be brutally hot and humid. Visitors in July and August not only contend with the heat as they sprint from building to building, but also must endure the city's heavy reliance on air conditioning that often reaches meat-locker chill. August, with its predictably oppressive heat, is the month when Washingtonians leave town in droves.

Washington's winter weather, on the other hand, is erratic. Balmy, mid-60s days are possible through December. While it often gets into the teens in January and February, midday temperatures can climb into the 40s and 50s. This is the season to beat the crowds.

March is tricky. While warm daytime temperatures are frequent, sometimes a large, moist air mass moving north from the Gulf of Mexico will collide with a blast of frigid air from Canada. The result is a big, wet snowfall that paralyzes the city for days. (It should be noted, in all fairness, that the *prediction* of snow can paralyze D.C.)

Washington weather can run the gamut from subzero (rarely), to mild (most of the winter, some of the summer, and most of the spring and fall), to scorchingly hot and unbearably humid (most of July and August). See the boxed table, on page 35, of the city's average monthly temperatures, in degrees Fahrenheit.

Avoiding Crowds

In general, popular tourist sites are busier on weekends than weekdays, Saturdays are busier than Sundays, and summer is busier than winter. The best days for avoiding big crowds at Washington's most popular attractions are Monday through Wednesday. Crowds begin to increase as the week progresses, with the volume of visitors peaking on Saturday. During the busiest tourist seasons, spring and summer, major Washington tourist attractions are always crowded between 9:30 a.m. and 3 p.m. For people in town on business, this tourist influx means heavier traffic, congested airports, a packed Metro . . . and a tough time finding a convenient hotel room.

Driving in weekday rush hours, featuring at least 100,000 frantic, short-tempered bureaucrats clawing their way to office or home, should be avoided at all costs. On weekends, the same government workers and their families become tourists, often creating midday traffic snarls during the warmer months.

If you're driving to Washington, try to time your arrival on a weekend or during a non–rush hour time—before 7 a.m. or during a rather narrow window that opens around 9:30 a.m. and starts to close quickly around 3 p.m. Afternoon traffic doesn't begin to clear up until at least 6:30 p.m. Friday afternoon rush hours are the worst: Don't even think of driving near D.C. until after 8 p.m.

Trying to Reason with the Tourist Season

Whether you're in town on business or pleasure, it's a good idea to be aware of when the big crowds of tourists are likely to be jamming up the Metro, the sidewalk, or the place you've picked for lunch.

The best time to avoid crowds entirely is in winter. On weekdays especially, the Mall is nearly deserted and museums, monuments, and normally crowd-intensive hot spots like the Capitol are nearly empty—except for the people who work there. Furthermore, the relative scarcity of tourists in the off-season eliminates the worst of D.C.'s traffic gridlock, except during peak rush hours.

After the winter doldrums, crowds begin picking up in late March and peak in early April, when the Japanese cherry trees along the Tidal Basin bloom and Washington is flooded with visitors. Mammoth throngs pack the Mall, and it's elbow to elbow in the National Air and Space Museum. Because of the crowded conditions, we do not recommend touring Washington in the early spring.

Instead, if at all possible, delay your visit until late May or early June. Crowds are more manageable for a few weeks and the weather is usually delightful.

The tourist pace begins picking up again in mid-June as schools let out. July through mid-August are very crowded—and usually the weather is brutally hot and humid. Popular museums such as the Museum of Natural History, the National Air and Space Museum, and the National Museum of American History fill up with masses of elbow-to-elbow people, eating in restaurants becomes a stress-inducing ordeal, and the entire experience becomes exhausting. Driving conditions, never good in Washington, degenerate into gridlock—even on weekends—and the Metro is packed to rush-hour levels all day.

The throngs begin to thin during the last two weeks of August, when kids start returning to school. After Labor Day, the volume of visitors drops off significantly during the week, but weekends remain packed through October—though not as packed as in spring and summer. In November, tourist activity slows down dramatically.

After May and June, the best time to visit Washington is in the late fall and winter. While Thanksgiving Day brings hordes of visitors to popular sights on the Mall, car traffic is light and getting around town from November through March is easy. Winter visitors can't count on balmy weather, but crowds are virtually nonexistent and Washington's elaborate cultural season kicks into full swing. Plays, music, opera, and ballet fill the city's theaters and halls—the Kennedy Center, Arena Stage, the Shakespeare Theater at the Folger, the National Theater, Ford's Theatre, and the Library of Congress. Both business visitors and folks in town to tour the sights will find Washington a lot easier to get around in during the late fall and winter.

WASHINGTON'S AVERAGE MONTHLY TEMPERATURES

	High	Low		High	Low
January	42° F	27° F	July	87° F	68° F
February	44° F	28° F	August	84° F	66° F
March	53° F	35° F	September	78° F	60° F
April	64° F	44° F	October	67° F	48° F
May	75° F	54° F	November	55° F	38° F
June	83° F	64° F	December	45° F	30° F

The Longest Lines

Unlike Disney World, a tourist destination with which Washington shares some similarities, D.C. has only a handful of attractions that require enduring long queues—most notably, the U.S. Capitol and the FBI. Even at these, a little judicious planning can virtually guarantee you won't spend hours standing in line.

If your visit to Washington must coincide with the heavy tourist season, read on: There are ways to make it more tolerable, in spite of the record crowds jamming the Mall, the popular museums, eateries, public transportation, and highways. Check Part Five for detailed information on transportation, and Part Six for pages of sight-seeing tips.

Getting to Washington

Folks planning a trip to our nation's capital have some options when it comes to getting there: by car, train, or plane. Your distance from Washington—and your tolerance for hassles such as Capital Beltway gridlock and inconveniently located airports—will probably determine which mode of transportation you ultimately take. (See also Part Four, Arriving and Getting Oriented.)

Driving

A lot of people who live in the populous Eastern Seaboard or anywhere else within a 12-hour drive of D.C. automatically jump in the family car when embarking on a vacation to Washington. And no wonder: Even though gasoline prices have increased, a nearly complete interstate highway system makes the car trip both easy and inexpensive. The problem, however, is when you arrive in Washington . . . or, to be more exact, when you hit the notorious Capital Beltway that surrounds the city in the Maryland and Virginia suburbs. Arrive on a weekday morning between 7 a.m. and 10 a.m. or in the afternoon from 3 p.m. to 7 p.m. and you'll discover why Washington has a reputation for traffic congestion rivaled only by New York and Los Angeles: Traffic inches along during rush hours and is astonishingly heavy the rest of the day and on warm-weather weekends as well. It only gets worse the closer you get to the Mall. Washington's peculiar geography and eighteenth-century street layout, coupled with unremitting urban and suburban growth, makes touring by car almost impossible. Street parking near popular tourist sights is severely limited, and parking garages, while plentiful in downtown D.C., are expensive and often inconvenient. Our recommendation: If at all possible, leave the car at home. Washington's air and rail connections are excellent, and its Metro subway system is one of the best in the world. And where the Metro won't take you—Georgetown, Mount Vernon, and the Washington National Cathedral come to mind—plentiful cabs and commercial touring outfits will. If you do drive, arrive on a weekend to miss the worst traffic, or very late or early on a weekday. Stay at a hotel with off-street parking and within easy walking distance to a Metro station. Use public transportation and leave the car parked through most of your stay.

AMTRAK PASSENGER TRAIN SERVICE TO WASHINGTON

City	Distance	Hours	Frequency
NORTHEAST			
Philadelphia	115 miles	1.5–2 hours	more than 1 per hour
New York City	225 miles	3–4.5 hours	more than 1 per hour
Boston	400 miles	8–9.75 hours	11 per day
SOUTH			
Richmond	110 miles	2 hours	8 per day
Newport News	187 miles	4 hours	2 per day
Raleigh-Durham	305 miles	6 hours	2 per day
Charlotte	376 miles	8.5–10 hours	2 per day
Charleston, S.C.	503 miles	9–9.5 hours	2 per day
Atlanta	633 miles	13.5 hours	1 per day
Birmingham	799 miles	18 hours	1 per day
New Orleans	1,155 miles	25–36 hours	1 per day
Jacksonville	753 miles	13.5–15 hours	3 per day
Tampa	996 miles	18 hours	1 per day
Orlando	1,129 miles	16.5–18.5 hours	2 per day
Miami	1,166 miles	22.5–24 hours	3 per day
WEST			
Pittsburgh	300 miles	7.5 hours	1 per day
Cleveland	440 miles	11 hours	1 per day
Toledo	550 miles	13 hours	1 per day
Cincinnati	602 miles	14 hours	3 per week
Chicago	780 miles	18 hours	10 per week

Taking the Train

Washington's gleaming Union Station, recently refurbished and the city's most visited tourist attraction (the National Air and Space Museum is number two), is only one of the reasons that taking the train to D.C. is an excellent idea. Another is convenience: Folks living along the East Coast from Boston to Miami are served daily by Amtrak, and lots of people living east of the Mississippi are close to direct rail service into the nation's capital. (In some cases you can board the train in the evening and arrive in Washington in the morning.) From Union Station you're only minutes from a downtown hotel by cab. Because of the city's exasperating traffic—and a public transportation system that virtually eliminates the need for a car—it's the smart way to travel to Washington. We've provided a listing of some major cities with direct Amtrak passenger train service to Washington's Union Station (the frequency of service indicates the number of trains running in both directions).

For schedules and reservations, call Amtrak at (800) 872-7245 or visit www.amtrak.com.

A CALENDAR OF FESTIVALS AND EVENTS

Washington hosts a variety of special events throughout the year: fairs, celebrations, parades, shows, festivals, tours, film and jazz festivals, and ceremonies. What follows is a listing of some of D.C.'s most popular and well-known annual events. For exact dates, times, locations, and admission fees, call the phone numbers provided before your visit. For additional information on special events, log on to www.washingtonpost.com or www. washington.org before you hit town.

January

Opening of Congress The first week of January.

Robert E. Lee's Birthday Celebration. The birthdays of Revolutionary War Colonel Light Horse Harry Lee and his son, Robert E. Lee, are celebrated at the Lee-Fendall House and The Boyhood Home of Robert E. Lee in Alexandria, Virginia. Refreshments, period music, house tours. Admission fee. (703) 548-1789.

February

Mount Vernon Open House A wreath-laying ceremony at Washington's tomb is followed by a fife and drum corps performance on the green. Free. (703) 780-2000.

George Washington's Birthday Parade The nation's largest parade celebrating our first president takes place in Old Town Alexandria. Free. (703) 838-4200.

Frederick Douglass Birthday Tribute The birthday of the great African- American statesman, orator, and advocate of freedom for African Americans and other minorities is observed at the Frederick Douglass National Historic Site (Cedar Hill) in Anacostia. Free. (202) 426-5961.

March

Smithsonian Kite Festival Kite makers and flyers of all ages gather at the Washington Monument grounds to compete for prizes and trophies. Free. (202) 357-2700.

National Cherry Blossom Festival More than 6,000 Japanese cherry trees bloom from late March to early April, bringing springtime splendor to Washington. The Cherry Blossom Festival Parade features princesses, floats, and VIPs. Other events include free concerts, the Japanese Lantern Lighting Ceremony, the Cherry Blossom Ball, and an annual Marathon. The parade hot line is (202) 547-1500.

April

White House Spring Garden Tours Tour the beautiful gardens of the presidential home. Free. (202) 456-2200.

White House Easter Egg Roll For children ages 3–6 accompanied by an adult. Eggs and entertainment provided. Children of other ages gather on the South Lawn of the White House. Free. (202) 456-2200.

William Shakespeare's Birthday A day of music, theater, children's events, food, and exhibits at the Folger Shakespeare Library. Free. (202) 544-7077.

May

Washington National Cathedral Flower Mart Each year is a salute to a different country, with flower booths, entertainment, and decorating demonstrations. Free. (202) 537-6200.

National Law Enforcement Officers Memorial Candlelight Vigil Honors America's fallen law enforcement officers; official dedication of new names being added to the memorial, located on E Street between 4th and 5th Streets, NW. Free. (202) 737-3400.

Memorial Day Weekend Concert The National Symphony Orchestra performs on the West Lawn of the U.S. Capitol, kicking off the summer season. Free. (202) 619-7222.

Memorial Day Ceremonies at Arlington National Cemetery Wreath-laying ceremonies at the Kennedy grave site, a presidential wreath-laying at the Tomb of the Unknowns, and services at the Memorial Amphitheater featuring military bands and a presidential keynote address. Free. (202) 685-2851.

Memorial Day Ceremonies at the Vietnam Veterans Memorial Wreath-laying, speeches, military bands, and a keynote address. Free. (202) 619-7222.

Memorial Day Ceremonies at the U.S. Navy Memorial Wreath-laying ceremonies and an evening concert by the U.S. Navy Band. Free. (202) 737-2300.

June

Capital Jazz Fest Three days of live, contemporary jazz featuring top national acts, workshops, food, and juried crafts. Held in D.C.'s Maryland suburbs. Check out their website at www.capitaljazz.com. Admission fee. (301) 218-0404.

A CALENDAR OF FESTIVALS AND EVENTS *(continued)*

June (continued)

Dupont-Kalorama Museum Walk Day Celebration of collections by six institutions in the area. Activities include textile demonstrations, video programs, interactive tours, hands-on art programs, historic house tours, food, and crafts. Shuttle service provided. Free. (202) 667-0441.

Kemper Open Watch the biggest names in professional golf. Admission fee for spectators. (301) 469-3737.

July

Smithsonian Folklife Festival More than one million people attend this festival of American music, crafts, and ethnic foods on the National Mall each year. Free. (202) 357-2700.

National Independence Day Celebration (July 4) A full day of dramatic readings, a parade down Constitution Avenue, a demonstration of colonial military maneuvers, entertainment at the Sylvan Theatre, a concert by the National Symphony Orchestra, and a spectacular fireworks display over the Washington Monument. Free. (202) 619-7222.

Virginia Scottish Games Two-day annual Celtic festival with traditional Highland dancing, bagpiping, animal events, and fiddling competitions. Scottish foods, goods, and genealogy featured. Held at Episcopal High School, 3901 West Braddock Road, Alexandria, Virginia. Admission fee. (703) 912-1943.

Soap Box Derby Soap-box cars roll down Constitution Avenue between New Jersey and Louisiana Avenues in Capitol Hill. Free. (202) 237-7200.

August

U.S. Army Band's 1812 Overture Concert A concert and pageant at the Sylvan Theatre on the Washington Monument grounds. Free. (703) 696-3399.

Summer-Long Activities

U.S. Navy Memorial Concerts on the Avenue Series Beginning at 8 p.m. on Memorial Day and continuing each Tuesday evening at 8 p.m. through Labor Day. At the U.S. Navy Memorial on Pennsylvania Avenue. Free. (202) 433-2525.

C&O Canal Mule-Drawn Boat Rides (April through October) Mule-drawn barge rides in Georgetown and Great Falls, Virginia. Costumed Park Service guides accompany each 60-minute trip, telling the canal's history through stories and song. Admission fee. (301) 299-3613.

Military Band Summer Concert Series Outdoor concerts held every summer evening (except Saturdays), from Memorial Day through Labor Day, beginning at 8 p.m. Free. Concerts are held on a rotating basis on the steps of the U.S. Capitol, the Sylvan Theatre (on the grounds of the Washington Monument) and the Navy Memorial Plaza (on Pennsylvania Avenue). For the current schedule, call the service-band information lines: U.S. Army Band, (202) 696-3399; "The President's Own" Marine Band, (202) 433-4011; U.S. Navy Band, (202) 433-2525; U.S. Air Force Band, (202) 767-5658. In addition, the U.S. Army Band holds its "Twilight Tattoo" at 7 p.m. on the Ellipse (near the White House) on Wednesdays; (202) 685-2852. For more information on concerts, call (202) 685-4989 or visit www.army.mil/armyband.

Monday	U.S. Navy Band, U.S. Capitol, west side
Tuesday	U.S. Army Band, various locations U.S. Air Force Band, U.S. Capitol, west side U.S. Navy Band, Navy Memorial Plaza
Wednesday	Marine Band, U.S. Capitol U.S. Army Band "Twilight Tattoo" at 7 p.m. on the Ellipse .
Friday	U.S. Army Band, U.S. Capitol, west side U.S. Air Force Band, Sylvan Theatre
Sunday	Marine Band, Sylvan Theatre

September

Annual "Arts on Foot" Festival Museums, galleries, and shops in the 7th Street area open their doors to the public. Free. (202) 482-7271.

Black Family Reunion A weekend celebration of the African-American family offers headline performers, fun, food, and exhibits on the Mall. Free. (202) 737-0120.

Labor Day Weekend Concert The National Symphony Orchestra closes the summer season with an evening concert on the West Lawn of the U.S. Capitol. Free. (202) 619-7222.

Kalorama House and Embassy Tour Tour selected homes and embassies and the Woodrow Wilson House. Admission fee. (202) 387-4062, ext. 18.

Kennedy Center Prelude Festival The John F. Kennedy Center for the Performing Arts celebrates the arts with free concerts and performances. (202) 467-4600; www.kennedy-center.org.

A CALENDAR OF FESTIVALS AND EVENTS *(continued)*

October

Supreme Court in Session First Monday of October. Free. (202) 479-3000.

Taste of D.C. Festival The best of D.C.'s vast array of restaurant food and ethnic cuisine; one of the city's most popular outdoor festivals. Free admission; purchase tickets for food tastings. (202) 789-7000; www.washington.org.

Marine Corps Marathon An annual event that attracts thousands of world-class marathoners. Starts and finishes at the Iwo Jima Memorial in Arlington. Registration fee. (703) 784-2225.

White House Fall Garden Tours View the Rose Garden and the South Lawn to the sounds of a military band. Free. (202) 456-2200.

November

Veteran's Day Ceremonies (November 11) Arlington National Cemetery. Solemn ceremony with military bands to honor the nation's war dead. (202) 685-2951. Additional ceremonies at the Vietnam Veterans Memorial on the National Mall, (202) 619-7222; Mount Vernon, (703) 780-2000; and the U.S. Navy Memorial on Pennsylvania Avenue, (202) 737-2300. Free.

A Christmas Carol The Dickens holiday classic returns each year to Ford's Theatre. Admission fee. (202) 347-4833 or (800) 899-2367.

December

Pearl Harbor Day (December 7) Wreath-laying ceremony at the U.S. Navy Memorial on Pennsylvania Avenue to commemorate the attack on Pearl Harbor. Free. (202) 737-2300.

Flying

Washington, the seat of the federal government and probably the world's most powerful city, is understandably well served by the airline industry. The town boasts three airports, each with its own peculiarities. Reagan Washington National Airport is by far the most convenient, located a few miles south of D.C. on the Virginia side of the Potomac River. Yet its closeness to the city has resulted in some odd restrictions: Planes aren't allowed to fly over the White House and other sensitive places, so all approaches and takeoffs are routed over the Potomac River; no planes are

Holidays at Mount Vernon A re-creation of the authentic eighteenth-century holiday season. Visitors may tour the mansion's third floor, which is usually closed to the public. Admission fee. (703) 780-2000.

Scottish Christmas Walk Featuring a parade through Old Town, bagpipes, Highland dancers, old homes tours, and children's events. Free. (703) 838-4200.

An American Holiday Celebration A holiday music show by the U.S. Army Band at DAR Constitution Hall. Free, but tickets are required to assure seating. Write to: An American Holiday Celebration, Building 42, Ft. Leslie J. McNair, Washington, D.C. 20319-5050. Call (202) 685-2851 for information. Do not call or write until after September. Call (866) 239-9425 for reservations.

National Christmas Tree Lighting/Pageant of Peace The president lights the giant National Christmas Tree near the White House. Through the end of the year, the Ellipse is the site of nightly choral performances, a nativity scene, a burning yule log, and a spectacular display of lighted Christmas trees representing each state and territory. Free. (202) 619-7222.

Old Town Christmas Candlelight Tours Visit Ramsay House, Gadsby's Tavern Museum, the Lee-Fendall House, and the Carlyle House in Old Town Alexandria. Music, colonial dancing, period decorations, and light refreshments. Admission fee. (703) 838-4200.

allowed to take off or land late at night; only 37 large jets are allowed to land or take off an hour; and a "perimeter rule" restricts nonstop flights to and from National to a distance of 1,250 miles or less. With virtually no international connections, think of National as the "East Coast, short-hop" airport. If you can't get a direct flight into National from your hometown, consider making a connection that will get you into National. It will probably be faster—and certainly more convenient—than flying into either of the other two airports that serve Washington.

While Reagan is our first choice for travelers flying into D.C., its close proximity to the bustling city creates problems for the unwary flyer: It's incredibly congested by heavy traffic. Parking is expensive; long-term parking is a long bus ride away; and renting a car and driving into D.C. can be a drawn-out, frustrating experience. The good news: A new, $1 billion terminal should help reduce the curbside congestion. Cab fares to downtown are reasonable; free shuttles can get you to your hotel in a half-hour or so; and National has its own Metro stop.

Dulles International Airport, on the other hand, is rarely congested. No wonder: It's located in the boonies of Virginia, a solid hour from the city by car and with no direct public transportation downtown. Dulles is primarily known as an international hub, although domestic flights are on the increase (spurring a construction project that in 1996 doubled the main terminal's size to 1.1 million square feet). In a sly marketing move a few years back, Baltimore's Friendship Airport became Baltimore/Washington International Airport (BWI). It worked: 2000 was a record-breaking year for this ever-expanding air hub. Southwest, for example, has increased its low-cost service to 65 flights a day, attracting a lot of travelers to Washington who would otherwise drive. BWI is also aggressively pursuing an international market and opened a new, $110 million international pier in the fall of 1997. Yet this busy airport is still closer to Baltimore than to Washington, which means D.C.-bound tourists face at least a 50-minute car or van ride before the Washington Monument comes into view. Another option for folks arriving at BWI is to take the train: Maryland commuter rail service (called MARC) and Amtrak connect BWI to D.C.'s Union Station. The train ride takes almost an hour, though—hardly convenient for tourists itching to explore the marble edifices lining the Mall.

Part Two

Hotels

Deciding Where to Stay

On weekdays, driving and parking in downtown Washington are nightmarish. On weekends, there is less traffic congestion, but parking is extremely difficult, particularly in the area of the Mall. Because the best way to get around Washington is on the Metro, we recommend a hotel within walking distance of a Metro station. With two rather prominent exceptions, all of Washington's best areas, as well as most of the Virginia and Maryland suburbs, are safely and conveniently accessible via this clean, modern subway system. Only historic Georgetown and the colorful, ethnic Adams-Morgan neighborhood are off-line.

Unless you plan to spend most of your time in Georgetown, we suggest that you pick a hotel elsewhere in the city. If you lodge in Georgetown, you will be reduced to driving or cabbing to get anywhere else. Adams-Morgan, a great neighborhood for dining and shopping, does not offer much in the way of lodging. If you go to Adams-Morgan, especially at night, take a cab.

Some Considerations

1. When choosing your Washington lodging, make sure your hotel is situated in a location convenient to your recreation or business needs, and that it is in a safe and comfortable area. Please note that while it is not practical to walk to the Washington Convention Center (the major convention venue) from many of the downtown hotels, larger conventions and trade shows provide shuttle service.
2. Find out how old the hotel is and when the guest rooms were last renovated. Request that the hotel send you its promotional brochure. Ask if brochure photos of guest rooms are accurate and current.

3. If you plan to take a car, inquire about the parking situation. Some hotels offer no parking at all; some charge dearly for parking; and a few offer free parking.
4. If you are not a city dweller, or if you are a light sleeper, try to book a hotel on a more quiet side street. Ask for a room off the street and high up.
5. Much of Washington is quite beautiful, as is the Potomac River. If you are on a romantic holiday, ask for a room on a higher floor with a good view.
6. When you plan your budget, remember that there is a 14.5% hotel tax (including sales tax) in the District of Columbia.
7. Washington is one of the busiest convention cities in the United States. If your visit to Washington coincides with one or more major conventions or trade shows, hotel rooms will be both scarce and expensive. If, on the other hand, you are able to schedule your visit to avoid big meetings, you will have a good selection of hotels at reasonably competitive prices. If you happen to be attending one of the big conventions, book early and use some of the tips listed below to get a discounted room rate. To assist in timing your visit, we have included a convention and trade show calendar.

Getting a Good Deal on a Room

Though Washington, D.C., is a major tourist destination, the economics of hotel room pricing is driven by business, government, and convention trade. This translates to high "rack rates" (a hotel's published room rate) and very few bargains. The most modest Econo Lodge or Days Inn in Washington charges from $84 to $139 a night, and mid-range chains, such as Holiday Inn and Radisson, ask from $129 to $229.

The good news is that Washington, D.C., and its Virginia and Maryland suburbs offer a staggering number of unusually fine hotels, including a high percentage of suite properties. The bad news, of course, is that you can expect to pay dearly to stay in them.

In most cities, the better and more expensive hotels are located close to the city center, with less expensive hotels situated farther out. There is normally a trade-off between location and price: If you are willing to stay out off the interstate and commute into downtown, you can expect to pay less for your suburban room than you would for a downtown room. In Washington, D.C., unfortunately, it very rarely works this way.

In the greater Washington area, every hotel is seemingly close to something. No matter how far you are from the Capitol, the Mall, and downtown, you can bank on your hotel being within spitting distance of some bureau, agency, airport, or industrial complex that funnels platoons of business travelers into guest rooms in a constant flow. Because almost every hotel and motel has its own captive market, the customary proximity/price trade-off doesn't apply. The Marriott at the Beltway and Wisconsin Avenue, for example, is 30 to 40 minutes away by car from the Mall but stays full with visitors to the nearby National Institutes of Health.

Where the Hotel Discounts Are

Special Weekend Rates

Although well-located Washington hotels are tough for the budget-conscious, it's not impossible to get a good deal, at least relatively speaking. For starters, some hotels that cater to business, government, and convention travelers offer special weekend discount rates that range from 15 to 40% below normal weekday rates. You can find out about weekend specials by calling individual hotels or by consulting your travel agent.

Getting Corporate Rates

Many hotels offer discounted corporate rates (5 to 20% off rack). Usually you do not need to work for a large company or have a special relationship with the hotel to obtain these rates. Simply call the hotel of your choice and ask for their corporate rates. Many hotels will guarantee you the discounted rate on the phone when you make your reservation. Others may make the rate conditional on your providing some sort of bona fides, for instance a fax on your company's letterhead requesting the rate, or a company credit card or business card on check-in. Generally, the screening is not rigorous.

Preferred Rates

If you cannot book the hotel of your choice through a half-price program, you and your travel agent may have to search for a lesser discount, often called a preferred rate. A preferred rate could be a discount made available to travel agents to stimulate their booking activity, or a discount initiated to attract a certain class of traveler. Most preferred rates are promoted through travel industry publications and so are often accessible only through an agent.

We recommend sounding out your travel agent about possible deals. Be aware that the rates shown on travel agents' computerized reservations systems are not always the lowest rates obtainable. Zero in on a couple of hotels that fill your needs in terms of location and quality of accommodations, and then have your travel agent call for the latest rates and specials.

Hotel reps are almost always more responsive to travel agents because travel agents represent a source of additional business. There are certain specials that hotel reps will disclose *only* to travel agents. Travel agents also come in handy when the hotel you want is supposedly booked. A personal appeal from your agent to the hotel's director of sales and marketing will get you a room more than half of the time.

Half-Price Programs

The larger discounts on rooms (35 to 60%), in Washington or anywhere else, are available through half-price hotel programs, often called travel clubs. Program operators contract with an individual hotel to provide rooms at deep discounts, usually 50% off rack rate, on a "space available" basis. Space available in practice generally means that you can reserve a room at the discounted rate whenever the hotel expects to be at less than 80% occupancy. A little calendar sleuthing to help you avoid city-wide conventions and special events will increase your chances of choosing a time when the discounts are available.

Most half-price programs charge an annual membership fee or directory subscription charge of $25 to $125. Once enrolled, you are mailed a membership card and a directory listing participating hotels. Examining the directory, you will notice immediately that there are many restrictions and exceptions. Some hotels, for instance, "black out" certain dates or times of year. Others may only offer the discount on certain days of the week or require you to stay a certain number of nights. Still others may offer a much smaller discount than 50% off rack rate.

Programs specialize in domestic travel, international travel, or both. More established operators offer members between 1,000 and 4,000 hotels to choose from in the United States. All of the programs have a heavy concentration of hotels in California and Florida, and most have a very limited selection of participating properties in New York City or Boston. Offerings in other cities and regions of the United States vary considerably. The programs with the largest selections of Washington hotels are Encore, Travel America at Half Price (Entertainment Publications), International Travel Card, and Quest. Each of these programs lists between 4 and 50 hotels in the greater Washington area.

D.C. Half-Price Hotel Programs

Encore	(800) 638-0930; www.preferedtraveller.com
Entertainment Publications	(800) 285-5525; www.entertainment.com
International Travel Card	(800) 342-0558
Quest	(800) 638-9819

One problem with half-price programs is that not all hotels offer a full 50% discount. Another slippery problem is the base rate against which the discount is applied. Some hotels figure the discount on an exaggerated rack rate that nobody would ever have to pay. A few participating hotels may deduct the discount from a supposed "superior" or "upgraded" room rate, even though the room you get is the hotel's standard accommodation. Though hard to pin down, the majority of participating properties base discounts on the published rate in the *Hotel & Travel Index* (a quarterly reference work used by travel agents) and work within the spirit of their agreement with the program operator. As a rule, if you travel several times a year, your room rate savings will easily compensate you for program membership fees.

A noteworthy addendum: Deeply discounted rooms through half-price programs are not commissionable to travel agents. In practical terms this means that you must ordinarily make your own inquiry calls and reservations. If you travel frequently, however, and run a lot of business through your travel agent, he or she will probably do your legwork, lack of commission notwithstanding.

Wholesalers, Consolidators, and Reservation Services

If you do not want to join a program or buy a discount directory, you can take advantage of the services of a wholesaler or consolidator. Wholesalers and consolidators buy rooms, or options on rooms (room blocks), from hotels at a low, negotiated rate. They then resell the rooms at a profit through travel agents and tour packagers, or directly to the public. Most wholesalers and consolidators have a provision for returning unsold rooms to participating hotels, but they are disinclined to do so. The wholesaler's or consolidator's relationship with any hotel is predicated on volume. If they return rooms unsold, the hotel might not make as many rooms available to them the next time around. Thus, wholesalers and consolidators often offer rooms at bargain rates, at anywhere from 15 to 50% off rack, occasionally sacrificing their profit margin in the process, to avoid returning the rooms to the hotel unsold.

When wholesalers and consolidators deal directly with the public, they frequently represent themselves as "reservation services." When you call, you can ask for a rate quote for a particular hotel, or, alternatively, ask for their best available deal in the area where you prefer to stay. If there is a maximum amount you are willing to pay, say so. Chances are, the service will find something that will work for you, even if they have to shave a dollar or two off their own profit. Sometimes you will have to pay for your room in advance, with a credit card, when you make your reservation. Other times you will pay at the usual time, when you check out.

Hotel Discounters

Accommodations Express	(800) 444-7666
Capitol Reservations	(800) 847-4832
Central Reservation Service	(800) 950-0232
Hotel Discounts	(800) 715-7666; www.hoteldiscount.com
Hotel Reservations Network	(800) 964-6835
Quikbook	(800) 789-9887; www.quickbook.com
RMC Travel	(800) 782-2674 or (800) 245-5738; www.rmcwebtravel.com
Washington, D.C., Accommodations	(800) 503-3338

Bed-and-Breakfasts (B&Bs)

B&Bs offer a lodging alternative based on personal service and hospitality that transcend the sterile, predictable product of chain hotels; however, they can be quirky. Most, but not all, B&Bs are open year-round. Some accept only cash or personal checks, while others take all major credit cards. Not all rooms come with private baths. Some rooms with private baths may have a tub but not a shower, or vice versa. Some allow children but not pets; others, pets but not children. Many B&Bs provide only the most basic breakfast, while some provide a sumptuous morning feast. Still others offer three meals a day. Most B&Bs are not wheelchair accessible, but it never hurts to ask.

Because staying at a B&B is like visiting someone's home, reservations are recommended, though B&Bs with more than ten rooms usually welcome walk-ins. To help you sort out your B&B options, we recommend the following guides. Updated regularly, these books describe B&Bs in more detail than is possible in the *Unofficial Guide.*

Inspected, Rated, and Approved, Bed & Breakfasts and Country Inns, by Beth Burgreen Stuhlman, published by the American Bed & Breakfast Association. Covers the entire United States. Visit www.abba.com.

Bed & Breakfasts—Country Inns and The Official Guide to American Historic Inns, by Deborah Sakach, published by American Historic Inns, Inc. Covers the entire United States. To order, phone (949) 499-8070.

Recommended Country Inns, Mid-Atlantic and Chesapeake Region, by Suzi Forbes Chase, published by the Globe Pequot Press. Covers Virginia, Delaware, Maryland, Pennsylvania, New Jersey, New York, and West Virginia. To order, phone (800) 243-0495.

For Washington area B&B reservations, check the website located at www.bedandbreakfastdc.com, or call *Bed and Breakfast Accommodations Ltd.* at (202) 328-3510.

Helping Your Travel Agent Help You

When you call your travel agent, ask if he or she has been to Washington. If the answer is no, be prepared to give your travel agent some direction. Do not accept any recommendations at face value. Check out the location and rates of any suggested hotel and make certain that the hotel is suited to your itinerary.

Because some travel agents are unfamiliar with Washington, your agent may try to plug you into a tour operator's or wholesaler's preset package. This essentially allows the travel agent to set up your whole trip with a single phone call and still collect an 8–10% commission. The problem with this scenario is that most agents will place 90% of their Washington business with only one or two wholesalers or tour operators. In other words, it's the line of least resistance for them, and not much choice for you.

Travel agents will often use wholesalers who run packages in conjunction with airlines, like Delta's Dream Vacations or American's Fly-Away Vacations. Because of the wholesaler's exclusive relationship with the carrier, these trips are very easy for travel agents to book. However, they will probably be more expensive than a package offered by a high-volume wholesaler who works with a number of airlines in a primarily Washington market.

To help your travel agent get you the best possible deal, do the following:

1. Determine where you want to stay in Washington and, if possible, choose a specific hotel. This can be accomplished by reviewing the hotel information provided in this guide and by writing or calling hotels that interest you.
2. Check out the hotel deals and package vacations advertised in the Sunday travel section of the Washington Post. Often you will be able to find deals that beat the socks off anything offered in your local paper. See if you can find specials that fit your plans and include a hotel you like.
3. Call the hotels, wholesalers, or tour operators whose ads you have collected. Ask any questions you have concerning their packages, but do not book your trip with them directly.
4. Tell your travel agent about the deals you find and ask if he or she can get you something better. The deals in the paper will serve as a benchmark against which to compare alternatives proposed by your travel agent.
5. Choose from among the options that you and your travel agent uncover. No matter which option you elect, have your travel agent

book it. Even if you go with one of the packages in the newspaper, it will probably be commissionable (at no additional cost to you) and will provide the agent some return on the time invested on your behalf. Also, as a travel professional, your agent should be able to verify the quality and integrity of the deal.

If You Make Your Own Reservation

As you poke around trying to find a good deal, there are several things you should know. First, always call the specific hotel as opposed to the hotel chain's national toll-free number. Quite often, the reservationists at the national toll-free number are unaware of local specials. Always ask about specials before you inquire about corporate rates. Do not be reluctant to bargain. If you are buying a hotel's weekend package, for example, and want to extend your stay into the following week, you can often obtain at least the corporate rate for the extra days. Do your bargaining, however, before you check in, preferably when you make your reservations.

How to Evaluate a Travel Package

Hundreds of Washington package vacations are offered to the public each year. Packages should be a win/win proposition for both the buyer and the seller. The buyer has to make only one phone call and deal with just one salesperson to set up the whole vacation: transportation, rental car, lodging, meals, tours, attraction admissions, and even golf and tennis. The seller, likewise, has to deal with the buyer only once, eliminating the need for separate sales, confirmations, and billing. In addition to streamlining sales, processing, and administration, some packagers also buy airfares in bulk on contract like a broker playing the commodities market. Buying a large number of airfares in advance allows the packager to buy them at a significant savings from posted fares. The same practice is also applied to hotel rooms. Because selling vacation packages is an efficient way of doing business, and because the packager can often buy individual package components (airfare, lodging, etc.) in bulk at discount, savings in operating expenses realized by the seller are sometimes passed on to the buyer. In addition to being convenient, such packages can be exceptional values. In any event, that is the way it is supposed to work.

All too often, in practice, the seller cashes in on discounts and passes none on to the buyer. In some instances, packages are loaded up with extras that cost the packager next to nothing but inflate the retail price sky-high. As you may expect, the savings to be passed along to customers evaporate.

When considering a package, choose one that includes features you are sure to use. Whether you use all the features or not, you will certainly pay for them. Second, if cost is of greater concern than convenience, make a few phone calls and see what the package would cost if you booked its individual components (airfare, rental car, lodging, etc.) on your own. If the package price is less than the à la carte cost, the package is a good deal. If the costs are about the same, the package is probably worth buying just for the convenience.

If your package includes a choice of rental car or "airport transfers" (transportation to and from the airport), take the transfers unless you are visiting Washington for the weekend and don't plan to visit the Mall. During the weekend, it is relatively easy to get around by car as long as you don't visit the dreaded "monument alley." During the week, forget it; a car is definitely *not* the way to go. If you do take the car, be sure to ask if the package includes free parking at your hotel.

Tips for Business Travelers

The primary considerations for business travelers are affordability and proximity to the site or area where you will transact your business. Identify the zone(s) where your business will take you on the maps on pages 8 and 9, and then use the Hotel Chart in the back of the book to cross-reference the hotels located in that area. Once you have developed a short list of possible hotels that are conveniently located, fit your budget, and offer the standard of accommodations you require, you (or your travel agent) can make use of the cost-saving suggestions discussed earlier to obtain the lowest rate.

Lodging Convenient to Washington Convention Center

If you are attending a meeting or trade show at Washington Convention Center, look for convenient lodging in downtown Washington, where at least a half-dozen hotels are within walking distance. From most downtown hotels, Washington Convention Center is a five- to eight-minute cab or shuttle ride away. Parking is available at the convention center, but it is expensive and not all that convenient. We recommend that you leave your car at home and use shuttles and cabs.

The Washington Convention Center is about a two-and-a-half-block walk from the nearest Metro station. The walk passes through a section of town that is safe during daylight hours.

Commuting to Washington Convention Center from the suburbs or the airports during rush hour is something to be avoided if possible. If you want a room downtown, book early—very early. If you screw up and need a room at the last minute, try a wholesaler or reservation service, or one of the strategies listed below.

Convention Rates: How They Work and How to Do Better

If you are attending a major convention or trade show, it is probable that the meeting's sponsoring organization has negotiated "convention rates" with a number of hotels. Under this arrangement, hotels agree to "block" a certain number of rooms at an agreed-upon price for convention-goers. Sometimes, as in the case of a small meeting, only one hotel is involved. In the event of a large, citywide convention at Washington Convention Center, however, almost all downtown and airport hotels will participate in the room block.

Because the convention sponsor brings a lot of business to the city and reserves a large number of rooms, it usually can negotiate a volume discount on the room rates, a rate that should be substantially below rack rate. The bottom line, however, is that some conventions and trade shows have more clout and negotiating skill than others. Hence, your convention sponsor may or may not be able to obtain the lowest possible rate.

Once a convention or trade show sponsor has completed negotiations with participating hotels, it will send its attendees a housing list that includes all the hotels serving the convention, along with the special convention rate for each. When you receive the housing list, you can compare the convention rates with the rates obtainable using the strategies covered in the previous section. If the negotiated convention rate doesn't sound like a good deal, you can try to reserve a room using a half-price club, a consolidator, or a tour operator. Remember, however, that many of the deep discounts are available only when the hotel expects to be at less than 80% occupancy, a condition that rarely prevails when a big convention is in town.

Here are some tips for beating convention rates:

1. Reserve early. Most big conventions and trade shows announce meeting sites one to three years in advance. Get your reservation booked as far in advance as possible using a half-price club. If you book well before the convention sponsor sends out its hotel list, chances are much better that the hotel will have space available.
2. If you've already got your convention's housing list, compare it with the list of hotels presented in this guide. You might be able to find a hotel not on the convention list that better suits your needs.
3. Use a local reservation agency or consolidator. This strategy is useful even if, for some reason, you need to make reservations at the last minute. Local reservation agencies and consolidators almost always control some rooms, even in the midst of a huge conven-

tion or trade show. (See our section on wholesalers and consolidators on pages 49–50.)

4. Book a hotel somewhat distant from the convention center but situated close to the Metro. You may save money on your room rate, and your commuting time underground to the convention center will often be shorter than if you take a cab or drive from a downtown hotel.
5. Stay in a bed and breakfast, either downtown or near a Metro line. Bed and Breakfast Accommodations Ltd., at (202) 328-3510, or www.bedandbreakfastdc.com, can help you locate one.

Hotel/Motel Toll-Free Numbers

For your convenience, we've listed on the next page the toll-free numbers, including TDDs (Telecommunication Device for the Deaf) for the following hotel and motel chains' reservation lines:

Hotels and Motels: Rated and Ranked

What's in a Room?

Except for cleanliness, state of repair, and decor, most travelers do not pay much attention to hotel rooms. There is, of course, a discernable standard of quality and luxury that differentiates Motel 6 from Holiday Inn, Holiday Inn from Marriott, and so on. In general, however, hotel guests fail to appreciate that some rooms are better engineered than others.

Contrary to what you might suppose, designing a hotel room is (or should be) a lot more complex than picking a bedspread to match the carpet and drapes. Making the room usable to its occupants is an art, a planning discipline that combines both form and function.

Decor and taste are important, certainly. No one wants to spend several days in a room where the decor is dated, garish, or even ugly. But beyond the decor, certain variables determine how "livable" a hotel room is. In Washington, D.C., we have seen some beautifully appointed rooms that are simply not well designed for human habitation. The next time you stay in a hotel, pay attention to the details and design elements of your room. Even more than decor, these are the things that will make you feel comfortable and at home.

It takes the *Unofficial Guide* researchers about 40 minutes to inspect a hotel room. Here are a few of the things we check that you may want to start paying attention to:

HOTEL/MOTEL TOLL FREE NUMBERS

Best Western	(800) 528-1234 U.S. & Canada (800) 528-2222 tdd
Comfort Inn	(800) 228-5150 U.S. (800) 22-3323 TDD
Courtyard by Marriott	(800) 321-2211 U.S. (800) 228-7014 TDD
Days Inn	(800) 325-2525 U.S. (800) 329-7155 TDD
Doubletree and Doubletree Guest Suites	(800) 222-8733 U.S. & Canada (800) 528-9898 TDD
Econo Lodge	(800) 424-4777 U.S.
Embassy Suites	(800) 362-2779 U.S. & Canada (800) 458-4708 TDD
Fairfield Inn by Marriott	(800) 228-2800 U.S.
Hampton Inn	(800) 426-7866 U.S. & Canada (800) 451-4833 TDD
Hilton	(800) 445-8667 U.S (800) 368-1133 TDD
Holiday Inn	(800) 465-4329 U.S. & Canada (800) 238-5544 TDD
Howard Johnson	(800) 654-2000 U.S. & Canada (800) 544-9881 TDD
Hyatt	(800) 233-1234 U.S. & Canada (800) 228-9548 TDD
Loew's	(800) 235-6397 U.S. & Canada
Marriott	(800) 228-9290 U.S. & Canada (800) 228-7014 TDD
Quality Inn	(800) 228-5151 U.S. & Canada (800) 228-3323 TDD
Radisson	(800) 333-3333 U.S. & Canada (800) 906-2200 TDD
Ramada Inn	(800) 228-3838 U.S. (800) 228-3232 TDD
Renaissance	(800) 468-3571 U.S. & Canada (800) 228-7014 TDD
Residence Inn by Marriott	(800) 331-3131 U.S. (800) 228-7014 TDD
Ritz-Carlton	(800) 241-3333 U.S. (800) 228-7014 TDD
Sheraton	(800) 325-3535 U.S. & Canada
Wyndham	(800) 822-4200 U.S.

Room Size While some smaller rooms are cozy and well designed, a large and uncluttered room is generally preferable, especially for a stay of more than three days.

Temperature Control, Ventilation, and Odor The guest should be able to control the temperature of the room. The best system, because it's so quiet, is central heating and air conditioning, controlled by the room's own thermostat. The next best system is a room module heater and air conditioner, preferably controlled by an automatic thermostat, but usually by manually operated button controls. The worst system is central heat and air without any sort of room thermostat or guest control.

The vast majority of hotel rooms have windows or balcony doors that have been permanently secured shut. Though there are some legitimate safety and liability issues involved, we prefer windows and balcony doors that can be opened to admit fresh air. Hotel rooms should be odor-free and smoke-free, and should not feel stuffy or damp.

Room Security Better rooms have locks that require a plastic card instead of the traditional lock and key. Card and slot systems allow the hotel to change the combination or entry code of the lock with each new guest who uses the room. A burglar who has somehow acquired a room key to a conventional lock can afford to wait until the situation is right before using the key to gain access. Not so with a card and slot system. Though the largest hotels and hotel chains with lock and key systems usually rotate their locks once each year, they remain vulnerable to hotel thieves much of the time. Many smaller or independent properties rarely rotate their locks.

In addition to an entry lock system, the door should have a deadbolt and preferably a chain that can be locked from the inside. A chain by itself is not sufficient. Doors should also have a peephole. Windows and balcony doors should have secure locks.

Safety Every room should have a fire or smoke alarm, clear fire instructions, and preferably a sprinkler system. Bathtubs should have a nonskid surface, and shower stalls should have doors that either open outward or slide side-to-side. Bathroom electrical outlets should be high on the wall and not too close to the sink. Balconies should have sturdy, high rails.

Noise Most travelers have been kept awake by the television, partying, or amorous activities of people in the next room, or by traffic on the street outside. Better hotels are designed with noise control in mind. Wall and ceiling construction are substantial, effectively screening out routine noise. Carpets and drapes, in addition to being decorative, also absorb and muffle sounds. Mattresses mounted on stable platforms or sturdy bed frames do not squeak even when challenged by the most passionate lovers. Televisions enclosed in cabinets, and with volume governors, rarely disturb guests in adjacent rooms.

In better hotels, the air conditioning and heating system is well maintained and operates without noise or vibration. Likewise, plumbing is quiet and positioned away from the sleeping area. Doors to the hall, and to adjoining rooms, are thick and well fitted to better keep out noise.

Darkness Control Ever been in a hotel room where the curtains would not quite come together in the middle? In cities where many visitors stay up way into the wee hours, it's important to have a dark, quiet room where you can sleep late without the morning sun blasting you out of bed. Thick, lined curtains that close completely in the center and extend beyond the dimensions of the window or door frame are required. In a well-planned room, the curtains, shades, or blinds should almost totally block light at any time of day.

Lighting Poor lighting is an extremely common problem in American hotel rooms. The lighting is usually adequate for dressing, relaxing, or watching television, but not for reading or working. Lighting needs to be bright over tables and desks and alongside couches or easy chairs. Since so many people read in bed, there should be a separate light for each person. A room with two queen beds should have an individual light for four people. Better bedside reading lights illuminate a small area, so if you want to sleep and someone else prefers to stay up and read, you will not be bothered by the light. The worst situation by far is a single lamp on a table between the beds. In each bed, only the person next to the lamp will have sufficient light to read. This deficiency is often compounded by light bulbs of insufficient wattage.

In addition, closet areas should be well lit, and there should be a switch near the door that turns on lights in the room when you enter. A seldom seen but desirable feature is a bedside console that allows a guest to control all or most lights in the room from the bed.

Furnishings At bare minimum, the bed(s) must be firm. Pillows should be made with nonallergenic fillers and, in addition to the sheets and spread, a blanket should be provided. Bedclothes should be laundered with a fabric softener and changed daily. Better hotels usually provide extra blankets and pillows in the room or on request and sometimes use a second top sheet between the blanket and the spread.

There should be a dresser large enough to hold clothes for two people during a five-day stay. A small table with two chairs, or a desk with a chair, should be provided. The room should be equipped with a luggage rack and a three-quarter- to full-length mirror.

The television should be color, be cable-connected, and ideally have a volume governor and remote control. It should be mounted on a swivel base and preferably enclosed in a cabinet. Local channels should be posted on the set, and a local TV program guide should be supplied.

The telephone should be touchtone, conveniently situated for bedside use, and should have, on or near it, easily understood dialing instructions and a rate card. Local white and yellow pages should be provided. Better hotels have phones in the bath and equip room phones with long cords.

Well-designed hotel rooms usually have a plush armchair or a sleeper sofa for lounging and reading. Better headboards are padded for comfortable reading in bed, and there should be a nightstand or table on each side of the bed(s). Nice extras in any hotel room include a small refrigerator, a digital alarm clock, and a coffeemaker.

Bathroom Two sinks are better than one, and you cannot have too much counter space. A sink outside the bath is a great convenience when one person dresses as another bathes. Sinks should have drains with stoppers.

Better bathrooms have both tub and shower with a nonslip bottom. Tub and shower controls should be easy to operate. Adjustable shower heads are preferred. The bath needs to be well lit and should have an exhaust fan and a guest-controlled bathroom heater. Towels should be large, soft, and fluffy, and provided in generous quantities, as should hand towels and washcloths. There should be an electrical outlet for each sink, conveniently and safely placed.

Complimentary shampoo, conditioner, and lotion are a plus, as are robes and bathmats. Better hotels supply their bathrooms with tissues and extra toilet paper. Luxurious baths feature a phone, a hair dryer, sometimes a small television, or even a jacuzzi.

Vending There should be complimentary ice and a drink machine on each floor. Welcome additions include a snack machine and a sundries (combs, toothpaste) machine. The latter are seldom found in large hotels that have 24-hour restaurants and shops.

Room Ratings

To separate properties according to the relative quality, tastefulness, state of repair, cleanliness, and size of their standard rooms, we have grouped the hotels and motels into classifications denoted by stars:

★★★★★	*Superior Rooms*	Tasteful and luxurious by any standard
★★★★	*Extremely Nice Rooms*	What you would expect at a Hyatt Regency or Marriott
★★★	*Nice Rooms*	Holiday Inn or comparable quality
★★	*Adequate Rooms*	Clean, comfortable, and functional without frills (like a Motel 6)
★	*Super Budget*	

Star ratings in this guide do not necessarily correspond to ratings awarded by Mobil, AAA, or other travel critics. Because stars have little relevance when awarded in the absence of commonly recognized standards of comparison, we have tied our rating to expected levels of quality established by specific American hotel corporations.

Star ratings apply to *room quality only* and describe the property's standard accommodations. For most hotels and motels a "standard accommodation" is a hotel room with either one king bed or two queen beds. In an all-suite property, the standard accommodation is a one- or two-room suite. In addition to standard accommodations, many hotels offer luxury rooms and special suites that are not rated in this guide. Star ratings for rooms are assigned without regard to whether a property has restaurant(s), recreational facilities, entertainment, or other extras.

In addition to stars (which delineate broad categories), we also employ a numerical rating system. Our rating scale is 0–100, with 100 the best possible rating and 0 (zero) the worst. Numerical ratings are presented to show the difference we perceive between one property and another that may be in the same star category. Rooms at the Morrison House, the Washington Court Hotel, and the Washington Renaissance Hotel, for instance, are all rated as ★★★★ (four stars). In the supplemental numerical ratings, the Morrison House and the Washington Court Hotel are rated 88 and 87, respectively, while the Washington Renaissance Hotel is rated 83. This means that within the four-star category, the Morrison House and the Washington Court Hotel are comparable, and that both have somewhat nicer rooms than the Washington Renaissance Hotel.

The location column identifies the greater Washington area (by zone) where you will find a particular property.

How the Hotels Compare

Cost estimates are based on the hotel's published rack rates for standard rooms. Each "$" represents $50. Thus, a cost symbol of "$$$" means a room (or suite) at that hotel will cost about $150 a night.

Below is a hit parade of the nicest rooms in town. We've focused strictly on room quality and excluded any consideration of location, services, recreation, or amenities. In some instances, a one- or two-room suite can be had for the same price or less than that of a hotel room.

If you used previous editions of this guide, you may notice that many of the ratings and rankings have changed. These changes reflect the inclusion of new properties, as well as guest room renovations or improved maintenance and housekeeping in previously listed properties. A failure to properly maintain guest rooms or a lapse in housekeeping standards can negatively affect the ratings.

Finally, before you begin to shop for a hotel, take a hard look at this letter we received from a couple in Hot Springs, Arkansas:

We cancelled our room reservations to follow the advice in your book [and reserved a hotel room highly ranked by the Unofficial Guide*]. We wanted inexpensive, but clean and cheerful. We got inexpensive, but [also] dirty, grim, and depressing. I really felt disappointed in your advice and the room. It was the pits. That was the one real piece of information I needed from your book! The room spoiled the holiday for me aside from our touring.*

Needless to say, this letter was as unsettling to us as the bad room was to our reader. Our integrity as travel journalists, after all, is based on the quality of the information we provide our readers. Even with the best of intentions and the most conscientious research, however, we cannot inspect every room in every hotel. What we do, in statistical terms, is take a sample: We check out several rooms selected at random in each hotel and base our ratings and rankings on those rooms. The inspections are conducted anonymously and without the knowledge of the management. Although it is unusual, it is certainly possible that the rooms we randomly inspect are not representative of the majority of rooms at a particular hotel. Another possibility is that the rooms we inspect in a given hotel are representative but that by bad luck a reader is assigned a room that is inferior. When we rechecked the hotel our reader disliked, we discovered that our rating was correctly representative but that he and his wife had unfortunately been assigned to one of a small number of threadbare rooms scheduled for renovation.

The key to avoiding disappointment is to snoop around in advance. We recommend that you ask for a photo of a hotel's standard guest room before you book, or at least get a copy of the hotel's promotional brochure. Be forewarned, however, that some hotel chains use the same guest room photo in their promotional literature for all hotels in the chain; a specific guest room may not resemble the brochure photo. When you or your travel agent call, ask how old the property is and when your guest room was last renovated. If you arrive and are assigned a room that does not live up to the brochure's promises, demand to be moved to another room.

HOW THE HOTELS COMPARE

Hotel	Zone	Quality Rating	Star Rating	Cost $=50
The Ritz-Carlton	6	98	★★★★★	$$$$$$$$$
The Westin Grand	5	95	★★★★½	$$$$$$$-
Ritz-Carlton Pentagon City	11	94	★★★★½	$$$$$$$
Watergate Hotel	6	94	★★★★½	$$$$
Hay-Adams Hotel	3	93	★★★★½	$$$$$$$$$$$+
Park Hyatt	5	93	★★★★½	$$$$$$$-
St. Regis	3	93	★★★★½	$$$$+
Willard Inter-Continental	3	93	★★★★½	$$$$$$$$$$$-
Jefferson Hotel	3	92	★★★★½	$$$$$$$$
Renaissance Mayflower Hotel	3	92	★★★★½	$$$$
Four Seasons Hotel	5	91	★★★★½	$$$$$$$$-
Westin Fairfax	6	91	★★★★½	$$$$$$$+
Hotel Topaz	6	90	★★★★½	$$$$$-
Loew's L'Enfant Plaza	1	90	★★★★½	$$$+
Sheraton Premiere Tysons Corner	11	90	★★★★½	$$$$$
Hotel Helix	7	89	★★★★	$$$-
Hotel Madera	6	89	★★★★	$$$
The Hotel George	2	89	★★★★	$$$$$$$$-
Washington Monarch Hotel	5	89	★★★★	$$$$$$$-
J.W. Marriott Hotel	3	88	★★★★	$$$$$$$-
Morrison-Clark Inn	7	88	★★★★	$$$$-
Omni Shoreham Hotel	7	88	★★★★	$$$$-
Sofitel Lafayette	3	88	★★★★	$$$$$$$-
Washington Terrace Hotel	7	88	★★★★	$$$+
Embassy Suites Tysons Corner	11	87	★★★★	$$$$-
Hotel Monaco	3	87	★★★★	$$$$$$-
Hyatt Arlington	11	87	★★★★	$$$$-
Madison Hotel	3	87	★★★★	$$$$$+
Morrison House	11	87	★★★★	$$$$-
One Washington Circle Hotel	4	87	★★★★	$$$-
Washington Court Hotel	3	87	★★★★	$$$$$
Embassy Suites Downtown	6	86	★★★★	$$$$-
St. Gregory Luxury Hotel & Suites	6	86	★★★★	$$$$$-
The Wyndham Washington	3	86	★★★★	$$$$-
Courtyard Crystal City	11	85	★★★★	$$$$+
Doubletree Hotel Crystal City	11	85	★★★★	$$$

HOW THE HOTELS COMPARE *(continued)*

Hotel	Zone	Quality Rating	Star Rating	Cost $=50
Embassy Row Hilton	6	85	★★★★	$$$+
Embassy Suites Alexandria	11	85	★★★★	$$$$-
Embassy Suites Chevy Chase	7	85	★★★★	$$$$
Grand Hyatt Washington	3	85	★★★★	$$$$+
Hotel Rouge	6	85	★★★★	$$$$-
Residence Inn Bethesda	10	85	★★★★	$$$-
Sheraton Suites Alexandria	11	85	★★★★	$$$+
The Melrose Hotel	5	85	★★★★	$$$$-
Embassy Suites Crystal City	11	84	★★★★	$$$+
Georgetown Inn	5	84	★★★★	$$$$-
Hyatt Regency Bethesda	10	84	★★★★	$$$$+
Residence Inn Pentagon City	11	84	★★★★	$$$$+
River Inn	4	84	★★★★	$$$-
Washington Renaissance Hotel	3	84	★★★★	$$$$$$
Washington Suites Pennsylvania Ave.	5	84	★★★★	$$$$$-
Capitol Hilton	3	83	★★★★	$$$$$+
Churchhill Hotel	6	83	★★★★	$$$$
Doubletree Hotel Tysons Corner	11	83	★★★★	$$$+
Marriott Crystal Gateway	11	83	★★★★	$$$
Marriott Tysons Corner	11	83	★★★★	$$+
Marriott Wardman Park Hotel	7	83	★★★★	$$$$$$-
St. James	4	83	★★★★	$$$$+
Four Points Sheraton Pentagon	11	82	★★★½	$$$+
Hilton Alexandria at Mark Center	11	82	★★★½	$$-
Hotel Monticello	5	82	★★★½	$$$$$
Hyatt Regency Capitol Hill	3	82	★★★½	$$$-
Hyatt Regency Crystal City	11	82	★★★½	$$$+
Residence Inn Thomas Circle	3	82	★★★½	$$$$$
Washington Marriott Hotel	6	82	★★★½	$$$$$+
Wyndham City Center	6	82	★★★½	$$$$+
Arlington Virginia Hilton	11	81	★★★½	$$$-
Marriott Hotel Bethesda	10	81	★★★½	$$$$$
Washington National Airport Hilton	11	81	★★★½	$$$-
Bethesda Court Hotel	10	80	★★★½	$$$$-
Holiday Inn Select Old Town	11	80	★★★½	$$$$$
Marriott Crystal City	11	80	★★★½	$$$$+

HOW THE HOTELS COMPARE *(continued)*

Hotel	Zone	Quality Rating	Star Rating	Cost $=50
Residence Inn Dupont Circle	6	80	★★★½	$$$$-
Washington Hilton & Towers	6	80	★★★½	$$$$-
Courtyard Embassy Row	6	79	★★★½	$$$
Hotel Lombardy	4	79	★★★½	$$$+
Latham Hotel Georgetown	5	79	★★★½	$$$$-
Marriott Hotel Key Bridge	11	79	★★★½	$$$$
Radisson Barceló Hotel	6	79	★★★½	$$+
Tabard Inn	6	79	★★★½	$$$$-
Washington Suites Alexandria	11	79	★★★½	$$$
Courtyard New Carrollton	10	78	★★★½	$$$+
Hilton Garden Inn	3	78	★★★½	$$$-
Holiday Inn Arlington	11	78	★★★½	$$$$-
Lincoln Suites	3	78	★★★½	$$$+
Courtyard Rosslyn	11	77	★★★½	$$$$-
Courtyard Washington	6	77	★★★½	$$$-
Hawthorn Suites Hotel	11	77	★★★½	$$$-
Hotel Washington	3	77	★★★½	$$$+
Crowne Plaza National Airport	11	76	★★★½	$$$$+
Holiday Inn Bethesda	10	76	★★★½	$$+
Holiday Inn Georgetown	7	76	★★★½	$$$$
Sheraton Crystal City	11	76	★★★½	$$$$$-
Sheraton National Hotel	11	76	★★★½	$$-
Carlyle Suites Hotel	6	75	★★★½	$$$+
Four Points Sheraton Downtown	3	75	★★★½	$$$$
Marriott Metro Center	3	75	★★★½	$$$$$$
Radisson Plaza Hotel Old Town	11	75	★★★½	$$+
Savoy Suites Hotel	7	75	★★★½	$$$+
State Plaza Hotel	4	75	★★★½	$$$-
Best Western New Hampshire Suites	6	74	★★★	$$$+
Courtyard Alexandria	11	74	★★★	$$$+
Embassy Square Summerfield Suites	6	74	★★★	$$$
Holiday Inn Rosslyn at Key Bridge	11	74	★★★	$$$+
Kalorama Guest House	6	74	★★★	$$$-
The Governor's House	6	74	★★★	$$$$+
Channel Inn Hotel	1	72	★★★	$$$-
Crowne Plaza	3	72	★★★	$$$$$$-

HOW THE HOTELS COMPARE *(continued)*

Hotel	Zone	Quality Rating	Star Rating	Cost $=50
Days Inn Crystal City	11	72	★★★	$$+
Four Points Sheraton Bethesda	10	72	★★★	$$$$-
Holiday Inn Silver Spring	10	72	★★★	$$$$-
Hilton of Silver Spring	10	70	★★★	$$$-
Holiday Inn Central	7	70	★★★	$$$+
Phoenix Park Hotel	2	70	★★★	$$$$+
Sheraton Pentagon South	11	70	★★★	$$$$$-
Holiday Inn Capitol	3	69	★★★	$$$+
Holiday Inn Hotel and Suites	11	69	★★★	$$$$-
Holiday Inn Chevy Chase	10	68	★★★	$$$$-
Holiday Inn National Airport	11	68	★★★	$$+
Holiday Inn on the Hill	3	68	★★★	$$$+
Hampton Inn Alexandria	11	67	★★★	$$+
Holiday Inn Downtown	3	67	★★★	$$$$+
Quality Inn Iwo Jima	11	67	★★★	$$-
Washington Plaza Hotel	3	66	★★★	$$$$-
Best Western Tyson's Westpark	11	64	★★½	$$+
Comfort Inn Washington Gateway	11	63	★★½	$$$-
Jurys Normandy	6	63	★★½	$$+
Quality Inn College Park	10	63	★★½	$$-
Red Roof Inn Downtown	3	63	★★½	$$$-
Adam's Inn	7	62	★★½	$$
Holiday Inn and Suites	11	62	★★½	$$$-
Best Western Key Bridge	11	61	★★½	$$$-
American Inn of Bethesda	10	60	★★½	$$+
City Center Hotel	7	60	★★½	$$
Comfort Inn Arlington	11	60	★★½	$$$+
Comfort Inn Tysons Corner	11	60	★★½	$$$+
Embassy Inn	6	59	★★½	$$$-
Best Western Pentagon	11	56	★★½	$$$-
Comfort Inn Landmark	11	56	★★½	$$-
Days Inn Connecticut Ave	7	56	★★½	$$+
Windsor Park Hotel	6	56	★★½	$$+
Best Western Capitol Hill	3	53	★★	$$$-
Days Inn Alexandria	11	52	★★	$$
Econo Lodge National Airport	11	52	★★	$$-

THE HOTELS LISTED BY ZONE

Hotel	Zone	Quality Rating	Star Rating	Cost $=50
Channel Inn Hotel	1	72	★★★	$$$-
Loew's L'Enfant Plaza	1	90	★★★★½	$$$+
Phoenix Park Hotel	2	70	★★★	$$$$+
The Hotel George	2	89	★★★★	$$$$$$$$-
Best Western Capitol Hill	3	53	★★	$$$-
Capitol Hilton	3	83	★★★★	$$$$$+
Crowne Plaza	3	72	★★★	$$$$$$-
Four Points Sheraton Downtown	3	75	★★★½	$$$$
Grand Hyatt Washington	3	85	★★★★	$$$$+
Hay-Adams Hotel	3	93	★★★★½	$$$$$$$$$$+
Hilton Garden Inn	3	78	★★★½	$$$-
Holiday Inn Capitol	3	69	★★★	$$$+
Holiday Inn Downtown	3	67	★★★	$$$$+
Holiday Inn on the Hill	3	68	★★★	$$$+
Hotel Monaco	3	87	★★★★	$$$$$$-
Hotel Washington	3	77	★★★½	$$$+
Hyatt Regency Capitol Hill	3	82	★★★½	$$$-
J.W. Marriott Hotel	3	88	★★★★	$$$$$$$-
Jefferson Hotel	3	92	★★★★½	$$$$$$$$
Lincoln Suites	3	78	★★★½	$$$+
Madison Hotel	3	87	★★★★	$$$$$+
Marriott Metro Center	3	75	★★★½	$$$$$$
Red Roof Inn Downtown	3	63	★★½	$$$-
Renaissance Mayflower Hotel	3	92	★★★★½	$$$$
Residence Inn Thomas Circle	3	82	★★★½	$$$$$
Sofitel Lafayette	3	88	★★★★	$$$$$$$-
St. Regis	3	93	★★★★½	$$$$+
The Wyndham Washington	3	86	★★★★	$$$$-
Washington Court Hotel	3	87	★★★★	$$$$$
Washington Plaza Hotel	3	66	★★★	$$$$-
Washington Renaissance Hotel	3	84	★★★★	$$$$$$
Willard Inter-Continental	3	93	★★★★½	$$$$$$$$$$-
Hotel Lombardy	4	79	★★★½	$$$+
One Washington Circle Hotel	4	87	★★★★	$$$-
River Inn	4	84	★★★★	$$$-
St. James	4	83	★★★★	$$$$+

THE HOTELS LISTED BY ZONE *(continued)*

Hotel	Zone	Quality Rating	Star Rating	Cost $=50
State Plaza Hotel	4	75	★★★½	$$$-
Four Seasons Hotel	5	91	★★★★½	$$$$$$$$-
Georgetown Inn	5	84	★★★★	$$$$-
Hotel Monticello	5	82	★★★½	$$$$$
Latham Hotel Georgetown	5	79	★★★½	$$$$-
Park Hyatt	5	93	★★★★½	$$$$$$$-
The Melrose Hotel	5	85	★★★★	$$$$-
The Westin Grand	5	95	★★★★½	$$$$$$$-
Washington Monarch Hotel	5	89	★★★★	$$$$$$$-
Washington Suites Pennsylvania Ave.	5	84	★★★★	$$$$$-
Best Western New Hampshire Suites	6	74	★★★	$$$+
Carlyle Suites Hotel	6	75	★★★½	$$$+
Churchhill Hotel	6	83	★★★★	$$$$
Courtyard Embassy Row	6	79	★★★½	$$$
Courtyard Washington	6	77	★★★½	$$$-
Embassy Inn	6	59	★★½	$$$-
Embassy Row Hilton	6	85	★★★★	$$$+
Embassy Square Summerfield Suites	6	74	★★★	$$$
Embassy Suites Downtown	6	86	★★★★	$$$$-
Hotel Madera	6	89	★★★★	$$$
Hotel Rouge	6	85	★★★★	$$$$-
Hotel Topaz	6	90	★★★★½	$$$$$-
Jurys Normandy	6	63	★★½	$$+
Kalorama Guest House	6	74	★★★	$$$-
Radisson Barceló Hotel	6	79	★★★½	$$+
Residence Inn Dupont Circle	6	80	★★★½	$$$$-
St. Gregory Luxury Hotel & Suites	6	86	★★★★	$$$$$-
Tabard Inn	6	79	★★★½	$$$$-
The Governor's House	6	74	★★★	$$$$+
The Ritz-Carlton	6	98	★★★★★	$$$$$$$$$
Washington Hilton & Towers	6	80	★★★½	$$$$-
Washington Marriott Hotel	6	82	★★★½	$$$$$+
Watergate Hotel	6	94	★★★★½	$$$$
Westin Fairfax	6	91	★★★★½	$$$$$$$+
Windsor Park Hotel	6	56	★★½	$$+
Wyndham City Center	6	82	★★★½	$$$$+

THE HOTELS LISTED BY ZONE ***(continued)***

Hotel	Zone	Quality Rating	Star Rating	Cost $=50
Adam's Inn	7	62	★★½	$$
City Center Hotel	7	60	★★½	$$
Days Inn Connecticut Ave	7	56	★★½	$$+
Embassy Suites Chevy Chase	7	85	★★★★	$$$$
Holiday Inn Central	7	70	★★★	$$$+
Holiday Inn Georgetown	7	76	★★★½	$$$$
Hotel Helix	7	89	★★★★	$$$-
Marriott Wardman Park Hotel	7	83	★★★★	$$$$$$-
Morrison-Clark Inn	7	88	★★★★	$$$$-
Omni Shoreham Hotel	7	88	★★★★	$$$$-
Savoy Suites Hotel	7	75	★★★½	$$$+
Washington Terrace Hotel	7	88	★★★★	$$$+
American Inn of Bethesda	10	60	★★½	$$+
Bethesda Court Hotel	10	80	★★★½	$$$$-
Courtyard New Carrollton	10	78	★★★½	$$$+
Four Points Sheraton Bethesda	10	72	★★★	$$$$-
Hilton of Silver Spring	10	70	★★★	$$$-
Holiday Inn Bethesda	10	76	★★★½	$$+
Holiday Inn Chevy Chase	10	68	★★★	$$$$-
Holiday Inn Silver Spring	10	72	★★★	$$$$-
Hyatt Regency Bethesda	10	84	★★★★	$$$$+
Marriott Hotel Bethesda	10	81	★★★½	$$$$$
Quality Inn College Park	10	63	★★½	$$-
Residence Inn Bethesda	10	85	★★★★	$$$-
Arlington Virginia Hilton	11	81	★★★½	$$$-
Best Western Key Bridge	11	61	★★½	$$$-
Best Western Pentagon	11	56	★★½	$$$-
Best Western Tyson's Westpark	11	64	★★½	$$+
Comfort Inn Arlington	11	60	★★½	$$$+
Comfort Inn Landmark	11	56	★★½	$$-
Comfort Inn Tysons Corner	11	60	★★½	$$$+
Comfort Inn Washington Gateway	11	63	★★½	$$$-
Courtyard Alexandria	11	74	★★★	$$$+
Courtyard Crystal City	11	85	★★★★	$$$$+
Courtyard Rosslyn	11	77	★★★½	$$$$-
Crowne Plaza National Airport	11	76	★★★½	$$$$+

THE HOTELS LISTED BY ZONE *(continued)*

Hotel	Zone	Quality Rating	Star Rating	Cost $=50
Days Inn Alexandria	11	52	★★	$$
Days Inn Crystal City	11	72	★★★	$$+
Doubletree Hotel Crystal City	11	85	★★★★	$$$
Doubletree Hotel Tysons Corner	11	83	★★★★	$$$+
Econo Lodge National Airport	11	52	★★	$$-
Embassy Suites Alexandria	11	85	★★★★	$$$$-
Embassy Suites Crystal City	11	84	★★★★	$$$+
Embassy Suites Tysons Corner	11	87	★★★★	$$$$-
Four Points Sheraton Pentagon	11	82	★★★½	$$$+
Hampton Inn Alexandria	11	67	★★★	$$+
Hawthorn Suites Hotel	11	77	★★★½	$$$-
Hilton Alexandria at Mark Center	11	82	★★★½	$$-
Holiday Inn and Suites	11	62	★★½	$$$-
Holiday Inn Arlington	11	78	★★★½	$$$$-
Holiday Inn Hotel and Suites	11	69	★★★	$$$$-
Holiday Inn National Airport	11	68	★★★	$$+
Holiday Inn Rosslyn at Key Bridge	11	74	★★★	$$$+
Holiday Inn Select Old Town	11	80	★★★½	$$$$$
Hyatt Arlington	11	87	★★★★	$$$$-
Hyatt Regency Crystal City	11	82	★★★½	$$$+
Marriott Crystal City	11	80	★★★½	$$$$+
Marriott Crystal Gateway	11	83	★★★★	$$$
Marriott Hotel Key Bridge	11	79	★★★½	$$$$
Marriott Tysons Corner	11	83	★★★★	$$+
Morrison House	11	87	★★★★	$$$$-
Quality Inn Iwo Jima	11	67	★★★	$$-
Radisson Plaza Hotel Old Town	11	75	★★★½	$$+
Residence Inn Pentagon City	11	84	★★★★	$$$$+
Ritz-Carlton Pentagon City	11	94	★★★★½	$$$$$$$
Sheraton Crystal City	11	76	★★★½	$$$$$-
Sheraton National Hotel	11	76	★★★½	$$-
Sheraton Pentagon South	11	70	★★★	$$$$$-
Sheraton Premiere Tysons Corner	11	90	★★★★½	$$$$$
Sheraton Suites Alexandria	11	85	★★★★	$$$+
Washington National Airport Hilton	11	81	★★★½	$$$-
Washington Suites Alexandria	11	79	★★★½	$$$

Good Deals and Bad Deals

Having listed the nicest rooms in town, first by qualtiy then by location, let's reorder the list to rank the best combinations of quality and price in a room—in other words, its value. Using a mathematical formula that factors in a hotel's quality and star ratings as well as the rack rate, we derive a list of hotels ranked by value. As before, the rankings are made without consideration of location or the availability of restaurants, recreational facilities, entertainment, or amenities. We list only the top 30 hotel values because, as consumers, value-concious readers are simply concerned with finding the best deals.

We use the hotels' rack rates as a level playing field, so to speak, when calculating value. However, most hotels offer special rates and incentives; they also increase rates to capitalize on periods of peak demand. If you're looking for a room on short notice most times of the year, then the value chart below should serve you well. If, however, you're planning a value-concious vaction well in advance, use the chart as a guide but by no means as a substitute for the advice listed under "Getting a Good Deal on a Room," on page 46.

A reader recently complained to us that he had booked one of our top-ranked rooms in terms of value and had been very disappointed in the room. We noticed that the room the reader occupied had a quality rating of ★★½. We remind you that the value ratings are intended to give you some sense of value received for dollars spent. A ★★½ room at $90 may have the same value rating as a ★★★★ room at $200, but that does not mean the rooms will be of comparable quality. Regardless of whether it's a good deal or not, a ★★½ room is still a ★★½ room.

Listed below are the best room buys for the money, ordered without regard to quality or star ratings. Note that sometimes a suite can cost less than a hotel room.

THE TOP 30 BEST DEALS IN WASHINGTON, D.C.

Hotel	Zone	Quality Rating	Star Rating	Cost $=50
1.Sheraton National Hotel	11	76	★★★½	$$-
2. Hilton Alexandria at Mark Center	11	82	★★★½	$$-
3. Marriott Tysons Corner	11	83	★★★★	$$+
4. Hotel Helix	7	89	★★★★	$$$-
5. One Washington Circle Hotel	4	87	★★★★	$$$-
6. Residence Inn Bethesda	10	85	★★★★	$$$-
7. Radisson Plaza Hotel Old Town	11	75	★★★½	$$+
8. River Inn	4	84	★★★★	$$$-
9. Loew's L'Enfant Plaza	1	90	★★★★½	$$$+
10.. Hotel Madera	6	89	★★★★	$$$
11. Doubletree Hotel Crystal City	11	85	★★★★	$$$
12. Marriott Crystal Gateway	11	83	★★★★	$$$
13. Holiday Inn Bethesda	10	76	★★★½	$$+
14. Radisson Barceló Hotel	6	79	★★★½	$$+
15. Embassy Suites Crystal City	11	84	★★★★	$$$+
16. Watergate Hotel	6	94	★★★★½	$$$$
17. Quality Inn Iwo Jima	11	67	★★★	$$-
18. Hilton Garden Inn	3	78	★★★½	$$$-
19. Renaissance Mayflower Hotel	3	92	★★★★½	$$$$
20. Doubletree Hotel Tysons Corner	11	83	★★★★	$$$+
21. Courtyard Washington	6	77	★★★½	$$$-
22. Washington Terrace Hotel	7	88	★★★★	$$$+
23. Hyatt Regency Capitol Hill	3	82	★★★½	$$$-
24. Washington National Airport Hilton	11	81	★★★½	$$$-
25. Arlington Virginia Hilton	11	81	★★★½	$$$-
26. State Plaza Hotel	4	75	★★★½	$$$-
27. Embassy Row Hilton	6	85	★★★★	$$$+
28. Embassy Suites Chevy Chase	7	85	★★★★	$$$+
29. Sheraton Suites Alexandria	11	85	★★★★	$$$+
30. Omni Shoreham Hotel	7	88	★★★★	$$$$-

Hotel	Star Rating	Zone	Street Address
Adam's Inn	★★½	7	1744 Lanier Place, NW Washington, DC 20009
American Inn of Bethesda	★★½	10	8130 Wisconsin Avenue Bethesda, MD 20814
Arlington Virginia Hilton	★★★½	11	950 N. Stafford Street Arlington, VA 22203
Best Western Capitol Hill	★★	3	724 3rd Street, NW Washington, DC 20001
Best Western Key Bridge	★★½	11	1850 N. Fort Myer Drive Arlington, VA 22209
Best Western New Hampshire Suites	★★★	6	1121 New Hampshire Avenue, NW Washington, DC 20037
Best Western Pentagon	★★½	11	2480 S. Glebe Road Arlington, VA 22206
Best Western Tyson's Westpark	★★½	11	8401 Westpark Drive McLean, VA 22102
Bethesda Court Hotel	★★★½	10	7740 Wisconsin Avenue Bethesda, MD 20814
Capitol Hilton	★★★★	3	1001 16th Street, NW Washington, DC 20036
Carlyle Suites Hotel	★★★½	6	1731 New Hampshire Avenue, NW Washington, DC 20009
Channel Inn Hotel	★★★	1	650 Water Street, SW Washington, DC 20024
Churchhill Hotel	★★★★	6	1914 Connecticut Avenue, NW Washington, DC 20009
City Center Hotel	★★½	7	1201 13th Street, NW Washington, DC 20005
Comfort Inn Arlington	★★½	11	1211 N. Glebe Road Arlington, VA 22201
Comfort Inn Landmark	★★½	11	6254 Duke Street Alexandria, VA 22312
Comfort Inn Tysons Corner	★★½	11	1587 Spring Hill Road Vienna, VA 22182
Comfort Inn Washington Gateway	★★½	11	6111 Arlington Boulevard Falls Church , VA 22044
Courtyard Alexandria	★★★	11	2700 Eisenhower Avenue Alexandria, VA 22314
Courtyard Crystal City	★★★★	11	2899 Jefferson Davis Highway Arlington, VA 22202
Courtyard Embassy Row	★★★½	6	1600 Rhode Island Avenue, NW Washington, DC 20036

Local Phone	Fax	Toll-Free Reservations	Rack Rate	No. of Rooms	On-Site Dining	Pool
(202) 745-3600	(202) 319-7958	(800) 578-6807	$$	27		
(301) 656-9300	(301) 656-2907	(800) 323-7081	$$+	76	✔	✔
(703) 528-6000	(703) 528-4386	(800) HILTONS	$$$-	208	✔	✔
(202) 842-4466	(202) 842-4831	(800) 528-1234	$$$-	58	✔	
(703) 522-0400	(703) 524-5275	(800) HOLIDAY	$$$-	178	✔	✔
(202) 457-0565	(202) 331-9421	(800) 762-3777	$$$+	76		
(703) 979-4400	(703) 685-0051	(800) 426-6886	$$$-	206	✔	✔
(703) 734-2800	(703) 734-0521	(800) 937-8376	$$+	346	✔	✔
(301) 656-2100	(301) 986-0375	(800) 874-0050	$$$$-	75		
(202) 393-1000	(202) 639-5784	(800) HILTONS	$$$$$+	540	✔	
(202) 234-3200	(202) 387-0085	(800) 964-5377	$$$+	170	✔	
(202) 554-2400	(202) 863-1164	(800) 368-5668	$$$-	100	✔	✔
(202) 797-2000	(202) 462-0944	(800) 424-2464	$$$$	144	✔	
(202) 682-5300	(202) 371-9624	(888) 250-5396	$$	100	✔	
(703) 247-3399	(703) 524-8739	(800) 228-5150	$$$+	126	✔	
(703) 642-3422	(703) 642-1354	(800) 228-5150	$$-	150	✔	✔
(703) 448-8020	(703) 448-0343	(800) 228-5150	$$$+	250		
(703) 534-9100	(703) 534-5589	(800) 228-5150	$$$-	111		✔
(703) 329-2323	(703) 329-6853	(800) 321-2211	$$$+	176	✔	
(703) 549-3434	(703) 549-7440	(800) 847-4775	$$$$+	268	✔	✔
(202) 293-8000	(202) 293-0085	(800) 321-2211	$$$	156	✔	✔

Hotel	Star Rating	Zone	Street Address
Courtyard New Carrollton	★★★½	10	8330 Corporate Drive Landover, MD 20785
Courtyard Rosslyn	★★★½	11	1533 Clarendon Boulevard Rosslyn, VA 22209
Courtyard Washington	★★★½	6	1900 Connecticut Avenue, NW Washington, DC 20009
Crowne Plaza	★★★	3	1001 14th Street NW Washington, DC 20005
Crowne Plaza National Airport	★★★½	11	1489 Jefferson Davis Highway Arlington, VA 22202
Days Inn Alexandria	★★	11	110 S. Bragg Street Alexandria, VA 22312
Days Inn Connecticut Ave	★★½	7	4400 Connecticut Avenue, NW Washington, DC 20008
Days Inn Crystal City	★★★	11	2000 Jefferson Davis Highway Arlington, VA 22202
Doubletree Hotel Crystal City	★★★★	11	300 Army Navy Drive Arlington, VA 22202
Doubletree Hotel Tysons Corner	★★★★	11	7801 Leesburg Pike Falls Church, VA 22043
Econo Lodge National Airport	★★	11	2485 S. Glebe Road Arlington, VA 22206
Embassy Inn	★★½	6	1627 16th Street, NW Washington, DC 20009
Embassy Row Hilton	★★★★	6	2015 Massachusetts Avenue, NW Washington, DC 20036
Embassy Square Summerfield Suites	★★★	6	2000 N Street, NW Washington, DC 20036
Embassy Suites Alexandria	★★★★	11	1900 Diagonal Road Alexandria, VA 22314
Embassy Suites Chevy Chase	★★★★	7	4300 Military Road, NW Washington, DC 20015
Embassy Suites Crystal City	★★★★	11	1300 Jefferson Davis Highway Arlington, VA 22202
Embassy Suites Downtown	★★★★	6	1250 22nd Street, NW Washington, DC 20037
Embassy Suites Tysons Corner	★★★★	11	8517 Leesburg Pike Vienna, VA 22182
Four Points Sheraton Bethesda	★★★	10	8400 Wisconsin Avenue Bethesda, MD 20814
Four Points Sheraton Downtown	★★★½	3	1201 K Street, NW Washington, DC 20005

Local Phone	Fax	Toll-Free Reservations	Rack Rate	No. of Rooms	On-Site Dining	Pool
(301) 577-3373	(301) 577-1780	(800) 321-2211	$$$+	150		✔
(703) 528-2222	(703) 528-1027	(800) 321-2211	$$$$-	162	✔	✔
(202) 332-9300	(202) 328-7039	(800) 321-2211	$$$-	146	✔	✔
(202) 682-0111	(202) 682-9525	(800) 637-3788	$$$$ $$-	318	✔	
(703) 416-1600	(703) 416-1615	(800) 2 CROWNE	$$$$+	308	✔	✔
(703) 354-4950	(703) 354-4950	(800) 325-2525	$$	200		✔
(202) 244-5600	(202) 244-6794	(800) 325-2525	$$+	155		
(703) 920-8600	(703) 920-2840	(800) 325-2525	$$+	247	✔	✔
(703) 416-4100	(703) 416-4147	(800) 222-TREE	$$$	632	✔	✔
(703) 893-1340	(703) 847-9520	(800) 222-TREE	$$$+	404	✔	✔
(703) 979-4100	(703) 979-6120	(800) 424-4777	$$-	160		✔
(202) 234-7800	(202) 234-3309	(800) 423-9111	$$$-	38		
(202) 265-1600	(202) 328-7526	(800) HILTONS	$$$+	196	✔	✔
(202) 659-9000	(202) 429-9546	(800) 424-2999	$$$	250		✔
(703) 684-5900	(703) 684-1403	(800) EMBASSY	$$$$-	268	✔	✔
(202) 362-9300	(202) 686-3405	(800) EMBASSY	$$$$	198	✔	✔
(703) 979-9799	(703) 920-5947	(800) EMBASSY	$$$+	267	✔	✔
(202) 857-3388	(202) 293-3173	(800) EMBASSY	$$$$-	318	✔	✔
(703) 883-0707	(703) 883-0694	(800) EMBASSY	$$$$-	232	✔	✔
(301) 654-1000	(301) 654-0751	(877) 795-7842	$$$$-	163	✔	✔
(202) 289-7600	(202) 789-0173	(888) 625-5144	$$$$	265	✔	✔

Hotel	Star Rating	Zone	Street Address
Four Points Sheraton Pentagon	★★★½	11	2480 S. Glebe Road Arlington, VA 22206
Four Seasons Hotel	★★★★½	5	2800 Pennsylvania Avenue, NW Washington, DC 20007
Georgetown Inn	★★★★	5	1310 Wisconsin Avenue, NW Washington, DC 20007
The Governor's House	★★★	6	1615 Rhode Island Avenue, NW Washington, DC 20036
Grand Hyatt Washington	★★★★	3	1000 H Street, NW Washington, DC 20001
Hampton Inn Alexandria	★★★	11	4800 Leesburg Pike Alexandria, VA 22302
Hawthorn Suites Hotel	★★★½	11	420 North Van Dorn Street Alexandria, VA 22304
Hay-Adams Hotel	★★★★½	3	One Lafayette Square, NW Washington, DC 20006
Hilton Alexandria at Mark Center	★★★½	11	5000 Seminary Road Alexandria, VA 22311
Hilton Garden Inn	★★★½	3	815 14th Street, NW Washington, DC 20005
Hilton of Silver Spring	★★★	10	8727 Colesville Road Silver Spring, MD 20910
Holiday Inn and Suites	★★½	11	2460 Eisenhower Avenue Alexandria, VA 22314
Holiday Inn Arlington	★★★½	11	4610 N. Fairfax Drive Arlington, VA 22203
Holiday Inn Bethesda	★★★½	10	8120 Wisconsin Avenue Bethesda, MD 20814
Holiday Inn Capitol	★★★	3	550 C Street, SW Washington, DC 20024
Holiday Inn Central	★★★	7	1501 Rhode Island Avenue, NW Washington, DC 20005
Holiday Inn Chevy Chase	★★★	10	5520 Wisconsin Avenue Chevy Chase, MD 20815
Holiday Inn Downtown	★★★	3	1155 14th Street, NW Washington, DC 20005
Holiday Inn Georgetown	★★★½	7	2101 Wisconsin Avenue, NW Washington, DC 20007
Holiday Inn Hotel and Suites	★★★	11	625 First Street Alexandria, VA 22314
Holiday Inn National Airport	★★★	11	2650 Jefferson Davis Highway Arlington, VA 22202

Local Phone	Fax	Toll-Free Reservations	Rack Rate	No. of Rooms	On-Site Dining	Pool
(703) 682-5500	(703) 682-5505	(800) 325-3535	$$$+	120	✔	✔
(202) 342-0444	(202) 944-2076	(800) 819-5053	$$$$$ $$$+	196	✔	✔
(202) 333-8900	(202) 625-1744	(800) 424-2979	$$$$-	95	✔	
(202) 296-2100	(202) 463-6614	(800) 821-4367	$$$$+	150	✔	✔
(202) 582-1234	(202) 637-4781	(800) 233-1234	$$$$+	900	✔	✔
(703) 671-4800	(703) 671-2442	(800) HAMPTON	$$+	130		✔
(703) 370-1000	(703) 751-1467	(800) 368-3339	$$$-	184		✔
(202) 638-6600	(202) 638-2716	(800) 223-5652	$$$$$ $$$$$+	143	✔	✔
(703) 845-1010	(703) 845-7662	(800) HILTONS	$$-	500	✔	✔
(202) 783-7800	(202) 783-7801	(800) HILTONS	$$$-	300	✔	✔
(301) 589-5200	(301) 563-3832	None	$$$-	231	✔	✔
(703) 960-3400	(703) 329-0953	(800) HOLIDAY	$$$-	197	✔	✔
(703) 243-9800	(703) 527-2677	(800) HOLIDAY	$$$$-	221	✔	✔
(301) 652-2000	(301) 652-4525	(877) 888-3001	$$+	267	✔	✔
(202) 479-4000	(202) 479-4353	(800) HOLIDAY	$$$+	528	✔	✔
(202) 483-2000	(202) 797-1078	(800) 248-0016	$$$+	212	✔	✔
(301) 656-1500	(301) 656-5045	(800) HOLIDAY	$$$$-	216	✔	✔
(202) 737-1200	(202) 783-5733	(800) HOLIDAY	$$$$+	212	✔	✔
(202) 338-4600	(202) 338-4458	(800) HOLIDAY	$$$$	296	✔	✔
(703) 548-6300	(703) 684-7782	(877) 732-3318	$$$$-	178	✔	✔
(703) 684-7200	(703) 684-3217	(800) HOLIDAY	$$+	280	✔	✔

Hotel	Star Rating	Zone	Street Address
Holiday Inn on the Hill	★★★	3	415 New Jersey Avenue, NW Washington, DC 20001
Holiday Inn Rosslyn at Key Bridge	★★★	11	1900 N. Fort Myer Drive Arlington, VA 22209
Holiday Inn Select Old Town	★★★½	11	480 King Street Alexandria, VA 22314
Holiday Inn Silver Spring	★★★	10	8777 Georgia Avenue Silver Spring, MD 20910
The Hotel George	★★★★	2	15 E Street, NW Washington, DC 20001
Hotel Helix	★★★★	7	1430 Rhode Island Avenue, NW Washington, DC 20005
Hotel Lombardy	★★★½	4	2019 I Street, NW Washington, DC 20006
Hotel Madera	★★★★	6	1310 New Hampshire Avenue, NW Washington, DC 20036
Hotel Monaco	★★★★	3	7th and F Streets, NW Washington, DC 20004
Hotel Monticello	★★★½	5	1075 Thomas Jefferson Street, NW Washington, DC 20007
Hotel Rouge	★★★★	6	1315 16th Street, NW Washington, DC 20036
Hotel Topaz	★★★★½	6	1733 N Street, NW Washington, DC 20036
Hotel Washington	★★★½	3	Pennsylvania Avenue, NW at 15th Washington, DC 20004
Hyatt Arlington	★★★★	11	1325 Wilson Boulevard Arlington, VA 22209
Hyatt Regency Bethesda	★★★★	10	One Bethesda Metro Center Bethesda, MD 20814
Hyatt Regency Capitol Hill	★★★½	3	400 New Jersey Avenue, NW Washington, DC 20001
Hyatt Regency Crystal City	★★★½	11	2799 Jefferson Davis Highway Arlington, VA 22202
J.W. Marriott Hotel	★★★★	3	1331 Pennsylvania Avenue, NW Washington, DC 20004
Jefferson Hotel	★★★★½	3	1200 16th Street, NW Washington, DC 20036
Jurys Normandy	★★½	6	2118 Wyoming Avenue, NW Washington, DC 20008
Kalorama Guest House	★★★	6	1854 Mintwood Place, NW Washington, DC 20009

Local Phone	Fax	Toll-Free Reservations	Rack Rate	No. of Rooms	On-Site Dining	Pool
(202) 638-1616	(202) 638-0707	(800) 638-1116	$$$+	343	✔	✔
(703) 807-2000	(703) 522-7480	(800) 368-3408	$$$+	306	✔	✔
(703) 549-6080	(703) 684-6508	(800) 368-5047	$$$$$	227	✔	✔
(301) 589-0800	(301) 587-4791	(800) HOLIDAY	$$$$-	220	✔	✔
(202) 347-4200	(202) 346-4213	(800) 576-8331	$$$$$ $$$-	139	✔	
(202) 462-7777	(202) 332-3519	(800) 368-5690	$$$-	184	✔	✔
(202) 828-2600	(202) 872-0503	(800) 424-5486	$$$+	126	✔	
(202) 296-7600	(202) 293-2476	(800) 368-5691	$$$	82	✔	
(202) 628-7177	(202) 628-7277	(800) 649-1202	$$$$ $$-	184	✔	
(202) 337-0900	(202) 333-6526	(800) 388-2410	$$$$$	47		
(202) 232-8000	(202) 667-9827	(800) 221-2222	$$$$-	137	✔	
(202) 393-3000	(202) 785-9581	(800) 424-2950	$$$$$-	99	✔	
(202) 638-5900	(202) 638-1595	(800) 424-9540	$$$+	344	✔	
(703) 525-1234	(703) 875-3393	(800) 233-1234	$$$$-	302	✔	
(301) 657-1234	(301) 657-6453	(800) 233-1234	$$$$+	381	✔	✔
(202) 737-1234	(202) 737-5773	(800) 233-1234	$$$-	834	✔	✔
(703) 418-1234	(703) 418-1289	(800) 233-1234	$$$+	685	✔	✔
(202) 393-2000	(202) 626-6991	(800) 228-9290	$$$$ $$$-	772	✔	✔
(202) 347-2200	(202) 331-7982	(800) 368-5966	$$$$ $$$$	100	✔	
(202) 483-1350	(202) 387-8241	(800) 424-3729	$$+	75		
(202) 667-6369	(202) 319-1262	None	$$$-	29		

Hotel	Star Rating	Zone	Street Address
Latham Hotel Georgetown	★★★½	5	3000 M Street, NW Washington, DC 20007
Lincoln Suites	★★★½	3	1823 L Street, NW Washington, DC 20036
Loew's L'Enfant Plaza	★★★★½	1	480 L'Enfant Plaza, SW Washington, DC 20024
Madison Hotel	★★★★	3	1177 15th Street, NW Washington, DC 20005
Marriott Crystal City	★★★½	11	1999 Jefferson Davis Highway Arlington, VA 22202
Marriott Crystal Gateway	★★★★	11	1700 Jefferson Davis Highway Arlington, VA 22202
Marriott Hotel Bethesda	★★★½	10	5151 Pooks Hill Road Bethesda, MD 20814
Marriott Hotel Key Bridge	★★★½	11	1401 Lee Highway Arlington, VA 22209
Marriott Metro Center	★★★½	3	775 12th Street, NW Washington, DC 20005
Marriott Tysons Corner	★★★★	11	8028 Leesburg Pike Vienna, VA 22182
Marriott Wardman Park Hotel	★★★★	7	2660 Woodley Road, NW Washington, DC 20008
The Melrose Hotel	★★★★	5	2430 Pennsylvania Avenue, NW Washington, DC 20037
Morrison House	★★★★	11	116 S. Alfred Road Alexandria, VA 22314
Morrison-Clark Inn	★★★★	7	1015 L Street, NW Washington, DC 20001
Omni Shoreham Hotel	★★★★	7	2500 Calvert Street, NW Washington, DC 20008
One Washington Circle Hotel	★★★★	4	One Washington Circle, NW Washington, DC 20037
Park Hyatt	★★★★½	5	24th Street at M Street, NW Washington, DC 20037
Phoenix Park Hotel	★★★	2	520 N. Capitol Street, NW Washington, DC 20001
Quality Inn College Park	★★½	10	7200 Baltimore Boulevard College Park, MD 20740
Quality Inn Iwo Jima	★★★	11	1501 Arlington Boulevard Arlington, VA 22209
Radisson Barceló Hotel	★★★½	6	2121 P Street, NW Washington, DC 20037

Local Phone	Fax	Toll-Free Reservations	Rack Rate	No. of Rooms	On-Site Dining	Pool
(202) 726-5000	(202) 348-1800	(800) LATHAM-1	$$$$-	143	✔	✔
(202) 223-4320	(202) 223-8546	(800) 424-2970	$$$+	99		
(202) 484-1000	(202) 646-4456	(800) 635-5065	$$$+	370	✔	✔
(202) 862-1600	(202) 785-1255	(800) 424-8578	$$$$$+	353	✔	
(703) 413-5500	(703) 413-0192	(800) 228-9290	$$$$+	345	✔	✔
(703) 920-3230	(703) 271-5212	(800) 228-9290	$$$	697	✔	✔
(301) 897-9400	(301) 897-0192	(800) 228-9290	$$$$$	399	✔	✔
(703) 524-6400	(703) 524-8964	(800) 228-9290	$$$$	588	✔	✔
(202) 737-2200	(202) 347-5886	(800) 228-9290	$$$$$$	456	✔	✔
(703) 734-3200	(703) 734-5763	(800) 228-9290	$$+	392	✔	✔
(202) 328-2000	(202) 234-0015	(800) 228-9290	$$$$$$-	1465	✔	✔
(202) 955-6400	(202) 955-5765	(800) 822-4200	$$$$-	239	✔	
(703) 838-8000	(703) 684-6283	(800) 367-0800	$$$$-	45	✔	
(202) 898-1200	(202) 289-8576	(800) 332-7898	$$$$-	54	✔	
(202) 234-0700	(202) 265-7972	(800) THE-OMNI	$$$$-	836	✔	✔
(202) 872-1680	(202) 887-4989	(800) 424-9671	$$$-	149	✔	✔
(202) 789-1234	(202) 457-8823	(800) 233-1234	$$$$ $$$-	223	✔	✔
(202) 638-6900	(202) 393-3236	(800) 824-5419	$$$$+	150	✔	
(301) 864-5820	(301) 864-5820	(800) 221-2222	$$-	154		✔
(703) 524-5000	(703) 522-5484	(800) 221-2222	$$-	141	✔	✔
(202) 293-3100	(202) 857-0134	(800) 333-3333	$$+	300	✔	✔

Hotel	Star Rating	Zone	Street Address
Radisson Plaza Hotel Old Town	★★★½	11	901 N. Fairfax Street Alexandria, VA 22314
Red Roof Inn Downtown	★★½	3	500 H Street, NW Washington, DC 20001
Renaissance Mayflower Hotel	★★★★½	3	1127 Connecticut Avenue, NW Washington, DC 20036
Residence Inn Bethesda	★★★★	10	7335 Wisconsin Avenue Bethesda, MD 20814
Residence Inn Dupont Circle	★★★½	6	2120 P Street, NW Washington, DC 20037
Residence Inn Pentagon City	★★★★	11	550 Army Navy Drive Arlington, VA 22202
Residence Inn Thomas Circle	★★★½	3	1199 Vermont Avenue, NW Washington, DC 20005
Ritz-Carlton Pentagon City	★★★★½	11	1250 S. Hayes Street Arlington, VA 22202
River Inn	★★★★	4	924 25th Street, NW Washington, DC 20037
Savoy Suites Hotel	★★★½	7	2505 Wisconsin Avenue, NW Washington, DC 20007
Sheraton Crystal City	★★★½	11	1800 Jefferson Davis Highway Arlington, VA 22202
Sheraton National Hotel	★★★½	11	Columbia Pike & Washington Blvd. Arlington, VA 22204
Sheraton Pentagon South	★★★	11	4641 Kenmore Avenue Alexandria, VA 22304
Sheraton Premiere Tysons Corner	★★★★½	11	8661 Leesburg Pike Vienna, VA 22182
Sheraton Suites Alexandria	★★★★	11	801 N. St. Asaph Street Alexandria, VA 22314
Sofitel Lafayette	★★★★	3	806 15th Street, NW Washington, DC, 20005
St. Gregory Luxury Hotel & Suites	★★★★	6	2033 M Street Washington, DC 20036
St. James	★★★★	4	950 24th Street, NW Washington, DC 20037
St. Regis	★★★★½	3	923 16th Street & K Street, NW Washington, DC 20006
State Plaza Hotel	★★★½	4	2117 E Street, NW Washington, DC 20037
Tabard Inn	★★★½	6	1739 N Street, NW Washington, DC 20036

Local Phone	Fax	Toll-Free Reservations	Rack Rate	No. of Rooms	On-Site Dining	Pool
(703) 683-6000	(703) 683-7597	(800) 333-3333	$$+	258	✔	✔
(202) 289-5959	(202) 289-0754	(800) RED-ROOF	$$$-	197	✔	
(202) 347-3000	(202) 776-9182	(800) HOTELS-1	$$$$	660	✔	
(301) 718-0200	(301) 718-0679	(800) 331-3131	$$$-	187		✔
(202) 466-6800	(202) 466-9630	(800) 331-3131	$$$$-	107		
(703) 413-6630	(703) 418-1751	(800) 331-3131	$$$$+	299		✔
(202) 898-1100	(202) 898-1110	(800) 331-3131	$$$$$	202		
(703) 415-5000	(703) 415-3781	(800) 241-3333	$$$$ $$$	345	✔	✔
(202) 337-7600	(202) 337-6520	(800) 424-2741	$$$-	126	✔	
(202) 337-9700	(202) 337-3644	(800) 944-5377	$$$+	150	✔	
(703) 486-1111	(703) 769-3970	(888) 625-5144	$$$$$-	220	✔	✔
(703) 521-1900	(703) 521-2122	(888) 625-5144	$$-	415	✔	✔
(703) 751-4510	(703) 751-9170	(888) 298-2054	$$$$$-	193	✔	✔
(703) 448-1234	(703) 893-8193	(888) 625-5144	$$$$$	437	✔	✔
(703) 836-4700	(703) 548-4518	(888) 625-5144	$$$+	247	✔	✔
(202) 737-8800	(202) 730-8500	(800) SOFITEL	$$$$ $$$-	237	✔	
(202) 223-0200	(202) 223-0580	(800) 829-5034	$$$$$-	154	✔	
(202) 457-0500	(202) 659-4492	(800) 852-8512	$$$$+	195	✔	✔
(202) 638-2626	(202) 879-2058	(800) 562-5661	$$$$+	197	✔	
(202) 861-8200	(202) 659-8601	(800) 424-2859	$$$-	224	✔	
(202) 785-1277	(202) 785-6173	None	$$$$-	40	✔	

Hotel	Star Rating	Zone	Street Address
The Ritz-Carlton	★★★★★	6	1150 22nd Street, NW Washington, DC 20037
Washington Court Hotel	★★★★	3	525 New Jersey Avenue, NW Washington, DC 20001
Washington Hilton & Towers	★★★½	6	1919 Connecticut Avenue, NW Washington, DC 20009
Washington Marriott Hotel	★★★½	6	1221 22nd St. and M Street, NW Washington, DC 20037
Washington Monarch Hotel	★★★★	5	24th and M Street, NW Washington, DC 20037
Washington National Airport Hilton	★★★½	11	2399 Jefferson Davis Highway Arlington, VA 22202
Washington Plaza Hotel	★★★	3	10 Thomas Circle, NW Washington, DC 20005
Washington Renaissance Hotel	★★★★	3	999 Ninth Street, NW Washington, DC 20001
Washington Suites Alexandria	★★★½	11	100 S. Reynolds Street Alexandria, VA 22304
Washington Suites Pennsylvania Ave.	★★★★	5	2500 Pennsylvania Avenue Washington, DC 20037
Washington Terrace Hotel	★★★★	7	1515 Rhode Island Avenue, NW Washington, DC 20036
Watergate Hotel	★★★★½	6	2650 Virginia Avenue, NW Washington, DC 20037
Westin Fairfax	★★★★½	6	2100 Massachusetts Avenue, NW Washington, DC 20008
The Westin Grand	★★★★½	5	2350 M Street, NW Washington, DC 20037
Willard Inter-Continental	★★★★½	3	1401 Pennsylvania Avenue, NW Washington, DC 20004
Windsor Park Hotel	★★½	6	2116 Kalorama Road, NW Washington, DC 20008
Wyndham City Center	★★★½	6	1143 New Hampshire Avenue, NW Washington, DC 20037
The Wyndham Washington	★★★★	3	1400 M Street, NW Washington, DC 20005

Local Phone	Fax	Toll-Free Reservations	Rack Rate	No. of Rooms	On-Site Dining	Pool
(202) 835-0500	(202) 974-5505	(800) 241-3333	$$$$$ $$$$	300	✔	✔
(202) 628-2100	(202) 879-7918	(800) 321-3010	$$$$$	266	✔	
(202) 483-3000	(202) 232-0438	(800) HILTONS	$$$$-	1123	✔	✔
(202) 872-1500	(202) 872-1424	(800) 228-9290	$$$$$+	418	✔	✔
(202) 429-2400	(202) 457-5010	(877) 222-2226	$$$$ $$$-	415	✔	✔
(703) 418-6800	(703) 418-3763	(800) HILTONS	$$$-	386	✔	✔
(202) 842-1300	(202) 371-9602	(800) 424-1140	$$$$-	339	✔	✔
(202) 898-9000	(202) 789-4213	(800) 228-9898	$$$$$$	800	✔	✔
(703) 370-9600	(703) 370-0467	(877) 736-2500	$$$	225	✔	✔
(202) 333-8060	(202) 955-5765	(877) 736-2500	$$$$$-	239	✔	
(202) 232-7000	(202) 332-8436	(800) 222-TREE	$$$+	219	✔	
(202) 965-2300	(202) 337-7915	(800) 424-2736	$$$$	235	✔	✔
(202) 293-2100	(202) 293-0641	(800) 325-3535	$$$$ $$$+	206	✔	
(202) 429-0100	(202) 429-9759	(888) 625-5144	$$$$ $$$-	263	✔	✔
(202) 628-9100	(202) 637-7326	(800) 327-0200	$$$$$$ $$$$-	340	✔	
(202) 483-7700	(202) 332-4547	(800) 247-3064	$$+	43		
(202) 775-0800	(202) 331-9491	(800) WYNDHAM	$$$$+	353	✔	
(202) 429-1700	(202) 785-0786	(800) WYNDHAM	$$$$-	400	✔	

Part Three

Visiting Washington on Business

Not All Visitors Are Headed for the Mall

While most of the more than 21 million people who come to Washington each year are tourists, not everyone visiting the city has an itinerary centered around the Mall. In fact, almost 1.5 million visitors are convention-goers attending shows at the Washington Convention Center, located in downtown Washington. In addition, as the seat of the United States government, the city draws another 4.5 million visitors from around the world who fly in to conduct business with both federal agencies and a wide array of private organizations headquartered here.

The city is also a center of higher education. The District is home to George Washington University, Georgetown University, American University, Howard University, and the Catholic University of America, among others. As a result, Washington attracts a lot of visiting academics, college administrators, and students and their families.

In many ways, the problems facing business visitors on their first trip to Washington don't differ much from the problems of folks in town intent on hitting the major tourist attractions. People visiting on business need to locate a hotel that's convenient, want to avoid the worst of the city's traffic, face the same problems getting around an unfamiliar city, must figure out how to buy a Metro ticket, and want to know the locations of the best restaurants. This book can help.

For the most part, though, business visitors aren't nearly as flexible about the timing of their visit as folks who pick Washington as a vacation destination. While we advise that the best times for coming to D.C. are spring and fall, the necessities of business may dictate that January is when you pull into town—or, even worse, early April, when the city is mobbed for the Japanese cherry blossom festivities.

Yet much of the advice and information presented in the *Unofficial Guide* is as valuable to business visitors as it is to tourists. As for our recommendations on seeing the city's many sights . . . who knows? Perhaps you'll be able to squeeze a morning or an afternoon out of your busy schedule, grab this book, and spend a few hours exploring some of the attractions that draw the other 17 million people who visit Washington each year.

The Washington Convention Center

In the fall of 1998, ground was broken for a new $800 million Washington Convention Center, located two blocks from the existing center at Mount Vernon Square. The building, slated to open March 2003, has more than 2 million square feet of space, including 725,000 square feet of exhibit space, a half-million square feet of contiguous space, and 70 meeting rooms totaling 150,000 square feet. It's the largest building in D.C.

The new Washington Convention Center is a four-level structure located seven blocks from the White House on a 17-acre site bounded by Mount Vernon Place, 9th, N, and 7th Streets, NW. The center contains 56 meeting rooms (some divisible), 3 ballrooms, and 5 exhibit halls with 151,000 square feet, 194,000 square feet, 128,000 square feet, 111,000 square feet, and 119,000 square feet of space, respectively. The Center provides all food and beverage services on the premises, including catered meal and brand restaurants like Wolfgang Puck's and Starbucks.

For both exhibitors and attendees, the Washington Convention Center looks like it will be an excellent site for a meeting or trade show. Large and small exhibitors can set up their exhibits with a minimum of effort. Forty-two loading docks and huge bay doors make unloading and loading quick and simple for large displays arriving by truck. Smaller displays transported in vans and cars are unloaded in the same area, entering from N Street. Equipment can be carried or wheeled directly to the exhibit area. The exhibit areas and meeting rooms are well marked and easy to find. For more information, call (202) 789-1600, (800) 368-9000 or visit www.dcconvention.com.

Lodging within Walking Distance of the Convention Center

While participants in citywide conventions lodge all over town, a couple of hotels are within easy walking distance of the Convention Center: the Grand Hyatt (phone (202) 582-1234) and Crowne Plaza (phone (202) 682-0111). The Grand Hyatt, directly across the street from the Center, features 900 rooms and 65 suites. The Crowne Plaza, two blocks away at Metro Center, has 318 rooms, each supplied with a minibar, and 40 suites.

Other hotels within a few blocks of the Washington Convention Center are:

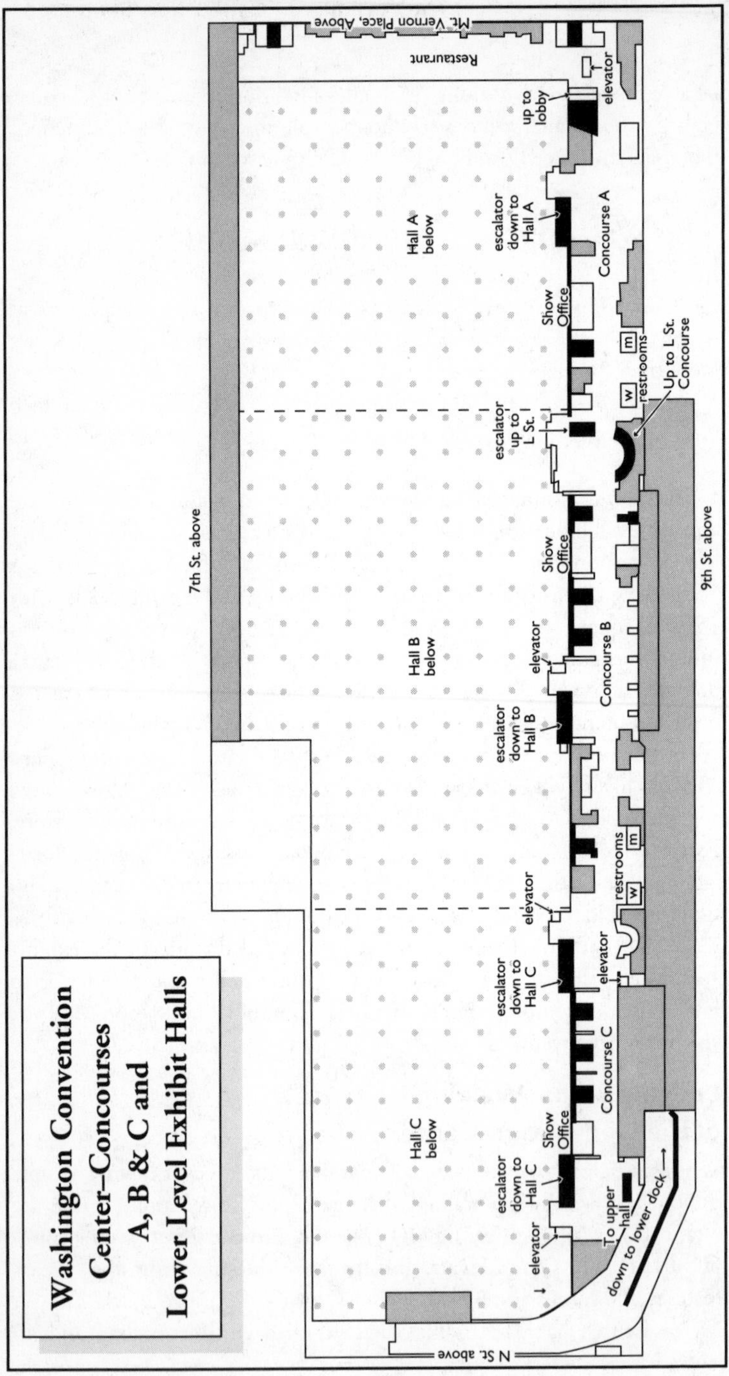
Washington Convention Center–Concourses A, B & C and Lower Level Exhibit Halls
Mt. Vernon Place, Above
Restaurant
elevator
up to lobby
Hall A below
escalator down to Hall A
Show Office
Concourse A
restrooms
m
w
Up to L St. Concourse
escalator up to L St.
7th St. above
9th St. above
Show Office
Hall B below
elevator
Concourse B
escalator down to Hall B
restrooms
m
w
elevator
elevator
escalator down to Hall C
Concourse C
Hall C below
Show Office
escalator down to Hall C
To upper hall
down to lower dock
elevator
N St. above

Washington Convention Center–Street Level, Rooms 101–160

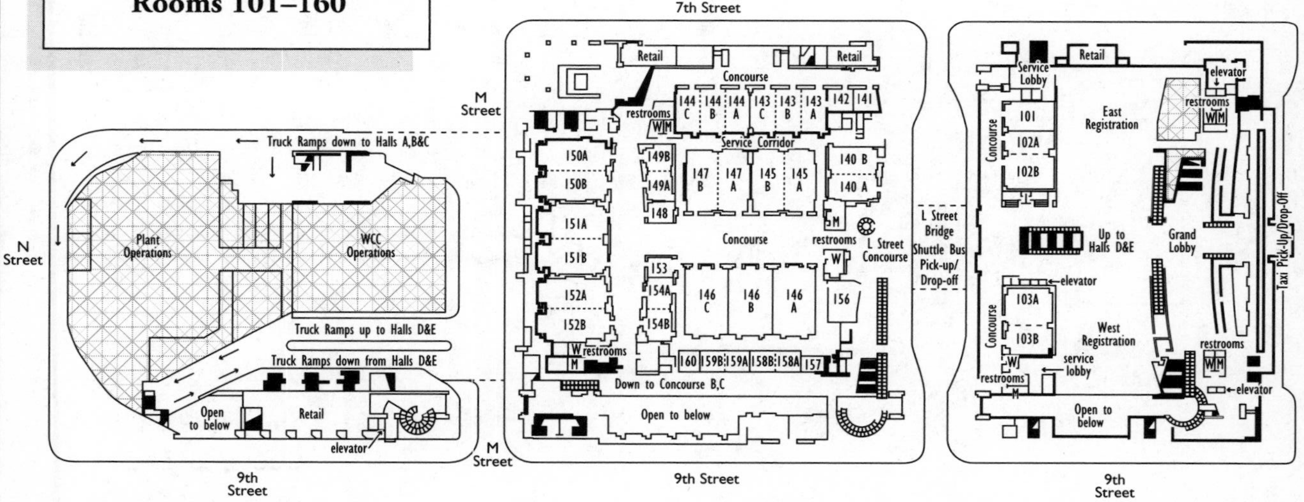

Washington Convention Center—Level Two, Halls D & E and Rooms 201–210

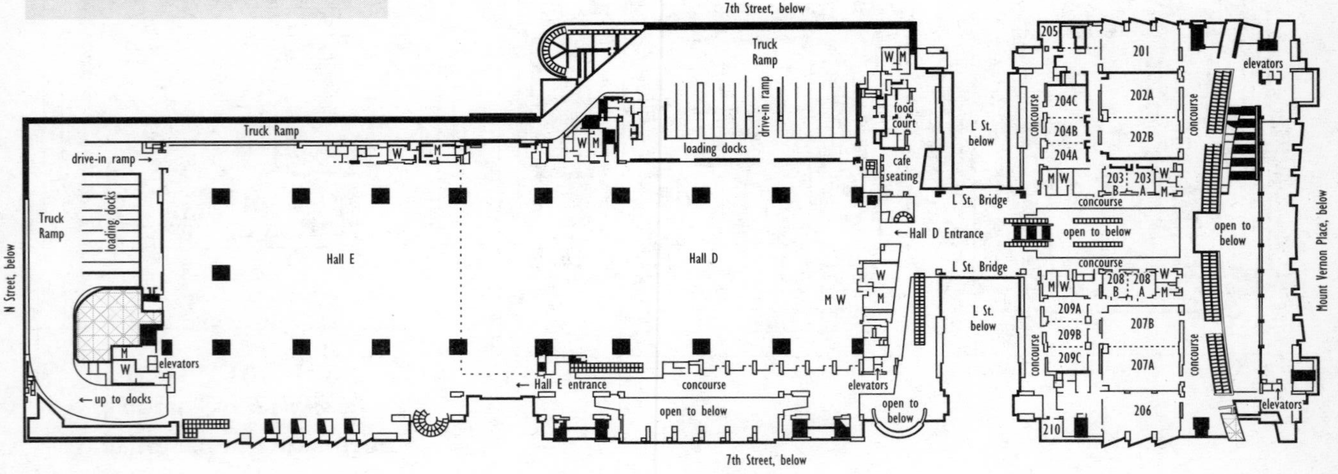

Washington Convention Center–Level Three, Ballroom and Rooms 301–306

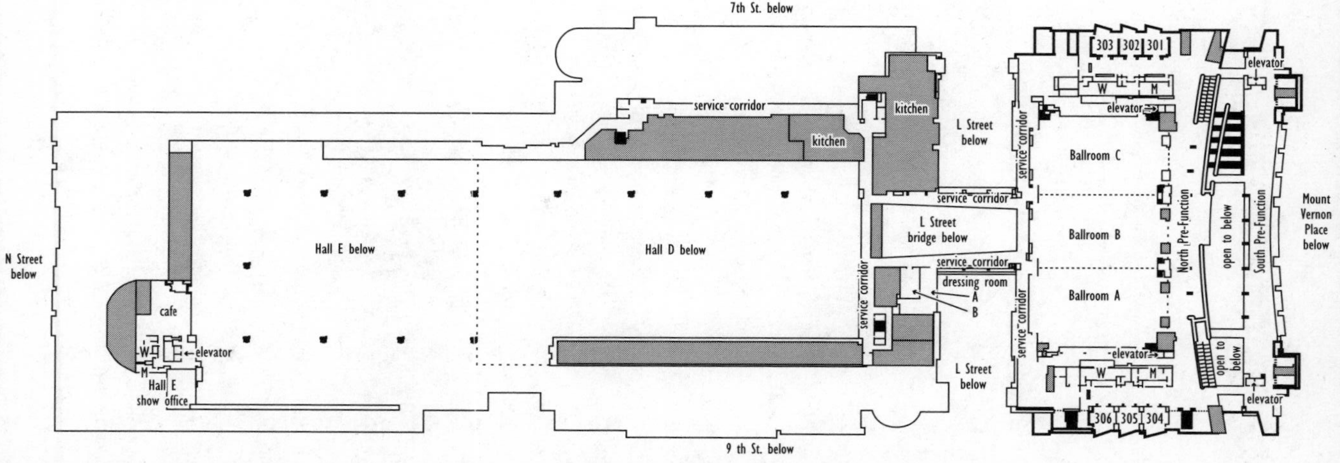

A CONVENTION CENTER CALENDAR

The city's considerable convention business (1.5 million delegates in 2001) can make it hard to get a hotel room in and around the city. Use the following list of major 2003 and 2004 convention dates to plan your trip to Washington.

Dates	Convention/Event	Attendees
2003		
Jan. 3–7	Association of American Law Schools	3,000
Jan. 3–5	American Economic Assn./ Allied Social Sciences	8,000
Jan. 28–31	ComNet	42,000
Mar. 10–12	National Managed Health Care Congress	6,000
Mar. 20–31	U.S. Figure Skating Association	20,000
Apr. 3–5	New York State United Teachers	6,000
Apr. 8–10	FOSE Info Technology Forum	60,000
Apr.29–May 1	Internet Service Provider	15,000
May 7–11	National Association of Home Builders	3,000
May 15–17	North American Society of Pacing and Electrophysiology	7,000
May 19–22	American Society for Microbiology	13,500
June 3–5	A/E/C Systems	25,000
June 5–7	American Occupational Therapy Associations	5,000
June 8–15	American Association of Health Plans	4,500
June 17–20	American Physical Therapy Association	4,000
June 20–27	Biotechnology Industry Association	7,000
July 12–19	Smart Meetings	3,000
July 22–24	Trade Show Exhibitors Association	4,000
Aug. 9–16	SHARE International	5,000
Sept. 3–4	Hospitality Sales and Marketing Association International	3,000
Sept. 5–7	Natural Products Exposition	20,000
Sept. 16–18	Transcatheter Cardiovascular Theraputics	12,000
Sept. 26–29	Congressional Black Caucus	8,000

Dates	Convention/Event	Attendees
Oct. 5–8	Association of the U.S. Army	20,000
Oct. 16–18	National Automatic Merchandising Association	7,450
2004		
Jan. 27–30	ComNet	42,000
Feb. 7–10	American Academy of Dermatology	17,500
Feb. 19–21	International Travelgoods, Leather and Accessories Show	7,000
Mar. 1–3	National Managed Health Care Congress	11,000
Mar. 16–18	FOSE	60,000
Apr. 18–20	Federation of American Societies/ Experimental Biology	18,000
May 25–27	American Society for Training and Development	18,000
June 5–8	International Dairy Deli Bakery Association	8,000
June 13–16	Drug Information Association	9,000
June 19–22	Newspaper Association of America	10,500
June 20–22	Electrical Apparatus Service Association	3,400
July 3–6	National Education Association	17,000
July 9–18	American Federation of Teachers	5,000
Aug. 4–8	Unity: Journalists of Color	8,000
Sept. 8–11	Congressional Black Caucus	8,000
Sept. 8–9	Affordable Meetings Exhibition	3,000
Sept. 16–24	National Postal Forum	8,000
Sept. 30–Oct. 2	Transcatheter Cardiovascular Therapeutics	12,000
Oct. 11–13	American Health Information Management Association	3,800
Oct. 15–17	Natural Products Exhibition	20,000
Oct. 24–27	Association of the U.S. Army	20,000
Oct. 31–Nov. 4	American Society for Microbiology	12,000
Nov. 8–10	American Public Health Association	12,000
Dec. 4–8	American Society for Cell Biology	8,000

Hotel	*Rooms*	*Suites*	*Distance*
Marriott	456	3	1 block
Red Roof Inn	197	none	3 blocks
J.W. Marriott	772	23	4 blocks
Willard Intercontinental	307	33	8 blocks

See our "Tips for Business Travelers" on page 53 for more on lodging.

Parking at the Convention Center

While there's no parking in the Washington Convention Center itself, the surrounding area offers 15 parking lots and garages within a 3-block walk. Daily rates run as high as $10 but average around $7.

Metro Center, one of Washington's 83 subway stations, is two blocks away from the Washington Convention Center and offers conventioneers an easy alternative to driving and parking in downtown D.C. On the red line, Metro Center is three stops from Union Station, making it convenient for people who opt to come in by train. Metro Center can be entered from the Grand Hyatt Hotel's lobby, directly across the street from the Convention Center.

Cabs and Shuttles to the Convention Center

Large, citywide conventions often provide complimentary bus service from major hotels to the Convention Center. If you are staying at a smaller hotel and wish to use the shuttle bus, walk to the nearest large hotel on the shuttle route. In addition, cabs are relatively cheap and plentiful in Washington. The Metro, D.C.'s subway system, is clean, safe, and fast; the nearest station is Metro Center, two blocks from the Convention Center.

Lunch Alternatives for Convention and Trade Show Attendees

Prices of food from the Convention Center's food service are on the high side, but convention attendees needn't feel trapped: Plenty of good eating establishments are within a few blocks. Directly across the street on 11th Street, NW, is the Capitol City Brewing Company, a pub featuring burgers and like fare. Washington's Chinatown is a block away; the area is packed with good, cheap eateries, including the China Doll at 627 H Street, NW, (202) 289-4755, and Go Lo's at 604 H Street, NW, (202) 347-4656. For a quiet business lunch, the Old Ebbitt Grill at 675 15th Street, (202) 347-4800, should fill the bill. For more exotic tastes, try the Moroccan fare at Marrakesh at 617 New York Avenue, (202) 393-9393, or the Burmese cuisine at Burma, 740 6th Street, (202) 638-1280. For fast food, choose from Hardee's, McDonald's, Taco Bell Express, and the Shops at National Place, a three-level mall located at 13th and F Streets, NW, that features a food court.

Part Four

Arriving and Getting Oriented

Coming into the City

By Car

If you drive, you will most likely arrive on one of three freeways: Interstate 95 from the north, I-95 from the south, or I-70 from the northwest. Other routes that converge in Washington are I-66 from the west (which links with I-81 in Virginia's Shenandoah Valley), US 50 (which hooks up with Annapolis, Maryland, US 301, and Maryland's Eastern Shore), and the Baltimore-Washington Parkway, which parallels I-95 between the two cities' beltways.

All these routes have one common link: They connect with Washington's Capital Beltway, a ribbon of concrete encircling the city. Now for an introduction to how unfriendly D.C. freeways can be to unsuspecting motorists: Part of the Beltway is numbered both I-95 and I-495. Why? Since I-95 doesn't cut directly through Washington (the way it does in Richmond to the south and Baltimore to the north), it's rerouted along the southern half of the Beltway. It's quite confusing to visitors, and it's only the first of many Washington driving horrors you'll encounter.

Drivers coming from the north and I-70 and headed downtown should take the Beltway to the Baltimore-Washington Parkway and exit south. Bear right onto New York Avenue where the Parkway splits; it goes straight to downtown, near Union Station.

From the south and west, motorists can take either I-66 or I-395 (what I-95 becomes after it crosses inside the Beltway). Both get you across the Potomac and into D.C. near the center of the tourist hubbub.

Our advice to drivers unfamiliar with Washington is to sit down with a map before you leave home and carefully trace out the route to your destination. If you need to make a phone call or two for directions, do it

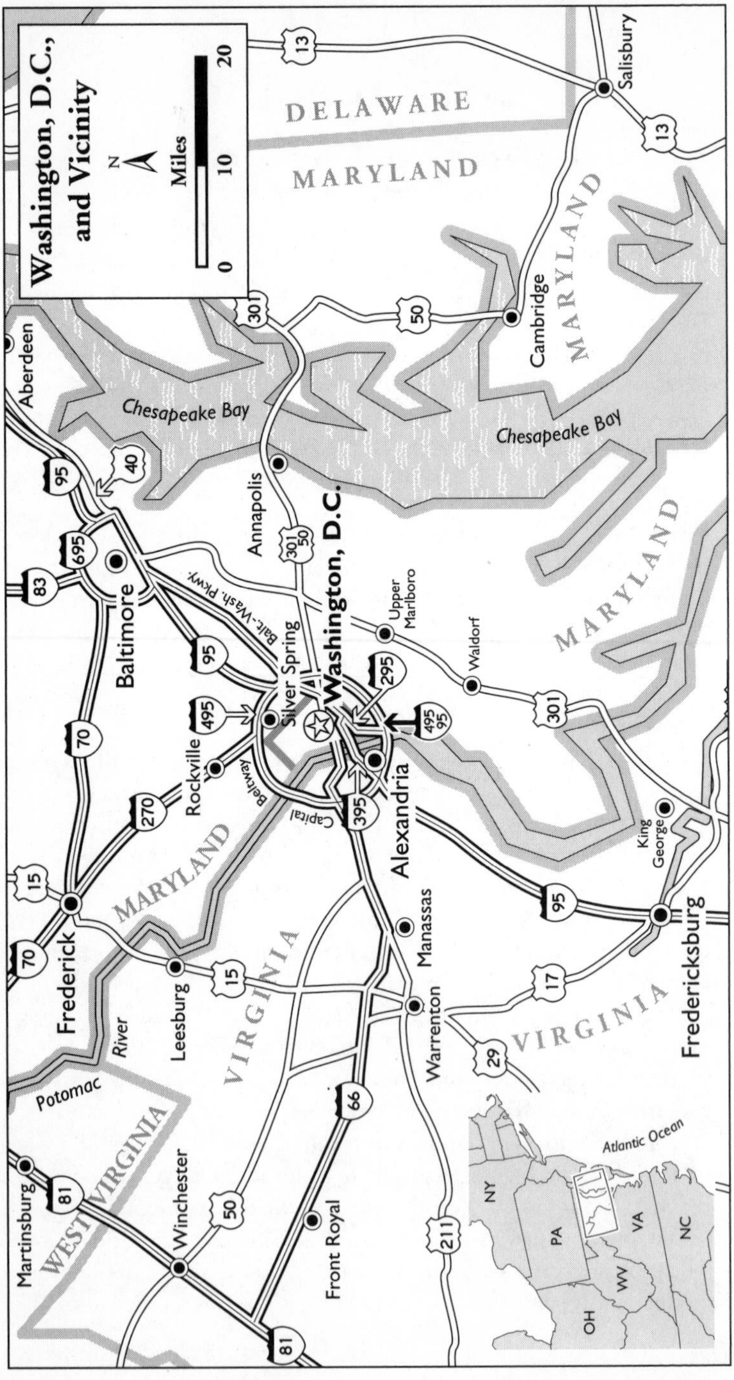
Washington, D.C., and Vicinity
N
Miles
0
10
20
DELAWARE
MARYLAND
VIRGINIA
WEST VIRGINIA
Chesapeake Bay
Potomac River
Aberdeen
Baltimore
Annapolis
Cambridge
Salisbury
Frederick
Rockville
Silver Spring
Washington, D.C.
Upper Marlboro
Waldorf
Alexandria
Capital Beltway
Balt.-Wash. Pkwy.
Manassas
Leesburg
Warrenton
King George
Fredericksburg
Martinsburg
Winchester
Front Royal
95
695
83
70
40
13
50
301
495
295
270
15
395
66
81
211
29
17
Atlantic Ocean
NY
PA
OH
WV
VA
NC

then. And don't try to fight the weekday rush hour traffic (6:30–9:30 a.m. and 3–7 p.m.).

By Plane

Reagan Washington National Airport While Washington officially has three major airports, this is the most convenient by far for domestic flyers, just a few miles south of the city on the Virginia side of the Potomac. Don't ask a friend to pick you up: Parking is terrible at this cramped facility. A courtesy van service can whisk you from the Virginia side of the Potomac.

A new $1 billion, 1-million-square-foot main terminal that opened in the summer of 1997 improved National's notorious reputation as a cramped, hard-to-get-in-and-out-of airport. The new terminal features seamless connection between ground transportation, parking, buses, and D.C.'s subway. (It also boasts a food court, 32 elevators, 26 escalators, 12 baggage carousels, dozens of retail stores, and a great view of the nation's capital across the Potomac River.) Along with 6,500 new parking spaces, new roadways, and expanded curb space and travel lanes (8 lanes for lower-level baggage claims, 5 lanes for upper-level ticket counters), the new facility makes things much easier for travelers.

Nearly 5,000 parking spaces are housed in a new parking garage directly across from the new terminal and are reached via moving sidewalks. Two new Metro mezzanines connect D.C.'s subway system to the terminal via two pedestrian bridges spanning the airport's roads. Two ground transportation centers located on the baggage claim level provide information on Metro, taxi service, SuperShuttle vans, and rental cars.

Cab fares to nearby downtown Washington are reasonable ($12–17). SuperShuttle shared-service vans leave every 15 (or fewer) minutes to any destination in the D.C. area. Fares range from $18–22 to any address in Washington and from $12 to more than $30 in the Virginia and Maryland suburbs. Three SuperShuttle ticket counters are located at National; look for the "Washington Flyer/SuperShuttle" signs posted throughout the airport. For more information, exact fares, and reservations for return pick-up to National, call (800) BLUE VAN (258-3826).

Dulles International Airport Foreign flights arrive at Dulles, although AirTran (formerly ValuJet) and Western Pacific have increased the airport's domestic traffic volume considerably in the last few years. Reflecting that growth is Dulles's recent main terminal expansion, which doubled the size of the building to 1.1 million square feet. Yet Dulles remains the least convenient of the three airports serving Washington. Located in the rolling Virginia countryside beyond the suburbs, Dulles is about a 45-minute drive from downtown—longer during rush hour. Use the Dulles Access Road, which connects with the Capital Beltway and I-66.

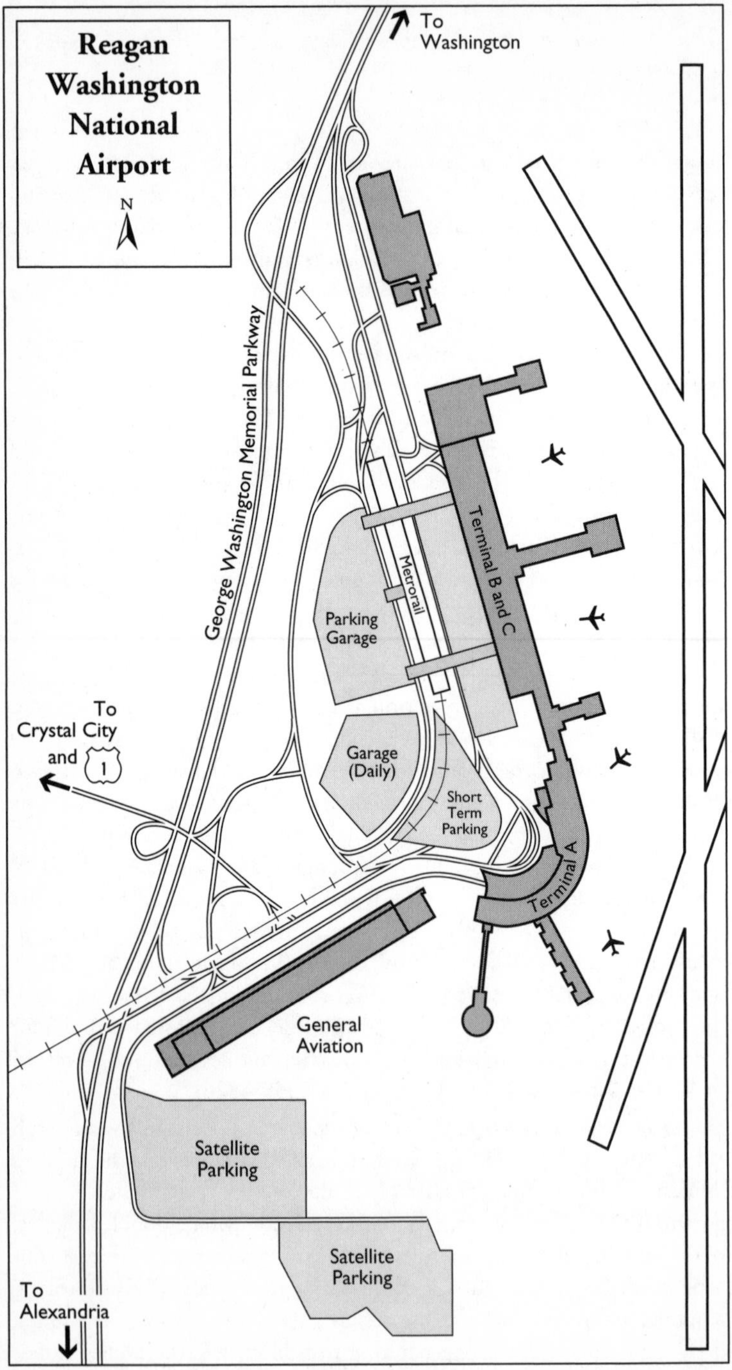
Reagan
Washington
National
Airport
N
To
Washington
George Washington Memorial Parkway
Metrorail
Terminal B and C
Parking
Garage
Garage
(Daily)
Short
Term
Parking
Terminal A
To
Crystal City
and
1
General
Aviation
Satellite
Parking
Satellite
Parking
To
Alexandria

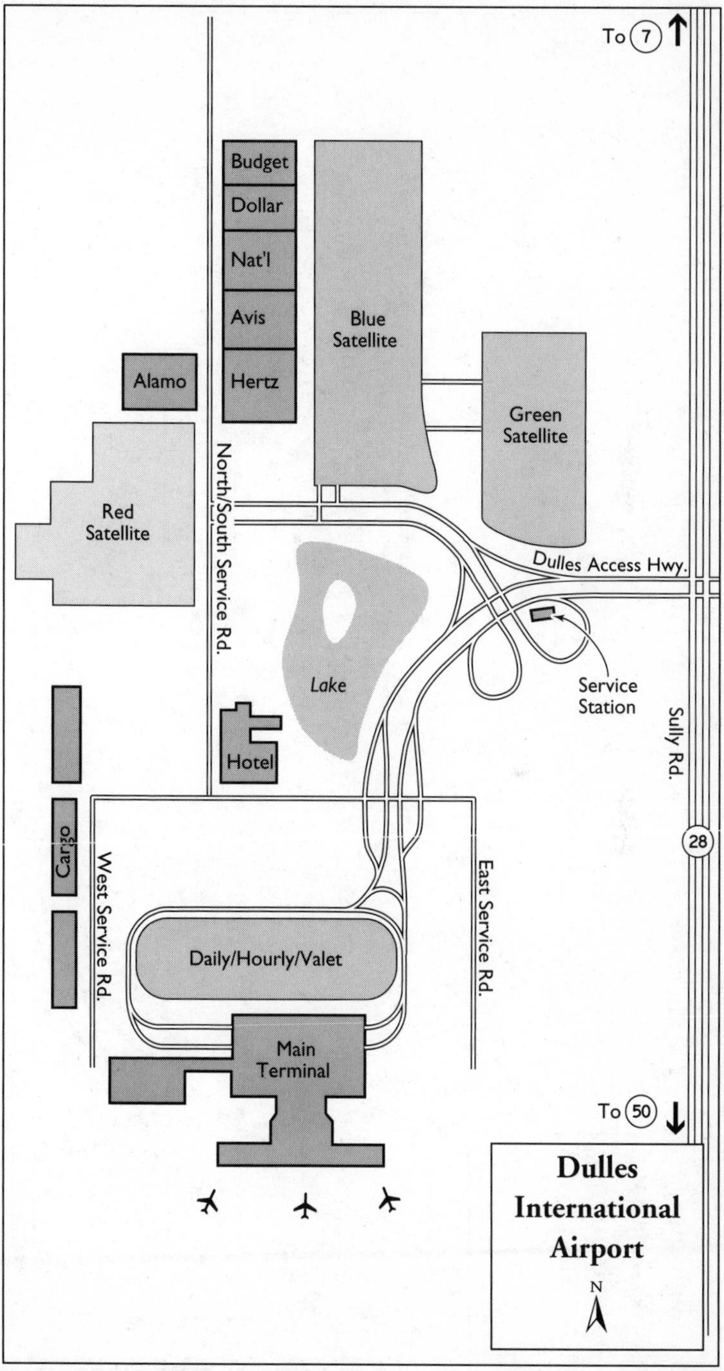
To 7
Budget
Dollar
Nat'l
Avis
Hertz
Alamo
Blue Satellite
Green Satellite
Red Satellite
North/South Service Rd.
Dulles Access Hwy.
Lake
Service Station
Sully Rd.
Hotel
28
Cargo
West Service Rd.
East Service Rd.
Daily/Hourly/Valet
Main Terminal
To 50
Dulles International Airport
N

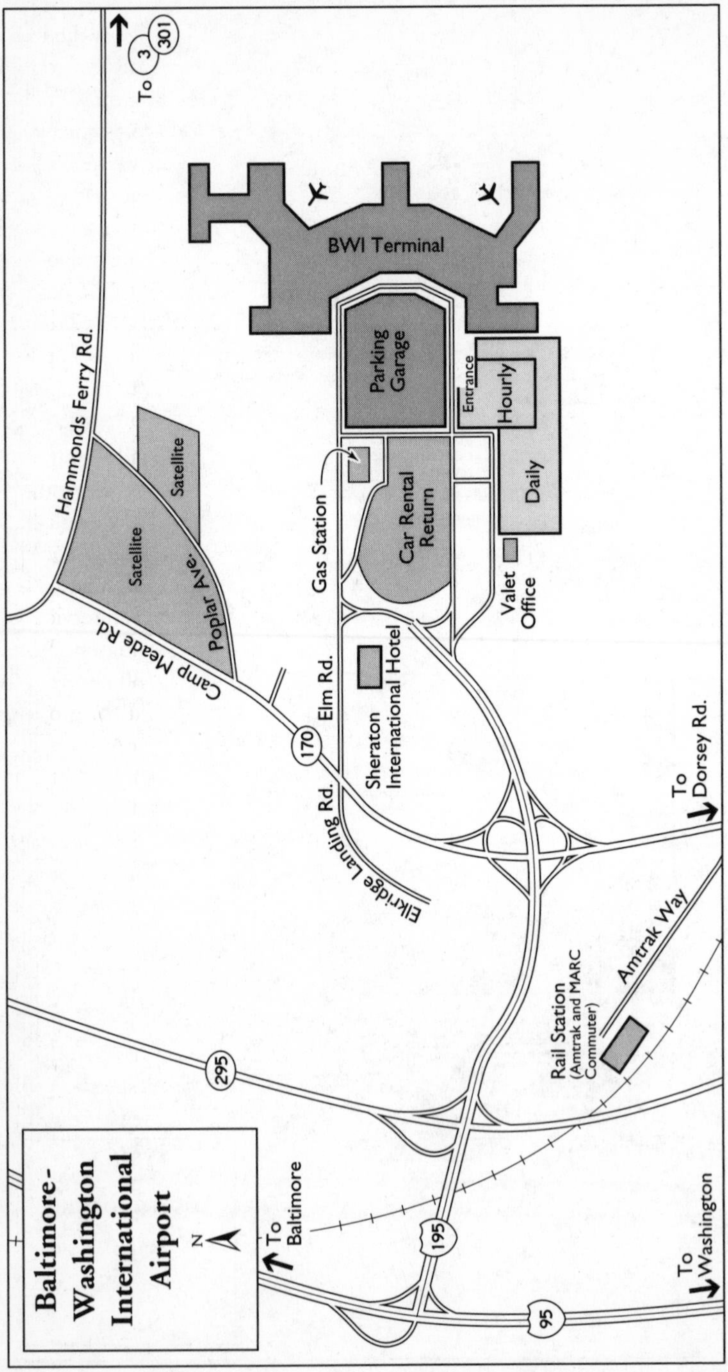
Baltimore-Washington International Airport
N
To Baltimore
To Washington
95
195
295
Rail Station (Amtrak and MARC Commuter)
Amtrak Way
To Dorsey Rd.
Elkridge Landing Rd.
170
Camp Meade Rd.
Elm Rd.
Sheraton International Hotel
Poplar Ave.
Satellite
Satellite
Hammonds Ferry Rd.
Gas Station
Car Rental Return
Valet Office
Daily
Hourly
Entrance
Parking Garage
BWI Terminal
To 3 301

From the gate, go to the lower level and claim your baggage at the baggage carousels. Then proceed out of the terminal on the ground level to the curb, where you can meet someone picking you up or find ground transportation out of the airport. The Washington Flyer shuttle to the West Falls Church Metro station leaves about every 30 minutes weekdays ($8 one-way, $14 round-trip) and every 30 minutes on weekends; it's a 22-minute bus trip to the subway station. SuperShuttle shared-ride vans will take you anywhere in the D.C. metropolitan area; there's usually about a 30-minute wait and fares range from $7 to more than $40 to the downtown area (typically $22 for the first person and $10 for each additional person). For more information, exact fares, and reservations for pickup for your return trip to Dulles, call SuperShuttle at (800) BLUE VAN (258-3826). Cab fare to downtown D.C. can run more than $50 one-way.

Baltimore-Washington International BWI, located 10 miles south of Baltimore's Inner Harbor, is about a 50-minute drive from downtown Washington; allow lots more time during rush hour. From the gate area, descend to the luggage pickup belts, which are located next to the ground-level doors. If someone is picking you up, they can meet you outside the baggage claim area at the curb. SuperShuttle offers van service to the Washington Convention Center in downtown Washington. Vans leave on the hour from 6 a.m. to 7 p.m. daily; the fare is $30 per person one-way (children under age 6 ride free). Tickets are sold at the ground transportation desk on the lower level in Pier C. No reservations are required for service from the airport to downtown D.C.; for reservations for the return trip to BWI or for more information, call (800) BLUE VAN (258-3826). Cab fares to downtown D.C. start at around $55 one-way. In addition, BWI offers train service to Washington's Union Station via MARC commuter trains on weekdays (cheap) and Amtrak on weekends and holidays (expensive).

By Train

Union Station Located near Capitol Hill, Union Station is the central Amtrak connecting point in Washington. From here, trains go out all over the country. For most routes you can choose either a speedy Acela Express, Metroliner or a regular train. Once inside the newly restored train station, you can jump on the Metro, located on the lower level. But not so fast! The station itself is full of delights—small shops, cafes, and even a theater complex. To reach cabs, limousines, buses, and open-air tour trolleys, walk through Union Station's magnificent Main Hall to the main entrance.

A Geographic Overview of Washington

City and Two States

Washington, D.C., is a city of more than 500,000 people located near the southern end of the East Coast megalopolis stretching from Boston to Richmond. George Washington chose the city's site, where the Anacostia River flows into the Potomac, upriver from his Mount Vernon plantation. Maryland and Virginia donated wedges of land from both sides of the Potomac to make the 100-square-mile diamond called the District of Columbia. In 1846, Virginia snatched its lands back; today, the planned city of Washington sits on the former Maryland acreage on the river's east bank.

Washington proper is surrounded by bustling, congested suburbs. Across the Potomac, Arlington County, the town of Alexandria, and Fairfax County crowd D.C. from the south and west, while the Maryland counties of Montgomery and Prince George's surround Washington's northwestern and eastern borders. All the suburbs surrounding D.C. are experiencing exponential growth. Rockville, for example, a few miles north of the D.C. line, has become Maryland's second-largest city, after Baltimore.

Washington's most important geographical feature, the Potomac River, is a natural impediment to both tourists and suburban commuters. The few bridges that cross the river from Virginia to Washington are rush-hour bottlenecks. While driving across the border to the Maryland suburbs is nominally easier, D.C.'s intense traffic and concentration of government and tourist sites near the river make for a long trek into Maryland.

D.C.'s Street Plan

While Washington's reputation as a tough city to get around in is well deserved—at least for first-time visitors—the city's layout is actually fairly logical. Downtown streets are arranged in a grid, with numbered streets running north/south and lettered streets going east/west. The loose cannons in the scheme are streets named after states, which cut across the grid diagonally and meet in traffic circles that are the nemesis of Washington drivers.

Our advice: Ignore the state-named streets on your map and you'll discover the underlying logic of the system. If your destination is, in fact, on a street named after a state, the underlying grid of number- and letter-named streets will get you there and can even help you locate your block. An example: A popular destination for both tourists and power seekers is 1600 Pennsylvania Avenue, NW. Since this well-known street snakes a course from the poor neighborhoods of Southeast Washington through downtown and into Georgetown, pinpointing an exact address is tough. The clue, however, is in the street address: The White House is near the intersection of Pennsylvania Avenue and 16th Street. *Note:* The two blocks of Pennsylvania Avenue immediately in front of the White House are closed to vehicles.

Finding Your Way

Once you get the hang of it, finding your way around Washington is a snap. You'll have a head start if you know the basics of how D.C. is arranged. The roughly diamond-shaped city's four corners point north, south, east, and west. Inside the diamond, Washington is laid out in a rectilinear gridlike plan and divided into four pie-wedge-shaped quadrants: Northwest (NW), Northeast (NE), Southwest (SW), and Southeast (SE); in the center of the pie is the U.S. Capitol building. Separating the quadrants and running in compass directions from the Capitol are North Capitol Street, East Capitol Street, and South Capitol Street. What happened to West Capitol Street? It's the Mall, which runs west from the Capitol to the Potomac River.

Within each quadrant, numbered streets run north-south, and lettered streets run east-west. Addresses on lettered streets give a clue to the numbered cross street at the end of the block. For example, the National Building Museum at 401 F Street, NW, is located on F Street between 4th and 5th Streets, NW.

Surprise: Washington has four 1st Streets, four E Streets, and so on, one for each quadrant. As a result, addresses must bear designations such as NW to prevent utter confusion. The good news for short-term visitors is that they can virtually ignore the quadrants: virtually all tourist sights, hotels, restaurants, and nightlife are in Northwest Washington. Northeast and Southeast Washington, with the exception of the middle-class enclave of Capitol Hill, are predominantly poor and less commercially developed, while tiny Southwest is mostly middle-class.

Avenues are named after states (Connecticut, Massachusetts, Wisconsin, etc.) and cut diagonally across the street grid. Some are major thoroughfares and do a good job of disrupting the traffic pattern. Downtown, the avenues meet at circles and squares, the most noteworthy of which are:

- *Dupont Circle* (Connecticut, Massachusetts, and New Hampshire Avenues)
- *Washington Circle* (New Hampshire and Pennsylvania Avenues)
- *Scott Circle* (Massachusetts and Rhode Island Avenues, and 16th Street)
- *Mount Vernon Square* (Massachusetts and New York Avenues)

Here's a rundown of some major roads that visitors will encounter in the city:

- *Pennsylvania Avenue* runs from Southeast and Capitol Hill through downtown and into Georgetown. The two blocks of Pennsylvania Avenue immediately in front of the White House are closed to vehicles.
- *Wisconsin Avenue* starts in Georgetown and leads north to the Maryland suburbs.
- *Connecticut Avenue* runs from Lafayette Square, in front of the White House, through Dupont Circle, past the National Zoo, and into Chevy Chase, Maryland.
- *16th Street, NW,* heads due north from the White House through Adams-Morgan and merges with Georgia Avenue in the Maryland suburbs.
- *K Street, NW,* is a major east-west downtown business artery.
- *Constitution* and *Independence Avenues* run east-west along the Mall.
- *New York Avenue* is a major artery that runs from the White House to Northeast Washington and turns into US 50 and the Baltimore-Washington Parkway.
- *14th Street, SW,* is a major point of egress to and from the Virginia suburbs.
- *Massachusetts Avenue* runs from Union Station through Dupont Circle, up Embassy Row, and past Washington National Cathedral and American University on its way to Maryland.

Things the Natives Already Know

The Metro: An Introduction

The first section of Washington's clean, modern, safe, and efficient subway system opened in 1976, just in time for the nation's bicentennial celebrations. As the five-line system has expanded over the years, the rave reviews keep coming. All of the stations follow the same brown-and-beige color scheme, with high, curved ceilings made of square concrete panels that fade into the distance. Monotonous, maybe, but the stations are safe and make the lives of visitors infinitely easier.

The trains themselves are clean, quiet, carpeted, virtually crime free, and air-conditioned. They run so often that carrying a schedule isn't really necessary. With two notable exceptions (trendy Georgetown and hip Adams-Morgan), the Metro delivers visitors within a comfortable walking distance of everywhere they might want to go inside the city and into the suburbs.

Even if, like a lot of Americans, you're not comfortable with the idea of relying on public transportation, Washington provides a strong argument for seriously reconsidering your love affair with your car. The Metro system is easy, even fun, to ride. There's really no excuse not to use it. Later, in Part Five, we include a chapter on how.

Taxis

Washington's cab fares are low, but the fare system is weird: Fares are based on zones, not a meter. You can go 2 blocks from one zone to another and be charged more than for a 12-block ride within one zone. It helps to know the zones.

Washington has more cabs per capita than any other American city. But other than for schlepping your luggage to and from National Airport or Union Station, or dining out in subway-free Georgetown and Adams-Morgan, cabs are superfluous, thanks to the Metro. Take the train instead.

In our experience, Washington cabbies are polite and friendly. Yet it's a good idea to ask for a receipt at the beginning of the ride, just to let the driver know that you're not some inexperienced out-of-towner and you won't tolerate being charged for a roundabout route through many zones. Most sight-seeing attractions and hotels are in Zone 1. (The strange hows, whats, and wheres of taxi travel in D.C. are discussed in more detail in Part Five.)

Traffic

If at all possible, avoid driving during your stay in Washington. If you arrive by car, make sure your hotel has parking and is either within walking distance to a Metro station (more on that in Part Five) or offers convenient shuttles to one. Park your car and, with few exceptions, don't plan on moving it until you leave.

Here's why: Driving in Washington is infuriating, and trying to park your car near major tourist sites and government buildings is usually hopeless. The city is a bewildering mix of traffic circles, diagonal boulevards, and one-way streets that change direction depending on the time of day. To make matters worse, some avenues change names for no apparent reason. And the volume of traffic? The *Washington Post* doesn't call its regular traffic column "Dr. Gridlock" for nothing.

One last note: You'll see a lot of cars with cute red, white, and blue license plates imprinted with the word "Diplomatic." The driver of such a car is associated with a foreign embassy and has diplomatic immunity from many local laws—including traffic violations. Give these cars a wide berth. (We cover driving in more detail in Part Five.)

The Neighborhoods

Arguably, Washington is the most important city in the world. When most people think of D.C., they conjure up an image of the Mall, anchored by the U.S. Capitol at the east end and the Lincoln Memorial on the other. On its east end alone, the Mall features at least 11 major museums and attractions. In the center is the Washington Monument, with the White House just to the north.

While there's much to see and do on the Mall, visitors who don't get beyond the two-mile strip of green are missing a lot of what this vibrant, international city has to offer: brick sidewalks in front of charming colonial-era row houses in Georgetown, the bohemian cafes of Adams-Morgan, stately townhouses and mansions near Dupont Circle, the glitter and overflowing street life in the "new downtown" along K Street, NW. At the very least, a foray off the Mall can elevate your trip beyond the level of an educational grade-school field trip and give you a taste of the lively city itself. All the neighborhoods that follow are safe for visitors to explore on foot, except where noted. For more details on zones, see page 7, "Geographic Zones."

Adams-Morgan (in Zone 6)

An ethnic neighborhood with a heavy emphasis on the Hispanic and African, Adams-Morgan is where young and cool bohemians migrated after the price of real estate zoomed around Dupont Circle in the 1970s and 1980s. While it doesn't offer much in the way of large museums or monuments, the neighborhood is full of ethnic restaurants, eclectic shops, and nightclubs. Parking, alas, is a severe problem: Adams-Morgan isn't served by the Metro. Don't let that stop you; take a cab.

Dupont Circle (in Zone 6)

Dupont Circle is the center of one of the city's most fashionable neighborhoods, where you'll find elegantly restored townhouses, boutiques, restaurants, cafes, bookstores, and art galleries. A stroll down Embassy Row (along Massachusetts Avenue) leads past sumptuous embassies and chancellories, as well as some of Washington's best visitor attractions: Anderson House, the Phillips Collection, Woodrow Wilson House, and the Islamic Center. You can recognize an embassy by the national coat-of-arms or flag; a pack of reporters and TV cameras may indicate that international unrest has erupted somewhere in the world.

Capitol Hill (in Zone 2)

The neighborhood surrounding the Capitol is a mix of residential and commercial, with plenty of restored townhouses and trendy bars. Called "The Hill" by natives, here congressional staffers, urban homesteaders, and poor people commingle—sometimes not so successfully: Street crime can be a problem. Blocks can change character abruptly from one end to the other, but if you don't wander far from the Capitol itself you'll be okay.

Downtown (in Zone 3)

Directly north of the Mall is "old downtown," full of department stores, government office buildings (including the FBI), shops, street vendors, hotels, restaurants, two Smithsonian museums, Ford's Theatre, a tiny Chinatown, and the Washington Convention Center. To the west is "new downtown," the glittery glass and steel office buildings where D.C.'s legions of lobbyists and lawyers do their thing. Both areas offer visitors plenty of choices for shopping, dining, and sight-seeing.

Foggy Bottom (in Zone 4)

Located west of the White House, Foggy Bottom got its name from the swampy land on which it was built. Today, it's home to George Washington University, the U.S. Department of State ("Foggy Bottom" is journalese for "State"), the Kennedy Center, and the Watergate. Closer to the Mall, massive government office complexes such as the Department of the Interior and the Federal Reserve crowd the White House.

Georgetown (in Zone 5)

A river port long before Washington was built, Georgetown is now the epitome of swank. From a distance, Georgetown is immediately identifiable by its skyline of spires. The neighborhood of restored townhouses is filled with crowded bars and shops, and the streets pulse with crowds late into the night. An overflow of suburban teens on weekends makes for traffic congestion that's intense, even by Washington standards; lack of a Metro station only makes it worse. Georgetown University marks the neighborhood's western edge. The Chesapeake and Ohio Canal and its famous towpath begin in Georgetown and follow the Potomac River upstream for 184 miles to Cumberland, Maryland. When you've had enough of the city, rent a bike and see how far you can get.

Upper Northwest (in Zone 7)

Here's where the Washington National Cathedral, the National Zoo, the Hillwood Museum, the city's best private schools, and its wealthiest citizens are found. Without clear boundaries to separate them, Tenleytown, Glover Park, Woodley Park, and Cleveland Park are full of Victorian houses that are homes to members of Congress, rich lobbyists, and attorneys. Attention, joggers: This is where you go for a nighttime run.

Rock Creek Park (in Zone 7)

It's not a neighborhood but a managed forest in the heart of Washington well worth knowing about. Hikers, joggers, in-line skaters, equestrians, mountain bikers, and anyone wishing an escape from the city can get away here. In the summer, it's ten degrees cooler than the rest of the city.

The Southwest Waterfront (in Zone 1)

A fascinating array of private yachts is on view in Washington's waterfront area, a stretch along Maine Avenue that features marinas, seafood restaurants, and the Wharf Seafood Market, where visitors can sample fresh fish and Chesapeake Bay delicacies such as oysters on the half shell.

Here's where you can take a scenic river cruise to Mount Vernon on the *Potomac Spirit.* It's easy to get to the waterfront: Take the subway to the Waterfront Metro station.

Anacostia (in Zone 9)

The city's first suburb today sits in the midst of a war zone of drive-by shootings, drug dealing, and random violence. When Washington is called "Murder Capital of the U.S.," the reference is usually to a large swath of Northeast and Southeast Washington across the Anacostia River from downtown. While Anacostia is well off the beaten tourist path, there are two attractions visitors should take the time to explore: Cedar Hill, the home of nineteenth-century abolitionist Frederick Douglass, and the Smithsonian's Anacostia Museum. Either drive or ride special tourist buses (not public transportation) to visit these attractions.

Customs and Protocol

Dress In spite of its status as a world capital, Washington is a fairly relaxed town under the surface. The city's laid-back Southern heritage and the vestiges of an inferiority complex relative to older East Coast cities mean that Washingtonians, by the way they dress and socialize, aren't an ostentatious crowd. For men, suits and ties remain the uniform of work, while most women stick to power suits with padded shoulders in neutral colors for office wear.

Tourists have diplomatic immunity from this dreary dress code, however. In daytime and around the major tourist areas, it's perfectly okay to look the part: If it's hot, wear a T-shirt and bermudas as you stroll the Mall with three cameras around your neck. You won't be alone.

For forays up Connecticut Avenue and into Georgetown, though, leave the cameras and loud Hawaiian print shirts in your hotel room. The crowds are better dressed and hipper, and if you don't follow suit, you'll really stand out in the crowd.

Washington, we're glad to report, is quite informal after 5 p.m.—which makes it easy on visitors. With few exceptions, men needn't worry about going out to a restaurant without a tie, and women can feel comfortable wearing slacks. If there's a casual, after-work uniform in this city, it's probably the preppie look: chinos, Docksiders, and an Izod shirt for men and similar attire for women.

Eating in Restaurants Washington, as an international city, is full of inexpensive ethnic restaurants—Ethiopian, Thai, Vietnamese, Lebanese, Greek, Afghani . . . the list goes on. Most are casual and you needn't feel intimidated about unfamiliar menus—just ask the waiter or waitress for a recommendation. Since Washington doesn't take itself as seriously as, say, New York, you won't be made to feel uncomfortable in a Japanese restaurant if you request a spoon for your miso soup. Expect to be elbow to elbow with other diners in the crowded eateries, since dining out seems to be a full-time activity for a lot of Washingtonians.

Tipping Is the tip you normally leave at home appropriate in Washington? The answer is yes. Just bear in mind that a tip is a reward for good service. Here are some guidelines:

Porters, Redcaps, and Bellmen	At least 50 cents per bag and $2–3 for a lot of baggage.
Cab Drivers	15% of the fare. Add an extra dollar if the cabby does a lot of luggage handling.
Valet Parking	A dollar.
Waiters	15–20% of the pretax bill.
Bartenders	10–15% of the pretax bill.
Chambermaids	A dollar a day.
Checkroom Attendants in Restaurants or Theaters	A dollar per garment.

Going Where the Locals Go During the week, you'll have to get away from the Mall or the Washington Convention Center if you want to rub shoulders with native Washingtonians. But not too far—Capitol Hill bars and restaurants are crowded with congressional aides, lobbyists, secretarial staff, and even the odd congressperson or two. During the lunch hour on weekdays (but not weekends and holidays), L'Enfant Plaza is jammed with bureaucrats from the myriad concrete-enclosed agencies located south of Independence Avenue.

North of the White House, the "new downtown" (roughly from 15th Street, NW, west to Rock Creek Park) is an area of glass-enclosed office buildings where lawyers, lobbyists, and other professionals ply their trades—and take their clients to lunch. Dupont Circle, formerly Washington's bohemian quarter, remains headquarters to Washington's artist, international, and gay communities.

How Not to Look Like a Tourist If it's important to you not to look like A Visitor on Holiday in Our Nation's Capital, we offer the following advice:

1. Never say "Washington"—it's "D.C." to the natives. If you must say the full name of the city, pronounce it "Worshington."
2. Be obsessive, if not maniacal, about the Redskins.
3. For men, wear a coat and tie, and carry a briefcase at all times. For women, wear power suits with padded shoulders.
4. Tuck a *Washington Post* under your arm and march up Connecticut Avenue with a determined stride.
5. Be blasé about Washington's tourist attractions: Deny ever going to the Mall except in the company of small children.

6. Clutch an espresso, latte, or cappuccino in one hand and a just-baked, multigrain olive loaf in the other: The natives are wild about fresh bread and coffee bars.

Tips for the Disabled

Washington is one of the most accessible cities in the world for the disabled. The White House, for example, has a special entrance on Pennsylvania Avenue for visitors arriving in wheelchairs, and White House guides usually allow visually handicapped visitors to touch some of the items described on tours. Each Metro station is equipped with an elevator, complete with Braille number plates.

All Smithsonian museum buildings are accessible to wheelchair visitors, as are all museum floors. For a copy of "Smithsonian Access" call (202) 357-2700 or (202) 357-1729 (TTY). Folks headed to the National Zoo can get a copy of the Zoo Guide for Disabled Visitors by calling (202) 673-4717 or (202) 673-4823 (TTY). The Lincoln and Jefferson Memorials and the Washington Monument are equipped to accommodate disabled visitors. Most sight-seeing attractions have elevators for others who want to avoid a lot of stair climbing. See our section "People with Special Needs" on page 134 in Part Five for more information.

The Local Press

Washington is a city of news junkies, and the *Washington Post* is the opiate of choice. Visitors should make a point of picking up Friday's edition, which includes the paper's "Weekend" section. It's loaded with information on things to do in and around Washington; if you can, grab a copy of a Friday *Post* on your way into town for the weekend.

The *Washington Times,* D.C.'s other daily newspaper, offers a more conservative slant on national and world events.

City Paper, a free weekly "alternative" newspaper, is another good source of information on arts, theater, clubs, popular music, and movie reviews. It's available from street-corner vending machines and stores all over town.

The *Washingtonian,* a monthly magazine, is strong on lists (top 10 restaurants, etc.) and provides a calendar of events, dining information, and feature articles.

Where/Washington is one of several free publications that list popular things to do around town.

Visitors looking for the latest information on Washington theater, nightlife, restaurants, special exhibitions, and gallery shows in advance of their trip should call or write:

Where/Washington Magazine, 1225 19th Street, NW, Suite 510, Washington, D.C. 20036-2411. Phone (202) 463-4550.

The *Washingtonian,* 1828 L Street, NW, Suite 200, Washington, D.C. 20036. Phone (202) 331-0715.

Telephones

The Washington area is served by three area codes: (202) inside the District, (703) in the Northern Virginia suburbs across the Potomac River, and (301), which connects you with the Maryland suburbs. To dial out of D.C. to suburbs beyond the city's limits, it's necessary to dial the right area code. While calls to Arlington, Alexandria, and most of Fairfax County in Virginia and to Montgomery and Prince George's Counties in Maryland are dialed as if they're long distance, they are charged as local calls (50 cents from most pay phones).

Rest Rooms

Field researchers for the *Unofficial Guide* are selected for their reporting skills, writing ability . . . and small bladders. When we enter a marble edifice, you can be sure we're not just scrutinizing the layout, the flow of the crowd, and the aesthetics: We're also nervously eyeing the real estate for the nearest public facility where we can unload that second cup of coffee.

So how does Washington rate in the rest room department? Actually, pretty well. That's because of the huge number of museums, monuments, federal office buildings, restaurants, bars, department stores, and hotels that cover the city. Most rest rooms are clean and conveniently located.

Leading any list of great rest room locations should be the National Air and Space Museum on the Mall. For women who claim there's no justice in the world when it comes to toilet parity, consider this: There are three times as many women's rest rooms as there are men's rest rooms. "And the men don't seem to notice," says a female Smithsonian employee who works at the information desk.

Other facilities of note on the Mall include those at the National Gallery of Art, the Arthur M. Sackler Gallery, the Hirshhorn Museum and Sculpture Garden, and the National Museum of African Art. The rest rooms in the National Museum of Natural History are inconveniently located on a lower level. At the Arts and Industries Building, facilities are located far away from the front entrance. On the other hand, the rest rooms in The Castle, the Smithsonian's visitor center, are easy to find and usually not very crowded.

Virtually all the monuments are rest room–equipped, including the Lincoln and Jefferson Memorials and the Washington Monument. One notable exception is the White House, a place infamous for long lines. Downtown, hotels, restaurants, and bars are good bets. (The rest rooms off the huge lobby of the Stouffer Mayflower Hotel on Connecticut Avenue are both convenient and elegant.) Avoid the few public rest rooms located in parks, such as the ones on the grounds of the Washington Monument and at Dupont Circle; they're usually dirty. You won't find rest rooms in Metro stations, although a few stations are located in complexes that do provide rest rooms, including Union Station, Metro Center, Farragut North, and L'Enfant Plaza.

How to Avoid Crime and Keep Safe in Public Places

Crime in Washington

The combination of a widespread crack epidemic and the availability of high-powered weaponry put Washington on the map for a dubious distinction: "Murder Capital of the United States." Anyone who watches the evening news or reads a newspaper knows about Washington's grim murder rate. So the question arises, as you contemplate a trip to D.C.: Just how safe is Washington anyway? Am I going to end up just another statistic?

"It's very safe," says Officer Rod Ryan of D.C.'s Metropolitan Police Department, as long as you stay in proscribed areas. Ryan, a three-year veteran of the force who has worked special anticrime details around the Mall and popular tourist sites, explains, "Washington patrols its main visitor areas very strongly, because tourism is all the city has for income."

To get an idea of how much protection the average tourist or business visitor gets, consider this fact: It's not just Officer Ryan and the rest of D.C.'s finest patrolling the city. Contributing to the task are a number of other law enforcement agencies whose jobs include protecting visitors: The U.S. Park Police patrols the monuments, the U.S. Capitol Police protects the Capitol and the 20-square-block area around it, and the Secret Service patrols the area around the White House. Plus, the Metro has its own police force for protecting people riding public transportation. That's not all: Post-Sept. 11, a new network of security cameras has been added on the Mall by the Park Police and the Metropolitan Police has installed a network of security cameras in high-traffic areas such as Georgetown, Union Station and around the White House.

"Police are patrolling on bicycles, on horseback, on small motorcycles, on foot, and in unmarked cars," explains Officer Ryan. "And the Smithsonian has its own police force—highly trained federal officers—who patrol inside the buildings and around the grounds. Anyone who knows what he's looking for can spot five police patrols from anywhere on the Mall."

Statistics support his claim: D.C.'s overall crime rate has been declining steadily for the last decade, according to the Metropolitan Police. From a high of 454 homicides in 1994, the rate dropped to 242 in 2000. Halfway through 2002, the number of murders is up 25 percent compared to the previous year, but is on track to come in under 220 for the year. The overall crime rate is doing even better, down a half-percent over 2001—part of a steady, decade-long decline.

So, who's on the receiving end of all that automatic weapons fire? Most of the victims are either young drug dealers in shootouts with competitors or people involved in violent domestic disputes. Random murders are rare events in D.C., despite its reputation, and police say the odds here are about the same as anywhere else. Furthermore, the mayhem usually occurs in sections of the city visitors do not normally frequent: low-income, residential areas that are removed from the city center and business/tourist districts. The worst areas are in Northeast and Southeast Washington across the Anacostia River from downtown and the major visitor areas. You'd have to go to quite an effort to get there, even by mistake.

"Tourists should never wander across the bridge over the Anacostia River," says Officer Ryan, who should know: He leads a newly formed mountain bike patrol that has helped reduce street crime by 75% in one of the worst sections of Southeast Washington. "Visitors should stay within the boundaries of the Mall, Georgetown, upper Northwest, Dupont Circle, Adams-Morgan, and downtown."

Even Capitol Hill, which gained notoriety when a legislative aide was murdered on the street a few years ago, is as safe for visitors as any other area that out-of-towners frequent. Ryan explains, "Too many powerful congressmen live in Capitol Hill for it not to be well patrolled."

Starting in November 1997, visitors began seeing a new force making Washington safer and cleaner: Downtown SAM (Safety and Maintenance) Teams, easily recognized by their bright red attire. By cleaning streets and sidewalks, removing graffiti, and assisting visitors, SAM Teams are creating a safer environment downtown. According to the D.C. Metropolitan Police, in April 1998 downtown Washington saw a 54% drop in crime compared to April 1997, while more than 10,000 bags of garbage were collected and more than 25,000 workers and visitors were aided. Visitors are encouraged to stop a SAM Team member and ask for directions, get a restaurant recommendation, or get directions for finding a landmark.

Having a Plan

Random violence and street crime are facts of life in any large city. You've got to be cautious and alert and plan ahead. When you are out and about, you must work under the assumption that you must use caution because you are on your own; if you run into trouble, it's unlikely that police or anyone else will be able to come to your rescue. You must give some advance thought to the ugly scenarios that might occur, and consider both preventive measures that will keep you out of harm's way and an escape plan just in case. Not being a victim of street crime is sort of a survival-of-the-fittest thing. Just as a lion stalks the weakest member of the antelope herd, muggers and thieves target the easiest victim. Simply put, no matter where you are or what you are doing, you want potential felons to think of you as a bad risk.

On the Street For starters, you always present less of an appealing target if you are with other people. Second, if you must be out alone, act alert, be alert, and always have at least one of your arms and hands free. Felons gravitate toward preoccupied folks, the kind found plodding along staring at the sidewalk, with both arms encumbered by briefcases or packages. Visible jewelry (on either men or women) attracts the wrong kind of attention. Men, keep your billfolds in your front trouser or coat pocket or in a fanny pack. Women, keep your purses tucked tightly under your arm; if you're wearing a coat, put it on over your shoulder bag strap.

Here's another tip: Men can carry two wallets, including one inexpensive one, carried in your hip pocket, containing about $20 in cash and some expired credit cards. This is the one you hand over if you're accosted. Your real credit cards and the bulk of whatever cash you have should be in either a money clip or a second wallet hidden elsewhere on your person. Women can carry a fake wallet in their purse and keep the real one in a pocket or money belt.

If You're Approached Police will tell you that a felon has the least amount of control over his intended victim during the few moments of his initial approach. A good strategy, therefore, is to short-circuit the crime scenario as quickly as possible. If a felon starts by demanding your money, for instance, quickly take out your billfold (preferably your fake one) and hurl it in one direction while you run shouting for help in the opposite direction. The odds are greatly in your favor that the felon will prefer to collect your silent billfold rather than pursue you. If you hand over your wallet and just stand there, the felon will likely ask for your watch and jewelry next. If you're a woman, the longer you hang around, the greater your vulnerability to personal injury or rape.

Secondary Crime Scenes Under no circumstance, police warn, should you ever allow yourself to be taken to another location—a "secondary crime scene" in police jargon. This move, they explain, provides the felon more privacy and consequently more control. A felon can rob you on the street very quickly and efficiently. If he tries to remove you to another location, whether by car or on foot, it is a certain indication that he has more in mind than robbery. Even if the felon has a gun or knife, your chances are infinitely better running away. If the felon grabs your purse, let him have it. If he grabs your coat, come out of the coat. Hanging onto your money or coat is not worth getting mugged, raped, or murdered.

Another maxim: Never believe anything a felon tells you, even if he's telling you something you desperately want to believe, for example, "I won't hurt you if you come with me." No matter how logical or benign he sounds, assume the worst. Always, always, break off contact as quickly as possible, even if that means running.

In Public Transport When riding a bus, always take a seat as close to the driver as you can; never ride in the back. Likewise, on the subway, sit near the driver's or attendant's compartment. These people have a phone and can summon help in the event of trouble.

In Cabs While it is possible to hail a cab on the street in Washington, you are somewhat vulnerable in the process. Particularly after dusk, call a reliable cab company and stay inside while they dispatch a cab to your door. When your cab arrives, check the driver's certificate, which must, by law, be posted on the dashboard. Address the cabbie by his last name (Mr. Jones or whatever) or mention the number of his cab. This alerts the driv-er to the fact that you are going to remember him and/or his cab. Not only will this contribute to your safety, it will also keep your cabbie from trying to run up the fare.

If you are comfortable reading maps, familiarize yourself with the most direct route to your destination ahead of time. If you can say, "Georgetown via Wisconsin Avenue, please," the driver is less likely to run up your fare by taking a circuitous route so he can charge you for three zones instead of two.

If you need to catch a cab at the train station or at one of the airports, always use the taxi queue. Taxis in the official queue are properly licensed and regulated. Never accept an offer for a cab or limo made by a stranger in the terminal or baggage claim. At best, you will be significantly overcharged for the ride. At worst, you may be abducted.

Personal Attitude

While some areas of every city are more dangerous than others, never assume that any area is completely safe. Never let down your guard. You can be the victim of a crime, and it can happen to you anywhere. If you go to a restaurant or nightspot, use valet parking or park in a well-lighted lot. Women leaving a restaurant or club alone should never be reluctant to ask to be escorted to their car.

Never let your pride or sense of righteousness and indignation imperil your survival. This is especially difficult for many men, particularly for men in the presence of women. It makes no difference whether you are approached by an aggressive drunk, an unbalanced street person, or an actual felon, the rule is the same: Forget your pride and break off contact as quickly as possible. Who cares whether the drunk insulted you, if everyone ends up back at the hotel safe and sound? When you wake up in the hospital with a concussion and your jaw sewn shut, it's too late to decide that the drunk's filthy remark wasn't really all that important.

Felons, druggies, some street people, and even some drunks play for keeps. They can attack with a bloodthirsty hostility and hellish abandon that is beyond the imagination of most people. Believe us, you are not in their league (nor do you want to be).

Self-Defense

In a situation where it is impossible to run, you'll need to be prepared to defend yourself. Most policemen insist that a gun or knife is not much use to the average person. More often than not, they say, the weapon will be turned against the victim. Additionally, concealed firearms and knives are illegal in most jurisdictions. The best self-defense device for the average person is Mace. Not only is it legal in most states, it is nonlethal and easy to use.

When you shop for Mace, look for two things: It should be able to fire about eight feet, and it should have a protector cap so it won't go off by mistake in your purse or pocket. Carefully read the directions that come with your device, paying particular attention to how it should be carried and stored, and how long the active ingredients will remain potent. Wearing a rubber glove, test-fire your Mace, making sure that you fire downwind.

When you are out about town, make sure your Mace is someplace easily accessible, say, attached to your keychain. If you are a woman and you keep your Mace on a keychain, avoid the habit of dropping your keys (and the Mace) into the bowels of your purse when you leave your hotel room or your car. The Mace will not do you any good if you have to dig around in your purse for it. Keep your keys and your Mace in your hand until you have safely reached your destination.

Carjackings

With the recent surge in carjackings, drivers also need to take special precautions. "Keep alert when you're driving in D.C. traffic," Officer Ryan warns. "Keep your doors locked, with the windows rolled up and the air conditioning or heat on. In traffic, leave enough space in front of you so that you're not blocked in and can make a U-turn. That way, if someone approaches your car and starts beating on your windshield, you can drive off." Store your purse or briefcase under your knees when you are driving, rather than on the seat beside you.

Ripoffs and Scams

First-time visitors to the Mall stepping off the escalator at the Smithsonian Metro are often confronted by fast-talking men who try to sell them museum brochures. Don't fall for it; the brochures are free in Smithsonian museums—and the fast-talkers are trying to rip you off.

Another scam that visitors need to watch out for is the well-dressed couple who claim their car broke down and they need $5 for train fare. Refer them to a cop for help and move on.

More Things to Avoid

When you do go out, walk with a minimum of two people whenever possible. If you have to walk alone, stay in well-lit areas that have plenty of people around. And don't walk down alleys. It also helps not to look like a tourist when venturing away from the Mall. Don't wear a camera around your neck, and don't gawk at buildings and unfold maps on the sidewalk. Be careful about whom you ask for directions. (When in doubt, shopkeepers are a good bet.) Don't count your money in public, and carry as little cash as possible. At public phones, if you must say your calling card number to make a long-distance call, don't say it loud enough for strangers around you to hear. And, with the exception of the Mall, avoid public parks after dark. In particular, don't go to Rock Creek Park at night.

Help May Be Closer Than You Think

While walking in Washington, try to be aware of public and federal facilities. If, despite your precautions, you are attacked, head for any federal office building for help. The entrances are all patrolled by armed guards who can offer assistance.

While this litany of warnings and precautions may sound grim, it's really commonsense advice that applies to visitors in any large American city. Keep in mind that Washington's reputation for crime is enhanced by the worldwide media attention the city gets: Local news in Washington is really national news. Finally, remember that 21 million visitors a year still flock to the nation's capital, making it one of the most visited destinations in the United States. The overwhelming majority encounter no problems with crime during their Washington visit.

The Homeless

If you're not from a big city or haven't visited one in a while, you're in for a shock when you come to Washington. It seems that every block in the city is filled with shabbily dressed people asking for money. Furthermore, along the Mall, near the national monuments, on downtown sidewalks, and in parks and gardens, you will see people sleeping in blankets and sleeping bags, their possessions piled up next to them. On crowded Georgetown streets filled with opulent shops, homeless women with small children beg for money. Drivers in cars are approached at stoplights by men carrying Magic-Marker-on-cardboard signs reading "Homeless—Will Work for Food." Virtually every Metro exit is choked with clusters of people begging for money.

Who Are These People? "Most are lifelong D.C. residents who are poor," according to Joan Alker, assistant director of the National Coalition for the Homeless, an advocacy group headquartered in Washington. "The people you see on the streets are primarily single men and women. A disproportionate number of them are minorities and people with disabilities—they're either mentally ill, or substance abusers, or have physical disabilities."

Are They a Threat to Visitors? "No," Ms. Alker says. "Studies done in Washington show that homeless men have lower rates of conviction for violent crimes than the population at large. We know that murders aren't being committed by the homeless. I can't make a blanket statement, but most homeless people you see are no more likely to commit a violent crime than other people."

Should You Give the Homeless Money? "That's a personal decision," Ms. Alker says. "But if you can't, at least try to acknowledge their existence by looking them in the eye and saying, 'No, I can't.'" While there's no way to tell if the guy with the Styrofoam cup asking for a handout is really destitute or just a con artist, no one can dispute that most of these people are what they claim to be: homeless.

Ways to Help It's really a matter for your own conscience. We confess to being both moved and annoyed by these unfortunate people: moved by their need and annoyed that we cannot enjoy the nation's capital without running a gauntlet of begging men and women. In the final analysis, we found that it is easier on the conscience and spirit to get a couple of rolls of quarters at the bank and carry an overcoat or jacket pocket full of change at all times. The cost of giving those homeless who approach you a quarter really does not add up to all that much, and it is much better for the psyche to respond to their plight than to deny or ignore their presence.

There is a notion, perhaps valid in some instances, that money given to a homeless person generally goes toward the purchase of alcohol or drugs. If this bothers you excessively, carry granola bars for distribution or buy some inexpensive gift coupons that can be redeemed at a McDonald's or other fast-food restaurant for coffee or a sandwich.

We have found that a little kindness regarding the homeless goes a long way, and that a few kind words delivered along with your quarter or granola bar brighten the day for both you and your friend in need. We are not suggesting a lengthy conversation or prolonged involvement, just something simple like, "Sure, I can help a little bit. Take care."

Those moved to get more involved in the nationwide problem of homelessness can send inquiries—or a check—to the National Coalition for the Homeless, 1012 14th Street, NW, Suite 600, Washington, D.C. 20005-3471; (202) 737-6444; www.nationalhomeless.org.

Keep It Brief Finally, don't play psychologist. All the people you encounter on the street are strangers. They may be harmless, or they may be dangerous. Either way, maintain distance and keep any contact or encounter brief. Be prepared to handle street people in accordance with your principles, but mostly, just be prepared. If you have a druggie in your face wanting a handout, the last thing you want to do is pull out your wallet and thumb through the twenties looking for a one-dollar bill. As the sergeant on *Hill Street Blues* used to say, be careful out there.

Part Five

Getting around Washington

Driving Your Car: A Really Bad Idea

Traffic Hot Spots

Here's some bad news for anyone considering driving to our nation's capital: Washington is legendary for its traffic congestion. Let's start with the Capital Beltway (I-495 and I-95), which encircles the city through the Virginia and Maryland suburbs: It's guaranteed to be logjammed on weekdays from 7 a.m. to 9:30 a.m. and again from 3 p.m. to 7 p.m. Unremitting suburban growth and geography confound the best efforts of traffic engineers to alleviate the congestion.

Inside the Beltway, the situation only gets worse. The few bridges that connect Washington and Virginia across the Potomac River are rush-hour bottlenecks. Interstates 66 and 395 in Virginia have restricted car-pool lanes inbound in the morning and outbound in the evening. Inside the District, Rock Creek Parkway becomes one-way during rush hour, and major thoroughfares such as Connecticut Avenue switch the direction of center lanes to match the predominant flow of traffic at different times of day. Downtown, the city's traffic circles can trap unwary motorists and reduce drivers to tears or profanity. Pierre L'Enfant's eighteenth-century grand plan of streets and avenues that intersect in traffic circles is a nightmare for twentieth-century motorists.

First-time drivers to Washington should map out their routes in advance, avoid arriving and departing during rush hour, and then leave the car parked throughout their stay. Lunch-hour traffic can be equally ferocious, and don't think that weekends are immune from traffic snarls: Washington's popularity as a tourist mecca slows Beltway traffic to a crawl on Saturdays and Sundays in warm weather. If there's any good news about driving in Washington, it's this: After evening rush hour subsides, getting around town by car is pretty easy.

Parking

If you ignore our advice about driving in Washington (we repeat: don't) and battle your way downtown by car, you'll find yourself stuck in one of those good news/bad news scenarios. The good news: There are plenty of places to park. The bad news: Virtually all the spaces are in parking garages that charge an arm and a leg. Figure on $12 a day or $5 an hour, minimum.

Think you can beat the system by finding street parking? Go ahead and try, but bring a lot of quarters—and plenty of patience. Most metered parking is restricted to two hours—not a long time if you're intent on exploring a museum or attending a business meeting. And D.C. cops are quick to issue tickets for expired meters. Also, a lot of legal spaces turn il-legal during afternoon rush hour.

In popular residential neighborhoods such as Georgetown and Adams-Morgan, parking gets even worse at night. Unless you've got a residential parking permit—not likely if you're from out of town—street parking is limited to from two to three hours, depending on the neighborhood. The parking permits are prominently displayed in the cars of area residents.

If you're tempted to park illegally, be warned: D.C. police are grimly efficient at whisking away cars parked in rush-hour zones, and the fines are hefty. (If your car is towed, call the D.C. Department of Public Works at (202) 727-1010; if you're not sure if it was towed, call (202) 727-5000.) Incredibly, there's free parking along the Mall beginning at 10 a.m. weekdays; the limit is three hours. Needless to say, competition for the spaces is fierce.

Riding the Metro: A Really Good Idea

A Clean, Safe Alternative

It should be clear by now that visitors who would prefer to spend their time doing something productive rather than sit in traffic jams shouldn't drive in or around Washington. Thanks to the Metro, visitors can park their cars and forget them. Five color-coded subway lines connect downtown Washington to the outer reaches of the city and beyond to the Maryland and Virginia suburbs. It's a clean, safe, and efficient system that saves visitors time, money, and shoe leather as it whisks them around town. Visitors to Washington should use the Metro as their primary mode of transportation.

The trains are well maintained and quiet, with carpeting, cushioned seats, and air conditioning. The stations are modern, well lighted, and usually spotless, and they are uniformly constructed with high, arching ceilings paneled with sound-absorbing, lozenge-shaped concrete panels.

Bronze pylons (*left*) identify Metro stations; colored stripes at top show the line or lines served by that station.

Metro system and neighborhood maps (*below*) are located in the mezzanine of each station, as are automated Farecard vending machines (*bottom*).

The wide-open look of the stations has been criticized as sterile and monotonous, but the design may explain why the Metro has maintained a crime-free reputation: There's no place for bad guys to hide. In addition, the entire system is monitored by closed-circuit TV cameras, and each car is equipped with passenger-to-operator intercoms, as are rail platforms and elevators. And cars and stations are nearly graffiti free.

The Metro (nobody calls it Metrorail, its real name) transports more than half a million passengers a day along 103 miles of track and through 83 stations. Currently, one line extension and three new stations are under construction and scheduled for completion in late 2004. It's a world-class engineering marvel.

Trains operate so frequently that carrying a schedule is unnecessary. During peak hours (weekdays 5:30 a.m. to 9:30 a.m. and 3 p.m. to 8 p.m.), trains enter the stations every three to six minutes. During off-peak hours, the interval increases to an average of 12 minutes; it can go to 20 minutes on weekends. To maintain the intervals throughout the year, the Metro adds and deletes trains to compensate for holidays and peak tourist season. Hours of operation are 5:30 a.m. to midnight weekdays, and 8 a.m. to 2 a.m. on weekends and holidays.

How to Ride the Metro

Finding the Stations

Many (but, unfortunately, not all) street signs in Washington indicate the direction and number of blocks to the nearest Metro station. Station entrances are identified by brown columns or pylons with an "M" on all four sides and a combination of colored stripes in red, yellow, orange, green, or blue that indicate the line or lines serving that station. Since most stations are underground, users usually descend on escalators to the mezzanine or ticketing part of the station. At above-ground and elevated stations outside of downtown Washington, the mezzanine is most often on the ground level. At the kiosk located there, pick up a system map with quick directions on how to use the Metro.

Purchasing a Farecard

Next comes the tricky part: You must determine your destination and your fare ahead of time because the ticketing system is automated. Walk up to the backlit, color-coded map located in each mezzanine and find the station nearest your ultimate destination. Then look on the bottom of the map, where an alphabetized list of stations reveals both the fare (peak and off-peak) and the estimated travel time to each. Peak fares, usually more expensive, are in effect from 5:30 a.m. to 9:30 a.m. and from 3 p.m. to 8 p.m. weekdays. Unless you're traveling from a suburban station to downtown, or from one suburb to another, one-way fare is typically $1.10 (non-rush hour). A final note: Before you walk away from the map, make a mental note of the last station of the train that you plan to board, even though you're probably not traveling that far. The name of your train's final destination is the name of the train, thus the key to locating the right platform—the one whose trains are going in the right direction. (See photographs starting on page 122.)

Farecard Vending Machines

Those big vending machines lining the walls of the mezzanine don't dispense sodas. Instead, they swallow your money and issue farecards with magnetic stripes that get you in and—this is crucial—out of Metro stations. Once you get your card, hang onto it.

Buying a farecard works like this: Walk up to the farecard vending machine and look for the numeral "1" on the left side at eye level. (We'll call this **Step 1**.) This is where you insert bills and/or coins. If your destination is, say, a $1.10 fare, and you're making a round-trip, insert $2.20 into the machine. As the money slides in, look at the middle of the machine for the numeral "2" (**Step 2**), where a digital readout registers the amount you've shoved into the contraption.

Machines that accept paper money invariably screw up, and these machines are no exception. They often spit back bills they don't like, so try smoothing wrinkled bills before inserting them and choose new, unfrayed greenbacks over bills that are worn. Inserting coins is nearly foolproof, but not very practical if you're riding the Metro a lot.

Our advice is to cut down on using these infernal machines as much as possible by plugging in $5, $10, or even $20 at once, which means you're buying a ticket that can last several days or longer. The computerized turnstiles print the remaining value on the farecard after each use, which lets you know when it's time to buy a new one. A major drawback, of course, is the possibility of losing the farecard while it's still worth a few bucks. If you value your time at all, take the risk. Below the digital readout at Step 2 are white "plus" and "minus" buttons that let you adjust the readout to the exact fare you wish to purchase. For example, if your round-trip fare is $2.20 and you inserted a $5 bill, toggle the readout from $5 down to $2.20 by repeatedly pushing the "minus" button. (If you overshoot, push the "plus" button to increase the value.) Then look to the right side of the machine and the numeral "3" (**Step 3**), and press the button that reads "Press for Farecard." If all goes well (and, in all fairness, it usually does), out pops your farecard and your change—in this case, $2.80 in change; the machines don't dispense bills. (We *told* you to buy a $5 farecard.)

The farther out you get from downtown, the fewer farecard machines line the walls of the mezzanines—which usually isn't a problem at these

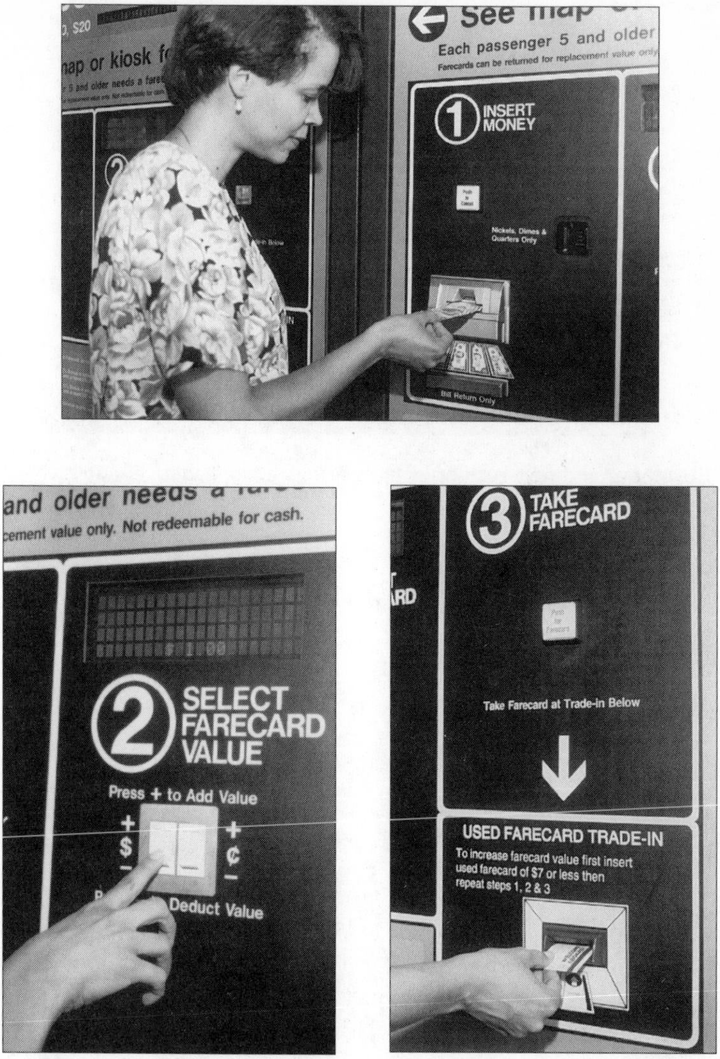

Step 1 (*top*): To purchase a farecard, insert bills and/or coins.
Step 2 (*bottom left*): Use toggle switches to add or decrease the farecard's value. Plug in enough cash to buy at least a round-trip ticket (or more, if desired).
Step 3 (*bottom right*): Press the "Push for Farecard" button; the farecard appears at the "Used Farecard Trade-In" slot.

Rush hour and non-rush hour fares are listed alphabetically at each station's kiosk (*top*).

Automated faregates, which control access in and out of spacious Metro stations, are located near the kiosk. The woman pictured here is exiting the station. (*below*)

less busy stations. For balky machines that won't take your money, or for any problem at all, help is only a few steps away at the kiosk located at each station near the faregate. Inside is a breathing human being who will help. Don't be shy.

One last warning: If the farecard machine accepts $20 bills, keep in mind that the maximum amount of change the machine can spit out is $4.95—which means you're stuck buying a farecard with a minimum value of $15.05.

New Talking Fare Machines

Recently, Metro installed new talking express farecard vending machines at 46 mezzanines in the system's busiest stations; look for the name *Passes/Farecards* across the top. An optional audio button lets you hear a voice guide you through the steps to purchase farecards, which removes much of the confusion and is a real boon to visually impaired riders.

The new machines let you buy up to $200 worth of farecards with a top denomination of $45. You can also purchase the $5 one-day pass, valid for unlimited rides after 9:30 a.m. weekdays and all day on weekends and holidays (a very good deal that we recommend most visitors take advantage of). Currently, you can charge your farecard purchases to VISA, Discover, and MasterCard. *Note:* Most users will want to press button two, for a single farecard, to begin the card purchase process.

Entering the Station

With your farecard firmly in hand, you are now authorized to enter the Metro station. Hold the card in your right hand with the brown magnetic stripe facing up and on the right. Walk up to one of the waist-high faregates with the green light and white arrow near the kiosk (not the faregates that read "Do Not Enter"—they are for passengers exiting the station) and insert your card into the slot, where it is slurped into the bowels of the Metro. As the gate opens, walk through and grab your card as it is regurgitated from the slot at the top of the gate. All this happens in less than a second. Place the farecard in a safe place; if you lose it, you must pay the maximum fare when you exit.

Finding the Train Platform

Once you're past the faregate, look for signs with arrows and the name of your intended line's end station that point toward the platform where your train will arrive. At an underground station, you will descend on an escalator or stairs to the train platform; at an above-ground station, you will ascend to the platform. You can reconfirm that you're on the correct side of the platform by reading the list of stations printed on the pylon located there and finding your destination. If your destination is listed, you're on the right track; departing trains go in one direction only. Stand in the red-tiled area to wait for the next train.

Boarding the Train

As a train approaches a station, lights embedded in the floor along the granite edge of the platform begin flashing. As the train comes out of the tunnel, look for a sign over the front windshield that states the train's destination and line (blue, red, green, orange, or yellow). The destination, but not the color, is also shown on the side of the train. Double-check to make sure the approaching train is the one you want.

If it's the right train, approach the doors, but stand clear to let departing passengers exit the train. Then move smartly; the train stops for only a few seconds, then chimes will indicate that the doors are about to close. If you're rushing to catch a train and hear the chimes, don't attempt to board. Unlike elevator doors, the train doors won't pop open if you lean on them—and they exert a lot of pressure. Wait for the next train.

Inside, take a seat or, if you're a first-time Metro user, study the system map located near the doors. The trains all have real operators who announce the next station over a PA system and give information for transferring to other lines (sometimes you can even hear them over the din). It's better to study the map and read the signs mounted on the cavernous station walls at each stop.

Exiting the Station

As the train enters your station, move toward the doors. When you step off the train, look for stairs or escalators on the platform and walk toward them. Some stations have two or more exits, but the signs on the walls of the stations aren't always clear about where each exit goes. If you know which exit you want (for example, at the Smithsonian station most tourists want the Mall exit, not Independence Avenue), look for that sign and follow the arrow.

At the top of the escalator or stairs, walk toward the mezzanine area, get your farecard ready, and repeat the same procedure you used to enter the Metro system (card in right hand, magnetic stripe up and on the right, insert in slot). If you bought exact fare, you won't get your card back, but the gate will open and a little sign will flash "Exact Fare." You're on your way. If your farecard still has money left on it, it pops up as the gate opens and the sign flashes "Take Farecard." Do same; exit station.

If your farecard doesn't have enough value to cover your trip, the gate won't open and the card will pop back out. You need to take it to an "Exitfare" machine somewhere just behind you. (Invariably ten people are lined up behind you when this happens, creating the equivalent of a minor Beltway backup.) The reddish-colored Exitfare machines look like

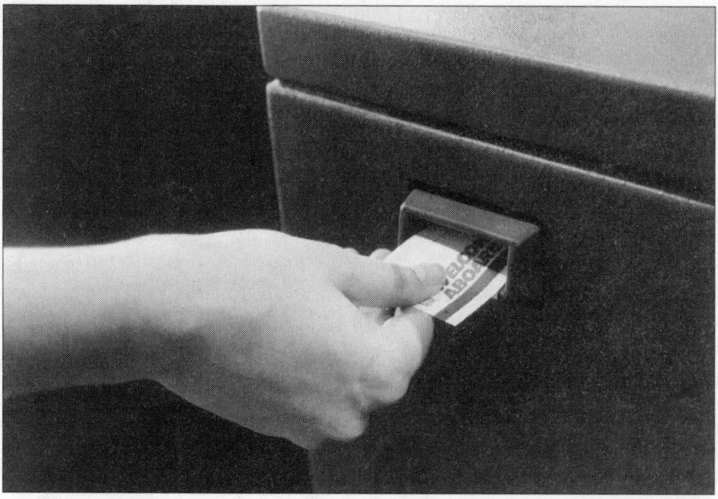

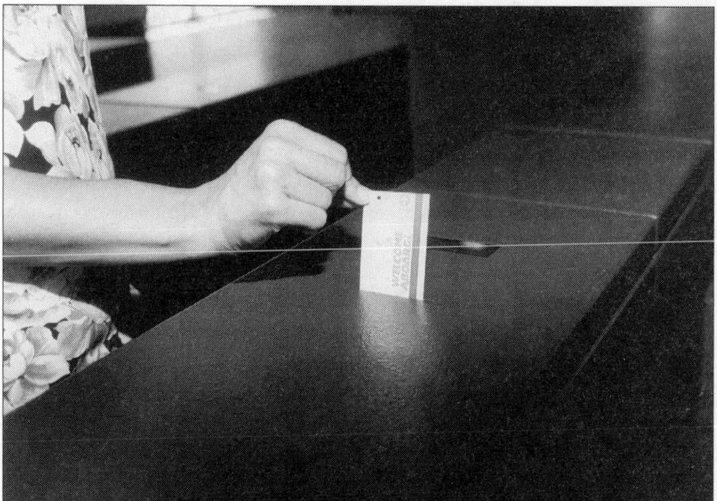

When entering or exiting, insert the farecard (face up with the magnetic strip on the right) into the slot on the front of the faregate (*top*). The farecard reappears at the top of the faregate (*bottom*); remove it and the faregate opens. On new faregates for disabled people, the farecard reappears at the front of the gate.

Note: Remember to hang on to the farecard—you need it to exit the system.

their brothers, the farecard machines. Insert your card and immediately the digital readout displays the exact amount of moolah it needs so you can exit the station. (Don't make my mistake: The machine asked for 40 cents and I stuck a $5 bill into it. I got $4.60 in change back.) Plug in the coins; the farecard reappears; grab it; insert same into the faregate, which swallows it and sets you free.

Changing from One Line to Another

Sooner or later—probably sooner—you will need to transfer from one Metro line to another. Metro Center is the Big Enchilada of the transfer stations, where the red, orange, and blue lines converge in downtown Washington. Other transfer stations tourists are likely to hit are Gallery Place–Chinatown (red, yellow, and green); L'Enfant Plaza (yellow, blue, orange, green); Rosslyn (orange and blue); and Pentagon (yellow and blue).

To transfer, you don't use your farecard. Simply exit your train, take the escalator to the correct platform, and reboard. Try to listen to the PA system as your train enters the station: The driver recites where the different lines are located in the approaching station (for example, "Transfer to the red line on the lower level"). If you can't hear the driver's instructions, look for the color-coded pylons with arrows that point toward the platforms, and look for the one with your destination listed on it.

The Gallery Place–Chinatown station is especially complicated. Frequently, you're routed down and up escalators to reach your platform. Keep your eyes up for signs overhead that state reassuring messages such as "Red Line–Wheaton Straight Ahead."

Metro Foibles and How to Cope

Boarding the Wrong Train

Unless you're concerned about being ten minutes or so late for your meeting with the president, boarding a train going in the wrong direction isn't a big problem. Simply get off at the next station, and if the platform is located between the tracks, go to the other side of the platform to wait for the next train running in the opposite direction, and board it. If both sets of tracks run down the center of the station, take the escalator or stairs and cross the tracks to the other side, where you can catch the next train going the other way.

If you realize you've boarded the wrong *color* train (say, the orange train to Vienna, Virginia, instead of the blue train to Van Dorn Street), just get off at the next station, stay on the same platform, and take the next blue line train.

What to Do with Farecards Worth 50 Cents

After a few days in Washington, you may start accumulating farecards that don't have enough value for even a one-way trip. Don't throw them away! Instead, next time you're using the Metro go up to a farecard vending machine in the mezzanine and insert the old farecard into the slot on the right side of the machine where it says "Trade In Used Farecard." Its value will be displayed on the digital readout at Step 2. Feed the machine money at Step 1, futz with the "plus" and "minus" buttons, and press the white "Push for Farecard" button to get a new card that includes the value on your old card.

If, Like Joe, You're Color Blind

Joe's heart sank the first time he tried to figure out Washington's Metro system: Like a few other men, he is afflicted with red-green color blindness. To his eyes, the Metro's red and green lines look nearly identical in color, and the orange line looks a lot redder than it ought to. The only lines on the system map he could distinguish by color were the blue and yellow ones.

The solution is to fixate on the names of the stations at the ends of the lines. That way, the red line becomes the "Wheaton/Shady Grove" line, while the green line is the "U Street–Cardozo/Anacostia" line. It's harder at first, but you'll end up with a distinct advantage over those who blindly follow colored signs: Knowing a line's end station is helpful when you've got to make a split-second decision on whether or not to board a train that's almost ready to depart the station. For instance, if you enter the Dupont Circle Metro and want to go to Union Station, you need to board the red line train heading toward Wheaton—not Shady Grove. So, sooner or later, you'll get familiar with the end stations anyway.

Discounts and Special Deals

Children Up to two children under age five can ride free when accompanied by a paying passenger.

Senior Citizens and People with Disabilities Reduced fares are available for qualified senior citizens; call (202) 637-7000 for more information. People with disabilities can call (202) 962-1245 for information on reduced fares. A new service called "Metro Mobility Link" supplies people with disabilities with specialized information about Metro stations, including general features of each station, the location of Braille signs, whether the station has a center or side platform, and other disabled-accessible features. The number is (202) 962-6464.

The Metro is a tourist attraction in its own right, featuring the longest escalator in the Western Hemisphere: the 230-foot, mezzanine-to-

When the value of a farecard drops below $1, trade it in for a new one at a farecard machine (*top*).

Emergency intercoms (*bottom*) are located on all station platforms.

platform-level behemoth at the Wheaton Metro in suburban Maryland. If that's a little out of the way, the Dupont Circle Metro's escalator is nearly as long. If escalators terrify you or you are wheelchair-bound, all stations are equipped with elevators. But it's a good idea to check at a station kiosk and confirm that the elevator at your destination station is in operation. To find the elevator, look for the wheelchair symbol near the station entrance.

Fare Discounts If you plan on using the Metro more than once or twice a day, call Metrorail at (202) 637-7000 to find out what discounts are in effect during your visit. A high-value farecard of $20 or more garners a 10% bonus. A Metrorail One-Day Pass lets you ride from 9:30 a.m. till midnight for $5 weekdays, and all day on weekends and holidays; it's the way to go if you plan to ride the subway to several locations in one day. Commuters can save money by purchasing passes that let them ride anywhere, anytime, for two weeks. Discount passes are available at the Metro Center sales office and from the new talking farecard machines installed in busier Metro Stations. Discount passes are also sold at many Safeway, Giant, and SuperFresh grocery stores.

Free Information For a free visitor information kit that includes a Metro system map, specific information on getting to Smithsonian museums and other attractions, and information on driving to suburban Metro stations, call this number: (202) 637-7000. The computer literate can get up-to-the-minute Metro information on the Internet at www.wmata.com. You can also purchase tickets in $10, $15, and $20 increments.

A Note about Metrobus

Washington's extensive bus system, known as Metrobus, serves Georgetown, downtown, and the suburbs. Racks recently installed on metro buses as part of the new Bike-on-Bus program further increase commuter flexibility. There is no additional charge for passengers with bicycles. However, with 400 routes and more than 1,500 buses, Metrobus is an extremely complicated system to figure out how to use. As a result, we feel that visitors to Washington should leave Metrobus to the commuters and stick to the Metro. For the few places that the Metro doesn't reach—notably Georgetown and Adams-Morgan—we recommend taking a cab.

Bus Transfers

If, despite our advice, you plan to transfer from the Metro to a Metrobus in D.C. or Virginia, get a free transfer before you board the Metro train from the machine located next to the escalator in the mezzanine of the station that you entered. You also need to pick up a bus transfer at the

White Flint, Twinbrook, and New Carrollton suburban stations to qualify for reduced parking fees on weekdays; look for signs in the station.

Taxis

Washington taxis are plentiful and relatively cheap. They're also strange. Instead of a metered fare system, fares are figured on a map that splits the city into 5 zones and 27 subzones; the base fare for one zone is $4. A zone map and fare chart are posted in all legal cabs but probably won't mean much to first-time visitors—or most residents, for that matter. If you're concerned about getting ripped off, request a receipt before you start the ride. That way the driver knows he's got no defense in an overcharging claim.

The cab system has other quirks. Drivers can pick up other fares as long as the original passenger isn't taken more than five blocks out of the way of the original destination. That's good news if you're the second or third rider and it's raining; it's not so hot if you're the original passenger and trying to catch a train.

To eliminate the possibility of a ride in a poorly maintained cab or one driven by a recent immigrant who is as unfamiliar with the city as you are, stick to the major cab companies. Some of the independents are illegal yet still carry the markings and roof light of a seemingly legitimate cab. One way to spot a fly-by-night taxi is to check for hubcaps. If there aren't any, pass that one by.

Major D.C. Taxi Companies

Capitol	(202) 546-2400
Diamond	(202) 387-6200
Yellow Cab	(703) 522-2222

People with Special Needs

Washington is one of the most accessible cities in the world for folks with disabilities. With the equal-opportunity federal government as the major employer in the area, Washington provides a good job market for disabled people. As a result, the service sector—bus drivers, waiters, ticket sellers, retail clerks, cab drivers, tour guides, and so on—are somewhat more attuned to the needs of people with disabilities than service-sector employees in other cities. It doesn't hurt that a number of organizations that lobby for handicapped people are headquartered in Washington.

The Metro, for example, was designed to meet federal standards for accessibility. As a result, the stations and trains provide optimal services to a wide array of people with special requirements. Elevators provide access to the mezzanine, or ticketing areas platform, and street level; call the Metro's 24-hour elevator hot line at (202) 962-1825 to check if the elevators at the stations you plan to use are operating.

The edge of the train platform is built with a 14-inch, smooth, light gray, granite strip that's different in texture from the rest of the platform flooring so that visually impaired passengers can detect the platform edge with a foot or cane. Flashing lights embedded in the granite strip alert hearing-impaired passengers that a train is entering the station. Handicapped-only parking spaces are placed close to station entrances. While purchasing a farecard is a strictly visual process (unless the station is equipped with the new talking vending machines), visually impaired passengers can go to the nearby kiosk for assistance. Priority seating for senior citizens and passengers with disabilities is located next to doors in all cars.

Visitors with disabilities who possess a transit ID from their home city can pick up a courtesy Metro ID that provides substantial fare discounts; the ID is good for a month. Go to Metro Headquarters, 600 5th Street, NW, from 8 a.m. to 4:30 p.m. weekdays to pick one up; call (202) 962-1245 for more information. If you want to ride the Metro to get there, the nearest station is Gallery Place. For a free guide with information on Metro's rail and bus system for the elderly and physically disabled, call (202) 637-1328. "Metro Mobility Link" is a new help line for people with disabilities. Call (202) 962-6464 for basic as well as more specialized information on Metro stations.

The Smithsonian and the National Park Service, agencies that run the lion's share of popular sights in Washington, offer top-notch services to folks with disabilities. Designated handicapped parking spaces are located along Jefferson Drive on the Mall. Museums are equipped with entrance ramps, barrier-free exhibits, elevator service to all floors, and accessible rest rooms and water fountains. Visually impaired visitors can pick up large-print brochures, cassette tapes and recorders, and raised-line drawings of museum artifacts at many Smithsonian museums. The National Air and Space Museum offers special tours that let visitors touch models and artifacts; call (202) 357-1400 for information.

Hearing-impaired visitors to the National Air and Space Museum can arrange tours with an interpreter by calling (202) 357-1400 or (202) 357-1505 (TTY). Public telephones in the museum are equipped with amplification, and the briefing room is equipped with audio loop. For a copy of the Smithsonian's "A Guide for Disabled Visitors," call (202) 357-2700 or (202) 357-1729 (TTY).

The Lincoln and Jefferson Memorials and the Washington Monument are equipped to accommodate disabled visitors. Most sight-seeing attractions have elevators for seniors and others who want to avoid a lot of stair climbing. The White House, for example, has a special entrance on

Pennsylvania Avenue for visitors arriving in wheelchairs, and White House guides usually allow visually handicapped visitors to touch some of the items described on tours.

Tourmobile offers a special van equipped with a wheelchair and scooter lift for handicapped visitors. The van visits all the regular sites on the tour; in fact, visitors can usually specify what sites they want to see in any order and the van will wait until they are finished touring. The service is the same price as the standard Tourmobile rate, $18 for adults and $8 for children. Call (202) 554-7020 at least a day in advance to reserve a van. Information available at www.tourmobile.com

In spite of all the services available to disabled visitors, it's still a good idea to call ahead to any facility you plan to visit and confirm that services are in place and that the particular exhibit or gallery you wish to see is still available.

Foreign visitors to Washington who would like a tour conducted in their native language can contact the Guide Service of Washington. See "The Guide Service of Washington" on page 159.

Part Six

Sight-Seeing Tips and Tours

Plan before You Leave Home

There are several good reasons why you should take the time to do some planning before coming to Washington to tour its sights. First of all, Washington is a big, sprawling city that covers a lot of real estate. The National Mall, for example, is two miles long—and there's more to Washington beyond that long expanse of green. Spending a poorly planned day traipsing back and forth from monument to museum to federal building to monument can waste a lot of time, energy, and shoe leather.

But it's not only Washington's physical size that makes planning a must: It's the mind-boggling number of tourist attractions that are available. Even if your vacation is a week long, be prepared to make some hard choices about how many sights you can fit into your itinerary. If your visit is shorter, say only two or three days, it's even more imperative that you have a firm idea of what you want to see. Attempting to see too much during your allotted time is exhausting: Your visit becomes a blur of marble monuments and big rooms. As with most large-scale projects, a little research can go a long way in making your trip more pleasurable.

Our recommendation is to do some soul-searching and try to reach some decisions about what your interests are before you leave for Washington. Are you curious about how the government spends all your tax money? Have you always wanted to gaze up at the solemn figure of Lincoln in his marble memorial? Do you love antiques? Are you a military buff? Does technology fascinate you? Do you love exploring art museums? Gardens? Historical houses? Washington offers places to explore for people with all these interests. Yet neither this guide nor any other can tell you what your interests are. You gotta do your homework.

Some more advice: To help winnow your choices, get as much written information as you can before you leave—and read it. To supplement this guide, you can get information concerning Washington tourist attractions, hotels, and recreation at the public library and travel agencies, or by calling or writing any of the profiled attractions.

Web surfers and the computer literate will be glad to know that Washington now has its own website. It offers a comprehensive guide to D.C. hotels that's searchable by location and price, restaurants searchable by neighborhood, tour information, and a quarterly calendar of special events and festivals. The Internet address is www.dcvisit.com.

Thinking in Categories

Visitors to Washington are often thrown into large groups of tourists as they visit famous and popular edifices such as the Washington Monument, the U.S. Capitol, and the White House. Unless you've made prior arrangements for a VIP tour or Uncle Milt is a congressional staffer, you'll be craning your neck under the Capitol dome with 49 other tourists as you listen to your tour guide's spiel. Our advice: Go with the flow, relax, and enjoy the tour. But not everything you do while in Washington has to turn into a group traipse.

Question: How do you avoid the big crowds that clog the major tourist attractions?

Answer: By organizing your visit around things that interest you.

By charting your own course, you get off the beaten track and visit places that offer higher quality tours than the canned presentations given in the better known attractions. Often, you find yourself visiting places with small groups of people who share your interests. In short, you have more fun.

By following your own interests, you can make some intriguing discoveries as you visit Washington:

- A collection of miniature Revolutionary soldiers fighting a mock battle (Anderson House).
- A four-sided, colonial-era mousetrap that guillotines rodents (Daughters of the American Revolution building).
- A tropical rain forest located just off the Mall (Organization of American States building).
- A space capsule you can climb into (Navy Museum).
- Fabergé eggs encrusted with diamonds (Hillwood Museum).
- The tomb of the only president buried in Washington (National Cathedral).
- A garden filled with flowers mentioned in the plays of William Shakespeare (the Folger Shakespeare Library).
- A pub that shows how typical colonial-era Americans lived (Gadsby's Tavern..

As you travel around Washington, you'll discover sights like these and many others that most visitors miss. To help you on your way, we've selected major categories and listed the best destinations for visitors to explore. As you read the list, keep in mind that many attractions overlap. For example, the National Air and Space Museum appeals to both technology and military buffs, while the Woodrow Wilson House is interesting to history fans, lovers of the decorative arts, and folks curious about how the high and mighty conducted their day-to-day lives in the 1920s.

Government

- Bureau of Engraving and Printing
- Federal Bureau of Investigation
- Ronald Reagan Building
- U.S. Capitol
- U.S. Department of the Treasury
- U.S. Supreme Court
- Voice of America

Monuments and Memorials

- African-American Civil War Memorial
- Arlington Cemetery
- Black Revolutionary War Patriots Memorial
- Franklin Delano Roosevelt Memorial
- George Mason Memorial
- Iwo Jima Memorial
- Kennedy Center
- Korean War Veterans Memorial
- Lincoln and Jefferson Memorials
- National Law Enforcement Officers Memorial
- Navy Memorial
- U.S. Holocaust Memorial
- Vietnam Veterans Memorial
- Washington Monument Museum
- Women in Vietnam Memorial

Historic Places

- Arlington House
- Chesapeake and Ohio Canal
- Decatur House
- Ford's Theatre
- Frederick Douglass House
- Georgetown
- Mount Vernon
- The Octagon
- Old Stone House
- Old Town Alexandria
- U.S. Capitol
- Woodrow Wilson House

Art Museums

- Art Museum of the Americas (at the Organization of American States)
- Corcoran Gallery of Art in the Arts
- Dumbarton Oaks National Portrait Gallery
- Freer Gallery of Art
- Hirshhorn Museum and Sculpture Garden
- Phillips Collection
- Renwick Gallery
- National Gallery of Art
- National Museum of African Art
- National Museum of Women
- Sackler Gallery

History

- Anacostia Museum
- Arlington House
- Bethune Museum and Archives
- Chesapeake and Ohio Canal

History *(continued)*

- Decatur House
- Folger Shakespeare Library
- Georgetown
- International Spy Museum
- Lincoln Museum (in Ford's Theatre)
- Mount Vernon
- National Air and Space Museum
- National Archives
- National Cryptologic Museum
- National Museum of American History
- National Portrait Gallery
- Old Town Alexandria
- U.S. Holocaust Memorial Museum

Children

- Bureau of Engraving and Printing National
- Capital Children's Museum
- Federal Bureau of Investigation
- Museum of Natural History
- National Air and Space Museum
- National Aquarium
- National Geographic Society's Explorers Hall
- National Museum of American History
- National Postal Museum
- National Wildlife Visitor Center
- National Zoological Park
- Old Post Office Pavilion
- Washington Monument
- Washington Navy Yard

Decorative Arts and Antiques

- Anderson House
- Christian Heurich Mansion
- Daughters of the American Revolution Museum and Period Rooms
- Decatur House
- Dumbarton Oaks
- Hillwood Museum
- Mount Vernon
- The Octagon
- Old Town Alexandria
- Textile Museum
- Tudor Place
- U.S. Department of State Diplomatic Reception Rooms

Military

- Anderson House
- Arlington National Cemetery
- Black Revolutionary War Patriots Memorial
- Iwo Jima Memorial
- National Air and Space Museum
- National Cryptologic Museum
- Smithsonian's Garber Facility*
- U.S. Navy Memorial
- Vietnam Veterans Memorial
- Washington Navy Yard
- Women in Vietnam Memorial

**A National Air and Space Museum storehouse that houses aircraft from both World Wars.*

Gardens

- Bishops Garden at Washington National Cathedral
- Constitution Gardens
- Dumbarton Oaks
- Enid A. Haupt Garden (behind the Castle on the Mall)
- Folger Shakespeare Library
- Franciscan Monastery

Gardens *(continued)*

- Hillwood Museum
- Kenilworth Aquatic Gardens
- Meridian International Center
- Mount Vernon
- National Arboretum
- National Gallery of Art Sculpture Garden
- Tudor Place
- U.S. Botanic Garden

Architecture

- Constitution Hall
- Daughters of the American Revolution Museum
- Hirshhorn Museum
- House of the Temple
- Kennedy Center
- Library of Congress (Jefferson Building)
- Meridian International Center
- National Archives
- National Building Museum
- National Gallery of Art (East Building)
- National Postal Museum
- Old Post Office Pavilion
- Ronald Reagan Building
- U.S. Capitol
- U.S. Supreme Court
- Union Station
- Washington National Cathedral
- Washington Monument

Places of Worship

- Adas Israel Synagogue at the Lillian and Albert Small Jewish Museum
- Franciscan Monastery
- Islamic Center
- National Shrine of the Immaculate Conception
- Pope John Paul II Cultural Center
- St. John's Episcopal Church (across from the White House)
- Washington National Cathedral

African-American

- African-American Civil War Memorial
- Anacostia Museum
- Bethune Museum and Archives
- Black Revolutionary War Patriots Memorial
- Frederick Douglass House (Cedar Hill)
- Lincoln Memorial
- National Museum of African Art
- National Museum of American Art

Technology

- Arts and Industry Building
- Goddard Space Flight Center
- International Spy Museum
- National Air and Space Museum
- National Building Museum
- National Cryptologic Museum
- National Museum of American History
- National Museum of Health and Medicine
- National Postal Museum
- Washington Navy Yard

Great Views

- Arlington House (Arlington National Cemetery)
- Iwo Jima Memorial
- Kennedy Center
- Lincoln and Jefferson Memorials
- Mount Vernon
- Old Post Office Pavilion
- Washington Monument
- Washington National Cathedral

Outdoors

- Chesapeake and Ohio Canal
- Great Falls Park
- Mount Vernon Trail
- National Wildlife Visitor Center
- Potomac Park
- Rock Creek Park
- Roosevelt Island

Great Places to Walk When You're Sick of Museums

- Cathedral Avenue between Connecticut Ave. and Washington National Cathedral
- anywhere along Connecticut Avenue
- the bike path along the Potomac from the Kennedy Center to Georgetown
- Dupont Circle
- Embassy Row (Massachusetts Avenue northwest of Dupont Circle)
- Fort McNair and the Southwest
- Georgetown
- Kenilworth Aquatic Gardens
- The Mall
- National Arboretum
- National Zoo

Putting Your Congressperson to Work

A letter to a representative or senator well in advance of your trip (six months is not too early) can bring a cornucopia of free goodies your way: reservations on VIP tours of the Supreme Court, the FBI, and the Bureau of Engraving and Printing that can save you hours of time waiting in line, as well as getting you on longer, more informative tours. In addition, your eager-to-please congressperson (he or she wants your vote) can provide timely information about hotels, restaurants, shopping, and special events. It's all free. Just be sure to include the exact dates of your visit.

Here's why you must send off your letter as soon as you know the dates that you'll be in Washington: Senators and House members are limited in the number of spaces on VIP tours they can provide to constituents. Since all the legislators get the same number of passes, reason dictates that the farther away your state is from Washington, D.C., the better chance you have of getting on a coveted VIP tour. For example, Maryland legislators, some of whose constituents can literally jump on the Metro to reach D.C., are often booked five and six months in advance for the popular White House VIP tours. But if you're from South Dakota, chances are your congressperson will be able to get you reservations during your visit.

There is a downside to the VIP tours: Some of them take place very early, usually before the regular, nonreserved tours begin. For example, Bureau of Engraving and Printing VIP tours depart at 8 a.m. Monday through Friday. The upside: If you're touring in the spring and summer, you've already resigned yourself to early starts to beat the worst of the crowds anyway. Another myth shattered: The VIP tours still require waiting in line. But the tours are longer and, unlike the unreserved version, guided.

How do you reserve a VIP tour? Write a letter to your senator or representative at his or her home office or the one in Washington. For senators, the Washington address is U.S. Senate, Washington, D.C. 20510. For House members, address your letter to the U.S. House of Representatives, Washington, D.C. 20515. Again, don't forget to include the dates you'll be visiting Washington.

A Sample Letter

25 October 2003

The Honorable [*your congressperson or senator's name*]
U.S. House of Representatives (or U.S. Senate)
Washington, D.C. 20515 (or 20510 for the Senate)

Dear Mr. or Ms. [*your congressperson or senator's name*],

During the week of [*fill in your vacation date*] my family and I will be visiting Washington to tour the major attractions on the Mall, Capitol Hill, and downtown. I understand your office can make reservations on VIP tours for constituents.

Specifically, I would like tours for the White House, the Bureau of Engraving and Printing, and the FBI during that week. I'll need four reservations for each tour. If at all possible, please schedule our tours in the middle of our week.

In addition, I'd appreciate any other touring information on Washington you can send me. Thanks in advance for your help.

Yours truly,
[*Your name*]

Operating Hours

By and large, Washington's major attractions keep liberal operating hours, making it easy for visitors to plan their itineraries without worrying about odd opening and closing times. There are, however, a few exceptions. Of all the major tourist attractions, the Bureau of Engraving and Printing keeps the weirdest hours: closed in the afternoon and not open seven days a week.

Smithsonian museums are open every day from 10 a.m. to 5:30 p.m. During the summer, hours may be extended into the evening if operating budgets allow. The Bureau of Engraving and Printing allows visitors to view its money-printing operation Monday through Friday from 9 a.m. to 2 p.m. and again from 5 p.m. to 7:30 p.m. in the summer (a free time-ticket system is in effect in the spring and summer).

Most monuments, on the other hand, are open 24 hours a day. Our recommendation is to visit the Lincoln and Jefferson Memorials after dark. Lit up by floodlights, the marble edifices appear to float in the darkness, and the Reflecting Pool and Tidal Basin dramatically reflect the light. It's much more impressive than by day—and a lot less crowded. The Washington Monument now has a time-ticket system that eliminates long lines.

While many sights are open every day, a lot of Washington attractions close on federal holidays: January 1, Martin Luther King Jr. Day (the third Monday in January), Presidents' Day, Memorial Day, Independence Day, Labor Day (the first Monday in September), Columbus Day (the second Monday in October), Veterans Day, Thanksgiving, and Christmas Day (when virtually everything except outdoor monuments and Mount Vernon is closed).

Rhythms of the City

Although it's impossible to be specific, the ebb and flow of crowds follows a pattern throughout the day and the week at major tourist attractions. By being aware of the general patterns, you can sometimes avoid the worst of the crowds, traffic congestion, and long lines.

Mornings are slow, and the quietest time to visit most museums and sights is when they open. As lunchtime approaches, the number of people visiting a popular attraction begins to pick up, peaking around 3 p.m. Then the crowds begin to thin, and after 4 p.m. things start to get quiet again. It follows that the best times to visit a wildly popular place like the National Air and Space Museum is just after it opens and just before it closes. Conversely, when the crowds are jamming the Museum of Natural History during the middle of the day, expand your cultural horizons with a visit to the Sackler and Freer Galleries, or the National Museum of African Art. They are rarely, if ever, crowded.

Among days of the week, Monday, Tuesday, and Wednesday see the lowest number of visitors. If you visit the Washington Monument, the Bureau of Engraving and Printing, the National Air and Space Museum, the National Museum of American History, and the National Museum of Natural History, try to do so early in the week. Attempt to structure your week so that Thursday, Friday, and the weekend are spent visiting sights that are away from the Mall.

If You Visit During Peak Tourist Season

The key to missing the worst of the crowds in spring and summer is to get a hotel close to a Metro station, park the car, and leave it. Then decide what is most important for you to see, and get to those places early.

An example: You've miraculously secured a convenient D.C. hotel room in early April. From your in-town window, Washington is laid out before you—and for most of the day, it's a view of gridlocked motor coaches, school buses, families in cars, angry commuters, and jammed sidewalks. Everyone but the commuters is drawn by the Japanese cherry trees in bloom along the Tidal Basin and the Reflecting Pool on the Mall.

But don't rush out the door and join the throngs on their way to see the trees. Because it's early (say, 7 a.m.), your plan is to hit the sights that you want to see before the crowds arrive. So walk to the nearby Metro station and take the train to the Smithsonian station. From there, it's a 10-minute stroll to the Washington Monument—and at 7:30, you're near the front of the line when the kiosk that distributes time tickets opens. By 9 a.m., you're out of the marble obelisk and on your way to the nearby Bureau of Engraving and Printing. At the ticket office on Raoul Wallenberg Place, pick up a time ticket for a tour of the money-printing facility that begins at 1:30 p.m. From there, it's a short walk to the Jefferson Memorial and those famous trees.

At 10 a.m, you stroll toward the Mall for a visit to the National Air and Space Museum as it opens. At 10:15, you join a free, guided tour. At 11 a.m., you're back on your own again to explore some corners of the museum that interest you.

By noon, the crowds are starting to fill the museum, so you leave Air and Space in search of a bite to eat. If it's a weekday, L'Enfant Plaza, only one subway stop away from the Smithsonian station, has a wide array of eateries. Then it's an easy walk to the Bureau of Engraving and Printing to see the stacks of money.

By 2 p.m., you have already visited three of the world's most popular attractions during peak season with almost no waiting in line. Now you can spend the afternoon exploring a wide range of attractions that never get crowded, even when Washington is besieged by tourists in the spring: the Freer Gallery, the Hirshhorn Museum, the Vietnam Veterans Memorial, the Corcoran Gallery, or the DAR Museum, just to name a few.

Intragroup Touring Incompatibility: What It Is and How to Avoid It

The incidence of "Intragroup Touring Incompatibility" (members of the same group having strongly conflicting interests or touring objectives) is high in Washington, thanks to the city's wide variety of touring attractions. An example: Some people would be happy never to leave the

National Air and Space Museum; a lot of other folks find that after an hour or two of staring at old airplanes and spacecraft, it's time to move on.

Children, at the other extreme, haven't the patience or inclination for all the reading required by the exhibits and fizzle out after a couple of hours of touring D.C. museums. In fact, even grown-ups should consider a touring plan that puts reading-intensive attractions such as self-guided museum tours at the beginning of the day, and take guided tours in the afternoon, where you're spoon-fed information by a guide and you can put your brain on autopilot.

A touring plan made up before your arrival in Washington can help your group avoid the worst manifestations of intragroup incompatibility. If your group contains, for example, a real "Rocket George," let him linger at the National Air and Space Museum while the rest of you move on to another Mall attraction. Arrange a meeting place later in the day where you can all regroup; both you and Rocket George will be happier.

Washington with Children

Most adult visitors to Washington experience a rush of thrill and pride on viewing the U.S. Capitol, the Washington Monument, and the White House. And, for most of us, those are feelings that hold up well over repeat visits to the nation's capital. In fact, a fascination for the city often begins on a first visit to Washington in grade or high school and can continue through adulthood.

The Ten Most Popular Sights for Children

1. National Air and Space Museum
2. National Zoological Park
3. The Capital Children's Museum
4. National Museum of Natural History
5. Bureau of Engraving and Printing
6. Federal Bureau of Investigation
7. National Museum of American History
8. National Geographic Society's Explorers Hall
9. Washington Navy Yard
10. Washington Monument

So it follows that Washington is one of the most interesting, beautiful, and stimulating cities in the world for children and young people. Where else can kids see the president's house, touch a moon rock, feed a tarantula, and view a city from the top of a 555-foot marble obelisk?

Luckily, most popular Washington tourist destinations for kids offer a lot to hold an adult's attention, too—which means you don't have to worry about parking the kids someplace while you tour a museum. For example, as your kids marvel at the dinosaur skeletons in the Museum of Natural History or feed that giant spider, you can be fantasizing over the Hope Diamond. Even so, on a Washington vacation with small children, anticipation is the name of the game. Here are some things you need to consider:

Age Although the big buildings, spaciousness, and thrill of Washington excite children of all ages, and while there are specific sights that delight toddlers and preschoolers, Washington's attractions are generally oriented to older kids and adults. We believe that children should be a fairly mature nine years old to get the most out of popular attractions such as the National Museum of Natural History and the U.S. Capitol, and a year or two older to get much out of the art galleries, monuments, and other federal buildings around town.

Time of Year to Visit If there is any way to swing it, avoid the hot, crowded summer months. Try to go in late September through November, or mid-April through mid-June. If you have children of varying ages and your school-age kids are good students, consider taking the older ones out of school so you can visit during the cooler, less-congested off-season. Arrange special study assignments relating to the many educational aspects of Washington. If your school-age children can't afford to miss any school, take your vacation as soon as the school year ends in late May or early June. Nothing, repeat, nothing will enhance your Washington vacation as much as avoiding the early spring and summer months.

Building Naps and Rest into Your Itinerary Washington is huge and offers more attractions than you can possibly see in a week, so don't try to see everything in one day. Tour in the early morning and return to your hotel midday for a swim (if your hotel has a pool; see below) and a nice nap. Even during the fall and winter, when the crowds are smaller and the temperature more pleasant, the sheer size of D.C. will exhaust most children under eight by lunchtime. Go back and visit more attractions in the late afternoon and early evening.

Where to Stay The time and hassle involved in commuting to and from downtown Washington and its surrounding neighborhoods will be lessened if you can afford to stay inside the District and near a Metro station. But even if, for financial or other reasons, you lodge outside of Washington, it remains imperative that you get small children off of the Mall for a few hours to rest and recuperate. Neglecting to relax and unwind is the best way we know to get the whole family in a snit and ruin the day (or the entire vacation).

With small children, there is simply no excuse for not planning ahead. Make sure you get a hotel, in or out of Washington, within a few minutes' walk to a Metro station. Naps and relief from the frenetic pace of touring Washington, even in the off-season, are indispensable. While it's true that you can gain some measure of peace by finding a quiet spot near the Tidal Basin to relax, there is no substitute for returning to the familiarity and security of your own hotel. Regardless of what you have heard or read, children too large to sleep in a stroller will not relax and revive unless you get them back to your room.

Another factor in choosing a hotel is whether or not it has a swimming pool. A lot of visitors to D.C. assume that, like those in most destinations, Washington hotels automatically come with a pool. Alas, it ain't necessarily so. A swimming pool, especially in warmer weather, can be a lifesaver for both you and your kids. So if a refreshing dip is important to your family, be sure to ask before making hotel reservations.

Be in Touch with Your Feelings While we acknowledge that a Washington vacation can be a capital investment (pardon the pun), remember that having fun is not necessarily the same as seeing everything. When you and your children start getting tired and irritable, call time out and regroup. Trust your instincts. What would really feel best right now? Another museum, a rest break with some ice cream, going back to the room for a nap? *The way to protect your investment is to stay happy and have a good time, whatever that takes.* You do not have to meet a quota for experiencing every museum on the Mall, seeing every branch of government, walking through every monument, or anything else. It's your vacation; you can do what you want.

Least Common Denominators Remember the old saying about a chain being only as strong as its weakest link? The same logic applies to a family touring Washington. Somebody is going to run out of steam first; when they do, the whole family will be affected. Sometimes a cold Coke and a rest break will get the flagging member back into gear. Sometimes, however, as Marshall Dillon would say, "You just need to get out of Dodge." Pushing the tired or discontented beyond their capacity is like driving on a flat tire: It may get you a few more miles down the road but you will be sorry in the long run. Accept that energy levels vary among individuals and be prepared to respond to small children or other members of your group who poop out. *Hint:* "After we've driven a thousand miles to take you to Washington, you're going to ruin everything!" is not the right thing to say.

Setting Limits and Making Plans The best way to avoid arguments and disappointments is to develop a game plan before you go. Establish some general guidelines for the day and get everybody committed in advance. Be sure to include:

1. Wake-up time and breakfast plans.
2. What time you need to depart for the part of Washington you plan to explore.
3. What you need to take with you.
4. A policy for splitting the group up or for staying together.
5. A plan for what to do if the group gets separated or someone is lost.
6. How long you intend to tour in the morning and what you want to see, including fall-back plans in the event an attraction is too crowded.
7. A policy on what you can afford for snacks, lunch, and refreshments.
8. A target time for returning to your hotel for a rest.
9. What time you will return to touring D.C. and how late you will stay.
10. Plans for dinner.
11. A policy for shopping and buying souvenirs, including who pays: Mom and Dad or the kids.

Be Flexible Having a game plan does not mean forgoing spontaneity or sticking rigidly to the itinerary. Once again, listen to your intuition. Alter the plan if the situation warrants. Be prepared to roll with the punches.

Overheating, Sunburn, and Dehydration In the worst of Washington's hot and humid summers, the most common problems of smaller children are overheating, sunburn, and dehydration. A small bottle of sunscreen carried in a pocket or fanny pack will help you take precautions against overexposure to the sun. Be sure to put some on children in strollers, even if the stroller has a canopy. Some of the worst cases of sunburn we have seen were on the exposed foreheads and feet of toddlers and infants in strollers. To avoid overheating, rest at regular intervals in the shade or in an air-conditioned museum, hotel lobby, or federal building.

Do not count on keeping small children properly hydrated with soft drinks and water fountain stops. Long lines often make buying refreshments problematic, and water fountains are not always handy. What's more, excited children may not inform you or even realize that they're thirsty or overheated. We recommend using a stroller for children six years old and under, and carrying plastic water bottles.

Blisters Blisters and sore feet are common for visitors of all ages, so wear comfortable, well-broken-in shoes and two pairs of thin socks (preferable to one pair of thick socks). If you or your children are unusually susceptible to blisters, carry some precut Moleskin bandages; they offer the best possible protection, stick great, and won't sweat off. When you feel a hot spot, stop, air out your foot, and place a Moleskin over the area before a blister forms. Moleskin is available by name at all drugstores. Sometimes small children won't tell their parents about a developing blister until it's too late. We recommend inspecting the feet of preschoolers two or more times a day.

Health and Medical Care If you have a child who requires medication, pack plenty, and bring it in a carry-on bag if you're flying to Washington. A bottle of liquid Dramamine will come in handy to fight off car sickness or motion sickness, which can affect kids who are normally fine in a car but may get sick in a plane, train, or boat.

A small first-aid kit, available at most pharmacies, will handle most minor cuts, scrapes, and splinters and is easy to pack. Grown-up and children's strength aspirin or Tylenol, a thermometer, cough syrup, baby wipes, a plastic spoon, a night light, and pacifiers will round out a small kit of health-related items for people traveling with children or infants.

Be sure to carry proof of insurance and policy numbers with you. If possible, check with friends or relatives before you leave for Washington to get the name of a pediatrician who practices locally; it could save a lot of time thumbing through the yellow pages if a youngster should fall ill. For emergency treatment, dial 911 or go to the emergency room of the nearest hospital.

Major D.C. Hospitals

Children's National Medical Center
111 Michigan Avenue, NW
(202) 745-5000

George Washington University Medical Center
901 23rd Street, NW
(202) 994-10000

Georgetown University Medical Center
3800 Reservoir Road, NW
(202) 784-2000

Sunglasses If you want your smaller children to wear sunglasses, it's a good idea to affix a strap or string to the frames so the glasses won't get lost and can hang from the child's neck while indoors.

If You Become Separated Before venturing out of your hotel room, sit down with your kids and discuss what they should do if they get separated from you while touring a museum, monument, or federal building.

Tell them to find a uniformed guard and ask for help. Point out that the main entrance of most Washington attractions has an information desk where they should go if they temporarily get separated.

We suggest that children under age eight be color-coded by dressing them in purple T-shirts or equally distinctive attire. It is also a good idea to sew a label into each child's shirt that states his or her name, your name, and the name of your hotel. The same thing can be accomplished less elegantly by writing the information on a strip of masking tape: Hotel security professionals suggest that the information be printed in small letters and that the tape be affixed to the outside of the child's shirt five inches or so below the armpit.

The Ten Least Popular Sights for Children

1. National Gallery of Art–West Building
2. Library of Congress
3. U.S. Supreme Court
4. Pentagon
5. Kennedy Center
6. Dumbarton Oaks museum
7. National Portrait Gallery
8. Folger Shakespeare Library
9. Textile Museum
10. Renwick Gallery

Rainy Days Rainy days and Mondays can get you down—even while on vacation—and cooped-up children suffer even worse. Museums and galleries are obvious choices during inclement weather (as you can tell from the crowds), but don't rule out some other options to keep children entertained when the sun doesn't shine or if you're museumed-out. Catch a movie at Union Station's nine-screen cinema complex or take the Metro to Alexandria's Torpedo Factory, where 150 craftsmen work and sell their creations Tuesday through Sunday. And don't forget that age-old panacea for boredom—shopping. Union Station, the Old Post Office Pavilion, the Shops at National Place, and Georgetown Park are all indoor shopping centers with interesting specialty stores. If you run out of ideas, check the *Washington Post* "Weekend" section for inspiration.

Of course, some attractions can bore active kids to tears—even if it's raining outside. An entire afternoon in the National Gallery of Art can be deadly to eight-year-olds. The best plan is to reward your youngsters for their patience with a trip to someplace really special when the weather clears. The National Zoo should top the list. And you'll enjoy it, too.

A final tip that can help you and your kids weather a storm: Stay in a hotel with an indoor pool; on rainy days, kids love getting wet indoors.

Washington's Top 20 Tours

With only a few exceptions (such as the FBI), it isn't absolutely necessary to join a group tour while visiting Washington's attractions. Simply explore on your own, letting your curiosity and interests be your guide. This strategy works well in a large museum such as the National Museum of Natural History—dinosaur skeletons? an insect zoo? the Hope Diamond? Take your pick. At selected locations, though, it can be a nice change of pace to have an expert lead you by the hand and—who knows?—even enlighten you. What follows is a highly arbitrary list of guided tours that the authors of the *Unofficial Guide* think do a splendid job at introducing visitors to their respective attractions. For addresses and phone numbers for the following attractions, see the listings in Part Ten.

1. U.S. Department of State Diplomatic Reception Rooms One of the advantages of taking tours that require advance reservations is that the tour guides are top-notch. The guide we encountered on this tour of the $90 million rooms housed on the eighth floor of this otherwise humdrum building really knew her stuff, from the art on the walls to the historical significance of the impressive furniture that fills these spectacular, ornate rooms.

2. U.S. Capitol Alas, post-September 11, visitors are prohibited from wandering the halls of the Capitol and must arrive *very* early to pick up a time-ticket for a guided tour (that day only). Stick close to your guide so you can hear his or her comments about the artwork on display and the history of the building.

3. Washington National Cathedral While this is an easy place to just wander around in, don't do it: Take the free tour. The docent (or museum guide) who led our group of out-of-towners showed enthusiasm, a real concern for her charges, and a deep knowledge of the cathedral. She also mentioned the free organ demonstration that followed the tour, which we stayed for. It turned out to be the highlight of our day.

4. Library of Congress This tour is led by a knowledgeable tour guide who takes your group to the Jefferson Building's magnificent Main Reading Room, one of the most beautiful interiors in D.C. And don't miss the 12-minute video that explains the mission of the world's largest library.

5. Daughters of the American Revolution (DAR) Museum and Period Rooms Our tour of the period rooms (there are 33, but no one sees them all on one tour) was led by a poised young woman who really knew her history—and her decorative arts. She also was well informed on the handsome building that serves as DAR headquarters: A special railroad spur was built to bring the massive, solid-marble columns on the front of the building to the site. For antique lovers, this tour is about two hours of bliss.

6. The Phillips Collection The 45-minute tour highlights the best items in the modern art collection and puts them in the context of the wealthy collector who founded the museum. The guides know their art and manage to tie together different art periods as they talk about the paintings. The comfortable Phillips is a welcome contrast to Mall megamuseums. Guided tours are free and offered on Wednesdays and Saturdays.

7. Hillwood Museum Our only complaint about the reservation-only guided tour was its length—two hours. But it will fascinate anyone interested in the decorative arts, antiques, jewelry, porcelain, paintings, furniture . . . the list goes on. But following Hillwood's recent renovation, visitors may also wander at will on self-guided tours; the choice is yours. It's a breathtaking collection, and you'll tour in small groups led by knowledgeable guides.

8. National Air and Space Museum Dedicated space cadets and unapologetic Star Trek fanatics should take the free, one-hour tour (offered daily at 10:15 a.m. and 1 p.m.; meet at the information desk in the main lobby). It's a good introduction to this sprawling—and most visited in the world—museum.

9. U.S. Department of the Treasury This reservation-only, behind-the-scenes tour lets visitors feel like they're really seeing something special. The interior of the building was recently renovated: The tour takes you through sumptuous offices and corridors restored to their mid-nineteenth-century opulence. (*Note:* For security reasons, tours have been suspended until further notice.)

10. The Voice of America (VOA) We liked this small, off-the-beaten-track tour. Most of the visitors who go are from foreign countries and listen to Voice of America broadcasts at home. (Listening to the VOA in the United States requires a shortwave radio.) You'll also see a four-panel mural painted by noted artist Ben Shahn in the early 1940s. And the broadcast studios are really neat.

11. Arlington National Cemetery Tourmobile does a good job of transporting visitors around 612-acre Arlington National Cemetery. The thought of trying to see all the sights in the cemetery on foot makes our feet hurt. The tour bus stops at the Kennedy gravesite, the Tomb of the Unknowns, and Arlington House, where you can linger as long as you like, since you have unlimited boarding privileges to the buses that come about every 15 minutes.

12. The Kennedy Center This leisurely tour of the sumptuous performing arts center and JFK memorial gives visitors a behind-the-scenes look at Washington's cultural life, as well as a chance to linger over some of the artwork donated to the center from countries around the world. The 360° view of Washington from the center's roof terrace is a knockout.

13. The National Portrait Gallery (*Note:* Currently closed for renovations, this museum is scheduled to reopen in 2004 or 2005.) What would have been an aimless ramble through this downtown art museum turned into an informative tour. On a whim, we asked the guard at the information desk when the next guided tour left. The answer: "Whenever you're ready." So we received a tour from a docent who's the wife of an admiral and really knows her history. The moral: Don't be afraid to ask for the free tour, which is available by request between 10 a.m. and 3 p.m. weekdays and from 11 a.m. to 1:30 p.m. weekends. Scheduled tours are also offered on weekends at 11:15 a.m. and 1 p.m. Call (202) 275-1738 for details.

14. Decatur House A half-hour tour of this Federalist home brings early Washington to life as the tour guide explains what life was like when Stephen Decatur lived here in 1819. Upstairs, visitors get a glimpse of how upper-crust Washington society, including President and Mrs. Kennedy, were entertained by later owners of the house.

15. Woodrow Wilson House A video narrated by Walter Cronkite primes you for a detailed tour of the house where President Wilson retired after leaving the White House. He was the only president to live in Washington after leaving office. The house preserves elements of Wilson's day-to-day life, including an ancient movie projector he used and his meticulously kept basement kitchen.

16. Cedar Hill The nineteenth-century home of abolitionist Frederick Douglass is a find. Our well-informed guide provided a detailed commentary on Douglass's life and times, including pointing out intimate details such as Douglass's barbells on the floor next to his bed. A late afternoon visit is almost like stepping back into the nineteenth century because the house is preserved as it was when Douglass died in 1895: There's no electricity, and the gathering shadows in the house evoke the past. Be sure to see "The Growlery," a small, one-room structure behind the main house Douglass declared off-limits to the household so that he could work alone.

17. The Franciscan Monastery The 45-minute tour includes a beautiful, recently restored church and replicas of shrines in the Holy Land. But the real treat is hair-raising stories of Christian martyrs told by your guide as you wind your way through a replica of Roman catacombs.

18. Mount Vernon Visitors can choose from a number of guided tours that give insight into life on an eighteenth-century plantation—including how the slaves owned by America's first president lived. Plus, the river vista has been preserved and visitors get a view that closely resembles the one George enjoyed more than 200 years ago. Not everyone who comes to Washington (the city) makes it to Mount Vernon, located 16 miles down the Potomac. But you should.

19. Gadsby's Tavern After seeing nothing but sumptuousness and 20-foot ceilings in Washington's magnificent edifices, it's a relief to make the short trek to Alexandria and see how average Americans lived and worked in the eighteenth century. The tour of this tavern gives a glimpse of how most people traveled, ate, and slept during the period when Alexandria was a major port—and Washington didn't exist.

20. FBI Headquarters This popular tour follows a rigid formula executed with military precision and features lots of static displays. But is it good? The young women leading the tour recited a series of canned presentations that sounded memorized. Most of the exhibits are inert displays of guns, drug paraphernalia, fingerprinting methods, and old "most wanted" posters. We suspect it's the demonstration of automatic weapons fire at the end of the tour—and the chance to hear a real FBI special agent talk and answer questions—that makes this tour so popular.

Taking an Orientation Tour

First-time visitors to Washington can't help but notice the regular procession of open-air, multicar tour buses—"motorized trolleys" is probably a more accurate term—that prowl the streets along the Mall, the major monuments, Arlington Cemetery, downtown, Georgetown, and Upper Northwest Washington. These regularly scheduled shuttle buses drop off and pick up paying customers along a route that includes the town's most popular attractions. Between stops, passengers listen to a tour guide talk about the city's monuments, museums, and famous buildings. The guides also suggest good places to eat and drop tidbits of interesting—and often humorous—Washington trivia. Our advice: If this is your first trip to Washington, take one of the tours early in your visit.

Here's why: Geographically, Washington is a spread-out city. Attempting to hoof it to Capitol Hill, the Washington Monument, and the Lincoln and Jefferson Memorials in one day amounts to cruel and unusual punishment to the body—especially your feet. Throw in a hot and humid Washington afternoon and a few cranky kids, and it's a recipe for vacation meltdown.

Think of the narrated shuttle-bus tours that cruise Washington as a special transportation system that not only gets you to the most popular sights, but also provides a timely education on the city's size and scope. The money you pay for your ticket allows unlimited reboarding privileges for that day, so you can get off at any scheduled stop and reboard a later bus (they run at 20- to 30-minute intervals).

The three guided tours that operate on a regular route in the city—Tourmobile, Old Town Trolley, and Gray Line's Li'l Red Trolley—are good values.

Tourmobile has the National Park Service franchise and shuttles its open-air, articulated buses to 18 sights around the Mall, Capitol Hill, and Arlington Cemetery from 9:30 a.m. to 4:30 p.m. For tour information, call (202) 554-5100. Ticket booths are located at Arlington Cemetery, the Lincoln Memorial, and the Washington Monument, but you can board at any red-and-white Tourmobile stop sign on the route and pay the driver ($18 adults, $8 children ages 3–11). The company also runs narrated tours to Mount Vernon (four hours; $25 adults, $12 for children ages 3 to 11; fee includes admission to the estate) and to the Frederick Douglass National Historical Site in Anacostia (two-and-a-half hours; $7 adults, $3.50 for children ages 3 to 11), mid-June through Labor Day and in February, Black History Month.

Old Town Trolley takes visitors to the Mall, downtown Washington, Dupont Circle, posh Northwest Washington, Embassy Row, and Georgetown. If you're staying at one of the following hotels, you can hop on board and be dropped at your door: Hyatt Regency, Grand Hyatt, Marriott Metro Center, J.W. Marriott, Hotel Washington, Capitol Hilton, Holiday Inn Capitol Hill, and the Washington Hilton. Tickets ($24 adults, $12 for children ages 4 to 12) can be purchased from the driver or at ticket booths located at most of the stops. The tours begin at 9 a.m. and run on the half-hour until 4:30 p.m. For more information, call (202) 832-9800.

Gray Line's Li'l Red Trolley features "hop on–hop off" service at the Mall, Capitol Hill, Chinatown, Dupont Circle, Adams-Morgan, Embassy Row, Georgetown, Foggy Bottom, Arlington Cemetery, and the Waterfront. The two-hour circuit operates on a half-hour schedule year-round; the fare is $28 for adults and $14 for children ages 3–11. Hotels on the 18-stop route include the Holiday Inn Capitol Hill, Willard Hotel, Mayflower Hotel, Washington Hilton, Marriott Wardman Park,

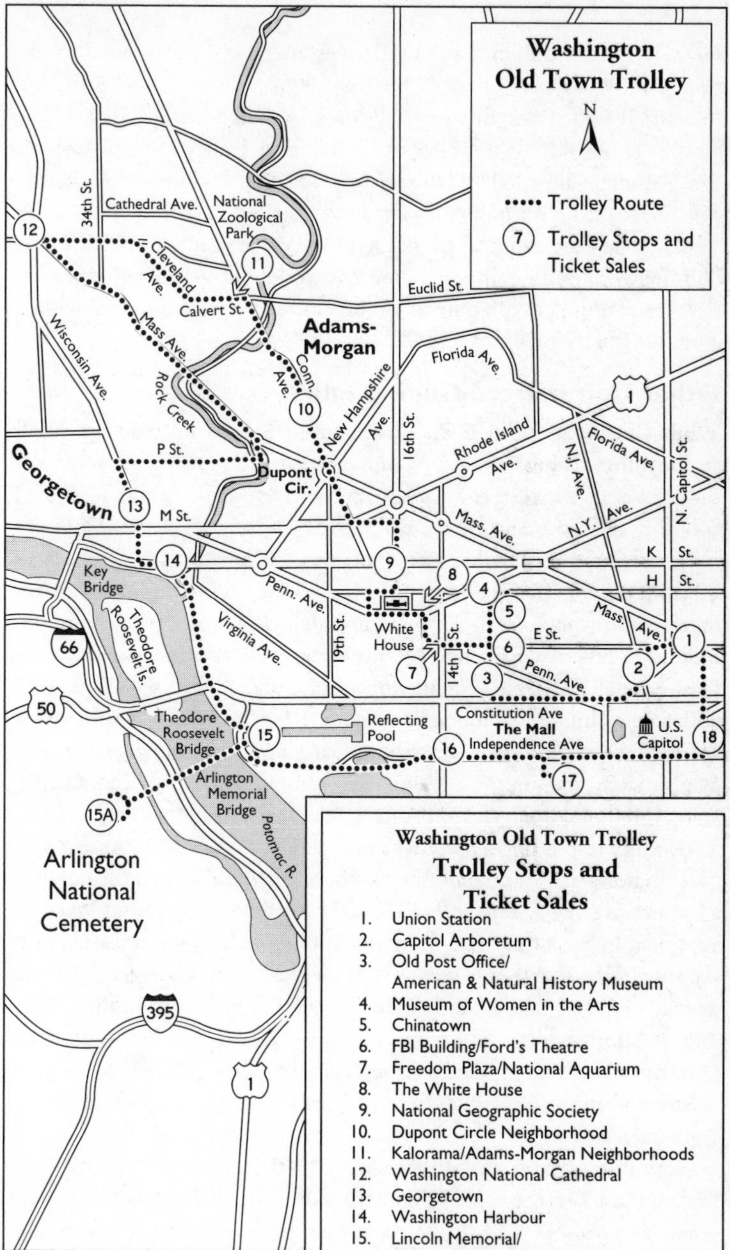

Washington Old Town Trolley

Trolley Stops and Ticket Sales

1. Union Station
2. Capitol Arboretum
3. Old Post Office/ American & Natural History Museum
4. Museum of Women in the Arts
5. Chinatown
6. FBI Building/Ford's Theatre
7. Freedom Plaza/National Aquarium
8. The White House
9. National Geographic Society
10. Dupont Circle Neighborhood
11. Kalorama/Adams-Morgan Neighborhoods
12. Washington National Cathedral
13. Georgetown
14. Washington Harbour
15. Lincoln Memorial/ Vietnam Veterans Memorial

15A. Arlington National Cemetery

16. Washington Monument/Holocaust Museum
17. Air & Space Museum/Smithsonian Mall
18. U.S. Capitol/Library of Congress

Holiday Inn on the Hill, and the Renaissance D.C. For more information, call (800) 862-1400 or (202) 289-1995.

Hint: If you didn't drive to Washington and don't have a car, take advantage of Old Town Trolley or the Li'l Red Trolley to visit Washington National Cathedral and Georgetown; neither is close to a Metro station, and getting off now can save on cab fare or shoe leather later. Old Town Trolley also offers a "Monuments by Moonlight" tour, which visits illuminated monuments and memorials while tour guides tell ghost stories. Tours begin at 7:30 p.m. at Union Station and last about two hours. The cost is $25 for adults and $13 for children ages 4 to 12.

Other Commercial Guided Tours

While Tourmobile, Old Town Trolley, and Li'l Red Trolley do a good job at shuttling visitors around Washington's major tourist attractions, a number of other local companies offer more specialized tours. Here's a run-down of some tours that are a little different.

Gray Line offers a wide variety of narrated bus tours in and around Washington. Half-day, all-day, and overnight tours take visitors to Washington's most popular sights, including the Mall museums, government buildings, Embassy Row, and Mount Vernon and Alexandria in Virginia. Gray Line also offers a "Washington After Dark" tour to see monuments and federal buildings flooded in lights, a black heritage tour, trips to Harpers Ferry and the Gettysburg battlefield, multilingual tours of Washington, and tours of Monticello and Williamsburg. Tours depart from Union Station; call (202) 289-1995 for more information.

Go amphibious on a **DC Ducks** tour. The narrated, 90-minute tour of Washington's sights and monuments features 30 minutes on the Potomac as you cruise in a restored 1942 DUKW, created during World War II to supply ships in areas that didn't have ports. The tour finishes up at Gravely Point, where it feels like you can almost touch the jets overhead as they land and take off at National Airport. The cost is $25 for adults and $13 for children 4–12. No reservations accepted; the tours leave Union Station hourly, March through late October.

Spirit Cruises, located at Pier 4, 6th and Water Streets, SW, takes visitors on boat tours of the Potomac River spring through fall. The star attraction is the half-day cruise to Mount Vernon, where the boat docks and you can tour the mansion and grounds. Call (202) 554-8000 or visit www.spiritcruises.com for information and rates on lunch, dinner, and moonlight dance party cruises aboard an air-conditioned luxury ship.

Odyssey III cruises the Potomac River year-round, offering Sunday jazz brunches, lunch and dinner cruises, and midnight cruises. Two-hour and three-hour trips feature live music, entrees and desserts prepared on board by a four-star chef, and views of Washington from outside decks and through the ship's glass ceilings. Prices range from $35 to $84 per person; prices for children under age 11 are half the adult rates for lunch cruises only. Jackets are recommended for gentlemen on dinner cruises. *Odyssey* departs from the Gangplank Marina, 6th and Water Streets, SW, near the Waterfront Metro station on the green line. For more information and reservations, call (800) 946-7245 or (202) 488-6000.

The Cruise Ship *Dandy* departs Old Town Alexandria for dinner cruises that feature after-dinner dancing. Sights along the way include the floodlit Capitol dome. Dinner cruises start at $67.50 per person. Call (703) 683-6076 for information and schedules, or visit their website at www.dandydinnerboat.com.

GNP's Scandal Tours will reinforce every evil thought you ever had about Washington and those who rule. It's a comedy review on wheels—not a sight-seeing tour—and makes stops at, predictably enough, the Watergate complex, the White House (where 494 of Bill Clinton's close personal friends spent the night in the Lincoln Bedroom), and the Tidal Basin, where a powerful member of Congress once went skinny-dipping with a stripper. Seventy-five-minute public tours depart Saturdays at 1 p.m., April through Labor Day, from 12th Street and Pennsylvania Avenue, NW. Tickets are $30 and reservations are required; call (202) 783-7212 for more information or check out the website at www.gnpcomedy.com. Private charters are available year-round.

Bike the Sites offers a new and calorie-burning way to see Washington, D.C.'s history and architecture: by bicycle. Two licensed guides lead daily tours averaging three hours. Bicycles, helmets, water, snacks, and all necessary equipment are provided on the rides. Tours include the Capital Sites Tour ($40) and the Mount Vernon Ride ($85). For more information, call (202) 966-8662, or visit www.bikethesites.com.

The Guide Service of Washington, the oldest and largest in D.C., offers private, customized VIP tours led by licensed guides. For foreign visitors, guides are available who speak your native tongue. Four-hour tours start at $155, plus transportation, regardless of the size of your group. Call (202) 628-2842 for more information.

Children's Concierge designs custom itineraries for families and provides interactive ways for kids to get involved in Washington's cultural and historical sights. This is not a tour service; for information and rates, call (301) 948-3312.

Optimum Adult Touring Plan

An Optimum Touring Plan in Washington, D.C., requires a thoughtful itinerary, a minimum of five days in town (i.e., not including travel time), a surprisingly modest amount of money (most attractions are free), and a comfortable pair of walking shoes. It also requires a fairly prodigious appetite for marble edifices, huge museums, and historical trivia. We will provide an itinerary; the rest is up to you.

With an Optimum Touring Plan, you can see the various attractions in and around Washington without facing huge crowds on the Mall, sitting in restaurants and shops that are jammed to capacity, or trudging through heat and humidity during sweltering afternoons.

Since an Optimum Touring Plan calls for seeing a lot of different parts of D.C., it makes for easier logistics if you stay at a hotel that's in the city and close to a Metro station. But even if your hotel is in the suburbs, you can still use the day-by-day plan as long as you can walk to the Metro. You'll lose some time commuting, but you may save some money on hotel rates. You'll lose even more time if you have to drive to a Metro station and park (see pages 167–168). Once you get in your car and start driving around in D.C., you're defeating the purpose of the Optimum Touring Plan, and you'll know it. We repeat: Don't drive in the city.

If you plan to visit Washington during the busiest months (see pages 34–36), you need to get up early to beat the crowds. Getting free "time tickets" for the Washington Monument and Bureau of Engraving and Printing is basically incompatible with sleeping in. If you want to sleep late and enjoy your touring experience, visit Washington in the fall or winter, when crowds are smaller. The Optimum Touring Plan assumes your visit is during the busy season.

We do not believe there is one ideal itinerary. Tastes, levels of energy, and basic perspectives on what is interesting or edifying vary. This understood, what follows is our personal version of an optimum Washington vacation week.

Before You Go

1. Write your congressperson as far in advance as possible for VIP tour reservations and a packet of free information on visiting Washington.
2. Determine which of the attractions that appeal to you require advance reservations, select one or two that most interest you, and make them for the afternoon of Day 3 at the same time you write your congressperson.
3. Read through all your information and make an informal list of sights that you and your family want to see during your Washington stay.
4. Break in a pair of thick-soled walking shoes.

On-Site

DAY 0

1. Arrive and get settled. Explore the features and amenities of your hotel.
2. If you get checked in by 3 p.m., go to the Mall and visit the Castle, the Smithsonian's visitor center. (If you're not within walking distance, this is an opportunity to get familiar with the Metro. Read our chapter on how it works and take the red line to the Smithsonian station.) Since crowds start to thin in the late afternoon, you may have time to duck into the National Air and Space Museum or the National Museum of Natural History after viewing the orientation film in the Castle.
3. Take the Metro to Dupont Circle for dinner at the Thai, Japanese, or Greek restaurant of your choice. When you get back to your hotel, check with the desk to find the nearest stop for boarding either the Li'l Red Trolley or Tourmobile sight-seeing tours. This will save you time in the morning.

DAY 1

1. After breakfast at your hotel, board one of the sight-seeing buses for an orientation tour of Washington. The driver sells tickets.
2. Stay on the bus for a complete circuit, which takes about an hour and a half (two hours for Li'l Red Trolley; Old Town Trolley tickets are only good for one complete tour). You'll gain a good overview of Washington's huge number of attractions, which will help you decide what sights you want to see this trip—and which ones can wait for another visit.
3. For lunch, get off the tour bus at Union Station, an architectural masterpiece, and head for the lower-level food court. Over lunch, decide what stops you want to make from the bus this afternoon.
4. Reboard your tour bus at Union Station. In deciding where to get off next, consider an attraction that's not convenient to your hotel. On Li'l Red Trolley, both Georgetown and Washington National Cathedral are good choices. On Tourmobile, consider the Arlington National Cemetery tour. Another hint: Some of the guides on the buses really know their stuff regarding sights, restaurants, and strategies on how to tour D.C. Ask them for suggestions. Tour until dinnertime.
5. Return to your hotel. For dinner, take a cab to Georgetown. After dinner, take in a stroll and some nightlife.

DAY 2

1. An early start: Get to the Mall by 7 a.m. and pick up "time tickets" to the White House, the Washington Monument, and the Bureau of Engraving and Printing.
2. After lunch, return to your hotel for a nap or a dip in the pool.
3. Around 3 p.m. take the Metro to Dupont Circle, where you can window-shop, stroll down Embassy Row, and stop in Anderson House, a sumptuous mansion and museum. Then have dinner in one of the many restaurants nearby.

DAY 3

1. Get in line for the FBI tour by 8 a.m. Then hit one of the popular Mall museums right away, before the crowds show up: Air and Space, American History, or Natural History.
2. After lunch, concentrate on some of the best art galleries in the world—the National Gallery of Art and the Hirshhorn Museum and Sculpture Garden. Or take the tour of the U.S. Department of State's Diplomatic Reception Rooms or one of the other reservation-only tours that you set up before the trip. If a few hours off your feet sounds attractive, consider taking in the five-story IMAX movie at the Air and Space Museum.
3. Take the Metro to Gallery Place for dinner in Chinatown. Then take the Metro to the Federal Triangle station and go to the Old Post Office Pavilion for dessert and a spectacular night view of Washington from the 315-foot-high clock tower. Afterwards, go to a jazz or blues club.

DAY 4

1. Sleep in from your night on the town. In the morning tour Capitol Hill: the U.S. Capitol (arrive at the kiosk by 7:15 a.m. to pick up tickets), the Supreme Court, and the Library of Congress. Eat lunch at a Capitol Hill cafe.
2. If it's a scorching summer day, consider one of these options after lunch: downtown's National Museum of American Art/National Portrait Gallery or the DAR Museum. Around 4 p.m., take the Metro to Woodley Park and walk or take a cab to the National Zoo. For dinner, pick from the many restaurants in Woodley Park. Hit the sack early: You'll be tired.

DAY 5

1. Either drive or take the 8:30 a.m. Gray Line bus or the 10 a.m. Tourmobile to Mount Vernon, George Washington's estate on the Potomac River. If you drive, leave before 7:30 a.m. or after 9:30 a.m. to avoid the worst rush-hour traffic.
2. Visit Old Town Alexandria for lunch and more eighteenth-century Americana. Stop in the Torpedo Factory to shop for unique arts and crafts.
3. If you're visiting in the summer, start your evening with a free military band concert. These are held on a rotating basis at 8 p.m. at either the U.S. Navy Memorial (Archives/Navy Memorial Metro), the steps of the U.S. Capitol (Capitol South Metro), or the Sylvan Theatre, located on the grounds of the Washington Monument (Smithsonian Metro). Afterwards, take the Metro to the Waterfront station and walk to a Maine Avenue seafood restaurant for dinner.

The Red Line Tour

When things are really hectic down on the Mall—we especially have in mind spring and summer weekends, when the crowds are at their worst—consider exploring a wide range of tourist attractions along the Metro's red line. You'll avoid the worst of the throngs packing the city, yet still see some of the best sights in Washington. Here's a list of sights you can see, station by station:

1. Union Station: Capital Children's Museum, National Postal Museum, U.S. Supreme Court, U.S. Capitol, Folger Shakespeare Library, Library of Congress
2. Judiciary Square: National Building Museum, National Law Enforcement Officers Memorial
3. Gallery Place/Chinatown: National Museum of American Art, National Portrait Gallery, Ford's Theatre, Chinatown
4. Metro Center: National Museum of Women in the Arts
5. Farragut North: National Geographic Society's Explorers Hall
6. Dupont Circle: Phillips Collection, Anderson House, Islamic Center, Woodrow Wilson House, Textile Museum
7. Woodley Park/Zoo or Cleveland Park: National Zoo, Washington National Cathedral (Both require some walking, however.)

Touring Strategies

Attractions Grouped by Metro Station

With the exception of the Red Line Tour, we don't recommend structuring your visit around attractions located near Metro stations. But we do think a list of tourist attractions located within walking distance of Metro stations can help make a last-minute touring selection to fill in part of a morning or afternoon—and maybe save you a buck or two in Metro fares. A warning: Although this list shows what attractions are closest to a Metro station, some sights could be as far as 20 minutes away by foot. An example: While the Foggy Bottom/GWU Metro is the closest to the Lincoln Memorial, it's still about a three-quarter-mile hike.

RED LINE

Brookland/CUA The National Shrine of the Immaculate Conception, the Franciscan Monastery (10- and 20-minute walks, respectively)

Union Station Capital Children's Museum, National Postal Museum, the U.S. Supreme Court, the U.S. Capitol, Senate office buildings, Folger Shakespeare Library

Judiciary Square National Building Museum, National Law Enforcement Officers Memorial, the Lillian and Albert Small Jewish Museum

Gallery Place/Chinatown National Portrait Gallery (currently closed for renovations), National Museum of American Art (currently closed for renovations), Chinatown, National Building Museum, Washington Convention Center, Ford's Theatre, the FBI

Metro Center National Museum of Women in the Arts, U.S. Department of the Treasury, the Washington Convention Center, the Shops at National Place

Farragut North Swank shops on Connecticut Avenue, National Geographic Society's Explorers Hall

Dupont Circle Shops and restaurants, Embassy Row, the Phillips Collection, Anderson House, the Islamic Center, Woodrow Wilson House, the Textile Museum, House of the Temple

Woodley Park/National Zoo National Zoo, Washington National Cathedral, Adams-Morgan (*Note:* The Zoo is about a 10-minute walk; Adams-Morgan is about 15 minutes away on foot; and the Cathedral is a half-hour stroll.)

Van Ness/UDC Intelsat, Hillwood Museum (20-minute walk)

BLUE AND ORANGE LINES

Capitol South Library of Congress, House office buildings, Capitol Hill restaurants, the U.S. Capitol, Folger Shakespeare Library, the U.S. Supreme Court

Federal Center, SW U.S. Botanic Garden, the National Air and Space Museum

L'Enfant Plaza Shops and restaurants, the National Air and Space Museum, the Hirshhorn Museum and Sculpture Garden, the Arts and Industries Building

Smithsonian The National Mall, the Freer and Sackler Galleries, the National Museum of African Art, the Bureau of Engraving and Printing, the National Museum of Natural History, the National Museum of American History, the Washington Monument, the Smithsonian Castle visitor center, the Tidal Basin, the Jefferson Memorial (20-minute walk), FDR Memorial (20-minute walk), the U.S. Holocaust Memorial Museum

Federal Triangle The Old Post Office Pavilion, the National Aquarium, the FBI, Pennsylvania Avenue, National Museum of American History, National Museum of Natural History, the White House Visitors Center, Visitor Information Center (in the Ronald Reagan Building)

McPherson Square The White House, the *Washington Post* building, Lafayette Park

Farragut West Decatur House, Renwick Gallery, the Old Executive Office Building, the White House, the Corcoran Gallery of Art, the DAR Museum, the Ellipse, the Octagon

Foggy Bottom/GWU The Kennedy Center, the U.S. Department of State's Diplomatic Reception Rooms, Vietnam Veterans Memorial, Korean War Veterans Memorial, the Reflecting Pool, the Lincoln Memorial, the FDR Memorial, Georgetown (20- to 30-minute walk)

Arlington National Cemetery Arlington National Cemetery, the Lincoln and FDR Memorials (across Memorial Bridge)

Pentagon The Pentagon (closed to visitors)

Reagan Washington National Airport Reagan Washington National Airport

King Street Old Town Alexandria (15-minute walk), shops and restaurants, the Torpedo Factory (20-minute walk), the George Washington National Masonic Memorial

YELLOW LINE

Gallery Place/Chinatown National Portrait Gallery (currently closed for renovations), National Museum of American Art (currently closed for renovations), Chinatown, National Building Museum, Washington Convention Center, Ford's Theatre, the FBI

Archives/Navy Memorial The National Archives, the U.S. Navy Memorial, the National Gallery of Art, the National Museum of Natural History

GREEN LINE

Waterfront Washington's Potomac River waterfront area (restaurants, marinas, and river cruises), Fort McNair, Arena Stage

Seeing Washington on a Tight Schedule

Many visitors do not have five days to devote to visiting Washington. They may be en route to other destinations, or may live within a day's drive, making later visits practical. Either way, efficient, time-effective touring is a must. Such visitors cannot afford long waits in line to see attractions or spend hours trying to find a place to park the family car.

Even the most efficient touring plan will not allow the visitor to visit the Mall, Capitol Hill, and Georgetown in one day, so plan on allocating at least an entire day to the Mall (but not just museums), and devoting your remaining days to other parts of Washington that appeal to you.

One-Day Touring

A comprehensive tour of Washington is literally impossible in a day. But a day trip to Washington can be a fun, rewarding experience. Pulling it off hinges on following some basic rules.

A. Determine in Advance What You Really Want to See

What are the categories that appeal to you most? If it's government, spend your day on Capitol Hill. If it's exploring museums, visit the Mall. If you like trendy shops and a sophisticated ambience, go to Georgetown or Dupont Circle.

B. Select an Area to Visit

For example, if visiting the U.S. Capitol is your goal, look at what other nearby attractions on Capitol Hill or the east end of the Mall interest you. That way you won't waste time and steps.

C. Arrive Early! Arrive Early! Arrive Early!

This is the single most important key to efficient touring and avoiding big crowds. First thing in the morning, lines are short at the Bureau of

Engraving and Printing and the Washington Monument's ticket kiosk. You can visit three famous Washington attractions in one or two hours that would take an entire afternoon if you arrived at noon. Eat breakfast before you arrive so you will not have to waste your prime touring time sitting in a crowded restaurant.

D. Avoid Bottlenecks

Helping you avoid bottlenecks and big crowds is what this guide is all about. Bottlenecks occur as a result of crowd concentrations in the absence of crowd management. Concentrations of hungry people create bottlenecks at restaurants during the lunch and dinner hours; concentrations of visitors heading toward the best known monuments, memorials, museums, and government buildings create elbow-to-elbow crowds during afternoons. Avoiding bottlenecks involves knowing when and where large concentrations of visitors begin to occur.

In addition, daytrippers need to avoid the agony of driving in D.C. traffic if they expect to have any fun and see enough Washington attractions to make the trip worthwhile. There are two ways to do it:

1. Park Your Car in the Suburbs In suburban Maryland and Virginia, the Metro extends to the Beltway and beyond, eliminating the need for you to battle Washington traffic, as well as saving you time, money, and stomach acid. On weekends, Metro users park for free at any suburban station. During the week, unless you arrive before 7 a.m., your choice of suburban Metro stations is limited to five: Vienna (on I-66 in Virginia, which fills by 8 a.m.); New Carrollton (on the Beltway in Maryland); Greenbelt (also on the Beltway in Maryland); Shady Grove (off I-270 in Maryland); and Silver Spring (inside the Beltway in Maryland). We recommend that you park at a Maryland station, unless you can make it to a Virginia station very early. From the outermost suburbs, it's about a 20-minute, stress-free train ride to the Mall.

New Carrollton has plenty of parking, plus a parking garage for overflow. Take Beltway Exit 19B (US 50 west) and follow the signs to the Metro. Go to the second parking lot, where you can park all day for $2.25 (free on weekends). If it's filled, park in the five-level garage for $7 all day. On weekdays, make sure to pick up a bus transfer in the station on your return trip to qualify for the low parking rate.

Greenbelt is an easy Metro station to reach for daytrippers from Baltimore and other points north. Take I-95 or the Baltimore-Washington Parkway south to the Capital Beltway, go south about two miles and get off at Exit 24, which goes to the Greenbelt Metro station. All-day parking is $1.75 during the week, free on weekends. Take the train to the Fort Totten station (which is temporarily the end of the line) and transfer to the red line train to Shady Grove, which takes you downtown.

Shady Grove also has plenty of parking for daytrippers. From I-270 near Gaithersburg, take Exit 9 (marked "Sam Eig Highway/Metro Station") to I-370 East, which takes you directly to the station. Metro parking is $1 for the day (free on weekends); if the Metro lots are filled, park in the nearby garage for $2.50.

Silver Spring is a somewhat less convenient option for daytrippers because it means a short drive inside the Beltway. But there's plenty of commercial parking close by. Take US 29/Colesville Road south from the Beltway and turn left onto Georgia Avenue in downtown Silver Spring; follow the signs to the Metro, loop past it, and park in one of the big parking garages. Parking is around $6 for the day.

2. Take the Train Taking the train to Washington is a snap for day visitors who live along the Eastern Seaboard from Richmond to Philadelphia. Amtrak, Maryland commuter (MARC), and Virginia Railway Express trains arrive at gleaming Union Station, located on the Metro's red line. You can be on the Mall minutes after getting off your train. From Union Station, visitors are only a few blocks' walk from the U.S. Capitol, the U.S. Supreme Court, the Library of Congress, the Folger Shakespeare Library, and the newest Smithsonian facility, the National Postal Museum.

From Virginia, Virginia Railway Express operates two commuter lines connecting Fredericksburg (to the south) and Manassas (to the west) with Union Station in downtown Washington. The 18-station system offers inbound service in the mornings and outbound service in the afternoons, Monday through Friday. For more information, call (703) 684-1001 or (800) RIDE VRE (743-3873) or visit www.vre.org.

MARC train service operates three lines connecting Washington with the Maryland suburbs: one to BWI airport, another to downtown Baltimore, and the third goes northwest along the Potomac River into western Maryland. For information and schedules for Amtrak, the national passenger train service, call (800) 872-7245 or visit www.amtrak.com. For express Metroliner information, call (800) 523-8720. By the way, Amtrak also provides weekend and holiday service along several of the lines used by MARC and Virginia Railway Express (but at a higher cost than the commuter services).

Excursions beyond the Beltway

If you've got the time or if your visit to Washington is a repeat trip, consider exploring some places outside the city. From the mountains to the west and the Chesapeake Bay to the east, there's plenty to see. Furthermore, a look at something that's not made of marble or granite can be a welcome relief to eyes wearied by the constant onslaught of Washington edifices and office buildings. Here are a few suggestions for day trips that Washington visitors can make beyond the Beltway.

Annapolis

Maryland's capital for more than 300 years, Annapolis is more than a quaint little town on the Chesapeake Bay—it's one of the biggest yachting centers in the United States. Acres and acres of sailboats fill its marinas. A steady parade of sailboats moves past the City Dock during the sailing season, April through late fall. You'll see oyster and crab boats that work the bay, in addition to pleasure boats, cruise ships, and old sailing ships.

Annapolis has been discovered and is now a major bedroom community for well-off Washingtonians. The town boasts fine restaurants, fancy shops, bars, and jazz clubs. On weekends during the summer, Annapolis is packed with visitors. The town is about a one-hour drive from Washington on US 50.

Baltimore

Steamed crabs, H. L. Mencken, the Orioles, and the National Aquarium are just a few of the reasons Washingtonians trek north one hour on a regular basis to this industrial city on the Chesapeake Bay. Washington's visitors have good reason to detour and discover the charms of Baltimore.

Daytrippers can explore the Inner Harbor, dominated by a bilevel shopping mall that's heavy on restaurants and boutiques. The National Aquarium features a tropical rain forest and a sea mammal pavilion—and it's a much larger attraction than the National Aquarium in Washington. Kids will love the Maryland Science Center and nearby Fort McHenry, where Francis Scott Key wrote the national anthem from a ship anchored offshore. If you've got the time, explore some other Baltimore attractions: the B&O Railroad Museum, the Edgar Allan Poe House, and the Babe Ruth House.

Shenandoah National Park

Although it makes for a long day, a drive to Shenandoah National Park in Virginia is a treat for outdoors-lovers, featuring some of the prettiest mountain scenery in the eastern United States. A drive along a portion of the 105-mile-long Skyline Drive takes visitors to a nearly endless series of mountain overlooks where you can get out of the car and walk on well-maintained trails. In early June, the mountain laurel blooms in the higher elevations, and in the fall, it's bumper-to-bumper as hordes of Washingtonians rush to see the magnificent fall foliage. It's about a two-hour drive from Washington, one-way.

Harpers Ferry National Historical Park

This restored nineteenth-century town at the confluence of the Shenandoah and the Potomac Rivers in West Virginia offers visitors history and natural beauty in equal doses. At the park's visitor center you can see a film about radical abolitionist John Brown's 1859 raid on a U.S. armory here, an event that was a precursor to the Civil War. Then you can tour a renovated blacksmith's shop, ready-made clothing store, and general store. A short hike to Jefferson Rock is rewarded with a spectacular mountain view of three states (Maryland, Virginia, and West Virginia) and two rivers (the Potomac and the Shenandoah). Thomas Jefferson said the view was "worth a voyage across the Atlantic." Luckily, the trip by car from Washington is only about 90 minutes.

A Tour of Civil War Battlefields

From the number of battlefield sites there, it would seem that the entire Civil War was fought in nearby Virginia, Maryland, and Pennsylvania—which is nearly the truth. Visitors with an interest in history and beautiful countryside can tour a number of Civil War sites within a day's drive of Washington.

Gettysburg, where the Union turned the tide against the South, is about two hours north of D.C. While the overdeveloped town is a testament to tourist schlock gone wild, the National Battlefield Park features a museum, a tower that gives sight-seers an aerial view of the battlefield, and many acres of rolling countryside dotted with monuments, memorials, and stone fences. It's a popular tourist destination and worth the drive.

The first battle of the Civil War took place at Bull Run near Manassas, on the fringe of today's Virginia suburbs. The **Manassas National Battlefield Park** features a visitor center, a museum, and miles of trails on the grounds.

The Confederate victory set the stage for the next major battle, at Antietam, across the Potomac River in Maryland. **Antietam National Battlefield,** near Sharpsburg, is the site of the bloodiest day of the Civil War: On September 17, 1862, there were 12,410 Union and 10,700 Confederate casualties in General Robert E. Lee's failed attempt to penetrate the North. The battlefield, about a 90-minute drive from Washington, is 15 miles west of Frederick, Maryland.

A number of later Union campaigns are commemorated at Fredericksburg and **Spotsylvania National Military Park** in Virginia, halfway between Washington and Richmond. Included in the park are the battlefields of Fredericksburg, Chancellorsville, the Wilderness, and Spotsylvania. The park is about an hour's drive south of D.C.

Helpful Hints

A Worst-Case Touring Scenario

Here's how *not* to visit Washington: On a weekday, load the kids in the family car, and arrive around 8 a.m.—the worst part of rush hour. Then battle your way downtown through bumper-to-bumper traffic, arriving at the Mall about 9:30, your nerves thoroughly frayed. Waste a half-hour looking for a parking space before giving up and shelling out $12 for a space in a parking garage. Next, troop over to the Washington Monument, where a sign in the window of the time-ticket kiosk informs you that the day's allotment of tickets has already been given out. Then go to the National Air and Space Museum, where it's packed shoulder-to-shoulder around the most popular exhibits.

Later, at the National Museum of Natural History, little Jimmy disappears into the bowels of the paleontological exhibits, and since you didn't agree on a designated meeting place, it takes 45 minutes to track him down. At 5 p.m., you and your family stagger back to the car, just in time to join the afternoon rush hour.

Amazingly, people do this all the time. But it doesn't have to be this way. Instead of hitting Beltway traffic at 8 a.m., leave a half-hour earlier and go to any suburban Metro station and park. Then it's a 20-minute trip by train downtown. You can be at the Washington Monument by 8 a.m. and pick up a time ticket while the line is short. Then pick up tickets for a tour of the Bureau of Engraving and Printing later in the morning at the ticket booth on Raoul Wallenberg Place. Next, visit the National Air and Space Museum.

After watching money being printed, eat lunch at the Old Post Office Pavilion, then take the Metro to Dupont Circle. There, you can visit the Phillips Collection, a really classy art gallery, and tour Anderson House, a sumptuous mansion. Next, go to the National Zoo in the late afternoon or early evening, when the temperature begins to drop and the animals get more active. Eat dinner at a restaurant near the Woodley Park Metro on Connecticut Avenue and then take the Metro back to your car.

The second scenario takes advantage of two things: an early start and no time wasted in traffic or searching for a parking space. It lets you visit at a leisurely pace and gives you the freedom to explore out-of-the-way and unusual sights you normally wouldn't take the time to see. It's the smart way to visit Washington.

Travel Tips for Tourists

The idea behind visiting any major tourist attraction is to have fun, and you can't do that if you're getting fatigued or crabby. Here are some touring tips you should review before your visit. They're really no more than commonsense rules for any type of outing:

1. *Drink Water.* You'll need to drink plenty, especially on hot, humid, sunny Washington afternoons. Dehydration can sneak up on you and cause physical problems which might ruin your vacation plans. So don't hesitate to drink more water than you think you'll need.
2. *Avoid Sunburn.* Protect sun-sensitive areas of your body. Shade your head and eyes with a hat. Wear sunglasses. Treat exposed skin with a sunscreen lotion—especially your face. And if you're wearing sandals, don't forget your feet. You don't have to go to the beach to get a really nasty burn on the tops of your feet!
3. *Pace Yourself.* Washington is filled with good places to sit in the shade and rest, and people-watching is part of the fun. Hunger, overheating, tension from fighting the crowds for hours, fatigue —each of these realities of touring and all of them together can combine to produce fussy kids and grumpy adults. You'll notice if someone else in your party is getting unpleasant to be around, but you may not recognize the symptoms in yourself unless you periodically make an effort to run a little self-check and think about your behavior. If you and your party can't salvage things with a rest and a food break, cut your day short and go back to your hotel for a swim, a nap—or a drink in the bar. Visiting Washington is not meant to be a test of your temper and patience, after all. You're here to have fun.
4. *Wear Comfortable Clothes.* This especially goes for shoes—shoes that cushion, shoes that are broken in, shoes that won't make your feet too hot. Wear clothing that protects you from the sun and permits the air to circulate around your skin and doesn't bind or chafe.
5. *Food Strategies.* Keep on good terms with your stomach, but don't let it dictate your trip. Eat a good breakfast before you set out for the day, then snack a lot while touring. Avoid lunch lines, especially those at overpriced museum cafeterias.
6. *Traveling with Teens.* Do yourself and them a favor: Send them off on their own for at least part of a day during your D.C. visit. Arrange to meet them at a specific time and place, and elicit a very firm and definite understanding about this meeting time and place. Give them a watch if they don't have one, a map, and the hotel number for emergencies.

Getting Touring Information When in Washington

In fall 1998, a new Visitor Information Center opened in the Ronald Reagan Building and International Trade Center at 1300 Pennsylvania Avenue, NW. It's the place to go for up-to-date information on attractions, hotels, restaurants, shops, cultural venues, and tourist services. The center is staffed by knowledgeable personnel and is stocked with free brochures and maps. Also on-hand are interactive information kiosks, and visitors can make hotel and restaurant reservations, as well as purchase souvenirs.

The 3,200-square-foot center is located on street level at the Wilson Plaza entrance of the Ronald Reagan Building, across the street from the Federal Triangle Metro station. This newest of huge federal buildings (no jokes, please, about the name) offers an extensive food court, public phones, and rest rooms, and is centrally located between the Mall and downtown. Hours of operation for the Visitor Information Center are Monday through Saturday, 8 a.m.–6 p.m. The phone number is (202) DC VISIT.

Designated Meeting Places

Families and groups touring together should designate a meeting spot in case members get separated. On the Mall, good places to link up are in front of the Castle (the Smithsonian visitor center) or in front of the domed National Museum of Natural History. The information desks located in most main museum lobbies are logical meeting places if the group separates. Downtown, it's easy to lose your sense of direction due to a scarcity of landmarks. A good designated meeting place would be a hotel lobby, a department store entrance, or a Metro station.

A Money-Saving Tip for Lunch

Where *not* to have lunch: The sidewalk food vendors on the Mall, the kiosk in front of the National Museum of Natural History, and the small restaurant down the hill from the Washington Monument charge about a dollar more for a hot dog than the street vendors you see everywhere off the Mall. Unless you're dying of hunger, walk to either Constitution or Independence Avenue, find a street vendor, and save yourself some dough. The hot dogs, by the way, are pretty good.

Where's the Smithsonian?

It's a common question fielded by the folks who staff the information desk in the Castle, the main visitor center for the Smithsonian Institution. The query is posed by first-time visitors who have the mistaken notion that the renowned museum complex is located in one building somewhere along the Mall. In reality, the Smithsonian is a complex of 14 museums and a world-class zoo, scattered around the city. In 2004, the Smithsonian's newest museum, the $110 million National Museum of the American Indian, will open on the Mall. In addition, the Institution operates the Cooper-Hewitt National Design Museum and the National Museum of the American Indian, both located in New York City. (Some folks are also surprised when they learn that the National Gallery of Art and the Holocaust Memorial Museum are not part of the Smithsonian complex.) In the list below is an alphabetical rundown of the Smithsonian's Washington facilities by location.

THE SMITHSONIAN'S FACILITIES

The Mall

- African Art Museum Air and Space Museum
- American History Museum
- Arts and Industries Building
- Hirshhorn Museum and Sculpture Garden
- Natural History Museum
- Postal Museum
- Sackler Gallery
- Smithsonian Institution Building Information Center

Downtown

- American Art Museum
- National Portrait Gallery
- Renwick Gallery

Upper Northwest

- National Zoo

Get Off the Mall!

A full day of traipsing from museum to museum along the Mall is exhausting and, for most folks, a pretty one-dimensional experience. After a while it starts to feel like a grade-school field trip—and, later, there's going to be a quiz. Is that a vacation? Snap out of it by breaking up the day and taking the Metro to any number of other fascinating destinations, including Dupont Circle, the waterfront, and the National Zoo. Or grab a cab and visit Georgetown, Adams-Morgan, or the Washington National Cathedral.

A Photography Tip

Washington, D.C., with its impressive memorials and federal buildings, is a photographer's mecca. But for a really spectacular shot of downtown Washington, go across the Potomac River to the Iwo Jima Memorial in Arlington, Virginia. Stand on the hill near the Netherlands Carillon and look toward the Lincoln Memorial. At dawn, the sun rises almost directly behind the U.S. Capitol. At dusk, the panorama of twinkling lights includes the Jefferson and Lincoln Memorials, the Washington Monument, and, more than two miles away, the U.S. Capitol.

How to Sneak on a Reservation-Only Tour at the National Archives

For the behind-the-scenes tour of the National Archives, most people call weeks in advance for reservations. If you didn't, however, take a chance and show up at the Pennsylvania Avenue entrance (across from 8th Street) at tour time. If there's a cancellation or a no-show, you're in. The free reserved tours begin at 10:15 a.m. and 1:15 p.m. daily and last about an hour and a half. On the reserved tour, you'll explore the building, including book stacks, the microfilm viewing rooms, and the exhibits and models that show how researchers preserve documents. The tour ends in the magnificent Rotunda, where the great documents are on display. (The building closed in July 2001 for two years of renovations.) For more information, call (202) 501-5205.

Getting a Free Pass to a National Gallery of Art Show

Most people call or stop by weeks in advance to get free "time tickets" that admit them to the wildly popular art exhibits regularly held in the National Gallery of Art's East Building. What most of them don't know is that hundreds of tickets per half-hour are reserved for folks like you. Tickets can be picked up any day a show is in progress. Just show up by noon on weekends or by 2 p.m. on weekdays at the ticket counter in the main lobby and come back later in the day to see the show.

An Informal Georgetown Tour of JFK Residences

Structure an informal walking tour around Georgetown by viewing—from the outside only, please—a few places where a great American statesman once lived. As a congressman and senator, John F. Kennedy lived in four different houses in Georgetown: 1528 31st Street, NW; 1400 34th Street, NW; 3271 P Street, NW; and 3307 N Street, NW. The last address is where the Kennedys lived just before moving to 1600 Pennsylvania Avenue, NW. For more information, call (301) 588-8999.

D.C. on the Air

Aside from the usual babble of format rock, talk, easy listening, and country music radio stations, Washington is home to a few radio stations that really stand out for high-quality broadcasting. Tune in to what hip Washingtonians listen to, as listed below:

Format	Frequency	Station
All news	1500	WTOP-AM
Bluegrass, folk, talk	88.5	WAMU-FM
Classical	570/103.5	WGMS-AM/FM
Classical, NPR	91	WETA-FM
Jazz	89.3	WPFW-FM

Format	Frequency	Station
Progressive rock	99.1	WHFS-FM
Progressive rock	103.1	WRNR-FM

How to Tell If the President Is Home

A flag flies over the White House when the president is in Washington. At night, one of the facades on the White House stays lit for the benefit of trench coat–clad TV news reporters who intone to the camera, "Live, from the White House . . ."

How to Tell If the House or Senate Is in Session

Look for a flag flying over the respective chamber of the U.S. Capitol to determine which, if either, house of Congress is in session. From the Mall, the Senate is to the left of the dome; the House of Representatives is on the right. At night, a light burns on top of the Capitol dome if Congress is in session.

Avoiding the Heat on a Sweltering Afternoon

On hot, humid D.C. afternoons, it's imperative to avoid long walks between sights; in fact, you shouldn't leave an air-conditioned building at all, if you can help it. On the Mall, one solution to touring on a hot day is to visit this trio of museums: the National Museum of African Art, the Arthur M. Sackler Gallery, and the Freer Gallery. The first two museums are built underground, so they're probably cool even during a power failure (dark, too). The three museums are connected by tunnels, eliminating the need to venture outside.

More good choices that will reduce the possibility of heat stroke include the Corcoran Gallery of Art, the Phillips Collection, and the National Gallery of Art. Another strategy is to visit museums next to each other (say, the National Museum of Natural History and the National Museum of American History). And don't plan any ambitious treks like a walk to the Jefferson Memorial from the Capitol, or from one end of the Mall to the other, when it's scorchingly hot outside.

D.C. after Dark

Touring Washington's monuments and memorials after dark offers dramatic views of both famous marble edifices and Washington itself. At night, the Jefferson and Lincoln Memorials float in pools of light; from the steps of the Lincoln Memorial, the Eternal Flame at the John F. Kennedy gravesite shimmers across the river in Arlington National Cemetery. The scene at the Vietnam Veterans Memorial is a moving experience as people hold flickering matches up to the reflective black marble surface, searching for names.

Capitol Hill: A Family Affair

Rather than just getting in line to tour the U.S. Capitol, give yourself and your kids a real civics lesson you'll all remember: Visit your congressperson or senator.

"Go to your member's office and get a pass to see the House and Senate in session," suggests one of the Capitol guards. "It's a real experience—and the kids will love it. And while you're there, ask for a special tour of the Capitol given by a member's staff person." House office buildings are across Independence Avenue from the Capitol building; Senate office buildings are across Constitution Avenue. Offices are open weekdays during normal business hours, and you don't need an appointment. If you don't know the name of your representative, go to either one of your senators' offices.

Where the Real Work of Congress Is Done

Most visitors who obtain gallery passes to the House or Senate in session are mildly disappointed: The scene is usually one member giving a speech to a nearly empty chamber, unless you happen to stumble in during a vote. Everyone else is at committee meetings, where the real work is done. Check the *Washington Post* "A" section for a list of legislative hearings open to the public, along with their time and location (always in one of the buildings near the Capitol).

Another Photo Tip

Across from the Mall near the Lincoln Memorial is the stately National Academy of Sciences on Constitution Avenue. Outside, Albert Einstein's statue is waiting for you to crawl into its lap so you can have your picture taken; it's a D.C. tradition.

Speeding through the Ubiquitous Metal Detectors

Walk-through metal detectors staffed by no-nonsense guards are standard equipment in virtually every federal building in Washington, including the U.S. Capitol, the Supreme Court, all Senate and House office buildings, and the National Archives. Men: To speed your way through, you should get in the habit of carrying all your change and keys in one place. When your turn comes to pass through the metal detector, dump it all into one of the bowls provided, and you'll avoid the tedious drill of passing through the door-sized detector a half-dozen times. (You'll also find out which metal-buckled belt not to wear when visiting government buildings.) Women have it easier: Just place your purse on the conveyor that shoots it through the X-ray machine, then walk through the detector.

Part Seven

Washington's Attractions

Where to Go

Visitors come to Washington from all over the world—and for a lot of different reasons. Some want to see how the U.S. government works (or, as some cynics say, *doesn't* work); others want to see the places where history happened; and many are drawn by the city's magnificent monuments and museums.

It's tough for a guidebook to decree to such a diverse group where they should spend their time. Is the National Gallery of Art better than the Air and Space Museum? The answer is yes—if your interests and tastes range more toward Van Gogh than von Braun.

Because we can't read your mind and tell *you* the top places you should visit on your trip to Washington, we'll do the next best thing: give you enough information so that you can quickly choose the places you want to see—with enough detail that you can plan your visit logically—without spending a lot of time (and energy) retracing your steps and standing in line.

Armed with enough information to make informed choices about how to spend your valuable time, you can avoid a common mistake a lot of visitors to D.C. make: hitting the Mall for a death march through a blur of Smithsonian museums, federal buildings, and monuments.

Time-Saving Charts

Because of the wide range of attractions in and around Washington—from a 500-foot marble obelisk on the Mall to collections of modern art—we've provided the following charts to help you prioritize your touring at a glance. In the first, you'll find attractions listed by type, allowing you to locate a particular attraction easily even if you don't know its location. In the second, attractions are listed by zone, allowing you to plan efficient touring in a given area. In each you'll find an authors' rating from one star (skip it) to five stars (not to be missed), and a brief description of the attraction. (Some like the Smithsonian's Anacostia Museum and Arts and Industries Building—which don't have permanent collections—weren't rated because exhibits change.) A few of the attractions require advance reservations. Each attraction is individually profiled later in this section.

ATTRACTIONS BY TYPE

Attraction	Description	Zone	Rating
Cemeteries			
Arlington National Cemetery	largest U.S. military cemetery	1	★★★★
Churches/Houses of Worship			
Basilica of the Shrine of the Immaculate Conception	largest Catholic church in U.S.	8	★
Franciscan Monastery	restored church, catacombs, garden	8	★★
Islamic Center	exotic mosque	6	★½
Washington National Cathedral	6th largest cathedral in the world	7	★★★★★
Government Buildings Open for Tours			
Bureau of Engraving and Printing	where U.S. dollars, stamps get printed	1	★★
FBI	tour of G-men headquarters	3	★½
U.S. Capitol	where Congress meets	2	★★★★½
U.S. State Department Diplomatic Reception Rooms	decorative arts; reservation-only	4	★★★★★
U.S. Supreme Court	nation's highest court	2	★★★★
Voice of America	radio studios	1	★★½
Washington Navy Yard	3 military museums and U.S. Navy destroyer; reservations only	9	★★½
Historic Buildings and Homes			
Christian Heurich House Mansion	lavish Guilded Age home	6	★★★
Decatur House	early D.C. residence near White House	1	★★½
Ford's Theatre/ Petersen House	where Lincoln was assassinated and died	3	★★½
Frederick Douglass National Historic Site	preserved Victorian mansion	9	★★★½

ATTRACTIONS BY TYPE *(continued)*

Attraction	Description	Zone	Rating
Historic Buildings and Homes (continued)			
House of the Temple	Masonic temple modeled on an ancient wonder	6	★
Meridian International Center	two mansions, galleries, gardens	6	★★½
Mount Vernon	George Washington's river plantation	11	★★★★★
The Octagon	early D.C. home and museum	1	★★½
Old Town Alexandria	restored colonial port town	11	★★★★
Society of the Cincinnati	lavish mansion and Revolutionary War museum	6	★★★★
Union Station	beaux-arts palace, food court, shopping mall	2	★★★½
Woodrow Wilson House	final home of 28th president	6	★★★½
Libraries			
Folger Shakespeare Library	Bard museum and theater	2	★★
Library of Congress	world's largest library	2	★★★★
Monuments and Memorials			
Jefferson Memorial	classical-style monument on Tidal Basin	1	★★½
Lincoln Memorial	memorial to 16th president on Reflecting Pool	1	★★★
Old Post Office Tower	a great view and a food court	1	★★★½
Roosevelt Memorial	open-air memorial to FDR	1	★★★½
Vietnam Veterans Memorial	U.S. soldier memorial on the Mall	1	★★★½
Washington Monument	500-foot memorial to first U.S. president	1	★★½
Museums and Galleries			
Anacostia Museum	African-American history and culture	9	N/A
Arts and Industries Building	changing special exhibitions	1	N/A
B'nai B'rith Klutznick Museum	Jewish folk and ceremonial art	3	★★½

ATTRACTIONS BY TYPE *(continued)*			
Attraction	**Description**	**Zone**	**Rating**
Museums and Galleries (continued)			
Capitol Children's Museum	touchy-feely for kids	2	★½
Corcoran Gallery of Art	modern and classical art and antiques	1	★★½
DAR Museum	decorative U.S. arts and antiques	1	★★★½
Freer Gallery of Art and Printing	Asian and American art	1	★★★★
Hillwood Museum	mansion with fabulous art treasures	7	★★★★½
Hirshhorn Museum	modern art	1	★★★★★
International Spy Museum	spook exhibits	3	★½
NASA/Godard Space Flight Center	space flight museum	10	★★½
National Air and Space Museum	chronicles manned flight	1	★★★★★
National Aquarium	fish tanks in a basement	1	★½
National Building Museum	architectural marvel and exhibits	3	★★★½
National Cryptologic Museum	NSA spook museum	10	★
National Gallery of Art –East	20th-century art	1	★★★★★
National Gallery of Art –West	Euro and American classical art	1	★★★★★
National Geographic Society	high-tech exhibition for kids	3	★★
National Museum of African Art	traditional arts of Africa	1	★★
National Museum of American History	historical and social collections	1	★★★★★
National Museum of Health and Medicine	medical museum	7	★★
National Museum of Natural History	treasure chest of natural sciences	1	★★★★½
National Museum of Women in the Arts	modern and classical art by women	3	★★★½
National Postal Museum	philately and exhibits	2	★★★
Phillips Collection	first U.S. modern art museum	6	★★★★
Renwick Gallery	American crafts and decorative arts	1	★★

ATTRACTIONS BY TYPE *(continued)*

Attraction	Description	Zone	Rating
Museums and Galleries (continued)			
Sackler Gallery	Asian art	1	★★½-
Smithsonian Building (The Castle)	museum information and display	1	★★★★
Textile Museum	textile arts	6	★★
U.S. Department of Interior	old-fashioned museum of parks, outdoors	4	★
U.S. Holocaust Memorial Museum	graphic memorial to WWII holocaust	1	★★½
Parks, Gardens, and Zoos			
Dumbarton Oaks and Gardens	mansion/museum and a beautiful garden	5	★★★★
Kenilworth Aquatic Gardens	national park for water plants	9	★★★
National Wildlife Visitor Center	museum on 13,000-acre wildlife refuge	10	★★½
National Zoological Park	world-class zoo in a wooded setting	7	★★★★½
U.S. Botanic Garden	huge greenhouse and living museum on Mall	2	★★★
U.S. National Arboretum	444-acre collection of trees, flowers, herbs	8	★★½
Theaters/Performances			
JFK Center for Performing Arts	stunning performing arts center on Potomac	4	★★

ATTRACTIONS BY ZONE

Attraction	Description	Rating
Zone 1 The Mall		
Arlington National Cemetery	largest U.S. military cemetery	★★★★
Arts and Industries Building	changing special exhibitions	N/A
Bureau of Engraving and Printing	where U.S. dollars, stamps get printed	★★
Corcoran Gallery of Art	modern and classical art and antiques	★★½
DAR Museum	decorative U.S. arts and antiques	★★★½
Decatur House	early D.C. residence near White House	★★½
Freer Gallery of Art and Printing	Asian and American art	★★★★
Hirshhorn Museum	modern art	★★★★★
Jefferson Memorial	classical-style monument on Tidal Basin	★★½
Lincoln Memorial	memorial to 16th president on Reflecting Pool	★★★
National Air and Space Museum	chronicles manned flight	★★★★★
National Aquarium	fish tanks in a basement	★½
National Gallery of Art-East	20th-century art	★★★★★
National Gallery of Art-West	Euro and American classical art	★★★★★
National Museum of African Art	traditional arts of Africa	★★
National Museum of American History	historical and social collections	★★★★★
National Museum of Natural History	treasure chest of natural sciences	★★★★½
The Octagon	early D.C. home and museum	★★½
Old Post Office Tower	a great view and a food court	★★★½
Renwick Gallery	American crafts and decorative arts	★★
Roosevelt Memorial	open-air memorial to FDR	★★★½
Sackler Gallery	Asian art	★★½
Smithsonian Building (The Castle)	museum information and display	★★★★

ATTRACTIONS BY ZONE *(continued)*

ATTRACTION	DESCRIPTION	RATING
Zone 1 The Mall (continued)		
U.S. Holocaust Memorial Museum	graphic memorial to WWII holocaust	★★½
Vietnam Veterans Memorial	U.S. soldier memorial on the Mall	★★★½
Voice of America	radio studios	★★½
Washington Monument	500-foot memorial to first U.S. president	★★½
Zone 2 Capitol Hill		
Capitol Children's Museum	touchy-feely for kids	★½
Folger Shakespeare Library	Bard museum and theater	★★
Library of Congress	world's largest library	★★★★
National Postal Museum	philately and exhibits	★★★
U.S. Botanic Garden	huge greenhouse and living museum on Mall	★★★
U.S. Supreme Court	nation's highest court	★★★★
Union Station	beaux-arts palace, food court, shopping mall	★★★½
U.S. Capitol	where Congress meets	★★★★½
Zone 3 Downtown		
B'nai B'rith Klutznick Museum	Jewish folk and ceremonial art	★★½
FBI	tour of G-men headquarters	★½
Ford's Theatre/ Petersen House	where Lincoln was assassinated and died	★★½
International Spy Museum	spook exhibits	★½
National Building Museum	architectural marvel and exhibits	★★★½
National Geographic Society	high-tech exhibition for kids	★★
National Museum of Women in the Arts	modern and classical art by women	★★★½
Zone 4 Foggy Bottom		
JFK Center for Performing Arts	stunning performing arts center on Potomac	★★
U.S. Department of Interior	old-fashioned museum of parks, outdoors	★

ATTRACTIONS BY ZONE *(continued)*		
ATTRACTION	**DESCRIPTION**	**RATING**
Zone 4 Foggy Bottom (continued)		
U.S. State Department Diplomatic Reception Rooms	decorative arts; reservation-only	★★★★★
Zone 5 Georgetown		
Dumbarton Oaks and Gardens	mansion/museum and a beautiful garden	★★★★
Zone 6 Dupont Circle/Adams–Morgan		
Christian Heurich House Mansion	lavish Guilded Age home	★★★
House of the Temple	Masonic temple modeled on an ancient wonder	★
Islamic Center	exotic mosque	★½
Meridian International Center	two mansions, galleries, gardens	★★½
Phillips Collection	first U.S. modern art museum	★★★★
Society of the Cincinnati	lavish mansion and Revolutionary War museum	★★★★
Textile Museum	textile arts	★★
Woodrow Wilson House	final home of 28th president	★★★½
Zone 7 Upper Northwest		
Hillwood Museum	mansion with fabulous art treasures	★★★★½
National Museum of Health and Medicine	medical museum	★★
National Zoological Park	world-class zoo in a wooded setting	★★★★½
Washington National Cathedral	6th-largest cathedral in the world	★★★★★
Zone 8 Northeast		
Basilica/Immaculate Conception	largest Catholic church in U.S.	★
Franciscan Monastery	restored church, catacombs, garden	★★
U.S. National Arboretum	444-acre collection of trees, flowers, herbs	★★½
Zone 9 Southeast		
Anacostia Museum	African-American history and culture	N/A
Frederick Douglass National Historic Site	preserved Victorian mansion	★★★½

ATTRACTIONS BY ZONE ***(continued)***

Attraction	Description	Rating
Zone 9 Southeast (continued)		
Kenilworth Aquatic Gardens	national park for water plants	★★★
Washington Navy Yard	3 military museums and U.S. Navy destroyer; advance reservation only	★★½
Zone 10 Maryland Suburbs		
NASA/Godard	space flight museum	★★½
National Cryptologic Museum	NSA spook museum	★
National Wildlife Visitor Center	museum on 13,000-acre wildlife refuge	★★½
Zone 11 Virginia Suburbs		
Mount Vernon	George Washington's river plantation	★★★★★
Old Town Alexandria	restored colonial port town	★★★★

Zone 1: The Mall

Arlington National Cemetery

Type of Attraction The largest military cemetery in the United States. Guided and self-guided tours.

Location Across the Potomac from Washington via Arlington Memorial Bridge, which crosses the river near the Lincoln Memorial.

Nearest Metro Station Arlington Cemetery

Admission Free

Hours Every day: April–September, 8 a.m.–7 p.m.; October–March, closes at 5 p.m.

Phone (703) 607-8052

When to Go Before 9 a.m. in spring and summer.

Special Comments Don't underestimate the ferocity of Washington summer afternoons; in hot weather, get here early.

Overall Appeal by Age Group

Pre-school ★	Teens ★★★	Over 30 ★★★★
Grade school ★★	Young Adults ★★★★	Snr. citizens ★★★★

Author's Rating Beyond tourism. ★★★★

How Much Time to Allow Two hours

Description and Comments It's not fair to call a visit to Arlington National Cemetery mere sight-seeing; as Americans, our lives are too intimately attached to the

200,000 men and women buried here. They include the famous, the obscure, and the unknown: John F. Kennedy, General George C. Marshall, Joe Louis, Abner Doubleday, and Oliver Wendell Holmes are among them. Sights located in the cemetery's 612 rolling acres include the Tomb of the Unknowns (guarded 24 hours a day; witness the changing of the guard on the hour from October to March, and on the half-hour the rest of the year), memorials to the crew of the space shuttle *Challenger,* the Iran Rescue Mission Memorial, and Arlington House, built in 1802. With the ease of touring provided by Tourmobile, Arlington Cemetery should be on every first-time visitor's list of things to see.

Touring Tips To avoid the worst of Washington's brutal summer heat and humidity, plan to arrive as early as possible. Private cars are not allowed inside, but there's plenty of parking near the visitor center at $1.25 an hour for the first three hours, then $2 an hour. Take the Metro instead. Although you can wander around the cemetery on your own, the narrated Tourmobile tour is informative and saves wear and tear on your feet—and at $5.25 for adults and $2.50 for children under age 12, it's a good deal. The ticket allows you to get off at all the major sites and reboard at your leisure. The shuttle tours leave the visitor center (where tickets are sold) about every 15 to 20 minutes. If you're touring the Mall by Tourmobile, transferring to the cemetery tour is free for that day only. If you want to tour the cemetery by shuttle bus on a different day, don't pay $18 for another full-circuit ticket. Just take the Metro to the Arlington Cemetery station, walk the short distance to the visitor center, buy the cemetery-only ticket, and save a few bucks. Finally, bathrooms are located in the visitor center. But don't come to Arlington Cemetery when you're hungry: There's no place to eat.

Other Things to Do Nearby The Pentagon is the next stop on the Metro. The Iwo Jima Memorial and the Netherlands Carillon are about a 20-minute walk from Arlington House (down Custis Walk and through Weitzel Gate). Two new attractions are an easy two-block walk from the Rosslyn Metro (one station away on the Metro): Freedom Park is a 1.6-acre park that features a memorial to nearly 1,000 journalists who died or were murdered on the job and a big chunk of the Berlin Wall; Newseum is a $50 million, 72,000-square-foot journalism museum. The nearest restaurants via the Metro are in Rosslyn and Pentagon City.

Arts and Industries Building (a Smithsonian museum)

Type of Attraction A museum highlighting temporary exhibitions. A self-guided tour.
Location 900 Jefferson Drive, SW, on the Mall.
Nearest Metro Station Smithsonian
Admission Free
Hours 10 a.m.–5:30 p.m.; closed Christmas Day.
Phone (202) 357-2700; (202) 357-1729 (TTY)
When to Go Anytime
Special Comments All the exhibits are on one level.
Overall Appeal by Age Group *Because the museum features special exhibitions that change throughout the year, it's not possible to rate it by age group.*
Author's Rating Because it features only temporary exhibitions, it's not possible to rate the museum.
How Much Time to Allow 30 minutes to an hour

Description and Comments The Arts and Industries Building was the original home of the Smithsonian after it was built in 1879–81. Formerly it housed the anthropological and scientific specimens now in the National Museum of Natural History across the Mall, industrial arts and technology items now in the National Museum of American History, artworks now in the National Museum of American Art and the National Portrait Gallery (both downtown), and aircraft exhibits currently displayed in the National Air and Space Museum. Today the museum features temporary exhibitions.

Touring Tips Some people call this a great "warm up" museum that gets you ready for the larger Smithsonian institutions; it's friendly and not overpowering.

Other Things to Do Nearby The Hirshhorn and the Air and Space Museum are next door. The Museum of Natural History (the one with the dome) is directly across the Mall. Tired of museums? Jump on the Metro, get off at Capitol South, and explore Capitol Hill. The Metro is also the fastest way to reach two good restaurant locales: L'Enfant Plaza (on weekdays) and the Old Post Office Pavilion (anytime).

Bureau of Engraving and Printing

Type of Attraction The presses that print U.S. currency and stamps. A guided tour.
Location Raoul Wallenberg Place (formerly 15th Street) and C Street, SW (two blocks south of the Mall).
Nearest Metro Station Smithsonian
Admission Free
Hours Monday–Friday, 8:30 a.m.–3 p.m. Closed on federal holidays and weekends. The ticket office, located on Raoul Wallenberg Place, opens at 8 a.m. No tickets are required; first come, first served. A valid ID is required. No bookbags, backpacks, or any sharp objects are allowed. Go to the 14th Street side of the building to enter.
Phone (202) 874-3019; (202) 874-3188 for a recording
When to Go The earlier, the better. During peak season, try to arrive on Monday by 8 a.m. (or earlier) and pick up tickets at the ticket office. See "Hours" above.
Special Comments Small children may have trouble looking over the ledge and down into the press rooms below.

Overall Appeal by Age Group

Pre-school ★★	Teens ★★★★	Over 30 ★★★★
Grade school ★★★★	Young Adults ★★★★	Snr. citizens ★★★★

Author's Rating After the novelty of seeing all that cash fades, it's just a printing plant. ★★
How Much Time to Allow About an hour when the ticket system is in effect. In the early fall, when the line snakes out the front door and up 14th Street, figure on at least two hours. Count on about 15 minutes for every 100 people ahead of you in line.

Description and Comments This is a 35- to 45-minute guided tour through the rather cramped and elevated glass-lined corridors that go over the government's immense money and stamp printing plant. Visitors look down and gape at the printing presses that crank out the dough and at pallets of greenbacks in various stages of completion. The sign some wag hung on a press, however, says it all: "You have never been so close yet so far away." Kids love this place, so it's a tourist site families should plan on hitting, even if you're only in town for a short period.

Touring Tips Arrive early—this is one of D.C.'s most popular attractions. In early spring and summer, get to the ticket booth before 8 a.m. on Monday to avoid disappointment. The ticket office distributes about 80 tickets for every tour starting at 10-minute intervals between 9 a.m. and 1:40 p.m. When all tickets are gone, the ticket office closes until the following Monday at 8 a.m. After picking up your tickets, come back for your tour and meet near the ticket office on Raoul Wallenberg Place, where you will be escorted into the building. You have about a 30-minute grace period if you're running late. For a unique souvenir, check out the bags of shredded money for sale in the visitor center at the end of the tour. For a VIP guided tour, contact your congressperson's office at least two months before your trip. The VIP tours are conducted at 8 a.m., Monday through Friday. Bathrooms are located inside the building where the tour begins.

Other Things to Do Nearby As you exit the building on Raoul Wallenberg Place, the Tidal Basin is a short walk to the left: Benches, tables, a lot of greenery, and the calming effect of water make it a great spot to unwind or eat lunch—or rent a paddleboat. And there's a great view of the Jefferson Memorial. Other sights close at hand are the Holocaust Memorial Museum, the Washington Monument, and the new seven-and-a-half-acre memorial to President Franklin D. Roosevelt. The $52 million series of gardens, sculptures, and granite walls are located between the Lincoln and Jefferson Memorials along the Potomac River and the Tidal Basin. There aren't a lot of places to eat nearby, however.

Corcoran Gallery of Art

Type of Attraction A museum that primarily features American art from the colonial period to the present. A self-guided tour.
Location 17th and E Streets, NW, a half-block west of the White House.
Nearest Metro Stations Farragut West and Farragut North
Admission $5 for adults, $3 for seniors and students, $1 for students 13-18, and $8 for families. Free on Mondays and after 5 p.m. on Thursdays.
Hours Wednesday–Monday, 10 a.m.–5 p.m.; Thursday, till 9 p.m.; closed Tuesdays, Christmas Day, and New Year's Day.
Phone (202) 639-1700 or (888) CORCORAN (toll free)
When to Go Anytime
Special Comments Free 45-minute tours are offered daily at noon, Thursdays at 7:30 p.m., and Saturdays and Sundays at 10:30 a.m. and 2:30 p.m.

Overall Appeal by Age Group

Pre-school —	Teens ★★	Over 30 ★★★
Grade school ★	Young Adults ★★½	Snr. citizens ★★★

Author's Rating Art snobs will feel at home. ★★½
How Much Time to Allow Two hours

Description and Comments Frank Lloyd Wright called this beaux arts museum "the best designed building in Washington." Inside are works by John Singer Sargent, Mary Cassatt, and Winslow Homer, among others. There's also an abundance of cutting-edge contemporary art. It's a big place with a wide range of periods and styles, so you're bound to see something you like.

Touring Tips Maybe it's because of the art school next door, but this museum has a distinctly serious atmosphere. It's not a place to drag little Johnny and Sally, who would rather be looking at dinosaur bones in the National Museum of Natural History. For a delightful Sunday museum excursion, take this Smithsonian staffer's suggestion: Begin with brunch in the Corcoran's stunning cafe. Afterwards, take a leisurely tour of the art museum and then stroll over to the Renwick Gallery for more first-class art—and, perhaps, some shopping in the Renwick's excellent museum shop. It's a great, laid-back way to spend the day ... and you won't be battling the crowds besieging the mega-museums on the Mall. The Corcoran's cafe hours are 11 a.m. to 2 p.m. (and 8 p.m. on Thursdays). Reservations are suggested; call (202) 639-1786.

Other Things to Do Nearby Duck into the Organization of American States and enter a rain forest: A courtyard filled with palm trees and the sound of falling water awaits you. Walk up the staircase and peek into the opulent Hall of the Americas. The Octagon, one of the earliest Federal-period houses in the United States, is a block to the east; Dolley Madison entertained there after the Brits burned the White House in 1814. For lunch, stroll up 17th Street toward Pennsylvania Avenue. Le Sorbet, around the corner on G Street, can supply a sandwich and drink for less than $5. Another block north is McDonald's.

Daughters of the American Revolution (DAR) Museum

Type of Attraction The 33 period rooms are a cornucopia of decorative arts and antiques. A self-guided museum tour and a guided tour.
Location 1776 D Street, NW, across from the Ellipse.
Nearest Metro Station Farragut West
Admission Free
Hours Monday–Friday, 9:30 a.m.–4 p.m.; weekends, 9:30 a.m.–4 p.m. The museum is closed on Saturday, federal government holiday weekends, and for two weeks in April. Guided tours of the period rooms are available Monday through Friday from 10 a.m.–2:30 p.m., and 9 a.m.–4:30 p.m. on weekends. Tours leave approximately every 45 minutes.
Phone (202) 879-3241
When to Go Anytime
Special Comments Expect to do a lot of stair climbing on the tour. You can't enter the rooms, and only two or three visitors at a time can squeeze into doorways to peer inside.

Overall Appeal by Age Group

Pre-school —	Teens ★★★½	Over 30 ★★★½
Grade school ★	Young Adults ★★	Snr. citizens ★★★★½

Author's Rating A must-see for lovers of antiques and decorative arts. ★★★½
How Much Time to Allow Two hours

Description and Comments This beaux arts building, completed in 1910, is a knockout. The huge columns that grace the front of the building are solid marble; a special railroad spur was built to transport them to the building site. The DAR Museum, predictably enough, emphasizes the role of women throughout American history and includes fine examples of furniture, ceramics, glass, paintings, silver, costumes, and textiles. It's a small museum filled with everyday items out of America's past. From the interior of a California adobe parlor of 1850, to a replica of a 1775 bedchamber in Lexington, Massachusetts, to the kitchen of a nineteenth-century Oklahoma farm family, the period rooms display objects in a context of both time and place. Kids will get a kick out of the four-sided mousetrap that guillotines rodents, the foot-controlled toaster, and the sausage stuffer that looks like an early nineteenth-century version of a NordicTrack machine.

To make the museum more attractive to children accompanying parents on the period-rooms tour, docents drop kids off at the Touch Area on the third floor. While their parents tour nearby period rooms, kids can play with authentic eighteenth- and nineteenth-century toys and objects, including miniature Chippendale tables and chairs, real powder horns, butter molds, candle snuffers, and flags. The museum and period rooms are sleepers that a lot of visitors to Washington overlook. But for lovers of antiques and decorative arts, the rooms provide visitors an opportunity to view beautiful objects in authentic period settings.

Touring Tips Finding the entrance is a bit tough, although the DAR building itself is easy enough to find. At D and 17th (across from the Ellipse), walk about half a block down D Street; the museum and tour entrance is on the side of the building. During the busy spring and summer, the period room tours can get crowded, especially on weekends, so try to arrive before noon.

Other Things to Do Nearby Walk up the marble steps and into the American Red Cross building to see the Memorial Windows, reputed to be the largest suite of Tiffany windows still in their original location (except for in churches). Their theme is ministry to the sick and wounded. Next door to DAR, the lobby of the Organization of American States building is a bit of a tropical paradise; around back is the Art Museum of the Americas, a small gallery featuring art from Latin America and the Caribbean (open Tuesday through Saturday, 10 a.m. to 5 p.m.; admission is free). Head up 17th Street toward Pennsylvania Avenue to find a large selection of restaurants.

Decatur House

Type of Attraction One of Washington's earliest surviving important residences. A guided tour.
Location 748 Jackson Place, NW, across from Lafayette Park.
Nearest Metro Stations Farragut West, Farragut North
Admission Free
Hours Tuesday–Friday, 10 a.m.–3 p.m.; weekends, noon–4 p.m. Closed Mondays and Thanksgiving and Christmas Days.
Phone (202) 842-0920
When to Go Anytime
Special Comments The tour involves descending a steep, curving staircase.

Overall Appeal by Age Group

Pre-school ★	Teens ★	Over 30 ★★
Grade school ★	Young Adults ★★	Snr. citizens ★★½

Author's Rating An interesting yet narrow slice of early Americana. ★★½
How Much Time to Allow 1 hour

Description and Comments Stephen Decatur was a naval war hero who defeated the Barbary pirates off the shores of Tripoli (ring a bell?) during the War of 1812. If he hadn't been killed in a duel, some say he might have been president. No doubt he built this house in 1819 with presidential aspirations in mind: It's close to the White House. The first floor is decorated in authentic Federalist style and displays Decatur's furnishings and sword. The formal parlors on the second floor reflect a later Victorian restyling. Famous statesmen who resided in the building include Henry Clay, Martin Van Buren, and Edward Livingston.

Touring Tips If you're on a tight schedule, this isn't the place to be blowing your time. But it's an okay rainy-afternoon alternative that gives insight into the early days of Washington.

Other Things to Do Nearby The Renwick Gallery is around the corner on Pennsylvania Avenue; next to it is Blair House, where foreign dignitaries stay. Decatur House faces Lafayette Park, frequent site of political demonstrations, once home to many homeless, and predictably filled with statues. Across the street is the White House.

Freer Gallery of Art (a Smithsonian museum)

Type of Attraction A museum featuring Asian and American art. A self-guided tour.
Location Jefferson Drive at 12th Street, SW, on the Mall.
Nearest Metro Station Smithsonian
Admission Free
Hours Daily, 10 a.m.–5:30 p.m.; closed Christmas Day.
Phone (202) 357-4880; (202) 357-1729 (TTY)
When to Go Anytime
Special Comments This 70-year-old gallery reopened in 1993 after a 4.5-year, $26 million renovation.

Overall Appeal by Age Group

Pre-school ★	Teens ★★½	Over 30 ★★★½
Grade school ★★	Young Adults ★★★	Snr. citizens ★★★★

Author's Rating Gorgeous art on a human scale in a setting that's not overwhelming. ★★★★
How Much Time to Allow One to two hours

Description and Comments Well-proportioned spaces, galleries illuminated by natural light, and quiet serenity are the hallmarks of this newly renovated landmark on the Mall. And the art? It's an unusual blend of American paintings (including the world's most important collection of works by James McNeill Whistler), and Asian paintings, sculpture, porcelains, scrolls, and richly embellished household items. Charles Lang Freer, the wealthy nineteenth-century industrialist who bequeathed this collection to the Smithsonian, saw similarities of color and surface texture in the diverse assemblage. Surrender to the gallery's tranquility and you may, too.

Touring Tips An underground link to the nearby Arthur M. Sackler Gallery creates a public exhibition space, as well as convenient passage between the two museums. Don't miss the Peacock Room, designed by James McNeill Whistler; it's widely considered to be the most important nineteenth-century interior in an American museum.

Once the dining room of a Liverpool shipping magnate, it was installed in the Freer Gallery after Freer's death. The ornate room was painted by Whistler to house a collection of blue and white Chinese porcelains. Following a restoration that removed decades of dirt and grime, the room has been restored to its original splendor. Free walk-in tours of the Freer are available every day (except Wednesday) at 11 a.m.

Other Things to Do Nearby The Sackler Gallery, the National Museum of African Art, and the Enid A. Haupt Garden are within a few steps of the Freer Gallery. Directly across the Mall are the National Museum of American History and the National Museum of Natural History. Walk up the Mall toward the Capitol to reach the Arts and Industries Building, the Hirshhorn Museum, and the National Air and Space Museum. For lunch, take the Metro to either L'Enfant Plaza (if it's a weekday) or the Old Post Office Pavilion (anytime).

Hirshhorn Museum and Sculpture Garden (a Smithsonian museum)

Type of Attraction A museum of modern art. A self-guided tour.
Location 7th Street and Independence Avenue, SW, on the Mall.
Nearest Metro Stations Smithsonian, L'Enfant Plaza
Admission Free
Hours Daily, 10 a.m.–5:30 p.m.; closed Christmas Day. Sculpture Garden open from 7:30 a.m. until dusk daily.
Phone (202) 357-2700; (202) 633-8043 (TTY)
When to Go Anytime
Special Comments The Hirshhorn is a lot of people's favorite art museum on the Mall.

Overall Appeal by Age Group

Pre-school ★	Teens ★★★	Over 30 ★★★★★
Grade school ★★	Young Adults ★★★★	Snr. citizens ★★★★★

Author's Rating An outrageous collection of twentieth-century art; don't miss it. ★★★★★

How Much Time to Allow Two hours

Description and Comments The art found inside is often as bizarre as the circular building that houses it. Works by modern masters such as Rodin, Winslow Homer, Mary Cassatt, and Henry Moore line the easy-to-walk galleries. The outdoor sculpture garden (set below Mall level) contains works by Rodin, Giacometti, and Alexander Calder, among many others. The sculpture offers a refreshing contrast to the marble palaces that line the Mall. If you visit only one modern art gallery on your visit, make it the Hirshhorn.

Touring Tips Guided tours of the Hirshhorn are offered at 10:30 am and noon, Monday through Friday, and at noon and 2 p.m. on weekends. During the summer months, additional docent-led tours are sometimes added. The museum's outdoor cafe is open for lunch during the summer only.

Other Things to Do Nearby Two nearby museums, Arts and Industries and Air and Space, offer startling contrasts to the Hirshhorn's treasures. A less jarring experience may be the National Gallery of Art's East Wing, also featuring modern art. The best bets for lunch are L'Enfant Plaza (on weekdays) and the Old Post Office Pavilion (anytime). In the summer, the Hirshhorn has an outdoor self-service cafe featuring sandwiches, salads, and great sculpture.

Jefferson Memorial

Type of Attraction A classical-style monument to the author of the Declaration of Independence and the third U.S. president. A self-guided tour.
Location Across the Tidal Basin from the Washington Monument.
Nearest Metro Stations L'Enfant Plaza, Smithsonian
Admission Free
Hours Always open; staffed from 8 a.m.–11:45 p.m., except on Christmas Day.
Phone (202) 426-6841
When to Go For the best views, go at night or when the cherry trees along the Tidal Basin are in bloom.
Special Comments The view from the steps and across the Tidal Basin is one of the best in Washington.

Overall Appeal by Age Group

Pre-school ★	Teens ★★★	Over 30 ★★★
Grade school ★★	Young Adults ★★★	Snr. citizens ★★★

Author's Rating A favorite at night, but not convenient. ★★½
How Much Time to Allow 30 minutes

Description and Comments The neoclassical, open-air design of this monument reflects Jefferson's taste in architecture. Because it's somewhat off the tourist path, it's usually less crowded than the monuments on the Mall.

Touring Tips Park interpreters staffing the monument frequently give talks and can answer questions about Jefferson and the monument. Visitors can walk to the memorial along the rim of the Tidal Basin from Independence Avenue or along 14th Street, SW.

Other Things to Do Nearby The Bureau of Engraving and Printing and the Holocaust Memorial Museum are both on 14th Street. In 1997, a $52 million memorial to President Franklin D. Roosevelt opened on a 7.5-acre site located between the Lincoln and Jefferson Memorials. The Tidal Basin is great for paddleboating. L'Enfant Plaza has an underground shopping mall with many places to eat (but not on weekends, when most of the restaurants are closed).

Lincoln Memorial

Type of Attraction A classical-style memorial to the 16th American president. A self-guided tour.
Location At the west end of the Mall.
Nearest Metro Stations Smithsonian, Foggy Bottom/GWU
Admission Free
Hours Always open. Rangers on duty from 8 a.m.–11:45 p.m., except Christmas Day.
Phone (202) 426-6841
When to Go For the best views, visit in the early morning, at sunset, or at night.

Special Comments At night, facing west across the Potomac River, you can see the eternal flame at John F. Kennedy's grave.

Overall Appeal by Age Group

Pre-school ★★	Teens ★★★	Over 30 ★★★
Grade school ★★★	Young Adults ★★★	Snr. citizens ★★★

Author's Rating Both solemn and scenic. ★★★
How Much Time to Allow 30 minutes

Description and Comments To see what the Lincoln Memorial looks like, just pull out a penny. Yet a visit to this marble monument inspires awe. Historic events took place on the steps: Black soprano Marian Anderson sang here in 1939 after being barred from Constitution Hall; Martin Luther King Jr. gave his "I Have a Dream" speech here in 1963. The Lincoln Memorial anchors the Mall and should be on anyone's must-see list.

Touring Tips The new Legacy of Lincoln museum in the memorial's basement is worth a peek. You'll find exhibits about demonstrations held at the memorial and a video recounting the building's history. The Lincoln Memorial's location at the west end of the Mall near the river, however, puts this marble edifice at a distance from any lunch spots except for overpriced Mall hot dog vendors, so eat first. Bathrooms are located on the memorial's ground level.

Other Things to Do Nearby The Vietnam Veterans Memorial and the Reflecting Pool are directly across from the Lincoln Memorial. The National Academy of Sciences on Constitution Avenue features science exhibits (open Monday through Friday, 9 a.m. to 5 p.m.; free). Outside, tourists can crawl into the lap of an Albert Einstein statue to have their picture taken; it's a D.C. tradition. A $52 million memorial to President Franklin D. Roosevelt opened in 1997 on a 7.5-acre site located on the Tidal Basin between the Lincoln and Jefferson Memorials. If you hike a few blocks up 23rd Street or 17th Street, you'll find an alternative to those hot dog vendors.

National Air and Space Museum (a Smithsonian museum)

Type of Attraction A museum that chronicles the history of manned flight. A self-guided tour.
Location On the south side of the Mall near the U.S. Capitol.
Nearest Metro Stations Smithsonian, L'Enfant Plaza
Admission Free
Hours 10 a.m.–5:30 p.m.; closed Christmas Day. Depending on the shape of the federal budget, hours may be extended during the summer.
Phone (202) 357-2700; (202) 357-1729 (TTY)
When to Go Before noon or after 4 p.m.
Special Comments If you want to get tickets for the five-story-high IMAX theater, make the box office on the main floor your first stop. Some special exhibits require passes; check with the information desk in the main lobby.

Overall Appeal by Age Group

Pre-school ★★★★	Teens ★★★★★	Over 30 ★★★★★
Grade school ★★★★★	Young Adults ★★★★★	Snr. citizens ★★★★

Author's Rating Absolutely not to be missed. ★★★★★

How Much Time to Allow Two hours minimum—and you still won't see it all. If possible, try to spread your tour of the museum over two or more visits.

Description and Comments This museum is the most visited in the world, drawing about nine million visitors a year. Entering from the Mall, visitors can touch a moon rock and gaze up at the Wright Brothers' plane, the *Enola Gay*, and the *Spirit of St. Louis*, which Lindbergh flew across the Atlantic in 1927. Everywhere you look is another full-size wonder. The only drawback to this museum is its size—going to every exhibit becomes numbing after a while. If your length of stay allows it, try to split your time here into at least two visits. But it's a must-see for virtually anyone—not just airplane buffs and space cadets. The newly remodeled ground floor has new flight simulators. Five are tied to exhibits in the museum, giving visitors the chance to fly a World War I plane flown by Eddie Rickenbacker, Amelia Earhart's Lockheed Vega, and more. At the Einstein Planetarium, the starry sky has been replaced by digital projectors, which transport images from space and cast them out onto the 70-foot dome.

Touring Tips If you don't have an unlimited amount of time to wander around, try this strategy: After leaving the main lobby, work your way over to Space Hall, where you can tour Skylab and check out the Apollo-Soyuz spacecraft. For more insight into the exhibits, take one of the free, one-hour guided tours starting at 10:15 a.m. and 1 p.m. daily, beginning at the information desk in the main lobby. While you'll never have to stand in line to get into the National Air and Space Museum, you can avoid a few major bottlenecks by staying away from Skylab, the moon rock, and the cafeteria around lunchtime. Three exhibits also worth hitting early to avoid lines: "How Things Fly" (an interactive gallery that teaches the basic principles of flight), "Space Race" (examines the Cold War competition for outer space between the United States and the former Soviet Union), and "Beyond the Limits" (computers in aviation and space).

Other Things to Do Nearby To escape the worst of the crowds, try a stroll through the fragrant U.S. Botanic Garden, located a block east of the National Air and Space Museum. For lunch, the on-site cafeteria and restaurant feature a great view of the Capitol and expensive, run-of-the-mill dining. Best bet on weekdays: L'Enfant Plaza, where you can dine elbow-to-elbow with Washington bureaucrats in an underground mall with a wide range of eateries. The entrance is south of the Mall on 10th Street, SW, between D and E Streets. On weekends and holidays, Capitol Hill (with its wide array of restaurants, bars, and cafes) and the Old Post Office Pavilion are good bets. In the summer, check out the Hirshhorn Museum's self-service cafe, where you can dine al fresco with great art.

National Aquarium

Type of Attraction The oldest aquarium in the United States. A self-guided tour.

Location In the basement of the Department of Commerce building on 14th Street, NW.

Nearest Metro Station Federal Triangle

Admission $3.50

Hours Daily, 9 a.m.–5 p.m.; closed Christmas Day.

Phone (202) 482-2826; (202) 482-2825 (recording)

When to Go Anytime

Special Comments A cool, dark oasis on a sweltering summer afternoon.

Overall Appeal by Age Group

Pre-school ★★★★	Teens ★★★	Over 30 ★★
Grade school ★★★★	Young Adults ★★	Snr. citizens ★★

Author's Rating A basement full of fish tanks. ★½

How Much Time to Allow One hour

Description and Comments Essentially a long room lined with big fish tanks in the basement of an office building, this aquarium is not in the same league with other, newer fish and dolphin emporiums that are springing up all over (such as the one in Baltimore). But children will love it. Small and lacking crowd-pleasing sea mammals, the aquarium figures as a minor exhibit for filling in the odd hour or to escape from a sweltering afternoon. Otherwise, spend your valuable touring time elsewhere.

Touring Tips Sharks get fed at 2 p.m. on Monday, Wednesday, and Saturday; the piranhas get their meals at 2 p.m. on Tuesday, Thursday, and Sunday.

Other Things to Do Nearby The Washington Monument, the National Museum of American History, and the Old Post Office Pavilion are within a few minutes' walk. The Commerce Department cafeteria, open Monday through Friday from 9 a.m. to 2 p.m., offers good, cheap fare: a soup and salad bar, pizza and pasta, a grill, a deli, and hot entrees. You can get a whole pizza that will feed a family of four for less than $10.

National Archives

Type of Attraction The magnificent rotunda where the Declaration of Independence and U.S. Constitution are displayed. A self-guided tour. *Note:* The building is closed to visitors (but not researchers) until the summer of 2003 for renovations.

Location 7th Street and Constitution Avenue, NW, on the Mall.

Nearest Metro Station Archives

Admission Free

Hours April 1–Labor Day, Exhibition Hall open every day, 10 a.m.–9 p.m.; September–March 31, 10 a.m.–5:30 p.m.; closed Christmas Day.

Phone (202) 501-5205

When to Go Before noon or after 4 p.m. during spring and summer.

Special Comments Small children may need a lift to see the documents; skip it if the line is long. In July 2001, the building closed for two years to renovate the rotunda and exhibit area.

Overall Appeal by Age Group

Pre-school ★	Teens ★★½	Over 30 ★★★
Grade school ★★	Young Adults ★★★	Snr. citizens ★★★

Author's Rating A letdown. ★½

How Much Time to Allow 30 minutes

Average Wait in Line per 100 People ahead of You 20 minutes

Description and Comments In addition to trying to decipher the faint and flowing script on the sheets of parchment mounted in bronze and glass cases, visitors can stroll through a temporary exhibit of photos and documents covering various aspects of Americana. Most visitors seem as fascinated by the written description of the elaborate security system that lowers the sacred documents into a deep, nuclear-explosion-proof vault each night as they are by seeing the charters themselves—and you can't even see the contraption. While the 75-foot-high rotunda is impressive, most people are surprised at how little there is to see inside this huge building. In fact, there *is* a lot more to see—but you've got to call in advance to arrange a tour. If the line to get in is long, skip it and come back later. It's really not worth the wait.

Touring Tips Some visitors say the documents on display in the exhibition areas outside the rotunda are more interesting—and certainly easier to read—than the better known parchments under the big dome. For a behind-the-scenes view of the workings of the National Archives, arrange to take a reserved tour. During spring and summer, four weeks' notice is recommended. Or take a chance and show up at the Pennsylvania Avenue entrance (across from 8th Street, NW) at tour time. If there's a cancellation or a no-show, you're in. The reserved tours begin at 10:15 a.m. and again at 1:15 p.m. Monday through Friday and last about an hour and a half. On the reserved tour, visitors take a tour of the building, including the stacks, microfilm viewing rooms, and exhibits and models that show how researchers preserve documents. The tour ends at the Rotunda. Oh, and don't miss the gift shop, where the best-selling item is a photograph of President Nixon and Elvis Presley embracing. It's a scream.

Other Things to Do Nearby Pick a Smithsonian museum you haven't seen yet and dive in. Several good restaurants popular with folks who work in the museums along the Mall are located across Pennsylvania Avenue from the National Archives on Indiana Avenue, NW.

National Gallery of Art: East Building

Type of Attraction A museum housing twentieth-century art and special exhibitions. A self-guided tour.

Location 4th Street and Constitution Avenue, NW, on the Mall.

Nearest Metro Stations Archives, Judiciary Square, Smithsonian

Admission Free

Hours Monday–Saturday, 10 a.m.–5 p.m.; Sundays, 11 a.m.–6 p.m.; closed Christmas and New Year's Days.

Phone (202) 737-4215

When to Go Anytime

Special Comments Usually referred to as the "East Wing" of the National Gallery. Visitors with disabilities may park in available spaces in front of the building. Introductory tours are offered daily and last about an hour; for times, call (202) 842-6247. No luggage, backpacks, bookbags, or other personal bags allowed.

Overall Appeal by Age Group

Pre-school ★	Teens ★★★	Over 30 ★★★★★
Grade school ★★	Young Adults ★★★★★	Snr. citizens ★★★★★

Author's Rating Even the building is a great work of art. ★★★★★

How Much Time to Allow Two hours

Description and Comments Both the interior and exterior of this I. M. Pei–designed building are spectacular, so it's worth a visit even if you hate modern art. Outside, the popular 1978 building consists of unadorned vertical planes. Inside, it's bright, airy, and spacious. Look for art by modern masters such as Picasso, Matisse, Mondrian, Miró, Magritte, Warhol, Lichtenstein, and Rauschenberg. The exhibits change constantly, so there's no telling which of these is on display.

Touring Tips Occasionally, temporary exhibits (such as a recent Van Gogh show) are extremely popular and may require a free "time ticket" that admits you on a certain day at a specific hour. You may pick up such tickets in advance; tickets are available as much as a month before a show opens. If you don't have a ticket on the day you visit the East Wing, you're not completely out of luck: A number of tickets are set aside every day for distribution that day only. If you want one, arrive at the ticket counter on the main floor by noon (or 2 p.m. during the week). Then come back later to see the exhibit. When you exit the museum, turn left and check out the high, knife-edge exterior corner wall of the gallery, near the Mall—it's almost worn away from people touching their noses to it.

The new, more than six-acre National Gallery Sculpture Garden opened in the spring of 1999 on the Mall adjacent to the West Building. Works from the gallery's permanent collection, as well as temporary exhibits, grace the symmetrical garden, its central pool, and the circle of linden trees. A variety of shade trees provide welcome relief in the summer, while the central pool serves as a public ice skating rink in the winter (as it has since the late 1960s).

Other Things to Do Nearby The West Wing, with its more traditional European art, is connected to the East Building by an underground concourse. The Capitol and the U.S. Botanic Garden are close by, as well as the National Archives. The Cascade Cafe/Buffet, a cafeteria along the concourse, may be the best official Mall eatery, featuring a classy selection of food and an espresso bar. Otherwise, the Old Post Office Pavilion, the Sculpture Garden's Pavillion Cafe, and L'Enfant Plaza (weekdays only) offer the best food choices nearby.

National Gallery of Art: West Building

Type of Attraction Museum featuring European and American art from the thirteenth through the nineteenth centuries. Self-guided and guided tours.

Location 6th Street and Constitution Avenue, NW, on the Mall.

Nearest Metro Station Archives

Admission Free

Hours Monday–Saturday, 10 a.m.–5 p.m.; Sundays, 11 a.m.–6 p.m. Closed Christmas and New Year's Days.

Phone (202) 737-4215

When to Go Anytime

Special Comments Introductory tours are offered daily and last about an hour. For times, call (202) 842-6247. It's usually referred to as the "West Wing" of the National Gallery.

Overall Appeal by Age Group

Pre-school ★	Teens ★★★	Over 30 ★★★★★
Grade school ★★½	Young Adults ★★★★	Snr. citizens ★★★★★

Author's Rating Art with a capital "A." ★★★★★

How Much Time to Allow Two hours for a light skimming, but you could spend a week.

Description and Comments This is where you find the heavy hitters: Dutch masters such as Rembrandt and Vermeer, plus Raphael, Monet, and Jacques-Louis David, just to name a few. And it's all housed in an elegant neoclassical building designed by John Russell Pope. It's a world-class art museum; first-time visitors should make at least one stop.

The new Micro Gallery, 13 computer stations featuring high-tech computers and 20-inch touchscreen color monitors, provides visitors with images and information on about 1,700 paintings, sculptures, and decorative arts; 650 artists; and more than 530 art-related subjects. Modeled after a similar system at the National Gallery in London, the Micro Gallery lets visitors with little or no computer experience expand their appreciation of the gallery's permanent collection. You can even create a personal tour of the museum and print a map showing the locations of works of art you've selected. The Micro Gallery is located on the main floor near the Mall entrance.

Touring Tips Most of the museum's paintings are hung in many small rooms, instead of a few big ones, so don't try to speed through the building or you'll miss most of them. When museum fatigue begins to set in, rest your feet in one of the atriums located between the museum's many galleries. If you plan on dragging kids through this massive place, try bribing them with a later trip to the National Zoo.

Some temporary exhibits require a free time ticket that admits you on a certain day at a specific hour. You may pick up such tickets in advance; they are available as much as a month before a show opens. If you don't have a ticket on the day you want to visit the West Wing, you're not completely out of luck: A number of tickets are set aside every day for distribution that day only. If you want one, arrive at the ticket counter on the main floor by noon (or 2 p.m. on a weekday). Then come back later to see the exhibit.

Other Things to Do Nearby Take the connecting corridor (an underground concourse) to the gallery's East Building. The Air and Space Museum is directly across the Mall, while the National Archives are in the other direction, across Constitution Avenue. Probably the best museum cafeteria on the Mall is located along the concourse. The Pavilion Cafe at the National Gallery's Sculpture Garden (located next door, across form the National Archives) has indoor and outdoor seating. Otherwise, L'Enfant Plaza (an underground shopping mall loaded with restaurants and fast food places; weekdays only) and the Old Post Office Pavilion (anytime) are your best bets for lunch.

National Museum of African Art (a Smithsonian museum)

Type of Attraction A museum specializing in the traditional arts of Africa. A self-guided tour.

Location 950 Independence Avenue, SW, on the Mall near the Castle (the Smithsonian Institution building).

Nearest Metro Station Smithsonian

Admission Free

Hours Daily, 10 a.m.–5:30 p.m.; closed Christmas Day.

Phone (202) 357-4600; (202) 357-4814 (TTY)

When to Go Anytime

Special Comments Provides a quiet respite when other Mall attractions are jammed; an excellent museum shop.

Overall Appeal by Age Group

Pre-school ★	Teens ★★	Over 30 ★★½
Grade school ★★	Young Adults ★★½	Snr. citizens ★★½

Author's Rating Exquisite sculpture and fascinating household items. ★★

How Much Time to Allow One hour

Description and Comments This relatively new subterranean museum, which opened in 1987, is paired with the Sackler Gallery, a museum of Asian art, and separated by an above-ground garden. Inside is an extensive collection of African art in a wide range of media, including sculpture, masks, household and personal items, and religious objects. Intellectually, this museum transports museum-goers far away from the Mall. It's an okay destination for older children, teens, and adults looking for some non-European cultural history and art. This museum is a great alternative on hot or crowded days in Washington.

Touring Tips One-hour guided tours are given at 1:30 p.m. Monday through Thursday and at 11 a.m. and 1 p.m. on weekends. And don't miss the excellent museum shop, where you'll find textiles, jewelry, scarves and sashes, wood carvings, and a wide selection of African music on tape, CD, and video.

Other Things to Do Nearby This museum is twinned with the Arthur M. Sackler Gallery, and even connects with it below ground—a nice feature on a sweltering Washington afternoon. If the weather's mild, stroll the Enid A. Haupt Garden, which separates the two museums at ground level. Neither museum has a cafeteria; the closest places featuring good selections and reasonable prices are L'Enfant Plaza (weekdays) and the Old Post Office Pavilion (anytime).

National Museum of American History (a Smithsonian museum)

Type of Attraction An extensive collection of artifacts reflecting the American experience—historical, social, and technological. A self-guided tour.

Location 14th Street and Constitution Avenue, NW, on the Mall.

Nearest Metro Stations Smithsonian, Federal Triangle

Admission Free

Hours Daily, 10 a.m.–5:30 p.m.; extended summer hours depend on budget restraints. Closed Christmas Day.

Phone (202) 357-2700; (202) 357-1729 (TTY)

When to Go To avoid the worst crowds, visit before noon and after 3 p.m.

Special Comments The immensity of this museum almost demands that visitors try to see it in more than one visit.

Overall Appeal by Age Group

Pre-school ★★★	Teens ★★★★★	Over 30 ★★★★★
Grade school ★★★★	Young Adults ★★★★★	Snr. citizens ★★★★★

Author's Rating A collection of national treasures; don't miss it. ★★★★★

How Much Time to Allow Two hours on a first pass; it would take a week to see it all.

Description and Comments Three exhibit-packed floors feature such treasures as the original Star-Spangled Banner, steam locomotives, a Model T Ford, a pendulum three stories high that shows how the earth rotates, a collection of ball gowns worn by First Ladies, and Archie Bunker's chair. If you can't find something of interest here, you may need mouth-to-mouth resuscitation. For a lot of people, this ranks as their favorite Mall museum. No wonder: It offers viewers a dizzying array of history, nostalgia, technology, and culture. And kids love it. It's a must-see for virtually all visitors.

Touring Tips At most museums, you look at *stuff,* but a lot of the collection at American History is arranged so that viewers can learn about *people* in the context of their times. To see what we mean—and to help you organize yourself in this bewilderingly large museum—make it a point to see these exhibits: the First Ladies' Exhibition; Field to Factory (about the migration of Southern rural African Americans to northern cities); and a collection of objects about television that includes Archie Bunker's chair, Fonzie's jacket, one of Mr. Rogers' sweaters, Oscar the Grouch (of *Sesame Street* fame), and for baby boomers, some items from the *Howdy Doody Show.* Check at the information desk for a schedule of tours (usually at 10 a.m. and 1 p.m. daily), demonstrations, concerts, lectures, films, and other activities put on by the museum staff. Some final hints: A lot of people touring the museum on their own overlook the Hall of Transportation in the museum's east wing, which features an excellent collection of cars, trains, and motorcycles. Car aficionados will love it. Kids (and most adults) enjoy the Science in American Life exhibit, the Hands-on Science Center, and the Hands-On History Room.

Other Things to Do Nearby Within a short walk are the Washington Monument, the National Aquarium, the Old Post Office Pavilion, and the National Museum of Natural History. Almost directly across the Mall are the Freer and Sackler Galleries and the National Museum of African Art. And, yes, the American History Museum has a cafeteria and an ice cream parlor.

National Museum of Natural History (a Smithsonian museum)

Type of Attraction America's treasure chest of the natural sciences and human culture. A self-guided tour.

Location On the Mall at 10th Street, NW, and Constitution Avenue.

Nearest Metro Stations Smithsonian, Archives, Federal Triangle

Admission Free; IMAX admission is $7.50 for adults and $6 for seniors and children under age 17.

Hours 10 a.m.–5:30 p.m.; open until 8:00 p.m. during the summer months; closed Christmas Day.

Phone (202) 357-2700; (202) 357-1729 (TTY)

When to Go Before noon and after 4 p.m. Free weekday highlight tours are offered at 10:30 a.m. and 1:30 p.m., Monday through Thursday, and at 10:30 a.m. on Friday. Meet in the rotunda.

Special Comments In the Discovery Room, kids ages 4 years and up can touch nearly everything. Hours are Tuesday through Friday, noon to 2:30 p.m.; weekends, 10:30 a.m. to 3:30 p.m. Make the popular Discovery Room your first stop and pick up free time tickets; tour the rest of the museum and return at the time stamped on your ticket.

Overall Appeal by Age Group

Pre-school ★★★★	Teens ★★★★½	Over 30 ★★★★★
Grade school ★★★★★	Young Adults ★★★★★	Snr. citizens ★★★★★

Author's Rating The displays of huge dinosaur fossils and the world's best known gem make this museum a classic. ★★★★½

How Much Time to Allow Two hours is enough time to see the really cool stuff, but you could easily spend an entire day here.

Description and Comments Distinguished by its golden dome and the towering bull elephant in the rotunda, the Museum of Natural History is a Washington landmark. It's also a bit old-fashioned, with long halls filled with dioramas, display cases, and hanging specimens that reflect the Victorian obsession with collecting things. This museum, along with Air and Space across the Mall, is immensely popular with families, and for a good reason—folks of all ages and tastes will find fascinating things to see here.

In September 1997, the Janet Annenberg Hooker Hall of Geology, Gems, and Minerals opened, showcasing the museum's world-class gem and mineral collection. It's part of an ongoing $8.5 million museum renovation, which includes an IMAX theater specializing in nature films. The gem hall features interactive computers, animated graphics, film and video presentations, and hands-on exhibits. In addition to the 45.52-carat Hope Diamond, the space features meteorites, emeralds, a 23,000-carat topaz, crystals, a walk-through mine, a re-creation of a cave, and a plate tectonics gallery showing how the earth's surface shifts.

A new mammal hall will open in 2003. State-of-the-art-dioramas will explain mammalian evolution, and hands-on activities will be available to hold kids' interests.

Touring Tips After entering through the big doors at the Mall entrance, bear right to see the dinosaur skeletons. Then ascend to the second floor to gaze upon the supposedly cursed Hope Diamond and to explore the new hall. If you're not put off by crawling critters, stop by the Insect Zoo, which features a wide array of (live) bugs. Special exhibits are located on the ground level (Constitution Avenue entrance).

Other Things to Do Nearby The National Museum of American History is next door; across the Mall are the Hirshhorn Museum, the Arts and Industries Building, the Museum of African Art, and the Sackler and Freer Galleries; the National Archives is across Constitution Avenue. A convenient choice for lunch is the Old Post Office Pavilion, about a block away on 12th Street or the Pavilion Cafe, located in the National Gallery Sculpture Garden. The fast-food kiosk in front of the museum on the Mall is overpriced: If you crave a hot dog, walk over to Constitution Avenue, find a street vendor, and save a buck.

The Octagon

Type of Attraction One of the first great homes built in Washington; a museum showcasing American architecture and historic preservation. A guided tour.
Location 1799 New York Avenue, NW.
Nearest Metro Station Farragut West
Admission $5 for adults; $3 for students and seniors
Hours Tuesday–Sunday, 10 a.m.–4 p.m.; closed Mondays, Thanksgiving, Christmas and New Year's Days.

Phone (202) 638-3221
When to Go Anytime
Special Comments One long staircase leads to the second-floor exhibition galleries.

Overall Appeal by Age Group

Pre-school ★	Teens ★★	Over 30 ★★½
Grade school ★½	Young Adults ★★½	Snr. citizens ★★½

Author's Rating Another interesting, yet narrow, slice of early Washington history. ★★½
How Much Time to Allow One hour

Description and Comments This elegant building is where President James Madison and First Lady Dolley Madison took up temporary residence after the British burned the White House during the War of 1812. Built in 1801 (when Washington was mostly swamp), this early Federalist building recently underwent a $5 million, six-year renovation; it's owned by the American Architectural Foundation. Period rooms on the first floor offer visitors a glimpse of how the upper crust lived in the early days of Washington; the coal stoves in the entrance hall are original. The former bedrooms upstairs are now galleries displaying temporary exhibits on architecture and design.

Touring Tips Interpreters give half-hour tours of the building that provide additional glimpses into the past—and tell fascinating anecdotes about the building and the city's early days. For example, President Madison signed the Treaty of Ghent, which ended the war that had driven him from the White House, in the upstairs parlor. Later the building served as a girls' school and was subdivided into ten apartments before it was acquired by the American Architectural Foundation in 1899.

Other Things to Do Nearby The Corcoran Gallery of Art is a block away. The Renwick Gallery and the White House are also close by. Walk up 17th Street for a selection of fast-food places and restaurants.

Old Post Office Tower and Pavilion

Type of Attraction A multi-ethnic food court in a spectacular architectural setting; home of the second-best view in Washington; trendy shops. A guided tour (of the tower).
Location 12th Street and Pennsylvania Avenue, NW.
Nearest Metro Station Federal Triangle
Admission Free
Hours During the summer, retail stores are open Monday–Saturday, 10 a.m.–9 p.m., and Sunday, noon–7 p.m. In the winter, stores are open Monday–Saturday, 10 a.m.–7 p.m., and Sunday, noon–6 p.m. Summer food court hours are Monday–Saturday, 10 a.m.–9 p.m., and Sunday, noon–8 p.m.; the food court closes an hour earlier the rest of the year. From Easter Sunday through Labor Day, the tower is open 8 a.m.–10:45 p.m.; the rest of the year it's open 10 a.m.–5:45 p.m.
Phone (202) 289-4224; (202) 606-8691 for the tower
When to Go Anytime to take the glass elevator up the clock tower; beat the worst of the crowds in the food court after 1 p.m.

Special Comments This is the place to come when they run out of time tickets at the Washington Monument. The food court is a favorite stop for tour buses, making it difficult at times to find a table.

Overall Appeal by Age Group

Pre-school ★★★	Teens ★★★★	Over 30 ★★★
Grade school ★★★★	Young Adults ★★★	Snr. citizens ★★★

Author's Rating A great view and a lifesaver for tourists who hate the overpriced, crummy food served in most museums. ★★★½

How Much Time to Allow One hour for the clock tower

Description and Comments This fine old building, a Pennsylvania Avenue landmark, was slated for demolition, but preservationist groups intervened to save it. Today, the 315-foot clock tower offers a spectacular view of Washington, while the multiethnic food court occupies a stunning, glass-roofed architectural space ten stories high. It offers a complete tourist experience for people of all ages: a view to kill for (through large plate glass windows, not tiny windows like at the Washington Monument), great food, and a shopping mall. And with its proximity to the Mall and White House, the Pavilion is a convenient place to visit for a quick lunch or snack.

Touring Tips It's elbow to elbow in the small elevator to the observation deck. Beware of groups of screaming teenagers in the food court—it's a popular destination for school groups. To reach the glass-enclosed elevators to the observation deck, go to the patio area in the food court. The National Park Service rangers on duty in the tower are a great source of advice about D.C. touring. Ask one to show you the lay of the land from the observation deck.

Other Things to Do Nearby Make faces at the groupers in the National Aquarium, see an agent rip off some rounds of automatic weapons fire at the FBI, or visit Ford's Theatre. If you can't find anything good to eat in the food court, it's time to go home.

Renwick Gallery (a Smithsonian museum)

Type of Attraction A museum dedicated to American crafts and decorative arts. A self-guided tour.

Location 17th Street and Pennsylvania Avenue, NW (diagonally across from the White House).

Nearest Metro Station Farragut West

Admission Free

Hours Every day, 10 a.m.–5:30 p.m.; closed Christmas Day.

Phone (202) 357-2700; (202) 357-1729 (TTY)

When to Go Anytime

Special Comments Don't expect an exhibition of hand-woven baskets: The museum features a wide array of mixed-media sculptures, tapestries, and constructions by major contemporary artists.

Overall Appeal by Age Group

Pre-school ★	Teens ★★	Over 30 ★★½
Grade school ★★	Young Adults ★★	Snr. citizens ★★½

Author's Rating An elegant setting, yet a bit dull. ★★
How Much Time to Allow One hour

Description and Comments Both the art and the Second Empire architecture of the mansion make this Smithsonian museum worth a stop when you're near the White House. Works on display are constructed in glass, ceramics, wood, fiber, and metal. But folks on a first-time visit to Washington or with children should skip it.

Touring Tips Glide up the Grand Staircase to enter the elegant Grand Salon, now an art gallery featuring floor-to-ceiling oil paintings, velvet curtains, and traditional furniture. On the same floor is the elegant Octagon Room, which faces the street and is used as exhibition space. The first floor hosts temporary exhibits.

Other Things to Do Nearby Next door is Blair House, where visiting foreign dignitaries stay; you can't get in, but look for Secret Service agents and diplomatic limos. A plaque on the wrought-iron gates honors a guard who saved President Truman from a would-be assassin. Around the corner on 17th Street is the closest McDonald's to the White House.

Franklin Delano Roosevelt Memorial

Type of Attraction A 7.5-acre, open-air memorial to the 32nd president of the United States. A self-guided tour.
Location West Potomac Park, between the Tidal Basin and the Potomac River.
Nearest Metro Station The Smithsonian (Independence Avenue exit) is about a brisk, 30-minute walk away. Other Metro stations even less convenient are Foggy Bottom and Arlington Cemetery (across Memorial Bridge in Virginia).
Admission Free
Hours Staffed daily, 8 a.m.–midnight, except on Christmas Day.
Phone (202) 426-6841
When to Go Anytime, except during inclement weather; the FDR Memorial is unenclosed.
Special Comments Folks old enough to have voted for FDR and disabled people may find it difficult to visit the memorial; nearby parking is scarce and the walk from the Nearest metro station is about a mile. One hundred and sixty unmetered parking spaces are located along Ohio Drive, SW, eastbound, and three lots with a total of 247 spaces are in East Potomac Park under the 14th Street bridges. Five handicapped spaces and one van space are located at the main entrance to the memorial on West Basin Drive. Except at off-peak times (before noon on weekdays and evenings), competition for the spaces is fierce. Other options for reaching the memorial include cabs and a water taxi.

Overall Appeal by Age Group

Pre-school ★★½	Teens ★★½	Over 30 ★★★½
Grade school ★★★	Young Adults ★★★	Snr. citizens ★★★★

Author's Rating Washington's newest presidential memorial successfully blends history, texture, drama, nostalgia, landscaping, and flowing water. The result is a dramatic and inspiring memorial to America's best loved twentieth-century leader. ★★★½
How Much Time to Allow 30 minutes to an hour

Description and Comments Unlike the nearby imposing marble edifices to Lincoln and Jefferson, the $52 million FDR Memorial on the Tidal Basin tells a story: In four open-air, interconnected "rooms" ("enclaves" or "tableaus" might be better words) that represent each of Roosevelt's four terms, his words are carved on granite walls, bronze images depict the alphabet-soup of programs and agencies he created to help millions of Americans devastated by the Depression, and statues depict the average citizens whose lives he touched. One shows a man listening intently to a radio, evoking the days before television—and a time when FDR's strong and vibrant voice gave hope to Americans in his "fireside chats."

Roosevelt himself is represented in the third room in a larger-than-life bronze statue. The president is seated, his body wrapped in a cape, his face lined with weariness as he approaches the final year of his life. His Scottish terrier Fala is at his feet. The fourth room features a statue of Eleanor Roosevelt, widely regarded as America's greatest first lady for her services as a delegate to the United Nations and as a champion for human rights. This is the first memorial to honor a presidential wife.

Many elements work in harmony to make the memorial a success. Textures of South Dakota granite, brick, rough wood, and falling water combine with ornamental plantings and shade trees to create the ambience of a secluded garden rather than an imposing structure. This is not a "hands off" memorial: The slightly-larger-than-life figures of FDR and Mrs. Roosevelt, as well as statues of five men in an urban bread line and a rural couple outside a barn door, are placed at ground level. Visitors can easily drape an arm around the first lady, sit in Franklin's lap as he delivers a fireside chat, or join the men in line for a souvenir snapshot. The memorial's many waterfalls (FDR considered himself a Navy man) attract splashers with stepping stones while kids enjoy climbing on giant, toppled granite blocks inscribed with the words "I hate war." As a result, visitors to the new memorial, both young and old, seem to enjoy themselves.

Touring Tips While you can enter the memorial (dedicated in May 1997) from either end, try to start your tour at the official entrance so you can stroll through the outside rooms in chronological order. That's not a problem if you're walking to the memorial from the Lincoln Memorial. But folks trekking from 14th Street and the Jefferson Memorial should resist the temptation to enter the memorial by continuing along the Tidal Basin and entering at the information center and bookstore. Rest rooms are located at both entrances. The memorial is a nice spot for an impromptu picnic by the water, so bring a lunch.

Other Things to Do Nearby The Lincoln, Korean War, and Jefferson Memorials are relatively close; just wear comfortable walking shoes and keep in mind that distances along the Tidal Basin and Mall are deceiving. The Bureau of Engraving and Printing and the Holocaust Memorial Museum are located on Raoul Wallenberg Place, on the east side of the Tidal Basin just beyond the Jefferson Memorial; both require picking up time tickets during the spring and summer (year-round at the Holocaust Museum). Hungry? Pack a lunch. The Holocaust Museum has a small cafe with a limited selection and is the closest place to grab something to eat. During warm weather, paddleboats are available for rent on the east side of the Tidal Basin, and a water taxi service shuttles tourists along the Potomac River from 11 a.m. to 6 p.m. daily.

The Arthur M. Sackler Gallery (a Smithsonian museum)

Type of Attraction A museum dedicated to Asian art from ancient times to the present. A self-guided tour.
Location 1050 Independence Avenue, SW, on the Mall near the Castle (the Smithsonian Institution building).
Nearest Metro Station Smithsonian
Admission Free
Hours Every day, 10 a.m.–5:30 p.m.; closed Christmas Day.
Phone (202) 357-2700; (202) 357-1729 (TTY)
When to Go Anytime
Special Comments A quiet respite when other Mall attractions are jammed with visitors.

Overall Appeal by Age Group

Pre-school ★	Teens ★★	Over 30 ★★½
Grade school ★★	Young Adults ★★½	Snr. citizens ★★½

Author's Rating Fabulous and exotic art. ★★½
How Much Time to Allow One hour

Description and Comments Descend through a granite-and-glass pavilion to view a collection of Asian (mostly Chinese) treasures, many of them made of gold and encrusted with jewels. The Sackler is full of exotic stuff that will catch the eye of older children, teens, and adults. Barring a strong interest in the Orient, however, first-time visitors on a tight schedule should visit the Sackler another time.

Touring Tips Stop at the information desk and ask about the guided tours offered throughout the day. The gift shop is an exotic bazaar, featuring paintings, textiles, ancient games, Zen–rock garden kits, and plenty of other Asian-influenced items. Free walk-in tours are offered daily (except Wednesday) at 11 a.m.

Other Things to Do Nearby The Sackler is connected with its twin, the Museum of African Art, below ground, so that's the logical next stop—especially if it's rainy or blazingly hot outside. A new underground corridor connects the Freer Gallery to the Sackler. None of these museums offers a cafeteria, but that's okay: Try either L'Enfant Plaza (weekdays) or the Old Post Office Pavilion (anytime). The only remaining problem is deciding what to eat.

Smithsonian Institution Building (the Castle)

Type of Attraction Information desks and displays, and a continuously running movie that introduces visitors to the vast number of Smithsonian museums.
Location 1000 Jefferson Drive, SW, on the Mall.
Nearest Metro Station Smithsonian
Admission Free
Hours Every day, 9 a.m.–5:30 p.m.; closed Christmas Day.
Phone (202) 357-2700; (202) 357-1729 (TTY)
When to Go Anytime
Author's Rating A must for first-time Mall visitors. ★★★★
How Much Time to Allow 30 minutes

Description and Comments This red brick building—you can't miss it—contains no exhibits. The Castle serves as an information center that will help you save time and trouble and reduce the frustration that comes from visiting the Smithsonian's large and perplexing museum complex. Step into one of the two theaters to see the 20-minute film. It's a bit long but gives a good idea of what each museum has to offer. Then you can talk to someone at the information desk for specific directions and advice (including multilingual assistance). A nifty map exhibit on the east wall lights up the location of each of the museums on the Mall, as well as other popular D.C. sights, when you press the corresponding button.

U.S. Holocaust Memorial Museum

Type of Attraction A museum and memorial presenting the history of the persecution and murder of six million Jews and others by Nazi Germany during World War II. A self-guided tour.

Location 100 Raoul Wallenberg Place, SW (formerly 15th Street), near the Mall between the Washington Monument and the Bureau of Engraving and Printing. Entrances are on Raoul Wallenberg Place and 14th Street.

Nearest Metro Station Smithsonian (Independence Avenue exit)

Admission Free

Hours Every day, 10 a.m.–5:30 p.m.; closed Christmas Day and Yom Kippur.

Phone (202) 488-0400

When to Go After favorable publicity generated large crowds following its opening in the spring of 1993, the Holocaust Museum went to a "time ticket" system to eliminate long lines at its permanent exhibits. While the ticket office opens at 10 a.m., plan on getting in line no later than 9 a.m. to be sure of getting a ticket (which are given out for that day only). If you want to be sure of getting on a morning tour during the busy spring and summer months, get in line by 8:30 a.m. For advance tickets, call (800) 400-9373.

Special Comments According to Holocaust Museum officials, the main exhibit is inappropriate for children under age 11—and we agree. However, a special exhibit on the museum's first floor, "Daniel's Story: Remember the Children," is designed for visitors age 8 and older. It gives a child's perspective on the Holocaust, but without the shocking graphics of the permanent exhibit. No tickets are required for the special, non-permanent exhibitions. Tickets can also be ordered in advance through Tickets.com. Call (800) 400-9373; or order online at www.tickets.com.

Overall Appeal by Age Group

Pre-school —	Teens ★★	Over 30 ★★★½
Grade school ★½	Young Adults ★★★	Snr. citizens ★★★★

Author's Rating As its designers intended, the Holocaust Museum is ugly, forbidding, and grim—and delivers a stern message about the evils of racial persecution. It also packs an emotional punch that may not fit some folks' vacation plans. ★★½

How Much Time to Allow One and a half to two hours

Description and Comments This $168 million museum utilizes stunning, high-tech audiovisual displays, advanced computer technology, and a model of a Nazi death camp to deliver a message about one of the darkest periods in human history. But that's not all. As part of the museum experience, museum-goers are cast as "victims" of Nazi brutality. Visitors receive an identity card of a real Holocaust victim matched to their sex and age—a demographic double. The building attacks the emotions of visitors in other, more subtle, ways. The interior of the museum, while spotless, is relentlessly industrial and forbidding—pipes are exposed and rough surfaces of brick and concrete are cold and unwelcoming. Diagonal walls in the exhibition areas create a disorienting effect. Ghostly shapes pass overhead on glass-bottomed walkways, suggesting Nazi prison guards patrolling a camp. (Actually, they are visitors walking on footbridges linking the permanent exhibit spaces.) Every moment spent inside the museum is orchestrated to impart the horror of Nazi persecution.

While many exhibits focus on Jewish life prior to the Holocaust and the political and military events surrounding World War II, the most disturbing displays are graphic depictions of Nazi atrocities. Large TV screens scattered throughout the exhibits present still and motion pictures of Nazi leaders, storm troopers rounding up victims, and life inside Jewish ghettos. Some of the TV screens are located behind concrete barriers to prevent younger (and, inadvertently, shorter) visitors from seeing them. They show executions, medical experiments on Jewish prisoners, and suicide victims. It's very strong, grim stuff.

Touring Tips Given the unrelenting horror of its subject matter, the Holocaust Museum is at best sobering and, at worst, depressing. There's no bright gloss to put on a museum chronicling the systematic murder of six million people . . . and anyone visiting the Holocaust Museum during a vacation should keep that in mind before placing it on his or her touring agenda, especially if traveling with small children.

Other Things to Do Nearby The Holocaust Memorial Museum occupies some prime real estate near the Mall, the Bureau of Engraving and Printing, the Washington Monument, the Tidal Basin, the FDR Memorial, and the Jefferson Memorial, so finding things to do before or after a tour of the museum is easy. The Museum Annex on Raoul Wallenberg Place has a small deli/cafe that's expensive but convenient.

Vietnam Veterans Memorial

Type of Attraction A memorial to U.S. soldiers who died in Vietnam.
Location On the west end of the Mall near the Lincoln Memorial.
Nearest Metro Station Foggy Bottom/GWU
Admission Free
Hours Every day, 8 a.m.–11:45 p.m.
Phone (202) 426-6841
When to Go Anytime
Special Comments At night this memorial is especially moving as people light matches to search for names inscribed on the wall.

Overall Appeal by Age Group

Pre-school ★	Teens ★★	Over 30 ★★★★
Grade school ★★	Young Adults ★★★	Snr. citizens ★★★★

Author's Rating Deeply moving. ★★★½
How Much Time to Allow 30 minutes

Description and Comments This long, narrow wall of polished black stone is inscribed with the names of the more than 58,000 Americans who died in Vietnam.

Many visitors to the memorial make rubbings of loved ones' names, while others leave flowers, military medals, letters, and gifts along the base of the wall. The wall, a black rift in the earth, packs an emotional wallop.

Touring Tips At both ends of the wall visitors will find books that list the inscribed names and the panel number to help them locate an inscription.

Other Things to Do Nearby The Lincoln Memorial, the Reflecting Pool, the $18 million Korean War Veterans Memorial, and Constitution Gardens are close by. Across from the Mall, the National Academy of Sciences features science exhibits and a statue of Albert Einstein with a lap that's large enough to sit in for picture-taking. For food, walk up 23rd Street toward Foggy Bottom and an assortment of restaurants and carryouts.

Voice of America

Type of Attraction The U.S. Government's overseas radio broadcasting studios. A guided tour.

Location Tours meet at the C Street entrance between 3rd and 4th Streets, SW.

Nearest Metro Station Federal Center SW

Admission Free; reservations are required and no groups larger than 20 people are allowed

Hours The 45-minute tours are Monday–Friday at 10:30 a.m., 1:30 p.m., and 2:30 p.m., except holidays.

Phone (202) 619-3919

Special Comments A "must" for news junkies.

Overall Appeal by Age Group

Pre-school —	Teens ★	Over 30 ★★
Grade school ★	Young Adults ★★	Snr. citizens ★★

Author's Rating Fascinating and informative. ★★½

How Much Time to Allow 45 minutes

Description and Comments After a short video about the VOA, the knowledgeable tour guide walks you through some of the agency's 34 studios, where you see and hear radio announcers reading newscasts in languages such as Arabic, Estonian, and Urdu. Worldwide, the VOA operates more than 100 shortwave radio transmitters, and all broadcasts originate in this building. You'll also see some murals painted by noted artist Ben Shahn in the 1940s. But mostly this is a tour for people interested in media and world events; it would bore most children silly.

Touring Tips You should call to reserve a place on a tour, but individuals and small groups won't have trouble joining a tour by just showing up a few minutes before a scheduled departure.

Other Things to Do Nearby The U.S. Botanic Garden is around the corner on Maryland Avenue, SW, and the Mall is two blocks away. For lunch, try the L'Enfant Plaza underground shopping mall, which on weekdays is usually jammed with bureaucrats looking for good, cheap food—and finding it. But don't go on weekends: Most restaurants are closed and the place is dead. Capitol Hill has a wide assortment of restaurants and cafes; another good choice for off-the-Mall eating is the Old Post Office Pavilion.

Washington Monument

Type of Attraction A monument to the first U.S. president.
Location On the Mall between 15th and 17th Streets, NW.
Nearest Metro Station Smithsonian
Admission Free
Hours Every day, 9 a.m.–5 p.m. The monument may be closed in thunderstorms and during periods of sustained high winds (not out of fear that the giant obelisk will tumble, but to protect visitors waiting in line on this exposed hilltop).
Phone (202) 426-6841
When to Go At 7:30 a.m. to pick up a time ticket.
Special Comments Skip this one in bad weather—the view can be lousy. The Park Service operates a "time ticket" system to eliminate the long lines that used to wrap three times around the base of the monument. Pick up the free tickets (a maximum of six per person) at the kiosk located on 15th Street on the edge of the monument grounds. Then return at the time stamped on your ticket for the trip up the elevator later that day; kiosk hours are 8 a.m. until all 1400 tickets run out. Show up five minutes before the time printed on your ticket. With only 150 tickets given out per half hour, all the tickets are usually gone by 9:30 a.m. on busy days and by 1:30 p.m. on slow days; early morning tickets go first. Tickets can be reserved in advance for a fee by calling (800) 967-2283 or over the Internet: www.reservations.nps.gov. There's a $1.50 service charge per ticket . . . and if it's raining or the view's socked in by clouds, too bad. Refunds are given only if the monument is closed.

Overall Appeal by Age Group

Pre-school ★★★★	Teens ★★★★★	Over 30 ★★★★★
Grade school ★★★★★	Young Adults ★★★★★	Snr. citizens ★★★★★

Author's Rating Obligatory for first-time visitors. ★★★★★
How Much Time to Allow Once you make it to the top, 30 minutes on the cramped observation deck can seem like an eternity.

Description and Comments At the top you're 500 feet up, and D.C.'s absence of other tall buildings (it's a law) guarantees a glorious, unobstructed view of Washington—if it's not raining. For most people, a first-time trip to Washington isn't complete without an ascent of this famous landmark. Yet most of them are surprised when they reach the cramped observation deck: You almost have to elbow your way to the tiny windows to see anything. The view, however, is great. Nobody's ever disappointed once they see it.

Touring Tips The new, year-round "time ticket" system eliminates three-hour waits in line for the elevator trip to the top of the monument, which reopened in the summer of 2000 after renovations. (The wait in line is now reduced to about half an hour for most visitors.) Bathrooms are located behind the outdoor amphitheater on the monument grounds and the snack bar near the ticket kiosk, but use them only in desperate situations: They are usually dirty. A nearby snack bar is overpriced; during the week, try the the food courts in the Old Post Office Pavilion and the Ronald Reagan Building.

Other Things to Do Nearby You're at the heart of tourist Washington: At hand are the Bureau of Engraving and Printing, the Holocaust Memorial Museum, the

National Museum of American History, and the National Aquarium. At one end of the Mall is the Lincoln Memorial; the U.S. Capitol is at the other. If it's a nice day and you're museumed-out, explore the stretch of the Mall between the Washington Monument and the Lincoln Memorial. Much of it is tree-lined, tranquil, and not nearly as crowded as the east end of the Mall (toward the U.S. Capitol).

The White House

Type of Attraction The official residence of the president of the United States. Closed to visitors, except for organized school groups.
Location 1600 Pennsylvania Avenue, NW.
Nearest Metro Stations Federal Triangle
Comments Public tours of the White House were discontinued in 2001 and will not resume in the foreseeable future. Tours of the White House are currently available to school and youth groups grades 1–12 and organized military and veteran groups. Group requests should be submitted through one's Congressional representative. These self-guided tours are scheduled 7:45 a.m. to 10:30 a.m., Tuesday through Saturday.

Zone 2: Capitol Hill

Capital Children's Museum

Type of Attraction A touchy-feely museum for kids. A self-guided tour.
Location 800 3rd Street, NE (behind the Union Station parking garage).
Nearest Metro Station Union Station
Admission $7; $5 for seniors; free for children ages 2 and under. Half-price on Sundays before noon.
Hours Every day, 10 a.m.–5 p.m. daily; closed Mondays, except for Monday holidays; closed New Year's, Thanksgiving, and Christmas Days.
Phone (202) 675-4120; (202) 675-4125 for a recording
When to Go Anytime except Tuesday mornings, which are reserved for large groups.
Special Comments The museum is located in a borderline neighborhood. Either drive or take the Metro to Union Station, where you can grab a cab for the short ride.

Overall Appeal by Age Group

Pre-school ★★★★★	Teens ★★	Over 30 ★
Grade school ★★★★	Young Adults ★½	Snr. citizens ★

Author's Rating Poor location and a bit shabby. ★½
How Much Time to Allow To justify the rather steep admission fee, plan on staying at least three or four hours. You'll still have to drag the kids away.

Description and Comments On the outside it looks like a large school, but the inside is loaded with interactive exhibits that will keep youngsters fascinated for hours. Neato attractions include a cave you can walk through (complete with dripping noises); TV, radio, and animation studios; voice synthesizers; a maze built for ankle biters; and computers that quiz kids. Alas, this museum is a bit worn around the edges. On our visit, a lot of the exhibits were closed or not working, and some of the equipment (such as personal computers) was outdated. But smaller children probably won't notice. A great place to reward tots dragged through boring Mall museums.

Touring Tips Plan your visit around lunch at nearby Union Station, since there's nothing else close by. Again, the neighborhood is marginal, so walk in a group, take a cab, or drive. Combine a visit to the Capital Children's Museum with a stop by the National Postal Museum and be a real hero to your kids.

Other Things to Do Nearby Union Station is a combination transportation hub, shopping mall, theater complex, and food emporium. The food court is pricey but casual, and you're sure to find something you like.

Folger Shakespeare Library

Type of Attraction A museum and library dedicated to the Bard. A self-guided tour.
Location 201 East Capitol Street, SE.
Nearest Metro Stations Capitol South, Union Station
Admission Free
Hours Monday–Saturday, 10 a.m.–4 p.m.; tours at 11 a.m. daily, and 11 a.m. and 1 p.m. on Saturday; closed on federal holidays.
Phone (202) 544-4600
When to Go Anytime
Special Comments The library is available only to accredited scholars.

Overall Appeal by Age Group

Pre-school —	Teens ★½	Over 30 ★★
Grade school ★	Young Adults ★★	Snr. citizens ★★

Author's Rating Dull. ★★
How Much Time to Allow One hour

Description and Comments The Folger House is the world's largest collection of Shakespeare's printed works, as well as a vast array of other rare Renaissance books and manuscripts. But unless you're a scholar doing research, you can't see any of it. Instead, stroll the Great Hall, featuring hand-carved, oak-paneled walls and priceless displays from the museum's collection. You may also visit the three-tiered Elizabethan theater, with walls of timber and plaster and carved oak columns. The Folger is an incongruous attraction that holds appeal only for people with a love of language, Merrie Olde England, and the theater. But it's worth a peek on a second or third trip to Capitol Hill.

Touring Tips Guided tours of the building, exhibits, and the Elizabethan garden are conducted daily at 11 a.m. Special tours of the garden, featuring herbs and flowers grown in Shakespeare's time, are held every third Saturday from April through October at 10 a.m. and 11 a.m. At the west end of the building, a statue of Puck from *A Midsummer Night's Dream* generally presides over a fountain and pool, but is presently under repair. The Folger doesn't have much of interest for kids, unless yours have a fondness for gardens or exhibits on Elizabethan England.

Other Things to Do Nearby The Folger is directly behind the Library of Congress, which sits in front of the U.S. Capitol. The Supreme Court is less than a block away. Walk south on 2nd Street, SE, to find a wide array of restaurants and cafes. The sixth-floor cafeteria in the Library of Congress's Madison Building is a cheap lunch option.

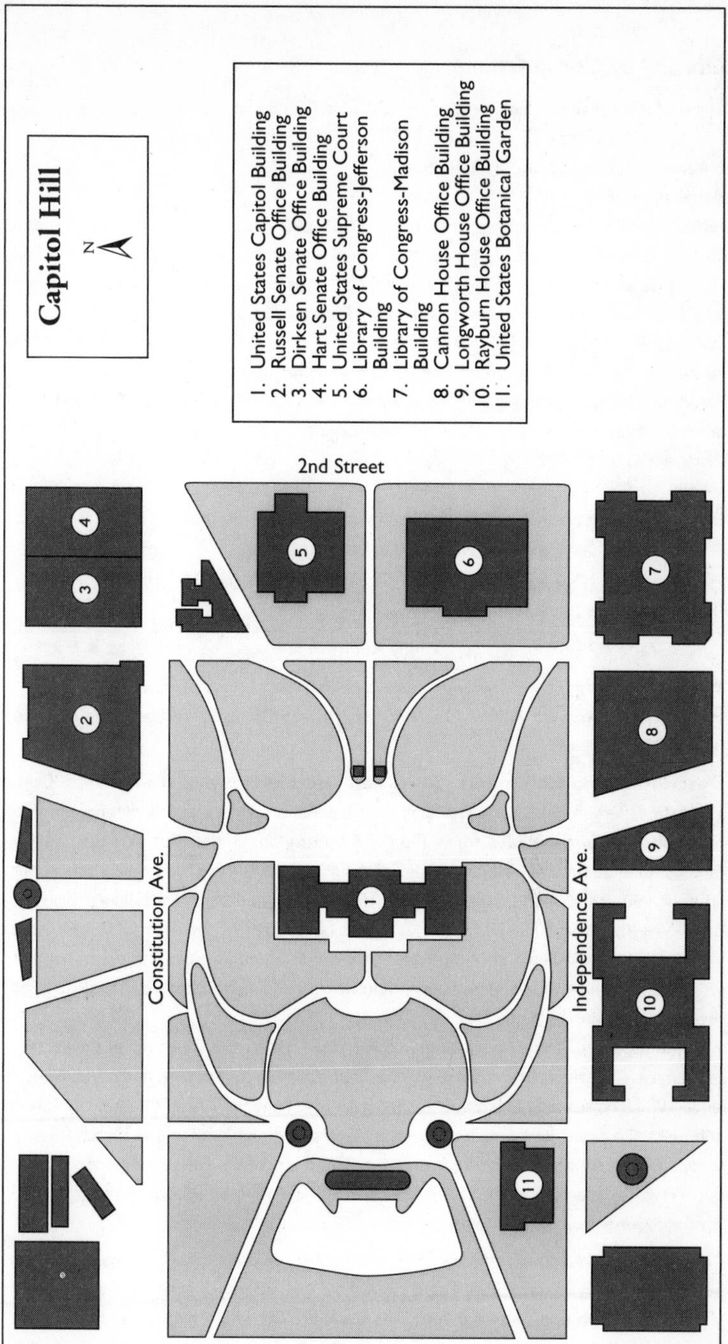
Capitol Hill
N
1. United States Capitol Building
2. Russell Senate Office Building
3. Dirksen Senate Office Building
4. Hart Senate Office Building
5. United States Supreme Court
6. Library of Congress-Jefferson Building
7. Library of Congress-Madison Building
8. Cannon House Office Building
9. Longworth House Office Building
10. Rayburn House Office Building
11. United States Botanical Garden
2nd Street
Constitution Ave.
Independence Ave.
3rd Street
1
2
3
4
5
6
7
8
9
10
11

Library of Congress

Type of Attraction The world's largest library. Guided and self-guided tours.
Location 1st Street, SE, on Capitol Hill.
Nearest Metro Station Capitol South
Admission Free
Hours Exhibition areas in the newly restored Jefferson Building are open Monday–Saturday, 10 a.m.–5:30 p.m.; the library is closed Sundays, federal holidays, and Christmas and New Year's Days. The Visitors Theater in the Jefferson Building shows a free 12-minute film on the library's mission. Free guided tours are offered Friday and Saturday, at 10:30 a.m., 11:30 a.m., 1:30 p.m., 2:30 p.m., and 4 p.m. Groups are limited to 40 people; sign up for any tour (for that day only) at the Information Desk located in the visitor center (on the ground floor on the west side of the Jefferson Building). Pick up your tickets ten minutes before the tour begins.
Phone (202) 707-8000
When to Go Anytime
Special Comments A trip to the library might not be on most folks' vacation itinerary, but consider making an exception in this case.

Overall Appeal by Age Group

Pre-school —	Teens ★★	Over 30 ★★★½
Grade school ★	Young Adults ★★★	Snr. citizens ★★★★

Author's Rating Impressive and informative. ★★★★
How Much Time to Allow One hour for the guided tour and another hour to browse the exhibits.

Description and Comments Three huge structures make up the Library of Congress: the Jefferson, Madison, and Adams Buildings. For an understanding of what goes on here, take one of the guided tours. (To get the most out of the tour, first see the 12-minute video about the varied workings of the library.) After the tour, which lasts about an hour, you can look at other exhibits in the Jefferson and Madison Buildings on your own. Who should go? The Library of Congress holds strong appeal for folks interested in books, academic research, American history, and antiquities. On the other hand, it won't interest many kids, and most first-time visitors on a tight schedule shouldn't waste their valuable touring time here.

In the spring of 1997 a permanent exhibit called "American Treasures of the Library of Congress" marked the reopening of the Thomas Jefferson Building, under renovation since 1984. The rotating exhibition in the Great Hall features 200 of the library's rarest and most significant items, such as Thomas Jefferson's rough draft of the Declaration of Independence, Abraham Lincoln's first and second drafts of the Gettysburg Address, Wilbur Wright's telegram to his father announcing the first heavier-than-air flight, and Bernard Hermann's manuscript score for the film classic *Citizen Kane*.

Touring Tips Although the Library consists of three buildings, visitors enter at the Jefferson Building on 1st Street. The tour, with its well-informed guide, is the way to go if you have the time and interest. *Note:* The tours are extremely popular, and it's a good idea to arrive early during the spring and summer to sign up for a tour later in the day. Tickets are available for that day only.

A permanent exhibit on copyright located on the fourth floor of the Madison Building features the original Barbie and Ken dolls, Dr. Martin Luther King Jr.'s "I Have a Dream" speech, and the statue of the "Maltese falcon" used in the famous film of the same name. More temporary exhibits are located on the sixth floor. Library materials available here go way beyond books. For instance, the Library of Congress has an extensive collection of recorded music, broadcast material, and films. While ostensibly these research materials are for "serious" researchers only, almost anyone with a strong interest in, say, the recordings of Jimmy Durante can find valuable information and hear rare recordings. For musical material, go to the Recorded Sound Reference Center, located on the first floor of the Madison Building, where helpful librarians are ready to assist.

Other Things to Do Nearby The U.S. Capitol, Supreme Court, and Folger Library are all within a block or two. Capitol Hill abounds with nearby lunch spots, not the least of which is right here. The sixth-floor cafeteria in the Madison Building is popular with congressional staffers, and it's a good deal for visitors, who can grab a bite to eat here from 12:30 p.m. to 3 p.m.

National Postal Museum (a Smithsonian museum)

Type of Attraction Displays from the largest philatelic collection in the world and exhibits about the social, historical, and technological impact of the U.S. postal system. A self-guided tour.
Location Washington City Post Office building, 2 Massachusetts Avenue, NE, next to Union Station.
Nearest Metro Station Union Station
Admission Free
Hours Every day, 10 a.m.–5:30 p.m.; closed Christmas Day.
Phone (202) 357-2991; (202) 633-9849 (TTY)
When to Go Anytime
Special Comments The Smithsonian's newest museum (opened summer 1993).
Overall Appeal by Age Group

Pre-school ★½	Teens ★★	Over 30 ★★½
Grade school ★★★	Young Adults ★★	Snr. citizens ★★½

Author's Rating Nifty. And the building that houses the museum is stunning. ★★★
How Much Time to Allow One to two hours

Description and Comments It's more interesting than it sounds—even if you're not one of America's 20 million stamp collectors. Kids will love the real airplanes hanging from the ceiling in the atrium, plus hands-on fun like the chance to sort mail on a train and track a letter from Kansas to Nairobi. Exhibits are arranged so that children and adults are entertained while they're in relative proximity to each other. Themes focus on the history of mail service, how the mail is moved, the social importance of letters, and the beauty and lore of stamps. Serious collectors can call in advance for appointments to see any stamp in the museum's world-class collection or to use the extensive library.

Touring Tips Due to its small size (at least when compared to museums on the Mall), it's easy to whiz through it in a half-hour or so. And because it's right across the street from Union Station, many folks will find it convenient to drop in while waiting for a train. Docent-led "drop-in" tours are available at 11 a.m. and 1 p.m. daily.

Other Things to Do Nearby The Capital Children's Museum is only a few blocks away, making a full day of kid-oriented museum-hopping a distinct possibility—without going near the Mall. Union Station's food hall can satisfy any food craving.

Union Station

Type of Attraction A spectacular interior space housing a transportation hub, upscale shops, a theater complex, and a food court.

Location Massachusetts Avenue and North Capitol Street, NE.

Nearest Metro Station Union Station

Admission Free

Hours Shops open Monday–Saturday, 10 a.m.–9 p.m.; Sunday, noon–6 p.m.

Phone (202) 289-1908

When to Go Anytime

Special Comments The food court's fare is on the expensive side, but the vast selection justifies the extra cost.

Overall Appeal by Age Group

Pre-school ★	Teens ★★★	Over 30 ★★★½
Grade school ★★	Young Adults ★★★½	Snr. citizens ★★★½

Author's Rating A beaux arts palace and a great lunch stop. ★★★½

How Much Time to Allow One hour to wander; longer for shopping or eating.

Description and Comments The Main Hall, with a 90-foot barrel-vaulted ceiling, is breathtaking. Shops run the gamut: chic clothing stores, The Great Train Store, bookstores, Brookstone, the Nature Company—more than 100 altogether. In the food court you'll find everything from sushi to ribs, while a nine-screen cinema complex offers solace on a rainy day. First-time visitors to D.C. shouldn't miss this magnificent structure. With more than 23 million visitors a year, Union Station is the most-visited tourist attraction in Washington (the National Air and Space Museum is number two).

Touring Tips Union Station is a great jumping-off point for touring Washington. Capitol Hill is a few blocks away (step out the front and walk toward the big dome), and Tourmobile, Gray Line, and Old Town Trolley tours stop in front. Monday through Friday, Maryland commuter trains (called MARC) regularly shuttle between D.C. and Baltimore, stopping at points between (a roundtrip from Baltimore is $10.25). Virginia Railway Express shuttles commuters and daytrippers from Fredericksburg, Manassas, and points in between to Union Station weekdays. To top it off, there's a Metro station in the basement. It's hard to believe that Washington functioned before Union Station's rebirth (at a cost of more than $100 million) in 1988.

Other Things to Do Nearby The Capital Children's Museum is only a few blocks away. Kids will love it, but either walk in a group or take a cab: The neighborhood is marginal. The Postal Museum is next door to Union Station; the U.S. Capitol, the Supreme Court, and the Library of Congress are close.

U.S. Botanic Garden

Type of Attraction A permanent collection of tropical, subtropical and desert plants housed in a stunning, fully renovated, 38,000-square-foot greenhouse. A self-guided tour.
Location 1st Street and Maryland Avenue, SW (on the Mall near the U.S. Capitol)
Nearest Metro Stations Federal Center, SW
Admission Free
Hours Every day, 9 a.m.–5 p.m.
Phone (202) 225-8333
When to Go Anytime
Special Comments Skip it on a sweltering summer afternoon.

Overall Appeal by Age Group

Pre-school ★	Teens ★★	Over 30 ★★★
Grade school ★½	Young Adults ★★½	Snr. citizens ★★★★

Author's Rating An excellent and comprehensive collection of plant life. ★★★
How Much Time to Allow 30 minutes

Description and Comments The Conservatory, a building that reflects the grand manner of Victorian architecture (even though it was constructed in the 1930s), houses a living museum on the Mall. The central jungle depicts an abandoned plantation in a tropical rainforest under a dome that rises to 93 feet. Other sections display orchids, ferns, cacti, and other types of plants in naturalistic settings. While people with green thumbs will want to put these gardens on their first-visit itinerary, most folks will just want to know it's nearby for a quiet break from more hectic sights along the Mall. You can sit down here, relax, read a book—or just do nothing in a magnificent setting.

Touring Tips Before or after strolling though this giant greenhouse, visit Frederic Bartholdi Park, located across Independence Avenue from the Conservatory and named for the designer of the Statue of Liberty. The park features displays of bulbs, annuals, and perennials. The focal point is Bartholdi Fountain, originally exhibited at the 1876 Centennial Exhibition in Philadelphia.

Other Things to Do Nearby The National Air and Space Museum and the Hirshhorn Museum and Sculpture Garden are close, as is the U.S. Capitol (although to tour the building requires time tickets handed out early each morning). L'Enfant Plaza, about five blocks away, has a shopping mall loaded with restaurants and fast-food outlets.

U.S. Capitol

Type of Attraction The building where Congress meets. Guided tours only.
Location East end of the Mall.
Nearest Metro Stations Capitol South, Union Station
Admission Free
Hours The building is open Monday–Saturday, 9 a.m.–4:30 p.m., for guided tours only. Pick up free tickets at the Capitol Guide Service kiosk on the curving sidewalk southwest of the Capitol (the Mall side, near the U.S. Botanic Garden). Ticket distribution begins at 8:15 a.m.; if you want one of the 450 tickets (good for that day only), arrive by 7:15 a.m.

Phone (202) 225-6827 for a recording; (202) 225-3121 for the Capitol switchboard
Special Comments After closing to the public after September 11, the Capitol reopened to guided tours only in December 2001. A shuttle is available from the ticket kiosk to the Capitol. Prohibited items include knifes, pointed objects, pepper spray, duffle bags, backpacks, aerosol cans, and bottles.

Overall Appeal by Age Group

Pre-school ★	Teens ★★★	Over 30 ★★★★½
Grade school ★★½	Young Adults ★★★★	Snr. citizens ★★★★★

Author's Rating Interesting and beautiful. ★★★★½
How Much Time to Allow One hour for the tour.

Description and Comments The U.S. Capitol manages to be two things at once: an awesome monument to democracy and one of the most important places in the world, as the frequent presence of reporters and film crews outside attests. The rather brief public tour, however, takes visitors through only a small part of the Capitol: the Rotunda and a few other rooms, which may include Statuary Hall, the House or Senate chambers (when they're not in session), and the low-ceilinged crypt. From the soaring Rotunda to the opulent rooms where the House and Senate meet, the Capitol is both physically beautiful and packed with historical significance. For first-time visitors, the tour is both awe-inspiring and relatively quick (after you've picked up tickets).

Touring Tips If your plans include viewing a session of Congress, don't make the time-consuming mistake thousands of other visitors make: coming to the Capitol without a gallery pass. Go first to the office of your senator or representative to pick one up. (Don't forget to ask for maps and other helpful touring goodies while you're there.) Don't know the name of your representative or of your senators? Then call (202) 224-3121 for help locating an office. The free tour is heavy on the history of the building, but if your group makes it to either the House or Senate chambers, you'll get a good rundown on how Congress operates. (Stick close to the guide if you expect to hear the entire spiel.)

Other Things to Do Nearby Explore the rest of Capitol Hill: The Supreme Court and Library of Congress face the Capitol's east front. On the other side, the east end of the Mall features the U.S. Botanic Garden and the East Wing of the National Gallery of Art. Capitol Hill is famous for its bars and restaurants. To find them, walk toward Constitution Avenue and past the Library of Congress's Madison Building, located between Independence Avenue and C Street, NE.

U.S. Supreme Court

Type of Attraction The nation's highest court. A self-guided tour.
Location One 1st Street, NE, across from the east front of the U.S. Capitol.
Nearest Metro Stations Union Station, Capitol South
Admission Free
Hours Monday–Friday, 9 a.m.–4:30 p.m. Free lectures are offered between 9:30 a.m. and 3:30 p.m. when the court isn't in session.
Phone (202) 479-3030
When to Go Anytime to tour the building. To see the Court in session, the public may attend oral arguments held Mondays, Tuesdays, and Wednesdays, 10 a.m. to 2 p.m.,

in two-week intervals from October through April; check the "A" section of the *Washington Post.*

Special Comments Seeing an oral argument here is probably your best chance of witnessing one of the three major branches of the government in operation while in D.C.

Overall Appeal by Age Group

Pre-school —	Teens ★★	Over 30 ★★★½
Grade school ★	Young Adults ★★★	Snr. citizens ★★★★

Author's Rating Extremely interesting and enlightening. ★★★★

How Much Time to Allow One hour to tour the building; plan on at least two hours total to see an oral argument.

Description and Comments This magnificent faux Greek temple is where the nine-member Supreme Court makes final interpretations of the U.S. Constitution and laws passed by Congress. When the Court's not in session, visitors may enter the stunning courtroom and hear a short lecture on its workings. An excellent 20-minute film explains the workings of the Supreme Court in more detail. On the ground floor is a small museum, a gift shop, a cafeteria, and a snack bar. A visit to the Supreme Court is a must for anyone interested in how the federal government works, or how the law works in general. Others should pass it up, although the building itself is impressive.

Touring Tips To see an oral argument, plan on arriving no later than 9 a.m. to get in line. Two lines form: a regular line, for those wishing to hear an entire argument (an hour), and a three-minute line, for folks who just want to slip in for a few moments. Bring quarters: You will have to place personal belongings like backpacks and cameras in coin-operated (quarters only) lockers. Security here is no-nonsense: Visitors pass through *two* X-ray machines before entering the courtroom, where very serious-looking security people patrol the aisles. Small children are not allowed in the courtroom during oral arguments.

Other Things to Do Nearby The U.S. Capitol, the Library of Congress, the National Postal Museum, and the Folger Shakespeare Library are all close by. The comfortable cafeteria on the ground level of the Supreme Court is one of the better government eateries. It's open for breakfast from 7:30 a.m. to 10:30 a.m. and for lunch from 11:30 a.m. to 2 p.m. except for 15-minute periods when only Court employees may enter. Capitol Hill is renowned for its many bars and cafes, many of which are a short walk up 2nd Street, SE.

Zone 3: Downtown

B'nai B'rith Klutznick National Jewish Museum

Type of Attraction A museum featuring Jewish folk and ceremonial art. A self-guided tour.

Location 2020 K St. NW, 7th Floor

Nearest Metro Stations Farragut North, Farragut West

Admission Suggested donation: adults, $3; seniors and children, $2. Reservations required

Hours Monday–Thursday, noon–3 p.m. and on Sundays; in all cases, by advanced appointment only.
Phone (202) 857-6583
When to Go Anytime
Special Comments This interim gallery of artifacts will serve as the museum's home as plans are developed for a new, enlarged museum.

Overall Appeal by Age Group

Pre-school ★	Teens ★½	Over 30 ★★½
Grade school ★½	Young Adults ★★	Snr. citizens ★★½

Author's Rating Small and tasteful, but inconveniently located. ★★½
How Much Time to Allow One hour

Description and Comments Although it's small, the Klutznick Museum features a wide variety of items, from 1,000-year-old coins to modern art. You'll also find the 1790 letter from President George Washington to a Newport, Rhode Island, synagogue. While you don't have to be Jewish to appreciate this attractive museum, for most folks it's not a main attraction.

Other Things to Do Nearby The National Geographic Society's Explorers Hall, a must-see for kids, is at 17th and M Streets, NW. For a limitless selection of eateries, just walk toward Connecticut Avenue.

Federal Bureau of Investigation

Type of Attraction FBI headquarters. A guided tour.
Location 10th Street, NW, at Pennsylvania Avenue. Visitor's entrance is at 9th and E Streets, NW.
Admission Free
Hours By appointment only; on Federal workdays only. Reservations are required and may only be made through Congressional representatives at least one month in advance. Currently, tours are only available to schools and childrens organizations and adult veteran groups.
Phone (202) 324-3447
Nearest Metro Stations Metro Center, Gallery, Archives, and Federal Triangle
When to Go As scheduled
Special Comments Children should try to stay close to the tour guide, since there's a lot of peering into crime labs through plate glass windows set at adult height.

Overall Appeal by Age Group

Pre-school ★★	Teens ★★★★½	Over 30 ★★★
Grade school ★★★★★	Young Adults ★★★★	Snr. citizens ★★★

Author's Rating A boring tour. ★½
How Much Time to Allow One hour

Description and Comments After a brief introductory video, the tour guide leads your group through a series of displays highlighting the Bureau's fabled history, with heavy emphasis on gangsters (look for John Dillinger's death mask), spies, and drug smugglers. Then you walk past FBI crime labs, with views through windows of technicians at work in DNA-, document-, and material-identification labs. There's also a collection of valuables confiscated in drug raids that includes expensive jewelry and a ten-foot, six-inch stuffed brown bear. This has long been one of the most popular tours in Washington. Families with school-age children should try to work out a visit—kids love it.

Touring Tips Call ahead and arrive early. Once you're inside, rest rooms are available before the tour begins.

Other Things to Do Nearby If the line at the National Archives is short (and it has reopened by your visit), scoot inside for a peek at the Declaration of Independence. Or go to the Old Post Office Pavilion for lunch in the food court and a trip to the clock tower for the second-best view in Washington. The International Spy Museum is also close by.

Ford's Theatre/Petersen House

Type of Attraction The restored theater where Abraham Lincoln was shot, and the house across the street, where he died. A self-guided tour.
Location 511 10th Street, NW.
Nearest Metro Station Metro Center, 11th Street exit
Admission Free
Hours Every day, 9 a.m.–5 p.m.; closed Christmas Day.
Phone (202) 426-6924
When to Go Anytime
Special Comments The theater (but not the museum) is closed to visitors on Thursday and Sunday afternoons, when matinees are in progress. It may also be closed on other afternoons when rehearsals are in progress.

Overall Appeal by Age Group

Pre-school ★	Teens ★★	Over 30 ★★½
Grade school ★½	Young Adults ★★½	Snr. citizens ★★★

Author's Rating An interesting, but small, museum; the theater is a reconstruction of the original interior. ★★½
How Much Time to Allow One hour

Description and Comments Don't miss the recently updated Lincoln Museum in the basement of the theater, featuring the clothes Lincoln was wearing the night he was shot and the derringer used to kill him. Across the street, Petersen House offers a glimpse of nineteenth-century Washington. Ford's Theatre, both the museum and where Lincoln was shot, is small. Unless you're a history buff, this is mostly a fill-in stop, at least for first-time visitors.

Touring Tips Start with the theater, then view the museum in the basement before crossing the street to Petersen House.

Other Things to Do Nearby The FBI, the International Spy Museum, the National Portrait Gallery, and the National Museum of American Art are all close. For lunch, it's four or five blocks to Chinatown, two blocks to the Old Post Office Pavilion, or just down the street to the Hard Rock Cafe.

International Spy Museum

Type of Attraction The history and gadgetry of espionage housed in Washington's newest museum. A self-guided tour.
Location 800 F St. N.W.
Nearest Metro Station Gallery Place
Admission $11 for adults, $9 for seniors, $8 for children 5-18, children under 5 free.
Hours Every day, 10 a.m.–8 p.m. April–October; until 6 p.m. November–March.
Phone (866) SPY MUSEUM (968-7386); (202) 654-0944
When to Go After the spook museum opened in the summer of 2002, lines stretched around the block throughout the day, signaling a minimum wait in line of 45 minutes (from the middle of the block on 9th Street) or longer. Either arrive at least a half-hour before 10 a.m. or plan to visit around 5 p.m. weekdays, when the there's usually no wait.
Special Comments There's a long, steep flight of stairs to descend about half way through the museum.

Overall Appeal by Age Group

Pre-school ★	Teens ★★½	Over 30 ★★★
Grade school ★★	Young Adults ★★★	Snr. citizens ★★★½

Author's Rating Spycraft meets Austin Powers: The museum is slick, manipulative and dodges some important moral questions (and historical failures) of U.S. intelligence operations. Otherwise, it's fun in an empty-headed sort of way (and located in city full of world-class museums, most of them free). ★½
How Much Time to Allow 90 minutes to 2 hours.

Description and Comments Since CIA headquarters across the Potomac in Langley isn't offering tours, this spanking new, $40 million, privately owned museum offers the next best thing: a look at the secret world of intelligence. More than 400 artifacts are on display, ranging from items dating from Biblical times to the modern age of terror. What you'll see: tools of the trade such as a lipstick pistol developed by the KGB, an Enigma cipher machine used by the Allies to break German secret codes during World War II, an Aston Martin DB 5 sports car decked out like the one used by James Bond in Goldfinger, and tributes to celebrity spies such as dancer Josephine Baker (who worked for the French resistance) and TV chef Julia Child (who worked for the OSS). What you won't see: Any mention of spectacular failures of U.S. intelligence, including how the CIA, NSA, DIA and other alphabet-soup spy agencies missed the fall of the Soviet Union and the Shah of Iran, and helped overthrow elected governments around the world. Alas, the museum's us-versus-them mentality spares visitors from the moral ambiguity of intelligence gathering. To get that insight, skip the museum and curl up with a novel by John LeCarre (a former spy).

Touring Tips This is one of those museums where visitors are herded into an elevator, taken to the second floor and everyone negotiates their way through narrow corridors—making it difficult to linger or backtrack against the human current. Keep that in mind as you tour.

Other Things to Do Nearby The National Portrait Gallery and the National Museum of American Art are across the street; currently under renovation, the museums reopen in 2003. Ford's Theatre/Petersen House (where Lincoln was assassinated/died) are a block over on 10th Street N.W. The booming downtown area is teeming with new restaurants. For classy Mexican cuisine, try Andele at 7th and D.

National Building Museum

Type of Attraction A museum dedicated to architecture and the construction arts that's an architectural marvel in its own right. Self-guided and guided tours.
Location 401 F Street, NW.
Nearest Metro Station Judiciary Square
Admission Free; suggested donation of $5 for adults
Hours Monday–Saturday, 10 a.m.–5 p.m.; Sunday, 11 a.m.–5 p.m. Closed Thanksgiving, Christmas, and New Year's Days.
Phone (202) 272-2448
When to Go Anytime
Special Comments Tours are given daily at 12:30 p.m., and additional tours are offered on Saturday at 11:30 a.m. and 1:30 p.m., and on Sunday at 1:30 p.m.

Overall Appeal by Age Group

Pre-school ★★	Teens ★★★	Over 30 ★★★½
Grade school ★★★	Young Adults ★★★½	Snr. citizens ★★★½

Author's Rating The Great Hall is eye-popping. ★★★½
How Much Time to Allow 45 minutes

Description and Comments The ideal way to visit this museum would be to walk in blindfolded, then have the blindfold removed. Rather unimposing on the outside, the Pension Building (as this museum is better known to Washingtonians) offers one of the most imposing interiors in Washington, if not the world. The Great Hall measures 316 feet by 116 feet, and at its highest point the roof is 159 feet above the floor. Eight marbleized Corinthian columns adorn the interior. It's a must-see, even if all you do is poke your head inside the door.

Touring Tips The exhibits in the museum are on the thin side: The main attraction is the building itself. But if you're interested in architecture and building construction, check out the permanent and temporary exhibits on the first and second floors. The new Courtyard Cafe is open weekdays, 11 a.m. to 3 p.m.

Other Things to Do Nearby The three-acre National Law Enforcement Officers Memorial is directly across from the National Building Museum's entrance on F Street. Engraved on blue-gray marble walls are the names of 12,500 law enforcement officers who died in the line of duty throughout U.S. history. Four groups of striking statues adorning the park each show a lion protecting her cubs.

The Lillian and Albert Small Jewish Museum at 701 3rd Street, NW, offers a glimpse into Washington's historic Jewish presence. The museum features temporary exhibits about the city's Jewish life, while the Adas Israel Synagogue on the second floor is listed in the National Register of Historic Places. Open Sunday through Thursday, noon to 4 p.m. Closed Saturdays and all major Jewish holidays; phone (202) 789-0900 for more information. Chinatown and a large selection of restaurants are only two blocks away.

National Geographic Society's Explorers Hall

Type of Attraction A small, high-tech exhibition that delights children. A self-guided tour.
Location 17th and M Streets, NW, four blocks north of the White House.
Nearest Metro Stations Farragut North, Farragut West
Admission Free
Hours Monday–Saturday, 9 a.m.–5 p.m.; Sundays and holidays, 10 a.m.–5 p.m.; closed Christmas Day.
Phone (202) 857-7588
When to Go Anytime
Special Comments The downtown exhibit is handy in an area that's spotty on entertaining things for kids to do.

Overall Appeal by Age Group

Pre-school ★★★	Teens ★★★½	Over 30 ★★
Grade school ★★★★	Young Adults ★★★	Snr. citizens ★★

Author's Rating Well-done exhibits that aren't overpowering. ★★
How Much Time to Allow One hour

Description and Comments It's like walking through a couple of National Geographic TV specials. Located on the first floor of the National Geographic Society's headquarters, this small collection of exhibits showcases weather, geography, astronomy, biology, exploration, and space science. It's also a bit heavy on quizzes that could prove embarrassing to adults. For example, Earth Station One is a 72-seat amphitheater that simulates orbital flight 23,000 miles above the earth. The interactive program lets kids punch buttons as they answer geography questions posed by the "captain."

Touring Tips Don't miss the extensive sales shop that offers books, videos, maps, and magazines. The courtyard on M Street is a great spot for a brown-bag lunch. Free films are shown on Tuesdays at noon.

Other Things to Do Nearby The still-imposing Russian embassy is around the corner on 16th Street; you can't go in, but check out the array of antennas on the roof.

National Museum of American Art (a Smithsonian museum)

This museum closed for major renovations in January 2000 and will not reopen until 2004 or 2005.

National Museum of Women in the Arts

Type of Attraction The world's single most important collection of art by women. A self-guided tour.
Location 1250 New York Avenue, NW.
Nearest Metro Station Metro Center
Admission $8 for adults; $3 for seniors, students, and children
Hours Monday–Saturday, 10 a.m.–5 p.m.; Sunday, noon–5 p.m. Closed Thanksgiving, Christmas, and New Year's Days.
Phone (202) 783-5000

When to Go Anytime
Special Comments Unfortunately, this beautiful museum is in an inconvenient location on the edge of downtown.

Overall Appeal by Age Group

Pre-school ★	Teens ★★½	Over 30 ★★★½
Grade school ★★	Young Adults ★★★	Snr. citizens ★★★½

Author's Rating Both the building and the art are superb. ★★★½
How Much Time to Allow One to two hours

Description and Comments This relatively new museum has a permanent collection of paintings and sculpture that includes art by Georgia O'Keeffe, Frida Kahlo, and Helen Frankenthaler, as well as art by women from the sixteenth century to the present. From the outside, it looks like any other office building along crowded New York Avenue. But inside the former Masonic Grand Lodge are striking architectural features such as a crystal chandelier, a main hall and mezzanine, and the Grand Staircase. The second-floor balcony hosts temporary exhibits; the third floor is where you'll find the permanent collection. Next door, a new annex that opened in the fall of 1997 allowed the museum to expand the amount of artwork on display, including sculpture and contemporary works by lesser known women artists. While this beautiful museum well off the beaten path deserves to be seen by more people, first-time visitors can wait and enjoy it on a later trip.

Touring Tips Take the elevator to the fourth (top) floor and work your way down. The mezzanine features an attractive cafe offering "light fare," and there's a gift shop on the ground floor.

Other Things to Do Nearby A block away is the old Greyhound Bus Station, now a fully restored Art Deco masterpiece; take a peek inside. The Capitol City Brewing Company brews beer on the premises and serves hearty fare like burgers to go with it.

National Portrait Gallery (a Smithsonian museum)

This museum closed for major renovations in January 2000 and will not reopen until 2004 or 2005.

Zone 4: Foggy Bottom

John F. Kennedy Center for the Performing Arts

Type of Attraction Both presidential memorial and D.C.'s performing arts headquarters. A guided tour for groups only.
Location New Hampshire Avenue, NW, and F Street.
Nearest Metro Station Foggy Bottom/GWU
Admission Free
Hours Every day, 10 a.m.–midnight.
Phone (202) 416-8340; (202) 416-8524 (TTY)
When to Go Free tours begin every 15 minutes; Monday–Friday, 10 a.m.–5 p.m., and on Saturday and Sunday, 10 a.m.–1 p.m.

Special Comments The leisurely tour lasts about 45 minutes but is easy on the feet: The Kennedy Center is well carpeted.

Overall Appeal by Age Group

Pre-school ★	Teens ★	Over 30 ★★½
Grade school ★	Young Adults ★★	Snr. citizens ★★★

Author's Rating So-so art, a huge building, and a great view. ★★
How Much Time to Allow One hour

Description and Comments The white rectilinear Kennedy Center facility boasts four major stages, a film theater, and a sumptuous interior shimmering with crystal, mirrors, and deep-red carpets. The Grand Foyer is longer than two football fields. Nations from around the world contributed art and artifacts on display in halls and foyers, such as African art, Beame porcelain, tapestries, and sculptures. If rehearsals aren't in progress, the tour includes peeks inside the intimate Eisenhower Theater, the Opera House (featuring a spectacular chandelier), and the Concert Hall, which seats 2,750. Admirers of JFK and culture vultures will love the tour, while kids will probably get bored. But you don't have to take the tour to enjoy the view; take the elevators to the roof terrace.

Touring Tips While the guided tour is leisurely and informative, the best way to visit the Kennedy Center is to attend a concert, play, or film. Before or after the event, go up to the seventh floor and stroll the roof terrace—the view at night is terrific. Free round-trip shuttle service from the Foggy Bottom Metro station is offered daily from 10 a.m. to midnight every 15 minutes. Also, don't miss the free performance given every day at 6 p.m. in the Grand Foyer.

Other Things to Do Nearby You can lunch or snack at the Kennedy Center's Encore Cafe without securing a second mortgage on your house, but the Roof Terrace Restaurant is expense-account priced. The infamous Watergate project is across G Street from the Kennedy Center and features expensive shops and restaurants, but you won't find any memorial to a certain burglary that occurred there in 1972. A biking and jogging path along the Potomac River is just below the Kennedy Center; follow it upriver to Thompson's Boat Center, which rents canoes and bikes. A little farther is Washington Harbour, an upscale collection of shops, restaurants, and condominiums, featuring life-size and lifelike sculptures of tourists, joggers, workers, and artists that add a bit of whimsy to scenic al fresco dining along the river. Hard-core walkers can continue along the path into Georgetown. Walk up Wisconsin Avenue and you enter a world of trendy shops, restaurants, and crowded sidewalks. Before you walk too far, remember that Georgetown lacks a Metro station to get you back to where you started.

U.S. Department of the Interior

Type of Attraction A museum located inside a square-mile chunk of government bureaucracy; a National Park Service office and a retail map outlet. A self-guided tour.
Location 1849 C Street, NW, between 18th and 19th Streets.
Nearest Metro Station Farragut West
Admission Free
Hours Weekdays, 8:30 a.m.–4:30 p.m., and every 3rd Saturday, 1 p.m.–4 p.m.; otherwise, closed weekends and federal holidays.
Phone (202) 208-4743

When to Go Anytime
Special Comments Go on a rainy day. Adults must show a photo ID to enter the building.

Overall Appeal by Age Group

Pre-school ★	Teens ★	Over 30 ★
Grade school ★★	Young Adults ★	Snr. citizens ★

Author's Rating Boring. ★
How Much Time to Allow 45 minutes

Description and Comments This six-wing, seven-story limestone edifice includes 16 acres of floors, two miles of corridors—and an old-fashioned museum. Dioramas of mines and geothermal power plants, Native American artifacts, and a historical exhibit of the National Park Service crowd the rather dark and quiet exhibit hall. This is definitely a rainy-day kind of a museum, unless you have a strong interest in national parks.

Touring Tips Outdoors-people and map-lovers shouldn't miss the U.S. Geological Survey map store, located off the lobby on the E Street side of the building. You can also load up on brochures on any (or all) U.S. national parks at the National Park Service office here. The Indian Craft Shop, across from the museum entrance, sells turquoise and silver jewelry, baskets, and other handicrafts made by Native Americans. The basement cafeteria can seat 1,200 people (open weekdays, 7 a.m. to 2:45 p.m.).

Other Things to Do Nearby The DAR Museum and the Corcoran Gallery of Art are around the corner on 17th Street; the Mall is about two blocks south. The Octagon, one of Washington's earliest and most elegant homes, is half a block north on 18th Street. For places to eat, head north up any numbered street toward Pennsylvania Avenue.

U.S. Department of State Diplomatic Reception Rooms

Type of Attraction The rooms where visiting foreign dignitaries are officially entertained. A guided tour.
Location 21st and C Streets, NW.
Nearest Metro Station Foggy Bottom/GWU
Admission Free
Hours Tours are given Monday–Friday at 9:30 a.m., 10:30 a.m., and 2:45 p.m., by reservation only.
Phone (202) 647-3241; fax (202) 736-4232; (202) 736-4474 (TDD)
Special Comments See what $90 million in decorative arts can buy. Children under age 12 are not permitted on the tour, nor are strollers, breifcases, or backpacks. Reservations are accepted up to 90 days in advance of your visit. A short, optional public affairs tour is offered after the main tour.

Overall Appeal by Age Group

Pre-school —	Teens ★★★½	Over 30 ★★★★★
Grade school —	Young Adults ★★★★	Snr. citizens ★★★★★

Author's Rating Although most tourists miss this, you shouldn't. ★★★★★
How Much Time to Allow One hour

Description and Comments While the State Department goes about its important work in a building with architecture best described as "early airport," the interiors on the eighth floor are something else entirely: A fabulous collection of 18th- and early nineteenth-century fine and decorative arts fills stunning rooms that are used daily to receive visiting heads of state and foreign dignitaries. This is a tour for almost anyone: antique and fine arts lovers, history buffs, and just casual visitors. It's also a sight that the overwhelming majority of D.C. tourists miss. First-time visitors should make the effort to get reservations well in advance of their trip. Then forget about visiting the White House.

Touring Tips By guided tour only; reservations are required and should be made at least four weeks in advance of your visit. Rest rooms are located near the waiting room and can be visited before and after the tour.

Other Things to Do Nearby The Lincoln Memorial and Vietnam Veterans Memorial are a short walk away, down 23rd Street to the Mall. The closest places to eat are a few blocks up 23rd Street, away from the Mall.

Zone 5: Georgetown

Dumbarton Oaks and Gardens

Type of Attraction A mansion/museum and a beautiful terraced garden. Self-guided tours.

Location 1703 32nd Street, between R and S Streets, NW, in Georgetown.

Admission $1 donation suggested for adults for the museum; $5 fee for adults, $3 for seniors and children for the gardens (April through October only, free the rest of the year)

Hours Museum hours are Tuesday–Sunday, 2 p.m. to 5 p.m. The garden is open (weather permitting) November–March, 2 p.m.–5 p.m., and until 6 p.m. the rest of the year. Closed on national holidays.

Phone (202) 339-6400

When to Go Anytime

Special Comments Don't be put off by the hushed surroundings—this is one of the best museums in Washington. There is, however, no eatery and picnics are not allowed.

Overall Appeal by Age Group

Pre-school —	Teens ★★½	Over 30 ★★★★
Grade school ★	Young Adults ★★★½	Snr. citizens ★★★★

Author's Rating Intimate and gorgeous. ★★★★

How Much Time to Allow Two hours

Description and Comments Most people associate Dumbarton Oaks with the conference held here in 1944 that led to the formation of the United Nations. Today, however, it's a research center for Byzantine and pre-Columbian studies owned by Harvard University. The Byzantine collection is one of the world's finest, featuring bronzes, ivories, and jewelry. The exquisite pre-Columbian art collection is housed in eight interconnected, circular glass pavilions lit by natural light. It's a knockout of a museum. Dumbarton Oaks Gardens is located around the corner on R Street. The terraced ten-acre garden is rated one of the top gardens in the United States, featuring an orangery, a rose garden, wisteria-covered arbors and, in the fall, a blazing backdrop of trees turning orange, yellow, and red. Dumbarton Oaks isn't the kind of museum with much appeal to small children, and some adults may not find much of interest in the collection due to its narrow focus. But combined with the adjacent gardens, it's a worthwhile place to visit when in Georgetown.

Touring Tips Because Dumbarton Oaks doesn't open its massive doors until 2 p.m., combine your visit with a morning trip to Georgetown. If it's raining the day you plan to visit, try to rearrange your schedule so you can come on a nice day; the gardens are terrific.

Other Things to Do Nearby Take a walking tour of Georgetown and see how lobbyists, politicians, media gurus, and other well-connected and monied denizens of Washington live. If you made advance reservations to see Tudor House, Dumbarton Oaks makes a great side trip. When you get hungry, turn left or right on Wisconsin Avenue and you won't have to go far to find an interesting restaurant or cafe. The Chesapeake and Ohio Canal, which starts in Georgetown, can offer near wilderness solace to weary tourists.

Zone 6: Dupont Circle/Adams-Morgan

The Christian Heurich House Mansion

Type of Attraction The lavish home of a wealthy turn-of-the-century Washington businessman. A self-guided tour.
Location 1307 New Hampshire Avenue, NW (two blocks south of Dupont Circle).
Nearest Metro Station Dupont Circle
Admission $3 for adults; $1.50 for students, seniors, and children
Hours Monday–Saturday, 10 a.m.–4 p.m. Research library hours are Wednesday through Saturday, 10 a.m.–4 p.m. Closed on federal holidays.
Phone (202) 785-2068
Special Comments Don't be put off by the grimy exterior.

Overall Appeal by Age Group

Pre-school —	Teens ★½	Over 30 ★★★
Grade school ★	Young Adults ★★½	Snr. citizens ★★★

Author's Rating An outrageous Gilded Age interior. ★★★
How Much Time to Allow One hour

Description and Comments It's doubtful that any amount of money could recreate what wealthy brewer Christian Heurich built in the early 1890s: a regal, 31-room mansion full of richly detailed mahogany and oak woodwork, elaborate plaster moldings, and a musician's balcony that lets live music be heard throughout the first floor. It may be the most opulent home open to the public in Washington. The building also serves as headquarters for the Historical Society of Washington and houses its library (for more information on the society, visit its webpage: www.hswdc.org). While most first-time visitors to Washington shouldn't feel obligated to spend time here, it's worth a look on a later trip. People who love decorative arts should put it on their "A" list.

Touring Tips The small garden behind the museum is a popular spot for a brown-bag lunch.

Other Things to Do Nearby Walk to Dupont Circle for a whiff of Washington's bohemian side: Trendy cafes, shops, bookstores, and restaurants crowd Connecticut Avenue. Expect to be panhandled about every 50 feet in fair weather; the street merchants crowding around the Metro entrances suggest a Middle East bazaar. *Note*: Good deals can be had.

House of the Temple

Type of Attraction A Masonic temple modeled after one of the Seven Wonders of the World. A guided tour.
Location 1733 16th Street, NW.
Nearest Metro Station Dupont Circle
Admission Free
Hours Guided tours Monday–Friday, 8 a.m.–2 p.m.
Phone (202) 232-3579
When to Go Anytime
Special Comments Unless you have an abiding interest in Freemasonry, the tour is way too long.

Overall Appeal by Age Group

Pre-school —	Teens ★	Over 30 ★
Grade school ★	Young Adults ★	Snr. citizens ★

Author's Rating Spectacular but cold. ★
How Much Time to Allow Two hours (less if you're willing to fib to the tour guide; see below).

Description and Comments The walls are 8 feet thick; the exterior is surrounded by 33 massive columns that support a magnificent pyramidal roof; and, inside, the Temple Room features a soaring 100-foot ceiling and 1,000-pipe organ. Unfortunately, with the exception of the exterior, you have to take an excruciatingly boring guided tour to see these goodies. You're guaranteed to be bored silly by displays of bric-a-brac and memorabilia belonging to long-dead Masonic leaders. There is one slightly bizarre treat: the J. Edgar Hoover Law Enforcement Room, a shrine to the Mason and lifelong FBI chief. But unless you're a rabid fan of J. Edgar, after about two minutes you'll be . . . bored.

Touring Tips Arrive around 1 p.m. on a quiet afternoon and tell the tour guide you've got to catch a train at 2:30. Then plead for an abbreviated tour, which he may grudgingly provide if there aren't any other tourists on-hand for a tour. But even reduced to an hour, the tour is too long.

Other Things to Do Nearby The House of the Temple is on the edge of a marginally safe neighborhood, so make a beeline toward Dupont Circle, where you'll find plenty to do. Six blocks west on S Street are the Textile Museum and the Woodrow Wilson House.

Islamic Center

Type of Attraction A mosque. A self-guided tour.
Location 2551 Massachusetts Avenue, NW.
Nearest Metro Station Dupont Circle

Admission Free
Hours Every day, 10 a.m.–5 p.m.; closed Fridays to non-Muslims between 1 p.m. and 2:30 p.m.
Phone (202) 332-8343
When to Go Anytime. Call ahead for a guided tour.
Special Comments The mosque enforces a strict dress code: Visitors must remove their shoes to go inside, and no shorts or short dresses are allowed. Women must cover their heads and wear long-sleeved clothing.

Overall Appeal by Age Group

Pre-school ★	Teens ★½	Over 30 ★★
Grade school ★½	Young Adults ★★★	Snr. citizens ★★

Author's Rating Exotic and surprisingly small. ★½
How Much Time to Allow 15 minutes

Description and Comments A brilliant white building and slender minaret mark this unusual sight on Embassy Row. Visitors must remove their shoes before stepping inside to see the Persian carpets, elegantly embellished columns, decorated arches, and huge chandelier. Alas, with America's focus on the Middle East and things Islamic, we were disappointed on our visit to the Islamic Center: It fell a little short on giving any useful insight into that troubled part of the world. The small bookstore next to the mosque was filled with Arabic texts and translations of the Koran, but no one was behind the counter to answer our questions. Though close to other tourist sights, the mosque seems to have missed an opportunity to educate D.C. visitors about Islam. Those with a strong interest in the Middle East should call a week in advance for the one-hour guided tour.

Touring Tips Make this small, exotic building a part of a walk down Embassy Row. But unless you have an interest in Islam, it's not worth going out of the way to see.

Other Things to Do Nearby Take a short walk and tour the Textile Museum and the Woodrow Wilson House. On Tuesday through Saturday afternoons, the opulent Anderson House is open. The Phillips Collection is an intimate modern art museum that's a refreshing change of pace from huge Mall museums.

Meridian International Center

Type of Attraction Two mansions designed by John Russell Pope; art exhibitions displayed in beautiful galleries; handsome gardens and a grove of linden trees. Guided and self-guided tours.
Location 1624 and 1630 Crescent Place, NW.
Admission Free
Hours Wednesday–Sunday, 2 p.m.–5 p.m. Closed Mondays, Tuesdays, and federal holidays. The cafe is open Monday–Friday, noon–2 p.m.
Phone (202) 939-5568
When to Go Anytime
Special Comments Call ahead of time or check Friday's "Weekend" section of the *Washington Post* to make sure the center isn't closed (due to a conference) and to find out what's on display in the galleries.

Overall Appeal by Age Group

Pre-school ★	Teens ★½	Over 30 ★★
Grade school ★½	Young Adults ★★	Snr. citizens ★★½

Author's Rating Grand architecture and a glimpse into the world of diplomacy. ★★½
How Much Time to Allow One hour

Description and Comments Two side-by-side mansions designed by John Russell Pope (architect of the Jefferson Memorial, the National Gallery of Art building, and other Washington treasures) make up the Meridian International Center, a nonprofit organization that promotes conferences, symposiums, lectures, and seminars and provides services to international visitors, diplomats, scholars, politicians, and others.

The 45-room Meridian House (1921) reflects an eighteenth-century French Louis XVI style of architecture, while the White-Meyer House (1911) is a salmon-color brick, Georgian-style mansion. Visitors are welcome to tour the ground floors of the gorgeous—though lightly furnished—buildings and the surrounding gardens. About five art exhibits a year rotate through the galleries of the White-Meyer House. The three-acre site, set off from the city by high, elegant walls, takes up an entire city block.

Touring Tips While folks who enjoy grand architecture won't need additional encouragement to visit these two distinguished buildings, others should plan on coming in the spring when the gardens are in bloom and an art exhibition is on display in the elegant galleries. A small cafe in the basement of the Meridian House (which recently underwent a two-year, $1.8 million restoration) offers coffee, tea, and lunch. For a guided tour of the property, just ask at the front desk in either building.

Other Things to Do Nearby Adams-Morgan, an eclectic multicultural neighborhood renowned for its ethnic eateries, is only two blocks away on 18th Street, NW.

Phillips Collection

Type of Attraction The first museum dedicated to modern art in the United States. A self-guided tour.
Location 1600 21st Street, NW.
Nearest Metro Station Dupont Circle
Admission Weekends: $10 for adults, $8 for seniors over age 62 and for full-time students. No charge for visitors under age 18. During the week, the museum suggests contributions at the same level.
Hours Tuesday–Saturday, 10 a.m.–5 p.m.; Sunday, noon–5 p.m. Open Thursday until 8:30 p.m. Closed New Year's Day, Fourth of July, Thanksgiving, and Christmas.
Phone (202) 387-2151
When to Go Anytime
Special Comments With lots of carpeting and places to sit, the Phillips Collection is a very comfortable museum to tour. A cafe on the ground floor is open Tuesday through Saturday from 10:45 a.m. to 4:30 p.m., and on Sunday noon to 4:30 p.m.

Overall Appeal by Age Group

Pre-school —	Teens ★★	Over 30 ★★★★
Grade school ★	Young Adults ★★★½	Snr. citizens ★★★★

Author's Rating One of the best art museums in Washington. ★★★★
How Much Time to Allow Two hours

Description and Comments Founded by Duncan Phillips, grandson of the founder of the Jones and Laughlin Steel Company, the Phillips Collection is set in the family's former mansion, which helps explain its intimate and comfortable feeling. The collection is too large for everything to be on display at once, so the art is constantly rotated. Expect to see works by Monet, Picasso, Miró, Renoir, and Van Gogh, among other modern masters. The large and ornate Music Room is as spectacular as the art hanging on its walls. If you've seen the Hirshhorn and the National Gallery of Art's East Wing, this should be on your agenda. It's a classy museum on a human scale.

Touring Tips The kids would probably prefer a trip to the zoo. Take advantage of the free, 45-minute guided tours given Wednesdays and Saturdays at 2 p.m. The well-informed guides do a good job of giving a context for the paintings and sculptures, the building, and its founder's taste in modern art.

Other Things to Do Nearby Cross Massachusetts Avenue and see another eye-popping mansion, the Anderson House (open Tuesday through Saturday from 1 p.m. to 4 p.m.). Dupont Circle hosts a myriad of cafes, restaurants, and fast-food joints to satisfy hunger pangs.

Society of the Cincinnati Museum at Anderson House

Type of Attraction A combination mansion and Revolutionary War museum. A self-guided tour.
Location 2118 Massachusetts Avenue, NW.
Nearest Metro Station Dupont Circle
Admission Free
Hours Tuesday–Saturday, 1 p.m.–4 p.m.; closed national holidays.
Phone (202) 785-2040
When to Go Anytime
Special Comments Children will love the Revolutionary War figurines fighting battles; older folks will marvel at the opulence.

Overall Appeal by Age Group

Pre-school ★	Teens ★★	Over 30 ★★★★
Grade school ★★	Young Adults ★★	Snr. citizens ★★★★

Author's Rating Robber-baron decadence. ★★★★

How Much Time to Allow One hour

Description and Comments This mansion along Embassy Row is a real sleeper that few visitors ever see. Built in 1906 by Larz Anderson, a diplomat, it's a reflection of fabulous turn-of-the-century taste and wealth. The two-story ballroom is a stunner; tapestries line the crystal chandeliered dining room; and paintings by Gilbert Stuart and John Trumbull hang in the billiard room. Anderson was a member of the Society of the Cincinnati, whose members are descendants of French and American officers who served in the Revolutionary Army. After his death, his widow donated the mansion to the society. Today the building serves the society as both headquarters and museum.

Even first-time visitors to D.C. should make the effort to see this spectacular mansion, which is located a block or so from Dupont Circle.

Touring Tips The first floor contains displays of Revolutionary War artifacts. On the second floor, the mansion remains as it was originally furnished, with eighteenth-century paintings, seventeenth-century tapestries from Brussels, and huge chandeliers.

Other Things to Do Nearby Take a walk along Embassy Row or browse the shops around Dupont Circle. Other sights within walking distance include the Phillips Collection (modern art), the Christian Heurich Mansion, the Textile Museum, and the Woodrow Wilson House.

Textile Museum

Type of Attraction A museum dedicated to textile arts. A self-guided tour.
Location 2320 S Street, NW.
Nearest Metro Station Dupont Circle
Admission Free; $5 donation suggested
Hours Monday–Saturday, 10 a.m.–5 p.m.; Sunday, 1 p.m.– 5 p.m. Closed federal holidays and December 24.
Phone (202) 667-0441
When to Go Anytime
Special Comments The museum is wheelchair-accessible but not barrier-free. Call ahead if you have special needs. Introductory tours are offered Wednesdays and weekends at 1:30 p.m., September through May.

Overall Appeal by Age Group

Pre-school —	Teens ★★	Over 30 ★★½
Grade school ★	Young Adults ★★½	Snr. citizens ★★★

Author's Rating Interesting, but small and esoteric. ★★
How Much Time to Allow One hour

Description and Comments Cloth, a mass-produced commodity in the West, no longer enjoys much prestige as an art form. But it's a different story in the rest of the world. The museum's collection ranges from countries as diverse as India, Indonesia, and China to Mexico, Guatemala, and Peru. Intricate designs and rich colors grace more than 14,000 textiles and 1,400 carpets dating from ancient times to the present day. Because the items can't be exposed to light for long periods of time, the exhibits are constantly rotated. This museum is much more interesting than it sounds—the rich colors derived from natural dye processes and elaborate details in the fabrics are subtly beautiful. Definitely for distinct tastes, but not to be missed if it appeals to you.

Touring Tips In the new second-floor Textile Learning Center, visitors can touch, feel, and examine textiles close up. It's an opportunity to get a better grip on how and why textiles are cultural carriers that reveal a lot about how people live. Don't miss the pleasant garden behind the museum. The gift shop is chock-full of books and items related to textiles and rugs.

Other Things to Do Nearby The Woodrow Wilson House is next door. The Islamic Center is around the corner on Massachusetts Avenue. In the other direction, S Street crosses Connecticut Avenue, where you can shop and dine to your heart's content.

Woodrow Wilson House

Type of Attraction The final home of the 28th U.S. president. A guided tour.
Location 2340 S Street, NW.
Nearest Metro Station Dupont Circle
Admission $5 for adults; $2.50 for students; $4 for seniors over age 62
Hours Tuesday–Sunday, 10 a.m.–4 p.m. Closed national holidays and Thanksgiving, Christmas, and New Year's Days.
Phone (202) 387-4062
When to Go To avoid a crowded tour during spring and summer, arrive before noon.
Special Comments Lots of stairs, including a steep, narrow descent down a back staircase.

Overall Appeal by Age Group

Pre-school ★	Teens ★★★	Over 30 ★★★½
Grade school ★★	Young Adults ★★★	Snr. citizens ★★★½

Author's Rating Interesting and informative. ★★★½
How Much Time to Allow One to two hours

Description and Comments After Woodrow Wilson left office in 1921, he became the only former president to retire in Washington, D.C.—and he did so in this house. The tour starts with a 25-minute video narrated by Walter Cronkite that puts this underrated president in perspective and fires you up for the tour. Ninety-six percent of the items in this handsome Georgian Revival townhouse are original, so visitors get an accurate picture of aristocratic life in the 1920s. On the tour you'll see Wilson's library (his books, however, went to the Library of Congress after his death), his bedroom, his old movie projector, and beautiful furnishings.

Touring Tips The basement kitchen is virtually unchanged from Wilson's day, with original items such as an ornate wooden icebox and a coal- and gas-fired stove. Peek inside the pantry, still stocked with items from the 1920s such as Kellogg's Corn Flakes ("wonderfully flavored with malt, sugar and salt"). This is another tour that gives visitors the feeling they've been somewhere special and off the beaten tourist track.

Other Things to Do Nearby The Textile Museum is next door. Embassy Row is around the corner on Massachusetts Avenue, and in the other direction, Connecticut Avenue bustles with shops and restaurants.

Zone 7: Upper Northwest

Hillwood Museum

Type of Attraction A mansion housing fabulous art treasures (guided or self-guided tours) and formal gardens on a 25-acre estate (guided and self-guided tours).
Location 4155 Linnean Avenue, NW.
Nearest Metro Station Van Ness/UDC. For a pleasant 20-minute walk, go south on Connecticut Avenue past the Star Trek-y Intelsat complex on the right, then turn left on Upton Street. Follow Upton to Linnean, turn right, and walk about a block to the estate entrance. Or grab a cab.

Admission $10 for the house tour ($8 for seniors,$5 for children and $5 for full-time students)

Hours Tuesday–Saturday, 9 a.m.–5 p.m. Closed Sunday, Monday, and major holidays.

Phone (202) 686-8500 or toll-free: 1-877-HILLWOOD; (202) 686-5807 for reservations

When to Go Spring is the most beautiful season to tour the house and gardens. But these are popular destinations for garden clubs, so you must secure reservations well in advance. Because of Hillwood's wooded location in Rock Creek Park, it's always five degrees cooler here in D.C.'s hot and humid summers.

Special Comments Self-guided audio tours are offered from 9:30 a.m. to noon, and from 2 p.m. to 5 p.m. A docent-led tour is offered daily from 12:30 p.m. to 2 p.m.; specify your preference when making reservations. A children's audio tour is also available ($5).

Overall Appeal by Age Group

Pre-school —	Teens ★★	Over 30 ★★★★½
Grade school —	Young Adults ★★★	Snr. citizens ★★★★½

Author's Rating Stunning. ★★★★½

How Much Time to Allow Two hours. The guided tour itself is over an hour but doesn't include the formal gardens and auxiliary buildings.

Description and Comments She was a girl from Michigan who inherited two things from her father: good taste and General Foods. That, in a nutshell, is the story of Marjorie Merriweather Post, who bought this Rock Creek Park estate in 1955. She remodeled the mansion, and filled it with exquisite eighteenth- and nineteenth-century French and Russian decorative art. "Fabulous" is required to describe the collection of Imperial Russian objects on display. Mrs. Post was married to the U.S. ambassador to Russia in the 1930s—a time when the communists were unloading "decadent," pre-Revolution art at bargain prices. Mrs. Post literally bought warehouse-loads of stuff: jewels, dinner plates commissioned by Catherine the Great, Easter eggs by Carl Fabergé, and chalices and icons. She then had the loot loaded onto her yacht, *Sea Cloud* (the largest private ship in the world), for shipment home. The very best of the booty is on display here. The tour provides a glimpse into Mrs. Post's lavish lifestyle.

Touring Tips Advance reservations are required to tour the mansion. Call at least two months in advance for a spring tour, although you may luck into a cancellation by calling a day or two before your planned visit. Children under age six are not admitted on the tour. Plan your visit so that you have enough time to stroll the gardens. The estate also has a cafe that serves lunch and tea, a gift shop, and a greenhouse you can tour. A "Behind the Scenes" tour is offered Wednesdays at 3 p.m., June through March (except the first Wednesday of the month; $10 per person). Visitors get a glimpse of Hillwood as it was run when Mrs. Post lived here by touring the fallout shelter, the massage room, the silver-polishing room, and other places not seen on the regular house tour. Reservations are suggested for the small cafe.

Other Things to Do Nearby Intelsat, near the Van Ness/UDC Metro station, looks like a building out of the late twenty-first century. That's no surprise, since the firm is an international conglomeration that produces satellites. The lobby features models and prototypes of its products hanging from the ceiling. For lunch, there are plenty of restaurants to choose from near the Metro station on Connecticut Avenue.

National Museum of Health and Medicine

Type of Attraction A medical museum. A self-guided tour.
Location On the grounds of Walter Reed Army Medical Center, located between 16th Street and Georgia Avenue, NW, near Takoma Park, Maryland.
Nearest Metro Station Takoma Park. If you have a car, drive.
Admission Free
Hours Every day, 10 a.m.–5:30 p.m. Closed Christmas Day.
Phone (202) 782-2200
When to Go Anytime
Special Comments Unless you're a health professional or harbor an intense interest in the history of medicine, this small but fascinating museum is simply too difficult to get to. Wait a few years until it relocates to the Mall.

Overall Appeal by Age Group

Pre-school —	Teens ★★½	Over 30 ★★½
Grade school ★★	Young Adults ★★½	Snr. citizens ★★½

Author's Rating Some excellent exhibits, but a bit unsettling. Though not as gruesome as it used to be, it's still not a place for the squeamish. ★★
How Much Time to Allow One hour

Description and Comments Excellent exhibits on the human body and the AIDS epidemic make this museum a worthwhile destination. Although there are still plenty of bottled human organs, skeletons, and graphic illustrations of the effects of disfiguring diseases, the emphasis has shifted from the bizarre to education. Exhibits on medicine in the Civil War and an extensive microscope collection (including huge electron microscopes) will probably have more appeal to physicians, scientists, and other health professionals. We're glad to report that the museum has improved the quality of its exhibits and its overall appearance since our first visit.

Touring Tips Finding this place can be tough. By subway, it's a brisk 15-minute walk to the museum from the Takoma Park Metro station. As you exit the station, turn right and walk under the railroad tracks, then turn right at Blair Road. Walk one block to Dahlia Street and turn left. Walter Reed is about six blocks straight ahead. The museum is directly behind the large white hospital building; you can walk around it on the left. If you're driving, enter the Walter Reed complex through the Dahlia Street gate on Georgia Avenue. The museum is located in the south end of Building 54 (behind the large white hospital building). There's a small parking lot next to the museum.

Other Things to Do Nearby Nothing recommended due to lackluster location.

National Zoological Park (part of the Smithsonian Institution)

Type of Attraction The Smithsonian's world-class zoo. A self-guided tour.
Location 3001 Connecticut Avenue, NW.
Nearest Metro Stations Woodley Park/National Zoo, Cleveland Park
Admission Free
Hours May 1–September 15. grounds are open 6 a.m.–8 p.m. and buildings are open 10 a.m.–6 p.m.; September 16–April 30, grounds are open 6 a.m.–6 p.m., and buildings

are open 10 a.m.–4:30 p.m. The Pollinarium and the invertebrate exhibits are closed Tuesdays.

Phone (202) 673-4800 (recording); (202) 673-4717 (during business hours; call if the weather is questionable)

When to Go Anytime. In the summer, avoid going during Washington's sweltering afternoons.—In the spring, avoid visiting between 10 a.m. and 2 p.m. weekdays, when many school buses full of children arrive.

Special Comments Many sections of the paths winding through the Zoo's 163 acres are steep.

Overall Appeal by Age Group

Pre-school ★★★★★	Teens ★★★★	Over 30 ★★★½
Grade school ★★★★★	Young Adults ★★★½	Snr. citizens ★★★½

Author's Rating A first-rate operation in a beautiful setting. ★★★★½

How Much Time to Allow Two hours just to see the most popular attractions; a whole day to see it all. Better yet, see the Zoo over several visits.

Description and Comments The National Zoo emphasizes natural environment, with many animals roaming large enclosures instead of pacing in cages. And it's all found in a lush woodland setting in a section of Rock Creek Park. Two main paths link the many buildings and exhibits: Olmstead Walk, which passes all the animal houses, and the steeper Valley Trail, which includes all the aquatic exhibits. They add up to about two miles of trail. The Zoo's nonlinear layout and lack of sight lines make a map invaluable; pick one up at the Education Building near the entrance for a buck. The most popular exhibits include the elephants, the great apes, the white tiger, the cheetahs, and the giant pandas, Tian Tian and Mei Xiang.

But for diversity and a good chance of seeing some animal activity, check out the Small Mammal House, the invertebrate exhibit (kids can look through microscopes), and the huge outside bird cages (the condors look the size of Volkswagens). If your visit to Washington is long enough to include forays away from the Mall, make this beautiful park part of your itinerary. Aside from a wide variety of wildlife on view, the wooded setting is a welcome relief from viewing too much marble downtown.

Touring Tips Plan to visit either early or late in the day. Animals are more active, temperatures are cooler—and crowds are thinner. During busy periods, some exhibits are subject to "controlled access" to prevent crowding; in other words, you may have to wait in line. If it is rainy, most of the indoor exhibits can be found along Olmstead Walk. Feedings and demonstrations occur throughout the day at the cheetah, elephant, seal, and sea lion exhibits; check at the Education Building for times.

Don't miss three new permanent exhibits: Pollinarium, Think Tank, and the Amazonia Science Gallery. Pollinarium, a lush garden housed in a 1,250-square-foot greenhouse, features hundreds of zebra long-wing butterflies that flutter around as visitors get a firsthand look at animal pollinators, plants, and the process of pollination. A glass-enclosed beehive gives an up-close glimpse of the activities of thousands of honeybees.

Think Tank, a 15,000-square-foot exhibit that opened in late 1995, attempts to answer the question, Can animals think? Scientists conduct demonstrations on language, tool use, and social organization. Displays, artifacts, graphics, and videos cover topics such as problem-solving ability, brain size, and language. Four animal species are featured in the exhibit: orangutans, Sulawesi macaque monkeys, hermit crabs, and leaf-cutter ants.

The new Amazonia Science Gallery explores the biological diversity of the Amazon rain forest; a biodiversity demonstration lab is equipped with a working electron microscope and with displays of living beetles, frog eggs, tadpoles, and boas. The two-meter-diameter "Geosphere" globe uses projectors, satellite imagery, and computer data to show seasonal changes, weather and land cultivation patterns, population distribution, and other factors that affect life on earth.

Other Things to Do Nearby If you've done the Zoo justice, your feet will hurt and your energy level will be too depleted for much else: Go back to your room. Lunch spots abound three blocks north on Connecticut Avenue; from there it's a short walk to the Cleveland Park Metro. But if you've got feet of steel, take the half-hour hike to the National Cathedral.

Washington National Cathedral

Type of Attraction The sixth-largest cathedral in the world. Guided and self-guided tours.

Location Massachusetts and Wisconsin Avenues, NW.

Nearest Metro Station The Woodley Park/National Zoo station is about a half-hour walk; drive or take a cab.

Admission Free; suggested donations are $3 for adults and $1 for children.

Hours September–April, Every day 10 a.m.–4:30 p.m.; May–August, weeknights only until 9 p.m.

Phone (202) 537-6200 and (202) 537-5596 for guided tour information

When to Go Anytime

Special Comments Take the optional 30- to 45-minute, docent-led tour.

Overall Appeal by Age Group

Pre-school ★	Teens ★★★½	Over 30 ★★★★★
Grade school ★★	Young Adults ★★★★★	Snr. citizens ★★★★★

Author's Rating A Gothic masterpiece. ★★★★★

How Much Time to Allow One hour

Description and Comments If you've been to Europe, you'll experience déjà vu when you visit this massive Gothic cathedral. It's a tenth of a mile from the nave to the high altar; the ceiling is 100 feet high. Don't miss the Bishop's Garden, modeled on a medieval walled garden, or the Pilgrim Observation Gallery and a view of Washington from the highest vantage point in the city. Small children may not enjoy being dragged around this huge cathedral, but just about anyone else will enjoy its magnificent architecture and stone carvings.

Touring Tips Docent-led tours are offered Monday through Friday from 10 a.m. to 3:15 p.m. and Sunday from 12:45 p.m. to 2:30 p.m. While the tours are free, suggested donations are $3 for adults and $1 for children. Remember to wear comfortable shoes. Try to catch the free organ demonstration given Wednesdays 1:15 to 3:15 p.m. Carillon recitals are given on Sundays; times vary so call ahead. You can also visit the grave of Woodrow Wilson, the only president buried in Washington. The Cathedral isn't well served by public transportation, but walking there takes you through safe, pleasant neighborhoods that are home to Washington's elite: It's about a half-hour stroll up Cathedral Avenue from the Woodley Park/National Zoo Metro.

Other Things to Do Nearby The National Zoo is about a half-hour walk from the National Cathedral, or take a cab. For lunch, walk two blocks north on Wisconsin Avenue to Cleveland Park and choose among Thai, Chinese, Mexican, and pizza restaurants. The best deals are at G.C. Murphy's, which features gyros, pita sandwiches, minipizzas, subs, pastries, and Italian coffee. Most items on the menu are under $5.

Zone 8: Northeast

Basilica of the National Shrine of the Immaculate Conception

Type of Attraction The largest Catholic church in the U.S. and the seventh-largest religious structure in the world. Guided and self-guided tours.

Location 4th Street and Michigan Avenue, NE, on the campus of the Catholic University of America.

Nearest Metro Station Brookland/Catholic University

Admission Free

Hours November 1–March 31, every day 7 a.m.–6 p.m.; until 7 p.m. the rest of the year. Guided tours are conducted Monday–Saturday, 9 a.m.–11 a.m. and 1 p.m.–3 p.m.; on Sunday 1:30 p.m.–4 p.m.

Phone (202) 526-8300

When to Go Anytime

Special Comments It's a huge cathedral and it requires a lot of walking.

Overall Appeal by Age Group

Pre-school ★	Teens ★	Over 30 ★
Grade school ★	Young Adults ★	Snr. citizens ★½

Author's Rating Sterile and cold. ★

How Much Time to Allow One hour

Description and Comments A huge, blue-and-gold onion dome lends Byzantine overtones to this massive cathedral, as does the wealth of colorful mosaics throughout its interior. Yet the architecture is lean and stark, and many of the figures in the mosaics and stained-glass windows look cartoonish. It's not in the same league with the awe-inspiring National Cathedral across town. Sure is big, though.

Touring Tips Skip the guided tour, which stops in every one of the dozens of chapels. Instead, grab a map at the information desk on the ground (crypt) level and enter Memorial Hall, which is lined with chapels. Then go up the stairs (or elevator) to the Upper Church.

Other Things to Do Nearby The Franciscan Monastery is a brisk, 20-minute walk away: Continue past the Metro station on Michigan Avenue to Quincy Street, turn right, and walk about four blocks. The Pope John Paul II Cultural Center, an interactive museum open to all faiths, is nearby. Call (202) 635-5400 for hours and directions. A free shuttle service to the center operates from the Brookland/CUA Metro station on weekends. The Basilica has a small cafeteria on the ground level; a better bet is the Pizza Hut on Michigan Avenue.

Franciscan Monastery and Gardens

Type of Attraction A working monastery. A guided tour.
Location 1400 Quincy Street, NE.
Nearest Metro Station Brookland/Catholic University. From the station exit, turn left, walk up to Michigan Avenue, turn left, and walk over the bridge. Continue on Michigan Avenue to Quincy Street, turn right, and walk four blocks.
Admission Free
Hours Guided tours on the hour Monday–Saturday, 9 a.m.–4 p.m. (except at noon daily and 9 a.m. on Tuesday); Sunday, 1 p.m.–4 p.m.
When to Go Anytime
Phone (202) 526-6800
Special Comments The tour involves negotiating many narrow, steep stairs and low, dark passageways. A limited number of wheelchairs are available for touring the church and upper grounds.

Overall Appeal by Age Group

Pre-school —	Teens ★★	Over 30 ★★
Grade school ★★½	Young Adults ★★	Snr. citizens ★★

Author's Rating Beautiful architecture, peaceful grounds—and kind of spooky. ★★
How Much Time to Allow One hour

Description and Comments Built around 1900 and recently restored, this monastery has everything you'd expect: quiet, contemplative formal gardens; a beautiful church modeled after the Hagia Sophia in Istanbul; and grounds dotted with replicas of shrines and chapels found in the Holy Land. What's really unusual is the sanitized crypt beneath the church, which is more Hollywood than Holy Land. (You almost expect to run into Victor Mature wearing a toga.) It's a replica of the catacombs under Rome and is positively—if inauthentically—ghoulish. As you pass open (but phony) grave sites in the walls, the guide narrates hair-raising stories of Christian martyrs eaten by lions, speared, stoned to death, beheaded, and burned at the stake. Shudder.

Touring Tips If you're driving, parking is easy. Two parking lots are located across from the monastery on 14th Street. If you're visiting Washington in the spring, the beautiful gardens alone are worth the trip.

Other Things to Do Nearby The Basilica of the National Shrine of the Immaculate Conception—let's catch our breath—is just past the Metro station on Michigan Avenue. For lunch, a Pizza Hut is conveniently located near the Metro.

U.S. National Arboretum

Type of Attraction A 444-acre collection of trees, flowers, and herbs. A self-guided tour.
Location Off New York Avenue in Northeast Washington.
How to Get There Drive. Take New York Avenue from downtown and enter on the service road on the right just past Bladensburg Road.
Admission Free

Hours Every day, 8 a.m.–5 p.m. The information center is open weekdays, 8 a.m.–4:30 p.m.; the gift shop is open weekdays, 10 a.m.–3:30 p.m., and weekends, 10 a.m.–5 p.m. The recently expanded National Bonsai and Penjing Museum is open daily 10 a.m.–3:30 p.m. Closed on Christmas Day.

Phone (202) 245-2726

When to Go In the spring, fields of azaleas are in bloom. The world-class bonsai collection is a treat all year. Late July and August feature blooming aquatic plants. For more information on what's in bloom visit www.ars-grin.gov/na/.

Special Comments The arboretum is mobbed in the spring; the rest of the year is usually tranquil.

Overall Appeal by Age Group

Pre-school ★	Teens ★½	Over 30 ★★½
Grade school ★½	Young Adults ★★	Snr. citizens ★★★

Author's Rating Interesting and beautiful; hard to get to. ★★½

How Much Time to Allow One hour to half a day.

Description and Comments With nine miles of roads and more than three miles of walking paths, the U.S. National Arboretum offers visitors an oasis of quiet and beauty for a drive or a stroll. Even people without green thumbs will marvel at the bonsai collection, whose dwarf trees are more like sculptures than plants. One specimen, a Japanese white pine, is 350 years old. Folks with limited time who aren't gardening enthusiasts, however, shouldn't spend their valuable touring hours on a visit.

Touring Tips Flowering dogwood and mountain laurel bloom well into May. The rest of the year, it's a fine place to go for a long walk. The surrounding neighborhoods aren't safe, so either drive or take a cab.

Other Things to Do Nearby The Kenilworth Aquatic Gardens are only a few minutes away by car.

Zone 9: Southeast

Anacostia Museum (a Smithsonian museum)

Type of Attraction A museum focusing on African-American history and culture. A self-guided tour.

Location 1901 Fort Place, SE, in Anacostia.

How to Get There For specific information on where to board the buses and for the schedule, stop at any museum information desk on the Mall or call (202) 287-3382.

To Drive From the Mall, take Independence Avenue east past the Capitol to 2nd Street, SE, where it is intersected by Pennsylvania Avenue. Bear right onto Pennsylvania Avenue and go to 11th Street, SE, and turn right. Cross the 11th Street Bridge and follow signs to Martin Luther King Jr. Avenue (left lanes). Follow MLK Avenue to Morris Road (third traffic signal) and turn left. Go up the hill to 17th Street, SE, where Morris Road becomes Erie Street. In about five blocks, Erie Street becomes Fort Place; the museum is on the right. Because this part of Southeast Washington is unsafe for pedestrians, we don't recommend taking public transportation.

Admission Free

Hours Every day, 10 a.m.–5 p.m.; closed Christmas Day.
Phone (202) 287-3306
When to Go Anytime. But either call first or pick up a brochure at the Castle on the Mall to find out what's on view before making the trip.
Special Comments This "neighborhood" museum features temporary, special exhibits; between shows, there is often very little to see, so call first.

Overall Appeal by Age Group *Since the museum features special exhibitions that change throughout the year, it's not really possible to rate this Smithsonian facility's appeal by age group.*
Author's Rating Again, temporary exhibitions make a rating impossible.
How Much Time to Allow One hour

Description and Comments Located on the high ground of old Fort Stanton, the Anacostia Museum features changing exhibits on black culture and history and the achievements of African Americans. Unfortunately for out-of-town visitors, it's in a location that's difficult to reach.

Touring Tips To save yourself the frustration of arriving between major shows, either call the museum first or pick up a flyer at the Castle on the Mall.

Other Things to Do Nearby Frederick Douglass National Historic Site is a short drive, but you should call in advance to make reservations for the house tour. Anacostia is a high-crime area. It's okay to drive through during daylight, but it's not an area we advise visitors to visit on foot or at night.

Frederick Douglass National Historic Site

Type of Attraction Cedar Hill, the preserved Victorian home of abolitionist, statesman, and orator Frederick Douglass. A guided tour by reservation only.
Location 1411 W Street, SE, in Anacostia.
How to Get There Drive; Anacostia is unsafe for pedestrians day or night. From the Mall, take Independence Avenue east past the U.S. Capitol to 2nd Street, SE, where it is intersected by Pennsylvania Avenue. Bear right onto Pennsylvania Avenue and go to 11th Street, SE, and turn right. Cross the 11th Street Bridge and go south on Martin Luther King Jr. Avenue to W Street, SE. Turn left and go four blocks to the visitor center parking lot on the right.

Another option during the summer and in February (Black History Month) is Tourmobile, which offers a three-hour guided tour to Cedar Hill. Call (202) 554-5100 or stop at a Tourmobile ticket booth at Arlington Cemetery, the Lincoln Memorial, or the Washington Monument to make reservations in person. Rates are $7 for adults and $3.50 for children.
Admission Free.
Hours Every day: October–April, 9 a.m.–4 p.m.; May–September, 9 a.m.–5 p.m. Closed New Year's, Thanksgiving, and Christmas Days.
Phone (202) 426-5961 and (800) 365-2267 for reservations
When to Go Anytime. While not required, it's a good idea to call and make reservations for the house tour.
Special Comments Do not take the Metro to Anacostia. The entire area is unsafe; Cedar Hill, administered by the National Park Service, is safe.

Overall Appeal by Age Group

Pre-school ★	Teens ★★★	Over 30 ★★★½
Grade school ★★	Young Adults ★★★	Snr. citizens ★★★½

Author's Rating Informative and interesting. ★★★½

How Much Time to Allow One hour

Description and Comments This lovely Victorian home on a hill overlooking Washington remains much as it was in Douglass's time. The former slave, who among other achievements became U.S. ambassador to Haiti, spent the final 18 years of his life in this house. Douglass lived here when he wrote the third volume of his autobiography, *Life and Times of Frederick Douglass*. For people interested in the history of the civil rights movement and genteel life in the late 1800s, Cedar Hill is a find. Our well-informed guide provided a detailed commentary on Douglass's life and times. Look for Douglass's barbells on the floor next to his bed. Most children, however, may find it dull.

Touring Tips A late afternoon visit is almost like stepping back into the nineteenth century, because the house is preserved as it was when Douglass died in 1895: There's no electricity, and the gathering shadows in the house evoke the past. Be sure to see "The Growlery," a small, one-room structure behind the main house that Douglass declared off-limits to the household so that he could work alone.

Other Things to Do Nearby The Anacostia Museum is a short drive. However, Anacostia, Washington's first suburb and an area rich in black history, is an area that's economically distressed and crime-ridden. It's okay to drive during daylight, but it's not a part of town to visit on foot or at night.

Kenilworth Aquatic Gardens

Type of Attraction A national park devoted to water plants. Self-guided tour.

Location 1900 Anacostia Drive, NE, across the Anacostia River from the National Arboretum.

How to Get There Drive. Go south on Kenilworth Avenue from its intersection with New York Avenue. Exit at Eastern Avenue and follow signs to the parking lot off Anacostia Avenue.

Admission Free

Hours Every day, 8 a.m.–4 p.m. (9 a.m.–4 p.m., April–September). Closed Thanksgiving, Christmas, and New Year's Days.

Phone (202) 426-6905

When to Go June and July to see hardy water plants; July and August to see tropical plants and lotus. On the third Saturday in July a water-lily festival is held. Year-round it's a great place for bird-watching.

Special Comments The gardens are located in a dangerous neighborhood. Don't take public transportation.

Overall Appeal by Age Group

Pre-school ★	Teens ★★	Over 30 ★★★
Grade school ★★	Young Adults ★★★	Snr. citizens ★★★

Author's Rating Unique. ★★★

How Much Time to Allow One hour

Description and Comments In addition to pools filled with water lilies, water hyacinth, lotus, and bamboo, the gardens teem with wildlife such as opossum, raccoon, waterfowl, and muskrats. It's an amazing place to visit on a clear summer morning.

Touring Tips Come in the morning, before the heat closes up the flowers. Don't take public transportation; the surrounding neighborhood is unsafe. Drive or go by cab.

Other Things to Do Nearby The National Arboretum is only a few minutes away by car.

Washington Navy Yard

Type of Attraction Three military museums and a U.S. Navy destroyer. Self-guided tours by reservation only; call (202) 433-6897.

Location 9th and M Streets, SE, on the waterfront.

Nearest Metro Station Eastern Market. Because this is an unsafe neighborhood any time of day, we recommend that visitors either drive (parking is available inside the gate) or take a cab.

Admission Free; reservations required for non-military personnel

Hours Monday–Friday, 10 a.m.–4 p.m. (until 5 p.m. Memorial Day through Labor Day). Closed weekends, Thanksgiving Day, Christmas Eve and Day, and New Year's Day.

Phone Navy Museum: (202) 433-4882; Marine Corps Historical Museum: (202) 433-3534 (closed Tuesdays); Navy Art Gallery: (202) 433-3815; *USS Barry*: (202) 433-3377 (open until 5 p.m. in the summer and until 4 p.m. in the winter; closed Monday and Tuesday).

When to Go Anytime. But unless you have military ID, advance reservations are required.

Special Comments A nice contrast to the look-but-don't-touch Mall museums.

Overall Appeal by Age Group

Pre-school ★	Teens ★★★	Over 30 ★★
Grade school ★★★½	Young Adults ★★	Snr. citizens ★★★

Author's Rating Hands-on fun for kids; informative for adults. ★★½

How Much Time to Allow Two hours

Description and Comments Exhibits in the Navy Museum include 14-foot-long model ships, undersea vehicles *Alvin* and *Trieste*, working sub periscopes, a space capsule that kids (and wiry adults) can climb in, and, tied up at the dock, a decommissioned destroyer to tour. The Marine Corps Historical Museum is less hands-on, featuring exhibit cases and Marine Corps mementos. The Navy Art Gallery is a small museum with paintings of naval actions painted by combat artists. A strong interest in the military is a prerequisite for making the trek to the Washington Navy Yard, and it's not a side trip that many first-time visitors make. But kids will love it. For current exhibition information visit www.history.navy.mil and click on "The Navy Museum."

Touring Tips Don't make our mistake—jumping off at the Metro's Navy Yard station and walking ten scary blocks to the Navy Yard entrance; drive or take a cab. It's too bad these museums are so far off the beaten path, because there's a lot here to see and do.

Other Things to Do Nearby Nothing recommended.

Zone 10: Maryland Suburbs

NASA/Goddard Space Flight Visitor Center (Zone 10D)

Type of Attraction NASA's 1,100-acre, campuslike facility in suburban Maryland, including a small museum and other buildings. Self-guided and guided tours.
Location Greenbelt, Maryland.
How to Get There Drive. From downtown Washington, drive out New York Avenue, which becomes the Baltimore-Washington Parkway (I-295). Take the MD 193 East exit, just past the Capital Beltway. Drive about two miles past the Goddard Space Flight Center's main entrance to Soil Conservation Road and turn left. Follow signs to the visitor center.
Admission Free
Hours Weekdays, 9 a.m.–4 p.m.; closed Thanksgiving, Christmas, and New Year's Days.
Phone (301) 286-8981
When to Go Anytime
Overall Appeal by Age Group

Pre-school ★	Teens ★★★	Over 30 ★★★
Grade school ★★★	Young Adults ★★★	Snr. citizens ★★★

Author's Rating Informative but not convenient for most visitors. ★★½
How Much Time to Allow One hour for the tours; two hours for the Sunday bus tours.

Description and Comments The small museum inside the visitor center is loaded with space hardware, including a space capsule kids can play in, space suits, and real satellites; think of it as a mini–National Air and Space Museum. Outside, some real rockets used to put the hardware into outer space are on display. While most folks will get their fill and then some of spacecraft at the museum on the Mall, a visit to NASA's Greenbelt facility is the icing on the cake for hard-core space cadets.

Touring Tips The small gift shop offers interesting NASA-related items such as postcards, 35mm color slides, posters, and publications. One-hour tours are given weekdays at 10 a.m., noon, and 2 p.m. On the first and third Saturdays of the month, model rocket launches are held on center grounds. Call the curator for details, (301) 286-9041.

Other Things to Do Nearby Drive through the adjacent Agricultural Research Center, a collection of farms where the U.S. Department of Agriculture studies farm animals and plants. The roads are narrow and quiet—it's a rural oasis in the heart of Maryland's suburban sprawl. The National Wildlife Visitor Center off nearby Powder Mill Road features nature displays and hiking paths.

National Cryptologic Museum (north of Zone 10D)

Type of Attraction A small museum offering a glimpse into the secret world of spies, national defense, and ciphers. A self-guided tour.
Location The National Security Agency, on the grounds of Fort George G. Meade, about 30 minutes north of Washington and east of Laurel, Maryland (Route 32 and the Baltimore-Washington Parkway).

Admission Free
Hours Weekdays, 9 a.m.–4 p.m. and the first and third Saturdays of the month. Closed federal holidays.
Phone (301) 688-5849
When to Go Anytime
Special Comments A very small museum that will only appeal to a narrow slice of Washington visitors.

Overall Appeal by Age Group

Pre-school —	Teens ★½	Over 30 ★½
Grade school ★	Young Adults ★½	Snr. citizens ★★

Author's Rating Gee, a real World War II German Enigma ciphering machine. Yet this tiny museum's greatest appeal may be its very existence: The National Security Agency (NSA) is the nation's largest spy organization—and its most secretive. ★
How Much Time to Allow One hour

Description and Comments Tourists are barred from Central Intelligence Agency headquarters in Langley, across the river from Washington in suburban Virginia. Yet all is not lost for visitors lusting for a peek into the world of cloaks and daggers. The ultra-hush-hush National Security Agency operates this tiny museum dedicated to codes, ciphers, and spies in a former motel overlooking the busy Baltimore-Washington Parkway.

All the displays are static; they include items such as rare books dating from 1526, Civil War signal flags, KGB spy paraphernalia, and the notorious Enigma, a German cipher machine (it looks like an ancient Underwood on steroids) whose code was "broken" by the Poles and British during World War II. (Spies, a film on code breaking during World War II, tells the story continuously on a TV in a small theater in the museum.)

Touring Tips Don't miss the "bugged" Great Seal of the U.S. that hung in Spaso House, the U.S. ambassador's residence in Moscow. (The microphone-equipped seal was uncovered in 1952.) The new high-tech room features spy devices used to guard against computer hackers. Outside, you get a glimpse of the huge NSA headquarters complex from Route 32. NSA is called "The Puzzle Palace" for its secretiveness and worldwide electronic eavesdropping capability. The agency's budget, by the way, is a secret.

Other Things to Do Nearby South on the Baltimore-Washington Parkway are the National Wildlife Visitor Center and the NASA/Goddard Space Flight Center (Powder Mill Road exit).

National Wildlife Visitor Center (Zone 10D)

Type of Attraction A museum featuring wildlife research exhibits located in a 13,000-acre national wildlife refuge about 30 minutes north of Washington. A self-guided tour.
Location Off Powder Mill Road, two miles east of the Baltimore-Washington Parkway, south of Laurel, Maryland.
Admission Free

Hours Every day, 10 a.m.–5:30 p.m. Closed Christmas Day.

Phone (301) 497-5760

When to Go Anytime. Weekends are busier than weekdays.

Special Comments You'll need a car to get here. Call ahead if you'd rather avoid large groups of schoolchildren on field trips. And there's no restaurant or snack bar on the premises.

Overall Appeal by Age Group

Pre-school ★★★★	Teens ★★★	Over 30 ★★½
Grade school ★★★★	Young Adults ★★½	Snr. citizens ★★½

Author's Rating Static exhibits and stuffed animals, but a tranquil setting in the heart of the hectic Washington-Baltimore corridor. ★★½

How Much Time to Allow One to two hours

Description and Comments This large, airy, new museum operated by the U.S. Department of the Interior is filled with attractive exhibits—dioramas, mostly—focusing on a wide range of wildlife and environmental topics. While the static displays won't accelerate the pulse rates of adults weary from traipsing through Smithsonian edifices on the Mall, children are fascinated by this place. Large dioramas on pollution, overpopulation, forest and ocean degradation, wildlife habitats, wolves, whooping cranes, and other endangered species demonstrate the value of wildlife research.

Touring Tips A "viewing pod" equipped with spotting scopes and binoculars lets youngsters (and adults) observe wildlife through a picture window overlooking acres of pond and natural wildlife habitat. If it's a nice day, enjoy the sights and sounds of real wildlife by taking a stroll on paved trails through woods and around ponds populated by geese, ducks, and other animals that find refuge on the refuge. Thirty-minute narrated tram rides with a wildlife interpreter are offered on weekends in the spring and fall and daily from the end of June through August. The cost is $3 for adults and $2 for seniors and $1 for children. On weekends documentary wildlife films are shown in the center's movie theater.

Other Things to Do Nearby The NASA/Goddard Space Flight Center in Greenbelt, Maryland, is only a few miles away; follow signs posted on Powder Mill Road near the Baltimore-Washington Parkway.

Folks looking for additional outdoor enjoyment and the opportunity to see more wildlife can drive a few miles north to the North Tract of the Patuxent Research Refuge; take the Baltimore-Washington Parkway north two exits to Route 198 east, drive one mile, and turn right onto Bald Eagle Drive to the Visitor Contact Station. The 8,100-acre tract features forest, wetlands, a wildlife viewing area (with an observation tower), and eight miles of paved roads for car touring and bicycling. There are another ten miles of graded gravel roads for hiking, mountain biking, and horseback riding. For more information, call (410) 674-3304.

The National Cryptologic Museum is located next to the huge National Security Agency complex near the intersection of the Baltimore-Washington Parkway and Route 32; drive north on the parkway a few miles and follow the signs. For a large selection of fast-food options, take the parkway north a few miles to Route 197.

Zone 11: Virginia Suburbs

Mount Vernon (south of Zone 11C)

Type of Attraction George Washington's eighteenth-century Virginia plantation on the Potomac River. A self-guided tour.

Location 16 miles south of Washington.

How to Get There To drive from Washington, cross the 14th Street Bridge into Virginia, bear right, and get on the George Washington Memorial Parkway south. Continue past National Airport into Alexandria, where the parkway becomes Washington Street. Continue straight; Washington Street becomes the Mount Vernon Memorial Parkway, which ends at Mount Vernon.

Tourmobile offers four-hour, narrated bus tours to Mount Vernon daily, April through October. Departures are at 10 a.m., 12 p.m., and 2 p.m. Tickets are $25 for adults and $12 for children ages 3 to 11. The price includes admission to Mount Vernon. Call Tourmobile at (202) 554-5100 for more information. Gray Line offers four-hour coach trips to Mount Vernon and Old Town Alexandria that depart daily at 8:30 a.m. from Union Station. No tours are scheduled on New Year's, Thanksgiving, and Christmas Days. Fares are $28 for adults and $14 for children. For more information, call Gray Line at (202) 289-1995 or visit www.grayline.com.

Admission $9 for adults; $8.50 for senior citizens age 62 and over; $4.50 for children ages 6 through 11

Hours Every day: April–August, 8 a.m.–5 p.m.; November–February, 9 a.m.–4 p.m.; March, September, and October, 9 a.m.–5 p.m. Open every day of the year, including Christmas Day.

Phone (703) 780-2000

When to Go Generally before 10 a.m., especially in hot weather. But sometimes tour and school buses arrive before the gates open, creating a line to buy tickets and tour the mansion. Come around 3 p.m. and you're sure to avoid the buses—and the lines. When longer hours are in effect, you must clear the grounds by 5:30 p.m.

Special Comments Mount Vernon is probably the only major D.C. attraction that opens at 8 a.m., making it a prime place to hit early in hot weather—if you have a car to get you there. During Christmas, the decorated mansion's seldom-seen third floor is open to the public.

Overall Appeal by Age Group

Pre-school ★★	Teens ★★★	Over 30 ★★★★★
Grade school ★★★★	Young Adults ★★★★½	Snr. citizens ★★★★★

Author's Rating Not to be missed. ★★★★★

How Much Time to Allow Two hours

Description and Comments Folks on a quick trip to Washington won't have time to visit Mount Vernon, but everyone else should. The stunning view from the mansion across the Potomac River is pretty much the same as it was in Washington's day. Unlike most historic sites in D.C., Mount Vernon gives visitors a real sense of how eighteenth-century rural life worked, from the first president's foot-operated fan chair (for keeping flies at bay while he read) to the rustic kitchen and outbuildings. Historic interpreters are stationed throughout the estate and mansion to answer questions and give visitors an overview of the property and Washington's life.

Mount Vernon is more than just a big house. Special 30-minute landscape and garden tours leave at 11 a.m., 1 p.m., and 3 p.m., April through October. "Slave Life at Mount Vernon" is a 30-minute walking tour to slave quarters and workplaces that starts at 10 a.m., noon, 2 p.m., and 4 p.m. daily, April through October. There's no additional charge for either tour.

Mount Vernon has opened several new attractions on the 30-acre plantation to help diffuse huge crowds that throng the mansion. The newest is a four-acre colonial farm site where visitors can view costumed interpreters using eighteenth-century farm methods and tools. Hands-on activities are available March through November, and wagon rides are offered on Fridays, Saturdays, and Sundays.

During the summer months, a "Hands-On History" area lets children handle eighteenth-century objects, play games such as rolling hoops, and learn about early American life; hours are 10 a.m. to 1 p.m. daily from Memorial Day through Labor Day. The estate's website, www.mountvernon.org, offers a historical primer for your visit.

Touring Tips Mount Vernon is *very* popular, and tourists pull up by the busload in the spring and summer months—sometimes before the grounds open. During the high tourist season, Monday, Friday, and Sunday mornings before 11 a.m. are the least busy periods. If you want to avoid big crowds, go around 3 p.m., but you must leave the grounds by 5:30 p.m. When crowds are small in the winter, visitors are frequently given guided tours of the mansion in groups of 20 to 30 people.

Other Things to Do Nearby Mount Vernon offers a snack bar, two gift shops, a post office, and a sit-down restaurant. Rest rooms can be found near the museum on the grounds or between the gift shop and snack bar near the entrance. Visit Old Town Alexandria on your way to or from Mount Vernon. To stop at Gadsby's Tavern is appropriate, because that's what George Washington used to do.

Old Town Alexandria (Zone 11C)

Type of Attraction A restored colonial port town on the Potomac River, featuring eighteenth-century buildings on cobblestone streets, trendy shops, bars and restaurants, parks, and a huge art center. Guided and self-guided tours.

Location In suburban Virginia, eight miles south of Washington.

Nearest Metro Station King Street

Admission Some historic houses charge $5 for admission. Admission to the Torpedo Factory Art Center, the Lyceum, and the George Washington Masonic National Memorial is free. Tickets that get you into three historic sites for $10 ($6 for children ages 11 to 17) are sold at Ramsay House, the main visitor center on King Street.

Hours Historic houses, shops, and the Torpedo Factory Art Center open by 10 a.m. and remain open through the afternoon.

Phone For more information on Old Town, call the Alexandria Convention & Visitors Association at (800) 388-9119 or (703) 838-4200. Press 4 for a recording of special events that's updated regularly.

When to Go Anytime

Special Comments The most scenic spot for a brown-bag lunch are the picnic tables located at the foot of 1st Street, on the Potomac River.

Overall Appeal by Age Group

Pre-school ★★	Teens ★★★	Over 30 ★★★★½
Grade school ★★★	Young Adults ★★★★½	Snr. citizens ★★★★½

Author's Rating A satisfying contrast to awesome D.C. ★★★★

How Much Time to Allow Half a day. If it's the second half, stay for dinner; Old Town Alexandria has a great selection of restaurants.

Description and Comments Alexandria claims both George Washington and Robert E. Lee as native sons, so history buffs have a lot to see. Topping the list are period revival houses that rival those in Georgetown, another old port up the river; Gadsby's Tavern (open Tuesday through Saturday, 10 a.m. to 5 p.m., April through September, and 1 p.m. to 5 p.m. on Sunday; guided tours at quarter of and quarter past the hour); Christ Church; and the Lee-Fendall House. This hip, revitalized city on the Potomac is crammed with exotic restaurants (Thai, Indian, Lebanese, Greek) and shops (art, jewelry, children's books, antiques, Persian carpets). And, unlike those in Georgetown, the eating and drinking establishments in Old Town aren't overrun by suburban teenagers on weekends.

Touring Tips As you exit the King Street Metro station, either board a DASH bus for a quick trip down King Street to Old Town (85 cents), or walk to your left and turn right onto King Street for a pleasant 15-minute stroll toward the river. The closest visitor center is at the Lyceum, where two exhibition galleries and a museum of the area's history are featured; from King Street, turn right onto Washington Street and walk a block. There's also a small museum featuring prints, documents, photographs, silver, furniture, and Civil War memorabilia. Farther down King Street on the left is Ramsay House, built in 1724 and now Alexandria's official visitor center, open daily from 9 a.m. to 5 p.m., except Thanksgiving, Christmas, and New Year's Days. Ramsay House makes a good starting point for a walking tour of Old Town Alexandria. The Torpedo Factory Art *Center* at the foot of King Street features more than 150 painters, printmakers, sculptors, and other artists and craftspeople. Visitors can watch artists at work in their studios housed in the former munitions factory. If you drive to Alexandria, park your car in a two-hour metered space, feed it a nickel or a dime, and go to a visitor center to pick up a pass that lets you park free for 24 hours in any two-hour metered zone inside Alexandria city limits (renewable once); you'll need your vehicle's license plate number. But parking is scarce and the King Street Metro is conveniently located.

Other Things to Do Nearby About a mile west of the center of Alexandria is the George Washington National Masonic Memorial. A free tour features a view from the 333-foot tower, Washington memorabilia, a 370-year-old Persian rug valued at $1 million, and more information about Masonry than you probably want. The tours are given Monday through Saturday on the half-hour in the mornings and on the hour in the afternoons; the Memorial is open daily, 9 a.m. to 5 p.m. Mount Vernon, George Washington's plantation on the Potomac, is eight miles downriver.

Part Eight

Dining and Restaurants

Experiencing Washington Cuisine

The New Washington Cookery

In the last 15 years, and even more rapidly over the past 5 years, Washington has evolved from an extremely predictable restaurant town, one in which dining out was more a matter of convenience and expense account than pleasure, to one of the country's top 10 culinary centers—a city where it's really fun to be a restaurant critic.

The sorts of heavy French and Italian and "continental" dishes that a generation of Washingtonians was inured to have been replaced by market-fresh, innovative, and even nutritionally informed recipes, many of them combining elements of the older classic cuisines (often lumped together as "modern eclectic" and a strong influence in the development of what is, for lack of a better term, described as "modern American"). Far beyond those cuisines are the scores of Vietnamese, Japanese, Indian, Chinese (of all regions), and Ethiopian establishments in the area, not just first-generation mom-and-pop immigrant eateries but professional, critically acclaimed restaurants. And the greater quantity of choices in all styles means better quality as well: The most recent boom in Thai food, has—like the successive explosions in other ethnic fare—educated diners to the delicacy as well as the potency of that cuisine, and chased many of the quickie, unauthentic kitchens out of business.

The ethnic-fare boom is almost certain to continue: National surveys show that younger consumers, "Generations X and Y," as marketers call them, are developing tastes for a variety of ethnic flavors early in life, and consider them as much a part of the American buffet as the Italian, Mexican, and Chinese—meaning Cantonese, primarily—older diners tend to stick to. And continued immigration naturally means greater cultural diversity, which is why there are increasing numbers of African and Russian restaurants in this country.

The Washington palate has become demanding enough (and, to be frank, the expense accounts have expanded sufficiently) to inspire a surprising number of restaurants from other dining capitals to open branches in the nation's capital, from New York's ultra-haute **Lespinasse** (closed since the sale of the St. Regis Hotel chain) and super-steakhouses **Angelo & Maxie's** (901 F Street, NW; (202) 639-9330), **Bobby Van's,** Michael's **jordan's,** and **Smith & Wollensky;** to L.A.'s haute-haute **Citronelle** (now Michel Richard's home base) and the more laid-back beefeaters' palace, **Nick and Stef's**; to Miami's **Ortanique;** to Boston's **Olives, Legal Seafood,** and **Pier 4.**

Though it's a 90-minute drive, Washingtonians gladly claim pride of place for the five-star **Inn at Little Washington** (the "Little," because it's in Washington, Virginia), whose chef, Patrick O'Connell, has been admired in print in every culinary journal of note.

And a different sort of Washington generation, a host of chefs who grew up in the kitchens of star chefs Roberto Donna, Jean-Louis Palladin, Mark Miller, Patrick O'Connell, and Yannick Cam, as well as the better hotel restaurants and those same old-time classicists, have kitchens and restaurants of their own. More collegial than contentious, these young chefs are developing a style that plays up regional flavors: Chesapeake Bay seafoods; Virginia, West Virginia, and Maryland game; and the wealth of organic produce and herbs being raised for this market. Organic-cooking maven Nora Poullion may not be able to claim all the credit for the number of menus with additive-free or heart-healthy entries, but as founder of a national organic network, the Chefs Collective, she has inspired many other chefs to demand the freshest ingredients. (And, of course, Washington is the home of the Center for Science in the Public Interest, the folks who went right on and told you that fettucine Alfredo was just as bad for you as you always knew it was.)

That an increasing number of these young chefs are choosing to remain in the D.C. area is itself proof of the audience's sophistication. Among them are Todd Gray of **Equinox,** Jacques Ford of **Matisse,** Damien Salvatore of **Persimmon,** Eric McCoy of **Cafe Bethesda,** Carolyn Bruder Ross of **La Bergerie,** Jason Tepper of **La Miche,** Martin Saylor of **Butterfield 9,** and Barbara Black of **Addie's,** all profiled here.

Even more intriguing is the number of chefs lured away from big-name eateries in Manhattan to positions in the nation's capital. Frank Morales, formerly of New York's Union Pacific, is now at the **Oval Room** just across Lafayette Park from the White House (Connecticut and H Streets, NW; (202) 463-8700). Jamie Leeds, a veteran of such Manhattan hot spots as Tribeca Grill and Union Square Cafe, created **15 ria** in the Washington Terrace Hotel (1515 Rhode Island Avenue, NW; (202)

742-0015). Gray Koonz protege Jon Mathieson quit **Lespinasse** to open **Poste** in the Hotel Monaco. And Mina Newman, formerly of **Layla** created a menu of hilariously irreverent recipes at **Restaurant Seven** in Tysons Corner (8571 Leesburg Pike/Route 7; (703) 847-0707). Just to name a few.

New Restaurant Districts

Along with the awakening of the Washington palate has come a rearrangement of the dining map. While Georgetown remains a busy shopping and nightlife area, it is no longer the dominant restaurant strip. The revitalized downtown arts district from the MCI Center at 7th Street west to about 10th Street north of Pennsylvania Avenue; the stunning renaissance of its near-neighbor, the midtown region from approximately 10th to 20th Streets between F and K; the ethnically mixed Adams-Morgan neighborhood; and the northwest suburbs—particularly the Asian polyglot neighborhoods of Wheaton and Bethesda, with their "golden triangles" of restaurants—have all emerged as livelier locations, with Gaithersburg and Germantown hot on their heels. At the same time, restaurant dining has become so diversified that one no longer needs to go to the "Little Saigon" neighborhood around Clarendon for very good Vietnamese cooking (although Adams-Morgan is still home to most of the Ethiopian restaurants); in fact, it's hard to imagine that anyone living in the Washington metropolitan area is more than a mile from five or six different ethnic restaurants.

Not surprisingly, given its long lobbying habits, Washington has also rediscovered the big steak and big-ticket business meals, and put the two together at the 21st century version of the saloon, the platinum-card chophouse. These are now so popular, and their formats so similar—prime beef, creamed spinach, Caesar salad, and hefty wine lists—that we have simply listed the biggest cow palaces below, under "More Recommendations," so that you can browse by location.

Scoping Out the Lunch Crowd

In the old days the price of a Washington meal proved its importance—and by implication, the diners'. These days the appeal of a D.C. restaurant rests more on a kitchen's imagination, its beer selection, its service, even its bottled water. Half the fun of lunching out is scoping out the midday clientele: power lunchers (at the old standbys and some well-kept secret spots), hour lunchers (very often at ethnic restaurants, which are rather quicker on the uptake than traditional white-linen establishments), flower lunchers (the remnants of the leisure class), and shower lunchers (those roving bands of office workers who seem always to be celebrating someone's great occasion but who want individual checks).

If you're not sure which kind of restaurant you've just walked into, glance around at the beverage glasses. Power lunchers are more likely to order a cocktail, hour lunchers a beer, flower lunchers wine, and shower lunchers soft drinks or pitchers with paper fans.

Brunch is back in fashion, not only on Sundays but on Saturdays, and not just eggy but ethnic; see the list of "Best Sunday Brunches" below.

Industry Trends

With the slowing of the 1990s stock market, and a few hints of economic "correction," Washington's restaurant industry has witnessed the effects of customer efforts to economize. Several of the finer establishments, caught between the pincers of exorbitant rent and declining expense-account business, have closed, most notably **Lespinasse** and its successor, **Timothy Dean's, Provençal,** and **Aquarelle.** There are still plenty of expensive menus, though, from which to choose. A few have down-scaled, and some of the most influential chefs in the area have opened what might be called "off-the-rack" restaurants (cafes and pizzerias) in addition to their designer rooms. More intriguing, some mixed-metaphor chefs are becoming partners: **Galileo** godfather Roberto Donna, who started the off-price trend with his Adams-Morgan kitchen **I Matti,** and the late, great Jean-Louis Palladin of **Watergate** fame, together created **Pesce.** Yannick Cam of **Provence** and Savio Racino of **Primi Piatti** founded **Provençal** and **Catalan** before splitting up. Donna also co-owns **Barolo;** the retro-trendy spaghetti gardens **Il Radicchio** and **Arucola;** and, with **i Ricchi** founder Francesco Ricchi, **Etrusco** on Dupont Circle and **Cesco** in Bethesda.

The 100 or so restaurant profiles that follow are intended to give you a sense of the atmosphere and advantages of a particular establishment as well as its particular cuisine. None should be taken as gospel, because one drawback of Washington's new appetite for adventure is that restaurants open and close—and promising chefs play musical kitchens—with breathtaking speed. This also means that we have for the most part profiled only restaurants that have been in operation for at least a year, or that have chefs with such strong track records that they are of special interest. Some very promising restaurants have been omitted because they were just opening at press time; other rather well-known ones may not have come up to scratch. (We tend to avoid chain restaurants, though it's not a hard-and-fast rule.) We have also in some cases given preference to establishments with subway access, though only as a balancing factor.

And, blame it on yuppie consciousness, gourmet magazine proliferation, or real curiosity, the increased interest in the techniques of cooking has also produced a demand for variety, constantly challenging presentations, and guaranteed freshness. Consequently, many of the fancier restaurants change their menus or a portion thereof every day, and more change seasonally, so the specific dishes recommended at particular places may not be available on a given night. Use these critiques as a guide, an indication of the chef's interests and strengths—and weaknesses, too. We'll tell you what's not worth trying.

The New Hotel Dining

When it comes to hotel dining rooms, Washington contradicts the conventional wisdom that hotel restaurants are not worth seeking out. In D.C. many of the better chefs are working in hotels. This is a mutually beneficial arrangement, allowing the chefs to concentrate on managing a kitchen, not a business, and providing an extra attraction to potential clients. Since Washington's hotels count on a great deal of expense-account business, they generally offer menus on the expensive side. In addition to the restaurants profiled, we recommend those at the Willard Hotel **(Willard Room),** the Hay-Adams Hotel **(Lafayette),** the Four Seasons **(Seasons), Jefferson Hotel** (currently getting a menu makeover by D.C. Coast and TenPenh chef Jeff Tunks), the **Morrison-Clark Inn**, the Watergate **(Jeffrey's at the Watergate),** the Hyatt Regency in Reston **(Market Street Grill),** Sofitel **(Cafe 15),** Washington Terrace **(15 ria),** the Hotel Monaco **(Posté),** Henley Park **(Coeur de Lion),** the Ritz-Carlton downtown **(Jockey Club),** the Stratford Motor Inn in Falls Church **(Cafe Rose),** the Fairmont **(The Bistro),** and the Mayflower **(Cafe Promenade),** as well as those noted in the description of the new downtown below.

The Inns and Outs

The Washington area is also blessed with some very fine country inns within a couple hours' drive. We have actually profiled only the nationally famous **Inn at Little Washington** in this edition, but in addition, if you're taking a longer vacation and want to see the countryside, we would recommend looking into such restaurants as **Antrim 1844** in Taneytown, **Willow Grove** in Orange, **Stone Manor** in Middleton, the **Turning Point Inn** in Urbana, **Four and Twenty Blackbirds** in Flint Hill, the **Hermitage Inn** in Clifton, and the **Ashby Inn** in Paris.

Diners' Special Needs

The following profiles attempt to address the special requirements of diners who use wheelchairs or leg braces. Because so many of Washington's restaurants occupy older buildings and row houses, options for wheelchair users are unfortunately limited. In most cases, wheelchair access is prevented right at the street, but many restaurants offering easy entrance to the dining room keep their rest rooms up or down a flight of stairs. In either case, we list them as having "no" disabled access. "Fair" access suggests that there is an initial step or small barrier to broach, or that passage may be a bit tight, but that once inside the establishment, dining is comfortable for the wheelchair user. Again, hotel dining rooms are good bets—the same wide halls and ramps used for baggage carts and deliveries serve wheelchair users as well. Newer office buildings and mixed shopping and entertainment complexes have ramps and elevators that make them wheelchair-accessible; the ones above subway stations even have their own elevators.

We have not categorized restaurants as offering vegetarian or other restricted diets because almost all Washington restaurants now offer either vegetarian entrees on the menu or will make low-salt or low-fat dishes on request, although some are particularly amenable to doing this, and we have said so. Use common sense: A big-ticket steakhouse is unlikely to have many nonmeat options (though many have become accustomed to making veggie plates), but since few countries in the world feature as much meat in their cuisine as America, most ethnic cuisines are good bets for vegetarians.

Places to See Faces

Washington may not really be Hollywood on the Potomac (so many movie stars come to town to lobby for their pet causes, it's getting close), but there are celebrity faces aplenty. Consequently, out-of-towners often list "famous people" right after the Air and Space Museum on the required-viewing list. Since being seen is part of the scene—and getting star treatment is one of the perks of being famous—celebrities tend to be visible in dependable places, particularly at lunch.

In the past couple of years, **Cafe Milano** has emerged as the single most celeb- and socialite-centric restaurant, with diplomats, royals, and even media-types. Ditto performers—the new decor is based on the best-known roles of regular Placido Domingo.

In this town, at least, politics not only makes strange bedfellows, it makes strange dining partners. Which may be why it wasn't all that odd that Democratic bad boy James Carville and his Republican commentator wife Mary Matalin tried opening their own neo-Southern restaurant, **West 24** (it didn't get enough bipartisan support). Top Democratic lobbyist Tommy Boggs and former GOP heavy Haley Barbour have more expertise in getting along; and their flagrantly pork-barrel sort of steakhouse, the **Caucus Room** (7th and D Streets; (202) 393-1300), is a hit. And now lobbyist Jack Abramoff has opened an upscale kosher spot called **Archives and Stacks** on Pennsylvania at 11th Street. The embassy staffers from various former-Soviet states—and their U.S. counterparts—show up at the Russian-retro **Mayim.**

The venerable steak-and-lobster **Palm** (1225 19th Street, NW; (202) 293-9091), with its wall-to-wall caricatures of famous customers and its bullying waiters, is still a popular media and legal-eagle hangout. **Butterfield 9**'s convenient proximity to both the White House and the National Press Building have made it a quick favorite for major media and network faces on the White House beat as well as celebs Judith Light, Pat Sajak, Tom Cruise, Reba McEntire, Wes Craven, Geraldo Rivera, and Dick Gregory. Talk show host Larry King, and those White House and Cabinet types not ducking him, often show up at **Max's of Washington** (1725 F Street, NW; (202) 842-0070).

The Capital Grille (601 Pennsylvania Avenue, NW; (202) 737-6200) is particularly well located; only a short stroll from the Capitol grounds, it serves as both boardroom and back room for the GOP. After the party's 1995 gala, a couple hundred of the black-tie guests dropped by the Grille for drinks and cigars. Only a few nights before, when a clutch of budget-crunching Republican senators had peeked in after last call, the general manager had rolled up his sleeves and grilled a couple dozen strategic burgers. The Grille gets its share of odd couples, too: Right-Republican Senator Launch Faircloth and liberal intellectual Senator Pat Moynihan once arrived for dinner, Faircloth announcing the pair to staff as "the red-neck and the aristocrat."

Galileo, the flagship restaurant of Washington's *capo di tutti capi* chef Roberto Donna, has its opposing political icons, Ted Kennedy and Bob Dole. **Restaurant Nora** was an early favorite of the Clintons and Gores; former Energy Secretary Hazel O'Leary, Bosnian peacemeister Richard C. Holbrooke, and Clinton insider Vernon Jordan like **Melrose**. The old-clubby **Monocle** (107 D Street, NE; (202) 546-4488), the unofficial transfer point between the Senate and its office buildings, draws the Republican money men—Alfonse D'Amato and Pete Domenici, chairmen of the Senate banking and finance committees, respectively, and John Kasich, chairman of the House budget committee.

The elegant Raj-redux **Bombay Club** across the street from the White House attracts presidential-advisor-cum-commentator George Stephanopoulos, Reno, and John Glenn. Senator Frank Lautenberg of New Jersey (who wrote the bill banning smoking on airlines), Stephanopoulos, D'Amato, and Bob Kerrey have taken the steak-and-stogie course at **Les Halles** (1201 Pennsylvania Avenue, NW; (202) 347-6848).

Pol-watchers should also check out **Two Quail** (320 Massachusetts Avenue, NE; (202) 543-8030) for congresswomen or **La Colline** for committee staffers. **Bullfeathers** is full of national committee staffers from both parties (410 1st Street, SE; (202) 543-5005). **The Hay-Adams** (16th and H Streets, NW; (202) 638-6600) is where the power breakfast was born, starring White House staff and federal bureaucrats.

Behind-the-scenes power-wielders, "spouses of," and social arbiters congregate at the Ritz-Carlton's **Jockey Club** (2100 Massachusetts Avenue, NW; (202) 835-2100).

Treasury and White House staff crowd the neighboring **Old Ebbitt Grill**, the **Occidental Grill** (1475 Pennsylvania Avenue, NW; (202) 783-1475), and **Georgia Brown's.** And, among the low-profile politicians and working press who frequent the **Market Inn,** especially in shad roe season, are rumored to be CIA and other professionals incognito (200 E Street, SW; (202) 554-2100).

World Bank and OAS suits lunch at **Taberna del Alabardero**; corporate write-offs go to the **Prime Rib** (2020 K Street, NW; (202) 466-8811) and the midtown **Morton's** (L Street and Connecticut; (202) 955-5997).

Chef Alison Swope's decision to go all modern-regional Mexican has made **Andale** a popular hangout for politicos de todas las Americas, including the Mexican and Canadian ambassadors and Senators Diane Feinstein of California and Kevin Brady of Texas. The black intelligensia, media, and sports stars (BET founder Robert Johnson, D.C. Mayor Anthony Williams, Redskins owner Dan Snyder, Capitals owner Ted Leonsis, and visiting celebs Morgan Freeman and Danny Glover) like **Ortanique.**

Oceanaire draws a lot of media faces, including CNN anchor Bernard Shaw and host Larry King, a host of ABC News staffers including John Cochran, pol-turned-commentator George Stephanopoulus, Sam Donaldson, and Chris Wallace; radio anti-hero Oliver North, as well as a number of athletes. (The downtown restaurants being so near the MCI Centre, any of them may sport a jersey or two.)

Tosca has become a sort of unofficial Democratic hangout: Regulars include many younger pros from the Kennedy/Shriver/Townsend clan as well as Senator Edward Kennedy (who prefers dining in the kitchen); presidential alter ego Martin Sheen of NBC's *The West Wing,* and power couple NBC reporter Andrea Mitchell and Federal Reserve Chairman Alan Greenspan.

The New Downtown Dining

The revival of the area between the power poles of the Capitol and the White House, with the new Convention Center and the MCI Centre sports arena in between, has produced an astonishing restaurant boom in the downtown area; after all, with all those lobbyists, politicians and sports fans, how could it miss?

Among the most promising new entries into the downtown dining scene are: **Zaytina** (701 Ninth Street, NW; (202) 638-0800), an upscale Middle Eastern tapas restaurant from the folks who brought you Jaleo and Cafe Atlantico; **Zola** (800 F Street, NW; (202) 654-0999) next to the International Spy Museum; **Finemondo** (1319 F Street, NW; (2020 737-3100), a sort of kebab house on the big steakhouse model and offering whole lambs on a day's notice; **Chef Geoff's** (1301 Pennsylvania Avenue, NW; (202) 464-4461); (801 Pennsylvania Avenue, NW; (202) 628-5900); and **Cafe 15** in the Sofitel Hotel, whose menu was created by Strasbourg's three-Michelin-star Antoine Westerman.

With the influx of boutique hotels has come also the boutique lounges, mostly named simply after the hotels themselves but often serving rather more upscale fare than the traditional bar bites. Longtime local chef John Wabeck was briefly executive chef for three of these (almost too hip) scenes at once, although he gave them slightly different personalities: the more Asian-fusion **Topaz Bar** (1722 N Street, NW; (202) 393-3000); the nuevo-Latino accented **Bar Rouge** (1315 16th Street, NW; (202) 232-8000); and **Helix** (1430 Rhode Island Avenue, NW; (202) 462-9001). Wabeck is now on the group's fourth new venture in a matter of months, the **Firefly Restaurant** alongside the Hotel Madera (1310 New Hampshire Avenue, NW; (202) 861-1310). (Actually, it's the fifth venture, as these four all belong to the same group that owns the Hotel Monaco.)

The Restaurants

Our Favorite Washington Restaurants

We have developed detailed profiles for the most interesting and reliable restaurants (in our opinion) in town. Each profile features an easily scanned heading that allows you, in just a second, to check out the restaurant's name, cuisine, star rating, cost, quality rating, and value rating.

Cuisine This is actually less straightforward than it sounds. A couple of years ago, for example, "pan-Asian" restaurants were generally serving what was then generally described as "fusion" food—Asian ingredients with European techniques, or vice versa. Since then, there has been a pan-Asian explosion in the area, but nearly all specialize in what would be street food back home: noodles, skewers, dumplings, and soups. Modern American sounds pretty broad, and it is—part "new continental," part "regional," and part "new eclectic." Like art, you know it when you see it. Where there are major subdivisions of cuisine, we have tried to put it in the most obvious place; Marcel's is Belgian-French, while Le Mannequin Pis is definitely Belgian. And Nuevo Latino is distinctly different from traditional Spanish or South American. Again, though, experimentation and "fusion" is ever more common, so don't hold us, or the chefs, to too strict a style.

Overall Star Rating The star rating is an overall rating that encompasses the entire dining experience, including style, service, and ambience in addition to the taste, presentation, and quality of the food. Five stars is the highest rating possible and connotes the best of everything. Four-star restaurants are exceptional, and three-star restaurants are well above average. Two-star restaurants are good. One star is used to indicate an average restaurant that demonstrates an unusual capability in some area of specialization—for example, an otherwise unmemorable place that has great barbecued chicken.

Cost To the right of the star rating is an expense description that provides a comparative sense of how much a complete meal will cost. A complete meal for our purposes consists of an entree with vegetable or side dish and choice of soup or salad. Appetizers, desserts, drinks, and tips are excluded.

Inexpensive	$14 and less per person
Moderate	$15–30 per person
Expensive	Over $30 per person

Quality Rating The food quality is rated on a five-star scale, five being the best rating attainable. The quality rating is based solely on the food served, taking into account taste, freshness of ingredients, preparation, presentation, and creativity. There is no consideration of price. If you want the best food available, and cost is not an issue, look no further than the quality ratings.

Value Rating If, on the other hand, you are looking for both quality and value, then you should check the value rating, also expressed in stars. The value ratings are defined as follows:

★★★★★	Exceptional value, a real bargain
★★★★	Good value
★★★	Fair value, you get exactly what you pay for
★★	Somewhat overpriced
★	Significantly overpriced

Locating the Restaurant Just below the heading is a designation for geographic zone. This zone description will give you a general idea of where the restaurant described is located. We've divided Washington, D.C., into the following 11 geographic zones:

Zone 1	The Mall
Zone 2	Capitol Hill
Zone 3	Downtown
Zone 4	Foggy Bottom
Zone 5	Georgetown
Zone 6	Dupont Circle/Adams-Morgan
Zone 7	Upper Northwest
Zone 8	Northeast
Zone 9	Southeast
Zone 10	Maryland suburbs
Zone 11	Virginia suburbs

The Maryland suburbs are divided into four smaller areas: Zones 10A (Bethesda) and 10B (Rockville-Gaithersburg) are bounded by the Potomac and Georgia Avenue and divided by the Beltway; Zone 10C is defined by 16th Street/Georgia Avenue, the District line, New Hampshire Avenue, and I-95 as a wedge that runs north from Silver Spring and that necessarily splits Wheaton down the middle; and Zone 10D reaches from the District line up New Hampshire and I-95 around to the Virginia line.

The Virginia suburbs are marked off more cleanly along I-66 and I-95/395 into three slices: Zone 11A covers Tysons Corner, McLean, Vienna, and Reston; Zone 11B includes Arlington, Annandale, and Fairfax; and Zone 11C is Alexandria, Old and otherwise. See pages 8–18 for detailed zone maps.

Payment We've listed the type of payment accepted at each restaurant using the following code: AmEx equals American Express (Optima), CB equals Carte Blanche, D equals Discover, DC equals Diners Club, MC equals MasterCard, JCB equals Japan Credit Bank, T equals Transmedia, and Visa is self-explanatory.

Who's Included Because restaurants are opening and closing all the time in Washington, we have tried to confine our list to establishments with a proven track record over a fairly long period of time. Franchises and national chains are rarely included, although local "chains," restaurant groups of three or four, may be. Newer or changed establishments that demonstrate staying power and consistency will be profiled in subsequent editions. Also, the list is highly selective. Noninclusion of a particular place does not necessarily indicate that the restaurant is not good, but only that it was not ranked among the best in its genre. Detailed profiles of individual restaurants follow in alphabetical order at the end of this part.

RESTAURANTS BY CUISINE, THEN STAR RATING

Cuisine and Name	Overall Rating	Price Rating	Quality Rating	Value Rating	Zone
American (see also Modern American)					
Old Ebbitt Grill	★★½	Mod	★★★½	★★★	3
Barbecue					
Old Glory	★★★	Mod	★★★★	★★★★	5
Rocklands	★★½	Inexp	★★★½	★★★	5, 11B
Belgian					
Le Mannequin Pis	★★★½	Mod	★★★½	★★★★	10C
Brazilian					
Grill from Ipanema	★★½	Mod	★★★	★★★	6

RESTAURANTS BY CUISINE, THEN STAR RATING *(continued)*					
Cuisine and Name	**Overall Rating**	**Price Rating**	**Quality Rating**	**Value Rating**	**Zone**
Burmese					
Burma	★★★	Inexp	★★★	★★★	3
Caribbean					
Ortanique	★★½	Exp	★★★	★★★½	3
Chinese					
Mark's Duck House	★★★½	Inexp	★★★★	★★★★	11B
Good Fortune	★★★	Inexp	★★★	★★★★	10B
Ethiopian					
Meskerem	★★★	Inexp	★★★★	★★★★★	6
Zed's	★★½	Mod	★★★	★★★★	5
French					
Gerard's Place	★★★★★	Exp	★★★★½	★★★	3
Citronelle	★★★★	Exp	★★★★	★★★½	5
Marcel's	★★★½	Exp	★★★★	★★★	6
Bistro Bis	★★★	Exp	★★★	★★★	3
L'Auberge Chez François	★★★	Exp	★★★★	★★★★★	11A
La Bergerie	★★★	Exp	★★★	★★★	11C
La Colline	★★★	Exp	★★★★	★★★★★	2
Jean-Michel	★★★	Mod	★★★	★★★	10A
Matisse	★★★	Exp	★★★★	★★★½	7
Bistro Lepic	★★½	Mod	★★★½	★★★	5
Bistro Français	★★½	Inexp	★★★½	★★★★	5
La Chaumière	★★½	Mod	★★★½	★★★★	5
La Miche	★★½	Exp	★★★	★★½	10A
Montmarte	★★½	Mod	★★★½	★★★½	2
Saveur	★★½	Mod	★★★★	★★★★	5
French (Provençal)					
La Côte D'Or Cafe	★★½	Exp	★★★½	★★★	11B
Greek					
Athenian Plaka	★★★	Mod	★★★½	★★★★	10A
Indian					
Bombay Bistro	★★★	Inexp	★★★★	★★★★★	10B,11B
Italian					
Maestro	★★★★	Very Exp	★★★★½	★★★	11A
Etrusco	★★★½	Mod	★★★★	★★★	6
Galileo	★★★½	Exp	★★★★★	★★★	6
Obelisk	★★★½	Exp	★★★★½	★★★★	6
Cafe Milano	★★★	Exp	★★★★	★★★★	5

RESTAURANTS BY CUISINE, THEN STAR RATING *(continued)*

Cuisine and Name	Overall Rating	Price Rating	Quality Rating	Value Rating	Zone
***Italian** (continued)*					
Cesco Trattoria	★★★	Mod	★★★★	★★★★	10A
i Ricchi	★★★	Exp	★★★★	★★★★	6
Teatro Goldoni	★★★	Exp	★★★★	★★★	3
Tosca	★★★	Exp	★★★½	★★★	3
Japanese					
Kaz Sushi Bistro	★★★★	Mod	★★★★½	★★★★	4
Sushi-Ko	★★★★	Mod	★★★★½	★★★★	5
Tako Grill	★★★★	Mod	★★★★½	★★★★	10A
Murasaki	★★★½	Exp	★★★★	★★★	7
Makoto	★★★	Mod	★★★★	★★★★	7
Matuba	★★★	Inexp	★★★★	★★★★	10A, 11B
Korean					
Woo Lae Oak	★★★	Mod	★★★½	★★★★★	11B
Lebanese					
Bacchus	★★★	Mod	★★★½	★★★★	6, 10A
Modern American					
The Inn at Little Washington	★★★★★	Exp	★★★★★	★★★★★	11B
Colvin Run Tavern	★★★★	Very Exp	★★★★½	★★★½	11A
Equinox	★★★★	Mod	★★★★	★★★½	3
Palena	★★★★	Exp	★★★★½	★★★★	7
Vidalia	★★★★	Exp	★★★★½	★★★★	6
Cafe Bethesda	★★★½	Exp	★★★★	★★★½	10B
Courduroy	★★★½	Exp	★★★★	★★★	3
D.C. Coast	★★★½	Exp	★★★★	★★★½	3
Butterfield 9	★★★	Exp	★★★★	★★★½	3
Elysium	★★★	Exp	★★★★	★★★★	11C
Geranio	★★★	Mod	★★★★	★★★	11C
Grapeseed	★★★	Exp	★★★★	★★★★	10
Melrose	★★★	Mod	★★★★	★★★	5
Old Angler's Inn	★★★	Exp	★★★½	★★½	10B
Persimmon	★★★	Mod	★★★★	★★★	10A
Addie's	★★½	Mod	★★★	★★★★	10B
Carlyle Grand Cafe	★★½	Mod	★★★½	★★★	11B
Greenwood	★★½	Exp	★★★★	★★★	7
New Heights	★★½	Mod	★★★½	★★★★	7
Nora	★★½	Mod	★★★½	★★★	6
Olives	★★½	Exp	★★★½	★★★	3
1789	★★½	Exp	★★★★	★★★	5
Tabard Inn	★★½	Mod	★★★★	★★★	6

RESTAURANTS BY CUISINE, THEN STAR RATING *(continued)*					
Cuisine and Name	**Overall Rating**	**Price Rating**	**Quality Rating**	**Value Rating**	**Zone**
Modern Mexican					
Andale	★★★	Mod	★★★	★★★	3
New Southwestern					
Red Sage	★★★	Exp	★★★★½	★★★★	3
Nuevo Latino					
Gabriel	★★½	Mod	★★★★	★★★★★	6
Cafe Atlantico	★★★	Mod	★★★½	★★★★	3
Jaleo	★★★	Mod	★★★★	★★★★	3
Pan-Asian					
Asia Nora	★★½	Mod	★★★★	★★★	6
TenPenh	★★★½	Exp	★★★★	★★★★★	3
Pizza					
Pizzeria Paradiso	★★★	Inexp	★★★★	★★★★★	6
Portuguese					
Tavira	★★★	Mod	★★★½	★★★★	10A
Seafood					
Kinkead's	★★★★	Exp	★★★★½	★★★	4
Sea Catch	★★★½	Mod	★★★★	★★★★	5
Black's Bar & Kitchen	★★★	Mod	★★★★	★★★★	10A
Oceanaire	★★★	Exp	★★★★	★★★★	3
Johnny's Half-Shell	★★½	Inexp	★★★½	★★★★★	6
Southern					
Georgia Brown's	★★½	Mod	★★★½	★★★	3
Spanish					
Taberna del Alabardero	★★★	Exp	★★★★	★★★	3
Tex-Mex					
Austin Grill	★★½	Inexp	★★★	★★★½	3, 5, 10A 11B, 11C
Thai					
Benjarong	★★★½	Inexp	★★★★	★★★★	10B
Busara	★★★½	Mod	★★★★	★★★★	5, 11A
Bangkok Garden	★★★	Inexp	★★★	★★★★	10A
Tara Thai	★★½	Mod	★★★½	★★★★★	10A, 10B, 11A, 11B
Turkish					
Cafe Divan	★★½	Mod	★★½	★★★½	5
Vietnamese					
Taste of Saigon	★★★	Mod	★★★★	★★★★★	10B, 11A

RESTAURANTS BY ZONE, THEN ALPHABETICAL

Zone and Name	Overall Rating	Price Rating	Quality Rating	Value Rating	Cuisine
Zone 2: Capitol Hill					
La Colline	★★★	Exp	★★★★	★★★★★	French
Montmarte	★★½	Mod	★★★½	★★★½	French
Zone 3: Downtown					
Andale	★★★	Mod	★★★	★★★	Southwest
Austin Grill	★★½	Inexp	★★★	★★★½	Tex-Mex
Bistro Bis	★★★	Exp	★★★	★★★	French
Burma	★★★	Inexp	★★★	★★★	Burmese
Tosca	★★★	Exp	★★★½	★★★	Italian
Butterfield 9	★★★	Exp	★★★★	★★★½	Mod. Am.
Cafe Atlantico	★★★	Mod	★★★½	★★★★	Latino
Courduroy	★★★½	Exp	★★★★	★★★	Mod. Am.
D.C. Coast	★★★½	Exp	★★★★	★★★½	Mod. Am.
Equinox	★★★½	Mod	★★★★	★★★½	Mod. Am.
Georgia Brown's	★★½	Mod	★★★½	★★★	Southern
Gerard's Place	★★★★★	Exp	★★★★½	★★★	French
Jaleo	★★★	Mod	★★★★	★★★★	Latino
Oceanaire	★★★	Exp	★★★★	★★★★	Seafood
Old Ebbitt Grill	★★½	Mod	★★★½	★★★	American
Olives	★★½	Mod	★★★½	★★★	Mod. Am.
Ortanique	★★½	Exp	★★★	★★★½	Caribbean
Red Sage	★★★	Exp	★★★★½	★★★★	Southwest
Taberna del Alabardero	★★★	Exp	★★★★	★★★	Spanish
Teatro Goldoni	★★★	Exp	★★★★	★★★	Italian
TenPenh	★★★½	Exp	★★★★	★★★★★	Pan-Asian
Zone 4: Foggy Bottom					
Kaz Sushi Bistro	★★★★	Mod	★★★★½	★★★★	Japanese
Kinkead's	★★★★	Exp	★★★★½	★★★	Seafood
Zone 5: Georgetown					
Austin Grill	★★½	Inexp	★★★	★★★½	Tex-Mex
Bistro Français	★★½	Inexp	★★★½	★★★★	French
Bistro Lepic	★★½	Mod	★★★½	★★★	French
Cafe Divan	★★½	Mod	★★½	★★★½	Turkish
Cafe Milano	★★★	Exp	★★★★	★★★★	Italian
Citronelle	★★★★	Exp	★★★★	★★½	French
La Chaumière	★★½	Mod	★★★½	★★★★	French
Melrose	★★★	Mod	★★★★	★★★	Mod. Am.
Old Glory	★★★	Mod	★★★★	★★★★	Barbecue
Rocklands	★★½	Inexp	★★★½	★★★	Barbecue

RESTAURANTS BY ZONE, THEN ALPHABETICAL *(continued)*

Zone and Name	Overall Rating	Price Rating	Quality Rating	Value Rating	Cuisine
***Zone 5: Georgetown** (continued)*					
Saveur	★★½	Mod	★★★★	★★★★	French
Sea Catch	★★★½	Mod	★★★★	★★★★	Seafood
1789	★★½	Exp	★★★★	★★★	Mod. Am.
Sushi-Ko	★★★★	Mod	★★★★½	★★★★	Japanese
Zed's	★★½	Mod	★★★	★★★★	Ethiopian
Zone 6: Dupont Circle/Adams Morgan					
Asia Nora	★★½	Mod	★★★★	★★★	Pan-Asian
Bacchus	★★★	Mod	★★★½	★★★★	Lebanese
Etrusco	★★★½	Mod	★★★★	★★★	Italian
Gabriel	★★½	Mod	★★★★	★★★★★	Latino
Galileo	★★★½	Exp	★★★★★	★★★	Italian
Grill from Ipanema	★★½	Mod	★★★	★★★	Brazillian
i Ricchi	★★★	Exp	★★★★	★★★★	Italian
Johnny's Half-Shell	★★½	Inexp	★★★½	★★★★★	Seafood
Marcel's	★★★½	Exp	★★★★	★★★	French
Meskerem	★★★	Inexp	★★★★	★★★★★	Ethiopian
Nora	★★½	Mod	★★★½	★★★	Mod. Am.
Obelisk	★★★½	Exp	★★★★½	★★★★	Italian
Pizzeria Paradiso	★★★	Inexp	★★★★	★★★★★	Pizza
Tabard Inn	★★½	Mod	★★★	★★★	Mod. Am.
Vidalia	★★★★	Exp	★★★★½	★★★★	Mod. Am.
Zone 7: Upper Northwest					
Greenwood	★★½	Exp	★★★★	★★★	Mod. Am.
Makoto	★★★	Mod	★★★★	★★★★	Japanese
Matisse	★★★	Exp	★★★½	★★★	French
Murasaki	★★★½	Exp	★★★★½	★★★★	Japanese
New Heights	★★½	Mod	★★★½	★★★★	Mod. Am.
Palena	★★★★	Exp	★★★★½	★★★★	Mod. Am.
Zone 10: Maryland Suburbs					
Addie's	★★½	Mod	★★★	★★★★	Mod. Am.
Athenian Plaka	★★★	Mod	★★★½	★★★★	Greek
Austin Grill	★★½	Inexp	★★★	★★★½	Tex-Mex
Bacchus	★★★	Mod	★★★½	★★★★	Lebanese
Bangkok Garden	★★★	Inexp	★★★	★★★★	Thai
Benjarong	★★★½	Inexp	★★★★	★★★★	Thai
Black's Bar & Kitchen	★★★	Mod	★★★★	★★★★	Seafood
Bombay Bistro	★★★	Inexp	★★★★	★★★★★	Indian
Cafe Bethesda	★★★½	Exp	★★★★	★★★½	Mod. Am.

RESTAURANTS BY ZONE, THEN ALPHABETICAL ***(continued)***

Zone and Name	Overall Rating	Price Rating	Quality Rating	Value Rating	Cuisine
Zone 10: Maryland Suburbs *(continued)*					
Cesco Trattoria	★★★	Mod	★★★★	★★★★	Italian
Good Fortune	★★★	Inexp	★★★	★★★★	Chinese
Grapeseed	★★★	Exp	★★★★	★★★★	Mod. Am.
Jean-Michel	★★★	Mod	★★★	★★★½	French
La Miche	★★½	Exp	★★★	★★½	10A
Le Mannequin Pis	★★★½	Mod	★★★½	★★★★	Belgian
Matuba	★★★	Inexp	★★★★	★★★★	Japanese
Old Angler's Inn	★★★	Exp	★★★½	★★½	Mod. Am.
Persimmon	★★★	Mod	★★★★	★★★	Mod. Am.
Rocklands	★★½	Inexp	★★★½	★★★	Barbecue
Tako Grill	★★★★	Mod	★★★★½	★★★★	Japanese
Tara Thai	★★½	Mod	★★★½	★★★★★	Thai
Taste of Saigon	★★★	Mod	★★★★	★★★★★	Vietnamese
Tavira	★★★	Mod	★★★½	★★★★	Portuguese
Zone 11: Virginia Suburbs					
Austin Grill	★★½	Inexp	★★★	★★★½	Tex-Mex
Bombay Bistro	★★★	Inexp	★★★★	★★★★★	Indian
Busara	★★★½	Mod	★★★★	★★★★	Thai
Busara	★★★½	Mod	★★★★	★★★★	Thai
Carlyle Grand Cafe	★★½	Mod	★★★½	★★★	Mod. Am.
Colvin Run Tavern	★★★★	Very Exp	★★★★½	★★★½	Mod. Am.
Elysium	★★★	Exp	★★★★	★★★★	Mod. Am.
Geranio	★★★	Exp	★★★★	★★★	Mod. Am.
L'Auberge Chez François	★★★	Exp	★★★★	★★★★★	French
La Bergerie	★★★	Exp	★★★½	★★★	11C
La Côte D'Or Cafe	★★½	Exp	★★★½	★★★	French
Maestro	★★★★	Mod	★★★★	★★★½	Italian
Mark's Duck House	★★★½	Inexp	★★★★	★★★★	Chinese
Matuba	★★★	Inexp	★★★★	★★★★	Japanese
Tara Thai	★★½	Mod	★★★½	★★★★★	Thai
Taste of Saigon	★★★	Mod	★★★★	★★★★★	Vietnamese
The Inn at Little Washington	★★★★★	Exp	★★★★★	★★★★★	Mod. Am.
Woo Lae Oak	★★★	Mod	★★★½	★★★★★	Korean

More Recommendations

The Best Afternoon Teas

Four Seasons Hotel 2800 Pennsylvania Avenue, NW (202) 342-0444
The Hay-Adams Hotel 16th and H Streets, NW (202) 638-6600
Henley Park Hotel 926 Massachusetts Avenue, NW (202) 638-5200
Jefferson Hotel 1200 16th Street, NW (202) 347-2200
Park Hyatt Hotel 24th and M Streets, NW (202) 955-3899
The Tea Cozy 119 South Royal Street, Alexandria (703) 836-8181
Teaism 400 Eighth Street, NW (202) 638-6010; 2009 R Street, NW (202) 667-3827

The Biggest Beef Steakhouses

Angelo & Maxie's 901 F Street, NW (202) 639-9330; 11901 Democracy Drive, Reston (703) 787-7766
Blackie's 1227 22nd Street, NW (202) 333-1100
Bobby Van's 809 15th Street, NW (202) 589-0060
Capital Grille 601 Pennsylvania Avenue, NW (202) 737-6200
Caucus Room Ninth and F streets, NW (202) 393-1300
District Chophouse & Brewery 509 7th Street, NW (202) 347-3434
Don Shula's 8028 Leesburg Pike/Route 7, Tysons Corner (703) 506-3256
Fleming's Steakhouse & Wine Bar 1960 Chain Bridge Road/Route 123 Tysons Corner (703) 442-8384
J. Gilbert's 6903 Old Dominion Drive, McLean (703) 893-1034
jordans 1300 Pennsylvania Avenue, NW (202) 589-1223
Max's of Washington 1725 F Street, NW (202) 842-0070
Morton's of Chicago 3251 Prospect Street, NW (202) 342-6258; 8075 Leesburg Pike/Route 7, Tysons Corner (703) 883-0800; L Street and Connecticut Avenue, NW (202) 955-5997; 1631 Crystal Square Arcade, Arlington (703) 418-1444; One Freedom Square, Reston Town Center, Reston (703) 796-0128
Nick & Stef's 601 F Street, NW (202) 661-5040
Palm 1225 19th Street, NW (202) 293-9091
Prime Rib 2020 K Street, NW (202) 466-8811
Ruth's Chris Steakhouse 1801 Connecticut Avenue, NW (202) 797-0033; 7315 Wisconsin Avenue, Bethesda (301) 652-7877; 2231 Crystal Drive, Crystal City (703) 979-7275
Sam & Harry's 1200 19th Street, NW (202) 296-4333
Smith & Wollensky's 1112 19th Street, NW (202) 466-1100

The Freshest Beers (Brewed On-site)

Brewer's Alley 124 N. Market Street, Frederick (301) 631-0089
Capitol City Brewing Co. 1100 New York Avenue, NW (202) 628-2222; 2700 South Quincy Street, Arlington (703) 578-3888
DuClaw Brewing Co. 16-A Bel-Air South Station Parkway, Bel Air (410) 515-3222

Franklin's Restaurant and Brewpub 5123 Baltimore Avenue, Hyattsville (301) 927-2740
Hops 3625 Jefferson Davis Highway, Alexandria (703) 837-9107
Gordon Biersch Brewery Restaurant 900 F Street, NW (202) 783-5454
John Harvard's Brewhouse 1299 Pennsylvania Avenue, NW (202) 783-2739
Old Dominion Brewing Co. 44633 Guilford Drive, Ashburn (703) 689-1225
Rock Bottom Restaurant & Brewery 7900 Norfolk Avenue, Bethesda (301) 652-1311
Summit Station Summit and Diamond Avenue, Gaithersburg (301) 948-4200
Sweetwater Tavern 14250 Sweetwater Lane, Centreville (703) 449-1100
Virginia Beverage Co. 607 King Street, Alexandria (703) 684-5397

The Best Burgers

The Brickskeller 1523 22nd Street, NW (202) 293-1885
Old Ebbitt Grill 675 15th Street, NW (202) 347-4801
Union Street Public House 121 South Union Street, Alexandria (703) 548-1785

The Most Entertaining Decor

Asia Nora 2213 M Street, NW; (202) 797-4860
Busara 2340 Wisconsin Avenue, NW (202) 337-2340; 8142 Watson Street, McLean (703) 356-2288
Filomena's 1063 Wisconsin Avenue, NW (202) 337-2782
P.F. Chang's 1716M International Drive (Tysons Galleria), McLean (703) 734-8996
Pizzeria Paradiso 2029 P Street, NW (202) 223-1245
Rain Forest Cafe Routes 7 and 123 (Tysons Corner Center), Tysons Corner (703) 821-1900
Red Sage 605 14th Street, NW (202) 638-4444
Restaurant Seven 8521 Leesburg Pike, Tysons Corner (703) 847-0707
Tara Thai 226 Maple Avenue West, Vienna (703) 255-2467;
4828 Bethesda Avenue, Bethesda (301) 657-0488;
12071 Rockville Pike (Montrose Crossing), Rockville (301) 231-9899;
4001 North Fairfax Drive, Ballston (703) 903-4999;
7501-C Leesburg Pike, Tysons Corner (703) 506-9788
Teatro Goldoni 1909 K Street, NW (202) 955-9494

The Best Family Dining

Cafe Deluxe 1800 International Drive, Tysons Corner (703) 761-0600
Generous George's 7031 Little River Turnpike, Annandale (703) 941-9600; 3006 Duke Street, Alexandria (703) 370-4303
Guapo's 4515 Wisconsin Avenue, NW (202) 686-3588; 9811 Washingtonian Boulevard (Rio Centre), Gaithersburg (301) 977-5655
Hard Rock Cafe 999 E Street, NW (202) 737-ROCK
Olney Ale House 2000 Sandy Spring Road (Route 108), Olney (301) 774-6708
Oodles Noodles 1120 19th Street, NW (202) 293-3138; 4907 Cordell Avenue, Bethesda (301) 986-8833
Radio Free Italy 5 Cameron Street (Torpedo Factory) (703) 683-0361

Rain Forest Cafe Routes 7 and 123 (Tysons Corner Center), Tysons Corner (703) 821-1900

The Best Pizza

Faccia Luna 2400 Wisconsin Avenue, NW (202) 337-3132;
23 Washington Boulevard, Alexandria (703) 838-5998;
2909 Wilson Boulevard, Arlington (703) 276-3099

Pizzeria Paradiso 2029 P Street, NW (202) 223-1245

Primi Piatti 2013 I Street, NW (202) 223-3600

Zio's 9083 Gaither Road, Gaithersburg (301) 977-6300

The Best Raw Bars

Blue Point Grill 600 Franklin Street, Alexandria (703) 739-0404

Oceanaire 1201 F Street, NW (202) 347-BASS

Kinkead's 2000 Pennsylvania Avenue, NW (202) 296-7700

McCormick's & Schmick's 11921 Freedom Drive, Reston (703) 481-6600;
7401 Woodmont Avenue, Bethesda (301) 961-2626;
1652 K Street NW (202) 861-2233;
8484 Westpark Drive/Route 2, Tysons Corner (703) 848-8000

Old Ebbitt Grill 675 15th Street, NW (202) 347-4801

The Sea Catch 1054 31st Street, NW (202) 337-8855

The Best Sunday Brunches

Cafe Atlantico 405 Eighth Street, NW (202) 393-0812 (Saturday only)

The Four Seasons Hotel Garden Terrace 2800 Pennsylvania Avenue, NW (202) 342-0444

Gabriel 2121 P Street, NW (next to Radisson Barceló Hotel) (202) 956-6690

Georgia Brown's 950 15th Street, NW (202) 393-4499

The Inn at Glen Echo MacArthur Boulevard and Clara Barton Parkway, Glen Echo (301) 229-2280

Jaleo 480 Seventh Street, NW (202) 628-7949; Elm and Woodmont Streets, Bethesda (301) 913-0003

The Kennedy Center Roof Terrace Virginia and New Hampshire Avenues, NW (202) 416-8555

Kinkead's 2000 Pennsylvania Avenue, NW (202) 296-7700

Melrose Park Hyatt Hotel, 24th and M Streets, NW (202) 955-3899

New Heights 2317 Calvert Street, NW (202) 234-4110

Old Angler's Inn 10801 MacArthur Boulevard, Potomac (301) 365-2425

Old Ebbitt Grill 675 15th Street, NW (202) 347-4801

The Best Sushi Bars

Chopsticks 1073 Wisconsin Avenue, NW (202) 338-6161

Ginza 1009 21st Street, NW (202) 833-1244

Kaz Sushi Bistro 1915 I Street, NW (202) 530-5500

Matuba 2915 Columbia Pike, Arlington (703) 521-2811;
4918 Cordell Avenue, Bethesda (301) 652-7449

Miyagi 6219 Curran Street, McLean (703) 893-0116

Momo Taro 16051 Frederick Road/Route 355, Rockville (202) 963-6868

Murasaki 4620 Wisconsin Avenue, NW (202) 966-0023
Niwano Hana 887 Rockville Pike (Wintergreen Plaza) (301) 294-0553
Sakana 2026 P Street, NW (202) 887-0900
Shiro-Ya 2512 L Street, NW (202) 659-9449
Sushi-Ko 2309 Wisconsin Avenue, NW (202) 333-4187
Sushi Taro 1503 17th Street, NW (202) 462-8999
Tachibana 6715 Lowell Avenue, McLean (703) 847-1771
Tako Grill 7756 Wisconsin Avenue, Bethesda (301) 652-7030
Tono Sushi 2605 Connecticut Avenue, NW (202) 332-7300
Yoko 2946-J Chain Bridge Road, Oakton (703) 255-6644
Yosaku 4712 Wisconsin Avenue, NW (202) 363-4453

The Best with Tables in the Kitchen

Bis 15 E Street, NW (202) 661-3899
Citronelle 3000 M Street, NW (Latham Hotel) (202) 625-2150
Galileo 1110 21st Street, NW (202) 293-7191
The Kennedy Center Roof Terrace Virginia and New Hampshire Avenues, NW (202) 416-8555
Maestro 700 Tysons Boulevard (Ritz-Carlton), Tysons Corner (703) 917-5498
Matisse 4934 Wisconsin Avenue, NW (202) 244-5222
Melrose 24th and M Streets, NW (Park Hyatt Hotel) (202) 955-3899
Restaurant Nora R Street and Florida Avenue, NW (202) 462-5143

The Best Views

America 50 Massachusetts Avenue, NE (Union Station) (202) 682-9555
Hotel Washington Roof 515 15th Street, NW (202) 638-5900
J.W.'s View 1401 Lee Highway (Key Bridge Marriott), Arlington (703) 243-1745
Lafayette 16th and H Streets, NW (Hay-Adams Hotel) (202) 638-2570
New Heights 2317 Calvert Street, NW (202) 234-4110
Perry's 1811 Columbia Road, NW (202) 234-6218
Sequoia 3000 K Street, NW (202) 944-4200
Tony & Joe's 3000 K Street, NW (202) 944-4545

The Best Wine Lists

Citronelle 3000 M Street, NW (in the Latham Hotel) (202) 625-1250
Colvin Run 8045 Leesburg Pike/Route 7, Tysons Corner (703) 356-9500
Corduroy 1201 K Street, NW (in the Four Points Hotel) (202) 589-0699
D.C. Coast 1401 K Street, NW (202) 216-6988
Galileo 1110 21st Street, NW (202) 293-7191
Gerard's Place 915 15th Street, NW (202) 737-4445
Grapeseed 4865-C Cordell Avenue, Bethesda (301) 986-9592
Inn at Little Washington Middle and Main streets, Washington, Virginia (540) 675-3800
Kinkead's 2000 Pennsylvania Avenue, NW (202) 296-7700
L'Auberge Chez Francois 322 Springvale Road, Great Falls (703) 759-3800
Maestro 700 Tysons Boulevard (Ritz-Carlton), Tysons Corner (703) 917-5498
Melrose 24th and M streets, NW (in the Park Hyatt Hotel) (202) 955-3899
Obelisk 2029 P Street, NW (202) 872-1180

Le Relais 1025-I Seneca Road (in Seneca Square), Great Falls (703) 444-4060
Seasons 2800 M Street NW (in the Four Seasons Hotel) (202) 944-2000
Signatures 801 Pennsylvania Avenue, NW (202) 628-5900
Taberna del Alabardero 1776 I Street, NW (202) 429-2200
Vidalia 1990 M Street, NW (202) 659-1990
Zola 800 F Street, NW (202) 654-0999)

Restaurant Profiles

ADDIE'S ★★½

MODERN AMERICAN | MODERATE | QUALITY ★★★ | VALUE ★★★★ | ZONE 10B

11120 Rockville Pike, Rockville; (301) 881-0081

Reservations Not available Saturday and Sunday**When to go** Late lunch, mid-week **Entree range** $9–27 **Payment** VISA, MC, AMEX, DC **Service rating** ★★★½ **Friendliness rating** ★★★★ **Parking** Free lot **Bar** Beer and wine **Wine selection** Good **Dress** Casual, informal **Disabled access** Good **Customers** Locals, area business

Lunch Monday–Friday, 11:30 a.m.–2:30 p.m.; Saturday, noon–2:30 p.m.
Dinner Monday–Thursday, 5:30–9:30 p.m.; Friday, 5:30–10 p.m.; Saturday, 5–10 p.m.; Sunday, 5–9 p.m.

Setting & atmosphere This is a simple suburban house turned into a cartoon fantasy, a family dine-in kitchen of the future past: rooms brightly painted primary blue, red, and yellow; collections of oddball clocks; plastic place mats; doorknobs mounted as coat hooks; and antique stoves as serving tables. And the simple white oval platters actually come as a pleasant surprise in this era of florid china.

House specialties Playful tastes starring the likes of grilled marinated quail and goat cheese (appetizer or entree-sized); seared scallops in mango sauce or black olive couscous and pesto; soft-shell crabs over linguini; crab cakes over polenta; ostrich with onion compote; cornmeal-crusted oysters with roasted corn and prosciutto; seared tuna with shrimp wontons.

Other recommendations Variations of pescado Andalucia, fish (halibut, bass, or rockfish) with mussels, potatoes, and merguez sausage stew; updated duck cassoulet; shrimp taco salad; grilled vegetables with real flavor.

Entertainment & amenities Outdoor seating (though with a close view of Rockville Pike traffic).

Summary & comments Owners Jeff and Barbara Black are simply having fun in the kitchen, and it shows: The food is trendy and smart without being overly showy; flavorings are distinctive but not overwhelming; salt is carefully considered. When the urge for comfort food strikes one of them, it's apt to be roast chicken or pork chops. Lunch is much simpler, geared to the working/shopping crowds from White Flint Mall across the street—sandwiches (including a fried oyster sandwich), chili, and salads. Though Jeff is usually tending their new restaurant, Black's Bar & Kitchen in Bethesda, both sensibilities—the comfy and the iconoclastic—are delightfully obvious in both.

ANDALE ★★★

MODERN MEXICAN | MODERATE | QUALITY ★★★ | VALUE ★★★ | ZONE 3

401 Seventh Street, NW; (202) 783-3133

Reservations Recommended **When to go** Monday nights for wine specials; Fridays for bar snacks; otherwise anytime **Entree range** $14–22 **Payment** VISA, MC, AMEX, DC, D **Service rating** ★★★ **Friendliness rating** ★★★★ **Parking** Valet, pay lots **Bar** Full service **Wine selection** Good **Dress** Business, casual **Disabled access** Good **Customers** Locals, embassy/government types, young cocktail nibblers

Lunch Monday–Saturday, 11:00 a.m.–3 p.m.
Dinner Monday–Thursday, 5–10 p.m.; Friday and Saturday, 5–11 p.m.

Setting & atmosphere The room is comfy but a little (intentionally) cartoonish, with big bold primary colors, bouncy booths, and overripe ladies on the wall.

House specialties Roast duck in chili-cinnamon-chocolate mole; chili- and garlic-marinated rib-eye; sea bass with ground–pumpkin seed sauce; crisp-fried pork carnitas with hot chili sauce; roast chicken with sour orange in banana leaves; griddled squash blossom and cheese quesadillas; achiote-marinated tuna with sour orange juice.

Other recommendations Cornmeal–black bean pancakes; oozing chili rellenos; shrimp and chili empenadas. Of the salsa dips, the smoked chipotle is the best; for bar-snacking, try the chili-toasted peanuts.

Summary & comments Chef Alison Swope has been into New Southwestern cuisine since before it was chic, but her interest gradually focused and sharpened on contemporary regional Mexican cuisine; having turned her daily specials into sequential explorations of those areas, she abruptly shut down and in less than a month transformed the Mark into Andale, which has quickly become the meeting place of international from all the Americas, North (and north of the border) to Central and South. This makes a good change of pace for vegetarians, too, as there are several veggie dishes and meat-free salads and noshes.

ASIA NORA ★★½

PAN-ASIAN | MODERATE | QUALITY ★★★★ | VALUE ★★★ | ZONE 6

2213 M Street, NW; (202) 797-4860

Reservations Recommended **When to go** Anytime **Entree range** $20–27 **Payment** VISA, MC, AMEX, D **Service rating** ★★★ **Friendliness rating** ★★★½ **Parking** Valet **Bar** Full service **Wine selection** Limited **Dress** Business, informal **Disabled access** No **Customers** Local, tourist, business

Dinner Monday–Friday 5:30–10:00 p.m. and Saturday, 5:30–10:30 p.m.; Sunday, closed.

Setting & atmosphere A small but very romantic two-story Indonesian jewel box (or fantasy boudoir) of a room, with carved wood, mirrors, and intriguing booths and balcony niches.

House specialties Rockfish with lemongrass and chilis; lacquered spit-roasted duck with a crêpe-light mushroom pancake and chili-hoisin sauce; salmon glazed with Japanese miso and served with ginger-flavored soba noodles.

Other recommendations Grilled "satays" of shiitake mushrooms and tofu; Asian veal-rice sausage; vegetable or seafood tempura; Vietnamese-style garden rolls with crabmeat, cilantro, mint, and peanut sauce; hot-and-sour coconut soup. At lunch, the "grill of the day" or Japanese-style bento box lunches. A selection of quality sakes and green teas.

Summary & comments This is a restaurant designed for dawdling. The menu, which is seasonally adjusted, is divided into "small dishes" of three or four bites each and larger dishes of six to eight bites, so that a series of different tastes can be shared. (Of course, this means that you can spend rather more money here if you want.) The dishes are more traditional in attitude than in strict recipes: Japanese udon noodles are topped with portobello mushrooms; salmon "tartare" is lightly pickled, like ceviche; and the tuna "sashimi" is seared, just as the flounder "sashimi" is dressed with sizzling-hot oil—a trick made famous by bicoastal star Nobu.

ATHENIAN PLAKA ★★★

GREEK | MODERATE | QUALITY ★★★½ | VALUE ★★★★ | ZONE 10A

7833 Woodmont Avenue, Bethesda; (301) 986-1337

Reservations Accepted **When to go** Anytime **Entree range** $9–16 **Payment** VISA, MC, AMEX, CB, DC, D **Service rating** ★★★ **Friendliness rating** ★★★ **Parking** Validated, free valet (weekends) **Bar** Full service **Wine selection** Limited **Dress** Informal, casual **Disabled access** Good **Customers** Locals

Open Monday–Thursday, 11:30 a.m.–10 p.m.; Friday and Saturday, 11:30 a.m.–11 p.m.; Sunday, 10:30 a.m.–10 p.m.

Setting & atmosphere A quietly proud little dining room, with fresh linen and greenery, plaster arches, and vivid travel-mag murals of the home country. (In fact, it shares ownership with the nearby La Panetteria Italian restaurant.) In good weather, tables are set up on the sidewalk.

House specialties Among entrees, veal baked with eggplant, wine, and two cheeses; exohikon (lamb sautéed with artichokes, calamata olives, and cheese, and then baked in phyllo); pan-fried baby squid. Among appetizers, a combination platter of calf's liver, sweetbreads, meatballs, sausage, and lamb (for two); eggplant stuffed with pine nuts, raisins, and tomato; pan-fried smelt.

Other recommendations Broiled red snapper; shrimp baked with tomatoes and feta; swordfish.

Summary & comments Don't let the suburban storefront location fool you; this is not your father's greasy Greek joint. The kitchen says it takes time to prepare dishes to order, and they mean it—it's a little slow, but it's right. A surprising number of these dishes are also available at lunch for a couple of dollars less.

AUSTIN GRILL ★★½

TEX-MEX | INEXPENSIVE | QUALITY ★★★ | VALUE ★★★½ | ZONES 3, 5, 10A, 11B, 11C

750 E Street, NW; (202) 393-3776
2404 Wisconsin Avenue, NW; (202) 337-8080
7278 Woodmont Avenue, Bethesda; (301) 656-1366
8430-A Old Keene Mill Center, West Springfield; (703) 644-3111
801 King Street, Old Town Alexandria; (703) 684-8969

Reservations For parties of 10+ **When to go** Late afternoon, late night **Entree range** $7–17 **Payment** VISA, MC, AMEX, DC, D **Service rating** ★★★ **Friendliness rating** ★★★ **Parking** Street **Bar** Full service **Wine selection** Fair **Dress** Casual **Disabled access** Poor, all bathrooms are upstairs **Customers** Local, student

Breakfast (West Springfield only) Saturday and Sunday, 10 a.m.–3 p.m.
Brunch Saturday and Sunday, 11 a.m.–3 p.m.
Lunch/dinner Monday, 11:30 a.m.–10:30 p.m.; Tuesday–Thursday, 11:30 a.m.–11 p.m.; Friday and Saturday, 11 a.m.–midnight; Sunday, 11 a.m.–10:30 p.m.

Setting & atmosphere Hot adobe pastels, Crayola-colored tile, buffalo and lizard stenciling, angular art-joke graphics, and Tex-Mex pun art and T-shirts in funky vinyl-booth roadhouse settings. Great Texas music on the PA. If not a mom-and-pop joint, it's a friends' franchise: One of the original prep cooks who started at age 19 in Georgetown became the head chef in Bethesda.

House specialties Potent quesadillas with chorizo or delicate ones with crabmeat; grilled fish of the day; real all-beef chunky chili; "Austin special enchilada" with three sauces; green chicken chili; grilled chili-rubbed shrimp and scallops; grilled fish; pork loin enchilada with mole sauce.

Other recommendations Margaritas; chili-flavored rib eye; pork chops adobado; eggs Benedict with jalapeño hollandaise (brunch); barbecued brisket.

Summary & comments The perfect antidote for designer chili cuisine (not that these are plain-Jane spots; in fact, they're corporate cousins of the slick-chic Jaleo). The original Georgetown branch made its first friends just from the smell of the smoker out back. The hot-hot sauces—a choice of four—were the local endorphin addict's drugs before chilis were cool, so to speak. Incidentally, the Springfield location has been experimenting with serving breakfast, but a fairly straight version.

BACCHUS ★★★

LEBANESE | MODERATE | QUALITY ★★★½ | VALUE ★★★★ | ZONES 6, 10A

1827 Jefferson Place, NW; (202) 785-0734
7945 Norfolk Avenue, Bethesda; (301) 657-1722

Reservations Suggested **When to go** Anytime **Entree range** $15–20 **Payment** VISA, MC, AMEX **Service rating** ★★½ **Friendliness rating** ★★ **Parking** Street, valet at dinner, free **Bar** Full service **Wine selection** Brief **Dress** Informal, casual **Disabled access** Jefferson Street (none), Norfolk Avenue (good) **Customers** Diplomats, locals, business

Lunch Monday–Friday, noon–2:30 p.m.
Dinner Monday–Thursday, 6–10 p.m.; Friday and Saturday, 6–10:30 p.m.; Sunday, 6–10 p.m.

Setting & atmosphere The D.C. location is a simple, pleasantly crowded English basement downtown; in Bethesda, it's a villa with carved screens, whitewashed walls, a sort of marketplace square layout, and a lively, gossipy atmosphere.

House specialties Mezze (or "maza" here–small servings to share of stuffed phyllo turnovers with spinach or cheese); kibbeh (a steak tartare with cracked wheat); zucchini pancakes; grilled sausages; stuffed baby eggplant; fried smelt; stuffed grape leaves; fragrant pilaf.

Other recommendations Lamb almost any fashion, including layered over a fried pita and yogurt or with eggplant; fried smelts; fatayer bel sbanegh, a spinach and coriander pastry; stuffed cabbage with pomegranate sauce; kebabs.

Summary & comments For whatever reason, the Bethesda location is more consistent, the specials are more interesting, and the food is just a little sprightlier; on the other hand, its popularity can make for a Casbah-style din. The Washington location has no separate nonsmoking section.

BANGKOK GARDEN ★★★

THAI | INEXPENSIVE | QUALITY ★★★ | VALUE ★★★★ | ZONE 10A

4906 St. Elmo Avenue, Bethesda; (301) 951-0670

Reservations Accepted on weekends **When to go** Anytime **Entree range** $7–19
Payment VISA, MC, AMEX, D **Service rating** ★★★½ **Friendliness rating** ★★★★
Parking Street, free lot after 7 p.m.; valet Thursday through Saturday **Bar** Full service
Wine selection House **Dress** Casual **Disabled access** Fair **Customers** Local, ethnic

Open Monday–Thursday, 11 a.m.–10:30 p.m.; Friday and Saturday, 11 a.m.–11 p.m.; Sunday, 11 a.m.–10 p.m.

Setting & atmosphere Small, cheery, and so crowded with brass and plaster animals—giraffes, elephants, temple foo dogs, peafowl, deer—that the enshrined young Buddha resembles a Thai Francis of Assisi. Enlarged and framed colorful Thai currency and portraits of the royal family are also prominent.

House specialties A rich, skin-and-fat duck in five-flavor sauce; fat "drunken" noodles with beef; hoy jawh (a crispy pork and crab appetizer cake); squid with basil and chili (unusual, almost purely squid and scarce vegetable filler); the tangy rather than searing seafood combination.

Other recommendations Soft-shell crabs in one of five sauces, including one very light version with asparagus and oyster sauce; steamed crab dumplings; shrimp in chili oil.

Summary & comments Though relatively low-profile amid the Thai boom—with Americans, that is; it's very popular within the Thai community—this family-run restaurant rewards regular attendance and obvious interest because some of the best dishes aren't on the English menu, but are available to anyone who knows to ask. A particularly delicious example is the "Thai steak tartare," a beef version of a Thai pork classic that is rich with garlic, cilantro, and basil and served with a steaming basket of "sticky rice" intended to be used as the utensil: Take a pinch of rice—about a tablespoon—slightly flatten it and grasp a bite of meat with it and pop the whole morsel into your mouth. At $7.95, it's a steal of a meal.

BENJARONG ★★★½

THAI | INEXPENSIVE | QUALITY ★★★★ | VALUE ★★★★ | ZONE 10B

855 Rockville Pike (Wintergreen Plaza), Rockville; (301) 424-5533

Reservations Suggested **When to go** Anytime **Entree range** $8–13 **Payment** VISA, MC, AMEX, DC, D **Service rating** ★★★ **Friendliness rating** ★★★★ **Parking** Free lot **Bar** Full service **Wine selection** House **Dress** Informal **Disabled access** Good **Customers** Local, ethnic

Open Monday–Thursday, 11:30 a.m.–10 p.m.; Friday and Saturday, 11:30 a.m.–10:30 p.m.; Sunday, 5–10 p.m.

Setting & atmosphere A simple but soothing room decorated with off-white grass wallpaper, pink linens, black lacquer chairs, and a few Thai carvings and figurines.

House specialties Duck with asparagus (in season); spicy duck and coriander salad; mussels steamed in lemongrass and spices; sliced beef filet in red wine sauce; fresh squid sautéed with chilis and basil; and the best pra pla mug—a sort of squid ceviche with lime juice and chilis—even in this Thai-smart town.

Other recommendations Steamed whole snapper with delicate scallions and ginger sauce or crispy fried flounder; spicy shrimp in red curry sauce; red curry duck; seafood combination chow foon noodles; a rattle-shaped chicken drummette appetizer stuffed with ground chicken and pork; soft-shell crabs in a choice of sauces; and a sort of barbecue beef in chili paste with scallions.

Summary & comments Benjarong (the name refers to a type of multicolored Thai porcelain) closed awaiting new digs, but the kitchen staff used the hiatus for a trip to Thailand to sharpen their skills. Many of the dishes here are Southern Thai, meaning the curries are creamier and there's a good pork satay on the menu. There are also several good vegetarian choices, including a delicately peppery sautéed watercress. If you're uncertain of spice levels, inquire; this is a hospitable and accommodating establishment.

BISTRO BIS ★★★

FRENCH | EXPENSIVE | QUALITY ★★★ | VALUE ★★★ | ZONE 3

15 E Street, NW; (202) 661-2700

Reservations Recommended **When to go** Late lunch, early or late dinner **Entree range** $17–23 **Payment** VISA, MC, AMEX, DC, D **Service rating** ★★★ **Friendliness rating** ★★★½ **Parking** Valet after 5:30, pay lot **Bar** Full service **Wine selection** Good **Dress** Business, informal **Disabled access** Good **Customers** Political/media biz, food trendies

Breakfast Daily, 7–10 a.m.

Brunch Saturday and Sunday, 11:30 a.m.–2:30 p.m.

Lunch Monday–Friday, 11:30 a.m.–2:30 p.m.
Dinner Daily, 5:30–10:30 p.m.

Setting & atmosphere Its name is short for "bistro," and like that offhand joke, it's sleek, chic, and a touch oblique, its long space divided into a series of step-down semi-detached dining "suites" off a hallway. The dark old Tiber Creek Pub has been transformed into a very blond-wood and etched-glass complex that somehow makes you feel that your companions may be billing you by the hour: zinc-topped bar, cigar-bar mezzanine with lobby-like chairs, and an almost voyeuristic display of exposed-steel kitchen countertop. Even the fireplace has changed from London pubby to L.A. clubby.

House specialties Intriguingly idiosyncratic semi-classic French fare: tangy steak tartare topped with cornichon fans and served on super-crisp garlic potato chips or escargot-artichoke ragoût in brioche (appetizers); pan-roasted monkfish wrapped in cured ham with apples and Calvados; pepper-crusted salmon; asute of rabbit with mustard sauce; braised veal short ribs; huge and tender scallops; and the more traditional bistro-esque steak 'n' fries, sweetbreads, duck confit, etc.

Other recommendations Roast poultry, in generous portions—a half-hen even at lunchtime. Game specials are carefully tended, too.

Summary & comments "Bis" can also mean an encore, but while this may be the second fine production from the team of Sallie and Jeff Buben of Vidalia (see later in this section), it resembles that neo-Southern favorite only in its refusal to see traditional fare as limiting. The quantity of food is not so unusual in this business-expense era, but the delicacy of seasoning and the staff's light hand with rich sauces make it hard to leave much on the plate. The all-French wine list has some fine bargains on it, especially for those willing to look beyond the warhorse burgundy or chablis labels.

BISTRO FRANÇAIS ★★½

FRENCH | INEXPENSIVE | QUALITY ★★★½ | VALUE ★★★★ | ZONE 5

3124 M Street, NW; (202) 338-3830

Reservations Recommended **When to go** Pre- or post-theater **Entree range** $15–26 **Payment** VISA, MC, AMEX, DC **Service rating** ★★★ **Friendliness rating** ★★★ **Parking** Street (validated parking for two hours) **Bar** Full service **Wine selection** House **Dress** Casual **Disabled access** Good **Customers** Local, ethnic

Open Sunday–Thursday, 11 a.m.–3 a.m.; Friday and Saturday, 11 a.m.–4 a.m.

Setting & atmosphere This old reliable hasn't changed much since the word "bistro" was new to Washington—hanging pots, rotisserie spits, frankly well-used flatware, and clanking trays. In other words, just right.

House specialties This is the sort of place where as nice as the menu is—especially Dover sole, coq au vin, quenelles of pike, its signature spit-roasted chicken—the daily specials are even better: for instance, duck confit, roast game birds, or lamb with artichokes.

Other recommendations The steak 'n' fries here is probably the standard against which all others should be measured. And there are fixed-price lunch and pre-theater menus for $18, including wine.

Summary & comments For all its many pleasures—its famous late-night service and the especially telling fact that many local chefs eat here after-hours—it sometimes seems as if this old favorite gets the Rodney Dangerfield treatment from the fashionable crowds.

BISTRO LEPIC ★★½

FRENCH | MODERATE | QUALITY ★★★½ | VALUE ★★★ | ZONE 5

1736 Wisconsin Avenue, NW; (202) 333-0111

Reservations Recommended **When to go** Anytime **Entree range** $14–21 **Payment** VISA, MC, AMEX, DC, D **Service rating** ★★★ **Friendliness rating** ★★★½ **Parking** Street **Bar** Full service **Wine selection** Good **Dress** Business, Friday casual **Disabled access** Good **Customers** Embassy-Row types, business, Georgetown local

Lunch Tuesday–Sunday, 11:30 a.m.–2:30 p.m.
Dinner Tuesday–Thursday, 5:30–10 p.m.; Friday and Saturday, 5:30–10:30 p.m.; Sunday, 5:30–9:30 p.m.
Setting & atmosphere This is a true bistro, one plain little room that seats about 40, with huge art reproduction murals on the wall and a view of the upper Georgetown street life. But it's currently undergoing a renovation to put a Provençal-feel wine lounge and "international tapas bar" for more casual moments upstairs.

House specialties Satisfying and for the most part traditional dishes such as cassoulet, the French casserole of white beans, sausage, and duck confit; calf's liver with olives and capers; chicken in the pot; and also more authentic and flavorful bistro fare, including braised veal cheeks and rich chicken stew.

Other recommendations Kidneys in mustard sauce; grilled fish; potato-crusted salmon.

Summary & comments This cheery room burst out in a blaze of publicity and got the usual Georgetown trend victims' rush; then the other shoe dropped, domestic discord arose, and the original staff split. The good news is, it's recovered well, and the fad audience has settled into real fans.

BLACK'S BAR & KITCHEN ★★★

SEAFOOD | MODERATE | QUALITY ★★★★ | VALUE ★★★★ | ZONE 10A

7750 Woodmont Avenue, Bethesda; (301) 652-6278

Reservations Recommended **When to go** Anytime **Entree range** $16–32 **Payment** VISA, MC, AMEX, DC **Service rating** ★★★ **Friendliness rating** ★★★½ **Parking** Pay lot, street meters, valet **Bar** Full service **Wine selection** Good house list **Dress** Business, casual **Disabled access** Yes **Customers** Local, business

Lunch Monday–Friday, 11:30 a.m.–2:30 p.m.
Dinner Monday–Thursday, 5–10 p.m.; Friday and Saturday, 5–11 p.m.; Sunday, 5–9:30 p.m.

Setting & atmosphere A funky/fun version of a Gulf Coast fish house, but a little cleaned up from its previous bayou/garage-chic incarnation: raw bar attached to the main bar and couch-slouch cocktail area; not too many fish-decor jokes and a partially glassed-off dining room; also a second-story deck for good weather.

House specialties "Campeche," a sort of crab-shrimp ceviche but served parfait-style with tomatoes and avocado; New Orleans chopped salad with roasted corn and grilled sweet potatoes topped with fried crawfish tails; braised duck enchilada with poblanos and cheese (all appetizers); tortilla-crusted snapper with black beans and rice plus wilted spinach; salmon with succotash; crispy duck breast with cheese grits.

Other recommendations Crabcakes; étouffées; seared tuna with pineapple and lime-cilantro vinaigrette; chili-rubbed pork rib chop. At happy hour, oysters and shrimp are extra cheap.

Summary & comments Jeff Black (see listing for Addie's, above) and executive chef David Craig range across and around the Gulf Coast for recipe ideas, saluting Mexico, New Orleans, San Luis Pass, TX, Siesta Key, FL, Perdido Beach, AL, and the Atchafalaya River Basin, LA. It's not the sort of place that seems ground-breaking . . . until it becomes one of your regular stops.

BOMBAY BISTRO ★★★

INDIAN | INEXPENSIVE | QUALITY ★★★★ | VALUE ★★★★★ | ZONES 10B, 11B

98 West Montgomery Avenue, Rockville; (301) 762-8798
3570 Chain Bridge Road, Fairfax; (703) 359-5810

Reservations Not accepted **When to go** Early evening, lunch buffet **Entree range** $7–17 **Payment** VISA, MC, AMEX, DC, D **Service rating** ★★★ **Friendliness rating** ★★★ **Parking** Free lot **Bar** Beer and wine **Wine selection** House **Dress** Casual **Disabled access** Yes **Customers** Local, ethnic, business

Lunch *Rockville:* Monday–Friday, 11 a.m.–2:30 p.m.; Saturday and Sunday, noon–3 p.m.; *Fairfax:* Monday–Friday, 11:30 a.m.–2:30 p.m.; Saturday and Sunday, noon–3 p.m.
Dinner *Rockville:* Sunday–Thursday, 5–9:30 p.m.; Friday and Saturday, 5–10 p.m.; *Fairfax:* Sunday–Thursday, 5–10 p.m.; Friday and Saturday, 5–10:30 p.m.

Setting & atmosphere Rockville's storefront family-style diner is made cheery in an almost Christmasy way, with red and green native costumes and gilded slippers hung on the wall along with strings of stuffed birds above wooden booths. Its newer offshoot is equally simple and comfy.

House specialties Tandoori chicken or, even better, tandoori salmon; lamb vindaloo, the hottest item on the menu; el maru (a bowlful of rice and crispy noodles with a texture between granola and trail mix); Goan fish curry with a golden sauce; many fine vegetarian choices, notably an aromatic clove-and-cinnamon-flavored okra curry and baingan bhartha (tandoori eggplant); roasted vegetables; mild chicken tikka or spicy chicken madras; oothapam (a South India "crêpe" of lentil and rice dough, stuffed with onions, tomatoes, and green peppers).

Other recommendations Lamb rogan josh or shish kebab; chicken or vegetable biryani; beef badam pasandra (an almond-spiked stew); a sampler platter with chicken tikka, rogan josh, cucumber raita, puri, lentils, and spinach or eggplant.

Summary & comments Located among the lawyers' warrens of historic Rockville, this squeeze-'em-in eatery started out as an Indians' Indian lunch spot, but the word leaked out. Now, even with three or four cooks working, you may have to wait at dinner for a table at the original location, which is the second good reason to go for the all-you-can-eat lunchtime buffet (at both branches). The first good reason is the price: $6.95 on weekdays and $8.95 on weekends. Meanwhile, the cooking keeps getting better. Preview the restaurant at www.bombaybistro.com. *Note:* The owners are opening an upscale regional Indian restaurant in Cleveland Park to be called Indigue.

BURMA ★★★

BURMESE | INEXPENSIVE | QUALITY ★★★ | VALUE ★★★ | ZONE 3

740 6th Street NW (upstairs); (202) 638-1280

Reservations Accepted **When to go** Anytime **Entree range** $6–8 **Payment** VISA, MC, AMEX, DC, D **Service rating** ★★★½ **Friendliness rating** ★★★ **Parking** Street **Bar** Beer and wine **Wine selection** House **Dress** Casual, informal **Disabled access** Yes, but call ahead **Customers** Ethnic South Asian, local, tourist

Lunch Monday–Friday, 11 a.m.–3 p.m.
Dinner Every day, 6–10 p.m.

Setting & atmosphere A modest and unobtrusive second-floor warren with only a handful of native art on the walls to advertise its ethnicity.

House specialties Kaukswe thoke, a tangy noodle dish with ground shrimp, cilantro, red pepper, and peanuts; pickled green tea leaf salad, a slightly sour, spicy slaw with caramelized onions and peanuts dressed in a green tea pesto; squid with ham and scallions; a chili-spiked tofu-and-shrimp stir-fry; and an almost soul-food version of mustard greens with shrimp, pork, or chicken.

Other recommendations Gold fingers, strips of squash-like calabash in a peppery dipping sauce; chili- and mango-flavored pork; a macrobiotic delight of substantial dried tofu with cruciferous veggies; roast duck (requires 24 hours' notice).

Summary & comments Using familiar ingredients from any Asian grocery, this Burmese holdout manages to turn out flavors surprisingly distinct from its near relatives: not so "fishy" (no fermented fish sauce or soy) or seafood-conscious as Vietnamese, less purely peppery and more sour-tangy than Thai, and with the concentrated tea and smoke background of classic Chinese and Japanese cuisine. Disabled patrons should call ahead to make sure the elevator is unlocked. Incidentally, this place is a remarkable bargain: Prices haven't changed in years. And it's fast—one of the best pre-concert stops in the MCI Centre/Shakespeare Theatre circuit.

BUSARA ★★★½

THAI | MODERATE | QUALITY ★★★★ | VALUE ★★★★ | ZONES 5, 11A

2340 Wisconsin Avenue, NW; (202) 337-2340
8142 Watson Street, McLean; (703) 356-2288

Reservations Recommended **When to go** Before 7:30 p.m. or after 9:30 p.m. **Entree range** $8–24 **Payment** VISA, MC, AMEX, DC, D **Service rating** ★★★½

Friendliness rating ★★★ **Parking** Street, lot, valet after 6 p.m. **Bar** Full service **Wine selection** Fair **Dress** Informal **Disabled access** No **Customers** Local, ethnic

Lunch *Georgetown and McLean:* Monday–Friday, 11:30 a.m.–3 p.m.; Saturday and Sunday, 11:30 a.m.–4 p.m.
Dinner *Georgetown:* Sunday–Thursday, 5–10:30 p.m.; Friday and Saturday, 5–11:30 p.m. *McLean:* Sunday–Thursday, 5–10:30 p.m.; Friday and Saturday, 5–11 p.m.

Setting & atmosphere These Thai siblings are aggressively and cheekily modern. The decor of molded hard black rubber, brushed steel, slate, and heavily lacquered flame-streaked tabletops looks as if it were created by a former hot rod customizer—not to mention the ice-blue neon overhead ("busara" means "blue topaz") and post-Pop art. Outside, a partially covered patio curves around a miniature, but elegant, Japanese garden with a fountain. The Tysons Corner branch is even brighter, and although it doesn't yet have a garden, it may in the future.

House specialties Rice-fattened eesan sausage with pork and cabbage; roasted quail with asparagus and oyster sauce; cellophane noodles with three kinds of mushrooms; fillet of sea trout with salmon mousse served on a banana leaf; marinated pork satay with both a tomato-peanut sauce and a chili-spiked vinegar dip; duck in red curry; Thai bouillabaisse in coconut milk; country-style lamb curry.

Other recommendations Tiger shrimp grilled over watercress; vegetarian pad thai; soft-shell crabs and whole flounder. The Tysons branch has a grill that turns out chicken, lean pork, and assorted fresh fish and shellfish as well.

Summary & comments These are Siamese grins with the emphasis on presentation as much as preparation and a lightened-up attitude toward greens and veggies that makes them crisp and filling. A wide variety of spicing is represented (the chili-pod symbols next to menu items are fairly reliable for gauging heat; the Tysons branch sticks to the more familiar stars), and extra sauces or peppers are easy to obtain. Even nicer, there is no MSG in anything.

BUTTERFIELD 9 ★★★

MODERN AMERICAN | EXPENSIVE | QUALITY ★★★★ | VALUE ★★★½ | ZONE 3

600 14th Street, NW; (202) 289-8810

Reservations Essential **When to go** Anytime, after theatre and arena starts **Entree range** $17–36 **Payment** VISA, MC, AMEX, DC, D **Service rating** ★★★★ **Friendliness rating** ★★★ **Parking** Pay lots, valet **Bar** Full **Wine selection** Good **Dress** Business, Friday casual **Disabled access** Good **Customers** Food trendies, business, media

Lunch Monday–Friday, 11:30 a.m.-2:30 p.m.
Dinner Sunday–Thursday, 5:30–10 p.m.; Friday and Saturday, 5–11 p.m.

Setting & atmosphere This former department store is now a sophisticated (if a little decorator-self conscious) double-decker apartment named for a telephone exchange in the super-suave "Thin Man" series, with walls painted persimmon and sage and hung with 1940ish fashion black-and-whites, banquettes covered in the Y2K-favorite leaf-print fabrics, and SoHo-chic exposed metal light fixtures.

House specialties The foie gras "pancake," with batter baked around the liver; crab cakes (with a bouquet of multicolored sauces); the red snapper "calzone" in crêpe wrapping; horseradish-crusted halibut with leeks and celeriac mousse; a fine roast cod with truffle-salt cod sauce and crab-corn chowder bed; panko-crusted fried calamari stuffed with chorizo and bedded on mashed avocado.

Other recommendations Bison hanger steak with tomato-anchovy sauce; grilled lamb chops with white bean ravioli; vegetarian specials; semi-straightforward seafood such as grilled salmon with smoked salmon knish and radish salad.

Summary & comments Chef Martin Saylor, once of the Hay-Adams and later of Martha's Vineyard, wants the savoir fare to match the decor's savoir faire, which means he occasionally exposes his creations to unnecessary trendiness (like the foie gras pancake, a great idea often ruined by poor timing that makes for dry, puffy batter). And he's still working out the distinction between assemblage and accompaniment. Still, there's no denying he's off to a hot start; only time will tell if his style has "legs." Note that despite the formal hours, there is light fare available all afternoon and until midnight.

CAFE ATLANTICO ★★★

NUEVO LATINO | MODERATE | QUALITY ★★★½ | VALUE ★★★★ | ZONE 3

405 8th Street, NW; (202) 393-0812

Reservations Recommended **When to go** Anytime **Entree range** $19–25 **Payment** VISA, MC, AMEX, DC **Service rating** ★★★ **Friendliness rating** ★★★ **Parking** Street; valet at dinner, $8 **Bar** Full service **Wine selection** *Wine Spectator* Award **Dress** Casual **Disabled access** Good **Customers** Local, ethnic

Lunch Monday–Friday, 11:30 a.m.–2.30 p.m.; Saturday, 11:30 a.m.–1:30 p.m.
Dinner Sunday–Thursday 5–10 p.m.; Friday and Saturday, 5–11 p.m.

Setting & atmosphere A very stylish salon, like the living room of an art collector: brilliant fabrics, large and vibrant paintings, loft-like balconies and windows, mosaics, and richly oiled wood. The clientele tends to match the decor—very vibrant, very "on," and frequently very loud.

House specialties Jerk quail with plantain "foam" and pigeon peas; grilled salmon with banana leaf goat cheese packets and wild mushrooms; seared sea bass with butternut squash, lentils, and chorizo stew; roast rabbit with apples, potatoes, and onions in red wine-coconut sauce.

Other recommendations The Saturday "Latin dim sum" brunch, 25 tapas-sized dishes for $19.95; or pre-theater dinner, $22.

Summary & comments Cafe Atlantico is riding two waves at once: location and cuisine. In the heart of the new arts-intelligentsia neighborhood around the Shakespeare Theatre and Lansburg Building, it's also the first major restaurant in this area to specialize in cocina nueva, the Latin version of New Continental—lighter fare, more fashionably presented, and, depending on your perspective, less homey and more expensive than the Central and South American originals. Founding chef Jose Andres Ramon has returned to the Jaleo kitchen (see below), but former sous chef Christy Velie has learned well his way with flavors—the modern Basque foams and essences—and is developing her own style with a bit more Caribbean heat.

CAFE BETHESDA ★★★★

MODERN AMERICAN | MODERATE | QUALITY ★★★★ | VALUE ★★★½ | ZONE 3

5027 Wilson Lane, Bethesda; (301) 657-3383

Reservations Recommended **When to go** Early evening **Entree range** $23–29 **Payment** VISA, MC, AMEX, DC, D **Service rating** ★★★★ **Friendliness rating** ★★★ **Parking** Street, valet **Bar** Full service **Wine selection** Fair **Dress** Business, casual **Disabled access** Not accessible **Customers** Bethesda establishment and their first-dating offspring

Lunch Tuesday–Friday, 11:30 a.m.–2 p.m.; Friday, 11:30 a.m.–2 p.m. and 5:30–10 p.m. **Dinner** Tuesday–Thursday, 5:30–9 p.m.; Friday and Saturday, 5:30–10 p.m.; Sunday, 5:30–9 p.m.

Setting & atmosphere Cafe Bethesda, which is an offshoot of the adjoining L'Academie de Cuisine, gives "cottage industry" new meaning: It's a small country cottage, all dove grey and Wedgewood blue with bright red geraniums in the window boxes and white linen and lace curtains inside. There are some tables outside in summer, which are best used after about 7 p.m. when the traffic noises lessen.

House specialties Halibut with porcini sauce; a double veal chop with truffle sauce; eggplant roulade; and especially nightly specials such as fresh morels stuffed with scallop mousse, crab-stuffed zucchini blossoms, or seared scallops over morels with caviar sauce.

Summary & comments A longtime standard, but mostly for older, more conservative patrons, it has been gradually but gracefully updating to a menu of classic ingredients and intelligent treatments. And it manages to be smart without being showy; grace notes such as sea beans aren't flaunted on the menu, just tipped into the mix.

CAFE DIVAN ★★½

TURKISH | MODERATE | QUALITY ★★½ | VALUE ★★★½ | ZONE 3

1834 Wisconsin Avenue, NW; (202) 338-1747

Reservations Helpful **When to go** Thursdays for whole marinated rotisserie **Entree range** $5–16 **Payment** VISA, MC **Service rating** ★★★★ **Friendliness rating** ★★★★ **Parking** Street **Bar** Liscense pending **Wine selection** License pending **Dress** Business, casual **Disabled access** Good **Customers** Locals, homesice Middle Eastern diplomats

Open Sunday–Thursday, 11 a.m.–10:30 p.m.; Friday and Saturday, 11 a.m.–11 p.m.

Setting & atmosphere A remarkably (and unusually) bright and sunny triangular corner, with windows winging out on both sides, with polished Brazilian cherry flooring, Turkish tile, and pomegranate accents.

House specialties Spicy sun-dried beef baked with tomatoes; sliced chicken breast with walnut sauce; eggplant-smothered lamb shank; the mezze platter of feta, hummus, taramasalata, and stuffed grape leaves. Donner kebab, the thin-sliced layers of marinated lamb and veal alternately rolled on a spit and grilled, is a weekend special at most Turkish restaurants, but here it's available at every meal.

Other recommendations Slahmacun (the Turkish flatbread pizza) topped with chopped lamb and tomatoes or a variety of toppings; manti (the beef-stuffed and yogurt-topped dumplings common to Eastern Asia); a lamb and chicken kebab combo.

Summary & comments While not the most accessible in terms of location—the busy stretch of upper Georgetown is rife with restaurants and diners (and residents) struggling for parking—Cafe Divan has made itself a neighborhood favorite by dint of cheery service and Turkish fare far beyond the oily standards.

CAFE MILANO ★★★

ITALIAN | EXPENSIVE | QUALITY ★★★★ | VALUE ★★★★ | ZONE 5

3251 Prospect Street, NW; (202) 333-6183

Reservations Helpful **When to go** Late lunch, late dinner **Entree range** Four courses, $35 **Payment VISA**, MC, AMEX, DC **Service rating** ★★★½ **Friendliness rating** ★★★½ **Parking** Street, pay lots **Bar** Full service **Wine selection** Good **Dress** Business, hip informal **Disabled access** Through rear entrance **Customers** Local, embassy

Lunch Monday–Saturday, 11:30 a.m.–2:30 p.m.
Dinner Monday–Wednesday, 4–11 p.m.; Thursday and Friday, 4 p.m.–midnight
Brunch Sunday, 11 a.m.–3 p.m.

Setting & atmosphere A cross between a haute couturier's salon and a Milan disco, with a subway map painted on the ceiling—and new a portrait of Placido Domingo as El Cid, too (all of which makes for interesting philosophical speculation on the direction Italian interests have taken since the days of the Sistine Chapel). At Bice, where owner Franco Nuschese was manager, the shadowboxes held wallpaper samples; here they frame the even hip-jokier designer ties—presumably from his closet, as he never seems to be wearing one—and limited-edition scarves. And the pastas are named after designers. There's a terrace for warm-weather dining and a prettier-than-usual long bar.

Other recommendations The $35 four-course special.

House specialties After falling off a bit, the pretty boy of the kitchen is back in shape with some trendy stuff (carpaccio of salmon, ostrich, and beef hot or cold); some addictive indulgences (quail breast salad with cheese crostini); unexpectedly deft pastas (stuffed with mushrooms or pumpkin, dressed with eggplant or broccoli rabe and sausage or truffles); and for the big boys, steaks and chops with real Italian flavor, no Chicago nakedness. There are even light little pizzas, and lighter courses are available late.

CARLYLE GRAND CAFE ★★½

MODERN AMERICAN | MODERATE | QUALITY ★★★½ | VALUE ★★★ | ZONE 11B

4000 South 28th Street, Arlington; (703) 931-0777

Reservations Recommended for 6 or more **When to go** Early evenings **Entree range** $12–20 **Payment** VISA, MC, AMEX **Service rating** ★★½ **Friendliness rating** ★★★ **Parking** Free lot, street **Bar** Full service **Wine selection** Good **Dress** Casual **Disabled access** Good **Customers** Locals

Open Sunday–Thursday, 11:30 a.m.–11 p.m.; Friday and Saturday, 11 a.m–midnight.

Setting & atmosphere Simple and attractive, though often over-bustly, a mix of black-and-white and pink paint upstairs, but bistro-style rather than Deco.

House specialties Porterhouse-cut lamb chops with minted papaya chutney; lobster pot stickers with a spicy ginger sauce; quick-smoked salmon with merlot sauce; sautéed scallops and rock shrimp with asparagus risotto; crab cakes; jambalaya pasta.

Other recommendations A smoked chicken and wild mushroom tamale with roasted chili sauce; shrimp and shiitake spring rolls; a big salad with seared rare tuna or shiitake-crusted tuna steak.

Summary & comments Chef Bill Jackson, who's popular with his peers as well as his patrons, is interested in providing varied and unobtrusively healthful food and air: It's a smoke-free zone, and there are plenty of heart-healthy options as well as hearty ones. He likes to mix and match styles, although it isn't fusion food, just fun. He believes in light spirits as well as light food: Consider his own description, "chef and fearless sailboarder," on the menu, and the name of his adjoining bread bakery, Best Buns. Note that while the downstairs area is open all afternoon and into the late hours, the more formal upstairs dining room closes between lunch and dinner and also shuts down earlier in the evening.

CESCO TRATTORIA ★★★

ITALIAN | MODERATE | QUALITY ★★★★ | VALUE ★★★★ | ZONE 10A

4871 Cordell Avenue, Bethesda; (301) 654-8333

Reservations Recommended **When to go** Lunch **Entree range** $11–22 **Payment** AMEX, VISA, MC **Service rating** ★★★½ **Friendliness rating** ★★★½ **Parking** Valet, street meter, or lot **Bar** Full service **Wine selection** Very good **Dress** Business, informal **Disabled access** Good **Customers** Food trendies, locals with occasions to celebrate, expense accounters

Lunch Tuesday–Friday, 11:30 a.m.–2:30 p.m.
Dinner Daily, 5:30–10 p.m.

Setting & atmosphere A faux-stone villa, with patio "walls" dividing the dining room into mini-courtyards, fresh flowers, and heavenly aromas.

House specialties Housemade pastas, such as spinach pappardelle with duck sauce or tagliatelle with wild mushrooms; risotto of the day; veal osso bucco in white wine; rabbit with black olives and sweet peppers; venison loin with dried fruit sauce and wild mushrooms; sautéed filet of beef with eggplant, tomato, and gorgonzola sauce; veal scallopine with black truffle sauce; warm baby octopus salad with potatoes, string beans, and black olives.

Other recommendations Braised squid with Swiss chard and green-lipped mussels (both appetizers); roasted pork chop with balsamic vinegar, raisins, and pine nuts.

Entertainment & amenities Covered patio dining.

Summary & comments Dinner here is like a quick trip to Florence. Francesco Ricchi, who also lent his name to I Ricchi and now runs the very fine Etrusco in Dupont Circle (both profiled later) is one of Washington's best Northern Italian chefs, and his partnership here with Galileo (et al.) chef Roberto Donna has given him back both clout and confidence. He is frequently here during the day but downtown at night. The Italian wine list is heavy-duty but not too heavy-handed, or high-priced.

CITRONELLE (aka Michael Richard's Citronelle) ★★★★

FRENCH | EXPENSIVE | QUALITY ★★★★ | VALUE ★★½ | ZONE 5

Latham Hotel, 3000 M Street, NW; (202) 625-2150

Reservations Required **When to go** Lunch, before 9 p.m. **Entree range** Lunch, $16–25; pre-set dinner, $70–115 **Payment** VISA, MC, AMEX, DC, D **Service rating** ★★½ **Friendliness rating** ★★★ **Parking** Valet **Bar** Full service **Wine selection** Good **Dress** Jackets at dinner **Disabled access** Excellent **Customers** Local, tourist, business

Breakfast Every day, 6:30–10:30 a.m.
Brunch 10:30 a.m.–3:30 p.m. on Easter, Mother's Day, and Thanksgiving
Lunch Monday–Friday, noon–2 p.m.
Dinner Sunday–Thursday, 6:30–10 p.m.; Friday, 6:30–10:30 p.m.; Saturday, 6–10:30 p.m.

Setting & atmosphere Using a series of small level shifts and cutaway ceilings, the designers of this pretty but not showy establishment have made the space seem both intimate and expansive. The upstairs lounge is classic flannel grey and green; the downstairs rooms have a more classic look. Clearly, the star attractions are the exposed kitchen and its six chefs, two preppers, and salad chef—and the show does go on, sometimes unreasonably slowly.

House specialties Although listed as French because of Chef Michel Richard, this could just as well be called "Modern American," "eclectic," or simply flamboyant. Among his greatest inspirations have been a faux osso bucco with veal cheeks and a potato "bone"; rabbit-and-foie gras-stuffed cannelloni; a very nutrition-of-the-millenium fricassee of sweetbreads, snails, and soybeans; rabbit puzzle dishes mixing loin, limb, and rack of ribs; sautéed foie gras; braised veal in various forms.

Summary & comments L.A. star chef Michel Richard has now made this his flagship, but it isn't clear whether even his presence can compensate for the remarkable prices and frequently uneven food. (It's sort of like that misconceived "mood wall," the big attraction of a $2 million facelift. Say what?) Still, when it's good, it's very very good. Real food-mag addicts should go for the six-course tasting menu—if they can write off the $115 tab.

COLVIN RUN TAVERN ★★★★

MODERN AMERICAN | VERY EXPENSIVE | QUALITY ★★★★½ | VALUE ★★★½ | ZONE 11A

8045 Leesburg Pike, Tysons Corner; (703): 356-9500

Reservations Recommended **When to go** Lunch, early dinner **Entree range** $21–37 **Payment** VISA, MC, AMEX, DC, D **Service rating** ★★★★ **Friendliness rating** ★★★★ **Parking** Valet **Bar** Full service **Wine selection** Good **Dress** Business, Friday casual **Disabled access** Good **Customers** Local power lunchers, business diners, platinum card romantics

Lunch Monday–Friday, 11:30 a.m.–2:30 p.m.

Dinner Monday–Thursdays, 5:30–10 p.m.; Friday and Saturday, 5:30–10:30 p.m.; Sunday, 5–9 p.m.

Setting & atmosphere This is something of a concept restaurant, where four regions—Nantucket, the Shenandoah, Charleston, and Maine—are each represented by decor areas and menu items. It's an unobstrusively good-looking restaurant, with a fireplace in the lounge and a gracious marble bar (which wraps around the wine room) and those "regional" touches (flagstone in the Shenandoah, etc.), but decor is background—a welcome relief, actually. This is a very busy neighborhood, so expect to adjust to peak hours.

House specialties Squab with potato gnocchi; Zinfandel-braised short ribs; veal cheeks; stuffed leg of lamb rolled to the table and sliced; and similar cart service for venison, rack of veal, lamb, and so on, depending on the market.

Other recommendations Pan-roasted rockfish; seared scallops with sherry-lemon; crispy sweetbreads; rabbit-foie gras terrine—and rabbit with sweetbreads.

Summary & comments A number of food and wine publications, in and outside the area, have already taken note of Colvin Run as one of Washington's best new restaurants, and with reason. It's the second child of chef Bob Kinkead of the eponymous Kinkead's downtown. And while he is not in the kitchen (and in fact the menu, under former Kinkead's sous-chef Jeff Gaetjen, is quite different, being in heavy carno-territory), he keeps a close eye on quality.

CORDUROY ★★★

MODERN AMERICAN | EXPENSIVE | QUALITY ★★★★ | VALUE ★★★ | ZONE 11A

8201 K Street, NW (in the Four Points Hotel); (202) 589-0699

Reservations Recommended **When to go** Anytime **Entree range** $18–26 **Payment** VISA, MC, AMEX, D **Service rating** ★★★½ **Friendliness rating** ★★★★ **Parking** Street, pay lots, valet **Bar** Full service **Wine selection** Very good **Dress** Business, Friday casual **Disabled access** Good **Customers** Business, food-conscious commuters

Breakfast Monday–Friday, 6:30–10:30 a.m.; Saturday and Sunday, 7–11 a.m.

Lunch Daily, noon–2:30 p.m.

Dinner Sunday–Friday, 5:30–10:30 p.m.; Saturday, 5:30–11 p.m.

Setting & atmosphere Dark and earthy—mahogany with wheat and eggplant accents—but hospitable, with views of the kitchen and the bar to provide bustle.

House specialties Goat cheese in potato-crust tarte over roasted red pepper coulis; charred tomato soup; pan-seared halibut with corn and chanterelles; buffalo with mushrooms; wild striped bass with chanterelles and Chinese long beans.

Other recommendations Soft-shell crabs and tangy unripe grapes; veal cheeks osso bucco; roast duck breast with turnips, bok choy and fig sauce.

Summary & comments Chef Tom Power has been through the kitchens of Citronelle and the Old Angler's Inn, but seems most at home with his own menu. He uses local and seasonal ingredients to good effect—thankfully, a growing movement in Washington—and even his more elaborate dishes have a becoming modesty of presentation, so they're easy for all comers to accept. And not everyone can roast a chicken—or fry French fries—really well. For solo diners, the bar menu ranges from casual salads to a nice lobster salad sandwich and a few pastas. (Note that weekend lunch is bar menu only.)

D.C. COAST ★★★½

MODERN AMERICAN | EXPENSIVE | QUALITY ★★★★ | VALUE ★★★½ | ZONE 3

1401 K Street, NW; (202) 216-5988

Reservations A virtual necessity **When to go** Late lunch, dinner **Entree range** $13–30 **Payment** VISA, MC, AMEX, DC, D, T **Service rating** ★★★½ **Friendliness rating** ★★★★ **Parking** Valet after 5 p.m. ($5 minimum), pay lots **Bar** Full service **Wine selection** Good **Dress** Business, informal **Disabled access** Good **Customers** Business, light tourists, better convention

Lunch Monday–Friday, 11:30 a.m.–2:30 p.m.

Dinner Monday–Thursday, 5:30–10:30 p.m.; Friday and Saturday, 5:30–11 p.m.; Sunday, closed.

Setting & atmosphere The restaurant's name is a sort of joke on chef Jeff Tunk's previous stints at Washington's "waterfront" River Club, New Orleans, and San Diego. The decor is a low-key pun to match, with a bronze mermaid, a gently rolling ceiling (the curl of which allows mezzanine diners a view of the bar and kitchen staff), fan-pleated sconces that could have been Neptune's cockle shells, and huge oval mirrors that make the reflected customers seem to swim in and out of your imagination.

House specialties The menu is as Calypso as the mermaid—Pacific Rim with a little mod-med on top: fresh half-shelled oysters topped with a sorbet of pickled ginger and sake; smoked lobster finished with a soy sauté; mushroom-crusted halibut; lobster bisque with lobster-stuffed dumplings; ravioli with duck or osso bucco. The wine list is interesting and moderately priced, and the wines by the glass are blessedly unpredictable and refreshing.

Other recommendations Soft-shell crabs and crab cakes; cornmeal-fried oysters.

Summary & comments This smart but not showy restaurant is balanced between two booming neighborhoods—the revived downtown business district and the reviving Convention Center/MCI Centre area—and on the 14th Street "fault line" of eateries drawing trend-savvy young types with expense accounts. Even better, it's a light-and-light alternative to downtown's preponderance of rich sauces and big-beef chophouses. For a quick spiritual pick-me-up, caviar by the ounce is available at the bar.

ELYSIUM AT THE MORRISON HOUSE ★★★

MODERN AMERICAN | EXPENSIVE | QUALITY ★★★★ | VALUE ★★★★ | ZONE 11C

116 South Alfred Street, Old Town Alexandria; (703) 838-8000

Reservations Recommended **When to go** Anytime **Entree range** Breakfast, $12–15; lunch, $13–18; dinner $21–31 (grill) or $61–67 (dining room) **Payment** VISA,

MC, AMEX, DC **Service rating** ★★★★ **Friendliness rating** ★★★½ **Parking** Valet, street **Bar** Full service **Wine selection** Very good **Dress** Jacket and tie (dining room), informal (grill) **Disabled access** No **Customers** Local, business, tourists

Breakfast Monday–Friday, 7–10 a.m. and Saturday, 8–10 a.m.
Lunch Monday–Saturday, 11:30 a.m.–2:30 p.m.; Sunday brunch noon–2 p.m.
Dinner Monday–Thursday, 6–10 p.m.; Friday and Saturday, 6–11 p.m.

Setting & atmosphere A lovely, newer, but Old Town–style inn, with a curving white marble stairway and various small, pretty dining rooms: some more formal with classic white linen, oil paintings, and definitely modern but stylish china; some more like libraries and old smoking rooms.

House specialties There is no menu as such; chef Gian Piero comes out to say pretty much what's on his mind and takes diner's serious allergies or prejudices into account. Given the shifting menu, it's hard to specify recommendations, but meat dishes, including ostrich, pork, and Cervena venison are beautifully handled. Duck—cured, roasted, glazed, or confit'd—is a favorite ingredient.

Summary & comments Under different chefs, different names, and different cuisines, this restaurant has wandered from fine to frustrating, but it's been riding high for the last couple of years. The menu changes frequently, which is good for those intrigued by market-fresh ingredients, but not all Washingtonians are so off-the-cuff, and some may find this a little overwhelming. In addition, some dishes seem more carefully considered and original than others. But there is no doubt that if you're at all food-savvy, the chef's menus—$61–67 for three or more courses, each including dessert and quite likely a little lagniappe from the kitchen—are as intriguing as any. And you can opt for a glass of wine or even a tasting flight recommended for each course as well.

EQUINOX ★★★½

MODERN AMERICAN | MODERATE | QUALITY ★★★★ | VALUE ★★★½ | ZONE 3

818 Connecticut Avenue, NW; (202) 331-8118

Reservations Recommended **When to go** Lunch **Entree range** $16–32 **Payment** VISA, MC, AMEX, DC **Service rating** ★★★★ **Friendliness rating** ★★★★ **Parking** Valet, street **Bar** Full service **Wine selection** Good **Dress** Business, casual **Disabled access** Good **Customers** Foodies, business

Lunch Monday–Friday, 11:30 a.m.–2 p.m.
Dinner Monday–Thursday, 5:30–10 p.m.; Friday and Saturday, 5:30–10:30 p.m.

Setting & atmosphere The best thing about the decor at Equinox is its unobtrusiveness: smart tailored shades of charcoal and matte metal like a chalk-stripe suit. (Actually, it's a good metaphor for chef Todd Gray's polished and reticent technique.) The glass-walled sidewalk area is particularly popular, though better in the evening, after the rush-hour traffic slows.

House specialties "Barbecued salmon" marinated in herbs and basted with a smoked pork-tomato-honey-vinegar sauce; bacon-wrapped pork tenderloin with golden figs, sautéed spinach and shallots; foie gras with rhubarb compote; soft-shelled crabs over fresh vegetable julienne; duck breast over a duck leg slaw; medallions of venison with butternut squash puree and oyster mushrooms; grilled quail.

Other recommendations The chef's six-course tasting menu of dishes not on the menu, for $60 ($85 with wines); grilled Argentinian beef on spinach with crispy shallot rings; pan-roasted mahi-mahi with gnocchi, cherry tomatoes, and pesto; cornmeal-crusted fluke with leeks, shrimp, and spicy tartar sauce (lunch).

Summary & comments Chef-owner Todd Gray spent many years as the on-site chef at Galileo, and that kitchen's consistently excellent reputation depended heavily on his work (in fact, his leaving in part forced Galileo honcho Roberto Donna to rededicate himself to the art of cooking as well as restauranteering). It must be pointed out, however, that now that he has his own head, he's not cooking Italian (or French, which he performed under Jean-Louis Palladin), but what he calls mid-Atlantic regional, heavy on fresh seafood and updated Chesapeake Bay flavors. The menu changes frequently, but in general, expect vegetables to be incorporated into the recipes, not relegated to the side; light sauces based on reductions and natural flavors; and a fondness for contrasting sweet and sour or rich and acid within a single dish—see the examples above. Still a new restaurant, it's moving up rapidly.

ETRUSCO ★★★½

ITALIAN | MODERATE | QUALITY ★★★★ | VALUE ★★★ | ZONE 6

1606 20th Street, NW; (202) 667-0047

Reservations Recommended **When to go** Anytime **Entree range** $12–19 **Payment** VISA, MC, AMEX, DC **Service rating** ★★★ **Friendliness rating** ★★★ **Parking** Valet **Bar** Full service **Wine selection** Good **Dress** Business, dressy, dressy casual **Disabled access** Good **Customers** Locals, business, foodies, food pros

Dinner Monday–Saturday, 5:30–10 p.m.

Setting & atmosphere A cool townhouse-turned-palazzo with conservatory wing, smooth plaster arches, zabaglione-yellow paint, and lurking plants.

House specialties Chargrilled fresh fish; raw fennel and blood orange salad; pappardelle with duck ragu (a signature); warm baby octopus salad with potatoes, matchstick green beans, and black olives; grilled squid; bread-crusted tuna with basil purée.

Other recommendations Ribolitta; potato-stuffed tortelli with veal ragu; white wine osso buco (another signature); veal-stuffed ravioli with wild mushrooms.

Summary & comments Chef-owner Francesco Ricchi is one of Washington's preeminent chefs: At I Ricchi, he and his former wife broke ground with simple and irresistible Tuscan cuisine; he also oversees Bethesda's Cesco (also profiled). His fine and unfussy technique makes ingredients speak for themselves, and they do, splendidly. Even risotto remembers its dignity here, neither mushy nor over-sauced.

GABRIEL ★★½

NUEVO LATINO | MODERATE | QUALITY ★★★★ | VALUE ★★★★★ | ZONE 6

2121 P Street, NW (Radisson Barceló Hotel); (202) 956-6690

Reservations Recommended **When to go** Brunch, happy hour **Entree range** $12–25 **Payment** VISA, MC, AMEX, DC, D **Service rating** ★★½ **Friendliness rat-**

ing ★★★ **Parking** Street, hotel valet **Bar** Full service **Wine selection** Good and affordable **Dress** Business, casual **Disabled access** Good **Customers** Business, local

Breakfast Monday–Friday, 6:30–10:30 a.m.; Saturday and Sunday, 7–10:30 a.m.
Brunch Sunday, 11 a.m.–3 p.m., seatings 11–11:30 a.m. or 1–1:30 p.m.
Dinner Tuesday–Thursday, 6–10 p.m.; Friday and Saturday, 6–10:30 p.m

Setting & atmosphere Sunny yellow paint, ochre and red art, and lots of wood and windows make this English basement seem like an enclosed courtyard.

House specialties Tapas: grilled quail stuffed with sausage; neo-Salvadoran pupusas with a crunchy cornmeal batter; scallops and spicy chorizo with cilantro and lime; figs stuffed with chorizo. Entrees: vegetable stew with rice croquettes; roast monkfish with caramelized oranges and corn fungus sauce; seared salmon with serrano ham and saffron-tomato broth.

Summary & comments The $9.25 happy-hour spread, 5–8 p.m. Wednesday through Friday, could easily pass for dinner. The real pig-out, so to speak, is Sunday brunch, complete with suckling pigs carved from the spit; paella; cassoulet; rolls, danishes, and pastries; cheese and fruit; vegetable and couscous salads; sardines and cold cuts; omelets; polenta and potatoes; roast beef, lamb, and ham; plus unlimited champagne and a whole dessert bar, all for $24.75. Holy mole!

GALILEO ★★★½

ITALIAN | EXPENSIVE | QUALITY ★★★★★ | VALUE ★★★ | ZONE 6

1110 21st Street, NW; (202) 293-7191

Reservations A must **When to go** Anytime **Entree range** $22–37 **Payment** VISA, MC, AMEX, CB, DC, D **Service rating** ★★★★ **Friendliness rating** ★★★½ **Parking** Lot, valet (dinner, except Sunday) **Bar** Full service **Wine selection** Excellent **Dress** Dressy, business **Disabled access** Good **Customers** Local, tourist, business, gourmet mag groupies

Lunch Monday–Friday, 11:30 a.m.–2 p.m.
Dinner Sunday–Thursday, 5:30–9:30 p.m.; Friday and Saturday, 5:30–10:30 p.m.

Setting & atmosphere A gracious stone and plaster palazzo with vaulted recessed booths.

House specialties Among the frequent offerings are game birds—squab, woodcock, guinea hen—and red game such as venison and wild hare. Sea urchin appears fairly often, usually caressing a delicate pasta, as do wild mushrooms or truffles. Even the bread sticks and loaves, which come in a half-dozen flavors, are to be savored. Sauces and presentations are rarely showy, and purées often stand in for cream.

Other recommendations Ravioli stuffed with scallops and served with black truffles, or stuffed with veal and topped with roasted foie gras; grilled rack of veal or venison; sweetbreads; grilled or roasted seafood; gnocchi.

Summary & comments Among the city's finest restaurants by any account, it had begun to suffer from a lack of attention by super-chef Roberto Donna's who co-owns a collection of Italian restaurants in town. However, Donna himself is cooking once again, although it's in the 30-seat *Laboratorio* in back. There, the 10- to 12-course menu, which goes up in price to $115, is a marvel of market-fresh ingenuity. He also offers the longest, best, and probably priciest Italian wine list in Washington, but with style. Regular customers get white-glove treatment; tourists (and obvious food-trend victims) may find the staff showily condescending, but precise nonetheless.

GEORGIA BROWN'S ★★½

SOUTHERN | MODERATE | QUALITY ★★★½ | VALUE ★★★ | ZONE 3

950 15th Street, NW; (202) 393-4499

Reservations Suggested **When to go** Anytime **Entree range** $12–20 **Payment** VISA, MC, AMEX, CB, DC, D **Service rating** ★★★½ **Friendliness rating** ★★★½ **Parking** Street; valet (after 6 p.m.), $6 **Bar** Full service **Wine selection** Very good **Dress** Business, informal **Disabled access** Good **Customers** Business, local, tourist

Brunch Sunday, 11:30 a.m.–2:30 p.m.
Lunch/dinner Monday–Thursday, 11:30 a.m.–10:30 p.m.; Friday, 11:30 a.m.–11:30 p.m.; Saturday, 5:30–11:30 p.m.; Sunday, 5:30–10:30 p.m.

Setting & atmosphere An almost too-sophisticated take on Southern garden district graciousness, with vinelike wrought iron overhead, sleek wood curves, and conversation nooks; window tables are prime.

House specialties Real Frogmore stew, with oysters, scallops, clams, shrimp, fish, and potatoes; fried (or grilled) catfish with black-eyed pea succotash; beautiful white shrimp, heads still on, with spicy sausage over grits; kitchen-sink sausage-chicken-shrimp gumbo. Look for unusual short-term specials such as squab and Australian yabbies.

Other recommendations Sugar and spice rubbed pork chop with maple-whipped mashed potatoes and sautéed green beans; pecan-crusted lamb chops with collard greens; fried chicken salad or duck confit–spinach salad.

Entertainment & amenities Live jazz at Sunday brunch.

Summary & comments This is not low-country cuisine (except perhaps for the high-octane planter's punch); it's haute country, updated versions of dishes you might have found in Charleston or Savannah. Presentation is distinctive without being showy, and portions are generous. Homesick Southerners can indulge in the fried chicken livers and the farm-biscuit-like scones and still look uptown. The wine list is all-American and fairly priced; barrel-aged bourbons and single-malt Scotches are available as well.

GERANIO ★★★

MODERN ECLECTIC | EXPENSIVE | QUALITY ★★★★ | VALUE ★★★ | ZONE 11C

722 King Street, Alexandria; (703) 548-0088

Reservations Recommended **When to go** Anytime **Entree range** $17–32 **Payment** VISA, MC, AMEX **Service rating** ★★★★ **Friendliness rating** ★★★★ **Parking** Street **Bar** Full service **Wine selection** Good **Dress** Business, casual **Disabled access** Not accessible **Customers** Local

Lunch Monday–Friday, 11:30 a.m.–2:30 p.m.
Dinner Monday–Saturday, 6–10:30 p.m.; Sunday, 5:30–9:30 p.m.

Setting & atmosphere A classic Old Town Alexandria townhouse, the exposed brick is softened by richly-colored still lifes. Decor also includes the odd hanging implement (a huge old grain scale), majolica-look flooring, and plastered walls painted a soft flaxen that deepens through the evening to a sage green.

House specialties Chilled rare moulard stuffed with foie gras and wrapped in blanched leeks; osso bucco with saffon risotto and broccoli rabe; lobster risotto with a half-lobster or lobster over polenta; seared rare tuna.

Other recommendations Oven-roasted veal chop with truffled mashed potatoes; seared salmon; mushroom lasagna of porchini tagliatelle layered with portobellos.

Summary & comments Chef-owner Troy Clayton, who trained with Jean-Louis Palladin, has managed to maintain the neighborhood hospitality of this Old Town beauty while completely refreshing and upscaling the menu. Dishes are complex in pairings but without gratuitous frills; this is a restaurant that remains quiet only by choice.

GERARD'S PLACE ★★★★★

FRENCH | EXPENSIVE | QUALITY ★★★★½ | VALUE ★★★ | ZONE 3

915 15th Street, NW; (202) 737-4445

Reservations Recommended (not available after 9:30 p.m. **When to go** Monday **Entree range** $19–42 **Payment** VISA, MC, AMEX, CB, DC **Service rating** ★★★ **Friendliness rating** ★★½ **Parking** Street; valet (evenings) **Bar** Full service **Wine selection** Good **Dress** Business, casual **Disabled access** Very good **Customers** Business, local, tourist

Lunch Monday–Friday, 11:30 a.m.–2:30 p.m.
Dinner Monday–Thursday, 5:30–10 p.m.; Friday and Saturday, 5:30–10:30 p.m.

Setting & atmosphere A quietly powerful room, painted simply in charcoal and terra-cotta and studded with a series of stark pencil lithographs.

House specialties The menu changes weekly, but look for any sweetbread or venison dish; perfectly poached lobster topped with a tricolor confetti of mango, avocado, and red bell pepper in lime-sauterne sauce; "foie gras of the sea" (known to sushi connoisseurs as ankimo or monkfish liver), lightly crusted and grilled rare, as rich as real foie gras but with a fraction of the calories and guilt; terrine of quail bound by quail liver; boned rabbit rolled and wrapped in Japanese seaweed; soft-shell crabs not with almonds but sweeter, unexpected hazelnuts.

Other recommendations Hearty bistro-max dishes such as pot-au-feu of cured duck and savoy cabbage; cod cheeks; braised oxtail; breast of duck with shepherd's pie of the leg. Or you can try the tasting menu: five courses for $59 or with wine for $94. A vegetarian tasting menu is also offered.

Entertainment & amenities On Monday, Gerard's Place waives not only the corkage fee on wines but the markup as well.

Summary & comments Gerard Pangaud prepares classic food, often long-cooked and incredibly tender, but unobtrusively lightened to modern nutritional standards and keyed to seasonal specialties. Presentation is discreet but stunning. Pangaud's restaurant in Paris earned two Michelin stars.

GOOD FORTUNE ★★½

CHINESE | INEXPENSIVE | QUALITY ★★★ | VALUE ★★★★ | ZONE 10B

2646 University Boulevard West, Wheaton; (301) 929-8818

Reservations Accepted **When to go** Anytime, late night **Entree range** $7–14 **Payment** VISA, MC **Service rating** ★★★ **Friendliness rating** ★★★★ **Bar** Full service **Parking** Street, free lot **Wine selection** House **Dress** Informal, casual **Disabled access** Good **Customers** Local, ethnic

Open Monday–Thursday, 11:30 a.m.–1 a.m.; Friday, 11:30 a.m.–2 a.m.; Saturday, 11 a.m.–2 a.m.; Sunday, 11 a.m.–1 a.m.

Setting & atmosphere This is not a particularly elaborate room, settling for "oriental" dining room chairs and a big golden temple on the banquet stage, a few lions, etc. But it's very spacious, as demonstrated by the number of large family groups and parties that dine simultaneously, as well as being a longtime contender for best Cantonese kitchen in town.

House specialties Unusual seafood dishes featuring squid (especially the one with sweet-sour mustard greens), sea anemone or sea cucumber, oysters, shrimp, conch, and fish maw; frog legs; duck; dim sum. For less adventurous tastes, there are plenty of noodle dishes, casseroles, and steamed or fried fish.

Other recommendations Chinese "barbecue," meaning roasted pork, duck, and chicken, available chopped into two-inch pieces as appetizers; whole crispy fish; hot pots.

Summary & comments This establishment has a huge menu of some 200 items, and many "standards," such as fried dumplings, aren't even listed, although available. Dim sum is served every day at lunch, although the weekend version is a little more extensive.

GRAPESEED ★★★

MODERN AMERICAN | EXPENSIVE | QUALITY ★★★★ | VALUE ★★★★ | ZONE 10A

4865-C Cordell Avenue, Bethesda; (301) 986-9592

Reservations Recommended **When to go** Early dinner, late on weekends **Entree range** $19–26 **Payment** VISA, MC, AMEX, DC, D **Service rating** ★★★ **Friendliness rating** ★★★ **Parking** Pay lots, street meters, valet **Bar** Full service **Wine selection** Very good **Dress** Business, casual chic **Disabled access** Narrow **Customers** Food trendies, locals, business

Dinner Monday–Thursday, 5–10 p.m.; Friday and Saturday, 5–11 p.m.; Sunday, 5–9 p.m.

Setting & atmosphere This sleek and unfussy space, with its removable front walls onto the sidewalk and its leggy distance to the partially exposed bar, makes two points immediately: The wine is up front, and the food goes right behind. Chef-owner Jeff Heineman has designed a modern tapas menu to match his impressive list of wines, all available by the glass, bottle, or even taste. Both "appetizers" and entrees, which can vary considerably in size and staying power, come listed as accompanying red wine or white, and the pairings are usually quite smart—unless the country's wine imports hit a snag, as they sometimes do. However, the staff is well prepared to make alternate recommendations.

House specialties Ethereal sweetbreads; crisp and delicate cornmeal-fried oysters; spice-dusted red snapper; luxuriant braised veal cheeks; turkey breast stuffed with fontina, almonds, and green olives (and the Sangiovese recommendation is just right); a witty and robust pepper-crusted filet mignon with oxtail ragoût.

Other recommendations Wild mushroom fricassee; "Portuguese stew" of clams, pork, shiitakes, and oranges; snails with hazelnuts; grilled rockfish with wild mushrooms and roasted corn; seared scallops with port; roast pork with white balsamic vinegar and grapes; seared duck with rosemary and lavender.

Summary & comments Allow some time to get the full impact of this menu. The list of dishes is so intriguing that it's difficult not to over-order, which won't at all bother your palate but may surprise you at check-out, especially as the wines can reach $10 a glass. Still, this is a delightful change of pace, a quick private seminar in new wines and forward thinking. It's almost certainly headed for a fourth star.

GREENWOOD ★★½

MODERN ECLECTIC | EXPENSIVE | QUALITY ★★★★ | VALUE ★★★ | ZONE 7

5031 Connecticut Avenue, NW; (202) 364-4444

Reservations Recommended **When to go** Anytime **Entree range** $18–32 **Payment** VISA, MC **Service rating** ★★★ **Friendliness rating** ★★★½ **Parking** Street **Bar** Full service **Wine selection** Good **Dress** Business, casual **Disabled access** Fair **Customers** Local

Dinner Tuesday–Sunday, 6–10 p.m.

Setting & atmosphere A leftover Asian exterior, but a very modern, almost Homeric wine-dark interior with hand-blown glass lighting. A long trestle-like (or, for Manhattanites, Asia de Cuba–style) table down the center has become a neighborhood cocktail-hour gathering spot.

House specialties The menu is short but changes frequently. The signature dish is a seared rare tuna with seasonal sides.

Other recommendations Roasted root vegetables and even fruits; simple but high-quality meat dishes.

Summary & comments This is chef Carole Greenwood's third eponymous venture, and in some ways the most individualistic of her famously personalized establishments. She refuses to serve the tuna steak any way but rare, is very chary with any substitutions, and so on. But with such a small and personalized menu, it's a question of "love it or leave it," so she's quickly established a strong, if select, following.

GRILL FROM IPANEMA ★★½

BRAZILIAN | MODERATE | QUALITY ★★★ | VALUE ★★★ | ZONE 6

1858 Columbia Road, NW; (202) 986-0757

Reservations Recommended on weekends **When to go** Early, especially Wednesday and Saturday; or after 10 **Entree range** $12–20 **Payment** VISA, MC, AMEX, DC, D **Service rating** ★★½ **Friendliness rating** ★★★ **Parking** Street **Bar** Full Service **Wine selection** Limited **Dress** Casual, informal **Disabled access** Good **Customers** Local, ethnic Brazilian, embassy

Dinner Monday–Thursday, 5–11 p.m.; Friday, 5 p.m.–midnight; Saturday, noon–midnight; Sunday, 4–11 p.m.
Brunch Saturday and Sunday, noon–4 p.m.

Setting & atmosphere Spare and nouveau; its Brazilian rosewood, slate mountainscape mirrors, and darkly tinted windows suggest a huge celebrity limo on cruise control, and the black artist palm trees look like the backdrop for a fashion shoot.

House specialties Feijoada, a black bean/smoked pork/collard greens stew served only on Wednesday and Saturday for dinner and Sunday all day (hence the crush); shellfish stews in either cilantro and pepper or palm oil and coconut sauces; carne de sol, a salt-cured, milk-resuscitated beef roast grilled and thinly sliced.

Other recommendations Grouper and leeks in phyllo dough; marinated grilled shrimp; a mug of smooth black bean soup spiked with cachaca (Brazilian liquor somewhere between rum and moonshine).

Summary & comments A young and lively atmosphere, especially after 10 p.m. when the bar gets busy and the music turns up. The caipirinha, a mix of fresh lime and cachaca, is particularly popular and potent. Because of the no-reservations policy, and a certain tendency of the Portuguese-speaking staff to prefer regular customers, the wait can be annoying—which also adds to the caipirinhas' popularity.

THE INN AT LITTLE WASHINGTON ★★★★★

MODERN AMERICAN | EXPENSIVE | QUALITY ★★★★★ | VALUE ★★★★★ | ZONE 11B

Middle and Main Streets, Washington, VA; (540) 675-3800

Reservations Required **When to go** Anytime **Entree range** Prix fixe: $98 during the week, Friday and Sunday $108, and Saturday $128 **Payment** VISA, MC **Service rating** ★★★½ **Friendliness rating** ★★½ **Parking** Free lot **Bar** Full service **Wine selection** Very good **Dress** Dressy, informal **Disabled access** Fair **Customers** Local, tourist

Dinner Monday–Thursday, 6–9:30 p.m.; Friday and Saturday, seatings at 5:30, 6, 9, and 9:30 p.m.; Sunday, seatings at 4, 4:30, 7, 7:30, 8, and 8:30 p.m.; Tuesday, closed except during May and October.

Setting & atmosphere An elegantly appointed but unfussy frame building with an enclosed garden (with many romantic seatings on the patio) and rich, hand-painted walls, velvet upholstery, and the clean glint of real crystal and silver in all directions.

House specialties The menu changes continually, but look for dishes such as seafood and wild mushroom risotto; veal or lamb carpaccio; tenderloin of beef that reminds you why that's such a classic entree; home-smoked trout; sweetbreads with whole baby artichokes; baby lamb morsels with lamb sausage alongside. And although the dinner is purportedly four courses, here, as at several other top-flight restaurants, there are apt to be extras along the way.

Other recommendations Soft-shell crabs however offered (usually respectfully simple); a signature appetizer of black-eyed peas and Smithfield ham topped with foie gras; that same ham, sliced thin as prosciutto, wrapped around fresh local figs; portobello mushroom pretending to be a filet mignon.

Summary & comments A culinary legend—it's been profiled in The *New Yorker* and selected by *Travel and Leisure* as the second-finest hotel in the U.S. and eighth in the world—the Inn at Little Washington is the capital's most popular distant dining destination. Chef Patrick O'Connell is a name to make magic with in gourmet (and gourmand) circles all over the country. O'Connell's strength is a sense of balance: Dishes are never overwhelmed or overfussy; local produce is emphasized (which guarantees freshness); and a lot of fine ingredients are allowed to speak for themselves, which is sadly rare. Everyone remembers his or her first passion here—homemade white chocolate ice cream with bitter chocolate sauce—and for some Washingtonians, driving down to the other Washington becomes an addiction, a compulsion. It's the single biggest reason (besides horses, perhaps) for the boom in yuppie commuting to the hills. Incidentally, for fans of Cam, it was O'Connell who bought up the wine cellar when Le Pavilion went bankrupt, and one can almost not regret it.

I RICCHI ★★★

ITALIAN | EXPENSIVE | QUALITY ★★★★ | VALUE ★★★★ | ZONE 6

1220 19th Street, NW; (202) 835-0459

Reservations Suggested; call after 9 a.m. on weekdays, after 10 a.m. on weekends **When to go** Lunch or early dinner **Entree range** $23–32 **Payment** VISA, MC, AMEX **Service rating** ★★★★ **Friendliness rating** ★★★★ **Parking** Street, garage, valet (dinner) **Bar** Full service **Wine selection** Fine **Dress** Dressy, business **Disabled access** Good **Customers** Business, local, tourist

Lunch Monday–Friday, 11:30 a.m.–2:30 p.m.
Dinner Monday–Saturday, 5:30–9:30 p.m.; Sunday, closed.

Setting & atmosphere This stone and terra-cotta-tile room evokes a villa courtyard with *Better Homes & Gardens* detailing—gilded magnolia branches draped in muslin, floral tiles, and heavy cloth. The woodburning stove makes the whole restaurant smell like fresh bread.

House specialties Brick-pressed grilled half-chicken; rolled florentine of pork and rabbit; pasta with hare; a miraculously light fritto misto; a mixed grill of sausage, quail, and veal; scottiaglia, a mixed platter of braised meats.

Other recommendations The risotto of the day; grilled fresh fish; the warm salad of shrimp, cannellini, and green beans; the punning "ricchi e poveni," roasted goat chops; thick winter soups; Tuscan toast slathered with chicken livers.

Summary & comments The oak-fired grill is the other fiery attraction, and the fresh breads and grilled meats and seafoods taste, with pure Tuscan assurance, of smoke and rosemary. (Like many of the finer restaurants in town, i Ricchi changes its menu seasonally and has moved beyond strictly regional fare, but the grill is always featured.) Despite its prime law-and-lobby location, i Ricchi is arguably the most affordable fancy Italian restaurant in town, although the competition is quickening.

JALEO ★★★

NUEVO LATINO | MODERATE | QUALITY ★★★★ | VALUE ★★★★ | ZONE 3

480 7th Street, NW; (202) 628-7949;

Reservations 5–6:30 p.m only **When to go** Early evening **Entree range** $10–25 **Payment** VISA, MC, AMEX, DC, D **Service rating** ★★★ **Friendliness rating** ★★★ **Parking** Street; valet after 5 p.m except on Sunday, $8 **Bar** Full service **Wine selection** Good **Dress** Business, casual **Disabled access** Good **Customers** Local, tourist

Brunch Sunday, 11:30 a.m.–3 p.m.
Lunch/dinner Sunday and Monday, 11:30 a.m.–10 p.m.; Tuesday–Thursday, 11:30 a.m.–11:30 p.m.; Friday and Saturday, 11:30 a.m.–midnight.

Setting & atmosphere A combination tapas bar, chic competition, and piazza, with bits of wrought iron, a lush suedelike gray decor, and a partial copy of the John Singer Sargent painting from which it takes its name.

House specialties Tapas—bite-sized appetizers (four to a plate) meant to help wash down glasses of sangria and sherry and pass hours of conversation. Among the best regulars: tuna carpaccio; grilled quail; spinach with apples, pine nuts, and raisins; salmon with artichokes; eggplant flan with roasted peppers; serrano ham and tomatoes on focaccia; and miniature lamb chops. Chef Jose Ramon Andre's daily specials and particularly seasonal rarities, frequently of shrimp or shellfish, are extremely good bets.

Other recommendations Sausage with white beans; grilled portobello mushrooms (getting to be a local staple); lightly fried calamari; paella.

Summary & comments Jaleo has taken tapas, a late-blooming bar fad, and built an entire menu around them—there are five times as many tapas as whole entrees. If you're with three or four people, you can just about taste everything in sight. (In fact, the first time, you may want to go extra slow: The plates look so small, and the palo cortada goes down so smoothly, that you can overstuff yourself without realizing it.) The bar does a heavy business, too, especially pre- and post-theater. It's already so trendy that if you really want to celeb-spot, go off rush hour; they're ducking the crowds. Jaleo's Bethesday location (7271 Woodmont Avenue; (301)913-0003) is now open in Maryland.

JEAN-MICHEL ★★★

FRENCH | MODERATE | QUALITY ★★★ | VALUE ★★★½ | ZONE 10A

10223 Old Georgetown Road (Wildwood Shopping Center), Bethesda;
(301) 564-4910

Reservations Recommended **When to go** Any time **Entree range** $17–25 **Payment** VISA, MC, AMEX, DC **Service rating** ★★★★ **Friendliness rating** ★★★

Parking Free lot **Bar** Full service **Wine selection** Good **Dress** Informal **Disabled access** Fair **Customers** Locals, business people

Lunch Monday–Friday, 11:30 a.m.–2:30 p.m.
Dinner Monday–Friday, 5:30–10 p.m.; Saturday and Sunday, 5:30–9 p.m.

Setting & atmosphere Though rather small, and limited by its position in a strip shopping mall, this is nevertheless a pretty little room: light, decorated with restraint, and subtly divided by glass to lower the volume and make up for the lack of a foyer.

House specialties This is really a place to go by the daily specials, which often nearly equal the menu; one night there were eight appetizers and as many entrees, including roasted pepper and fennel soup, rockfish with shrimp and baby lobster, veal kidneys, and terrine of duck foie gras. Otherwise, look for the likes of ravioli with wild mushrooms or spinach and duck sauce; bouillabaisse; classic country-French versions of veal scaloppine, lamb, and venison.

Other recommendations Grilled rockfish or grilled tuna with black olive sauce, mussels, calf's liver, soft-shell crabs, and lobster flamed with whiskey.

Summary & comments Jean-Michel was the partner and host of what was once considered a good "continental French" restaurant downtown, but somehow this relaxed, comfy version with its simplified dishes seems to suit him—as well as modern attitudes—better. There is little that's unfamiliar here, but that's part of what makes it easy to enjoy.

JOHNNY'S HALF SHELL ★★½

SEAFOOD | INEXPENSIVE | QUALITY ★★★★ | VALUE ★★★★★ | ZONE 6

2002 P Street, NW; (202) 296-2021

Reservations Not accepted **When to go** Pre- or post-rush **Entree range** $7–22 **Payment** VISA, MC, AMEX **Service rating** ★★★ **Friendliness rating** ★★★★ **Parking** Street, pay lots **Bar** Full service **Wine selection** Good **Dress** Business, casual **Disabled access** Not accessible **Customers** Locals, business

Lunch 11:30 a.m.–3 p.m.; light fare served from 3–5 p.m.
Dinner 5–10:30 p.m.; open until 11 p.m. on Friday and Saturday.

Setting & atmosphere Intentionally low-key, it hearkens back to the New Orleans–style oyster bars and Gulf Coast fish houses: Naugahyde, a marble-topped pull-up bar, and a no-reservations policy.

House specialties The New Orleans seafood gumbo and the Chesapeake seafood stew, one dark and dirty and the other light and sunny; an equally lighthearted take on Manhattan-style clam chowder; soft-shell crabs with corn pudding; fried oyster po' boys; a sort of deconstructed ceviche of tequila-cured salmon with avocados, tomatoes, and hot chilies.

Other recommendations Barbecued shrimp on cheese grits, a spicier "dirtier" version than the more genteel, creamy low-country dishes elsewhere in town; roasted littleneck clams; decadent crab imperial.

Summary & comments Executive chef Ann Cashion and co-owner John Fulchino are old friends to Washington foodies. This intentionally low-key seafood shack, dropped down in the middle of Dupont Circle, is a mini-getaway to the sort of old New Orleans bar that is becoming a rarity in the actual, tourist-crazy Big Easy: fried oyster, frigid beer, and the sort of couturier "comfort food" that Cashion is famous for. This is a perfect example of when "only" three stars means modesty of menu and delightful execution.

KAZ SUSHI BISTRO ★★★★

JAPANESE | MODERATE | QUALITY ★★★★½ | VALUE ★★★★ | ZONE 4

1915 I Street, NW; (202) 530-5500

Reservations Recommended **When to go** Anytime **Entree range** $12–20 **Payment** VISA, MC, AMEX, DC **Service rating** ★★★ **Friendliness rating** ★★★ **Parking** Pay lots **Bar** Beer and wine **Wine selection** Fair, several sakes **Dress** Business, casual **Disabled access** No **Customers** Food trendies, business

Lunch Monday–Friday. 11:30 a.m.–2 p.m.
Dinner Monday–Saturday, 6–10 p.m.

Setting & atmosphere A smart and savvy-funny room, with a mini-fountain wall in front, a smallish sushi bar in the rear, and abstract but oddly maguro-ish wallpaper.

House specialties Sake-poached scallops; lobster salad; glazed grilled baby octopus; spicy broiled green mussels; tuna carpaccio with waski-avocado sauce; "Japanese style duck confit" in miso; salmon belly with fennel and yogurt sauce; the signature sea trout "napoleon" of chopped fish tossed with peanuts, cilantro, and soy-ginger dressing and layered on crispy wontons.

Other recommendations Non-traditional sushi such as tuna with foie gras or with kalamata pesto; foie gras infused with plum wine; lobster with wasabi mayo; asparagus and roasted red pepper roll; portobello and sun-dried tomato roll.

Summary & comments Chef-owner Kaz Okochi earned many of his fans while working at Sushi-Ko, where he originated many of what he calls his "original small dishes." He is also fearless about mixing East and West, but not in the usual fusion forms, i.e., the tuna and foie gras. The quality of the more traditional sushi is first-rate, of course. But you can get good sushi in a number of places, as listed in the front of this chapter. So take Kaz's inventions for a spin. Note the number of intriguing vegetarian options as well.

KINKEAD'S ★★★★

SEAFOOD | EXPENSIVE | QUALITY ★★★★½ | VALUE ★★★ | ZONE 4

2000 Pennsylvania Avenue, NW; (202) 296-7700

Reservations Recommended (required for the dining room upstairs) **When to go** Anytime, Sunday brunch **Entree range** $20–40 **Payment** VISA, MC, AMEX, DC, D **Service rating** ★★★ **Friendliness rating** ★★★ **Parking** Valet at dinner, pay lots, meters **Bar** Full service **Wine selection** Good **Dress** Business, informal **Disabled access** Good **Customers** Business, local

Brunch Sunday, 11:30 a.m.–2:30 p.m.
Lunch Monday–Saturday, 11:30 a.m.–2:30 p.m.

Dinner Sunday–Thursday, 5:30–9:30 p.m.; Friday and Saturday, 5:30–10 p.m.

Setting & atmosphere Pleasantly restrained, ranging over two floors and divided into a series of elevated or glass-enclosed areas. The kitchen staff is visible upstairs, as is commonplace these days; it's a little less common to see chef-owner Robert Kinkead on the consumer side of the glass wall, barking at his cooks via headset like a football coach talking to the booth.

House specialties A melting chargrilled squid over polenta with tomato confit (appetizer); delicate grilled skate with a veal reduction; rockfish with artichokes; seared tuna with portobellos and flageolets; lobster specials; roast saddle of rabbit with crispy sweetbreads and fava bean–chanterelle ragoût.

Other recommendations Grilled squid, shrimp, and crab pupusa with pickled cabbage; Ipswich-style fried soft-shell clams and crab and lobster cakes (appetizers); grilled pork chop with savory bread pudding; sautéed cod cheeks; Sicilian swordfish with fennel, olives, currants, and arugula.

Entertainment & amenities Live jazz weeknights; nonsmoking raw bar.

Summary & comments This is arguably the best all-around restaurant in the city. Kinkead's style is simple and straightforward but not shrinking; his sauces are balanced but assured, designed to highlight the food, not the frills. Any available seafood can be ordered broiled or grilled, but "simply grilled" here is almost an oxymoron. And Kinkead, whose first fame came from his Nantucket restaurant, has installed a little home-away-from-home downstairs by way of a raw bar—plus first-rate chowder, soups, and salads. For those who count Mobil stars, Kinkead's has four.

L'AUBERGE CHEZ FRANÇOIS ★★★

FRENCH | EXPENSIVE | QUALITY ★★★★ | VALUE ★★★★★ | ZONE 11A

332 Springvale Road, Great Falls; (703) 759-3800

Reservations Required 4 weeks in advance **When to go** Summer evenings in good weather for the terrace **Entree range** $40–50 **Payment** VISA, MC, AMEX, DC, D **Service rating** ★★★★ **Friendliness rating** ★★★★ **Parking** Free lot **Bar** Full service **Wine selection** Very good **Dress** Dressy, business (jacket required for men at night) **Disabled access** Very good **Customers** Locals

Dinner Tuesday–Saturday, 5:30–9:30 p.m.; Sunday, 1:30–8 p.m.

Setting & atmosphere One of the most beloved and romantic dining sites in the area, a real country inn with exposed beams, a mix of views of Alsace (home of pater familias/executive chef Jacques Haeringer), only-a-family-could-love drawings, and a travel-brochure veranda. It's so widely known as an engagement and anniversary mecca that *Regrets Only,* Sally Quinn's semi–roman à clef about journalistic and political circles, included a rather improbable but dramatic tryst in the parking lot (in an MG with a stick shift, no less).

House specialties Classics such as rack of lamb ($49.50 for one, $98 for two), Châteaubriand for two ($98), and duck foie gras either sautéed with apples or "plain"; the true choucroute royal garni, with Alsatian sauerkraut, sausages, smoked pork, duck, pheasant, and quail; game in season, such as medallions of venison and roast duck; veal kidneys in a rich, mustardy sauce; sweetbreads with wild mushrooms in puff pastry; roasted boneless duck breast paired with the stuffed leg and fruit-dotted rice; seafood fricassee with shrimp, scallops, lobster, rockfish, and salmon in Riesling.

Other recommendations Various seafood and game pâtés; red snapper braised in beer; boneless rabbit stuffed with leeks and fennel; soft-shell crabs with extra crabmeat stuffed into the body; big scallops in a bright (but not overwhelming) tomato–bell pepper sauce.

Summary & comments Although theoretically L'Auberge falls into the "expensive" range, it ought to be called "moderate" to give a fair comparison. What look like entrees on the menu are really whole dinners, and with salads, fancy appetizers, and dessert—not to mention bread and cheese and a bit of sorbet—this is a lot of food. Although the two-to-four weeks' notice rule still applies, competition has increased, along with cancellations: It may be worth it to call in the late afternoon, especially during the week. You can't make reservations for the outdoor terrace, incidentally; just call to make sure it's open (about May through September) and then show up.

LA BERGERIE ★★★

FRENCH | MODERATE | QUALITY ★★★½ | VALUE ★★★★ | ZONE 11C

218 North Lee Street, Alexandria; (703) 683-1007

Reservations Recommended **When to go** Anytime **Entree range** $20–29 **Payment** VISA, MC, AMEX, DC, D **Service rating** ★★★★ **Friendliness rating** ★★★ **Parking** Street **Bar** Full service **Wine selection** Good **Dress** Business, informal **Disabled access** Good (via Thompson Alley) **Customers** Local, business

Lunch Monday–Saturday, 11:30 a.m.–2:30 p.m.
Dinner Monday–Thursday, 6–10:30 p.m.; Friday and Saturday, 6–11 p.m.

Setting & atmosphere Mostly exposed brick but with one romantic "Umbrellas of Cherbourg" dining room with elegant blue and gold wallpaper, classic chandeliers and banquettes, and booth seating.

House specialties The nightly specials are always a good bet, but look for pan-crisped sweetbreads with luxuriant chanterelle sauce, braised veal cheeks, osso bucco, veal pot au feau, duck confit, and duck breast with foie gras.

Other recommendations Even the vegetables here have spunk, so to speak: braised endive, artichoke hearts, celerian puree, and so on.

Summary & comments This longtime Basque kitchen has found new life, and an even greater earthiness, under chef Caroline Bruder Ross, who believes in stripping ingredients to their darkest, dankest core. (You might call this a real woman's kitchen.) This taste for the dark side means that most of her dishes are rich in a way that has little to do with cream or butter, but is rooty, musty, and fungal flavors. The prestantations are balanced and self-assured rather than showy. One could wish the wine list were less heavy and fusty in a different way, and the servers less old-fashionedly condescending. La Bergerie is on the second floor, so wheelchair users should turn into the alley alongside and enter the lobby where they may take the elevator.

LA CHAUMIÈRE ★★½

FRENCH | MODERATE | QUALITY ★★★½ | VALUE ★★★★ | ZONE 5

2813 M Street, NW; (202) 338-1784

Reservations Recommended **When to go** Anytime **Entree range** $15–25 **Payment** VISA, MC, AMEX, CB, DC **Service rating** ★★★ **Friendliness rating** ★★★ **Parking** Two-hour parking at Four Seasons Hotel (dinner), street **Bar** Full service **Wine selection** Good **Dress** Business, informal **Disabled access** Good **Customers** Local, embassy, business

Lunch Monday–Friday, 11:30 a.m.–3 p.m.
Dinner Monday–Saturday, 5:30–10:30 p.m.; Sunday, closed.

Setting & atmosphere After 25 years in the often tumultuous Georgetown culinary competition, the cooking in this big-beamed, in-town country inn, with its free-standing fireplace in the center and old iron tools on the wall, has a revived freshness, thanks to the new kitchen broom of chef Patrick Orange. And what goes around comes around: Bistro fare of owner Gerard Pain's sort is suddenly booming around him.

House specialties Oysters; seasonal specials of rabbit, choucroute, or venison (as uptown as medallions with chestnut puree or as down-home as pot pie); seafood crêpes or jumbo shad roe; bouillabaisse; traditional tripe à la mode in Calvados. Here, as at the Bistro Français across the street (see listing), the daily specials are even more amazing: terrine of duck foie gras or fresh foie gras with cassis; ostrich loin wrapped in bacon; bison osso buco; seared sea bass with portobello-turnip risotto.

Other recommendations Calf's liver or brains; sweetbreads with turnips and Jerusalem artichokes; medallions of ostrich with blood orange sauce; quenelles of pike in lobster.

Summary & comments Part of La Chaumière's charm is its weekly treats: Wednesday it's couscous, and Thursday, cassoulet. This is family-style food, and most of its regulars are treated like family. Actually, "regulars" is a key word here; La Chaumière hearkens back to the time when Georgetown was more neighborhood than shopping mall, and a lot of its customers feel as if they graduated into adult dinner-dating here. The fireplace is one of the area's hottest (sorry) soulful-gazing areas.

LA COLLINE ★★★

FRENCH | EXPENSIVE | QUALITY ★★★★ | VALUE ★★★★★ | ZONE 2

400 North Capitol Street, NW; (202) 737-0400

Reservations Recommended **When to go** Anytime **Entree range** $15–24 **Payment** VISA, MC, AMEX, CB, DC **Service rating** ★★★★ **Friendliness rating** ★★★★ **Parking** Garage, validation after 5 p.m. **Bar** Full service **Wine selection** Good **Dress** Casual, elegant **Disabled access** Good **Customers** Business, local, tourist

Breakfast Monday–Friday, 7–10 a.m.
Lunch Monday–Friday, 11:30 a.m.–3 p.m.
Dinner Monday–Saturday, 6–10 p.m.; Sunday and holidays, closed.

Setting & atmosphere This stubborn bistro-within-an-office-building has undergone a long-needed facelift (and menu brush-up); the main dining room is large, two-tiered, with nostalgic paintings, a mix of booths and tables, and French country-kitchen cupboards. A new carryout annex suggests the more competitive and lively attitude of its new management/kitchen team.

House specialties The menu tends to feature "specials" rather than set pieces, but look for foie gras and homemade pâté; lobster and shellfish fricassee; sweetbreads with wild mushrooms and baby artichokes; tripe; cool lobster salad; stuffed quail; venison tournedos. On the newer side, watch for shrimp ravioli in lemongrass broth; Thai-flavored calamari salad; smoked trout.

Other recommendations Roasted monkfish; poached cod; appetizers of smoked duck breast, wild mushroom ravioli, or spicy lamb-stuffed pastries.

Summary & comments La Colline manages to serve old-homey French food in such quantity (and with such hospitable style) that you'd expect the quality to fall off, but somehow it never does. The quantity of business of this Senate-side favorite also keeps the prices fairly steady, though they've crept up a little. Presentation is simple and untrendy, but exact: salmon or swordfish steaks on beds of vermouth-flavored sauce, sweetbreads bull's-eyed over concentric circles of bordelaise and herb wine deglaze. Game dishes and rowdy, hearty stews, along with the organ meats most Americans are still only discovering, are always good bets.

LA CÔTE D'OR CAFE ★★½

FRENCH (PROVENÇAL) | EXPENSIVE | QUALITY ★★★½ | VALUE ★★★ | ZONE 11B

6876 Lee Highway, Arlington; (703) 538-3033

Reservations Recommended **When to go** Anytime **Entree range** $20–30 **Payment** VISA, MC, AMEX, DC **Service rating** ★★★ **Friendliness rating** ★★½ **Parking** Street, lot **Bar** Full service **Wine selection** Good **Dress** Business, informal **Disabled access** Good **Customers** Local, business

Lunch Monday–Saturday, 11:30 a.m.–3 p.m.; Sunday, 11 a.m.–3 p.m.
Dinner Monday–Thursday, 5:30–10 p.m.; Friday and Saturday, 5:30–11 p.m.; Sunday, 5:30–9 p.m.

Setting & atmosphere Although seeming rather out of place at first glance—a stone's throw from I-66 and associated with a motel—this is a very pretty, three-room French townhouse with armchairs, attractive but not overly formal silver and porcelain, and lots of flowers and windows. The brightly decorated addition, called Le Salon Basque, has added a needed sense of cheer to what was sometimes a rather stuffy atmosphere.

House specialties Wild mushrooms with delicate duck "ham" (appetizer); grilled tuna with basil and tomato; rabbit stew with mustard sauce over pasta; entrecôte with bleu cheese sauce; loin of lamb; monkfish with mustard sauce. If you like cassoulet, the occasional special here is very good.

Other recommendations Bouillabaisse with lobster and powerful aïoli; steamed mussels; scallop and shrimp soup; calamari with salmon mousse.

Summary & comments This menu is part traditional country French, part southern French, and occasionally old-fashioned "continental," but all hearty and aromatic comfort food. Sometimes the seasoning can seem overpowering (especially if you've been gradually accustomed to "new" Americanized versions of continental food), but many people will find that one of its virtues. The message is sometimes mixed, however: Suburbanizing seems to have increased the staff's desire to seem uptown, so they can be patronizing in the way that used to give continental dining a bad name. A little more consistency from the kitchen, too, would bring in another star.

LA MICHE ★★½

FRENCH | EXPENSIVE | QUALITY ★★★ | VALUE ★★½ | ZONE 10A

7905 Norfolk Avenue, Bethesda; (301) 986-0707

Reservations Recommended **When to go** Anytime **Entree range** $18–27 **Payment** VISA, MC, AMEX, DC **Service rating** ★★★ **Friendliness rating** ★★★½ **Parking** Valet, street meters **Bar** Full service **Wine selection** Good **Dress** Business, informal **Disabled access** Not accessible **Customers** Local, business

Lunch Tuesday–Friday, 11:30 a.m.–2 p.m.
Dinner Monday–Saturday, 6–9:45 p.m.; Sunday, 5:30–8:30 p.m.

Setting & atmosphere The tone is somewhere between an old French inn and an upscale bistro, with white lace curtains, gleaming wood, flowers, and soft, well-laundered linens.

House specialties Sweetbreads; braised tripe in tomato-wine sauce; nicely viscous frog's legs; duck confit or grilled duck or almost any duck presentation.

Other recommendations Lobster over fresh pasta; Kobe beef onglet.

Summary & comments La Miche was a magnet in Bethesda long before the restaurant boom of the 1990s, and new chef-owner Jason Tepper knows better than to shake off all the old standbys; he's just shaking them out. The dishes are classically "provincial" in the best, as-you-like-it fashion: Look for the likes of duck liver and foie gras, cassoulet, snails, medallions of venison, etc., depending on the season.

LE MANNEQUIN PIS ★★★½

BELGIAN | MODERATE | QUALITY ★★★½ | VALUE ★★★★ | ZONE 10C

18064 Georgia Avenue, Olney; (301) 570-4800

Reservations Recommended **When to go** Early dinner or after 9 p.m. on weekends **Entree range** $15–$20 **Payment** VISA, MC, AMEX, D **Service rating** ★★½ **Friendliness rating** ★★★ **Parking** Free lot **Bar** Full service **Wine selection** Fair **Dress** Suburban casual, business **Disabled access** Good **Customers** Food trend saveurs, local

Dinner Tuesday–Thursday, 5–9:30 p.m.; Friday and Saturday, 5–10:30 p.m.; Sunday, 5–8:30 p.m.

Setting & atmosphere Named for the famously rude statue in Brussels (the one of the little boy relieving himself into the fountain), this is a combination 1950s rec room, bistro, and coquette's salon, with tacked-up plywood, sponged egg-yolk walls, heavy red drapes, and stunning abstract paintings by chef Bernard Dehaene's mother. And one other thing: Whenever the light in the men's room is turned on, the statue "tinkles."

House specialties Mussels, done a half-dozen ways (try the beer, leeks, and goat cheese broth); classic Belgian fries (called "pommes pailles," potato straws); endive salads; wood-roasted sea bass with capers, balsamic vinegar, and braised Belgian endive; oysters au gratin in champagne; veal chop with escargot; roast pork with salty-sour pickled figs and spinach; salmon medallions with red cabbage and leeks. Daily specials are especially intriguing; split yabbies (Australia crawfish) spread with cognac-anchovy butter; foie gras; Flemishized osso buco with caramelized onions and beer.

Other recommendations Side dishes of braised endive and mini-saucepans of Brussels sprouts; rich Belgian beers; fish of the day; rump steak with a choice of sauces.

Summary & comments Like its decor, and its unapologetically economical location in an unprepossessing strip mall, Le Mannequin Pis can be delightfully iconoclastic or bafflingly headstrong, especially when the very short staff gets overwhelmed by a full dining room. Occasional lapses in kitchen temper are not unknown, but it's of a piece with the restaurant's personality. Less entertaining are the infrequent lapses in kitchen performance, but with time, they're becoming rare. Now if Montgomery County would just keep up its end on the beer list . . .

MAESTRO ★★★★

MODERN ITALIAN | VERY EXPENSIVE | QUALITY ★★★★½ | VALUE ★★★ | ZONE 11A

700 Tysons Blvd. (in the Ritz-Carlton Hotel), Tysons Corner; (703) 917-5498

Reservations Highly recommended **When to go** Anytime **Entree range** Fixed price $54–76 **Payment** VISA, MC, AMEX, DC, D **Service rating** ★★★★½ **Friendliness rating** ★★★★ **Parking** Valet **Bar** Full service **Wine selection** Very good **Dress** Business, dressy **Disabled access** Very good **Customers** Local expense accounters, special occasions, hotel patrons

Breakfast Monday–Friday, 7–10:30 a.m.
Dinner Tuesday–Saturday, 6:30–9:30 p.m.

Setting & atmosphere This is a classic luxury hotel dining room—white linen, brocade upholstery, heavy silver, huge flowers, and charming silver animal centerpieces—but with an almost equally huge open kitchen, where prodigal chef Fabio Trabocchi and a bustling supporting cast prepare (and polish) the ornate presentations and send them out with old-fashioned European flourish.

House specialties Seared foie gras with blood orange sorbet; lobster ravioli with half-lobster tails; sweatbreads Milanese; osso bucco–stuffed agnolotti; wild turbot baked over fragrant saltwater hay; Dungeness crab and chanterelle ravioli; scallops in the shell with Jerusalem artichoke julienne; grilled baby lobster with black truffles.

Other recommendations A dry-aged veal chop in Amarone; roast squab with figs; any sea urchin presentation.

Summary & comments There are actually several menus (which are perhaps a little much of a muchness, but impressive): more traditional Italian, very mod-Italian, and three tasting menus of various sizes. While the cooking is sometimes a little erratic—paradoxically, when the room is less busy, which perhaps suggests the chef is less inspired—it's never less than elaborate, and when it's good, which admittedly is most of the time, it's truly stunning. And, Maestro has another master at hand: sommelier Vincent Feraud, the dean of Washington wine stewards.

MAKOTO ★★★

JAPANESE | MODERATE | QUALITY ★★★★ | VALUE ★★★★ | ZONE 6

4822 MacArthur Boulevard, NW; (202) 298-6866

Reservations Recommended **When to go** Anytime **Entree range** $10–30; tasting menu about $35 **Payment** VISA, MC **Service rating** ★★★★½ **Friendliness rating** ★★★ **Parking** Street **Bar** Full service **Wine selection** House **Dress** Business, casual **Disabled access** No **Customers** Ethnic Japanese, local, business

Lunch Tuesday–Saturday, noon–2:30 p.m.
Dinner Tuesday–Sunday, 6–10:30 p.m.

Setting & atmosphere A secret Japanese garden of a spot, hidden behind two wood doors (with a stone garden between where you exchange your shoes for bedroom slippers) and only two lines of diners long. The kitchen is, in effect, the decor: Slightly sunken behind what is now the sushi counter, the chefs busily stir, fry, and slice over the restaurant equivalent of a Pullman stove.

House specialties A fixed-price omakase (chef's choice) dinner based on the market and featuring courses of two to six bites each, but extraordinarily generous: up to seven courses of sashimi; sushi (perhaps four differnt pieces, like a tray of fine miniature desserts); grilled marinated fillet of fish (a choice); such delicate morsels as ankimo (monkfish liver) or rare duck breast with asparagus tips and sesame seeds; salmon with Chinese broccoli; large bowls of wheat-noodle soup; and sherbet.

Other recommendations Limited à la carte sushi, such as uni (sea urchin), toro, or fresh sardines; yakitori, skewer-grilled marinated chicken.

Summary & comments This is a tiny establishment—perhaps 30 seats, even counting the new sushi bar—which explains how the chefs are able to produce such exquisite and imaginative meals. For the greatest pleasure, order the tasting menu and experience kaiseki cuisine, the formal, Zen-derived technique that salutes both nature and art by using only fresh, seasonal ingredients and a variety of colors, textures, and cooking techniques. Be sure to show your appreciation by admiring each carefully presented dish as it arrives. Note that none of the seats have backs—they're just boxes with removable tops for storing purses, jackets, and cushion lids—and there is no separate nonsmoking area.

MARCEL'S ★★★½

FRENCH | EXPENSIVE | QUALITY ★★★★ | VALUE ★★★ | ZONE 6

2401 Pennsylvania Avenue, NW; (202) 296-1166

Reservations Recommended **When to go** Dinner **Entree range** $22–29 **Payment** VISA, MC, AMEX, DC **Service rating** ★★★ **Friendliness rating** ★★★ **Parking**

Valet, street meters, lots **Bar** Full service **Wine selection** Very good **Dress** Business, dressy casual **Disabled access** Very good **Customers** Business, foodies

Dinner Monday–Thursday, 5:30–10 p.m.; Friday and Saturday, 5:30–11 p.m.; Sunday, 5–10 p.m.

Setting & atmosphere Much of the sunniness—warm yellow paint, weathered wood, wrought iron, stone facades, flowers and pottery—of the former Provençal decor remains, though a little more restrained. The long marble bar is a showpiece, and the partially exposed (and elevated) kitchen is not so intrusive as elsewhere.

House specialties Game dishes in season, such as breast of squab on truffled risotto; pheasant and foie gras in white bean ragoût with winter vegetables or roulade of rabbit stuffed with sausage over caramelized cabbage. Also crispy duck breast with celeriac and duck confit; pan-fried skate; fennel- and coriander-seed-crusted salmon.

Other recommendations Seared scallops with lardons of applewood bacon; wild mushroom timbale; duck consommé with sweetbreads; a czarist-nostalgia luxury of potato blini with seared fennel, and coriander salmon, lobster sauce, and caviar.

Entertainment & amenities Outdoor tables in good weather; live piano music nightly except Sunday.

Summary & comments Chef-owner Robert Weidmaier, formerly of Cafe on M and Aquarelle, gives his menu a Belgian touch that provides a rootier, earthier flavor: confits, root vegetables (including the various endives, of course), artichokes, and flavorful but not heavy sausages. The service is very attentive, though at times a trifle "educational." Marcel, incidentally, is the owner's baby son.

MARK'S DUCK HOUSE ★★★½

CHINESE | INEXPENSIVE | QUALITY ★★★★ | VALUE ★★★★ | ZONE 11B

6184-A Arlington Boulevard, Falls Church; (703) 532-2125

Reservations Helpful **When to go** Late lunch, late dinner **Entree range** $6.50–15; whole duck $24 **Payment** VISA, MC **Service rating** ★★★ **Friendliness rating** ★★★ **Parking** Valet **Bar** Newly licensed **Wine selection** Basic **Dress** Casual **Disabled access** Yes **Customers** Mostly Asian, but food-savvy types from all over

Open Sunday–Thursday, 10 a.m.–midnight; Friday, 10 a.m.–1 a.m.; Saturday 10 a.m.–2 a.m.

Setting & atmosphere Pig's heads, swags of roasted ducks, tanks of live (for the moment, anyway) seafood—maybe this should be called Mark's Menagerie Diner: After all, there are some 400 items on the dinner menu, not to mention the 70 kinds of dim sum available every day from 10 a.m. to 3 p.m. On the other hand, it does sell as many as 100 ducks on a busy night—mostly Peking duck to non-Chinese customers and Cantonese roast duck, which is similar but with more of a fat layer—a Chinese delicacy—to the ethnic crowd.

House specialties Aside from the ducks: roast pork; stir-fried greens; black cod; spicy quail; noodle soups with seafood, duck, or pork; eggplant with bean curd and shrimp paste; chive dumplings; barbecued pork buns.

Other recommendations For those who enjoy offal and organs, there's plenty here, and often on the specials board: knuckles, tripe, tongues (duck and pork), kidneys, etc. Also look for whole frogs, not just the legs; small birds such as squab and quail; sea cucumber; steamed sea bass.

Summary & comments When this place is jumping, which is most of the time, the cacophony from large family groups can be deafening, and the service a little less patient than its usual high style; but theses are noises of great satisfaction. Don't go to Mark's for pedestrian dishes you can get elsewhere; experiment and enjoy. Eel is great stuff.

MATISSE ★★★

MODERN AMERICAN | EXPENSIVE | QUALITY ★★★★ | VALUE ★★★½ | ZONE 7

4934 Wisconsin Avenue, NW; (202) 244-5222

Reservations Recommended **When to go** Anytime **Entree range** $18–26 **Payment** VISA, MC, AMEX, DC, D **Service rating** ★★★½ **Friendliness rating** ★★★½ **Parking** Valet, street **Bar** Full service **Wine selection** Fair **Dress** Business, casual **Disabled access** Very good **Customers** Upscale neighbors, suburban romantics

Lunch Tuesday–Thursday, 11:30 a.m.–2:30 p.m.; Sunday, 11 a.m.–3 p.m.
Dinner Monday–Thursday, 5:30–10 p.m.; Saturday, 5–11 p.m.; Sunday, 5–9:30 p.m.

Setting & atmosphere The room is understated but stylish: whitewashed and raw brick walls, softened by buttercream lighting and elegant wrought iron chandeliers, a bar footrail, and stair banisters. Sidewalk seating is offered in good weather.

House specialties Seared scllops, peas, and fava beans in caramalized nage; grilled quail with tomato-wine sauce over truffle potato cake; crab-stuffed soft-shells with corn/fava salsa; butter-poached lobster "confit."

Other recommendations The "pizza du jour" is a light, crackery, Euro-style nibble that is a fine appetizer and a guaranteed child-pleaser.

Summary & comments Chef Jacques Ford, a local boy with five-star training (Le Bernadin, Inn at Little Washington), is working his way into a light, clean, and considered style, classic in the main but with an attention to detail that gives his presentations a casual elegance and individuality. The staff is extremely child-friendly. On the other hand, for cooking this nice, the wine list could be pumped up somewhat.

MATUBA ★★★

JAPANESE | INEXPENSIVE | QUALITY ★★★★ | VALUE ★★★★ | ZONES 11B, 10A

2915 Columbia Pike, Arlington; (703) 521-2811
4918 Cordell Avenue, Bethesda; (301) 652-7449

Reservations Accepted **When to go** Monday, when many menu items are $1 **Entree range** $9–16 **Payment** VISA, MC, AMEX **Service rating** ★★★ **Friendliness rating** ★★★★ **Parking** Street **Bar** Beer and wine only **Wine selection** House **Dress** Casual, informal **Disabled access** Fair **Customers** Local, ethnic

Lunch Monday–Friday, 11:30 a.m.–2 p.m.
Dinner Monday–Thursday, 5:30–10 p.m.; Friday and Saturday, 5:30–10:30 p.m.; Sunday, 5:30–10 p.m.

Setting & atmosphere Small and traditional but uncomplicated, with a lot of blond wood and a few woodblock reproductions. A new "rotary sushi bar" works something like old dim sum carts; you grab a plate and you're charged by the color of the empties you accumulate. Some sushi is only $1 or $1.50, half rolls are $3. For Friday or Saturday lunch, pick five pieces, plus soup and salad bar, for $7.95.

House specialties Oyaku donburi (the homey chicken-and-egg: literally, "parent and child") variation on chicken and rice stew not often seen after lunch; "wedding sushi" (a marriage of scallops and shrimp); soft-shell crab tempura in season.

Other recommendations Unagi donburi; grilled teriyaki squid; sea urchin; grilled fresh fish.

Summary & comments Matuba (pronounced "MAT-su-ba") in Arlington was one of the first Japanese restaurants in the area that Japanese patrons recommended, although being honest and dependable is not always enough to keep up in such a competitive market. It's the sort of place that rewards regular attention: For unfamiliar customers, sushi portions can be small in comparison to many other bars, though the quality is high; but known faces are treated generously. Many of the custom rolls are delicious; the Alaska roll mixes smoked salmon and scallops.

MELROSE ★★★

MODERN AMERICAN | MODERATE | QUALITY ★★★★ | VALUE ★★★ | ZONE 5

Park Hyatt, 24th and M Streets, NW; (202) 955-3899

Reservations Recommended **When to go** Anytime **Entree range** $20–34 **Payment** VISA, MC, AMEX, CB, DC, D **Service rating** ★★★ **Friendliness rating** ★★½ **Parking** Valet, street **Bar** Full service **Wine selection** Good **Dress** Business, informal **Disabled access** Good **Customers** Local, business

Open Monday–Friday, 6:30 a.m.–10:30 p.m.; Saturday and Sunday, 7 a.m.–10:30 p.m.

Setting & atmosphere At first glance, it's almost plain, but after so many overdecorated restaurants, it becomes soothing: a simple room, light and bright, with pastels, florals, marble, and magnificent flowers. Glass walls along two sides allow diners to look out toward fountains, cafe-style umbrella tables, flowering shrubs, and the herb garden.

House specialties Roasted twin medallions of pepper-crusted tuna and foie gras; signature dishes such as poached salmon with bok choy, and vanilla-and-cardamom-flavored vinaigrette and steamed lobster and angelhair pasta with mascarpone sauce. Among the appetizers: house-cured gravlax stuffed with crab and crème fraîche; shrimp ravioli with sweet corn and cracked black pepper; poached Thai-style calamari.

Other recommendations Grilled seafood (a variety each day); imaginative vegetarian options such as parsnip ravioli with truffled sunchokes and baby snow pea shoots.

Entertainment & amenities A quartet for dancing on Saturday nights; no corkage fee on Sunday nights.

Summary & comments Chef Brian McBride has a light-bright attitude toward cooking that is a perfect match for the atmosphere here; he's especially good with seafood, which dominates the menu. His sauces are complements, not covers, and although the attitude is generally classic, his combinations often provide a gentle surprise. (Occasionally he wants to cover too many bases at once, but that's an explorer's risk.) The chef's choice is usually five courses for about $60.

MESKEREM ★★★

ETHIOPIAN | INEXPENSIVE | QUALITY ★★★★ | VALUE ★★★★★ | ZONE 6

2434 18th Street, NW; (202) 462-4100

Reservations Suggested **When to go** Anytime **Entree range** $9–13 **Payment** VISA, MC, AMEX, DC **Service rating** ★★★ **Friendliness rating** ★★★ **Parking** Street **Bar** Full service **Wine selection** Minimal **Dress** Casual **Disabled access** Good **Customers** Locals, tourists

Open Sunday–Thursday, noon–midnight; Friday and Saturday, noon–1 a.m.

Setting & atmosphere Simple but cheerful, with "skylight" rays painted blue and white and Ethiopian-style seating (for the limber) on leather cushions at balcony basket-weave tables.

House specialties Kitfo (tartare with chili sauce, but it can be ordered lightly cooked, or you can have a similar hot chopped beef stew called kay watt); lamb tibbs (breast and leg meat sautéed with onions and green chilis); shrimp watt; beef or lentil and green chili sambussa (fried pastries); tikil gomen (cabbage, potatoes, and carrots in a gentle sauce).

Other recommendations Chicken or shrimp alicha for the spice-intimidated; zilbo (lamb and collard greens); a honey-wine version of kitfo called gored-gored.

Summary & comments There are three things novices need to know about Ethiopian food: First, it's eaten with the hands, using a spongy pancake called injera as plate, spoon, and napkin all in one; second, "alicha" is the name of the milder stew or curry preparation; and third, "watt" is the spicier one. Washington's many Ethiopian restaurants (there may be a dozen in Adams-Morgan alone) offer similar menus, in some cases without much distinction between stews, but Meskerem is one of the best. If you want a sampler—a tray-sized injera palette—order the "mesob" for $7.25. "Meskerem," incidentally, is the first month of the 13-month Ethiopian calendar, the one that corresponds to September, which in Ethiopia is the end of the rainy season and thus is akin to springtime.

MONTMARTRE ★★½

FRENCH | MODERATE | QUALITY ★★★½ | VALUE ★★★½ | ZONE 7

327 Seventh Street, NW; (202) 544-1244

Reservations Recommended **When to go** Early or late dinner **Entree range** $15–20 **Payment** VISA, MC, AMEX, DC **Service rating** ★★★★ **Friendliness rating** ★★★★ **Parking** Street **Bar** Full service **Wine selection** Short but good **Dress** Casual, business **Disabled access** Fair **Customers** Local

Lunch Tuesday–Friday, 11:30 a.m.–2:30 p.m.

Dinner Tuesday–Thursday, 5:30–10 p.m.; Friday and Saturday, 5:30-10:30 p.m.; Sunday, 5:30–9 p.m.

Setting & atmosphere This is the sort of place that makes "cozy" seem like part of the word "cafe," a single sunny-sponged room of about 50 seats with a tiny bar at the back, lively views of the sidewalk to the front and the kitchen to the rear, and elbow-to-elbow tables.

House specialties The signature dish here is slow-braised rabbit leg with olives and wide egg noodles in cream sauce, and it's hard to beat. Otherwise, look for hangar steak (onglet); fine pink calf's liver with baby bok choy and balsamic sauce; a very Parisian salad of frisee with fried gizzards and bacon lardons; cream of cauliflower soup with mussels; shrimp and lemon risotto; mussels with Ricard; sauteed monkfish over potato cake with anchovy butter.

Other recommendations Daily specials such as venison rib chops with braised endive and a guinea hen confit with Jerusalem artichokes.

Summary & comments This is one of the beneficiaries of the shake-up at Bistrot Lepic (the other is Petits Plats in Woodley Park), as the owners are alums of that hospitable cafe and of the longtime Provençal hangout, Lavandou in Cleveland Park. Its success as a neighborhood favorite is attested to by the fact that there are frequently crowds winding out the door.

MURASAKI ★★★½

JAPANESE | MODERATE | QUALITY ★★★★½ | VALUE ★★★★ | ZONE 7

4620 Wisconsin Avenue, NW; (202) 966-0023

Reservations Helpful **When to go** Anytime **Entree range** $9–27 **Payment** VISA, MC, AMEX, DC, D **Service rating** ★★★★ **Friendliness rating** ★★★★ **Parking** Street **Bar** Beer and Wine **Wine selection** Limited **Dress** Business, casual **Disabled access** Good **Customers** Ethnic Japanese, business

Lunch Monday–Friday, 11:30 a.m.–2:30 p.m; Saturday and Sunday, noon–2:30 p.m.
Dinner Monday–Thursday, 5:30–10: p.m.; Friday and Saturday, 5:30–10:30 p.m; Sunday, 5:30–9 p.m.

Setting & atmosphere Murasaki means "purple," but there isn't much of that hue in this elegantly spare room, which tends instead to a clean, partially Deco and only slightly "Asian" look using wood framing, cream walls, and a pleasant side patio. The grill and sushi bars, which run a long L around the rear of the room, are the focal points.

House specialties The real specialties (occult parts of sea creatures, delicate baked dishes, etc.) are not printed on the menu, since novice diners too often order dishes they then dislike, so Japanese connoisseurs should consult with the chef about favorite items. On the other hand, even lobster sashimi and lobster miso soup can tickle the trend-addicted. Also look for eggplant dengaku, soft-shell crabs tempura, miso-marinated sea bass; white tuna and uni sushi—in fact, any sushi here.

Other recommendations An assortment of seafood tempura that puts all Maine fisherman's platters to shame; and for unregenerate carnivores, pork teriyaki and (seared) beef sushi.

Summary & comments The chefs here are among the most respected by their peers, and the restaurant's proximity to the Japanese Embassy is probably no accident; large tables of Japanese diners and even wedding parties often crowd the dining room. Should Murasaki be booked, there is a very likeable, though more predictabe, Japanese restaurant just down the street called Yosaku that should please (4712 Wisconsin Avenue, NW; (202) 363-4453).

NEW HEIGHTS ★★½

MODERN AMERICAN | MODERATE | QUALITY ★★★½ | VALUE ★★★★ | ZONE 7

2317 Calvert Street, NW; (202) 234-4110

Reservations Recommended **When to go** Anytime **Entree range** $17–30 **Payment** VISA, MC, AMEX, DC, D **Service rating** ★★½ **Friendliness rating** ★★★ **Parking** Valet **Bar** Full service **Wine selection** Very good **Dress** Informal, business **Disabled access** Fair **Customers** Local

Brunch Sunday, 11 a.m.–2:30 p.m.
Dinner Sunday–Thursday, 5:30–10 p.m.; Friday and Saturday, 5:30–11 p.m.

Setting & atmosphere A small Woodley Park townhouse simply decorated and opened up to take advantage of the light and the glorious view down Connecticut Avenue to Dupont Circle.

House specialties The menu changes seasonally, but typical dishes include five-spice powder-rubbed and smoked duck; rice-crusted diver scallops with pea shoots or wild mushroom risotto; halibut with cabbage, duck confit and macadamia spring rolls; rockfish with watermelon relish; and slow-roasted flounder with escargot, prosciutto, and lentil ragoût.

Other recommendations "Light" red meats such as clove-crusted venison and grilled buffalo strip; vegetarian dishes such as a faux cannelloni—really phyllo dough stuffed with eggplant and artichokes.

Summary & comments This is a back-to-modern basics kitchen with an Asian slant and an even bigger Mediterranean wanderlust. Even nicer, several of the entrees can be ordered in appetizer portions (and wine in half bottles). Some people find its eclecticism off-putting, but currently it's strongly on track. The owner here, Umbi Singh, has a great eye for chefs (a half-dozen of whom have graduated to restaurants of their own) and a history of giving them room to stretch. The newest, R. J. Cooper, has worked in Atlanta, New York, and Alaska, and most recently ran the kitchen at the Oval Room.

NORA ★★½

MODERN AMERICAN | MODERATE | QUALITY ★★★½ | VALUE ★★★ | ZONE 6

2132 Florida Avenue, NW; (202) 462-5143

Reservations Recommended **When to go** Anytime **Entree range** $25–35 **Payment** VISA, MC, AMEX, personal checks **Service rating** ★★★½ **Friendliness rating** ★★★★ **Parking** Street, valet **Bar** Full service **Wine selection** Good **Dress** Business, casual **Disabled access** No **Customers** Locals

Dinner Monday–Thursday, 6–10 p.m.; Friday and Saturday, 5:30–10:30 p.m.; Sunday, closed.

Setting & atmosphere A pretty corner townhouse with exposed brick walls and a gallery of handicrafts, quilt pieces, and faux naif art in the dining rooms; an enclosed greenhouse balcony in the rear is the prettiest area.

House specialties The menu changes frequently, but look for shellfish, such as a lobster-shellfish pan roast; organ meats from additive-free animals; seared squab or tuna appetizers; home-cured gravlax or trout; veal or lamb; honey-and-spice-glazed pheasant; roasted salmon; vegetarian platters.

Summary & comments Nora, the neighborhood hangout of the Dupont Circle A and B lists, was haute organic before organic was chic. The back of the menu, which changes daily, lists the specific farms where the meat, produce, dairy products, and eggs—naturally low in cholesterol, according to the supplier—are raised. Nora's own all-edible flower and herb garden alongside the restaurant is indicative. The cost of acquiring such specialized ingredients is passed on, but not unreasonably. Nora was also ahead of the crowd by introducing alternative grains and pastas, and it was the first restaurant to make lentils that didn't taste like a Zen penance. Its only drawback is an odd tendency to weightiness—the meals sometimes feel heartier than they taste. Now that the Clintons and Gores have been publicized dining here, it has become more of a place to see faces—and a place to be seen.

OBELISK ★★★½

ITALIAN | EXPENSIVE | QUALITY ★★★★½ | VALUE ★★★★ | ZONE 6

2029 P Street, NW; (202) 872-1180

Reservations Recommended **When to go** Anytime **Entree range** Prix fixe five-course $58 **Payment** VISA, MC, DC **Service rating** ★★★★ **Friendliness rating** ★★★½ **Parking** Street **Bar** Full service **Wine selection** Good **Dress** Business, informal **Disabled access** No **Customers** Local, business

Dinner Tuesday–Saturday, 6–10 p.m.; Sunday and Monday, closed.

Setting & atmosphere A tiny room that's elegant and good-humored; the customers, staff, and accoutrements—not only the room's floral centerpiece and silver chest but the astonishingly light breadsticks and bottles of grappa—work intimately elbow to elbow.

House specialties Chef Peter Pastan has figured out the cure for overlong, overrich menus—he offers a fixed-price menu, four to five courses with only three or maybe four choices per course. Among typical antipasti: marinated anchovies and fennel; artichokes with goat cheese; caramel-soft onion and cheese tart; crostini; a thick soup; quail terrine; crispy fried cheese; polenta with gorgonzola; potato or rice balls. The *primi* course is apt to be seafood or pasta (red pepper noodles with crab and pungent chive blossoms; gnocchi with pesto; wheat noodles with rabbit ragoût) or soup; the *secondi,* veal (particularly tenderloin prepared with artichokes or chanterelles); fish (pompano with olives; black sea bass with grilled radicchio, grilled shrimp with herb puree); or perhaps game birds or a mixed grill. After that comes a fine bit of cheese, with or without a dessert course following. Whatever the price—it varies with the daily menu—it's a quality bargain in this town.

Summary & comments Pastan's hand is so deft he doesn't need to overdress anything; sauces are more like glazes, and pungent ingredients—olives, pine nuts, garlic, and greens—are perfectly proportioned to their dish. Above all, it shows the value of letting a chef who knows exactly what he likes do as he likes. Pastan, who also owns Pizzeria Paradiso next door, knows the value of a really good bread dough, more than one in fact.

OCEANAIRE SEAFOOD ROOM ★★★

SEAFOOD | EXPENSIVE | QUALITY ★★★★ | VALUE ★★★★ | ZONE 3

1201 F Street, NW; (202) 347-BASS

Reservations Recommended **When to go** Anytime **Entree range** $22–60 **Payment** VISA, MC, AMEX, D **Service rating** ★★★ **Friendliness rating** ★★★ **Parking** Valet, pay lots **Bar** Full service **Wine selection** Very good **Dress** Business, dressy casual **Disabled access** Good **Customers** Local business, boutique finance types, lobbyists

Open Monday–Thursday, 10 a.m.–10 p.m.; Friday, 10 a.m.–11 p.m.; Saturday, 5–11 p.m.; Sunday, 5–9 p.m.

Setting & atmosphere Inspired by the great ocean liners of the 1930s, the room is full of curved surfaces, gleaming cherry- and etched-wood dividers, brass-studded leather booths and heavy silver. The music is Big Band, the condiment tray includes oyster crackers, and the raw bar, with its leather-topped stools and great piles of oysters, is a trip in itself. So are the retro cocktails: side cars, Singapore slings, cosmopolitans, etc.

House specialties Oysters (up to a dozen varieties a day); even more kinds of fresh fish flown in daily from all directions (Arctic char, Alaskan sable, Hawaiian spearfish, Florida wahoo, North Atlantic cod), all available simply grilled; crab- and shrimp-stuffed gray sole; lobsters by the pound; a huge chilled seafood platter or, for fried seafood fans, the old-fashioned fisherman's platter. If "sushi-grade black grouper" is available, head straight for it.

Other recommendations Crabcakes; a "cocktail" of rock lobster–sized shrimp; the lobster cobb salad; Ipswich clam or oyster pan roast.

Entertainment & amenities The relish tray of pickled herring, carrot sticks, olives, radishes, giant capers, etc. This even comes with oysters, making a dozen at the bar the steal meal of the new century. In fact, if we were only rating on the oyster bar, Oceanaire would be five stars.

Summary & comments This is the seafood chain of the twenty-first century, the logical outcome (given the ever-increasing size of the portions, steakhouses and expense accounts) of the hefty surf vs. turf wars. Everything is huge, easily shared, and that goes double for desserts. (The retro look and retro extravagance partly explain some of the retro entrees, such as baked Alaska and oysters Rockefeller.) The asparagus is fat, the frills a little excessive, and you definitely pay for the quality—even some chophouse veterans might blink at the $22-per-pound tag on the lobsters—and some of the staff can be showily "informative," but for a seafood fan, it really is a luxury liner. And for those tired of only a swordfish option at the steak palace, it's funny to see the "not seafood" list hidden at the bottom: one chicken option, a filet mignon, or a cheeseburger.

OLD ANGLER'S INN ★★★

MODERN AMERICAN | EXPENSIVE | QUALITY ★★★½ | VALUE ★★½ | ZONE 10B

10801 MacArthur Boulevard, Potomac; (301) 299-9097

Reservations Required **When to go** Anytime **Entree range** $24–36 **Payment** VISA, MC, AMEX, CB, DC **Service rating** ★★★ **Friendliness rating** ★★★ **Parking** Free lot **Bar** Full service **Wine selection** Brief **Dress** Dressy, business, jacket and tie **Disabled access** No **Customers** Locals

Brunch Sunday, noon–2:30 p.m.
Lunch Tuesday–Saturday, noon–2:30 p.m.
Dinner Tuesday–Sunday, 6–9 p.m.; Monday, closed.

Setting & atmosphere A beautiful, old-fashioned inn above the river, with a blazing fireplace in the parlor bar downstairs and a huddle of small dining rooms up a narrow iron spiral staircase (and bathrooms out of the servants' quarters). The stone terrace and gazebo levels are open in good weather.

House specialties The menu changes seasonally, but frequently includes ostrich, foie gras, venison, and lobster. Also look for squab or duck dishes, caviar (either as an ingredient or in classic service), and fresh fish.

Other recommendations Ask for the chef's-choice menu (for the whole table only), which can be requested as vegetarian or seafood-only if you like.

Summary & comments This has always been a beautiful site, but its familiar weaknesses—haphazard service and hit-or-miss food—still threaten it occasionally, and the wine list's range doesn't keep up with its price range. The crowd, too, has changed a little: dressing down more, treating it more as a neighborhood restaurant than a special occasion "inn"—which may be the direction it's headed.

OLD EBBITT GRILL ★★½

AMERICAN | MODERATE | QUALITY ★★★½ | VALUE ★★★ | ZONE 3

675 15th Street, NW; (202) 347-4801

Reservations Recommended **When to go** Sunday brunch, after work for power-tripping **Entree range** $12–26 **Payment** VISA, MC, AMEX, DC, D **Service rating** ★★★ **Friendliness rating** ★★★ **Parking** Pay lots (validated after 5 p.m.) **Bar** Full service **Wine selection** Good **Dress** Business, informal **Disabled access** Very good (through G Street atrium) **Customers** Business, feds, locals, tourists

Breakfast Monday–Friday, 7:30–11 a.m.; Saturday, 8–11:30 a.m.
Brunch Saturday and Sunday, 8:30 a.m.–4 p.m.
Lunch/dinner Monday–Friday, 11 a.m.–midnight; Saturday and Sunday, 4 p.m.–midnight; Late night menu daily from midnight to 1 a.m.

Setting & atmosphere An updated old-boys' club, but with equal opportunity hospitality: a few horsey accoutrements (bridles, snaffles) in front, lots of greenery and etched-glass dividers in the main room, and a classic oyster bar.

House specialties Linguine with shrimp, basil, and fresh tomatoes; pork chops with homemade applesauce; black pepper–rubbed leg of lamb with papaya relish; old-fashioned pepperpot beef; steamed mussels; smoked salmon (a company signature) and smoked bluefish when available. Annually, during the brief halibut season in Alaska, the Old Ebbitt and its Clyde's cousins have a halibut celebration that is a command performance for seafood lovers. For brunch, fat old-style French toast and corned beef hash.

Entertainment & amenities Occasional piano music at happy hour.

Summary & comments This is one restaurant whose whole experience is somehow better than the food might indicate by itself. The Old Ebbitt—actually, the new Old Ebbitt for those who remember the fusty Back Bay–style original around the corner and its stuffed owls and scuffed bar rails—takes its White House neighborhood location seriously, but not too seriously. That is, it gives out pagers to patrons waiting for tables, but the staff democratically seats the ties and T-shirts side by side.

OLD GLORY ★★★

BARBECUE | MODERATE | QUALITY ★★★★ | VALUE ★★★★ | ZONE 5

3139 M Street, NW; (202) 337-3406

Reservations Parties of 6 or more only, for lunch or weekday dinner **When to go** Afternoon **Entree range** $9–21 **Payment** VISA, MC, AMEX, DC, D **Service rating** ★★½ **Friendliness rating** ★★★ **Parking** Pay lots, street **Bar** Full service **Wine selection** Minimal **Dress** Casual, informal **Disabled access** Good **Customers** Local, tourist

Brunch Sunday, 11 a.m.–3 p.m.
Lunch/dinner Monday–Thursday, 11:30 a.m.–2 a.m.; Friday and Saturday, 11:30 a.m.–3 a.m.; Sunday, 11 a.m.–2 a.m.; late-night menu available every day, 11:30 p.m. until closing.

Setting & atmosphere A chic and cheeky take on roadhouse diner decor with a sort of Six Flags theme: The state colors of Tennessee, Texas, Georgia, Kentucky, Kansas (which used to be Arkansas), and the Carolinas hang overhead, while each table is armed with bottles of six different barbecue sauces—mild, sweet, vinegary, multi-chilied, mustardy, tomatoey—named for the same seven states. A mix of old and new country and honky-tonk music plays on the PA.

House specialties Pork ribs or beef spareribs; "pulled" (shredded rather than chopped) pork shoulder; jerk-rubbed, roasted chicken; slow-smoked leg of lamb; smoked ham; various combinations or sandwich versions thereof. Daily specials often include pit-fired steaks or fresh seafood.

Other recommendations Pit-grilled burgers with cheddar and smoked ham; marinated and grilled vegetables; marinated, wood-grilled shrimp.

Entertainment & amenities Live music on Saturday.

Summary & comments This trendy finger-lickers' stop is surprisingly good, particularly when it comes to the sort of Southern side dishes that rarely travel well. The biscuits are fine (the cornbread isn't), and the hoppin' John—black-eyed peas and rice—is better than authentic. It's neither mushy nor greasy.

OLIVES ★★½

MODERN AMERICAN | MODERATE | QUALITY ★★★½ | VALUE ★★★ | ZONE 3

1600 K Street, NW; (202) 452-1868

Reservations Recommended **When to go** Lunch **Entree range** $20–35 **Payment** VISA, MC, AMEX, DC **Service rating** ★★★ **Friendliness rating** ★★★ **Parking** Street, pay lots, valet **Bar** Full service **Wine selection** Good **Dress** Business, Friday casual, casual **Disabled access** Good **Customers** Business, local after-hours

Lunch Monday–Friday, 11:30 a.m.–2:30 p.m.
Dinner Monday–Thursday, 5:30–10 p.m.; Friday and Saturday, 5:30–10:30 p.m.

Setting & atmosphere Metallic tones and natural textures in an elaborately designed group of "areas" on slightly raised levels (and down an open staircase), including a large and comfy (and consequently frequently crowded) lounge.

House specialties Lunch is a good bargain here—home-style pizzas, tuna tartare in cucumber molding over rock shrimp and chef Todd English's trademark goat cheese dumplings in black olive pasta—but with an occasionally slightly overdone affectation of humor, i.e. "ham 'n' cheese" sandwiches (smoked ham and provolone on onion focaccia with basil aïoli and bean salad).

Summary & comments This offshoot of English's Boston landmark can be too cute for comfort sometimes—the TV "monitors" in the kitchen are supposed to allow English to maintain quality control from afar, though it's hard to imagine how; and occasionally the staff will forget to tell you that both items you've ordered have the same sauce. But it's consistently improved.

ORTANIQUE ★★½

CARIBBEAN/NUEVO LATINO | EXPENSIVE | QUALITY ★★★ | VALUE ★★★½ | ZONE 3

730 11th Street, NW; (202) 393-0975

Reservations Helpful **When to go** Late for the scene **Entree range** $21–33 **Payment** VISA, MC, AMEX, D **Service rating** ★★★ **Friendliness rating** ★★★★ **Parking** Pay lot **Bar** Full service **Wine selection** Limited **Dress** Business, dance-clubbish, casual **Disabled access** Good **Customers** Latino and buppie business; under-30s cocktailers; some pre- and post-MCI Centre crowds

Lunch Monday–Friday, 11:30 a.m.–2:30 p.m.
Dinner Monday–Thursday, 5:30–10 p.m.; Friday and Saturday, 5:30–11 p.m.

Setting & atmosphere This is a good-looking and festive restaurant, with a wide-open atrium-style ceiling, trompe l'oeil vinery (including the eponymous Jamaican citrus), various little nooks and even a few "private" tables on the mezzanine made for being seen. The 350-gallon aquarium and its lanquid inhabitants are on closed-circuit TV and broadcast big on a barside screen. Formerly owned by BET founder Robert Johnson, Ortanique still has a black/entertainment contingent who dress to impress.

House specialties Several ceviches du jour (including conch with Scotch bonnet peppers and salt-cod "tater tots"); curried crab cakes; citrus-rum and teriyaki-flavored pan-sauteed grouper; spiced-rum and jerk-rubbed pork chops; more-tangy-than-sweet barbecued salmon; West Indian-style bouillabaisse in curried coconut broth; and a rich but fascinating jerk-rubbed foie gras over salad and duck confit with Grand Marnier "drizzle."

Other recommendations Spicy-fried calamari; sesame- and spice-marinated tuna with salsa; conch fritters.

Summary & comments The menu was designed by Miami star chef Cindy Hutson, who hand-trained the kitchen and checks back in regularly; and reflects what she calls here "cuisine of the sun," a West African, Caribbean, Floribbean fusion. Some people find the layered flavors excessive and even confusing, others love the byplay on the palate—though, oddly, none of the heat is *Miami Vice*–worthy. There's live music for dancing or just drinking Thursday through Sunday.

PALENA ★★★★

MODERN AMERICAN | EXPENSIVE | QUALITY ★★★★½ | VALUE ★★★★ | ZONE 7

3529 Connecticut Avenue, NW; (202) 537-9250

Reservations Recommended **When to go** Anytime **Entree price** $28 **Payment** VISA, MC, AMEX, DC, D **Service rating** ★★★½ **Friendliness rating** ★★★½ **Parking** Street, pay lot **Bar** Full service **Wine selection** Good **Dress** Business, casual **Disabled access** Good **Customers** Local up-and-comers; connected out-of-towners

Dinner Tuesday–Saturday, 5:30–10 p.m

Setting & atmosphere Deceptively low-key from the sidewalk, this is a long, lean, easy, cream-colored space leading back from a chic front lounge to a subtle garden that provides a pleasant light over the banquets.

House specialties Daring and generally delightful presentions such as lobster and beet salad, rabit rolled around a quail egg–greens stuffing; venison loin paired with braised short ribs; sautéed skate, or pig's ears en croquette (which points out the chef's unusually broad repetoire).

Other recommendations Carefully tended duck breast or sometimes sweet-gamey squab; red snapper in a Thai-inflected broth; meaty crab salad.

Summary & comments Chef and co-owner Frank Ruta has one of D.C.'s most impressive kitchen resumes, starting at the White House and working through the River Club, Obelisk, and Provence—hence the free eclecticism of his combinations. He and his co-owner, the equally prominent pastry chef Ann Amernick, bought what had been one of the previous Greenwood sites and actually upscaled the food while somehow smoothing the atmosphere, replacing personality with repose. (Both, of course, are desirable in dining circles.) The one quirk is the one-price-fits-all entree sizing.

PERSIMMON ★★★

MODERN AMERICAN | MODERATE | QUALITY ★★★★ | VALUE ★★★ | ZONE 10A

7003 Wisconsin Avenue, Bethesda; (301) 654-9860

Reservations Recommended **When to go** Weeknights **Entree range** $17–25 **Payment** VISA, MC, AMEX, DC **Service rating** ★★½ **Friendliness rating** ★★★½ **Parking** Street (metered), pay lots **Bar** Beer and wine **Wine selection** Small but good **Dress** Business, informal **Disabled access** Good **Customers** Older suburban couples, young conservative professionals

Lunch Monday–Saturday, 11:30 a.m.–2 p.m.
Dinner Monday–Saturday, 5:30–10 p.m.; Sunday, closed.

Setting & atmosphere A real storefront, which has survived various incarnations with its pressed-tin ceiling remarkably intact, now exotically sponged to match its ruby-ripe name and given a "brocade" glitter with clusters of gilt-frame mirrors.

House specialties A trio of tartares: tuna, salmon, and ceviche; barbecue chicken pot stickers with mango salsa and black beans; wasabi-fried oysters; mushroom and blue cheese–stuffed ravioli; crabcakes; pecan crusted rack of lamb; shiitake and hoisin crusted salmon.

Other recommendations That retro favorite, roast chicken with mashed potatoes and vegetable ragoût; grilled pork porterhouse with fried plantains; fish in general.

Entertainment & amenities A homemade pâté with the bread basket.

Summary & comments This simple but smart little eclectic American bistro—actually more mod/Med/fusion—might well fill the Georgetown-chic gap in Bethesda. In fact, chef-owner Damian Salvatore used to run the kitchen at Georgetown's rising star Tahoga, and the fact that the meat dishes tend to be less intriguing suggests he hasn't quite adjusted to the slightly older, more conservative crowds he seems to be drawing here—or isn't sure they've adjusted to him. And there's a little more attention paid to the presentation *on* the plate than of it—the kitchen is way ahead of the wait staff.

PIZZERIA PARADISO ★★★

PIZZA | INEXPENSIVE | QUALITY ★★★★ | VALUE ★★★★★ | ZONE 6

2029 P Street, NW; (202) 223-1245

Reservations Not accepted **When to go** Anytime, except around 8–10 p.m. **Entree range** $8–16 **Payment** VISA, MC, DC **Service rating** ★★★ **Friendliness rating** ★★★ **Parking** Street **Bar** Beer and wine **Wine selection** Limited **Dress** Casual **Disabled access** No **Customers** Local, tourist, student

Open Monday–Friday, 11:30 a.m.–11 p.m.; Saturday, 11 a.m.–midnight; Sunday, noon–10 p.m.

Setting & atmosphere As tiny as this upper room is, it's hilariously decorated, with trompe l'oeil stone walls opening at the "ruined roof" to a blue sky; columns with capitals of papier-mâché veggies; a woodburning stove painted like a smokestack; and semi-Impressionistic painted cardboard pizzas like Amish hexes around the walls (a sly comment on the mass-market competition, perhaps?).

House specialties Pizzas with four cheeses, or "the atomica" with salami, black olives, and hot peppers; zucchini, eggplant, peppers, and fresh buffalo mozzarella; mussels (surprisingly, yes); and potato with pesto sauce and parmesan.

Other recommendations Thick sandwiches made with focaccia, including roast lamb and roasted veggies; multimeat Italian subs; pork with hot peppers.

Summary & comments It may seem extravagant to give such high marks to a pizzeria, but pizza this good—shoveled in and out of the deep oven, with a splash of extra-virgin olive oil and a handful of cheese tossed on at the last moment—makes most American takeout blush. It's almost a re-definition of pizza. This restaurant also has real attitude—not commercial camp, just an irresistible New Wave nonchalance. No larger than its next-door sibling, Obelisk, Pizzeria Paradiso shoehorns them in and rolls them out at an astonishing but validating rate. A new location is now open at 3282 M Street, NW; (202) 337-1245.

RED SAGE ★★★

NEW SOUTHWESTERN | EXPENSIVE | QUALITY ★★★★½ | VALUE ★★★★ | ZONE 3

605 14th Street, NW; (202) 638-4444

Reservations Essential for dining room; not accepted in chili bar **When to go** Anytime **Entree range** $20–40 **Payment** VISA, MC, AMEX, DC, D **Service rating** ★★★ **Friendliness rating** ★★★ **Parking** Pay lots (validated) **Bar** Full service **Wine selection** Good **Dress** Dressy, informal **Disabled access** Excellent **Customers** Local, tourist, gourmet mag groupies

Lunch Monday–Friday, 11:30 a.m.–2 p.m. *Chili bar:* Monday–Saturday, 11:30 a.m.–11:30 p.m.

Dinner Monday–Friday, 5:30–9:45 p.m.; Saturday, 5–10:30 p.m.; Sunday, 5–10 p.m. *Chili bar:* Sunday, 4:30–11 p.m.

Setting & atmosphere A fun and funny $5-million-plus New Wave slant on Santa Fe chic, with cast-iron lizard door handles, plaster clouds with "lightning" in the chili bar, and $100,000 worth of glass etched with campfires and broncos.

House specialties Wild mushroom–Swiss chard ravioli; cinnamon-smoked or roasted quail with pecans and ham; wood-roasted duck; house-smoked salmon or tuna carpaccio with habanero pesto; bourbon rabbit; a vegetarian plate with poblano tamales and wood-roasted mushrooms; sausage of the day (venison, duck, rabbit, even wild boar); venison chili in the chili bar.

Other recommendations The Cubana Torta (griddled pork loin with ham and cheese); blue cornmeal oysters. Upstairs, the Border Cafe has a choice of fascinating salads, small chic pizzas, and at dinner breaks out into updated enchiladas (mushrooms and goat cheese), quesadilla (portobello, chipotle, BBQ brisket), burritos (spinach and portobello), tacos (catfish or salmon). Head for the border, indeed.

Summary & comments After the biggest preopening ballyhoo of the decade, and the inevitable deflation, Red Sage has found its feet, and its heat, gloriously in the hands of chef Marou Outtara. The roasted-chili cuisine made famous by owner Mark Miller is a pungent panoply rather than a painful blur: Each dish is seasoned with just the right flavor of pepper and to just the right degree, so that you are constantly astonished by the nuances. All meats and game are steroid-free. *Note:* At presstime, a new chef and menu were being installed.

ROCKLANDS ★★½

BARBECUE | INEXPENSIVE | QUALITY ★★★½ | VALUE ★★★ | ZONES 5, 11B

2418 Wisconsin Avenue, NW; (202) 333-2558
4000 North Fairfax Drive, Arlington; (703) 528-9663

Reservations Not accepted **When to go** Afternoon, late dinner **Entree range** $5–20 **Payment** VISA, MC, AMEX **Service rating** ★★½ **Friendliness rating** ★★★ **Parking** Limited street meters **Bar** None **Wine selection** None **Dress** Casual **Disabled access** No **Customers** Locals

Open *Georgetown:* Monday–Friday, 11:30 a.m.–10 p.m.; Saturday, 11 a.m.–10 p.m.; Sunday, 11 a.m.–9 p.m. *Arlington:* Monday and Tuesday, 11:30 a.m.–9 p.m.; Wednesday, 11:30 a.m.–10 p.m.; Thursday, 11:30 a.m.–11 p.m.; Friday and Saturday, 11:30 a.m.–midnight; Sunday, 11 a.m.–9 p.m.

Setting & atmosphere Its small storefront size, and the fact that most of the room is taken up by pit space, kitchen, and grill, mean that this is authentically a stand-up or bolt-and-carryout spot. There's only one communal service table and six or eight stools at the window counter, and the food is served in burger-shop paper dishes. The primary decor is supplied by the two wall cabinets of trendy pepper and super-hot chili sauces, chutneys, etc. The Arlington branch is really the kitchen partner of an auto dealership–turned–billiard parlor called, appropriately, the Car Pool.

House specialties Chopped-pork sandwiches (actually almost everything—including the marinated sliced lamb loin, trout, and catfish, but excepting the ribs and chicken wings, is served as a sandwich); racks in quarter, half, and full sizes; and frequently "exotic" meats or fresh fish such as salmon and swordfish.

Other recommendations Most of the old-style side dishes, such as the greens (mustard, turnip, etc., available in pints and quarts), potato salad, slaw, fresh green beans, and red beans and rice are very good. The corn pudding is more like Stovetop Stuffing, although there are those who swear by the Caesar salad: a yuppie-ish side dish, perhaps, and one that seems to go strangely with the crew, but hey, this is Glover Park, after all.

Summary & comments Amid the tidal wave of authentic (and only "authentic-style") pit barbecue, Rocklands might be considered a nouveau-retro meat counter, attracting both barbecue heads and food trendies. Owner John Snedden not only stocks a huge selection of super-hot chili sauces—and sets out several at a time for taste-testing—but he also likes to serve up meats more interesting than the usual pig.

He's experimented with elk, boar, venison, and ostrich, and he often throws out a whole carcass (of whatever) as happy-hour fare.

SAVEUR ★★½

FRENCH | MODERATE | QUALITY 84 | VALUE ★★★★ | ZONE 5

2218 Wisconsin Avenue, NW; (202) 333-5885

Reservations Recommended **When to go** Sunday brunch, late evening **Entree range** $18–24 **Payment** AMEX, VISA, MC **Service rating** ★★★★ **Friendliness rating** ★★★ **Parking** Street, pay lots **Bar** Full service **Wine selection** Good **Dress** Business, casual **Disabled access** Good **Customers** Foodies, local

Brunch Sunday, 11:30 a.m.–3 p.m.
Lunch Monday–Saturday, 11:30 a.m.–2:30 p.m.
Dinner Monday–Thursday, 5:30–10 p.m.; Friday and Saturday, 5:30–11 p.m.

Setting & atmosphere The building has been several restaurants, which have left bits of decor behind, such as the lariat-covered columns and the adobe-sunshine paint. On the other hand, the accent here is mainly that of Provençal, the sunshine capital of France, so neo Santa Fe styling and weathered shutters aren't all that strange.

House specialties Grilled and roasted seafood with unexpected sauces, such as halibut with grilled garlic stems and miso or fennel-crusted salmon with cumin-grilled shrimp; rack or leg of lamb with roasted garlic mousseline and cured olive jus—a sort of super-bistro "bird in a nest" with eggplant instead of toast nesting a roquefort–pine-nut "egg."

Other recommendations Bone quail with pheasant sausage, lentils, and prosciutto; wild mushroom risotto; duck breast and leg confit with caramelized champagne-mango glaze.

Summary & comments This kitchen can prepare some of the deftest and most deceptively simple French fare in a town studded with furbelows: creamy custards and mousselines, glitteringly green arugula-Key lime sauce for fish. He occasionally turns out a fusion-ish special (Japanese tuna in a sushi Caesar salad or blackened over fresh mustard greens), but the squid is still more likely to come with oil-cured olives and fresh parsley than hot chilies. Most of the Asian tone is visual: brilliant colors, delicate presentation, and delicate contrasts of texture. *Note:* While there is a separate area for smoking during the week, the entire restaurant is turned into a no-smoking zone on weekends.

SEA CATCH ★★★½

SEAFOOD | MODERATE | QUALITY ★★★★ | VALUE ★★★★ | ZONE 5

1054 31st Street, NW; (202) 337-8855

Reservations Recommended **When to go** Early **Entree range** $16–32 **Payment** VISA, MC, AMEX, DC, D **Service rating** ★★★ **Friendliness rating** ★★½ **Parking** Validated for 3 hours **Bar** Full service **Wine selection** Good **Dress** Casual, business **Disabled access** Good **Customers** Local, business

Lunch Monday–Saturday, noon–3 p.m.

Dinner Monday–Saturday, 5:30–10:30 p.m.; Sunday, closed.

Setting & atmosphere Sleekly elegant, with a white marble raw bar, polished-wood dining room with fireplace, and, in good weather, a balcony overlooking the Chesapeake & Ohio Canal.

House specialties House-smoked salmon and big-eye tuna; lobster specials, such as medallions over fettuccine or steamed lobster, mussels, oysters, clams, and shrimp; shrimp with saffron; soft-shell crabs with pesto; scallops with black olive and tomato tapenade; the low-fat, catfish-flavored Amazon fish called pirarucu.

Other recommendations A personal "off the menu" favorite is the lobster sashimi, which is only available when the raw bar isn't too busy. Fresh stone crab claws flown in from Maine are another seasonal treat.

Summary & comments This is an underrated seafood establishment particularly ideal for people who suffer from fear of frying. The key here is balance: The kitchen likes to play with its presentations, but not to the point where the quality or texture of the shellfish is obscured. Those who prefer the straighter stuff may order lobster steamed, grilled, broiled, baked, or poached; a variety of fresh fish (there is no freezer in the kitchen, proof of the chef's dedication to freshness) brushed with oil and grilled; or an updated surf-and-turf of tenderloin and crab-stuffed mushrooms. Ask for guidance with the wine list—it's much more interesting than the usual fish grill's selection. However, for dedicated carnivores, the Thai-marinated roast chicken or the steaks are very dependable. There is also a pre-theater menu for $18.95.

1789 ★★½

MODERN AMERICAN | EXPENSIVE | QUALITY ★★★★ | VALUE ★★★ | ZONE 5

1226 36th Street, NW; (202) 965-1789

Reservations Recommended **When to go** Anytime **Entree range** $18–36 **Payment** VISA, MC, AMEX, DC, D **Service rating** ★★★ **Friendliness rating** ★★★ **Parking** Valet **Bar** Full service **Wine selection** Good **Dress** Jacket required **Disabled access** No **Customers** Local, business, tourist

Dinner Sunday–Thursday, 6–10 p.m.; Friday, 6–11 p.m.; Saturday, 5:30–11 p.m.

Setting & atmosphere A meticulously maintained Federal townhouse with blazing fireplaces, polished silver, and historic poise; a certain formality is implied rather than expressed.

House specialties Pan-roasted lobster with ginger and cilantro; rockfish with carrots and fennel; halibut with mushrooms "bread pudding;" grilled barbecued duck breast with greens; venison medallions with black trumpet mushrooms.

Other recommendations Rack of lamb with feta-flavored potato au gratin; lobster risotto; three-way salmon appetizers (smoked, salt-cured, and tartare); pan-seared salmon with cherries.

Summary & comments This menu, inspired by seasonal availability, showcases regional game and seafood with care and respect. The kitchen aims to re-create and reclaim classic dishes—grilled quail with oysters and bacon, venison medallions, rack of lamb—and update them rather than invent novel treatments. In other words, it's more of a culinary tender of the flame than an innovator, which suits its old-money clientele. However, under the direction of chef Ris Lacoste, the kitchen is moving with increasing confidence into a middle ground, still classic but fresh. Vegetarian options are especially intriguing.

SUSHI-KO ★★★★

JAPANESE | MODERATE | QUALITY ★★★★½ | VALUE ★★★★ | ZONE 5

2309 Wisconsin Avenue, NW; (202) 333-4187

Reservations Recommended **When to go** Anytime **Entree range** $11–20 **Payment** VISA, MC, AMEX **Service rating** ★★★ **Friendliness rating** ★★★ **Parking** Street, valet (dinner only) **Bar** Full service **Wine selection** Good, particularly French **Dress** Business, casual **Disabled access** No **Customers** Local, ethnic

Lunch Tuesday–Friday, noon–2:30 p.m.
Dinner Monday–Friday, 6–10:30 p.m.; Saturday, 5–10:30 p.m.; Sunday, 5–10 p.m.

Setting & atmosphere A sleek twist on classic sushi bar decor downstairs, carefully unfrilly; more obviously modern—i.e., non-tradition-bound upstairs.

House specialties Any of the seasonal "small dishes," either traditional or contemporary, from Chefs Tetsuro Takanashi (who had his own chef's-choice restaurant in Tokyo) or Duncan Boyd, involving and often combining fish, both cooked and raw, with seaweeds, wild greens, grains, herbs, caviar, and sometimes unexpected American touches.

Other recommendations Sushi, especially seasonal dishes such as ankimo (monkfish liver) and toro (fatty tuna); broiled eel; soft-shell crabs; octopus salad; grilled fish; spring for real wasabi.

Summary & comments Thanks to its unusual seasonal dishes, Sushi-Ko attracts a broad, generally knowledgeable, and fairly affluent crowd. This has made it possible for owner Daisuke Utagawa and his chef team to offer a more flexible style of cooking, both traditional and improvisational—that is, based on market availability and traditional seasonal factors. However, while the "ordinary" sushi is reasonable, those specials can make dinner somewhat more pricey than a meal at most other sushi bars, so don't waste it on someone who's happy with grocery-store California roll. Utagawa is also intrigued with the notion of matching French wines and Japanese food, and offering higher quality sakes.

TABARD INN ★★½

MODERN AMERICAN | MODERATE | QUALITY ★★★ | VALUE ★★★ | ZONE 6

1739 N Street, NW; (202) 785-1277

Reservations Recommended **When to go** Anytime **Entree range** $10–32 **Payment** VISA, MC, AMEX, DC, D **Service rating** ★★★ **Friendliness rating** ★★★★ **Parking** Street **Bar** Full service **Wine selection** Good **Dress** Business, informal **Disabled access** No **Customers** Business, locals

Breakfast Monday–Friday, 7–10 a.m.; Saturday and Sunday, 7–9:30 a.m.
Brunch Saturday, 11 a.m.–2:30 p.m.; Sunday, 10:30 a.m.–2:30 p.m.
Lunch Monday–Friday, 11:30 a.m.–2:30 p.m.
Dinner Sunday–Friday, 6–10 p.m.; Saturday, 6–10:30 p.m.

Setting & atmosphere This almost theatrically old-English jumble of rooms has a courtyard at its heart (as all good English country inns should), a series of small dining rooms with surprisingly light-hearted decor (a garden-path mural up the stairs, for example), and a wood-lined library with couches and a fireplace, ideal for a winter afternoon, cocktail before dinner, or after-dinner cordial.

House specialties Smoked trout salad with goat cheese croutons; seared foie gras with green lentils and cherry-fig compote; roulade of duck ham, cured grouper, and smoked salmon with fennel (appetizers); grilled mahi-mahi with black bean salsa; grilled scallops with fava bean–pea-butterbean ragoût; roast duck breast with savoy cabbage and bacon; sautéed sweetbreads with saffron noodles and wild mushrooms.

Other recommendations Pumpkin ravioli with walnuts; grilled veal chop with wild mushroom risotto; grilled mullet with saffron onions, black olives, and tomatoes.

Summary & comments With the arrival of chef David Craig, formerly of Pesce, the Tabard has shaken off its longtime country-maiden air and lingering good-earth style in favor of a confident, almost brash late-1990s continental sophistication with free-form fusion and Mediterranean asides. That doesn't mean that it isn't rather subtly healthful, however—there's lots of grilling, roasting, and smoking going on here. The menu changes constantly, but not surprisingly, given his experience at Pesce, Craig can be counted on to give fish and shellfish both careful handling and buoyant supporting ingredients (see that roulade above). Portions are European-savvy as well—not American-sized but exactly enough.

TABERNA DEL ALABARDERO ★★★

SPANISH | EXPENSIVE | QUALITY ★★★★ | VALUE ★★★ | ZONE 3

1776 I Street, NW (entrance on 18th Street); (202) 429-2200

Reservations Recommended **When to go** Anytime for tapas, lunch for fixed-price meals **Entree range** $25–35 **Payment** VISA, MC, AMEX, DC, D, JCB **Service rating** ★★★★ **Friendliness rating** ★★★ **Parking** Free next door **Bar** Full service **Wine selection** Very good **Dress** Jacket and tie suggested **Disabled access** Good **Customers** Local, embassy, ethnic

Lunch Monday–Friday, 11:30 a.m.–2:30 p.m.
Dinner Monday–Saturday, 5:30–10:30 p.m.; Sunday, closed.

Setting & atmosphere Lace curtain and velvet old-world elegance, with ornate moldings and a magnificent private room (like a chapel) in the center.

House specialties Luscious lobster paella at night, as well as traditional paella and the pasta version called fideua (there is a variety of versions at lunch); venison; rabbit casserole or boneless rabbit and lobster medallions dealt alternately on the plate; duck confit; stuffed squid in ink; sweetbreads.

Other recommendations Daily specials, particularly game, and at least a half-dozen seafood specials every day; quail or pheasant; halibut with mussels.

Summary & comments This is a very old-world-style restaurant and quite dignified. Some people may find it weighty as well, though chef Josu Zubikarai is one of only two Basque chefs in Washington (Jaleo's José Rámon Andres is the other) and his specials are often a delightful surprise. One alternative is to dabble in Taberna's riches via the tapas menu, a selection of a dozen smaller sized dishes, including a serving of the paella, for $3.50 to $6.50 apiece (and you can linger as long as you like). Other choices include artichoke bottoms baked with ham; empanadas; grilled chorizo; poached calamari in a salad of sweet peppers. There is also a list of a dozen sherries by the glass and red or white sangria. Taberna now offers 10 set lunch menus, ranging from $28 to $38, making it a little quicker, if not less expensive. And it's also getting into the special-events trend, with wine dinners and imported guest chefs who show off Spanish regional cuisine with monkfish in saffron ragoût, cream of pumpkin porcini soup, etc.

TAKO GRILL ★★★★

JAPANESE | MODERATE | QUALITY ★★★★½ | VALUE ★★★★ | ZONE 10A

7756 Wisconsin Avenue, Bethesda; (301) 652-7030

Reservations Not accepted **When to go** Before 7 p.m. **Entree range** $8–18 **Payment** VISA, MC, AMEX **Service rating** ★★★★ **Friendliness rating** ★★★ **Parking** Street, public garages, free lot (dinner only) **Bar** Wine and beer **Wine selection** House **Dress** Casual, informal **Disabled access** Very good **Customers** Local, business

Lunch Monday–Friday, 11:30 a.m.–2 p.m.
Dinner Monday–Thursday, 5:30–10 p.m.; Friday and Saturday, 5:30–10:30 p.m.; Sunday, 5–9:30 p.m.

Setting & atmosphere A cool, hip, very 1990s-Tokyo room, a study in white, black, and scarlet, but with deft artistic touches (the flower arrangements) and almost hallucinatory "script" versions of Japanese verses hung on the walls. (The chefs, particularly the younger ones, are very Tokyo-stylish, too—check out the bleached and reddened hair.) The adjoining sake bar (where you may order food as well) is particularly smart.

House specialties Grilled jaw of yellowtail; ankimo (a monkfish liver pâté); soft-shell crabs tempura-fried and chopped into hand rolls.

Other recommendations Grilled whole red snapper or rainbow trout; glazed grilled eel; tiny candied whole octopus.

Summary & comments Of the three best Japanese restaurants in the area, each has a different slant: Makoto's (a very small hideaway on Macarthur Boulevard) is classic; Sushi-Ko's cutting-edge; and Tako's cool. In addition to some of the best and freshest sushi and sashimi in the area, Tako has a hot-stone grill called a robotai, on which whole fish, large shrimp, and a variety of fresh vegetables are cooked. The line of customers waiting to get in—the recent expansion notwithstanding—is the surest evidence of Tako's quality. Weekday lunches are a business special: soup, salad, rice, and a daily entree (orange roughy, chicken teriyaki, pork cutlet), plus six pieces of rolled sushi for $6.95.

And since several of the waitresses are vegetarian or vegan, Tako is especially well equipped to satisfy customers with special diets.

TARA THAI ★★½

THAI | MODERATE | QUALITY ★★★½ | VALUE ★★★★★ | ZONES 10A, 10B, 11A, 11B

4828 Bethesda Avenue, Bethesda; (301) 657-0488
12071 Rockville Pike (Montrose Crossing), Rockville; (301) 231-9899
4001 North Fairfax Drive, Ballston; (703) 903-4999
7501-C Leesburg Pike, Tysons Corner; (703) 506-9788
226 Maple Avenue West, Vienna; (703) 255-2467

Reservations Helpful **When to go** Weekdays **Entree range** $8–13 **Payment** VISA, MC, AMEX, DC, D **Service rating** ★★★ **Friendliness rating** ★★★½ **Parking** Free lot **Bar** Full service **Wine selection** House **Dress** Informal, casual **Disabled access** Fair **Customers** Ethnic, local

Lunch Monday–Friday, 11:30 a.m.–3 p.m.; Saturday and Sunday, noon–3:30 p.m.
Dinner Sunday–Thursday, 5–10 p.m.; Friday and Saturday, 5–11 p.m.

Setting & atmosphere "Tara" has nothing to do with the Old South. It means "blue," and these charming restaurants are marine blue and swimming in fantastical creatures and lacquered tables. The original Vienna branch is quite small, but so friendly that it seems cheerfully crowded rather than annoyingly so. The Bethesda branch draws a more mixed 20- and 30-something crowd to its cheeky murals, window-box bar, and chrome touches. The newest is the big Rockville branch—the gold-and-glitter look.

House specialties Whole fish, either fried with chili sauce or steamed in banana leaves with black mushrooms and ginger; soft-shell crabs; "wild" lamb curry; red curry beef; green eggplant curry with chicken.

Other recommendations Nua sawan (thin, dried but tender beef, fried and served with slaw—sort of Thai barbecue); honey-glazed duck. For a light meal or shared appetizer, try the "heavenly wings" (chicken drummettes scraped back into rattle shapes, stuffed with crab and green onion, then battered and fried).

Summary & comments Too much success is a two-edged sword: While the fare at the Vienna and Bethesda branches remains consistently good, some of the other branches, notably Rockville, are more erratic. The group also owns the promising Tara Asian, near the Rockville Metro, which serves pan-Asian fare.

TASTE OF SAIGON ★★★

VIETNAMESE | MODERATE | QUALITY ★★★★ | VALUE ★★★★★ | ZONES 10A, 11B

410 Hungerford Drive, Rockville; (301) 424-7222
8201 Greensboro Drive, McLean; (703) 790-0700

Reservations Accepted **When to go** Anytime **Entree range** $8–15 **Payment** VISA, MC, AMEX, CB, DC, D **Service rating** ★★★ **Friendliness rating** ★★★★ **Parking** Free lot **Bar** Full service **Wine selection** Limited **Dress** Informal **Disabled access** Good **Customers** Local, business, ethnic

Open Monday–Thursday, 11 a.m.–10 p.m.; Friday and Saturday, 11 a.m.–11 p.m.; Sunday, 11 a.m.–9:30 p.m.

Setting & atmosphere An intriguingly angular, sleek, gray-and-black-lacquer room slyly tucked into the back of a plain office building.

House specialties Stuffed baby squid; steamed whole rockfish served with rice crêpes and vegetables for rolling up; grilled pork meatballs, also served with crêpes and dipping sauce; caramelized soft-shell crabs (in season) with black beans; choice of seafoods—lobster, soft shells, scallops, or shrimp—in a house special black pepper sauce.

Other recommendations Cornish hen stuffed with pork; boneless roast quail; grilled pork with mushrooms, peanuts, and cellophane noodles; pho and other noodle soups in appetizer or entree sizes; rich venison curry.

Entertainment & amenities Patio dining in good weather.

Summary & comments The specials here are interesting dishes; it's as if the kitchen were as intrigued as the diners. The beef dishes are only fair, but the seafood and game bird entrees are particularly good. Some of the sauces are quite heavy, but if you stick to the steamed fish or bountiful soup choices, a Vietnamese dinner can be a dieter's dream.

TAVIRA ★★★

PORTUGUESE | MODERATE | QUALITY ★★★½ | VALUE ★★★★ | ZONE 10A

8401 Connecticut Avenue, Chevy Chase; (301) 652-8684

Reservations Recommended **When to go** Anytime **Entree range** $18–25 **Payment** AMEX, VISA, MC, DC **Service rating** ★★★ **Friendliness rating** ★★★ **Parking** Free lot **Bar** Full service **Wine selection** Fair **Dress** Business, casual **Disabled access** Good **Customers** Local, business

Lunch Monday–Friday, 11:30 a.m.–2:30 p.m.
Dinner Monday–Thursday, 5:30–10 p.m.; Friday and Saturday, 5–11 p.m.

Setting & atmosphere Named for a medieval fortress town (a good pun, considering it's in the basement of a bank, like a dungeon), it's made bright by sunny paint, a fireplace, heavy artisan pottery, and glass sconces—a sort of indoor patio with bar.

House specialties Grilled seafood (fresh sardines, squid); diced baby octopus with potatoes and olive oil; a tureen of mussels with tomato-sweet pepper broth; veal chops with sherry; clams with chorizo and prosciutto; grilled lamb chops. Don't miss the "french fries," really more like homemade potato chips.

Other recommendations Whole baked snapper; traditional salt cod shredded with straw potatoes, onions, and egg.

Summary & comments Although not terribly visible to traffic, Tavira is making itself indispensable in a neighborhood hungry for good food and a city ready for its mix of traditional Mediterranean and navy-trade fare. It's also a good place to test out "vinho verde," the "green wine" of Portugal, so called for its light, youthful quality and a fine complement to the sometimes oil- and garlic-strong food.

TEATRO GOLDONI ★★★

ITALIAN | EXPENSIVE | QUALITY ★★★★ | VALUE ★★★ | ZONE 3

1909 K Street, NW; (202) 955-9494

Reservations Recommended **When to go** Lunch; late dinner **Entree range** $16–34 **Payment** VISA, MC, AMEX, DC **Service rating** ★★★ **Friendliness rating** ★★★ **Parking** Valet, pay lots **Bar** Full service **Wine selection** Very good **Dress** Business, dressy, dressy casual **Disabled access** Good **Customers** Business, foodies

Lunch Monday–Friday, 11:30 a.m.–2 p.m.
Dinner Monday–Thursday, 5:30–10 p.m.; Friday and Saturday, 5–11 p.m.

Setting & atmosphere Take the word "teatro" seriously: This is a theatrical setting for a culinary performance. Mini-spots are trained on the plates like klieg lights on stars; the huge mirror over the bar reveals the show behind you; and the tables and booths are on their own "stages." And you'd better be dressed for the part: Not only are the other customers watching you, but the eyeholes of the masks on the wall and those of the photographed models (like the rest of the decor, half commedia dell' arte, half carneval) seem to be evaluating you. In other words, it's either exhilarating or over-the-top, depending on your mood.

House specialties Look for earthy but not heavy flavors: mushrooms (veal with porcinis and truffles, shiitake-stuffed cannelloni, lobster risotto with roasted tomatoes and truffle oil); squid ink (baby octopus and squid with black pasta, ink-braised cuttlefish); clams; black olives (on the seared tuna, the Argentinian beef, and the asparagus with capers and beet sauce); and the like. In colder weather, expect comfort dishes, again richer than weighty: braises, stews, ragus, chicken and morel "casserole."

Other recommendations If veal cheeks are on the specials, go straight for them. Also expect interesting risottos and good vegetarian options such as a parmesan basket filled with vegetables and served with three sauces.

Summary & comments Chef-owner Fabrizio Aielli is on his third eponymous restaurant, and that after years at Galileo with Roberto Donna. However, his particular accent is Venetian, and the squid and fried seafood dishes, such as the fritto misto, are among his personal prides. He gave the two kitchens slightly different personalities, this one (obviously) the more flamboyant, Osteria Goldoni the more traditional. That flamboyance opens Teatro up to some inconsistencies; but even the errors are interesting.

TENPENH ★★★½

PAN-ASIAN | EXPENSIVE | QUALITY ★★★★½ | VALUE ★★★★★ | ZONE 3

1001 Pennsylvania Avenue, NW; (202) 393-4500

Reservations Recommended **When to go** Early dinner or bar **Entree range** $14–27 **Payment** VISA, MC, AMEX, CB, DC, D **Service rating** ★★★★ **Friendliness rating** ★★★ **Parking** Valet, pay lots **Bar** Full service **Wine selection** Very good **Dress** Business, casual, dressy **Disabled access** Very good **Customers** Business, food trendies, media, pols

Lunch Monday–Friday, 11:30 a.m.–2:30 p.m.
Dinner Monday–Thursday, 5:30–10:30 p.m.; Friday and Saturday, 5:30–11 p.m.

Setting & atmosphere This is a famous old law-firm office building, and it looks it outside, but inside, TenPenh is like one of those simple Asian jewelry boxes that opens to reveal the subdued glitter of saffron and gold silk, patined Buddhas, hammered bronze flatware, teak lamps, curio trays as dessert buffets, incense coils dangling from the ceiling, and bamboo place mats. And no wonder: The owners took a three-week shopping trip to Bangkok, Hong Kong, Ho Chi Minh City, Macao, and Singapore to hand-pick $40,000 worth of furnishings.

House specialties Vietnamese spiced crispy quail; curried lump crabcakes; steamed shrimp-scallion dumplings; spicy wok-seared calamari; a sort of tempura-fried California roll (all appetizers); steamed striped bass with fennel, tomato, and shiitakes over somen noodles; macadamia- and panko-crusted halibut with mango-lime sauce; the signature Chinese smoked lobster with crispy fried spinach; red Thai curry prawns with pineapple.

Other recommendations Oysters with sake-pickled ginger granita (another signature); house-smoked salmon and wonton "Napoleon"; adobo chicken ravioli with pineapple relish; crispy fish of the day.

Entertainment & amenities Great amuse bouche, such as the Thai-spiked gazpacho.

Summary & comments The executive chef here is Jeff Tunks, also of D.C. Coast, and his fearless handling of seafood is at the heart of this fun-fare bazaar. Both the appetizer and entree lists run the gamut from simple to ornate, mild to spicy, light to heavy; it's really like dining in Bangkok, where the outdoor stalls are like a giant progressive dinner, only sitting in a mogul's tent. Not only is the wine list thoughtful, unusual, and affordable, there are several fine sakes to try as well.

TOSCA ★★★

ITALIAN | EXPENSIVE | QUALITY ★★★½ | VALUE ★★★ | ZONE 3

112 F Street NW; (202) 367-1990

Reservations Recommended **When to go** Lunch, late dinner **Entree price** $18–32 **Payment** VISA, MC, AMEX, DC, D **Service rating** ★★★½ **Friendliness rating** ★★★½ **Parking** Street, pay lots, valet **Bar** Full service **Wine selection** Good **Dress** Business, Friday casual **Disabled access** Good **Customers** Business (especially power-lunchers), pre-theatre, young trendy

Lunch Monday–Friday, 11:30 a.m–2:30 p.m.
Dinner Sunday–Thursday, 5:30–10:30 p.m.; Friday and Saturday, 11:30 a.m.–2:30 p.m.

Setting & atmosphere This is decor so cool many people find it cold—stony shades of gray and beige with only splashes of cream and teal—but it does have the effect of making the dishes themselves seem more vivid. If you are hungry for sensation, go for the tasting menu, five or six courses for $75.

House specialties Octopus salad with fennel and artichokes; heirloom tomato ravioli; fresh thyme taglierini with roasted lobster and green peas; asparagus and Parmesan-stuffed cappellacci with morel sauce; venison and leek tarte with sauteed Swiss chard; black sea bass roasted under fresh porcinis.

Other recommendations Fried crab- or mozzarella-stuffed zucchini blossoms; fresh pea and housemade pork sausage risotto; choice of fresh grilled seafoods.

Summary & comments Even in this newly-bustling restaurant neighborhood, Tosca stands out. D.C is rich in chefs who started out in the Galileo galley, and Cesare Lanfranconi is another; this especially shows in his combinations. Lunch is expensive but elaborate enough to be the meal of the day; try the fast pre-set lunch for $25. There is also a chef's table in the kitchen, which is particularly popular with Senator Ted Kennedy, among others, so reserve early and often.

VIDALIA ★★★★

MODERN AMERICAN | EXPENSIVE | QUALITY ★★★★½ | VALUE ★★★★ | ZONE 6

1990 M Street, NW; (202) 659-1990

Reservations Recommended **When to go** Anytime **Entree range** $20–32 **Payment** VISA, MC, AMEX, D **Service rating** ★★★★ **Friendliness rating** ★★★ **Parking** Street, garage, valet (dinner) **Bar** Full service **Wine selection** Very good **Dress** Business, dressy, casual **Disabled access** Good **Customers** Business, local, tourist

Lunch Monday–Friday, 11:30 a.m.–2:30 p.m.
Dinner Sunday–Thursday, 5:30–10 p.m.; Friday and Saturday, 5:30–10:30 p.m.

Setting & atmosphere Although this is actually a below-stairs establishment (disabled access is through the office lobby elevators), it's remarkably bright for a basement and as new–Southern Revival as a Martha Stewart magazine: sponged buttercup walls (the chef's wife's handiwork), dried flower wreaths, and stripped-wood banisters and dowels.

House specialties Depending on the season, the flavors are hearty or light, but the juxtapositions are always intriguing. Roasted sweetbreads with morels and a tang of bacon and chard or more delicately with lobster and vermouth; salmon seared in a fennel-seed crust; roasted squid stuffed with shrimp and chard or fried squid with blackened fennel; a Provençal-style round-bone lamb steak with artichokes, olives, and roast garlic; double "porterhouse" pork chop with pears and currants at dinner and a cornbread-and-sausage-stuffed chop at lunch.

Other recommendations Monkfish roasted in a mushroom crust; a lunchtime steak salad with arugula, fennel, and shiitakes; breast of duck with duck confit; squab "strudel" with morels and sour cherries; a seared but rare salmon appetizer with marinated scallops and Southwestern spices. For light fare, go into the Onion Bar and check out the $4 tapas.

Summary & comments Executive Chef Jeff Buben (and on-site chef Peter Smith) have just shaken up their menu, picking native American ingredients based on flavor rather than tradition. Though the name is Southern, the menu is fused with broader tastes. The luxuriant sauces aren't necessarily low-cal, but served with a light touch. Particularly if you dally over the big first-course salads. Vidalia can be a bargain.

WOO LAE OAK ★★★

KOREAN | MODERATE | QUALITY ★★★½ | VALUE ★★★★ | ZONE 11B

1500 South Joyce Street, Arlington; (703) 521-3706

Reservations Accepted, suggested on weekends **When to go** Anytime **Entree range** $10–20 **Payment** VISA, MC, AMEX **Service rating** ★★★★ **Friendliness rating** ★★★ **Parking** Free lot **Bar** Full service **Wine selection** Fair **Dress** Casual, informal **Disabled access** No **Customers** Ethnic, local

Open Every day, 11:30 a.m.–10:30 p.m.

Setting & atmosphere California Asian, this freestanding section of an apartment complex is a big curving slice of a room on stilts, with modernized versions of traditional wood-slat-and-rice-paper decor. All tables have barbecue grills built in.

House specialties Shin sun ro (a fancy hot pot—Korean shabu shabu—that requires 24 hours' notice); saeng sun jun (battered and grilled fish); bulgoki (the familiar sweet-soy beef barbecue); spicy fish stew in a pot; yook hwe bibimbap (marinated raw sirloin strips with spinach, bean sprouts, zucchini, etc., in sesame oil); boneless short rib cubes.

Other recommendations Beef liver, heart, tongue, and tripe for the more intrepid barbecuers; broiled salmon; sliced raw fish, cut in generous, steak-fry-sized pieces, not the thin Japanese layers. Modum yori, a combination grill platter, including a whole fish, shrimp, chicken, and beef, is a huge family meal but requires a day's advance notice.

Summary & comments This is not food to eat alone. The fun is barbecuing (or in the case of the many hot-pot dishes, dipping) with friends. Besides, many of the dishes are made for two, and the sashimi appetizer is so big—about 24 pieces, and cut Korean-style, meaning large—that it's either a meal or a first course for several. Many dishes cost less at lunch. The one real disappointment about this restaurant for non-Asian diners is that staffers frequently either doubt that you know what you're ordering or don't take it seriously; for example, even with the 24 hours' notice, it can be hit-or-miss whether you get your shin sun ro.

ZED'S ★★½

ETHIOPIAN | MODERATE | QUALITY ★★★ | VALUE ★★★★ | ZONE 5

1201 28th Street, NW; (202) 333-4710

Reservations Accepted **When to go** Anytime **Entree range** $10–16 **Payment** VISA, MC, AMEX, DC, D **Service rating** ★★★ **Friendliness rating** ★★★ **Parking** Street, pay lots **Bar** Full service **Wine selection** House **Dress** Casual, business **Disabled access** Not accessible **Customers** Ethnic, local

Open Every day, 11 a.m.–11 p.m.

Setting & atmosphere A deceptively simple Georgetown rowhouse outside, its whitewashed exterior gives way to a cool, shadowy world of wood screens and white linen, fresh flowers, formally dressed staff, musical instruments, and artifacts of Ethiopian culture.

House specialties Classic Ethiopian fare such as the chicken-hardboiled egg stew called doro watt; the spicy steak tartare called kitfo; the many vegetarian stews: carrots and cabbage, eggplant, and tomatoes; string beans and cauliflower; lentils, etc. Zed also offers some less familiar dishes, such as a whole fried fish in moderately spicy sauce, a purée of spiced roasted flax seeds; and a soul food-style mix of collard greens and beef.

Other recommendations Sautéed chicken strips; bulgar wheat; spicy lamb stew; a condiment of dried cottage cheese. Everything is preservative-free.

Summary & comments Zed Wondemu is the first word in Washington's Ethiopian establishments, in both senses: Her original site, several blocks to the west, was the first Ethiopian establishment to break out of the Adams-Morgan alley and it made converts of many local diners. Her cooking is notable for the quality of its injera, the sourdoughish pancake that is platter and utensil in one (see the entry for Meskerem for more details) and for the number of veggie dishes made with oil rather than the traditional clarified butter, making them vegan-friendly.

Part Nine

Shopping in Washington

Mall Shopping

It should come as no surprise that Washington, with one of the highest median household incomes in the nation and an increasingly diverse population, offers a wide variety of shopping opportunities. You can quite literally shop until you drop—virtually malled to death. On Saturday afternoons, roads leading to the shopping centers are as congested as commuter routes during rush hour. The stretch of I-95 south of Washington around the Potomac Mills factory outlet complex in Dale City—which has now surpassed even Colonial Williamsburg as the number one tourist attraction in Virginia—is nearly always backed up (see "Bargains" in the "Specialty Shops" section later in this part). Tysons Corner, just west of the Beltway, is so large it helped inspire one of the catch phrases of 1990s development, the "edge city." Tysons is a Siamese twin mall now, the original Tysons and the Galleria at Tysons II, and has its own brewpub, appropriately named the Edge City Brewery. The newer Leesburg Corner Premium Outlets on Route 7 west of Tysons Corner and the vast Arundel Mills, from the same folks who brought you the jam at Potomac Mills, are spreading the name-brand wealth around the region.

Suburban Malls

Most of the smaller suburban malls are probably similar to what you have back home, with a few notable exceptions. One is **The Fashion Centre** (phone (703) 415-2400) at Pentagon City in Arlington, Virginia—a beautiful conservatory-style building filled with 160 primarily high-end retailers: **Crate and Barrel,** the **Museum Company,** the **Wizards of the Coast, Macy's,** and **Nordstrom,** the Seattle-based clothing retailer renowned for its service and selection. It also opens onto the Ritz-Carlton Hotel, where you can have a very refreshing, elegant meal or high tea. The Pentagon City Metro stop, on the blue line, deposits shoppers right into the mall. The **Chevy Chase Pavilion** (phone (202) 686-5335), at the very north end of the District of Columbia on the border of Maryland, has a somewhat similar look and such new "chain-boutique" stores as **Gazelle** (wearable art), and **Everett Hall,** plus **J. Crew, Talbots,** and a **Georgette Klinger** salon. Like most malls, it has a food court, but it also has the a Starbucks Coffee and a Cheesecake Factory. It is also directly accessible by the Metro (the Friendship Heights station).

Catty-corner from the Pavilion is **Mazza Gallerie** (phone (202) 966-6114), a slightly quieter mall with **Neiman Marcus, Saks for Men, Williams-Sonoma, Ann Taylor, House of Villeroy and Boch, Harriet Kassman,** and a branch of the famed Boston discounter **Filene's Basement.** For emergencies, there is an American Express office on-site.

White Flint Mall (phone (301) 468-5777), north of Washington, also has a subway stop, although it's a block or so away; shuttle bus service is continuous. It houses **Bloomingdale's, Ann Taylor, Lord & Taylor,** a Cheesecake Factory restaurant (which hands out silent "beepers" so you can keep shopping while waiting for a table), as well as a better-than-average food court and a huge, three-story **Borders Books & Music. Dave & Buster's,** a vast virtual-reality sports/billiard/parlor/bar/casino/restaurant complex, dominates the top floor (see its profile in Part Six: Entertainment and Nightlife). There is also a European-style day spa, **Roxsan,** which offers everything from hairstyling to ornately painted (real or false) nails, mud baths, massages, and all-natural facials.

Tysons Corner (phone (903) 893-9400), although it does not have subway access, offers nearly 400 shops in two large arcades, including **Nordstrom, Lord & Taylor, Bloomingdale's, Brooks Brothers, Movado, Talbots for Women,** and the Washington Redskins official store. (The "Corner" fills up the neighborhood between Routes 7 and 123.) Just across the way is **Fairfax Square** (phone (703) 448-1830), a sort of mini-mall of super-label shops (see "Designer Clothing" in the "Specialty Shops" section) that whet your appetite for the platinum-card eateries such as Morton's of Chicago and the old-guard white linen Ritz-Carlton Hotel.

Malls in D.C.

There are fewer malls within city limits. **Georgetown Park** (phone (202) 298-5577), near the intersection of M Street and Wisconsin Avenue, is the most extravagant, featuring a lush Victorian design and some popular retailers: **Abercrombie & Fitch, Papillon, Crabtre & Evelyn, Ann Taylor, Ralph Lauren Polo, J. Crew, Sharper Image,** and the **White House/Black Market,** which stocks only cream, white, ecru, or sable clothes and accessories. It also includes a Benihana Japanese steak house with sushi bar, the original Clyde's of Georgetown, and a food court.

Two Washington landmarks have lately been reborn as shopping centers: the **Old Post Office Pavilion** and **Union Station.** The Pavilion, on Pennsylvania Avenue just north of the Smithsonian, is the place for stocking up on souvenirs; it also has a tower with a view that rivals the Washington Monument but with a fraction of the waiting line. Union Station, the city's restored train station on Massachusetts Avenue, is a grand beaux arts building whose glory is undiminished by its two-story arcade of shops, including **Ann Taylor, Nine West,** and **Jones New York** (handy for travelers who arrive short of clothes). Be sure to wander into the East Hall, which has kiosks selling one-of-a-kind jewelry, ethnic Russian and Afrocentric crafts, and other merchandise. The lowest level is a bustling food court, and there's more just outside the train track waiting areas. It also has a branch of the New York neo-soul food restaurant B. Smith's, a Pizzeria Uno, Red's steakhouses, America (a restaurant that claims to have dishes from all 50 states), a couple of elevated-view bars, and a multiplex cinema. The Pavilion is very near the Federal Triangle Metro stop; Union Station's Metro stop is an escalator-ride down.

And although it's a couple of blocks from the Metro Center stations, most tourists will want to look into the **Shops at National Place** (F Street, SW, between 13th and 14th Streets; (202) 662-1212), which has a **Sharper Image, Banana Republic, Victoria's Secret,** and a couple of cafes. For free, you get to watch for political and media celebrities while you window shop; the building also houses the National Press Club.

Great Neighborhoods for Window-Shopping

If malls make you crazy, Washington has a number of neighborhoods made for window-shopping.

Georgetown

In Georgetown, the city's largest walk-and-shop district, most of the clothing stores, both franchise and boutique, are centered along the two main drags, M Street and Wisconsin Avenue—notably, **Commander Salamander** (1420 Wisconsin Avenue, NW; (202) 337-2265); **Max Azria BCBG** (3210 M Street, NW; (202) 333-2224); **Betsey Johnson** (1319 Wisconsin Avenue, NW; (202) 338-4090); plus the now ubiquitous **Banana Republic** (phone (202) 333-2554) and **Benetton** at the intersection of Wisconsin Avenue and M Street; and **Urban Outfitters** (3111 M Street, NW; (202) 342-1012). Thanks to the crowds of teens and twentysomethings that hang out on Georgetown's sidewalks on weekends, many of these keep late hours for impulse shopping. These are also the two main restaurant strips. Shops for antiques, both formal and more offbeat, stretch up Wisconsin past R Street, interspersed with collections of artwork, books, and shoes; see the section on "Antiques" in the "Specialty Shops" section.

Georgetown also has more than a few shops specializing in one-of-a-kind crafts—including art glass at **Maurine Littleton** (1667 Wisconsin Avenue, NW; (202) 333-9307); ceramics at **America Studio** (2906 M Street, NW; (202) 965-3273); and jewelry and wooden crafts at **Appalachian Spring** (1415 Wisconsin Avenue, NW; (202) 337-5780). **A Mano** (1677 Wisconsin; (202) 298-7200) lays out fine French linens, faience, and majolica plates for the fanciest breakfast in bed ever. For more traditional gifts, old-line Georgetowners prefer **Little Caledonia** (1419 Wisconsin Avenue, NW; (202) 333-4700).

Just off M Street near the Key Bridge park, in an alley at 33rd street, the **Cady Alley** complex holds a number of high-end furnishings stores, luxury bath fitters, kitchen specialists, and even antique marble floors from the Holy Land. But the specialty collector fascinated by late 19th- and early 20th-century decorative arts will find a paradise on M Street; see "Decorative Arts," page 350.

Adams-Morgan and U Street

Historically, Adams-Morgan and U Street (or the "new-U" neighborhood, as it's known now) had little connection. Adams-Morgan began as a wealthy white residential area adjoining the still-exclusive Kalorama but, with "white flight" to the suburbs after the unrest of the 1960s, emerged as the heart of the Hispanic and then Ethiopian communities. Over the past 15 or 20 years, it has developed into an eclectic nightlife and dining area, especially along 18th Street. U Street, though at the north end of the Shaw neighborhood, was the closest thing Washington had to a Harlem, thanks to its national-circuit jazz and vaudeville venues and the proximity of Howard University. An even more direct victim of the riots, it had sadly deteriorated and only began to revive a decade ago, thanks partly to some timely government investment and partly to a wave of young couples willing to invest in renovating the old townhouses as restaurants and small businesses.

In recent years, these two ethnically heterogenous areas have become increasingly popular with younger, hip, and international crowds. Three even more encouraging developments—the emergence of 14th Street as a center for small theaters and of U Street for nightclubs; the opening of the U Street-Cardozo subway station; and the commercial ripple effects from the construction of the MCI Center sports/entertainment arena and the new Convention Center to the south—have increased that area's visibility and pedestrian traffic even more. And thanks to their hip, entrepeneurial habituees, Adams Morgan and U Street are becoming intriguing window-shopping destinations as well.

Although the two neighborhoods have not completely met in the middle, they are beginning to send out tendrills of development toward one another. (However, the area can still be somewhat edgy late at night.)

In between Adams-Morgan's melting pot of restaurants (and its quite serious and expensive antique stores) are African and Hispanic (and Rasta) clothing stores and craft boutiques, racks of Mexican wedding dresses, religious icons, and perhaps a medicinal herb or two. **Ampofo** (18th and Belmont streets, NW; (202) 387-1069) is half-collection, half-shop; sometimes owner Heather Ampofo can scarcely bear to part with the African masks, chairs, crafts, and textiles she acquires.

For SoHo bohos, **Niagara** (2423 18th Street, NW; (202) 332-7474) is a cavern club for the label-conscious, a basement-level boutique of designs from Milk Fed (Sofia Coppola) and scents from Demeter (including "Altoids" and "Bourbon"). A few doors up is **All About Jane** (2438 18th Street; (202) 797-9710), stocking tees for the too-too trendy.

For architectural remnants—mantels, stained or leaded glass windows, chandeliers, door handles, and columns—check out the **Brass Knob** (2311 18th Street, NW; (202) 332-3370); the **Brass Knob Backdoors Warehouse** a parking lot away (2329 Champlain Street, NW; (202) 265-0587), which holds the clawfoot tubs, radiators, and sinks; and the innovative furnishings at the four-story **Skynear & Co.** (2122 18th Street, NW; (202) 797-7160), which stocks hand-painted pillows, repro armoires and red China cabinets, whimsical wrought iron, acrobatic light fixtures, and the like. (The Gen-X, smart-set stuff is in the basement.)

And although it's a little south of the main drag, **Simply Home** (1811-B 18th Street, NW; (202) 986-8607) is anything but the suburban catalogue shop it sounds; it's a Thai famly business, and the direct Bangkok-to-D.C. wares include silk throws, bamboo rice bowls, ceramics, chopsticks, and even cabinets.

Four blocks east of Simply Home are **Home Rule** (1807 14th Street, NW; (202) 797-5544), one of those shops that has figured out that home accessories don't have to be humorless, and **Go Mama Go!** (1809 14th Street, NW; (202) 299-0850), which stocks smaller-scale but eye-catching ethnically-flavored furnishings perfect for the chic dorm room, condo, or loft. A block north, **McKay's Antiques** (1902 14th Street, NW; (202) 265-4345) tends to focus on the small accents, while **Ruff & Ready** (1908 14th Street, NW; (202) 667-7833) is a more old-fashioned neighborhood antique store, which also offers increasingly desirable garden antiques.

The heaviest concentration of stores along U Street is between 16th and 13th streets, where the entrance to the subway is. **Urban Essentials** (1330 U Street, NW; (202) 299-0640) puts the emphasis on "urban," as in cool: a soft drink machine-turned-CD rack, modular storage containers, mod-design home office pieces, etc. **Goodwood** (1428 U Street, NW; (202) 986-3640), on the other hand, says "country," specializing in nineteenth-century Anerican furniture, including Arts & Crafts andirons and stained glass, but at Sunday auction prices.

Habitat (1510 U Street, NW; (202) 518-7222) deals in primarily Mexican crafts and jewels. The gifts and collectibles at **Weathered Classics** (1517 U Street, NW; (202) 238-0404) aren't faux-weathered (and aren't generally "weathered" at all) but a mix of old and new, Mission and modern. The African and African-American decorative arts and accessories, sculpture, and ceremonial items at **Zawadi Gallery** (1524 U Street, NW; (202) 232-2214), like those as Ampofo, range from the fine and expensive to the simply attractive and affordable. **Millennium Decorative Arts** (1528 U Street, NW; (202) 483-1218) is one of several retro-kitsch shops (and eateries) in new-U, mixing Waring blenders and fondue pots with the real retro stuff such as Eames chairs and a Saarinen pedestal table.

Fans of vintage clothing and accessories in the 1950s–1970s range should cruise the three stories at **Meep's** (1520 U Street NW; (202) 265-6546). And for moderate-income Imeldas, **Wild Women Wear Red** specializes in what it calls "funky, functional footwear for women," striking but well-made shoes, sandals, and boots at affordable prices (1512 U Street NW; (202) 387-5700).

Note than some of the shops in the U Street neighborhood are open only on weekends or toward the latter part of the week.

Dupont Circle

Dupont Circle is for shoppers looking to enrich the mind—it's full of art galleries, espresso bars, and bookstores (see "Specialty Shops"). Most of these are on the north side of the circle: The art galleries are generally clustered along R Street in the two blocks just west of Connecticut Avenue (leading you gently toward the **Phillips Collection**). The **Chao Phraya Gallery** (2009 Columbia Road, a half-block east of Connecticut Avenue; (202) 745-1111), showing Chinese and Southeast Asian art and antiques, is a few blocks north.

West of the circle near the Phillips Collection is the **Geoffrey Diner Gallery** (1730 21st Street, NW; (202) 483-5005), which specializes in American and British arts and crafts furniture, including Stickley and Mission, and Deco and Nouveau pieces. **Affrica** (2010½ R Street, NW; (202) 745-7272) offers African textiles, masks, figurines, and currency. **Marston-Luce** (1314 21st Street, NW; (202) 333-6800) is a Francophile's dream, but open by appointment only. (Their Georgetown store at 1651 Wisconsin Avenue is open to the public.)

South of the circle, on Connecticut Avenue, NW, between N and K Streets, are high-end retailers such as **Ralph Lauren Polo; Burberry's; Hugo Boss; Zoran; Betsey Fisher; Rizik's;** a prominent local women's shop, **Pampillonia Jewelers,** which specializes in antique and estate pieces; and a branch of London's **Thomas Pink** haberdasher in the Mayflower Hotel. There is also a fine estate jewelry shop called the **Tiny Jewel Box,** and just over at 18th and M is **Alan Marcus & Co.** (1200 18th Street, NW, 10th floor; (202) 331-0671), which discounts big name watches, pens, crystal, and silver.

Chevy Chase

At the northwest edge of D.C., where it blends into Montgomery County, Maryland, well-heeled shoppers love the stretch of Wisconsin Avenue from about Jenifer Street to Park Avenue. With two malls—**Mazza Gallerie** and **Chevy Chase Pavilion**—and lots of freestanding boutiques, there is much browsing and spending to do. Among the shops are: **Neiman Marcus, Jackie Chalkley, Gazelle** (a great spot for wearable art), **Joan and David, Pottery Barn, Tiffany, Lord & Taylor, Saks Fifth Avenue, Saks-Jandel** and **Rosendorf-Evans** furriers, **Gucci, Versace, The Right Stuff, Cartier,** and other couture clothiers (see "Designer Clothing," page 351). There are also jewelry and antique shops.

Bethesda

Bethesda, Maryland, which is just beyond Chevy Chase, has become not only one of the major restaurant centers in the Washington area but also a magnet area for fine rugs, art and antiques, books, tobacconists, vintage and consignment clothing (which, in an area as prosperous as this, means everything from faux pearls to furs), and trendy home furnishings. **Urban Country** (7801 Woodmont Avenue; (301) 654-0500) is crammed with painted, faux-distressed, and gilded furniture, desktop accessories, ceramics, linens, glass, and flatware; they also custom-upholster. But these days, the Bethesda boomers, like those in Adams-Morgan, are generally looking East. Just across the street from Urban Country, at 4827 Fairmont Avenue, is **Tribal Arts,** selling decorative pieces from Central Asia. **Ancient Rhythms,** about two blocks away (7920 Woodmont Avenue; (301) 652-2669) specializes in Southeast Asian (particularly Phillipine and Indonesian) and African-style furniture, jewelry, tapestry, and accessories of wood, art paper, and metalwork. Similarly opulent and/or "primitive" furnishings from Turkey, Nepal, the Balkans, India, and China fill the nearby **Terra Cognita** (7920 Norfolk Avenue; (301) 907-3055). Across from that is **Foreign Accents** (7917 Norfolk Avenue; (301) 294-9292), which deals in goods from Greece and trendy Monaco. **Muleh** (4731 Elm Street; (301) 941-1174) offers both real and reproduction antiques from Africa, Southeast Asia, and the Middle East. **Watana Rosewood Furniture** (4715 Cordell Avenue; (301) 656-0400) is another direct-from-the-Thai-in-laws operation. And **Bartley Tile Concepts** (6931 Arlington Road; (301) 913-9113) sells hand-painted tiles, marble, and slate, both new and salvaged. **Lomay-Schnitzel Antiques** (6826 Wisconsin Avenue; (301) 656-1911) is an old and respected source of English, French, and continental pieces, both original and fine reproduction.

Among art galleries are **Allyson Louis** (7200 Wisconsin Avenue; (301) 656-2877); **Capricorn Galleries** (10236 River Road; (301) 765-5900); and **Marin-Price** (7022 Wisconsin Avenue; (301) 718-0622). Particularly fine art glass is available—one might almost say on exhibit—at the **Glass Gallery** (4720 Hampden Lane; (301) 657-3478). **ZYZYX** mixes and matches art glass and ceramics with better production pieces (10301-A Old Georgetown Road; (301) 493-0297).

Capitol Hill

On Capitol Hill most shops are in the vicinity of Eastern Market—an actual market where vendors set up tables selling produce, baked goods, and flea market bric-a-brac—located on 7th Street between Pennsylvania and Independence Avenues, SE. There, amid the restaurants and bars, are secondhand clothing shops and first-rate crafts stores. Around the old Eastern Market building on 8th just north of Pennsylvania Avenue, you can browse through a variety of antiques stores and boutiques, as well as farmers' produce and fresh poultry stands. There's a pottery co-op upstairs at the Market itself.

Old Town Alexandria

Old Town Alexandria, Virginia, is a walker's delight, too, with shops clustered up, down, and around King Street, most of them selling antiques, crafts, and home furnishings. Wayne Fisher's **American Design** (114 South Royal Street; (703) 836-6043) specializes in charming old toys, pottery, tools, and painted wood ornaments as well as furniture. This trendy indoor-outdoor look is spotlighted at **Egerton Gardens** (1117 King Street; (703) 548-1197).

Other good poking-around spots include **Random Harvest** (810 King Street; (703) 548-8820), **Wooden Village Teak** (1218 King Street; (703) 299-5033), the **Old Colony Shop** (222-B South Washington Street; (703) 548-8008), and **Robert Bentley Adams** (405 South Washington Street; (703) 549-0650).

Specialty Shops

Antiques

Serious antique-seekers get out of town—driving an hour or more to the countryside of Maryland, Virginia, West Virginia, or Pennsylvania for the bargains. Frederick, Maryland, about an hour north of Washington, is particularly popular with area antiquers. The biggest single group is at the 125-dealer **Emporium Antiques** (112 East Patrick Street, Frederick; (301) 662-7099), though walking the Main Street neighborhood and the streets just off it will turn up plenty of others. But you will find treasures—though few bargains—in and around Washington. The largest concentration of such shops is on **"Antique Row"** in Kensington, Maryland, about four miles from the D.C. line. There are more than 50 antique dealers on **Howard Avenue,** with smaller shops east of Connecticut Avenue and larger warehouses west of Connecticut. **Sparrows** (4115 Howard Avenue; (301) 530-0175) specializes in late eighteenth- to early nineteenth-century French and French Revival pieces, including fine Deco and Nouveau. **Paris-Kensington** specializes in smaller bronze figurines, clocks, silver, and porcelain. **Desbois Antiques de France** (4080B Howard Avenue; (301) 897-9560) take the formal approach, as does **Huret Antiques** (4106 Howard Avenue; (301) 530-7551) which helpfully explains its periods, rules, epochs, and styles for less practiced customers. **J'antiques** (10429 Fawcett Street; (301) 942-0936) offers silver flatware and filigree, fine estate jewelry, and Limoges. Not surprisingly, there's even a restaurant called Cafe Monet.

In Georgetown and Alexandria, you'll find a variety of shops selling collectibles from the past three centuries. Among Georgetown's best (in geographically ascending order) are **Gore-Dean Antiques** (1529 Wisconsin Avenue, NW; (202) 625-1776); **David Bell Antiques** (1655 Wisconsin Avenue; (202) 965-2355); and **Miller & Arney** (1737 Wisconsin Avenue; (202) 338-2369). One Georgetown favorite is **Christ Child Opportunity Shop** (1427 Wisconsin Avenue, NW; (202) 333-6635), where, on the second floor, you'll find silver, china, paintings, and other cherishables on consignment from the best Georgetown homes. (See the neighborhood profiles earlier in this part.)

The best antiques in Alexandria are in **Old Town** along Washington Street and in the 4000 block of King Street: Check out **Studio Antiques & Fine Art** (524 North Washington Street; (703) 548-5253), and **Washington Square Antiques** (689 South Washington Street; (703) 836-3214). The **Thieves' Market** in Alexandria (8101 Richmond Highway; (703) 360-4200) has scores of booths with good used rugs, antique furniture, and jewelry.

Art

One of the city's most concentrated selection of art for sale—traditional, modern, photographic, and ethnic—can be found around Dupont Circle. The best are centered on a sort of crossraods of Connecticut Avenue and R Street and spreads a couple of blocks in each direction, especially R Street around 20th and 21st Streets, where there are a dozen galleries within two blocks. Gallery openings are generally on the first Friday of the month.

However, a renaissance of independent artists and co-ops has made the 7th Street area just north of Pennsylvania Avenue the SoHo of D.C. Among the important stops are the **Zenith Gallery** (413 7th Street, NW; (202) 783-2963), which specializes in photography, new art, and neon; the **Touchstone Co-op** (406 7th Street, NW; (202) 347-2787); and the **Lansburg Building** (406 7th Street, NW), a former department store that has been transformed into a three-story assortment of art and photography spaces. The 7th Street neighborhood opens every third Thursday of the month for a free gallery crawl; meet at the in the lobby of the Goethe-Institute (814 7th Stree NW; (202) 661-7589) at 6:30 p.m.

Similarly, the art galleries of **Canal Square** in Georgetown stay open late every third Friday, with jazz and hors d'oeuvres and wine for patrons. Another popular source for art is the **Torpedo Factory Art Center** in Old Town Alexandria (105 N. Union Street; (703) 838-4565), where 150 artists in a range of media—painting, sculpture, jewelry, and more—have set up studios. You can buy their work, or simply watch them create. For the gallery-cafe tours of Old Town, which are on the second Thursday of each month, gather at Gallery West at 205 S. Union Street.

Bargains

Washington may have its million-dollar houses, expense-account restaurants, and pricey private schools, but it also has a surprising number of discount outlets. Savvy shoppers never pay full price for their Coach bags, their Lancôme cosmetics, or their Polo dress shirts.

Nowadays, even the relatively affluent D.C. area is surrounded by big-name, bargain-price supermalls. To the south is **Potomac Mills Mall** in Dale City, VA—one of the world's largest outlet malls. Just 45 minutes south of D.C., off I-95, this 250-store mall (phone (800) VA-MILLS) gets more visitors each year than any other Virginia tourist attraction—even more than Colonial Williamsburg. It's nearly impossible to hit all of the stores, which include the popular **IKEA** (Swedish furniture store) and outlets for **Nordstrom, Eddie Bauer, Guess, Ann Taylor, Saks Off Fifth, Gap, Polo, Athlete's Foot, Brooks Brothers,** and **Benetton.**

To the west, perhaps 15 or 20 minutes past the various Tysons Corner malls at the intersection of Route 7 and the Route 15 Bypass is the **Leesburg Corner Premium Outlets** (241 Fort Evans Road, NE; (703) 737-

3071), a closet-heavy complex whose more famous designer names include **BCBG Max Aria, Bebe, Cole Haan, DKNY, Geoffrey Beene, Tommy Hilfiger, Polo Ralph Lauren, Kenneth Cole, Greg Norman, Perry Ellis, Kasper** and **Liz Claiborne,** along with **Jones New York, Barneys, Saks Off Fifth, Burberry, Movado,** and **Seiko.**

And northeast of town, off the Baltimore-Washington Parkway or Route 110 east of I-95, is **Arundel Mills** (7000 Arundel Mills Circle, Hanover, Maryland; (410) 540-5100). More than a million square feet of name brands that echo the other two but trump them with a 24-theater cinema you can park the kids at and a full-sized **Bass Pro Shops Outdoor World,** where you can exhaust them on the rock climbing wall.

If you can't make it to the suburbs except by Metro, Washington now has its first inside-the-Beltway off-price mall, **City Place** in Silver Spring, Maryland (phone (301) 589-1091). At the intersection of Colesville Road (Route 29) and Fenton Street, three blocks north of the Silver Spring Metro (red line), City Place's best assets are **Nordstrom Rack, Marshalls,** and its shoe outlets.

Bookstores

It's little wonder Washingtonians are well read: Almost everywhere you look, there is a bookstore. There are general-interest chains like **B. Dalton** and **Borders,** but the majority are small independents, many with narrow specialties such as art, travel, Russian literature, or mystery.

If you're in a book-browsing mood, you might take the red line to Dupont Circle or the orange line to Farragut West. Between these two Metro stops, along and just off Connecticut Avenue between S and I Streets, are some of the city's best bookstores. Walking south from S Street, NW, toward Dupont Circle, you'll hit the **Newsroom,** with an exhaustive stock of foreign-language periodicals (1803 Connecticut Avenue, NW; (202) 332-1489); **Lambda Rising,** a gay/lesbian bookshop (1625 Connecticut Avenue, NW; (202) 462-6969); and **Kramerbooks,** a bookstore and cafe that's quite the scene on weekends, when it's open 24 hours (1517 Connecticut Avenue, NW; (202) 387-1400). Right off the circle on P Street you'll find **Second Story Books,** a terrific source for used books (2000 P Street, NW; (202) 659-8884); and **Backstage,** which sells scripts and performing arts books (545 8th Street, SE; (202) 544-5744). Down side streets you can seek out **Olsson's Books and Records,** the city's most beloved general-interest book source, with a selective but broad inventory (1307 19th Street, NW; (202) 785-1133). One of the **Books-a-Million** stores is also on Dupont Circle between New Hampshire Avenue and P Street at about one o'clock (phone (202) 319-1374); it discounts the current *New York Times* hard- and paperback bestsellers at 30% off retail price.

Over by Farragut West you'll find volumes on the visual arts at **Franz Bader** (1911 I Street, NW; (202) 337-5440); travel guides at **The ADC Map Store** (1636 I Street, NW; (202) 628-2608); and literary criticism, biography, poetry, and a good general stock, as well as frequent Saturday afternoon readings at **Chapters** (1512 K Street, NW; (202) 347-5495). There is a fairly large **Borders** on L Street at 19th Street, though not as overwhelming as the flagship store in White Flint Mall; and a three-decker **Barnes and Noble** store, one of several recently opened in the Washington area, in Georgetown at M and 21st Streets.

And even Washingtonians tend to overlook the **Government Printing Office Bookstore,** which carries more than 15,000 books, pamphlets, and CD-ROMs as well as books of photographs—and sometimes the real things—from the Library of Congress (710 North Capitol Street; (202) 512-0132).

Another specialty bookstore can be found farther north on Connecticut Avenue, in the neighborhood known as Chevy Chase. **Politics & Prose** specializes in psychology, politics, and the works of local authors—and hosts many of their book-signing parties (5015 Connecticut Avenue, NW; (202) 364-1919), and in the Tenleytown Metro neighborhood is **Travel Books and Language Center** (4437 Wisconsin Avenue, NW; (202) 237-1322).

Decorative Arts

The south side of M Street between 28th and 30th Streets, NW, in Georgetown offers a staggering array of antiques and decorative arts, particularly rich in Art Deco, Art Nouveau, and Moderne pieces. **The Galerie Lareuse** (2820 Pennsylvania Avenue; (202) 338-1097) is a fine art gallery that specializes in twentieth-century prints and lithographs by Picasso, Miró, etc. At **Justine Mehlman** (2824 Pennsylvania Avenue; (202) 337-0613), you'll find silver, pewter and glass, and ceramic vases, the majority of them attributed, from Liberty arts and crafts and Nouveau artists; plus fine Victorian rings and earrings, enamel, intaglio, and even Bakelite.

Janis Aldridge, Inc. swings around the corner of 29th and M (2900 M Street, NW; (202) 338-7710), displaying floral paintings and still-lifes, handpainted furniture, tapestry cushions, and folk art as well as fine furniture. **Grafix** (2904 M Street, NW; (202) 342-0610) sells vintage posters—including Art Nouveau and Deco examples, antique hand-tinted maps, and collectible prints and illustration plates. A partitioned townhouse at 2918 M Street, NW, features **Michael Getz** (phone (202) 338-3811) and **Cherub Gallery** (phone (202) 337-2224) and gathers a collection of works by such artists and studios as Tiffany, Lalique, Daum, and Icart. Here you can find heavy wrought andirons, ivory-handled fish services and magnifying glasses, cream pitchers and perfume bottles, elegant cocktail shakers, nymphic candelabra, and ornate photo frames. In the back room is the largest collection of silver napkin rings outside a melting pot. **Keith Lipert** (2922 M Street, NW; (202) 965-9736) also displays art, glass, and silver, but its emphasis is on enamelware, ceramics, and heavier pieces.

Designer Clothing

In the free-spending 1980s, couture clothiers couldn't open shops fast enough in the Washington area. While the 1980s may be gone, most of the boutiques remain. And most are in "Gucci Gulch"—a row of chic shops extending from the 5200 to 5500 blocks of Wisconsin Avenue, from the upper edge of the District of Columbia right into Montgomery County, Maryland. Among the boutiques: **Saks Jandel, Hugo Boss, Jaeger, Georgette Klinger, Elizabeth Arden, Cartier, Saks Fifth Avenue, Relish, Versace, Harriet Kassman, Joan and David,** and **Gianfranco Ferre.** Also note the estate jewelry and silver at **Heller Jewelers.**

Virginia, too offers designer wares. Here, the gold-card crowd heads to **Fairfax Square,** a mall on Leesburg Pike in Tysons Corner that is home to **Tiffany & Company, Gucci, Fendi, Hermès,** and **Louis Vuitton.**

In the District proper, the grand old **Willard Hotel** on Pennsylvania Avenue, NW, houses a set of shops that includes **Chanel** and **Jackie Chalkley,** good for crafty clothing and art jewelry. Or try **Rizik's** at the corner of Connecticut Avenue and L Street for establishment-women's couture.

Insider Shops

Although the White House, the House of Representatives, and even Camp David have monogrammed and souvenir merchandise, it's available only to special staff. Outsiders who want to look like Washington insiders do have a few options, however.

The **NASA Exchange** gift shop (300 E Street, SW; (202) 358-0162) is for astronaut wannabes. It is open Monday to Friday, 8:15 a.m. to 4 p.m (closed during lunch, 1–2 p.m.).

A different sort of insider store is the **Counter Spy Shop** (1027 Connecticut Avenue, NW; (202) 887-1717), which has tiny cameras, bugging and taping trackers, night vision scopes, and protective clothing. Just look mysterious.

Museum Shops

Some of Washington's greatest finds are in its museum gift shops. A museum's orientation is a good guide to its shop's merchandise—prints and art books fill the **National Gallery of Art** shop; model airplanes and other toys of flight are on sale at the **Air and Space Museum.** The largest Smithsonian shops are at the **Museum of American History,** which sells toys, clothing, musical instruments, and recordings from countries highlighted in the exhibits; although all the museums have some items reflecting the collection.

Some good museum shops are often overlooked by tourists. The **National Building Museum** shop (phone (202) 272-2448), which sells design-related books, jewelry, and gadgets; the **Arts and Industries** shop (phone (202) 357-2700), a pretty, Victorian setting stocked with Smithsonian reproductions; the **Department of the Interior Museum's Indian Craft Shop** (phone (202) 208-4056), which sells one-of-a-kind creations at the museum and in Georgetown Park Mall; the **National Museum of African Art** shop (phone (202) 357-4600), a bazaar filled with colorful cloth and wooden ceremonial instruments such as hand drums and tambourines; the **Arthur M. Sackler Gallery** shop (phone (202) 357-4600), with cases full of brass Buddhas, Chinese lacquerware, jade and jasper jewelry, and porcelain; the **Renwick** shop, which stocks unusual art jewelry; the Shakespeare-lovers' treasure trove at the **Folger Library** (phone (202) 544-4600); and the newly expanded shop at the **John F. Kennedy Center for the Performing Arts** (phone (202) 357-4608), stocked with videos, opera glasses, and other gifts for performing arts lovers.

The **Decatur House Museum** (phone (202) 842-1856)has patriotic souvenirs emphasizing American history and architecture, and the expanded shop at **Mount Vernon** (phone (703) 799-6301)offers reproductions of Martha's cookbook, George's key to the Bastille, and period china and silver pattern's.

Oriental Rugs

Washington, D.C., offers the broadest selection of handmade oriental rugs available in the United States. In fact, there is so much competition here that prices are forced below what you would expect to pay for comparable quality in other American cities. Though shops are sprinkled all around the greater Washington area, the biggest concentration of reputable stores is located on Wisconsin Avenue from Friendship Heights to Bethesda.

Political Memorabilia

If you're a serious collector, no doubt you already know about stores selling political buttons and ribbons, autographed letters and photos, and commemorative plates and pens. If you're not a collector, these shops can be as fun to browse through as museums, except that you can touch things, buy them, and take them home. Two such shops, within walking distance of one another, are **Capitol Coin and Stamp** (1701 L Street, NW; (202) 296-0400) and **Political Americana** (1331 Pennsylvania Avenue, NW; (202) 737-7730), which also has a branch inside Union Station. **The Honest Abe Souvenir Company** (F and 10th Streets, NW; (202) 347-1021) has all sorts of Washingtonia, from tiny busts of Martin Luther King to D.C. snow globes and Georgetown T-shirts.

Prints and Photography

Although most dealers in fine photos are in Georgetown, one of the most prominent is the **Kathleen Ewing Gallery** (1609 Connecticut Avenue, NW, Suite 200; (202) 328-0955). Otherwise, visit the **Robert Brown Gallery** (2030 R Street, NW; (202) 483-4383); the **Ralls Collection** (1516 31st Street, NW; (202) 342-1754); and the **Govinda Gallery** (1227 34th Street, NW; (202) 333-1180), which specializes in photographs of and by rock 'n' rollers, from Annie Leibovitz to onetime Beatle-turned-artist Stu Sutcliffe and his photographer girlfriend Astrid Kirchherr. For prints and works on paper, visit the **Georgetown Gallery of Art** (3235 P Street, NW; (202) 333-6308); **Hemphill Fine Arts** (1027 33rd Street, NW; (202) 342-5610); and the **Spectrum Gallery** (1132 29th Street, NW; (202) 333-0954). For antique maps, botanical prints, and vintage cartoons, try the **Old Print Gallery,** also in Georgetown (1220 31st Street, NW; (202) 965-1818).

Salon Products

Although it seems as if every mall now has a Body Shop and several imitators, for the good stuff think about Georgetown: **Aveda** has a huge new spa/salon/store around the corner (1325 Wisconsin Avenue, NW; (202) 965-1325), offering body products from toners to massage oils, all made of only plant products—no artificial scents or coloring and no animal testing—and scented with the likes of rosemary, cinnamon, sesame, and almond oils. Soaps, bath salts, and oils are available by the ounce or bottle, not to mention facials, scrubs, and massages. There's sort of a "triptych" of cosmetic stores on M Street, starting with **MAC** (3067 M Street, NW; (202) 944-9771). **Blue Mercury** (3059 M Street, NW; (202) 965-1300) is both a spa and a Merle Norman for the new millennium, stocked with custom creams, exotic oils, and lipsticks named for film stars. Also, try the very hot French chain **Sephora,** where you can try on nearly a hundred brands of lipstick (3065 M Street; (202) 338-5644).

Watches

Washington's answer to Tourneau is **Alan Marcus & Co.**, which offers up to 50% off on Rolex, Patek Philippe, and Cartier, plus Lalique and Baccarat crystal and Montblanc pens (1200 18th Street, NW, Fifth Floor; (202) 331-0671).

Wine and Gourmet Foods

Georgetown has a branch of New York's famed **Dean & Deluca** (3276 M street, NW; (202) 342-2500), complete with cafe. **Mayflower Wines** joined forces with the **Sutton Place Gourmet** shops in 1992 to provide one-stop, fine-food shops in the greater Washington area. Each shop offers an excellent selection of wines and an impressive variety of gourmet and ethnic foods. The wine buyers travel abroad each year to select the stores' wine inventory and are particularly tuned in to Italian reds. Visitors to the stores from outside the District, Virginia, and Maryland can buy wine and have it shipped home. If you do not have time to shop in person, the **Sutton Place Gourmet** publishes a newsletter describing highly touted (and reasonably priced) wines. The newsletter also includes recipes. To receive the free newsletter call (301) 564-6006.

Another fine wine store, which invests in wine futures and offers a strong catalog, is **MacArthur Liquors** (4877 MacArthur Boulevard, NW; (202) 338-1433) in the Palisades neighborhood west of Georgetown. It's worth remembering that because of tax laws, wine for consumption is less expensive in stores like this within the District than in stores just over the border in Maryland or Virginia. Originally owned by the well-liked purveyor Addy Bassin, **MacArthur** is still often called "Bassin's" by Washington natives.

The family that brought you Crown Books and Trak Auto also owns a mega–wine and liquor warehouse line called **Total Beverage,** which has three Virginia stores, including one at the already bargain-heavy Potomac Mills. However, unless you plan to purchase in real bulk, you may do just as well in town Ther is no tax on alcohol in the District, making it a bargain compared to most jurisdictions.

Writing Implements

Fahrney's Pens (1317 F Street, NW; (202) 628-9525) has all the write stuff: For more than 70 years, Fahrney's has sold nothing but beautiful pens, including Watermans and Mont Blancs. White Flint Mall has a smaller shop but one well versed in the instant unblocking of recalcitrant fountain pens, **Bertram's Inkwell** (phone (301) 468-6936).

Part Ten

Entertainment and Nightlife

Washington Nightlife: More Than Lit-Up Monuments

Washington after-hours used to be an oxymoron. Public transportation set its clock by the bureaucracy, commuters had too far to go (and come back the next morning) to stay out late, and big expense account money was lavished on restaurants and buddy bars. Besides, Washingtonians suffered from a persistent cultural inferiority complex that had them running to buy tickets to see touring theatrical companies while not-so-benignly neglecting homegrown troupes.

Nowadays, though, the joke about "Washington after-hours" being an oxymoron is just that: a joke. It's not that there's too little nightlife around, it's that there's too much. Or too many. Washington is a polyglot of big-city bustlers, yuppies, diplomats, immigrants, CEOs, and college students; and every one of these groups is trying to create, and then integrate, their own circles. The fact that many overlap, and others evolve, means you can dabble in a little of everything.

Washington's legitimate theatrical community is underestimated but excellent; ballet, Broadway, and cabaret are almost constant presences, opera less so but increasingly frequent. At least some of the racetracks are open year-round; there are major- and minor-league sports teams at play in every season (see the "Spectator Sports" section). And nightclubs come in as many flavors as their patrons: discos, live music venues, comedy showcases, country dance halls, specialty bars, sports bars, espresso bars, singles scenes, and "second scenes" for re-entering singles. There are even a couple of strip joints around for boys' night sentimentalists and brewpubs for beer connoisseurs.

Just in the last couple of years, a kind of nightclub renaissance has revitalized whole neighborhoods, a shift that has been particularly visible downtown in areas that once were nearly deserted after rush hour, or at least after cocktail hour. The MCI Centre has sparked a development boom downtown; the "New U" corridor that originally centered on 14th and U Streets NW (and which now stretches to 9th or 10th) has begun to merge with the small-theatre strip, adding balance and interest. Adams-Morgan has regained vitality, thanks in part to the shift from Eurotrash posing to mambo-savvy swingers.

Among the more important musical addresses in the New U are the **9:30** club, the **Chi Cha Lounge,** and the **Black Cat** (all profiled); **Cada Vez** (1438 U Street, NW; (202) 667-2500); or for jazz swingers, **Utopia** (1418 U Street, NW; (202) 483-7669); **HR-57** (1610 14th Street, NW; (202) 667-3700); and on concert nights, the **Lincoln Theater** (1215 U Street, NW; (202) 328-6000). For being-scenery, there are **Bar Nun** (1327 U Street, NW; (202) 667-6680), with its soul and funk music but quiet storm alcoves; the **Saint** (1520 14th Street, NW; (202) 234-0886); **Republic Gardens** (1355 U Street, NW; (202) 232-2710); **Diversite** (1526 14th Street, NW; (202) 234-5740); and **Club U** (2000 14th Street, NW; (202) 3287-8859).

Adams-Morgan is a moveable feast, starting with **Rumba Cafe** (2443 18th Street, NW; (202) 588-5501) and moving toward the three-level **Heaven/Hell** (2327 18th Street, NW; (202) 667-4355); the multi-purpose restaurant/lounge **Felix** (2406 18th Street, NW; (202) 483-3549) and the even more ambitious culinary expeditions of the ever-changing **Cities** (2424 18th Street, NW; (202) 328-7194); the deep-dive **Dan's Cafe** (2315 18th Street, NW; (202) 265-9241); the 1950s gas station–look **Toledo Lounge** (2435 18th Street, NW; (202) 986-5416); the aptly named coffeehouse-bar hangout **Tryst** (2459 18th Street, NW; (202) 232-5500); **Madam's Organ**, with live blues, R&B, or bluegrass nightly (2461 18th Street, NW; (202) 667-5370); the **Blue Room** (2321 18th Street, NW; (202) 332-0800); salsa clasroom **Latin Jazz Alley** (1721 Columbia Road, NW; (202) 328-6190); the quintessential beer hall–basement rec room goof **Chief Ike's Mambo Room**, which also attracts one of the most (age, sex, and race) mixed crowds in town (1725 Columbia Road, NW; (202) 332-2211); **Pharmacy Bar** (2337 18th Street, NW; (202) 483-1200); **Habana Village** (1834 Columbia Road, NW; (202) 462-6310); and many others. Actually, you might end up back at the Bottom end for late-night refueling at the 18th and U Street **Duplex Diner** (phone (202) 265-7828.

Even more impressive is the millennial revival of downtown Connecticut Avenue, long a strictly commercial-business area, and one that regularly defeated attempts to go outside the expense-account restaurant envelope. These days, the five-star intersection at Connecticut, M, Jefferson and 18th Streets, NW, marks the junction of **MCCXXIII** and **Ozio** (both profiled); the swank all-white and sushi-chic (and smoker-friendly) hybrid dance hall **Dragonfly** (1215 Connecticut Avenue, NW; (202) 331-1775), **Andalus** (1214 18th Street, NW; (202) 785-9525), **Lucky Bar** (1221 Connecticut Avenue, NW; (202) 331-3733), **Club Five** (1214-B 18th Street, NW; (202) 331-7123); the underground bordello-decor **Red** (1802 Jefferson Place, NW; (202) 466-3475); **5** (1214-B 18th Street, NW; (202) 331-7123); and the **18th Street Lounge** (1212 18th Street, NW; (202) 466-3922). Sesto Senso, the designer-chic Italian restaurant above Andalus, just seems part of the complex. And if all that's too much for you, just turn up the street to the intentionally retro beer-bar **Big Hunt** (1345 Connecticut Avenue, NW; (202) 785-2333).

Live entertainment in Washington can be divided into three categories: legitimate theater, comedy, and live rock/pop/jazz/country music. The club profiles that follow focus on live music, comedy clubs, discos/dance clubs, and noteworthy after-hours scenes because they generally require no advance planning. (In some cases, live music venues might sell out particular performances, so call ahead.) Nightly schedules of live music clubs, comedy clubs, and theatrical productions, as well as listings of piano rooms, opera companies, movie showtimes, etc., are printed in the *Washington Post* Friday "Weekend" section and the free *Washington City Paper.*

Legitimate Theater

Washington boasts six major theatrical venues (ten if you count the Kennedy Center's five stages separately) and more than a half-dozen smaller residential and repertory companies, plus university theaters, small special-interest venues, and itinerant troupes. The Big Six are where national touring companies, classical musicians, and celebrity productions are most apt to show up, and they have the most complete facilities for handicapped patrons. They are also likely to be the most expensive.

On any given night at the **Kennedy Center for the Performing Arts,** you might see the resident National Symphony Orchestra under Leonard Slatkin or a visiting philharmonic in the 2,500-seat Concert Hall; a straight drama or classic farce in the 1,100-seat Eisenhower Theater; and a Broadway musical, kabuki spectacular, or premier cru ballet company in the 2,300-seat Opera House. The two smaller arenas, Terrace Theater and Theater Lab, share the third floor with the restaurant (which has a nice view if you can get it) and archives. Philip Johnson's steeply canted and gracious Terrace, a gift from the nation of Japan, houses experimental or cult-interest productions, specialty concerts, and showcases; in the Theater Lab, designed to accommodate the avant and cabaret, the semi-improvised murder farce *Sheer Madness* is halfway through its second decade. The Kennedy Center is at Virginia and New Hampshire Avenues, NW, next to the Watergate; the closest subway station is Foggy Bottom, and the Center operates a free shuttle from the station. For tickets and information, call (202) 467-4600 or visit www.kennedy-center.org.

The **National Theatre,** which was thoroughly, if a little showily, restored in Miami heat pastels a few years ago, is managed by the Shubert Organization, which not only books its touring Broadway productions there but more and more often uses it for pre-Broadway tryouts. The National is at 1321 Pennsylvania Avenue, NW, near the Federal Triangle or Metro Center subway stop. For information, call (202) 628-6161; for tickets, call (800) 447-7400 or visit www.nationaltheatre.org.

The **Shakespeare Theatre,** which moved in 1992 from its beloved but cramped home at the Folger Shakespeare Library into new digs in the grandly renovated Lansburg Building, now seats about 450. Each season it produces four classic plays, three by Shakespeare, and regularly corrals a few major stage and screen stars to headline. It also puts on free Shakespeare at the Carter-Barron amphitheater every summer. The Shakespeare Theater is at 450 Seventh Street, NW, near the Gallery Place subway stop; for information, (202) 547-1122; TTY (202) 638-3863; www.shakespearetheatre.org.

Ford's, where the balcony box in which Abraham Lincoln was shot remains draped in black (and spectrally inhabited, according to rumor), is a smallish (750-seat) but comfy venue that hosts primarily family fare such as the annual production of Dickens's *A Christmas Carol* and musicals and revues. Ford's is at 511 10th Street, NW (Metro Center subway); (202) 347-4833; www.fordstheatre.org.

The **Warner Theatre,** which survived a two-year restoration marathon, is now a rococo delight, complete with a few special boxes with food service. Although it is emphasizing more legitimate theatrical bookings and musicals, it still occasionally harkens back to the days when it was one of the nicer small-concert venues for popular music. The Warner is at 13th and E Streets, NW, near Federal Triangle or Metro Center; for information, call (202) 783-4000.

The tripartite **Arena Stage** is the most prestigious of Washington resident companies and was a prime factor in the rebirth of American regional theater. The Fichandler theater-in-the-round seats a little over 800; the Kreeger holds more than 500; and the tiny, pubbish Old Vat Room seats fewer than 200. Though it likes to show off its versatility (such as a dizzying reenactment of the Marx Brothers' "Coconuts" or the Flying Karamazov Brothers acting in *The Brothers Karamazov*), the Arena is dedicated and fearless, producing Athol Fugard as well as Tennessee Williams. The Arena is at 6th and Maine Avenue, SW—on the waterfront, which is also the Metro station; phone (202) 488-3300 or visit www.arena-stage.org.

Although many of these professional productions can be pricey and often sell out, the Ticket Place office in the Old Post Office Pavilion at

1100 Pennsylvania Avenue, NW (Federal Triangle Metro stop), sells half-price tickets (plus a service charge amounting to 10% of the face value) for same-day shows and concerts. Cash, traveler's checks, and debit cards are accepted. The Ticket Place is open Tuesday–Saturday from 11 a.m. until 6 p.m. tickets for Sunday and Monday shows are sold on Saturday when available; call (202) 842-5387 for a list of available tickets. The Kennedy Center also sells a limited number of same-day tickets at half price and offers half-price tickets for students, seniors, military, fixed-income families, and those with permanent disabilities. For more information, call (202) 467-4600. A limited number of standing-room passes at reduced prices and occasional returned seats may be available as well. (Several other ticket vendors in the area such as Top Centre sell tickets to area concerts and sporting events, but they usually impose a large service charge.)

Washington's "off-Broadway" theaters are clustered around the revitalized 14th Street, NW, neighborhood, specializing in new and cutting-edge works. Among the most intriguing are **Source Theater Co.** (1835 14th Street, NW; (202) 462-1073); **Woolly Mammoth** (1401 Church Street, NW; (202) 393-3939), which uses the Source space; and the **Studio Theater** (14th and P Streets, NW; (202) 332-3300). The smaller **Theater J** is just a few blocks away (1529 16th Street, NW; (202) 518-9400). On the Green Line, a nearby Metro station is located at 14th and U Streets called U Street-Cardozo.

One of the strongest "small" theaters is **Signature Theatre** in Arlington, which is getting some national reviews, especially of its Sondheim productions (3806 South Four Mile Run Drive; (703) 820-9771). **Horizons Theater: From a Woman's Perspective**, also in Arlington, mixes progressive, special-interest, and even cabaret shows; call (703) 243-8550. **The Center for the Arts at George Mason University,** (703) 993-ARTS, in Fairfax; the **Roundhouse Theater** in Bethesda (East-West Highway and Wisconsin Avenue; (301) 644-1100), just by the Bethesda Metro; and the picturesque country-inn **Olney Theater** in Olney (phone (301) 924-3400) are also professional stage shows. There are a few dinner theaters in the suburbs; if you're interested, check the Guide to the Lively Arts in the *Washington Post* Friday "Weekend" or Sunday "Show" sections, or look for a copy of *Washingtonian* magazine.

In general, Washington audiences have loosened their ties when it comes to theater attire. To some extent, the more "serious" a production is, the dressier the crowd, although jeans have become ubiquitous, particularly at the smaller, avant-garde companies. Opening nights are often black tie (or "creative black tie"), but you can go as you are. And incidentally, many of the nicer restaurants near the big-ticket venues offer pre-theater menus at fixed (and bargain) prices; be sure to inquire.

Comedy in Washington

Washington is full of jokes—and that's the first one. Capital comedians divide very roughly into three generations and styles: the cabaret performers (those "Washington institutions" whose satires are usually musical and relatively gentle); the sketch and improvisational troupes from the post-Watergate *Saturday Night Live* era; and the stand-up artists who are the anti-establishment baby-busters—in some cases, the urban guerrillas. The first two groups are almost unavoidably political; the stand-up comedians range from political podium to locker room.

The most famous of the cabaret comedians is PBS irregular **Mark Russell,** whose residency at the Omni Shoreham lasted about four senatorial terms and who still plays several weeks at a time at Ford's Theatre every year.

The most loyal opposition is offered by the **Capitol Steps,** a group of former and current Hill staffers who roast their own hosts by rewriting familiar songs with pun-ishing lyrics. In addition to entertaining at semiofficial functions (which may be one reason why their barbs are a tad blunted compared to some more outspoken satirists'), the Capitol Steps are a popular tourist attraction and perform every Friday and Saturday at the Ronald Reagan International Trade Building at 13th and Pennsylvania, NW; call (202) 312-1555. The Metro stop is Federal Triangle.

After a few years hiatus, **Comedy Sportz** has reformed and plays its *Whose Line Is It, Anyway*–style games Thursdays through Saturdays in the Metro-connected Ballston Common Mall (call (703) 486-HAHA).

The most successful sketch-humor troupe in Washington is **Gross National Product** (reservations at (202) 783-7212), an underground resistance movement that went above-ground after Reagan's election. Politics, especially the executive power structure, is its obsession: It skewers snoops, creeps, and veeps with gusto and, despite its long tenure, a hint of childish glee. Revues have titles like "Clintoons: The First Hundred Daze" and "A Newt World Order." Shows are about 90 minutes long, and since topicality is the name of the game, skits rise and fall with the state of the world. Performances are one-third to one-half improvisation. GNP's Saturday night shows (currently on an irregular basis at State Theatre) have become required recreation not only for unreconciled rat race victims but the newer, looser White House staff as well. GNP also operates one of Washington's more unique tour services, **Scandal Tours,** which takes sight-seers past such political landmarks as Gary Hart's townhouse; the Jefferson Hotel, where political gun-for-hire Dick Morris simultaneously sucked a prostitute's toes and directed the Democrats campaign strategy; and Fanne Fox's impromptu swimming pool, the Tidal Basin—an event retold by sex scandal veteran "Bob Packwood." Scandal Tours depart from the Old Post Office Pavilion Saturdays at 1 p.m. (reservations at (800) 758-TOUR; information at www.gnpcomedy.com).

The overbooking and overbuilding that made comedy shops the fast-food entertainment of the 1980s is giving way to more exclusive (or at least better-budgeted) clubs. The most reliable are the downtown franchise of the star-circuit **Evening at the Improv** and the cable-comic showcase's **Headliners** (both profiled). Hip, gay, and straight comedians of both sexes—Kate Clinton, Paula Poundstone, Dennis Miller, Judy Tenuta—do so well in Washington that many are regularly booked not into clubs but into mid-sized theatrical venues and colleges. Many nightclubs and restaurants offer comedy one night a week; check newspapers for specific listings.

In general, all clubs now follow a standard lineup: the opener, usually a local beginner who patters about ten minutes and also serves as emcee (and who, especially on open mike night, may mean the difference between a smooth production and a free-for-all); the "featured act," either an experienced journeyman or perhaps a second-rank national or cable TV performer, who does about 30 minutes; and the headliner, usually somebody with Letterman or Leno credits or at least a cable special, who performs about an hour.

Live Pop/Rock/Jazz

Although it isn't widely advertised, for some reason, Washington is a haven for music lovers of all types, and in the summer especially an astonishing amount of music is free to the public. From classical to college-radio rock, from hole-in-the-wall to the Washington Mall, you can hear it all. Credit for the rise in live-music clubs in the Washington area is split between the booming third-world community, used to later hours and different music styles; the large college and twentysomething population looking for entertainment, along with the thirtysomethings who started looking ten years ago; the increasing number of those twenty- and thirty- and even fortysomethings who live in the suburbs and don't want to go downtown for a good time; the more assertive gay and faux-prole communities seeking accommodation; and the fair number of stubborn musicians and underground entrepreneurs who have established venues and support networks for themselves and one another.

Jazz, of course, has a long history in Washington—in the 1930s and 1940s the U Street/Howard Theater corridor was known as the "Black Broadway" and rivaled Harlem. But after years of declining audiences and bankrupted clubs, jazz is reviving all around the area; and the number of young jazz musicians, black and white, classical and contemporary, is remarkable. In fact, the **Lincoln Theater** (not far from the U Street-Cardozo Metro at 1215 U Street, NW; (202) 328-6000), which used to be one of the most popular stops for nationally ranked performers, has been restored to its Georgian Revival glory and is beginning to feature jazz and pop shows again.

Among the best places to hear jazz are **Blues Alley** and **Takoma Station Tavern** (profiled); **Twins** (U Street; (202) 234-0072); the **Ritz-Carlton Arlington** (1250 South Hayes Street, Arlington; (703) 415-5000); the **Basin Street Lounge/219 Restaurant** (219 King Street, Alexandria, VA; (703) 549-1141); and **The Ice House Cafe** (760 Elden Street, Herndon, Virginia; (703) 437-4500). After a late Sunday brunch, stick around for evening jazz at the **Inn at Glen Echo** (next to Glen Echo Park on MacArthur Boulevard, Glen Echo; (301) 229-2280). In addition, many hotels have fine jazz pianists in their lounges.

The mega–rock concert venues tend to be sports arenas doing double duty: The new 20,000-plus-seat **MCI Center** downtown, home to the Washington Bullets basketball and Washington Wizards hockey teams; the 50,000-seat **RFK Stadium**, erstwhile home of the Redskins football team (which has the advantage of being accessible by Metro to the Stadium/Armory stop); and the all-purpose 10,000-seat **Patriot Center** college arena at George Mason in Fairfax, which also tends to carry the big-name country concerts. Tickets for these shows are usually available by phone from TicketMaster at (202) 432-7328, but beware: "Service charges" and handling fees have been known to reach $4.50 per ticket—not per order.

The most popular outdoor commercial venue is **Wolf Trap Farm Park** off Route 7 in Vienna, VA, which offers almost nightly entertainment—pop, country, jazz and R&B, MOR (middle-of-the-road) rock, and even ballet and Broadway musical tours—and picnicking under the stars during the summer at its Filene Center amphitheater. During the winter season, Wolf Trap shifts to its small but acoustically magnificent Barns, literally two rebuilt barns; among its best concerts are the annual Folk Masters series coordinated with the Smithsonian. Wolf Trap has started its own phone service called ProTix, which charges lower fees than TicketMaster (and thus has not incurred the wrath of any popular rock group); call (703) 218-6500 for Wolf Trap shows. On summer nights, the Metro operates a $4 roundtrip shuttle service from the West Falls Church station to the Filene Center, but watch your watch: The return shuttle leaves either 20 minutes after the final curtain or at 11 p.m., whichever is earlier, in order to ensure that riders don't miss the Metro.

Merriweather Post Pavilion in Columbia, MD, has the busiest pop/rock outdoor arena and specializes in old-favorite rock and pop tours, but it is some distance from Washington and can only be reached by car. (It also uses the ProTix network; see newspapers for current listings.) However, it has a new rival around the other side of the Beltway: the **Nissan Pavilion** outside Manassas, VA, which has 10,000 seats under cover and lawn seating for another 15,000 people. Operated by Cellar Door Productions, the largest booking agency on the east coast (and owners of the Bayou nightclub in Georgetown), the Nissan Pavilion is currently booking many of the same acts as MPP but uses the Ticket-Master network (phone (202) 432-7328). Like Merriweather Post, however, it can only be reached by car. The more progressive rock acts, which draw strong college and postgrad audiences, tend to be booked into college auditoriums such as George Washington University's **Lisner Auditorium** or **Smith Center**. National acts with limited audiences—R&B, gospel, soul, folk—are often booked into **DAR Constitution Hall** alongside the Ellipse. Check the newspaper listings for entertainers and phone numbers while you're in town. **George Mason University Center for the Arts,** which adjoins the Patriot Center, is a lovely new mid-sized venue for classical and jazz music and drama. Tickets available at (703) 218-6500 or www.tickets.com.

You will also find concerts at many Washington churches, including the **National Cathedral**; check the newspapers.

There are several fine outdoor music venues in the area, including **Freedom Plaza** at 14th and Pennsylvania Avenue near the White House, home to numerous free music and ethnic festivals during the summer, particularly the annual DC World Jazz Fest held during the Fourth of July celebrations. **Carter-Barron Amphitheatre** in Rock Creek Park hosts gospel, soul, jazz, and R&B concerts on summer weekends. Several other smaller city parks, museums, and federal building plazas stage concerts that are listed in the newspapers.

The Mall between the U.S. Capitol and the Washington Monument is the site of many festivals during the year, especially on such holidays as Memorial Day, the Fourth of July, and Labor Day, when the National Symphony Orchestra headlines family concerts. The Smithsonian's annual Festival of American Folklife, which features three or four different ethnic groups every year, also has music and dance parties every night; it runs from the weekend before the Fourth of July through the holiday itself.

The most important clubs booking national alternative rock acts are the **9:30** club, the **Black Cat** (both profiled), and the **Nation** on Capitol Hill near the Navy Yard Metro (Half and K Streets, SE; (202) 554-1500).

For folk, country, and bluegrass music, the most important venue is the **Birchmere** in Alexandria, VA (profiled), which boasts Mary Chapin Carpenter as favorite daughter. One of the increasingly important venues both for local and national bookings, plus the rare eccentric or cult oldie, is the **State Theater** in Falls Church (220 North Washington Street; (703) 237-0300).The new **Half Moon Bar-B-Q** in Silver Springs (8235 Georgia Avenue; (301) 585-1290) books local and national R&B, blues, Cajun and rockabilly—not surprising since it belongs to Marc Gretschel of **Twist and Shout** and **Phantasmagoria** in Wheaton, which books national Cajun/zydeco and deep-blues acts and front-line local groups. Piano bars are legion, but the best and most accomplished jazz is played at **Circle Bistro** (One Washington Circle; (202) 293-5390).

The best bets for acoustic, folk-rock, modern pop, or original music on just any old night are **Iota** (profiled), which is especially popular with local progressive pop/rock writers; **Uncle Jed's Roadhouse** in Bethesda (7525 Old Georgetown Road; (301) 913-0026); and the **Rhodeside Grill** in the hot new Clarendon neighborhood (1836 Wilson Boulevard, Arlington; (703) 243-0143). The last of the area's once-plentiful bluegrass spots is the **Tiffany Tavern** in Alexandria (1116 King Street; (703) 836-8844). "Coffeehouses" are flourishing (the folk music variety, not the cappuccino type, though they're booming, too), but many coffeehouse acoustic music events occur only monthly in area churches or schools; check the papers.

Irish bars do a flourishing business in Washington with the help of a resident community of performers. Among the pubs with live music—and almost always at least one fireplace—are the **Dubliner** (profiled); **Ireland's Four Provinces** (by the Cleveland Park Metro at 3412 Connecticut Avenue, NW; (202) 244-0860); **James Mackay's** downtown (L Street, NW; (202) 483-8008); **Nanny O'Brien's** across the street (3319 Connecticut Avenue, NW; (202) 686-9189); **Fado Irish Pub** (808 7th Street, NW; (202) 789-0066); the **Old Brogue** (760-C Walker Road, Great Falls, VA; (703) 759-3309); **Pat Troy's** (111 North Pit Street, Alexandria, VA; (703) 549-4535); and **Flanagan's** (near the Bethesda station at 7637 Old Georgetown Road, Bethesda, MD; (301) 986-1007), which also hosts the semiannual appearances of Irish veterans Tommy Makem and the Furey Brothers.

The local reggae acts generally play the **Grog & Tankard** (2408 Wisconsin Avenue, NW; (202) 333-3114), which is also local Deadhead Central; Dead diehards can also drop by **LuLu's** (profiled) on Monday nights and the State Theater on Thursdays.

Washington is also home to one other type of band: the **armed services bands**. From about Memorial Day to Labor Day, ensembles from the four branches perform Monday, Tuesday, Wednesday, and Friday at 8 p.m. at the east or west side of the Capitol; Tuesday, Thursday, Friday, and Sunday at 8 p.m. at various locations; and Tuesday at 8 p.m. at the Navy Memorial at 7th and Pennsylvania Avenue, NW. Call (703) 696-3399 or visit www.army.mil/armyband for details. Programs include patriotic/martial numbers, country, jazz, pop, and some classical music. You're welcome to bring brown bags, but alcohol is not permitted.

Swing Your Partner

Country and disco dancing have been big for years in Washington, but ethnic and folk dancing—klezmer, polka, contra, Cajun—as well as swing dance and big-band boogie are also popular, especially in the suburbs. Their venues are also nonthreatening and hospitable spots for singles, even novices, since many have pre-dance "workshops" for learning the steps, and all seem well supplied with tolerant and deft "leaders."

For swing dancing, the best bets are the **Washington Swing Dance Committee,** which holds Saturday night dances in all but the coldest weather at the grand deco Spanish Ballroom in the old Glen Echo amusement park in Bethesda, MD (information: (301) 492-6282); the **Clarendon Ballroom** (3185 Wilson Boulevard Arlington; (703) 469-2944); **Hollywood Ballroom** in Silver Springs (2126 Industrial Parkway; (301) 622-5494); the **Rock Around the Clock Club,** which holds dances twice a month at the Cherry Hill Park clubhouse in College Park, MD (information: (301) 897-8724); and **America** restaurant in Tyson's Corner (1961 Chain Bridge Road; (703) 847-6610), which hosts the Tom Cunningham Orchestra on Saturdays. The America branch in Union Station sometimes hosts bands, too; call (202) 682-9555. Various restaurants around town are experimenting with martini-lounge-swing nights during the week; check the local listings. Glen Echo hosts folk, Cajun, and contra dances every weekend; call the **Glen Echo** schedule hotline at (301) 492-6282 or contact the **Folklore Society of Greater Washington** at (202) 546-2228 or www.fsgw.org.

You can polka (and pile on the bratwurst) to your heart's content any Friday, Saturday, or Sunday at **Blob's Park,** a Bavarian-fantasy beer hall and polka pavilion in Jessup, Maryland, that holds 1,000 revelers and a five-man oompah band; for information, call (410) 799-0155 or visit www.blobspark.com.

For country, try **Nick's** in Alexandria (642 South Pickett Street; (703) 751-8900); **Chick Hall's** (4711 Kenilworth Avenue, Hyattsville; (301) 927-6310) or **Spurs** (2106 Crain Highway, Waldorf; (301) 843-9964).

For waltzing on a Sunday afternoon, head to **Glen Echo** or call (703) 978-0375. For Latin dancing, try **Bravo Bravo** (1001 Connecticut Avenue, NW; (202) 223-5330); **Diva** (1350 I Street, NW; (202) 289-7300); **Cuzco** (5831 Columbia Pike, Falls Church; (703) 845-1661); **Habana Village** in Adams-Morgan, which has salsa lessons on Wednesdays and Thursdays (1834 Columbia Road, NW; (202) 462-6310); or **Latin Jazz Alley,** also in Adams-Morgan, for lessons and dance Wednesday through Saturday (1721 Columbia Road, NW; (202) 328-6190).

For *Brady Bunch*–style 1970s retro, try **Polly Esther's,** a *Saturday Night Fever* revival club for white lipstick lovers open Thursday through Saturday (605 12th Street, NW; (202) 737-1970; and in the Rockville Doubletree Hotel at 1750 Rockville Pike, Rockville; (301) 881-7341).

The 20-to-40 crowd that's into Top 40 disco tends to hang out at **MCCXXIII** and **Platinum** (both profiled) and **DC Live** (932 F Street, NW; (202) 487-6675). The leading black/buppie draw is the **Ritz** (919 E Street, NW; (202) 638-2582), whose five rooms program house, R&B, techno, and contemporary jazz. Internationals head to **Dream** and **Zanzibar** (both profilied).

Ashes to Ashes

Here as in many other urban centers, cigars are the latest show of sophistication manqué. Aside from **Ozio** (profiled), the Grand Hyatt Hotel has jumped the trend-bar time warp and remodeled its old sports bar into **Butlers Cigar Bar** (10th and H Streets, NW; (202) 637-4765). Not far away is **Shelly's Back Room** (1331 F Street, NW; (202) 737-3003). And the wine bar at **Melrose** restaurant in the Park Hyatt Hotel is mixing its wines by the glass with a cigar menu (4th and M Streets, NW; (202) 955-3899).

Espresso and Eight-Ball

The two biggest trends in Washington are coffee bars and billiards parlors. At either you can spend not merely hours but whole evenings, and in a few cases, hang out virtually around the clock.

Many of the espresso bars are tiny walk-ins; some are mere service windows. But a couple are among the most interesting after-hours hangouts in the city, even if the patrons are the only "entertainment."

The biggest billiards parlors around are **Dave & Buster's** and **Buffalo Billiards** (both profiled); **Georgetown Billiards** (3251 Prospect Street, NW; (202) 965-7665); **Babe's** (near the Tenleytown Metro at 4600 Wisconsin Avenue, NW; (202) 966-0082); **Champion Billiards** (1776 East Jefferson Street, Rockville, MD; (301) 231-4949), which also serves food until 1 a.m. Sunday through Thursday, and until 3 a.m. on Friday and Saturday; and **CarPool** (4000 North Fairfax Drive, Arlington; (703) 532-7665), which has the specific attraction of serving barbecue from Rocklands (see its profile in Part Nine: Dining and Restaurants). Bethesda's Shark Club (4915 St. Elmo Avenue; (301) 718-4030) is another restaurant–dance club–pool hall complex that runs late

For funkier decor and a less formal atmosphere, try **Atomic Billiards** (3427 Connecticut Avenue, NW, at the Cleveland Park Metro; (202) 363-7665); **Bedrock Billiards** (1841 Columbia Road, NW; (202) 667-7665); or **Julio's** in Adams-Morgan (16th and U Streets, NW; (202) 483-8500).

True Brews

Washington has also discovered another fresh brew—beer. In fact, the entire Washington-Baltimore region has gone silly for suds. A boom in brewpubs and microbreweries has made it possible to support your local craft brewers in style and also to taste a huge number of recipes, from pilsners and lagers to stouts, porters, wheat ales, fruit beers, bocks, and seasonals. And most offer at least informal tours of the works, if you're intrigued.

Among the nearer brewpubs are the **Capital City Brewing Co.** branches near the Washington Convention Center (11th and H Streets, NW; (202) 628-2222), in the Village at Shirlington (2700 South Quincy Street, Arlington, VA; (703) 578-3888), and in the Postal Museum building (at Massachusetts Avenue and 1st Street, NW; (202) 842-2337), which are as much singles scenes as beer temples; and **John Harvard's Brewhouse**, a branch of a Cambridge, Massachusetts, favorite (13th and Pennsylvania Avenues, NW; (202) 783-2739). In Bethesda, the latest outpost of the Cap City group goes mug to mug with **Rock Bottom Brewery** at Old Georgetown Road and Woodmont Avenue; (301) 652-1311. Among other popular spots where vats are on view are **Summit Station** in Gaithersburg, MD (Summit and Diamond Avenues; (301) 948-4200); or **Old Dominion Brewing Co.** in Ashburn, VA (44633 Guilford Drive; (703) 724-9100), which is also the area's most successful microbrewing company. Baltimore also is big brew news. If you head up for an Orioles or Ravens game, try the English-style **Sisson's** ((410) 539-2093) or the German-style **Baltimore Brewing Co.** ((410) 837-5000, both only blocks from the stadium.

For more Washington suds stops, check the profile of the **Brickskeller** or the "Freshest Beer" restaurant list on pages 271–272.

The Sex Thing

Washington is not the singles capital of the world, but it does have many of the ingredients for a busy meat-market scene: frequent turnovers in power, a dozen colleges and universities, a continual influx of immigrants and corporate hires, and what until recently was considered a "recession-proof" economy.

The singles bars around Washington are relatively benign. Many of them are dance clubs as well, so there's something to do besides discuss astrological incompatibilities. The sports-bar habitués tend to be a little more flagrant in their appraisals of fresh talent, as are those in bars that cater to the fortysomething crowd.

The busiest singles strip in the District is midtown, just south and a bit west of Dupont Circle, especially around the intersection of 19th and M

Streets, where the **Sign of the Whale** (1825 M Street, NW; (202) 785-1110), **Rumours** (1900 M Street NW; (202) 466-7378), **Madhatter** (1831 M Street NW; (202) 833-1495), and **Mr. Day's** (1111 19th Street NW; (202) 296-7625) pack them in starting at happy hour. A few blocks west is Georgetown, so you can have a sort of progressive singles party.

The busiest singles bar for the older and cash-flow-confident crowd is the **Yacht Club of Bethesda** (profiled).

Suburban singles centers are easy to spot: Anything with a bar will do.

Although the District has been home to a strong gay community for many years, most clubs attract at least a slightly mixed, albeit unobtrusive crowd. However, there are many well-established gay nightspots, especially around Dupont Circle and Capitol Hill. Among the most popular are the Polo-label **JR's** (1519 17th Street, NW; (202) 328-0090) near Dupont Circle; the pointy-toe and big-buckle **Remington's** (near the Eastern Market station at 639 Pennsylvania Avenue, SE; (202) 543-3113), and the softcore leather-with-rhythm **DC Eagle** (near Gallery Place at 639 New York Avenue, NW; (202) 347-6025).

The hottest gay/lesbian dance clubs are the **Circle Underground** (1629 Connecticut Avenue, NW; (202) 462-5575), which offers a choice of loud bar, softer terrace bar, and dining room; **Chaos** (1603 17th Street, NW; (202) 232-4141), with its weekend drag-diva encores; **The Fireplace** (22nd and P Streets, NW; (202) 295-1293), with its two-way windows that turn prying eyes into entertainment; **Escalando**, a Tex-Mex bar with an Amateur Drag Show every Saturday at midnight (2122 P Street; (202) 822-8909); the far more low-key **Mr. P's** (2147 P Street; (202) 293-1064); Capital Hill's cowboy corral, **Remingtons** (639 Pennsylvania Avenue, SE; (202) 543-3113); **Badlands,** which has semi-steamy videos to go with the marathon mixes (Dupont Circle, 1415 22nd Street, NW; (202) 296-0505); and the predominantly lesbian **Hung Jury** (near Farragut West at 1819 H Street, NW; (202) 785-8181). **Ziegfeld's** is the most flamboyant of the hangouts, featuring uproarious and often astonishingly polished drag shows Thursday through Sunday (1345 Half Street, SE; (202) 554-5141). Although it's not in the safest neighborhood, Ziegfeld's will call you a cab when you're ready to leave.

If you can't dance but hate to eat alone, try the **Annie's Paramount Steak House** (1609 17th Street, NW; (202) 232-0395), or **Perry's** (1811 Columbia Road, NW; (202) 234-6218).

Finally, although the onetime red-light district around 14th Street was officially eradicated by redistricting and redevelopment, old habits die hard. North and east of the White House, and especially in the blocks around 13th and L, prostitutes not only parade past and proposition pedestrians but take advantage of traffic lights and stop signs to accost drivers. Periodically the police crack down on the scene, which is signalled by the overnight closing of streets in the neighborhood; but it makes only a temporary dent. The business also takes advantage of public transportation: Many of the hotel bars along the Metro are hangouts for soliciting singles—and humorously, they seem to prefer the red line, as if in tribute to "red-light" districts.

A few reminders: Although most prostitutes try to protect themselves from disease, both drug use and AIDS are pervasive. Second, many dates are actually bait, fronts for drug dealers who can more immediately endanger your health and safety. Besides, District police are fully familiar with the tricks of the trade, so we don't advise that you get involved. If you must look, don't touch—and keep your car doors locked.

For a somewhat less hands-on experience, there are a couple of relatively sedate strip joints downtown, including **Archibald's,** which is on the ground floor of the Comedy Cafe building off MacPherson Square (1520 K Street, NW; (202) 737-2662). **Good Guys,** above Georgetown, is an old favorite (2311 Wisconsin Avenue, NW; (202) 333-0128). And for the safest fantasy trips around, drop by Georgetown's funny/fantasy sex boutiques: the **Pleasure Place** (1063 Wisconsin Avenue, NW; (202) 333-8570), which offers videos, X-rated birthday cards, T-shirts, fishnet stockings, and the like; and its across-the-street-rival **Dream Dresser,** a fancy-silly X-rated Victoria's Secret, which dispenses leather and latex as well as lighter-hearted souvenirs and accoutrements (1042 Wisconsin Avenue, NW; (202) 625-0373).

More on the Safety Thing

There is only one safety tip to remember: You're never entirely safe. There is no guaranteed neighborhood in the area. In fact, we have left some otherwise deserving and successful clubs off the list because they're in questionable territory, even for savvy residents. The suburbs are generally okay, but even the ostensibly upscale areas of the District, such as Georgetown and Dupont Circle, are not immune to crime. It's best to leave nightclubs, especially after about 10 p.m., in company. Attach yourself to a group or ask the club management for an escort. It's also wiser to call a cab than to walk more than a block or so. (Mace, incidentally, is now legal in Maryland, Virginia, and the District of Columbia.)

And a final tip: If you believe in helping out the homeless (the staggering number of which you may find one of the less inspiring monuments to modern life in Washington), try stashing dollar bills or change in an outside pocket so that you can reach them without opening your wallet or purse.

NIGHTCLUBS BY ZONE

Nightclub	Description	Typical Cover
ZONE 1: The Mall		
Hard Rock Cafe	themed bar & grill with memorabilia	None
Zanzibar	upscale world-music disco	$10
ZONE 2: Capitol Hill		
Dubliner	traditional Irish pub	None
ZONE 3: Downtown		
The Improvisation	pro-circuit comedy dinner club	$12–15
Ozio	trendy martini and cigar lounge	None
Platinum	lavish, four-floor dance club	$5–14
ZONE 5: Georgetown		
Blues Alley	national-circuit jazz dinner club	$13–50
ZONE 6: Dupont Circle / Adams-Morgan		
Black Cat	live rock/pop venue with some DJs	$13–50
Brickskeller	vast beer selection and pub fair	None
Buffalo Billiards	singles bar with $5 per hour pool	None
Chi-Cha Lounge	relaxed Latino-jazz/cigar bar	None
Lulu's Night Club	Mardi–Gras themed singles bar	$5
MCCXXIII	pricey three-story hipster lounge	$10
ZONE 7: Upper Northwest		
9:30	big-name alternative/punk venue	$3–$30
Takoma Station Tavern	upscale jazz bar	$5
ZONE 8: Northeast		
Dream	four-story cocktail lounge/dance hall	$10
ZONE 9: Southeast		
Nation	multi-room dance club	varies
ZONE 10: Maryland Suburbs		
Dave & Buster's	adult game-room bar	$5, Sat.
Headliners	pro-circuit comedy dinner club	$10
Yacht Club of Bethesda	high-end singles bar/retro disco	$5–12
ZONE 11: Virginia Suburbs		
Birchmere	live folk/rockabilly bar & brewery	$8–10
Iota	tavern with live pop/roots rock	$4–10
Whitey's	neighborhood tavern/blues bar	varies

NIGHTCLUBS BY TYPE

Nightclub	Description	Zone	Cover
Bar & Grills/Buffets			
Dave & Buster's	adult game-room bar	10B	$5, Sat.
Hard Rock Cafe	bar & grill with memorabilia	1	None
Cigar bars			
Chi-Cha Lounge	relaxed Latino-jazz/cigar bar	6	None
Ozio	trendy martini and cigar lounge	3	None
Cocktail lounges			
MCCXXIII	pricey three-story hipster lounge	6	$10
Comedy Clubs			
Headliners	pro-circuit comedy dinner club	10A	$10
The Improvisation	pro-circuit comedy dinner club	3	$12–15
Dance Clubs			
Dream	four-story lounge/dance hall	8	$10
Nation	multi-room dance club	9	varies
Platinum	lavish, four-floor dance club	3	$5–14
Zanzibar	upscale world-music disco	1	$10
Live Jazz/Blues			
Blues Alley	national-circuit jazz dinner club	5	$13–50
Takoma Station Tavern	upscale jazz bar	7	$5
Whitey's	neighborhood tavern/blues bar	11B	varies
Live Pop/Rock			
Birchmere	live folk/rockabilly bar & brewery	11C	$8–10
Black Cat	live rock/pop venue, some DJs	6	$13–50
Iota	tavern with live pop/roots rock	11B	$4–10
9:30	big-name alternative/punk venue	7	$3–$30
Pubs/Brewhouses			
Brickskeller	vast beer selection and pub fair	6	None
Dubliner	traditional Irish pub	2	None
Singles Bars			
Buffalo Billiards	singles bar with pool tables	6	None
Lulu's Night Club	Mardi-Gras themed singles bar	6	$5
Yacht Club of Bethesda	high-end singles bar/retro disco	10A	$5–12

Profiles of Clubs and Nightspots

BIRCHMERE

LIVE FOLK, NEW ACOUSTIC, NEWGRASS, HIP ROCKABILLY/OUTLAW, LIGHT JAZZ AND COUNTRY, AND OCCASIONAL OFF-PEAK POP MUSIC

Who Goes There Gracefully aging boomers and a few recalcitrant rednecks; unreconciled folkies; local musicians

3701 Mt. Vernon Avenue, Alexandria; (703) 549-7500 Virginia suburbs, Zone 11C

Cover Varies with entertainment; roughly $8–20 **Minimum** None **Mixed drinks** $2.50–5 **Wine** $4.25 **Beer** $3.25–3.75 **Dress** A few suits, a lot of flannels, universal jeans, neo-farm country wear and boots of all sorts—cowboy, hiking, motorcycle **Food available** After years of getting by on potato chips, Birchmere patrons can now get serious tavern fare, including barbecue, burgers, and hot nibbles, from the folks at Union Street Pub and King Street Blues.

Hours Every day, 6–11:30 p.m. Shows start at 7:30.

What goes on This is one of the major clubs in town, the biggest for new acoustic and country acts especially, such as Rosanne Cash and hometown heroine Mary-Chapin Carpenter, plus cult regulars Jerry Jeff Walker and Delbert McClinton; old folk Tom Paxton and John Stewart; new femme fronters Kristin Hersh, Christine Lavin, and Maria Muldaur.

Setting & atmosphere The long-awaited new home for this venerable club has jumped from old-fashioned to new-fangled: not only a much more spacious 500-seat main stage but a cigar-martini bar (for the expected influx of trendy patrons?), a 150-seat side stage/cafe, a microbrewery on-site, and "real" pub food.

If you go Go early: Parking is tight (but free); the line is long; and seating is first-come, closest-in. If you're trying to eat light, eat elsewhere. Remember to take off your big hat so the folks behind you can see. And take thankful note of the sign that asks for quiet during performances: This really is a listening club. Visit www.birchmere.com for a schedule.

BLACK CAT

LIVE ROCK-POP VENUE WITH DJS FOR BACKUP

Who Goes There 20–40; locals and tourist music fans

1831 14th Street, NW; (202) 667-7960 Circle-Adams-Morgan, Zone 6

Cover Varies with entertainment **Minimum** None **Mixed drinks** $5–8 **Wine** $5–7 **Beer** $3–5 **Dress** Ranges from grungy to nightclub-hip, depending on the act **Food available** Vegan and vegetarian fair from the now-defunct Food for Thought menu

Hours Sunday–Thursday, 8 p.m.–2 a.m.; Friday and Saturday, 7 p.m.–3 a.m.

What goes on A mix of hot regional and early-national alternative rock, funky-punk, and high-ticket camp (El Vez, the "Mexican Elvis," etc.).

Setting & atmosphere The larger room holds 600, the rear room only about 100, so that's usually turned over to dance club on the weekends, with a mix of synth pop, Brit-indie and even some mod and cult garage.

If you go A who's-who of indie rock has passed through the Black Cat, so buy advance tickets for major concerts and expect some sweating crowds for louder acts.

BLUES ALLEY

NATIONAL-CIRCUIT JAZZ DINNER CLUB

Who Goes There 20–60; locals and tourists; other jazz pros; neo-jazz fans

1073 Wisconsin Avenue, NW (in the alley); (202) 337-4141 Georgetown, Zone 5

Cover Varies with entertainment; $13–50 **Minimum** Two drinks or $7 food **Mixed drinks** $3.95–7.50 **Wine** $3.50–5 **Beer** $3–5 **Dress** Jacket over jeans, business attire, musician chic **Food available** Full menu of semi-Creole food: gumbo, chicken, steak

Hours Every day, 6 p.m.–midnight.

What goes on When the big-name jazz performers come to town, this is where they play. And although many customers grumble about ticket prices, they pay anyway—partly because the acts require high guarantees, partly because Georgetown rents are high, and partly because so many other jazz clubs have folded.

Setting & atmosphere A fairly simple lounge, with exposed brick walls, a platform at one end and the bar at the other, and smallish dinner tables scattered between.

If you go Get there early; the line often goes around the block, and seating is first-come and squeeze-'em-together, even with reservations. The old and cramped rest rooms that are barely accessible upstairs are one drawback, and the ventilation can be another, but the acoustics are very good.

BRICKSKELLER

ENCYCLOPEDIC BEER RATHSKELLER

Who Goes There 21–45; students; former students; home brewers; beer fanatics

1523 22nd Street, NW; (202) 293-1885 Dupont Circle/Adams-Morgan, Zone 6

Cover None **Minimum** None **Mixed drinks** $2.75–4.75 **Wine** $3.25–4.50 **Beer** $2.75–54 **Dress** Jackets, jeans, khakis **Specials** Special drafts upstairs Fridays and Saturdays after 7 **Food available** The house specialty is buffalo; good pub food in general

Hours Monday–Thursday, 11:30 a.m.–2 a.m.; Friday, 11:30 a.m.–3 a.m.; Saturday, 6 p.m.–3 a.m.; Sunday, 6 p.m.–2 a.m.

What goes on Almost half a century ago, Maurice Coja put 50 kinds of beer, mostly bottled, in the basement of the Marifex Hotel and opened for business. Twenty years later, he had to give up kegs because room was so tight, and now, with 1,000 beers from all over the world offered at the same time, including over 100 microbrews, brands and cans are stuffed into every corner. The Brickskeller used to offer live music of the folk-rock variety but eventually realized the beer was sufficient entertainment. There are dart boards and a jukebox instead.

Setting & atmosphere A rabbit warren of rooms, with the main bar in the front and scuffed and hard-working tables snaking around between the dart boards. Feel free to strike up a conversation; the Brickskeller is unpretentious, college-bar friendly, and lively.

If you go Don't be shy; consult the staff. Beer is serious business here—three-liter bottles of Corsondonk go for $54—and you can learn a lot if you go slowly. Start light and work your way up to Samiclaus, a potent by-the-fireside beer of 14% alcohol. (The good news is the kitchen is open late, and the Subway is nearby.) Skip the mixed beer cocktails, or beer-tails; they're more novelty act than revelation.

BUFFALO BILLIARDS

PART BIZ-WHIZ POOL PARTY, PART SINGLES BAR (OVER 21 ONLY)

Who Goes There Junior associates; postgrads; bar pros

1330 19th Street, NW; (202) 331-7665 Dupont Circle/Adams-Morgan, Zone 6

Cover None **Minimum** None for bars or people-watching; to play, $5 per player per hour **Mixed drinks** $3.25–6 **Wine** $3.50–4 **Beer** $3.25–6.50 **Dress** Mix of officewear and jock chic; as many lace-ups as high-rises **Specials** Happy hour 4–8 p.m. weekdays; 1–7 p.m. weekends, with beer specials and wine and rail drinks for $2.50 **Food available** Mostly small plates—nachos, buffalo wings (of course), sandwiches—but also some fairly serious entrees such as tuna steak and trout

Hours Monday–Thursday, 4 p.m.–2 a.m.; Friday, 4 p.m.–3 a.m.; Saturday, 1 p.m.–3 a.m.; Sunday, 1 p.m.–1 a.m.

What goes on Parties circulate, singles practice their shots, and couriers wait for assignments.

Setting & atmosphere This is just one of a half-dozen upscale, all-the-modern-indulgences pool halls all over the area (see the section "Espresso and Eight-Ball" on p. 118), but it's one of the busiest and largest, the flagship of its owners' half-dozen parlors, with two entire rooms (one smoking, one nonsmoking) and vibrators to alert waiting customers to their tables. It's woodyish—Buffalo Bill-iards, get it?—but not too gadget-happy. And it's one level down from the street, which gives it a sort of old-fashioned speakeasy quality.

If you go Don't worry about your pool skills particularly, unless you're hoping to shark someone; a lot of the patrons are pleasure-seekers, not pros, and they won't be looking over your shoulder. The main thing is to watch where you're going: Don't knock someone else's cue or back into the player at the next table, and if that player lines up a shot first, it's his/her right of way, so to speak.

CHI-CHA LOUNGE

PART NEIGHBORHOOD CAFE, PART LATINO-CHIC JAZZ AND CIGAR LOUNGE WITH A FEW "EXOTIC" TOUCHES

Who Goes There 20–30 something regulars; Latino internationals

1624 U Street, NW; (202) 234-8400 Circle/Adams-Morgan, Zone 6

Cover None **Minimum** One drink or menu item **Mixed drinks** $4–7 **Wine** $4–6 **Beer** $3–5 **Dress** Business, light cocktail and nice casual; see below **Specials** Ask a server **Food available** "Modern Andean" fare, mostly tapas-sized snacks

Hours Sunday–Thursday, 5:30 p.m.–2 a.m.; Friday and Saturday, 5:30 p.m.–3 a.m.

What goes on This offbeat but endearing hangout, the "hacienda" of local entrepreneur Mauricio Fraga-Rosenfeld (Ozio, Gazuza, etc.), offers a few exotic indulgences to homesick internationals, such as the arguileh (hookah-like water pipes for smoking fruit-cured tobacco) for Middle Easterners, popped giant corn kernels and glasses of the eponymous chi-cha, a spicy, fruit and rice alcohol traditional in Latin America.

Setting & atmosphere Sort of rec-room casbah. "Couch potato" here means a little tamal snack on the sofa. The music is frequently live, and ranges from flamenco guitar to Latin jazz to Euro-jazz standards, and visiting pros such as the Gipsy Kings and Buena Vista Social Club have been known to drop in after their shows.

If you go The dress code is pretty much the formal standard nowadays: No hats for men, no athletic wear, no printed T's, no tanks, "no attitudes"—but no neckties, either, as per the owner's own preferences.

DAVE & BUSTER'S

ADULT ENTERTAINMENT À LA SPIELBERG—PART HIGH-TECH, PART RETRO-REGRESSIVE

Who Goes There Late-20s couples bored with disco; traveling salesmen nostalgic for Vegas; some computer geeks and groups of mixed-sex hangers looking for post-movie action

White Flint Mall, Bethesda; (301) 230-5151 Maryland suburbs, Zone 10B

Cover $5 weekends after 10 p.m. **Minimum** None **Mixed drinks** $5–7 **Wine** $3.50–5.75 **Beer** $2.75–5.25 **Dress** Upper shopping mall quality: casual, but no tanks, cutoffs, etc. **Specials** Half-price rail drinks and beer specials at happy hour **Food available** A full range of familiar upscale suburban fare: from artichoke dip and stuffed jalapeños to pastas, grilled salmon, Sante Fe chicken pizza, and ribs and rib-eyes

Hours Monday and Tuesday, 11 a.m.–midnight; Wednesday–Saturday, 11 a.m.–1 a.m.; Sunday, 11:30 a.m.–midnight.

What goes on This is a carnival of the business animals: a half-dozen pocket billiard tables, pinball and video games, a couple of simulated "19th hole" golf games, shuffleboard, and four full-size virtual-reality pods, interlinked for games and sports simulation. There are also casino games, with fully trained blackjack dealers and tables—but the poker chips are "on loan" only. No actual gambling is allowed. Everything is played by token in fact, except the virtual-reality pods. On Fridays and Saturdays, it's murder mystery dinner theater.

Setting & atmosphere This is unabashedly a bar as well as a playroom, with two sideline bars: the double-sided, 40-foot bar that partners the "midway" (a stretch of interactive video and carny attractions); and the elevated, square "Viewpoint" bar (not to mention the private "showroom" with its own stage, bar, dining tables, and even audio-visual equipment, which is bound to become the status CEO party room of D.C.).

If you go This is Dave & Buster's ninth such complex around the country, and they've got it down smooth. Besides offering nearly every sort of game, it has polished service, fairly strict rules about drinking and dressing, and even stricter rules about under-21-year-olds being with an adult. Even better in this cigar-crazed era, smoking is extremely limited (and even cigarettes only where allowed).

DREAM

FOUR-STORY MANHATTAN-STYLE SUPER-LOUNGE

Who Goes There *Friends, Sex in the City* sophisticates, Damon Wayans and even Seinfelds looking for love in all the lounge places

White Flint 1350 Oakie Street, NE; (202) 636-9030 Northeast Washington, Zone 8

Cover $10; sometimes free with promotion **Mixed drinks** $5–8 **Wine** $5–7 **Beer** $3–5 **Dress** Trendy; they hosted an Armani fashion show **Specials** Free cover early (before 11 p.m., give or take an hour) **Food available** Entrees like crabcakes and jerk chicken from Republic Gardens chef Lois Spencer

Hours Thursdays, 10 p.m.–2 a.m.; Fridays, 5 p.m.–3 a.m.; Saturdays, 8 p.m.–3 a.m.

What goes on Thursdays is usually international night, and the crowd is very mixed and elegant. Weekends are a mix of soul/R&B, hip-hop, and even a little trance, as the yuppie (Fridays) and buppie (Saturdays) level rises and falls. Sundays, as is traditional, goes gay.

Setting & atmosphere This is somewhere between a post-millennial Studio 54 and a luxury liner on land: magohany panelling, leather lounge chairs, plush carpeting and ambiance lighting. Besides the four dance halls, there's a billiard room, neary wall-to-wall bars and a deck for cooling down. The fourth floor is even available for private parties for a mere $5,000.

If you go Seriously dress to impress here; even P-Diddy would have to shed the jeans at this door. This is a "revitalizing" neighborhood, but there is valet parking or shuttle service from nearby secured lots.

DUBLINER

CLASSIC IRISH PUB

Who Goes There Hill workers, both upwardly mobile (staffers) and established (senators and lobbyists)

520 North Capitol Street, NW; (202) 737-3773 Capitol Hill, Zone 2

Cover None **Minimum** None **Mixed drinks** $3.25–6; Dubliner coffee is an Irish coffee with Bailey's added. **Wine** $4–5.50 **Beer** $3–4 **Dress** No cutoffs or tank tops **Specials** Reduced light-fare prices, 11 p.m.–1 a.m.; daily specials Monday–Friday for lunch and dinner **Food available** Irish pub classics, from stew to hot sandwiches

Hours Sunday–Thursday, 7 a.m.–2 a.m.; Friday and Saturday, 7 a.m.–3 a.m.

What goes on This is not the oldest Irish bar in town, but it has become the clan leader—centrally located, pol-connected, and providing the training ground for founders of a half-dozen other bars, including the semi-sibling-rival Irish Times next door. Fittingly, the Dubliner also has one of the most colorful histories, filled with romantic intrigue, boom-and-bust bank troubles, and riotous St. Patrick's week parties.

Setting & atmosphere Now part of the pricey and hunt-country gracious Phoenix Hotel complex, the Dubliner is filled with antiques, such as the 1810 hand-carved walnut bar in the back room. The front bar is louder and livelier, often populated by the surviving members of the Dubliner's Irish football and soccer teams; the snug is a discreet heads-together, take-no-names hideaway in the finest tradition; and the parlor is where the tweeds gather.

If you go Be sure to have at least one Guinness on draft: The Dubliner pours an estimated quarter-million pints a year. Drop by the Irish Times next door for a breather (the high ceilings carry smoke away) and the *Finnegans Wake* crazy quilt of literary and political conversation and intern rave downstairs. Then call a cab. Please.

HARD ROCK CAFE

SOUVENIR SHOP DISGUISED AS BARBECUE BAR

Who Goes There 12–55; tourists and locals; Hard Rock memorabilia collectors; air-guitar experts

999 E Street, NW; (202) 737-7625 The Mall, Zone 1

Cover None **Minimum** None **Mixed drinks** $7–18 **Wine** $6–15 **Beer** $3–7 **Dress** To be seen: pony-print leather, denim, sports or rock and roll tour jackets, business attire, creative black tie, Bermuda shorts (on tourists) **Food available** Surprisingly good

Hours Sunday–Thursday, 11 a.m.–11 p.m.; Friday and Saturday, 11 a.m.–1 a.m.

What goes on One of 100 Hard Rocks around the world, each of which takes its nickname from the site, this is the "Embassy" and sometimes the "Smithsonian of Rock 'n' Roll," taking its turn rotating the nearly 7,000 pieces of music history in the HRC collection. The souvenir shop, with its signature T-shirts, is as busy as the bar, which is often stand-in-line packed—a doorman passes judgment on the hopeful.

Setting & atmosphere This is ersatz nostalgia for the second Rolling Stone generation, with a bar designed like a piano, half of a pink Cadillac (sort of a franchise signature) hanging from the ceiling, and a lot of fed suits from nearby buildings trying to look cool. Hard Rock also makes a point of being Lollapalooza-era PC, supporting the Walden Project and nuclear freezes and hosting radio-chic benefits and post-concert VIP receptions, usually without the star.

If you go Pick up the guidebook, formally known as the "Hard Rock Cafe Self-Motivating Non-Nuclear-Powered Memorabilia Tour of the World's Foremost Rock 'n' Roll Museum" and start circling the balcony. Look for such treasures as Bo Diddley's first jerry-rigged electric guitar, Michael Jackson's glittering kneepad, and a stained-glass triptych featuring Elvis, Jerry Lee Lewis, and Little Richard.

HEADLINERS

PRO-CIRCUIT COMEDY CLUB

Who Goes There 18–50; suburban singles, young marrieds; comedy groupies; unbooked businessmen

Holiday Inn, 8120 Wisconsin Avenue, Bethesda; (301) 942-4242 Maryland suburbs, Zone 10A

Cover $10 on Saturday **Minimum** Two items **Mixed drinks** $3–6 **Wine** $3–6 **Beer** $2.25–4 **Dress** Anything goes **Food available** Full hotel menus, burgers to prime rib to seafood

Hours Shows start at 9 p.m.

What goes on One of the better regional performers and comic writers, Chip Franklin, books these clubs as well as doing feature duty; he brings in not only cable-friendly names but sharp, cutting-edge comics with brains. (Franklin's good connections and good taste are one reason he's stayed in business while so many other post-comedy-boom types have busted.) Like the Improv, Headliners largely eschews novices for full-time pros, although unlike the Improv, Headliners sticks to rotating performers every couple of nights.

Setting & atmosphere Nice but fairly simple rooms, with stages, brick backdrops, etc.

If you go You can expect three performers: the opener/emcee, a brief second banana, and the featured act. The hotel affiliation means that occasionally you may have a few over-cocktailed hecklers or loud talkers to overcome, but most of the time it's a good audience.

THE IMPROV

NATIONAL-CIRCUIT COMEDY CLUB

Who Goes There Visiting business types; 30ish suburbanites; 25–45 midlevel managers

1140 Connecticut Avenue, NW; (202) 296-7008 Downtown, Zone 3

Cover $12 Sunday–Thursday, $15 Friday and Saturday **Minimum** Two items **Mixed drinks** $4–6 **Wine** $3.50–6.50 **Beer** $3–4 **Dress** T-shirts with jackets, suits, casual yup attire **Specials** Tuesday, free admission to anyone wearing an Improv T-shirt ($12 in the lobby) **Food available** Full menu described as available before the 8:30 p.m. show, but light fare available whenever; standard one-size-fits-all menu with chicken cordon bleu, prime rib, catch of the day, Caesar salad, etc.

Hours Sunday–Thursday, 7–10:30 p.m.; Friday and Saturday, 6:30 p.m.–12:30 a.m. Shows at 8 p.m. (every day) and 10:30 p.m. (Friday and Saturday).

What goes on Standard Improv franchise fare: A short opening act, often local; a semi-established feature act; and a headliner from the national club/cable showcase circuit. However, like many comedy clubs, the Improv is increasingly dependent on extended bookings of more theatrical comics such as Rob "The Caveman" Becker or Jack Gallagher, who perform alone for 90 minutes or so.

Setting & atmosphere Again, this goes with the franchise—a "brick wall" stage sentimentally recalling the original no-frills Improvisation, and the black-and-white checkerboard floor and trim that is practically a logo design. TV screens hang overhead for those with obscured views, but they're not big enough to be terribly useful. The wait staff wear tux-material Bermuda shorts.

If you go Don't bother to come early, at least on weeknights, when being seated in order of arrival isn't apt to be a problem. Since latecomers are usually seated amongst the diners, you have no real reason to seek early reservations. Besides, nibbling through the appetizers list is a more satisfying experience than sitting down to dinner and then sitting through the show. The Improv, though below sidewalk level, has wheelchair access via the elevator in the building lobby.

IOTA

NEIGHBORHOOD TAVERN JOINT WITH SMART CONVERSATION AND LIVE NEW-POP ROOTS ROCK

Who Goes There Messengers; students; thirtysomething T-shirts; microbrew-savvy beer buddies; other musicians

2832 Wilson Boulevard, Arlington; (703) 522-8340 Virginia suburbs, Zone 11B

Cover $4–10, some shows free **Minimum** None **Mixed drinks** $3.20–9.75 **Wine** $3.50–4.50 **Beer** $2.80–8.50 **Dress** Jeans, with or without bolo; hog leathers; baggy athletic wear; and frayed button-down collars **Specials** Happy hour 5–8 p.m., $1 off rail and draft prices **Food available** Freestyle, eclectic pub food but far better than most: spicy lentil dip, quesadillas, veggie burgers with basil and roasted peppers, etc.

Hours Every day, 5 p.m.–2 a.m.

What goes on On a regular basis, this has the best lineup of acoustic rock, neo-roots, soft psychedelic, and eclectic melodic rock in town, and it's the quality of the people who run the shows, both before and behind the scenes, that makes it so. Steve Hagedorn holds the open mike on Wednesdays. When he's in town, this is where you're likely to find hometown favorite Kevin Johnson hosting songwriters' nights.

Setting & atmosphere In a time when a lot of Washington bars have an intentionally mismatched rec-room random look, Iota's decor is unusual but intelligent—murals, geometric eyecatchers chiseled into the exposed brick walls, and beams that show the age of the neighborhood (especially nice, since there's so little of it left otherwise). The room used to be only half this size, but giving the performers some extra elbow room has not made either the musicians or their audiences self-conscious.

If you go This is a good place to strike up a conversation at the bar before the music gets loud: You run into crossword puzzle freaks, novelists, doctoral candidates, musicians, roadies, and ponytails of the friendly sort. It's the sort of bar that makes hanging out a pleasure.

LULU'S NIGHT CLUB

MARDI GRAS SINGLES BAR/SEMI-OLDIES DISCO

Who Goes There 25–45; office fugitives; last-chance bachelorettes; former college jocks

1217 22nd Stree, NW; (202) 861-5858 Dupont Circle/Adams-Morgan, Zone 6

Cover $5 Friday and Saturday after 9 p.m. **Minimum** None **Mixed drinks** $3.75–5.50 **Wine** $3.50–4 **Beer** $3.50–4.50 **Dress** Georgetown prep, after-office hours, Cajun cowpunk **Specials** Happy hour with $2 appetizers and $2.25 beers, 5–8 p.m. weekdays **Food available** Gumbo, étouffée, po' boys, bar fare, sometimes crawfish and half-shells

Hours Sunday–Thursday, 5 p.m.–1:30 a.m.; Friday and Saturday, 5 p.m.–2:30 a.m.

What goes on This is a pack-'em-in lunch spot, catering to nearby office workers, but beginning at 4 p.m., when the Dixieland band "promenades" and the appetizer baskets begin to fry, it becomes a permanent party. In the three DJ areas, the music ranges from Top 40, for the early boomers who used to patronize the bar nearly 20 years ago when it was first called Déjà Vu, to techno and hip-hop. Actually, after the complex's recent removation, the lounge became Déjà Vu again, and dancing here really is déjà vu.

Setting & atmosphere A re-created corner of Bourbon Street, with the restaurant area authentically accessorized with wrought-iron balcony and the glittering carnival queen gown that the owner's mother, Lulu, wore in the 1962 Mardi Gras procession. There's a garden-style dining room reminiscent of Brennan's conservatory, and the multiple bar and informal dance rooms form a warren of exposed brick walls, bare-board floors, and mahogany bars.

If you go Try arriving during happy hour to avoid the cover and enjoy the specials.

MCCXXIII

GEN-X/GEN-TECHS VERSION OF CONSPICUOUS CHAMPAGNE CHIC

Who Goes There Embassy/buppie/Euro slicks; white collar/-tie associates; ambitious committee staff, trust fund babies

1223 Connecticut Avenue, N; (202) 822-1800 Circle-Adams-Morgan, Zone 6

Cover None early, about $10 after 10 on event nights **Minimum** 1 drink **Mixed drinks** $6–10 **Wine** $6–8 **Beer** $4–6 **Dress** One of the strictest dress codes around, and old-fashioned doormen to enforce it, so stalk the stalk as you talk the talk **Food available** Happy hours 5-9 p.m. Tuesdays, Thursdays and Fridays

Hours Monday–Thursday, 4 p.m.–2 a.m.; Friday, 4 p.m.–2 a.m.; Saturday, 6 p.m.–3 a.m.; Sunday, 8 p.m.–2 a.m.

What goes on Once the cocktail hour conventions are observed, the club goes showily swing-your-VIP, with a mix of disco, house, reggae and even Top 40 music.

Setting & atmosphere Now a three-story complex, MCCXXXIII (cute-speak for 1223, the street address) is industrial chic for the titanium-card crowd: caviar bar restaurant downstairs, champagne lounge upstairs, catwalk to glide over and now boudoir-style dance club-within-a-club on the third floor. You can even reserve your favorite couch. Sleek and breezy is the atmosphere, and that goes for the lit-within fabric dividers.

If you go Definitely hit the ATM; you'll need lavish tip cash as well as your credit cards. Remember that this is only one of a half-dozen hotspots at this intersection, including the subterranean Red and Andalu; see the description of the new 18th Street nightlife intersection in the introduction to this chapter.

NATION

THREE-RING CIRCUS OF THEATRICALLY PRODUCED DANCE-TILL-YOU-TRANCE MUSIC

Who Goes There 18–35; electronica fans, club kids, curious revelers

1015 Half Street, SE; (202) 554-1500 Southeast D.C., Zone 9

Cover Occasional **Minimum** None **Mixed drinks** $4–8 **Wine** $4–6 **Beer** $3–5 **Dress** Varies widely, from jeans and tees to outlandish clubwear **Food available** No

Hours Nightly, 7 p.m.–2 a.m. (officially)

What goes on Depending on the night, up to 2,000 fans of rave, synthpop, house, gay and even Goth events, with guest stints from international-circuit DJs and the odd drag queen.

Setting & atmosphere Counting the outdoor deck, three separate dance clubs operate with professional lighting, sound and mix equipment, with bars and lounge seating all about.

If you go Dress to your groove, which can mean anything from black leather to black Boss to black chiffon.

9:30

NATIONAL-NAME LIVE ALTERNATIVE, PROGRESSIVE, SEMI-PUNK ROCK MUSIC CLUB

Who Goes There 18–35; new music hopefuls; postgrads; young media and political types; couriers; cowpunks

815 V Street, NW; (202) 393-0930 Downtown, Zone 7

Cover Varies with entertainment, from $3 to as much as $30 **Minimum** None **Mixed drinks** $4–5.25 **Wine** $4.50 **Beer** $3.25–4.25 **Dress** Grunge, imitation grunge, rhinestone cowboy, leftover businesswear, knife-customized athletic wear, black jersey, black spandex, black denim, and black baggies **Food available** Tex-Mex and barbecue fare

Hours Sunday–Thursday, 7:30 p.m.–until close; Friday and Saturday, 9 p.m.–until close

What goes on "9:30" is the name, it used to be the address (before the former club moved into an old gospel music hall and radio broadcast site), and it used to be the showtime, but thanks to workday hangovers, mid-week music now starts at 8:30. This is one of Washington's most important clubs, the loss-leader indulgence of major concert promoter Seth Hurwitz, who, with daring and eclectic booking of breaking acts, fosters loyalty from new bands as their reputations rise. Promising local bands fight to get work as first acts here; a headliner contract is a real prize.

Setting & atmosphere A slightly trendy mix of leftover cornices, pilasters, virtue-of-necessity exposed steel trusses, and dropped lighting—but still theatrically dark, with great sight lines. The balconies are fine, and there are several bars, including one "quiet room" and a nostalgic, grungier one downstairs.

If you go Find out who's playing: The crowd that pays up for Ice T isn't the same as the one for Marshall Crenshaw or Happy Mondays—or They Might Be Giants, or even Anthrax. Never accuse Hurwitz of lacking a sense of humor.

OZIO

TREND-HAPPY, NEOCON MARTINI AND CIGAR LOUNGE

Who Goes There Ash-kissing Standard & Poor's and Rat Pack–chic wannabes, but with only standard pickup lines and a limited grasp of the inside-the-Beltway gossip they dish; nouveau riche-makers

1813 M Street, NW; (202) 822-6000 Downtown, Zone 3

Cover None **Minimum** None **Mixed drinks** $5–8 **Wine** $5–9 **Beer** $3.50–4 **Dress** European-cut jackets and Nicole Miller ties (especially the ones with martini glasses); imitation menswear or Eurotrash skinny-fits for women **Food available** "American tapas" that are more like Middle Eastern crostini, but interesting; a short menu of entrees, primarily steaks and seafood

Hours Monday–Thursday, 5 p.m.–2 a.m.; Friday, 5 p.m.–3 a.m.; Saturday, 6 p.m.–3 a.m.

What goes on Posturing for fun and profit. The name is Italian slang for "the act of doing nothing"—hanging, in other words. The action starts in a lounge lizard style, and gradually shifts into Euro-Latin and, on the highest levels (that's the third and fourth floors to you), hip-hop, house, and trance.

Setting & atmosphere This is actually what a cigar and martini lounge ought to look like: Tuscan red sponged walls; a sleek, glass-walled, walk-in cigar vault; lots of low, row cocktail tables for noshing and ashing, set off with recycled wrought-iron fencing and Deco-ish light fixtures designed to suggest the Paris Metro. It is, in fact, downstairs from the sidewalk, which makes even more atmospheric sense.

If you go Bring your gold and platinum cards: The martinis are long and strong and cost between $7.25 and $8.50, while the cigars run up to $30. There is one smoke-free dining room. And carry a lot of business cards, too: This is turning into a network center for up-and-coming lobbyists and credit card sharks.

PLATINUM

DISCO BALL GLITTERING IN THE MAIN HALL, LATIN SHARKSKIN GLITTERING IN THE BASEMENT

Who Goes There Younger internationals

915 F Street, NW; (202) 393-3555 Downtown, Zone 3

Cover Free early, then $5–15 **Minimum** None **Mixed drinks** $4–8 **Wine** $5–7 **Beer** $3–5 **Dress** Trendy **Specials** Vary **Food available** Sushi (what else?)

Hours Closed Sundays. There have been rumors of a closing and possible relocation, so call before you go.

What goes on Despite changing names a couple of times (Fifth Column, the Bank), this may have survived to become the grande dame of D.C. neo-discos, and is traditionally the entry-level club for would-be sophisticates. Thursday is College Night (ID gets you a discount), Friday is old-fashioned Ladies' Night (Cinderellas get in free till midnight), Saturday is just a trancy free-for-all. Tuesday and Sunday are heavier, with hip-hop the dominant beat.

Setting & atmosphere A fomer bank, Platinum still has the prosperous look, with a lavish chandelier and marble flooring and a sound system to match. Four floors counting the VIP lounge con fireplace, and balconies to be scene in. Concessions sell candy and cigars to both girls and guys.

If you go Dress code here, as with most the better clubs these days, so college studio or congressional aide, dump the faux-cool for the fashion chic. Get in before the witching hour to save money and shoetime outside. If the line's too long, check out the nearby VIP Club at 932 F, a new and very promising weekends-only annex from the same management.

TAKOMA STATION TAVERN

CLASSICALLY MINDED BUPPIE JAZZ BAR

Who Goes There 25–55; mixed media types; yuppies; buppies; other musicians

6914 4th Street, NW; (202) 829-1937 Upper Northwest, Zone 7

Cover $5 **Minimum** None **Mixed drinks** $4–8.50; their Long Island Iced Tea is strong enough to make you confuse your geography. **Wine** $3.50–7 **Beer** $3–5 **Dress** Suits and nice dresses; jeans, but with a jacket; no cutoffs; no tennis shoes **Specials** Happy hour 4–8 p.m. weekdays **Food available** Southern-style fried chicken, greens, meatloaf, ribs

Hours Sunday–Thursday, 4 p.m.–1:30 a.m.; Friday and Saturday, 4 p.m.–2 a.m.

What goes on Cocktail conversation here is loud, but once the performers—high-profile area pros and often national-rank musicians passing through who drop in to jam—begin, the attention level is pretty good. A true neighborhood joint owned by the taciturn Bobby Boyd, this bar was one of the nightspots that helped revitalize the untrendy side of Takoma Park without changing its character.

Setting & atmosphere This building, a former boxing gym, wears its age gracefully, with exposed brick, see-through room dividers that make the bar an integral part of the stage area, and just a handful of hanging plants.

If you go Don't be demonstrative, especially if you arrive early; the Boyds live on the nightside schedule and like to start mellow. Don't gawk at the media types who come in after production hours. Sunday is change-up night, with live reggae and a slightly younger crowd.

WHITEY'S

OLD REDNECK TAVERN/GOOD-EATS JOINT WITH LIVE BLUES

Who Goes There Old-timers; yuppie couples with blues joneses; frathouse beer buddies

2761 North Washington Boulevard, Arlington; (703) 525-9825 Virginia suburbs, Zone 11B

Cover None weekdays; varies weekends **Minimum** None **Mixed drinks** $3.15–4.20 **Wine** $3–4 **Beer** $2.65–3.50 **Dress** Jeans, with or without bolo; motorcycle leathers; athletic uniforms **Specials** Happy hour 4–7 p.m. (weekdays), noon–4 p.m. (Saturday and Sunday) with reduced prices **Food available** Legendary "broasted" chicken, home-style dinners, sandwiches, bar food

Hours Monday–Wednesday, 11 a.m.–1 a.m.; Thursday–Saturday, 8 a.m.–2 a.m.; Sunday, 8 a.m.–midnight.

What goes on Although Whitey's was for many years the best bar–blues roadhouse in the region—Sunday night jams were bywords and drew national-rank performers passing through town—neighborhood complaints about noise and parking (and overindulged patrons) gutted their live-music permit, so now Whitey's offers open mike (usually led by an area pro) on Tuesdays, and top local bands Thursday–Saturday. Pee Wee, the Wednesday-night DJ, has been spinning golden oldies for nearly 15 years.

Setting & atmosphere This is a real neighborhood tavern, whose neighborhood has upscaled around and past it, at least in some eyes. As neighbor and harmonica godfather Mark Wenner of the Nighthawks says, "We plant one bike outside and one official biker at the bar for atmosphere." It's a plain old wood and beer-sign bar with booths; a game room in the rear with dart board, pinball, shufflebowl, etc., and longneck regulars talking politics.

If you go Don't go by appearances; if you strike up a conversation, you'll discover this draws one of the most eclectic and politically opinionated crowds around. If you like the Dallas Cowboys, don't admit it. Tip well; since the kitchen keeps costs down, the waitresses don't always make what those at pricier nightspots do. Park legally—after 7 p.m. at the Country Club Cleaners—and don't litter; Whitey's doesn't need your help in alienating more neighbors.

YACHT CLUB OF BETHESDA

SECOND-CHANCE SINGLES BAR AND RETRO DISCO

Who Goes There 28–55; platinum cards and platinum blondes; the monied and the alimonied

8111 Woodmont Avenue, Bethesda; (301) 654-2396 Maryland suburbs, Zone 10A

Cover $5 Wednesday, $12 Friday and Saturday **Minimum** None **Mixed drinks** $3.95–4.50 **Wine** $3.65 **Beer** $3.65–4.25 **Dress** Dress as class advertisement; big earrings, gold chains—for women, too; jacket and tie required for men **Food available** Entrees, appetizers, and sandwiches

Hours Wednesday–Thursday, 7 p.m.–1 a.m.; Friday, 7 p.m.–2 a.m.; Saturday, 8 p.m.–2 a.m. Closed Sunday–Tuesday.

What goes on Upper, upper-middle, and upper-ambitious ring candidates in recession denial eye their conjugal options; close to 100 marital matches have been made here. This astonishingly successful mating pen, with its golden-oldies playlist and guest list to match, is the brainchild of longtime singles-bar spinmaster, flatter-patter DJ, and trend-shift sacrificial lamb Tommy the Matchmaker.

Setting & atmosphere A classy woodgrain, gray, and burgundy deco style that in fact does suggest the master suite of a luxury cruiser—but one that belongs to a sportsman past his prime. The name, and Curtis's use of the title "commodore," are metaphors for preferred rather than actual lifestyle, like wearing Polo sportswear. Or maybe it suggests the amount of booze that nightly goes down the hatch.

If you go Either line up before 8 p.m. or wait till about 11. This is the sort of place that confuses Gloria Vanderbilt with Coco Chanel; you can be rich and thin enough, but your dress can never be too little or too black. The Yacht Club boasts the only black-tie waiting line in Bethesda, which is sort of a self-fulfilling prophecy. If you don't dance (and many who do, shouldn't), get in line at the pool table. Or just plunk yourself down at the bar with a drink; the soft-hearted Curtis, an inveterate yenta, will have a candidate for your company in a flash.

ZANZIBAR

WORLD-BEAT DISCO

Who Goes There 23–45; trade law, embassy, and import reps; buppies, West African entrepreneurs, and Latin chic-sters

700 Water Street, SW; (202) 554-9100 The National Mall, Zone 1

Cover $10 after 7:00 on Friday and after 10:00 on Saturday **Minimum** None **Mixed drinks** $4.25–8.50 **Wine** $4.75 **Beer** $4.25–4.75 **Dress** Dress to impress or advertise success: European lapels, dresses with hip flounces, aerobic wear disguised as cocktail spandex; no T-shirts, jeans, or sneakers allowed **Specials** Free admission and hors d'oeuvres at happy hour, 5–7 p.m. Fridays and 9–10 p.m. Saturdays **Food available** Full West African menu

Hours Friday, 5 p.m.–3 a.m.; Saturday, 9 p.m.–4 a.m.; closed Sunday–Thursday.

What goes on Salsa, soca, soukous, samba salsa, reggae, and even go-go take turns—mostly on the turntable, but occasionaly with live bands. This is an expansively, expensively stylish singles bar, with potentially valuable networking as the undertone. The serious action starts after midnight; the visiting amateurs tend to turn pumpkin at 12.

Setting & atmosphere A sometime bureaucrats' business lunchspot, this is a long, underground wood and brick conference setup divided into larger and smaller areas, with a mahogany bar facing both and a lighted patio fountain outside the window.

If you go Be prepared to dance if you want to meet people; there's very little chatter at the bar unless you prove yourself (or are extremely well dressed). The downstairs is mostly restaurant, with great water views; the upstairs is nearly all dance floor. To go with the flow, move up and down both sides of the room; there is an unspoken tidal wave of unattached partners. *Note:* To simplify life, the tips are built into the drink prices, which makes them something more of a bargain.

Part Eleven

Exercise and Recreation

Working Out

Most of the folks on our *Unofficial Guide* research team work out routinely. Some bike, some run, some lift weights or do aerobics. While visiting Washington during the hot summer months, it didn't take long to figure out that exercising in the city's fearsome heat and humidity presented some problems.

The best months for outdoor exercise are March through June and October through December. In July and August, you must get up very early to beat the heat. January and February can bring quite cold weather, although snow isn't usually a problem. During the summer months, unless you get up very early, we recommend working out indoors.

Walking

With its wide-open spaces, Washington is made for walking. Security is very good along the Mall and Potomac Park, making for a safe walking environment at all hours of the day and night.

A long walk down the Mall and through East and West Potomac Parks offers grand views of the Lincoln, Jefferson, and FDR Memorials and the Washington Monument, as well as the Tidal Basin and the Potomac River. For a really long excursion, cross Arlington Memorial Bridge and explore Arlington National Cemetery. You can also walk north along the river past the Kennedy Center and the Thompson Boat Center and into Georgetown.

North of the Mall, downtown is not particularly interesting or aesthetically pleasing—and not too safe above New York Avenue. North of the White House, Connecticut Avenue offers unlimited window-shopping at the city's ritziest shops. South of the Capitol, Fort McNair is open to anyone who would like to stroll through well-kept grounds on a narrow peninsula where the Washington Channel and the Anacostia River meet the Potomac: Take the Metro to the Waterfront Station and walk straight

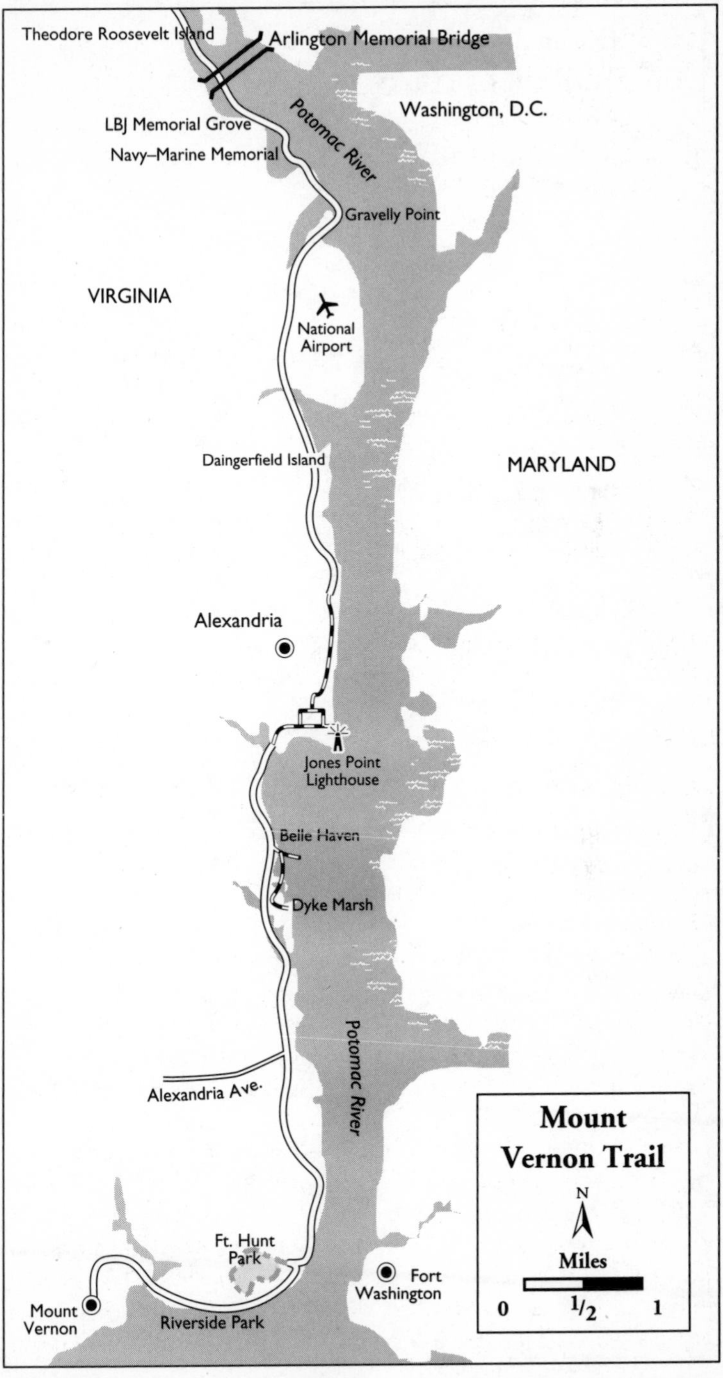
Theodore Roosevelt Island
Arlington Memorial Bridge
Washington, D.C.
Potomac River
LBJ Memorial Grove
Navy–Marine Memorial
Gravelly Point
VIRGINIA
National Airport
Daingerfield Island
MARYLAND
Alexandria
Jones Point Lighthouse
Belle Haven
Dyke Marsh
Potomac River
Alexandria Ave.
Ft. Hunt Park
Fort Washington
Mount Vernon
Riverside Park
Mount Vernon Trail
N
Miles
0
1/2
1

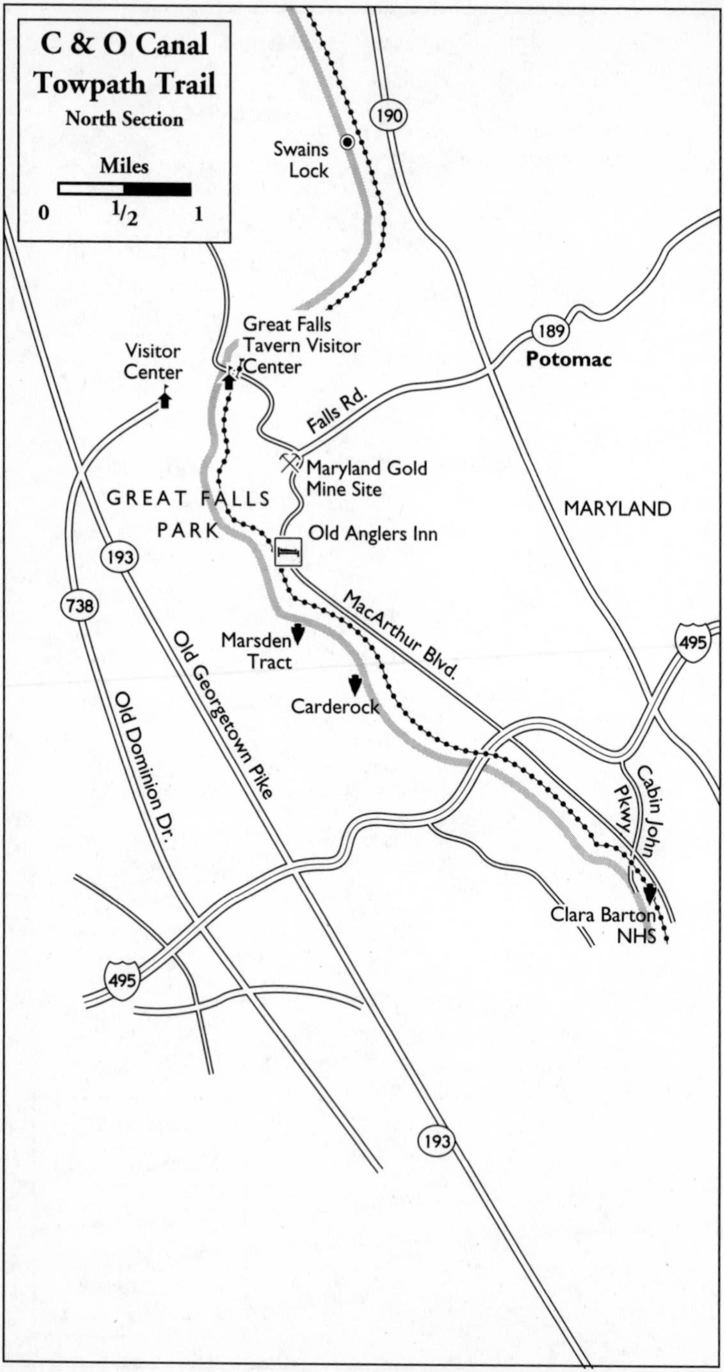
C & O Canal
Towpath Trail
North Section
Miles
0
1/2
1
190
Swains Lock
Great Falls Tavern Visitor Center
Visitor Center
189
Potomac
Falls Rd.
Maryland Gold Mine Site
GREAT FALLS PARK
MARYLAND
Old Anglers Inn
193
738
MacArthur Blvd.
Marsden Tract
Carderock
Old Georgetown Pike
Old Dominion Dr.
495
Cabin John Pkwy
Clara Barton NHS
495
193

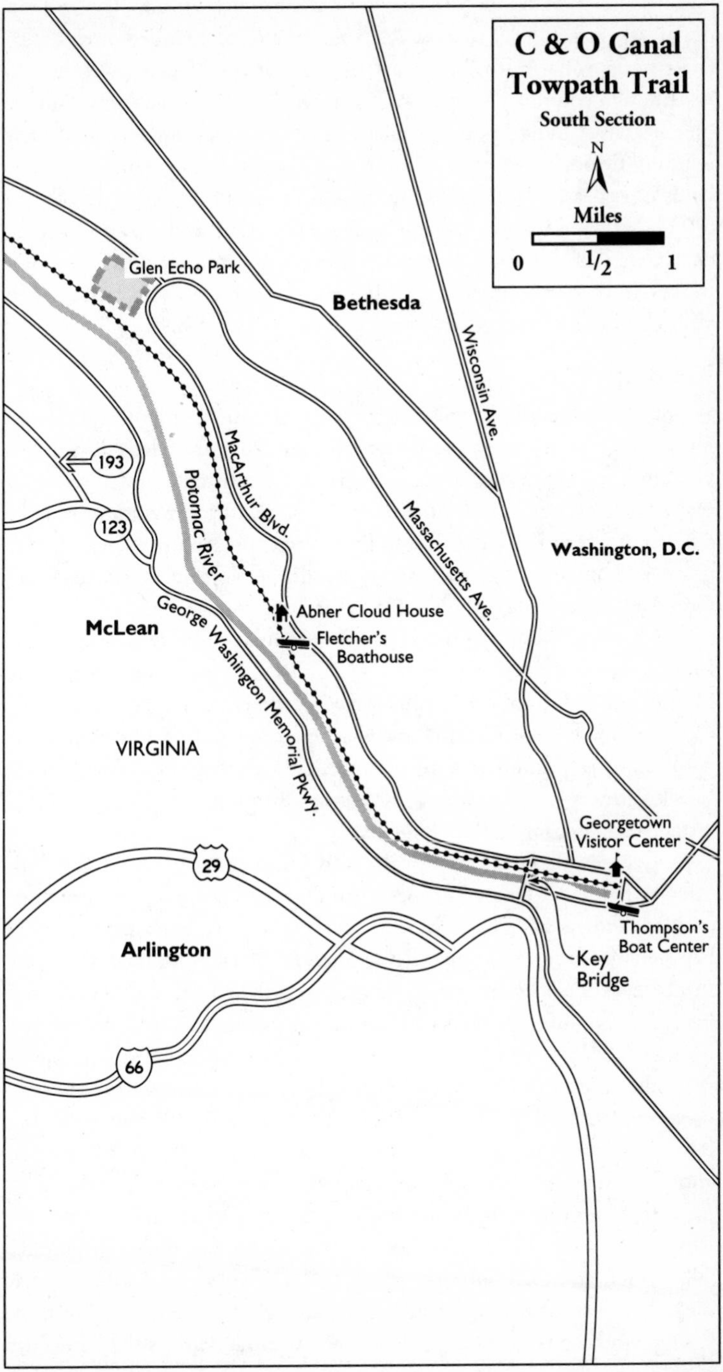
C & O Canal
Towpath Trail
South Section
N
Miles
0
1/2
1
Glen Echo Park
Bethesda
Wisconsin Ave.
193
MacArthur Blvd.
Massachusetts Ave.
Potomac River
123
Washington, D.C.
Abner Cloud House
McLean
George Washington Memorial Pkwy.
Fletcher's
Boathouse
VIRGINIA
Georgetown
Visitor Center
29
Thompson's
Boat Center
Arlington
Key
Bridge
66

down 4th Street, SW, to Fort McNair (not recommended after dark). Afterwards, you can stroll the waterfront marinas on Maine Avenue.

Although you must drive to get there, the U.S. National Arboretum in Northeast Washington offers walkers three and a half miles of easy trails winding through 444 acres of trees and flowers. In late April and May, fields of azaleas, flowering dogwood, and mountain laurel are in bloom.

The Mall and its surrounding areas are fairly flat, and distances can be deceiving there, making it easy to overextend yourself. Carry enough money to buy refreshments en route and for cab or Metro fare back to your hotel in case you get too tired to complete your walk.

Running

Washington's wealth of parks offers plenty of options to both casual and serious joggers. Most of the better running areas are relatively flat but visually stunning. Many of the best paths are centrally located, close to major in-town hotels and other attractions, making either a morning or late afternoon run easy to fit into a busy business or touring schedule. We don't recommend jogging at night; see the section on "How to Avoid Crime and Keep Safe in Public Places" in Part Four.

The heart of Washington and its most popular running location is the **Mall,** featuring packed-dirt paths. Nearby, the **Ellipse** (behind the White House) and the **Tidal Basin** offer paved pathways to run on.

Tree-shaded **Rock Creek Park** is a better bet during hot weather. A good starting point is where Connecticut Avenue crosses over Rock Creek Parkway in Northwest Washington. Run north to Pierce Mill and retrace your steps for a four-mile jog.

In Georgetown, the **Chesapeake and Ohio (C&O) Canal Towpath** offers what is probably the best running surface in town. Runners, cyclists, and hikers love this wide, dirt-pack trail that runs for miles between the scenic Potomac River and the canal. The river views are spectacular in places; the placid canal reflects the greenery alongside; and historic lockhouses and locks appear at regular intervals. Mileposts along the towpath keep you informed of your distance. Farther up, in Maryland, the enormous cataract at Great Falls attracts hikers and picnickers.

Another river route is the **Mount Vernon Trail,** a paved path that starts near the Lincoln Memorial, crosses Arlington Memorial Bridge, and goes downriver on the Virginia side of the Potomac for about 16 miles to Mount Vernon. Unless you're a marathoner, cut this run in half: Run to the airport and back, about seven and a half miles. In blustery fall, winter, and early spring weather, runners and cyclists will find that the better protected C&O Canal Towpath offers more protection from strong winds coming off the river. **West Potomac Park** is the best route in the spring, when the Japanese cherry trees are blooming around the Tidal Basin. Start near the Jefferson Memorial, head down Ohio Drive, and make the loop at the end of the park; if you've got any energy left, continue past the Jefferson Memorial and loop around the Tidal Basin. Go early in the morning to beat the crowds.

Getting to the Track

If your hotel is downtown, the Mall is the closest option you have without driving or taking the Metro. If you're staying along the Connecticut Avenue corridor, Rock Creek Park and the C&O Canal Towpath are your best bets. In Alexandria or Rosslyn, the Mount Vernon Trail and the Washington and Old Dominion Regional Park are popular paved running paths. In suburban Maryland, Greenbelt Park offers both paved and unpaved surfaces to run on, as well as a one-mile fitness trail outfitted with 20 exercise stations.

Swimming

Local waters are polluted to one degree or another, so stick to your hotel swimming pool. The closest saltwater beach is **Sandy Point State Park** in Maryland, about an hour's drive east on US 50 on the shores of the Chesapeake Bay. Atlantic Ocean beaches are a minimum three-hour drive; traffic tie-ups on summer weekends are horrendous as beachgoers funnel into the twin Chesapeake Bay bridges, where multihour backups are routine.

Free Weights and Nautilus

Almost all of the major hotels have a spa or fitness room with weight-lifting equipment. For an aerobic workout, most of the fitness rooms offer a Lifecycle, a Stairmaster, or a rowing machine.

Fitness Centers and Aerobics

Many Washington fitness centers are members-only and don't offer daily or short-term memberships. The few exceptions are all coed. **The Fitness Company,** located at 1339 Green Court (next to the Holiday Inn), features free weights, fixed weights, a full range of aerobic exercise equipment including a Stairmaster, rowing and cycling machines, and a full schedule of aerobics classes. Visitors with a hotel key can take advantage of the facilities for $10 a day. Call (202) 216-9000 for more information.

Washington Sports Club, at 1835 Connecticut Avenue, NW (across from the Hilton near Dupont Circle), offers much the same activities and services as The Fitness Company. The daily rate is $25. For more information, call (202) 332-0100.

On Capitol Hill, the **Washington Office Center Fitness Club** offers a full range of services, including free weights, fixed weights, aerobics classes, and cardiovascular workout equipment. The club, located at 409 3rd Street, SW, charges $10 a day. Call (202) 488-2822.

Tennis

Washington's two public tennis clubs are popular, making it difficult to get a court during peak hours without a reservation. The **Washington Tennis Center,** located at 16th and Kennedy Streets in Upper Northwest, offers 15 clay courts and 10 lighted hard courts during warm weather months. In winter, 5 indoor courts are available in addition to the 5 hard courts. The club accepts reservations up to a week in advance. The club is open from 7 a.m. to 11 p.m. and indoor rates begin at $24 an hour; outdoor rates begin at $4 an hour. A $28 spot-time deposit is optional. Call (202) 722-5949 for more information.

The **East Potomac Tennis Club,** located on Ohio Drive in East Potomac Park, features 5 indoor and 13 outdoor courts. Reservations for prime-time hours go fast, and you need to make reservations a week in advance. Players have a good chance of getting a court without reservations weekdays between 10 a.m. and 3 p.m. Rates range $22–30 an hour (indoor) and $5–8 an hour (outdoor). A credit card deposit is required. Call (202) 554-5962 for more information.

Recreational Sports: Biking, Hiking, Kayaking, and So On

Bicycling

Washington offers both on- and off-road cyclists a wide variety of bicycling, from flat and easy cruises along paved bike paths and the C&O Canal Towpath, to challenging terrain in the rolling countryside of nearby Virginia and Maryland.

In early spring and late fall, cyclists should wear riding tights and arm warmers to keep the chill off. From May through October, the temperatures range from comfortable to scorching—predictably the latter on summer afternoons. Listen to weather forecasts for predictions of afternoon thunderstorms in the late summer; they can be fearsome. Fall is the best season for cycling around Washington, with cool, crisp weather and a riot of color as the leaves turn in mid- to late October. Even in winter, Washington's mild climate offers at least a few days a month that are warm enough to induce cyclists to jump on their bikes.

A variety of bicycles are available for rent at **Thompson Boat Center** ($8 an hour or $25 a day; (202) 333-4861), located between the Kennedy Center and Georgetown on the Potomac, and **Fletcher's**

Boathouse ($4 an hour or $12 a day; (202) 244-0461), above Georgetown on Canal Road.

Road Biking

In downtown Washington, bicycling is better left to couriers. Unrelenting traffic congestion, combined with absent-minded tourists preoccupied with monuments and finding a cheap parking space, makes riding a bike on Washington's streets a brutal experience for all but the most hardened urban cyclists. Luckily, Washington is blessed with a network of bike paths that takes the terror out of riding a skinny-tired bike in—and out of—the city.

In terms of great scenery and enough distance to really get a workout, the **Mount Vernon Trail** is Washington's premier bike path. In addition to pedaling the 16 paved miles to Mount Vernon, cyclists can make side trips to Dyke Marsh wildlife habitat, explore fortifications at Fort Hunt, and see a 19th-century lighthouse at Jones Point Park.

Another good out-and-back ride is the **Washington and Old Dominion Railroad Regional Park (W&OD),** a 45-mile-long, paved linear bikeway that connects with the Mount Vernon Trail upriver of Arlington Memorial Bridge on the Virginia side of the Potomac. The trail intersects with a series of "bubble" parks in urban Northern Virginia and provides access to the rural Virginia countryside beyond the Capital Beltway. Both the Mount Vernon Trail and the W&OD trail are easily reached from Washington by bicycle by riding across the Arlington Memorial Bridge, at the Lincoln Memorial.

Road riders itching to see beautiful countryside outside the Washington metropolitan area (but within a day's drive) should go to either Middleburg, Virginia, or Frederick, Maryland. **Middleburg,** about 30 miles west of D.C., is in the heart of Virginia's horse country. Beautiful rolling countryside in the foothills of the Blue Ridge Mountains and low-traffic roads bordering thoroughbred horse farms make this area a fantastic place to spin the cranks.

Frederick, Maryland, is about an hour's drive north of Washington. North of town along US 15, covered bridges, narrow back roads, fish hatcheries, and mountain vistas evoke images of Vermont. To the south of Frederick, a 25-mile loop around **Sugar Loaf Mountain** is a favorite with local road cyclists.

Mountain Biking

Fat-tired cyclists can ride 184 miles one-way on the **Chesapeake and Ohio Canal Towpath,** beginning in Georgetown then following along the Potomac River upstream to Cumberland, Maryland. The hardpacked

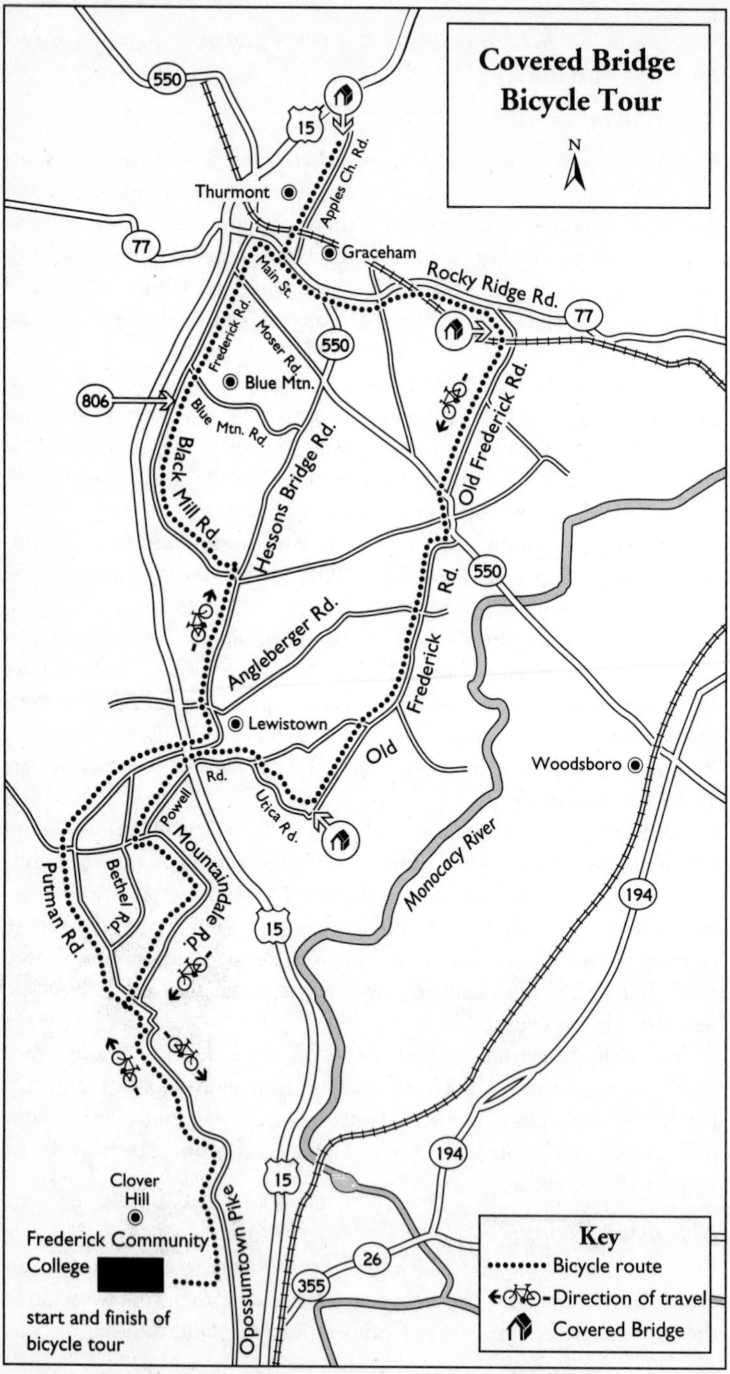
Covered Bridge
Bicycle Tour
N
Key
Bicycle route
Direction of travel
Covered Bridge
Frederick Community College
start and finish of bicycle tour
Clover Hill
Thurmont
Graceham
Blue Mtn.
Lewistown
Woodsboro
Apples Ch. Rd.
Main St.
Frederick Rd.
Moser Rd.
Blue Mtn. Rd.
Black Mill Rd.
Hessons Bridge Rd.
Rocky Ridge Rd.
Old Frederick Rd.
Angleberger Rd.
Old Frederick Rd.
Utica Rd.
Powell Rd.
Mountaindale Rd.
Putman Rd.
Bethel Rd.
Opossumtown Pike
Monocacy River
550
15
77
806
194
26
355

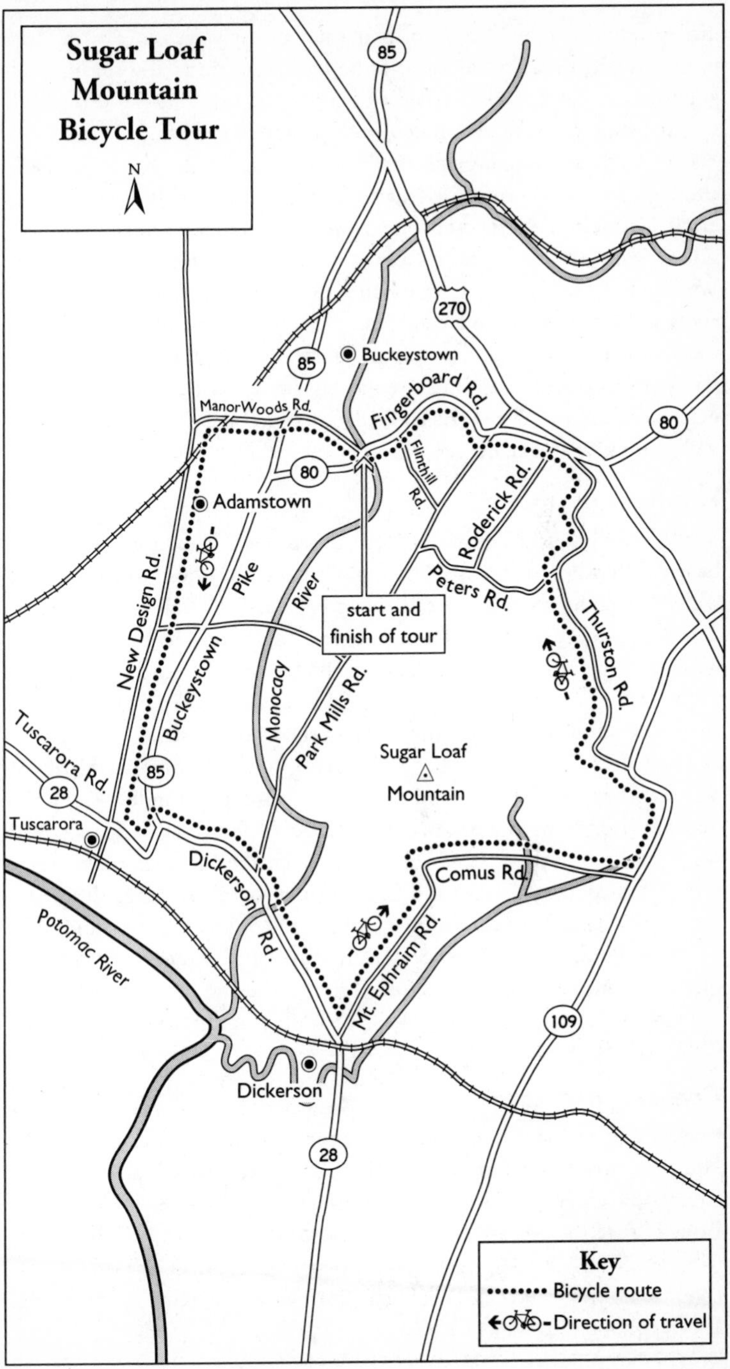
Sugar Loaf Mountain Bicycle Tour
N
85
270
85
Buckeystown
ManorWoods Rd.
Fingerboard Rd.
80
80
Flinthill Rd.
Adamstown
Roderick Rd.
Peters Rd.
New Design Rd.
Pike
River
start and finish of tour
Thurston Rd.
Buckeystown
Monocacy
Park Mills Rd.
Tuscarora Rd.
Sugar Loaf Mountain
85
28
Tuscarora
Dickerson Rd.
Comus Rd.
Potomac River
Mt. Ephraim Rd.
109
Dickerson
28
Key
Bicycle route
Direction of travel

dirt surface gives the illusion of being flat all the way; actually, the trip upriver is slightly uphill. Because of floods in the winter and spring, it's a good idea to call the National Park Service at (301) 739-4200 to make sure the section you're planning to ride is open to cyclists.

Hammerheads looking for challenging single-track and some steep climbing have to do some driving to find it, but it's worth it. The **Frederick Municipal Watershed** offers the best technical single-track this side of West Virginia—and it's a lot closer. Located an hour's drive from Washington near Frederick, Maryland, the 6,000-acre, mountaintop forest is riddled with narrow trails and well-maintained dirt roads. Since there are hardly any signs or trail markers, the Catoctin Furnace Quadrangle topographic map and a compass are a must. Local knowledge helps, too; call the **Wheel Base,** Frederick's pro bike shop, at (301) 663-9288 for maps and advice.

Hiking

While only about 15 minutes from downtown, **Theodore Roosevelt Island** is a wilderness oasis offering hikers a little over three miles of wide, flat paths through forests, swampy marshes, and rocky beaches. The park is located on the Potomac River across from the Kennedy Center and can be reached by car. Park in the area off the northbound lanes of the George Washington Memorial Parkway on the Virginia side of the river. A footbridge connects the Virginia shore to the island.

The C&O Canal, which begins in Georgetown, features a hardpacked dirt path that follows the Potomac River north for 184 miles. Along the way are river views, forest, and wildlife. At **Great Falls Park,** north of Washington on the Virginia side of the river, the Potomac roars over a series of steep, jagged rocks and flows through a narrow gorge. It's a dramatic scene and worth the trip. Hiking trails follow the river and offer views of Mather Gorge. Rock Creek Park in Northwest Washington offers 15 miles of hiking trails, plus bridle trails you can hike. Maps are available at the park headquarters, 3545 Williamsburg Lane, NW (phone (202) 895-6070).

Canoeing and Kayaking

Canoes and rowboats are available for rent on the C&O Canal and the Potomac River at **Thompson Boat Center,** located between the Kennedy Center and Georgetown (phone (202) 333-4861), **Fletcher's Boat House** located at Canal and Reservoir Roads above Georgetown (phone (202) 244-0461), and **Jack's Boats** on K Street in Georgetown (phone (202) 337-9642). Pedal boats for two can be rented at the **Tidal Basin** (phone (202) 484-0206).

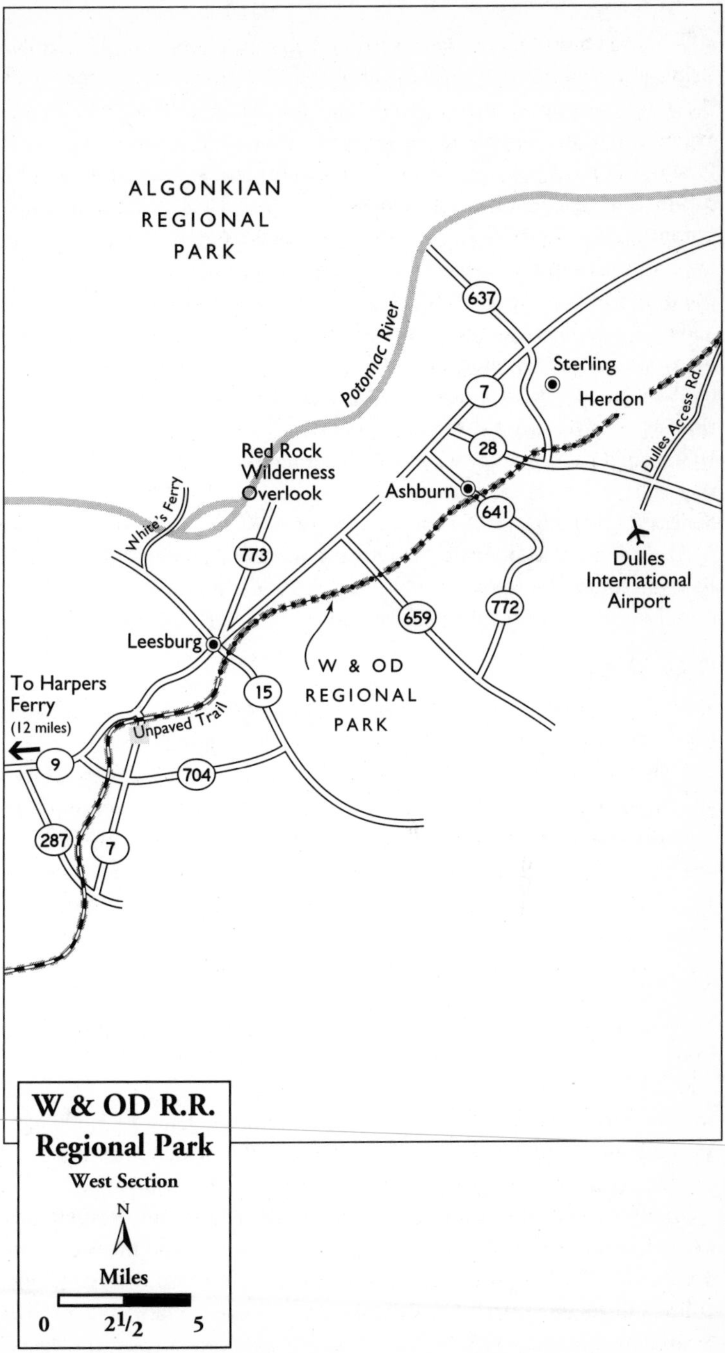
ALGONKIAN
REGIONAL
PARK
Potomac River
637
Sterling
7
Herdon
Dulles Access Rd.
28
Red Rock
Wilderness
Overlook
White's Ferry
Ashburn
641
773
Dulles
International
Airport
772
659
Leesburg
W & OD
REGIONAL
PARK
15
To Harpers
Ferry
(12 miles)
Unpaved Trail
9
704
287
7
W & OD R.R.
Regional Park
West Section
N
Miles
0
2 1/2
5

Whitewater enthusiasts need go only a few miles north of the Capital Beltway to find excellent Class I through Class VI rapids year-round on the **Potomac.** Local boaters boast that it's the best urban whitewater experience in the United States, featuring a very remote, wilderness feel. One of the most popular trips is the Class II Seneca rapids section. The put-in is at Violets Lock, located on River Road (MD 190), north of Potomac, Maryland. Violets Lock is also the take-out, meaning you don't have to run a shuttle: It's a round trip that lets you return to your starting point by paddling up the C&O Canal, about one and a half miles below Violets Lock. Below the Seneca Rapids, the river is very scenic, featuring many islands and no rapids. But you must make the next take-out on the left bank at Maryland's Great Falls National Park or become another statistic as the river drops through Great Falls.

Seasoned paddlers may want to try running the Class II/III-plus rapids that start below Great Falls and end at the Old Angler's Inn. As with Seneca Rapids, no shuttle is required: Park across the road from the Old Angler's Inn on MacArthur Boulevard on the Maryland side of the Potomac and follow the trail to the put-in. Paddle upstream on the C&O Canal to below Great Falls (at least 100 yards) for the return leg.

Boat Rides

Sixty-minute excursions leave Georgetown and Great Falls, VA, on the C&O Canal most days from April to mid-October. National Park Service guides wear 19th-century costumes, take the boat through a lock, and explain the history of the canal. Board and buy tickets near the Foundry Mall, below M Street at Thomas Jefferson Street, NW. Tickets are $8 for adults and $6 for seniors ages 62 and over, and $5 for children ages 4–14. Call (202) 653-5190 for current schedules and more information.

Skiing

Moderately good downhill ski slopes are within a couple hours' drive from Washington and offer dependable, machine-made snow and night skiing from November through March. **Whitetail,** a new $25-million ski area in nearby Pennsylvania, features a vertical drop of almost 1,000 feet, 14 trails, and plenty of lift capacity. Call (717) 328-9400 for information on ski packages, lodging, and lift rates.

Jointly owned **Ski Roundtop** and **Liberty Mountain Resort,** also located in south-central Pennsylvania, are about a two- to three-hour drive from Washington. Both offer 600-foot verticals, 13 trails, and 100% snowmaking. Call Ski Roundtop at (717) 432-9631 and Liberty Mountain Resort at (717) 642-8282 for lift rates, hours, and directions.

Horseback Riding

The **Rock Creek Park Horse Center** offers guided rides on the equestrian trails located in Rock Creek Park. Rates are $25 for an hour; reservations are required. The minimum age is 12. For those age 12 and under (and at least 30 inches tall), Rock Creek also offers pony rides for $15. The center, which is open all year, is located at Military and Glover Roads in Northwest Washington. The hours are Tuesday–Friday, noon–6 p.m.; Saturday and Sunday, 9 a.m.–5 p.m. Call (202) 362-0118 or visit www.rockcreekhorsecenter.com for more information.

Golf

Washington has three public golf courses operated on National Park Service land and open from dawn to dusk. Fees are $10 for 9 holes and $16 for 18 holes weekdays; weekends, the rates are $13 and $20, respectively. Reservations are not accepted. All three courses feature snack bars, pro shops, rental clubs, and gas cars ($13 for 9 holes, $20 for 18 holes).

East Potomac Golf Course, located in East Potomac Park across from Washington's waterfront area, offers one 18-hole course, two 9-hole courses, and an 18-hole miniature golf course. It's the busiest of the National Park Service courses; plan to arrive at dawn on weekends if you don't want to wait. East Potomac has wide-open fairways, well-kept greens, and great views of surrounding monuments. Call (202) 554-7660 for more information.

Langston Golf Course, at 26th Street and Benning Road, NE (near RFK Stadium), features an 18-hole course, including newly remodeled back-9 holes, and a driving range. Langston, the only public course with water holes, is located along the Anacostia River. For more information, call (202) 397-8638.

Rock Creek Golf Course is located at 16th and Rittenhouse Streets, NW, four and a half miles north of the White House on 16th Street. It offers duffers a hilly and challenging 18-hole course through rolling hills and wooded terrain. Call (202) 882-7332 for more information.

Spectator Sports

Alas, America's national pastime, baseball, is not played professionally in the nation's capital anymore. But Washingtonians have developed a fierce devotion to the **Baltimore Orioles,** only an hour north. Visitors to D.C. can make the trek by train to catch the Birds playing at home, Oriole Park at Camden Yards, near Baltimore's downtown Inner Harbor. Check the sports section of the *Washington Post* for information on home games and tickets.

However, if you're one of the growing number of fans of **minor-league baseball,** Washington is worth a minitour. The Class A **Frederick Keys** (named in honor of Francis Scott Key, a rural Maryland native) play in the historic town of Frederick, Maryland, about an hour to the northeast (call (301) 662-0013). The Class A **Potomac Cannons,** a farm team for the Cincinnati Reds, play just outside Fairfax County; call (703) 590-2311 for details.

The closest option for baseball is Prince George's County Stadium, where the **Bowie Baysox,** a Class AA team belonging to the same group as the Keys, have been steadily building a crowd. Both teams are associated with the Orioles, so they're sentimental favorites. Baysox tickets run only $14 for box seats, $10 for adults, and $8 for children ages 5–12. Call (301) 464-4880 for information.

For **professional basketball,** the **Washington Wizards** and the WNBA's **Mystics** (the league's highest-attendance team in 2002) play out of the MCI Center, located downtown near Gallery Place. For schedules and tickets, call TicketMaster at (202) 432-SEAT or visit the teams' respective websites: www.nba.com/wizards and www.wnba.com/mystics.

The **University of Maryland Terrapins** offer topflight **college basketball** at Comcast Center on the school's campus in suburban College Park. Call (301) 314-7070 for information. **Georgetown University** plays its home games at MCI Center; for ticket information call (202) 687-HOYA or (202) 432-SEAT.

Lots of luck getting tickets to see **professional football** in Washington: The **Washington Redskins** have sold out stadiums for years, and the team holds the reputation as the hardest ticket to acquire in pro sports. Still interested? Scalpers regularly charge three and four times the regular ticket price—and higher, if the 'Skins are playing Dallas.

In 1997, the Redskins moved from RFK Stadium to what is now FedEx Field in Landover. The stadium has nearly 80,000 seats, so tickets are slightly easier to obtain. Following suite, Baltimore built a new football stadium for the **Ravens,** née Cleveland Browns. For Redskins schedule and ticket information, call (301) 276-6800 or visit www.redskins.com. For the Ravens, call (410) 261-RAVE or visit www.ravenszone.com. Both teams sell tickets through TicketMaster, (202) 432-SEAT.

College football is another matter. The **Maryland Terrapins** play in Byrd Stadium at College Park (phone (301) 314-7064). The **Naval Academy** in Annapolis, Maryland, and **Howard University** in Washington also field teams; check the *Post* for home game information.

Washington's **professional hockey** team, the **Washington Capitals,** plays at the MCI Center in downtown D.C. near Gallery Place. For information, call (202) 628-3200.

Pro soccer comes to Washington when the **D.C. United** plays 16 home games each season (March through September) at RFK Stadium. Tickets for evening and Sunday afternoon games range from $22 to $55; call TicketMaster at (202) 432-SEAT to reserve individual game tickets. For schedule information, call (703) 478-6600.

Horse racing is available at a number of tracks around Washington; check the *Washington Post* to see which track is in season during your visit. Bus service from the city is usually available.

D.C. Area Horse Tracks	
Harness:	Rosecroft Raceway—Fort Washington, MD (301) 567-4000
Thoroughbred:	Bowie Race Course—Bowie, MD (301) 262-8111
	Charles Town Raceways—Charlestown, WV (304) 725-7001
	Laurel Race Course—Laurel, MD (301) 725-0400
	Pimlico Race Course—Baltimore, MD (410) 542-9400

Subject Index

Restaurant Index

Nightclub Index

Unofficial Guide to Washington Reader Survey

If you would like to express your opinion about Washington or this guidebook, complete the following survey and mail it to:

Unofficial Guide to Washington Reader Survey
PO Box 43673
Birmingham AL 35243

Inclusive dates of your visit: ____________________

Members of your party:	Person 1	Person 2	Person 3	Person 4	Person 5
Gender:	M F	M F	M F	M F	M F
Age:					

How many times have you been to Washington? ____________
On your most recent trip, where did you stay? ____________

Concerning your accommodations, on a scale of 100 as best and 0 as worst, how would you rate:

The quality of your room? ____ The value of your room? ____
The quietness of your room? ____ Check-in/check-out efficiency? ____
Shuttle service to the parks? ____ Swimming pool facilities? ____

Did you rent a car? ____________ From whom? ____________

Concerning your rental car, on a scale of 100 as best and 0 as worst, how would you rate:

Pick-up processing efficiency? ___ Return processing efficiency? ___
Condition of the car? ___ Cleanliness of the car? ___
Airport shuttle efficiency? ___

Concerning your dining experiences:

Including fast-food, estimate your meals in restaurants per day? ________
Approximately how much did your party spend on meals per day? ______
Favorite restaurants in Washington: ____________________

____

Did you buy this guide before leaving? ☐ while on your trip? ☐

How did you hear about this guide? (check all that apply)

Loaned or recommended by a friend ☐ Radio or TV ☐
Newspaper or magazine ☐ Bookstore salesperson ☐
Just picked it out on my own ☐ Library ☐
Internet ☐

Unofficial Guide to Washington Reader Survey *(continued)*

What other guidebooks did you use on this trip? ______________

On a scale of 100 as best and 0 as worst, how would you rate them?

Using the same scale, how would you rate *The Unofficial Guide(s)?*

____

Are *Unofficial Guides* readily available at bookstores in your area? ______

Have you used other *Unofficial Guides?* ______________

Which one(s)? ______________

Comments about your Washington trip or *The Unofficial Guide(s):*